Business Vocational A level

(formerly Advanced GNVQ)

second edition

Matthew Glew, Malcolm Surridge, Michael Watts and Stuart Merrills

Published by HarperCollins*Publishers* Limited
77–85 Fulham Palace Road
Hammersmith
London
W6 8JB

www.**Collins**Education.com
On-line support for schools and colleges

First edition first published 1996, reprinted 1997, 1998 and 1999
Second edition first published 2000
Reprinted 2000

ISBN 0 00 329104 9

British Cataloguing in Publication Data.
A cataloguing record for this publication is available from the British Library.

Almost all the case studies in this book are factual. However, the persons, locations and
subjects have been given different names to protect their identity. The accompanying
images are for aesthetic purposes only and are not intended to represent or identify
any existing person, location or subject. The publisher cannot accept any responsibility
for consequences resulting from this use, except as expressly provided by law.

Series commissioned by Charis Evans
Designed, edited and typeset by DSM Partnership
Cover designed by Patricia Briggs
Cover picture by Tony Stone
Picture research by Thelma Gilbert
Illustrations by Barking Dog Art
Cartoon by Alan Fraser
Index by Patricia Baker
Project managed by Paul Stirner, DSM Partnership
Production by Emma Lloyd-Jones
Printed and bound by Scotprint

www.**fire**and**water**.co.uk
The book lover's website

Contents

Acknowledgements

The authors would like to thank everybody involved in supporting them during the writing and production of this book.

In particular thanks go to Rachel Glew for additional research on Units 3 and 4 and to Mark Berrisford-Smith, of the HSBC's Business Economic Unit, for permission to reproduce the case study on pp. 142–3.

The authors and publisher would like to thank the following for permission to reproduce photographs and other material.

Ace Picture Library (pp. 120, 128)
Auto Express Picture Library (p. 75)
Bigcheese 200 (p. 224)
Bruce Coleman (pp. 145, 184)
Coloursport (p. 202)
Covent Garden Market Authority (p. 194)
Dyson Press Office (pp. 39, 152)
Empics Ltd (p. 78)
The Environmental Picture Library (p. 8)
Kay Wright (pp. 89, 227)

The Kobal Collection (p. 52)
Meadowhall Complex (p. 345)
Popperfoto/Reuters (pp. 51, 86, 204)
Rex Features (p. 192)
Robert Harding (pp. 5, 28, 57, 68, 83, 92, 96, 138)
Roger Scruton (pp. 6, 11, 13, 19, 21, 111, 150, 176, 190, 197, 328, 334)
Rover (p. 159)
Sally & Richard Greenhill (pp. 9, 60 left, 104, 117, 161, 201, 221, 332, 341)
SmithKline Beecham (pp. 29, 113)
The Stock Market (pp. 3, 56, 321)
Stone (pp. 54, 60 right, 61, 249)
Tesco (p. 149)
Trip (pp. 48, 229, 353)
Vauxhall/General Motors (p. 67)

Every effort has been made to contact copyright holders, but if any have been inadvertently overlooked, the publisher will be pleased to make the necessary arrangements at the first opportunity.

Author biographies

Matthew Glew is director of teaching and learning at North Hertfordshire College. He is actively involved in delivering Business GNVQ at all levels and is an external verifier for Edexcel. He has contributed to a wide range of business publications.

Malcolm Surridge is an experienced teacher and is involved in the delivery of GNVQ and vocational programmes at Advanced and Intermediate levels. He is principal examiner for AS level Business Studies with a major examining board and is writing assessment materials for the Vocational A level in Business.

Stuart Merrills is a full-time lecturer in business and finance at Great Yarmouth College. He has written extensively on a range of business subjects and is also an AEB examiner.

Michael Watts was a senior lecturer in further education for many years and is currently head of business studies and economics at St Christopher's School, Letchworth Garden City. He is also a visiting teacher at two other schools in North Hertfordshire. Michael has been an examiner for A level Economics and has contributed to a wide range of business publications.

Introduction

What is a vocational A level?

VOCATIONAL A LEVEL IS a qualification of the same standard as a traditional A level, but with a different focus. It used to be called an Advanced GNVQ, which stands for General National Vocational Qualification.

The Vocational A level qualification relates to the world of work and employment. In contrast to GCSEs and traditional A levels, which are based on knowledge and understanding of academic subjects, Vocational A levels are based on the ways in which people earn their living in business, in leisure and tourism, in hospitality and catering, and in many other areas of work.

Vocational A levels introduce you to a general area of work rather than to a particular job. You may have heard of NVQs (National Vocational Qualifications). These relate to the skills you need to undertake particular jobs. Vocational A levels, on the other hand, cover a broad area of work and are designed for people who are usually studying full-time at school or college, and are usually aged between 16 and 19.
GNVQ courses are also available at Foundation and Intermediate levels. These are equivalent to GCSEs.

How will I study?

If you have achieved an Intermediate GNVQ, you will already have a good idea of what it is like to study a Vocational A level. However, if you have taken GCSEs, you will find that studying for a Vocational A level is different in several ways from GCSE work, and from studying for traditional A levels.

First, as a Vocational A level student, you will take more responsibility for your own learning, for planning your work, for making your own investigations, and for keeping proper records of what you have done. Your tutor will play an important part in teaching you some of what you need to know and helping you to plan your work, to keep to your plan and to respond to problems and setbacks. However, in the end you have to take responsibility for your programme of study, just as you will take responsibility for your work when you are employed in the future.

Second, much of your learning will be acquired through carrying out your own enquiries and investigations, often in connection with assignments agreed with your tutor. These investigations can involve a wide range of tasks and activities, drawing on several

different sources of information. For example, you may:

- do research in libraries and resource centres
- visit work places and talk to the people currently employed in the business environment
- learn from visits by local employers and business people
- carry out surveys of people's activities, preferences and opinions
- study company brochures and gather information from press, television and internet reports
- study particular examples of people, places and companies that relate to your work
- learn from work experience with a local employer (if this can be arranged).

Overall, you will be actively investigating the real world of work and presenting your findings in various ways, including giving talks and presentations. All these activities develop skills which are essential in the world of work.

Third, two-thirds of your work will be assessed through assignments that you complete during the course, which you will assemble in a portfolio. Only one third will be assessed through tests.

The structure of the course

The structure of the Vocational A level in Business is quite simple. There are 12 units in the full award. Six are compulsory units; every student takes them. Each of the compulsory units is covered in this textbook. Six are optional units. Each awarding body has produced its own set of optional units and you will probably choose which of these to study. These optional units are not covered in this book, although you will find the information contained in the compulsory units a useful foundation for your optional unit work.

All units are the same size. To gain the full award you have to take all twelve units and your overall result is calculated on the basis of your performance in all of the units.

Since the new A levels have six units, your 12-unit Vocational A level is worth two traditional A levels. You may be able to take a six-unit Vocational A level award that is equivalent to one traditional A level.

Course specifications

Your tutor will give you a copy of the specifications for the units you will need in your course and will go through them with you. All units have the same basic characteristics. They are addressed directly to you, the student. They have three sections:

- **about this unit** – this briefly describes what the unit covers

- **what you need to learn** – this clearly states the knowledge, understanding and skills you need to complete the unit

- **assessment evidence** – this sets out the evidence you need to produce for the unit, including what you need to produce to get higher grades, and the tasks you will be set in the units which are assessed through tests.

The unit specifications are designed to let you know exactly what skills and knowledge you have to demonstrate to achieve the qualification.

How will I be assessed?

Four of your six compulsory units are assessed through a portfolio of evidence that you will compile. This portfolio of evidence is assessed by your tutors. The other two compulsory units – for the competitive business environment and finance, units 2 and 5 in this book – will be assessed by a test that is set and marked by the awarding body.

The portfolio is the heart of your course. Everything in it should be your own work and it must meet all the requirements set out in the assessment evidence sections of the unit specifications. It has to be carefully planned, organised and maintained, and it must have an index so that you can show how everything in it relates to the evidence requirements.

Evidence can take several forms. Much of it will be your own written work. However, some evidence will be provided by your tutor or some other person (maybe an employer) who has witnessed you taking part in a discussion, or dealing with a customer, or making a presentation. Your tutor, or other witness, must provide a written statement that you have reached the required standard.

Your portfolio of evidence may contain video or audio recordings of role plays, work experience and research activities. It may also include letters, photographs, computer printouts and graphics, sketches and plans.

You need to build up a separate portfolio for your key skills evidence

Vocational A levels are graded A to E, exactly like traditional A levels. You will be given a grade for each unit. These grades will then be combined to give your overall grade for the whole qualification. When you have completed the course successfully, you will be awarded a Vocational A level certificate from your awarding body. This will list all the units you have completed, with grades, and will also specify your grade for the whole qualification.

How this book is organised

The content, structure and features of *Business for Vocational A level* are designed to help you to get the most out of your course. The content directly matches all the underpinning knowledge that you will need to complete the compulsory units. The units in this book are organised into sections that make them easier to follow. Each section is packed with information, to help you learn in an active and stimulating way. You can identify each section within a unit by looking at the top right hand corner of every right hand page.

The special features include press and internet extracts, case studies and discussion points that will help you to develop your understanding of what you have been reading and to apply it to your own experience and studies. All special features are indicated by distinctive icons and banners. Discussion points stimulate you to reflect more fully about a topic.

Each section within a unit ends with a feature called build your learning. This lists the key words and phrases that you have covered and gives summary points for the section. Key words and phrases are also highlighted in blue where they first appear in the section.

Assessment guidance

You will find assessment guidance at the end of each of the four compulsory units These are based on the assessment criteria that you are required to meet in order to pass your Vocational A level. Check with your teacher before starting any assignment work that will contribute to your portfolio of evidence.

There is no assessment guidance for units two and five, the competitive business environment and finance, as these will be tested by your awarding body. However, case studies and sample questions are provided at the end of these units based on material that you are likely to be given in your external test.

Good luck with your course!

This unit provides an introduction to all types of businesses. It covers large and small firms, manufacturing businesses as well as those providing services. It includes businesses that sell their products in a single locality as well as multinational businesses that operate globally. It should provide you with a good insight into what is meant by the term business.

The unit starts by considering what firms are trying to achieve. What are their objectives? It looks at how businesses are affected by their objectives. The attitudes, values and beliefs of people working in a company seeking to maximise profits will be very different to those of a charity caring for deprived children. This unit explores the links between an organisation's objectives and its values and beliefs (known as the organisational culture).

Many different types of businesses exist. They can be categorised according to their legal structure. Your local corner shop may be operated as a sole trader, a business with a single owner, but you might buy most of your groceries at Tesco, one of the UK's largest retailers. This unit considers the legal structures required to create and operate businesses and the different legal forms that businesses can take.

There is an overview of the functions that take place within businesses. We outline the core functions of businesses: managing finance, production and human resources, as well as marketing, administration and research and development. These functions can be organised in various ways. Businesses adopt a number of structures: some have many levels of hierarchy, others have flatter structures with many employees operating at the same level within the organisation. We describe different organisational structures and consider the factors that influence the shape of an organisation.

Communication has been described as the lifeblood of business. We review the channels and forms that business communication can take. A recurring theme is the need to assess the value of effective communication and the ways in which it can contribute to the achievement of business objectives.

The final section of this unit covers production. This examines how businesses convert inputs, such as raw materials and labour services, into outputs, the finished goods and services. We consider the increasing importance of quality within business, distinguishing between quality control and quality assurance, and evaluate its contribution to an organisation's competitiveness.

1

Business at work

Contents

Business objectives

THE OBJECTIVES OF BUSINESSES can vary enormously. A charity's overriding objective might be to alleviate poverty in the developing world; on the other hand, many companies' major objective is to generate the maximum profits possible. An organisation's mission statement gives an indication of the purpose of the business and dovetails with the objectives the organisation sets itself.

Mission statements

Many organisations attempt to express the purpose of their being within a few sentences. These **mission statements** are intended to provide a sense of common purpose to direct and stimulate the organisation. This statement represents the vision or mission of the organisation. Mission statements change over time to reflect the changing competitive nature of the markets in which businesses sell.

Mission statements normally set out to answer the following questions.

■ What business is the organisation in?

■ Who is to be served?

■ What benefits are to be provided?

■ How are consumers to be satisfied?

Traditionally, businesses tended to operate almost exclusively in the interests of their shareholders and to seek to maximise profits. However, many businesses now have mission statements that reflect a desire to satisfy the needs of all their **stakeholders**, that is all the individuals or groups that have an interest or stake in a business and its activities. Employees, shareholders, managers, local residents and suppliers are all examples of stakeholders.

Many businesses have publicised their intention to attempt to meet the needs and desires of as many

---

Figure 1.1: The Co-operative Bank's mission statement

We, The Co-operative Bank Group, will continue to develop a successful and innovative financial institution by providing our customers with high quality financial and related services whilst promoting the underlying principles of cooperation which are ...

1 Quality and excellence

To offer all our customers consistent high quality and good value services and strive for excellence in all that we do.

2 Participation

To introduce and promote the concept of full participation by welcoming the views and concerns of our customers and by encouraging our staff to take an active role within the local community.

3 Freedom of association

To be non-partisan in all social, political, racial and religious matters.

4 Education and training

To act as a caring and responsible employer encouraging the development and training of all our staff and encouraging commitment and pride in each other and the Group.

5 Cooperation

To develop a close affinity with organisations which promote fellowship between workers, customers, members and employers.

6 Quality of life

To be a responsible member of society by promoting an environment where the needs of local communities can be met now and in the future.

7 Retentions

To manage the business effectively and efficiently, attracting investment and maintaining sufficient surplus funds within the business to ensure the continued development of the Group.

8 Integrity

To act with honesty and integrity and within legislative and regulatory requirements.

stakeholder groups as possible. This is not always easy to achieve, as satisfying one group can disadvantage another. The Co-operative Bank, as Figure 1.1 illustrates, promotes its positive ethical position. It has refused to invest in companies that pollute the environment or to trade with nations that have oppressive regimes. In taking this stance the bank has turned down a number of profitable investments; this policy may result in lower profits and dissatisfy some of its shareholders.

Discussion point

Do you think that the Co-operative Bank really believes in its ethical stance, or is it simply a tactic to attract more customers?

The British Airports Authority (BAA) is responsible for operating some of the UK's major airports. Its mission statement refers to customer needs, stressing safety, and to continuous improvement in financial performance and service quality. After a lengthy debate, BAA's management decided to add another clause to the mission statement committing the group to grow 'with the support and trust of our neighbours'.

▲ BAA restricts night flights into airports like Gatwick to reduce disturbance to local residents

Discussion point

Why might it be important for British Airports Authority, the company which operates most of the UK's major airports, to consider its neighbours? What benefits does BAA expect to get from changing its mission statement to refer to growth with the support and trust of its neighbours?

Objectives

Business objectives are medium- to long-term goals or targets that provide a sense of direction to the business. Objectives are normally measurable and have a stated timescale – for example, a business might have an objective to boost market share from 24 per cent to 33 per cent over the next four years. **Market share** simply measures the proportion of total sales in a particular market achieved by the business.

Companies may have a number of objectives. In general, the objectives pursued by a business tend to vary according to its size, ownership and legal structure. Small businesses are more likely to focus on survival as an objective as they tend to lack the financial resources to cope with adverse trading conditions. Larger businesses may aim to maximise profits, especially if they are public limited companies whose shareholders will want the highest possible return on their investments.

These objectives will reflect purpose of the business as expressed in the mission statement and they have a considerable impact on the way in which it operates. Figure 1.2 illustrates the interrelationship between a company's mission statement and its objectives.

Figure 1.2: The hierarchy of objectives

Mission statement

Organisation's purpose

Business objectives

Survival
Increasing market share

Divisional/departmental objectives

Support and contribute to the achievement of overall business objectives

The goals pursued by any business can be separated into primary and secondary objectives.

- Primary objectives are those that must be achieved if the business is to survive and be successful. These relate to issues such as profit levels and market share.

- Secondary objectives tend to measure the efficiency of the organisation. They may affect the chances of success, but only in the long term. Examples include administrative efficiency and labour turnover rates.

As businesses make efforts to consider all their stakeholders, customer care has assumed greater importance over recent years. As a result, improvements in customer care are often now classified as a primary objective.

Profit maximisation

Profit maximisation is likely to be an important objective for companies which are owned by shareholders. Profit, at is simplest, refers to the extent to which revenues exceed costs, so profit maximisation occurs when the difference between sales revenue and total costs is greatest.

Private sector companies, such as Tesco, Eastern Energy, Lloyds Bank and ICI, seek to maximise profits to provide high returns for their shareholders. High profit levels offer companies real advantages. They have funds to invest in improving products and production processes and they can use profits to launch new products. A positive record in terms of profitability can make it easier for a business to raise capital. Banks and other financial institutions will be more confident of receiving repayment of their loans. Potential shareholders will be attracted by the prospect of large dividends and rising share values.

In contrast to the companies which pursue a profit maximisation strategy, some firms are content to pursue a satisfactory level of profit. This is called satisficing. Satisficing is common among smaller firms, where the pursuit of higher profits may require the entrepreneur to work excessive hours.

Survival

Survival is an important objective for many businesses. It is particularly important when businesses are vulnerable such as:

- during their first few years of trading

- during periods of recession or intense competition

- at a time of crisis such as a hostile takeover.

Most recently established businesses have survival as an objective. This is because these businesses often have relatively few customers, have to spend heavily on advertising to attract customers and may have relatively inexperienced managers.

However, larger and long-established businesses can have survival as an objective. In 1999, the National Westminster Bank was subject to a number of takeover bids and in February 2000 finally succumbed to an improved offer from the Royal Bank of Scotland. The National Westminster Bank was aiming to survive as an independent organisation.

▲ Hostile takeover bids forced National Westminster Bank to pursue a – ultimately unsuccessful – survival strategy

In a different vein, textile firms William Baird and Daks Simpson have been hit by Marks and Spencer's decision not to place any further orders with these clothing manufacturers. The loss of such a valuable customer as Marks and Spencer has put the future of these companies in jeopardy. Their objective, at least in the short term, will be survival.

Increasing sales or market share

Growth increases the scale of a business, resulting in higher levels of output and more sales. Many businesses pursue growth strategies because their managers believe that this is essential for survival. If a firm grows, it might be able to attract more customers, earn higher profits and begin to establish itself in the market. Growth offers:

- increased returns for the owners of the business

- higher salaries (and more job security) for employees of the business

- a wider range of products for the business's existing and potential customers.

Growth can be an important target for managers. It is increasingly common for managers' pay packages to be a combination of shares and salary. Successful managers can earn substantial incomes by growing business, particularly if that is reflected in the company's share price. A record of managing growth also makes managers attractive to other businesses and can enhance their careers.

Price war in store

The purchase of Asda by American retailing giant Wal-Mart looks set to lead to a price war in the UK if other supermarkets respond to the challenge of cutting prices to American levels.

Major retailers such as Tesco and Sainsbury's have announced that they will respond, but believe that the announcement by Asda and Wal-Mart is really a publicity stunt.

Some leading retailers are concerned that cutting prices will put jobs at risk.

Adapted from *The Guardian*, 26 September 1999

Discussion point

How might retailers such as Sainsbury's and Tesco have to change their objectives as a result of Wal-Mart's take-over of Asda?

Figure 1.3: Share of UK grocery market, 1999

Tesco	22.00 %
Asda	16.53 %
Sainsbury's	16.50 %
Safeway	9.00 %

Source: Taylor Nelson Sofres, quoted in *Daily Telegraph*, 12 July 1999

Discussion point

The figures in Figure 1.3 measure sales by volume – that is, they measure the quantity of groceries sold. What other measures could be used to compare the share of the grocery market held by the major retailers? Which measure do you think is best?

Increasing market share is an important objective for some companies. It is likely to be a key objective any business operating in a market which is not growing. For example, the market for traditional beers in the UK is not growing – indeed there are signs that it may be declining. As the market is not increasing in size, brewers of traditional ales can only increase sales by taking market share from competitors.

Market share is also important for businesses that benefit considerably from producing on a large scale. They use expensive equipment, and unless they produce a large volume of output this is not used cost-effectively; valuable equipment is left idle for substantial amounts of time. The financial advantages of producing on a large scale are termed economies of scale. Where these economies exist, firms will attempt to take a greater share of the market. This allows them to manufacture their products more cheaply, and to sell them at a lower price, increasing their competitiveness.

Providing services to the community

A number of organisations provide services to the community. Examples include the National Health Service, schools and colleges. These organisations are part of the public sector – they are managed, directly or indirectly, on behalf of the government – yet they are a form of business. Their overriding objective is to provide the best possible service to the local community.

Successive governments have taken a number of actions in an attempt to enhance the quality of service provided by the health and education sectors.

- Schools, colleges and hospitals have been given greater control over their own affairs and, in particular, have been allowed to manage their own finances. The expectation is that this would lead to greater financial efficiency and higher quality services for local residents.

- The government has established bodies to inspect the quality of service provided by schools and colleges. Any institution found to be providing an inadequate quality of service has to implement action plans to reach the appropriate service standard. The government intends to extend this inspection mechanism to the health service.

Charitable and non-profit objectives

Charities have a high profile in the UK. Organisations such as Oxfam and Mencap are familiar to most people. Charities have a number of clear objectives:

- to raise the public's awareness of the cause that they support – Mencap, for example, campaigns in support of those suffering mental illness

- to raise funds to support their projects – Oxfam collects money to alleviate starvation, for example, it has spent heavily to assist the peoples of Ethiopia and Sudan in recent years.

Charities trade with the intention of earning as much revenue as possible to spend on their particular causes. Oxfam raises money to support its attempts to relieve famine across the world. Any surplus of revenue over expenditure on operating costs is used to raise further funds or is spent on providing relief for people in need.

Pressure groups operate in a similar way to charities. A **pressure group** is a collection of people who support a common cause. Well-known pressure groups such as Greenpeace and Friends of the Earth campaign to protect the environment. Less publicised are the activities of groups such as Compassion in World Farming (CIWF) which opposes the export of live animals.

Their objectives include bringing publicity to the causes they promote. For example, Greenpeace has gained much media attention for its protests over the UK trials of genetically modified crops. A carefully planned campaign has created considerable opposition to GM crops from the general public and has put pressure on the government to halt further testing until more research is completed. The GM campaign highlights the effectiveness of:

- direct action, including destroying test sites

- lobbying for support from individuals, companies and governments.

Pressure groups aim to increase the number of people who support their activities. This objective is often expressed in terms of increasing membership. Members

▼ By raising publicity for their causes, pressure groups seek to change the business objectives of companies

provide money through subscriptions and donations, and some may be prepared to support the cause through taking direct action.

Being seen to care for the environment is also an important objective for a number of businesses, and especially those who have great potential to cause environmental damage. Thus, oil companies such as Shell go to considerable lengths to publicise the ways in which they seek to avoid damaging the environment.

CASE STUDY

Shell's Pura Diesel

Diesel can offer several advantages over petrol. Fuel consumption is better and emissions of carbon dioxide – one of the gases linked to climate change – are about 15 per cent lower. Diesel engines also emit less carbon monoxide and fewer hydrocarbons than petrol engines.

But gains on some emissions typically means losses on others. Diesel engines currently emit more nitrogen and sulphur oxides, which are linked to smog, acid rain and particulates. So diesel isn't a totally environmentally friendly fuel.

However a new ultra-low sulphur diesel fuel known as Shell Pura Diesel is now available at more than 80 per cent of Shell Service Stations in the UK. Shell is the first UK retailer to make this type of diesel available across an extensive national network of service stations.

Shell Pura Diesel is six years ahead of its time as it already satisfies the European Union diesel specifications for 2005. The fuel, which replaces Shell Advanced Diesel, was launched following a successful trial at 140 sites around the M25 at the end of 1998.

Source: www.shell.co.uk

Discussion point

Developing Pura Diesel was very expensive. Suggest two reasons why Shell might have taken the decision to develop the new fuel. What other activities do oil companies engage in to present themselves as environmentally caring?

Developing a skilled workforce

One way a business can compete with its rivals is to have the most skilled workforce. A highly skilled workforce offers a number of competitive advantages:

- skilled workers are normally more productive, enabling businesses to operate more cheaply and more profitably

- training workers can increase their motivation and reduce the numbers seeking to leave the business

- a reputation for employee training can be a positive factor helping businesses to attract high calibre staff

- highly trained staff can provide customers with high quality service – this is particularly important in industries such as retailing.

▲ Many UK retailers believe that customer service provides an important competitive edge

Developing a skilled workforce is an important objective for businesses providing services. Retailers such as supermarkets and financial services businesses such as banks believe that providing high quality customer service is a way of differentiating their companies from competitors. Pursuing such an objective may assist in attracting more customers.

Discussion point

Why might customer service be an important issue for those providing services, such as retailers and banks? Why do you think that retailers might be happy to compete on the basis of the quality of customer service, rather than in other ways?

Customer service – the new competitive weapon

Over 53,000 staff at Tesco have recently completed a major retraining programme. This represents a further attempt by the UK's largest retailer to improve the quality of the service provided to shoppers in its stores. In the past managers have felt that Tesco staff have been too shy and unwilling to be positive in offering advice and support to customers. Hence the major drive to provide customers with a better experience.

Tesco is not alone in its belief that the way to attract more customers (and more profits) is to focus on developing and enhancing the relationship between staff and customers. Richard Branson's Virgin Group and the London-based sandwich bar chain Pret a Manger have increased sales and market share through high-quality customer care. Research in the United States in the early 1990s revealed that happy and committed staff results in happy and loyal customers. Research in the UK has shown that satisfied staff providing high quality service can increase sales at supermarkets by up to £200,000 per month.

Pret a Manger has designed a set of rules intended to produce the right psychological impact upon consumers. Research has shown that touching a customer's hand when returning change and saying something like 'see you soon' means customers leave with a better impression of the business. This also means that they are more likely to come back. All Pret a Manger employees have to follow the company's rules when dealing with customers.

Other employers do not wish to use such a regimented approach to contact with customers. Some believe that much of the relationship with employers is non-verbal. The way the employee stands, the amount of eye contact and facial expressions are all thought to be vital. The John Lewis Partnership tells its staff to deal with customers as they would wish to be treated themselves. Some UK managers believe that taking an American approach to customer care might involve too much showmanship and that this may prove to be unpopular with British shoppers who see it as superficial.

Observers of trends in Britain's high street note that the increasing importance of customer service is being reflected in mission statements. Previously they used to refer to efficiency and profitability. More modern statements explore the importance of the relationship between staff and customers. For many businesses in the service sector this is the most important focus.

Adapted from *The Guardian*, 28 October 1999

Producing high quality products

Just as many businesses seek to provide high quality service, a large number of businesses also have the provision of high quality products as an important objective. Companies such as Rolls Royce and Aga have reputations for supplying products that are well designed, carefully constructed and represent high quality. Acquiring a reputation for top quality can allow businesses to charge a premium price and to enjoy higher profits. Reputations for supplying quality products are jealously guarded.

Quality can come in a number of forms. The Body Shop has a reputation for providing environmentally friendly products. The company does not test any of its cosmetics on animals, does not exploit communities in the developing world and always uses sustainable sources for materials such as timber. In this way, The Body Shop has gained a reputation for quality in a rather different sense, its products are known for their environmental quality.

▲ The Body Shop has a reputation for environmental quality

Organisational cultures

Culture describes the values and beliefs of the people who make up an organisation. An organisation's culture will be displayed in the attitudes of its staff and the ways in which they interact with other people such as customers, suppliers and colleagues. It will also be shown by the way that decisions are taken and in the management style used throughout the organisation. It is, in short, the way an organisation does things.

Organisational cultures are neither static nor permanent. They develop over time in response to many factors. Various types of organisational culture exist and we shall describe the most common cultures using a categorisation developed by business guru Charles Handy in his 1993 book *Understanding Organisations*.

Role culture

Many businesses have traditionally operated in a bureaucratic manner, relying upon agreed procedures and strict hierarchy and roles within the organisation. Within these traditional or role cultures, employees are expected to behave conventionally. They are expected to follow the rules – individualism is discouraged. Some government departments and merchant banks operate with this type of culture. Role cultures are more likely to flourish in a stable and predictable environment.

Person-oriented culture

A person-oriented culture is characterised by a focus on fulfilling the needs of individuals within an organisation. It allows individuals freedom to shape their jobs and operate with a degree of independence. It is therefore appropriate when employees are highly skilled and motivated. This type of culture may exist within organisations staffed by professionals such as firms of accountants and solicitors.

Task culture

In some organisations, expert teams or groups are assembled to tackle particular problems or to complete projects. The focus is on solving problems. Task cultures attach importance to expertise, flexibility and creativity. Again, it is more appropriate when workers are highly skilled. A firm of management consultants might operate with a task culture, as its staff must tackle management problems in other businesses and provide solutions and ideas for improving performance.

Power culture

Power culture places considerable emphasis on personal charisma and risk-taking. It disregards procedures and values entrepreneurship. This type of culture is most common in small businesses, where a single person can have an overview of the entire organisation, and where risks are necessary if the business is to grow. As organisations get larger, it becomes more difficult to operate successfully with a power culture.

Change culture

A change culture can be highly valued in some circumstances. Change cultures are found in flexible, responsive organisations capable of adapting effectively and quickly to external stimuli. This culture can be a valuable advantage for a business operating in a highly competitive and rapidly changing market. It is a difficult culture to develop, as people do not respond well to change, particularly if it occurs regularly.

Factors influencing organisational culture

A variety of factors may shape the culture that exists within any organisation. It is normal for several influences to simultaneously determine the culture that exists within a business. However, many business analysts believe that the major determinant of culture is the external environment in which a business operates. We now look at different aspects of the external environment.

Economic influences

The economic and competitive environment in which an organisation operates is, arguably, the predominant factor affecting culture. If a business is providing goods or services in a market where customers expect high levels of customer service, then the organisation's culture will have to deliver high-quality service or the business will fail.

As the globalisation of business continues, many organisations now operate in international markets. This can encourage task and change cultures; global markets comprise many different elements and require a flexible and responsive organisational culture. Similarly, firms operating in markets with short product life cycles must be constantly innovative to develop the next generation of products, and they may adopt task cultures.

Competitive pressures have forced many businesses to move away from role cultures. Under a role culture great emphasis is given to an employee's position within the hierarchy. This was the situation within computer giant IBM in the 1980s. However, as IBM's competitors reduced costs and increased efficiency the company was forced to delayer – that is, reduce the number of levels of hierarchy in the business. Inevitably this changed the culture within IBM. In other UK sectors, privatisation has encouraged the replacement of role cultures in organisations such as the former water boards and British Gas.

The increasing size of modern business organisations – fed by mergers and takeovers – makes power cultures less common. Power culture places great responsibility on those at the centre of the organisation. Continuing to operate a power culture is more difficult as a business grows, as it becomes impossible for a single individual, or a small group, to effectively control the organisation.

Social and environmental influences

Businesses cannot remain immune from the changing views and values within society at large. As we discuss elsewhere in this unit, businesses have had to respond to the increasing demands from consumers for high-quality goods and services. This has weakened the influence of shareholders in shaping an organisation's culture.

Cultural and social values spur enterprise

Perceptions, not facts, drive entrepreneurial activity, according to a report by the London Business School. The study suggests that the major factor influencing whether businesses and individuals are entrepreneurial is perceptions of the available opportunities.

The report says that the most crucial promoters of enterprise are social values, which shape views of how many opportunities exist for businesses. The UK has relatively few business start ups because citizens are uneducated in enterprise and have few business skills. Furthermore, few people in the UK have the ambition to start their own businesses.

The UK comes well down a European league table of enterprise with businesses having a less entrepreneurial culture than those in other countries.

Adapted from *Daily Telegraph*, 20 December 1999

Discussion point

What benefits might the UK receive if its citizens are more entrepreneurial and its businesses develop a more entrepreneurial culture?

Society's views influence business in other ways. For example, increased public awareness of environmental issues has forced businesses to be aware of, and responsive to, the impact of their activities on the environment. This has affected the processes within many businesses as well as shaped the products they sell. Increased concern for the environment may encourage businesses to adopt task cultures.

Public opinion can also impact on businesses and their culture through the political process. Government legislation, framed in part in response to concerns raised by voters, affects the activities of private businesses in relation to advertising, employment and production, for example. Businesses may have to change the way they operate to comply with new legislation. Closer government regulation of businesses may discourage (or impede) power cultures and perhaps encourage a move towards role or task cultures.

Ethical influences

Ethics have played a more influential role in the activities of businesses in recent years. Legislation in respect of issues such as equal opportunities for all employees has played a part in this trend. However, a more ethical approach has also been encouraged to some extent by the expectations of businesses held by many groups in society.

Ethical factors have, perhaps, prompted moves away from person-oriented cultures. Ethical approaches demand that the values an organisation adopts are held by all employees, and reflected in their actions. The degree of individualism that may exist within a person-oriented culture makes it improbable that all employees act with the same ethical intentions. The changing demands on employees required by ethical approaches may not be easily introduced into a role culture.

Other influences

Internal factors play a role in shaping the structure and culture of an organisation. Perhaps the most influential factor is the history and tradition of a business. If, for example, a business has operated a role culture for some considerable time, then it may be difficult to change the company's culture. Individuals tend to resist change and it can be tricky to alter an organisation's culture.

The size of the business also is a factor. Small businesses are more likely to operate a power culture as it is possible for a single person to control such an organisation. The ownership of the organisation is also a determinant: organisations in the public sector are more likely to have role cultures, private sector businesses in highly competitive markets are more likely to find task cultures appropriate.

Culture and objectives

There are clear links between the culture of a business and the objectives that it may pursue. These relationships are set out in Figure 1.4 (see p. 14).

▼ Fairtrade's objectives include adopting an ethical approach in its dealings with suppliers in the developing world

Figure 1.4: Relationship between business culture and business objectives

Culture	Probable objectives
Power culture	Businesses with power cultures are likely to be small with strong, charismatic leaders. Their objectives will essentially be the objectives of those at the centre of the organisation: ■ survival ■ growth ■ profit maximisation ■ increasing market share.
Role culture	Organisations possessing a role culture will be more likely to be traditional and, perhaps, in the public sector. Their objectives will include: ■ providing services to the community ■ developing a skilled workforce ■ offering high quality products and services.
Task culture	Task culture is a way of getting things done and is appropriate for businesses in highly competitive and innovative industries. These business may seek to: ■ supply high-quality products and services ■ maximise profits ■ increase sales or market share ■ survive (maybe).
Person-oriented culture	Person-oriented culture places great importance on the individuals within the organisation. They are valued for their skills, their professionalism, their creativity and ingenuity. Organisations with this culture might: ■ provide services to the community ■ develop a skilled workforce ■ offer high-quality products and services.
Change culture	Not included in Handy's original categorisation, change cultures are valuable for businesses trading in highly competitive and flexible markets. Objectives include: ■ making a profit ■ increasing sales or market share ■ surviving.

BUILD YOUR LEARNING

Keywords and phrases

You should know the meaning of the words and phrases listed below. Go back through the last 11 pages of the unit to check or refresh your understanding as necessary.

- Business objectives
- Change culture
- Culture
- Economies of scale
- Market share
- Mission statements
- Person-oriented culture
- Power culture
- Pressure group
- Profit maximisation
- Role culture
- Satisficing
- Stakeholders
- Task culture

Summary points

- Businesses state their overall purpose in their mission statement. Commonly these statements reflect their desire to satisfy as many stakeholders as possible.

- Businesses pursue a range of objectives to help them to achieve their overall purpose as set out in their mission statement.

- Objectives vary according to the type of business. For example, a charity may pursue the objective of highlighting a particular social issue, a high street retailer may attempt to maximise profits.

- Organisational cultures influence both how firms behave and the objectives they pursue.

- Ethical issues have become much more influential over recent years. Many organisations attempt to pursue ethical objectives such as fair trading.

Types of businesses

BEFORE LOOKING AT DIFFERENT TYPES of businesses and the legal forms they can take, it is useful to begin with the important concept of **limited liability**. Regarded as a privilege, limited liability was first introduced in 1855 under the Limited Liability Act. It provides protection for the owners of the business – the **shareholders** – against unlimited personal loss. It is a major element in the legal structure of public and private companies. Partnerships and sole traders cannot benefit from limited liability. Figure 1.5 summarises which types of businesses can benefit from the privilege of limited liability.

With the protection of limited liability, a shareholder's financial liability is limited to the amount of capital that he or she has invested in the business. If a shareholder invests £20,000 in either a public or a private limited company and the company fails, all the shareholder can lose is that £20,000 investment.

There is one important caveat – any further funds promised by the shareholder are not protected by limited liability. If, say, £50,000 has been promised and only £35,000 has been contributed, the shareholder can be asked for the remaining £15,000. For example, when British Telecommunications was privatised, investors paid for their shares in three instalments. The first payment secured ownership of the shares; in the unlikely event of British Telecommunications failing at this time, shareholders would have been legally obliged to make the final two payments.

Business organisations which have no limited liability, such as partnerships and sole traders, must explore all ways of meeting liabilities. If a sole trader's business fails with significant sums owing to creditors, the trader may lose not just the business but also his or her house, car and personal possessions to meet as much of the debt as possible. The outcome is often bankruptcy.

Companies offering shares to the public to raise money know that limited liability is an important factor in attracting investors. It reduces the risk for individual investors and also attracts large-scale investment from financial institutions – pension funds, insurance companies, trade unions, etc. – which want to avoid taking excessive risks with their clients' or members' funds.

Not all companies choose to have limited liability. For example, a company limited by guarantee acquires the advantages of incorporation, but its members agree to meet specified sums in the event of failure. Many examination boards, for example, are limited by guarantee.

The three business sectors

Businesses within the UK economy can be classified into three sectors – the mutual, public and private sectors. Figure 1.6 sets out the type of organisations that can be found in each of the sectors. In this section, we examine in some detail the types of businesses that are to be found in each of the three sectors.

The private sector

The private sector encompasses businesses and organisations that are owned by individuals or groups of individuals.

Sole traders

A sole trader (or sole proprietor) exists where a single person owns a business. This is a very common form of organisation in the UK. Over recent years, the number

Figure 1.5: The scope of limited liability

Businesses with limited liability	Businesses without limited liability
Private limited companies	Sole traders
Public limited companies	Partnerships (except in special circumstances)
Cooperatives	

Figure 1.6: Structure of the UK economy

The mutual sector	The private sector	The public sector
Charities	Sole traders	Nationalised industries
Youth groups	Partnerships	Quangos
Life assurance societies	Private limited companies	Local government
Friendly societies	Public limited companies	Central government
Cooperative societies	Franchises	
Other non-profit making bodies		

of sole traders has grown significantly. There are several reasons for this trend including more opportunities to work for firms on consultancy basis and government support for self-employment. The sector continues to expand within the EU at some at 2.5 per cent annually.

Most sole traders work on their own. This need not be the case, and there is no theoretical reason why a sole trader cannot employ hundreds of staff and own several factories; however, in practice, it is unlikely that a single person could raise the amount of capital needed for this type of business. Typically sole traders are shopkeepers and market traders or they are self-employed in occupations such as plumbers, electricians, hairdressers and consultants. They are likely to trade in local or, at most, regional markets.

The essential feature of this type of business is that the sole trader has full responsibility for the financial control of his or her business, for meeting capital requirements and running costs, and full personal liability in the case of debt. He or she does not have the protection of limited liability. There is a minimum of legal regulation. However, if the business is not going to be run under the proprietor's name, then registration is required under the Business Names Act 1985.

Sole trader businesses are easy to set up. The sole trader has:

- responsibility for providing capital either from savings or a loan
- direct personal involvement
- unlimited liability
- independence
- entitlement to all of the profits but responsibility for all of the debts.

Partnerships

The Partnership Act 1890 and the Companies Act 1985 govern partnerships. The minimum membership is two partners and the maximum twenty, but the Companies

Act 1985 permits more practices of accountants and solicitors to have more than twenty partners. Mutual trust and confidence bind partners. They are jointly liable without limit (because partners do not benefit from limited liability) for each other's actions. Thus, one partner's decision or action binds the other(s). Every partner is entitled to participate in the management of the business, but some may choose not to do so. In this case, they are termed sleeping partners.

According to the Partnership Act 1890, a partnership dissolves on the death, resignation or bankruptcy of a partner, or on the agreed termination of the life and purpose of the business. In order to avoid disruption to the business, it is usual to draw up a deed of partnership to identify the ways in which the partnership will be operated. A deed might cover arrangements for sharing of profits, liabilities in case of debt, continuation after death or resignation of a member, and so on. In the absence of a deed (or partnership articles), partnership activity is governed by the 1890 Act.

The Limited Partnership Act 1907 allows a partnership to claim limited liability for some of its partners, but there must be at least one general partner who is fully liable for all debts and obligations of the practice. This is not a common type of organisation – it is easier and more advantageous to set up a limited company. It is unlikely that a single person would be willing to accept unlimited liability in these circumstances.

Partnerships exist mainly in the professions – doctors, lawyers, accountants and surveyors frequently run their organisations in the form of partnerships. This is an ideal legal structure as some professional bodies forbid their members to trade as companies. Furthermore, the professions rarely require large sums of capital to establish their practices and they do not therefore need to form a company to raise finance from investors. Partnerships normally operate in local or regional markets, though advances in information technology are allowing many professions to offer their services more widely. Solicitors, for example, use fax and e-mail to offer their services to customers throughout the UK. Some architectural partnerships undertake projects on a worldwide basis.

Companies

A company is defined as an association of persons that contributes money (or equivalent value in goods and assets) to a common stock, employ it in some trade or business, and share the profit or loss arising out of that business. Joint stock companies (as they are formally termed) are governed by and registered under the Companies Act 1985. A company has a separate legal identity from its members and can sue (or be sued) in its own name. There are two types of company: public companies and private companies. Both require a minimum of only two shareholders, and there is no upper limit on the number of shareholders. All companies enjoy the benefit of limited liability.

Private limited companies

Private limited companies are suitable for small and medium-sized operations. This type of business organisation is particularly suitable for family firms and for small enterprises involving just a handful of people. Private limited companies find it easier to attract capital because investors have the benefit of limited liability and this access to finance makes it simpler for the business to grow. In some highly specialised circumstances private limited companies may trade internationally; however, it is usual for this type of business to trade regionally and perhaps nationally.

Private limited companies:

- cannot advertise their shares for sale
- do not have their share prices quoted on stock exchanges
- always end their company name with the word limited
- may have a single director.

Some major and well-known businesses are operated as private companies. Perhaps the best-known example is Richard Branson's Virgin Group.

Public limited companies

The letters 'plc' at the end of its name distinguishes a public company from a private limited company. Most of Britain's famous businesses, such as Marks and Spencer, ICI, BP and Manchester United, are public limited companies. All companies with share prices quoted on the London Stock Exchange are public

limited companies. However, not all public limited companies are listed on the stock market; smaller public companies, unable to obtain a full listing on the London Stock Exchange, can trade their shares on the Alternative Investment Market (AIM).

To become a public limited company, a business must have an issued share capital of at least £50,000 and the company must have received at least 25 per cent of the nominal value of the shares. For example, if the shares are nominally worth 100p (that is, the face value), a company must have received a minimum of 25p per share. This regulation is designed to stop public limited companies setting up without sufficient capital. Public limited companies must also:

- be a company limited by shares
- have a memorandum of association with a separate clause stating that it is a public company
- publish an annual report and balance sheet
- ensure that its shares are freely transferable – they can be bought and sold (through stockbrokers, banks and share shops).

Quoted companies can be tracked each day by reference to the London Stock Exchange listings published in the financial pages of most newspapers.

Shares

A share is simply a certificate giving the holder ownership of part (or a share) of a company. Shareholders purchase shares. By selling large numbers of shares, companies can raise significant sums of capital. There are two main types of shares.

- Ordinary shares give a variable dividend from year to year. The dividend (a share of part of the company's profits) obviously varies according to how well the company has performed. Ordinary shares allow the shareholder a vote at the company's annual general meeting.
- Preference shares, as their name suggests, have priority over ordinary shares when it comes to paying dividends. If profits are small, holders of ordinary shares are likely to lose out and receive a very small dividend or even no dividend at all. Preference shareholders usually receive a fixed dividend.

Shares are a good way of raising capital but there are drawbacks. Shareholders have a say in the running of the company, so by selling too many shares owners can lose control of the company. Issuing shares is often administratively very expensive, which means it is only appropriate for raising very large sums of capital.

Public limited companies benefit greatly from their open access to funds. By being able to sell shares on the stock market, public limited companies experience fewer difficulties in raising capital than most other types of business. Not only can they arrange new share issues to raise capital, their high public profile also makes it easier to arrange loans from financial institutions. Because of this ability to raise enormous sums of capital, public limited companies usually have the financial resources to trade throughout the world and to compete in the toughest of markets overseas.

Registering a company

The Registrar of Companies oversees the registration procedure for companies. The Registrar must be satisfied that all statutory requirements have been fulfilled, and only then issues a **certificate of incorporation** which allows a company to start trading. It is an offence for a company to start trading or borrowing money until the certificate has been granted.

To receive a certificate of incorporation, the company provides details of its internal rules and external relationships. This information is contained within two documents, the memorandum of association and the articles of association.

The **memorandum of association** defines the constitution and powers of the company and the scope of its activities. It includes:

- the name of the company, including the word 'limited'

- the address of the company's registered office

- a statement of the company's aims

- the amount of capital the company wishes to raise

- a statement that the shareholders' liability is limited.

The articles of association govern the internal rules of the company. The articles are a contract between the company and its shareholders in respect of their ordinary rights as members. The document must provide the details of:

- the nominal capital

- when shareholders' meetings are to be held and how they are to be conducted

- the voting rights of members

- how profits and losses will be distributed

- the names of the directors

- how directors are appointed and the nature of their authority.

Franchises

A **franchise** is not a form of business organisation as such, but a way of managing and growing a business. Franchising covers a variety of arrangements under which the owner of a business idea grants other individuals or groups (known as franchisees) to trade using that name or idea. However, it is important to realise that a franchise can trade as a sole trader, a partnership or a private limited company. The legal form of business that is chosen will depend on the capital needed, the degree of risk, the number of people having a stake in the franchise and the personal preferences of the owner(s).

The person or organisation selling the idea (the franchisor) gains a number of advantages from the process of franchising. The franchisor gains an initial capital payment which, in the case of a McDonald's restaurant say, can be hundreds of thousands of pounds. The franchisor also normally receives a share of the profits generated by the franchise. Usually the franchisee benefits by being granted rights to an exclusive territory and support from the franchiser in the form of staff training, advertising and promotion.

Franchising is a cheap and quick way in which a business can grow. By the year 2004, it is estimated that 70 per cent of all new retail outlets in the US will be franchises. In the UK, the range of franchised activity is wide. It includes car dealerships, public houses, business service centres, doorstep milk deliveries, express delivery of parcels and fast food.

▲ Burger King has grown its business in the UK through franchising outlets

The mutual sector

The mutual sector comprises voluntary organisations and other mutual bodies. The **voluntary sector** is made up of non-profit making organisations such as charities and youth groups. The majority of the staff of voluntary organisations are unpaid volunteers. Other mutual organisations such as cooperative societies and friendly societies are also non-profit making, but employ a significant number of paid staff.

Cooperative societies

The cooperative movement contains a diversity of businesses – covering agriculture, engineering, retail and wholesale distribution, travel, funeral services, property, banking – organised in industrial and provident societies. The movement was established in Rochdale in 1844. Its essential purpose was to create a social organisation to offer protection from unfair trading practices and poverty. The ultimate aim was to establish a 'commonwealth' owning the means of production, distribution and exchange.

In recent years, there has been a renewal of interest in cooperative societies as an ideal business form for self-governing workshops such as studios of artists, designers and printers. There is an umbrella organisation, ICOM (Industrial Common Ownership Movement Ltd), which advises cooperative development agencies and workers' cooperatives. It has a sister organisation, ICOF (Industrial Common Ownership Finance Ltd).

The essential features of a cooperative society are:

- it is registered under the Industrial and Provident Societies Acts 1965–78 and the Companies Acts

- it has limited liability

- shares are not transferable, they can only be bought from or sold to the society

- membership is available on the purchase of one share with a nominal value of £1

- the maximum shareholding depends upon the rules of each society but it cannot exceed the £15,000 limit set by the law

- membership is voluntary and open

- society control is democratic, each member is permitted one vote regardless of shareholding

- there is equitable use of any surplus or profit

- a limited rate of interest is paid on capital.

Cooperative societies use various methods to distribute profits. After taxation and reserves, there is a distribution to members. Some money is put in a patronage fund to finance social and educational activities. Traditionally, retail societies paid members a dividend on purchases, but currently societies may choose one of fours ways of rewarding members:

- paying dividend on purchases

- issuing trading stamps

- paying interest on the share account

- issuing special offer vouchers for members.

Cooperatives, especially those in the retail sector, have faced intense competition over recent years. The increasing scale, access to capital and market dominance of supermarkets such as Tesco have meant that the cooperative stores have experienced problems in competing on prices, product range and facilities within store. The arrival of foreign retail businesses such as Wal-Mart is likely to increase these pressures.

Charities

Charities are run by full-time professionals and supported by a network of volunteers. There are more than 6,000 registered charities and voluntary organisations in the UK. They are financed by collections, flag days, donations, bequests and trading activities. Company sponsorship is also important, providing support such as rent-free accommodation, a minibus or the loan of a manager. The National Lottery also makes awards to charities.

In addition to charities, charitable trusts operate in both the private and public health and education sectors. These organisations operate as businesses but enjoy some tax advantages.

Friendly societies

Friendly societies were formed for the purpose of encouraging and managing savings to provide assistance to their members in time of need. Until the Welfare State was established, friendly societies were crucial to families that needed assistance during periods of illness or unemployment. In the 1930s, there were more than 3,000 societies, but today only a few hundred exist. Among the best known are the Royal Ancient Order of Buffaloes and the Ancient Order of Foresters. Governments continue to offer tax advantages to encourage saving with friendly societies.

Other mutual organisations

Some building societies and mutual life assurance businesses are non-profit making. Examples include the Portman Building Society and Standard Life Assurance Society. Mutual organisations have no shareholders and no owners. They operate solely in the interests of their customers (their members). Any surpluses they make are ploughed back into the business or paid to the organisation's members.

One famous example of a mutual organisation is the John Lewis Partnership, a leading retailer. John Lewis is a private company with a nominal share value of £100. It has four shareholders – the managing director has a 40 per cent holding and three trustees each hold a 20 per cent stake. The company has a structure that encourages staff participation and the profits are shared by the staff as bonuses.

▲ In spite of demutualisation, many small regional building societies remain

Most mutual societies in the UK have been under pressure to convert into public limited companies in a process known as **demutualisation**. Proponents for demutualisation have argued that building societies and life assurance companies are old fashioned, bureaucratic and ill prepared to compete in the modern world. They argue that converting to public limited companies would provide clearer objectives, such as to make profits for shareholders, and possibly better management. Members were seduced with large cash payments to approve the conversion of mutual societies to public limited companies.

The Norwich Union and the Halifax Building Society have demutualised, but there is little evidence to date that customers have received any long-term benefits from the change in ownership. However, the pressure for demutualisation is expected to continue.

CASE STUDY

Mutual admiration

About 30 million people in the UK are members of mutuals in one form or another. The mutual sector has a turnover of nearly £30 billion – a lot of money by anyone's standards. Much of our food comes from 550 agricultural cooperatives, with 243,000 members. Cooperatives produce 95 per cent of the UK's apples, 74 per cent of cauliflowers and most raspberries. Many of us still have mortgages with mutual building societies. Friendly societies are smaller than they were, but the largest 80 still have 4.76 million members and £11.4 billion under management.

A new economy is breeding new types of mutuals. Linux, the world's fastest growing software program, is available free of charge on the internet. Developed by Finnish student and adapted by other designers, nobody makes a profit from the program. Some parts of the mutual sector, particularly building societies, may be under pressure to convert to companies, but other areas are thriving.

Adapted from *The Guardian*, 27 June 1999

Discussion point

Why do people continue to invest in, and shop with, mutual organisations? What arguments might those running mutual organisations use when persuading potential customers to do business with them?

The public sector

The public sector comprises all organisations that are owned by the state. Public sector organisations might be controlled by central or local government and include organisations such as the Post Office, the National Health Service, universities and the few remaining nationalised industries (or public corporations). Despite the transfer of many activities from the public to the private sector, it remains a significant sector of activity within the UK economy.

Recent UK governments have sold many parts of the public sector, with industries such as coal mining and the railways now being owned and managed by private sector companies. This process of selling public sector organisations and assets to individuals and businesses in the private sector is known as **privatisation**. In addition to selling state-owned assets, the privatisation policy has also sought to introduce competition into sectors that were the province of state-owned monopolies. For example, private sector organisations can now operate bus services and manufacture and sell telephone equipment.

The privatisation programme was intended to raise large sums of money for the government, allowing it to reduce the rates of taxation. It was also intended to promote greater efficiency in industries such as coal mining, electricity generation and telephone services. Its success might be judged by the fact that countries throughout the world have imitated the UK's privatisation programme.

Central government

Central government comprises ministries and departments which establish policies and administer public services. Government activity has to be funded from taxation and other sources. It raises revenue from direct personal and corporate taxation, indirect taxes (VAT, customs and excise duties), sale of public assets (privatisation), motor vehicle tax, national insurance contributions and national savings. The government also borrows money. It issues gilt-edged stock, enabling private investors to loan money to the government. The European Union may make some financial contributions, particularly to assist declining areas (where, for example, traditional coal, steel and shipbuilding industries have declined or been closed) with employment creation projects.

Local government

Local government is an important part of country's democratic structure. Councils and local authorities are responsible for education, social services, police, fire, consumer protection, public transport, highways and many other local services within their own area. Local government is funded by council tax, government grants, loans and revenue generated by charges for services.

Local government is also funded through taxation on businesses. Business rates are levied on all commercial properties and paid to central government. This money is reallocated to local councils in accordance with a formula based on population and the level of services. District councils are the tax raising authorities.

Quangos

Quango stands for quasi-autonomous non-governmental organisation. The rationale for quangos is to provide some assistance to ministers and their departments in the formulation and application of policies. Lay people with particular expertise are appointed to quangos. There are some 40,000 public appointments to quangos; approximately 10,000 people are appointed or reappointed every year. The work can be unpaid or paid, and varies from one day a month to a full-time commitment. Examples of quangos include tribunals, public corporations (such as the BBC) and advisory bodies (on, for example, the environment, health and agriculture). Anyone wishing to work on a quango can submit an application to the Public Appointments Unit. The unit circulates a list to the various government departments responsible for the appointments.

Changing business ownership

Our analysis of the legal forms of business has been static. In the real world, private sector businesses regularly change their structure, particularly as they increase their size. For example, a business may start life as a sole trader, but if it grows it will adopt other legal forms, primarily to raise capital, but also to be able to hire expertise.

When businesses change their legal structure (or type of ownership) they have to take into account a number of implications. Businesses can gain significant privileges as they grow and adopt new legal structures. However, with these privileges come responsibilities.

Limited liability

One of the attractions for a business of moving from a non-corporate structure (sole trader or partnership) to a corporate structure (limited company) is that the business gets the advantage of limited liability. As we discussed earlier in this section, this means that the organisation's owners only put at risk the money they actually invest into the enterprise. They do not risk their entire personal wealth to meet all the company's debts.

A further significant benefit for businesses is that they are able to raise capital more easily under the protection of limited liability. Investors are more willing to purchase shares on the understanding that they only risk the sum they invest. Without this protection, the high degree of risk can put off potential investors.

Sources of finance

As businesses change their structures other and new sources of finance become available to them. Figure 1.7 summarises the key sources of finance available to different types of business. You can see, for example, a business converting to a corporate form and becoming a company can issue shares to raise capital. This is an important source of finance for businesses and a vital engine of growth.

Control of organisations

The control of business organisations inevitably becomes more complex as a business grows. The process of controlling a sole trader is simple. A single person owns the business, and that person takes all the decisions; he or she has complete control.

A partnership has slightly more complicated arrangements. Most partnerships have a deed of partnership setting out the amount of capital to be contributed by each partner and the proportion in which profits will be shared. The deed also states the proportion of any loss to be borne by each partner. Major decisions within partnerships involve debate and majority decisions, which is one of the reasons why partnerships are noted for their arguments. Responsibility is shared within partnerships: all partners are responsible for the decisions of any one partner. This can be significant in an organisation where partners are unlikely to have limited liability.

In companies, control is more complex. Considerable power and influence resides with the directors. There are two types of directors.

■ **Executive directors** are normally employees of the company, holding a senior managerial position. Directors are elected to the board of directors by the shareholders to represent their views in corporate decision-making.

■ **Non-executive directors** are not employed by the company and are usually only part-time appointments. They are selected for their particular expertise and, perhaps, their contacts and connections. Non-executive directors often include politicians, scientists and senior managers from other organisations.

In 1992, the Cadbury Committee proposed a voluntary agreement to extend and reinforce the role of non-executive directors in the control of companies in 1992. The intention was to encourage more ethical corporate decision-making following a series of business scandals. Business analysts have expressed doubts over the effectiveness of this reform.

Figure 1.7: Sources of finance

Type of business	Primary sources of finance
Sole trader	Own savings and those of family and friends
	Redundancy pay
	Inheritances
	Loans (but only for relatively small sums)
Partnership	Savings of partners as well as relatives and friends
	Inheritances
	Loans (somewhat easier for partners to arrange)
Private limited company	Selling shares (but requires approval of existing shareholders)
	Loans from banks and other financial institutions
	Business profits
Public limited company	Selling shares freely on the stock market
	Raising loans – public limited companies are able to use a variety of financial institutions
	Retained profits – this is a major source of finance for public limited companies
Non-profit making organisation	Surpluses from trading activities
	Grants from local and central government and other public bodies
	Donations from charities
	Support from other companies

The ultimate control of private and public limited companies lies, at least in theory, with the shareholders. A small private limited company might only have a handful of shareholders, all of whom would also be directors; each shareholder would have a direct say in the day-to-day operation of the business. In these circumstances power lies with the shareholder(s) who holds the majority of the shares. An individual owning over fifty per cent of the shares of a company is in control.

In some larger private limited companies and most public limited companies, shareholders elect directors (some of whom are employed by the company) to represent their views on the board of directors. The board takes all the important decisions within a limited company. Shareholders have an opportunity to vote on the performance of the board and the directors at a company's annual general meeting (AGM).

Discussion point

Obtain a company's annual report and accounts and look up the names and roles of the directors of the company. How many are executive and how many are non-executive directors? Looking at the description of the non-executive directors, can you explain why these particular people have been selected for the role?

Public limited companies can suffer from what is known as a **divorce of ownership from control**. This means that the people who own companies (the shareholders) do not necessarily control them. In theory, shareholders should be able to control companies by attending annual general meetings and voting on key issues and policies to determine the company's future strategy. In practice, this does not happen for a several reasons:

- many individuals with small holdings of shares do not attend meetings that may take place many miles away

- many shareholders have limited knowledge of business management and do not take an active role in AGMs even if they attend

- managing a modern, large company requires more regular involvement than most shareholders can make.

Effective control of larger companies therefore lies in the hands of the directors of the company. They have a day-to-day involvement with the company and a vested interest in its well-being. Although the shareholders own the business, the directors effectively control it.

Cooperatives and friendly societies are controlled in similar ways. The members of these organisations vote democratically on important decisions. The arrangements for voting reflect the socialist origins of cooperatives. Each member of the society has one vote irrespective of the amount of money that they have invested into the organisation.

The majority of organisations in the public sector have directors appointed to manage the business, set strategy and oversee daily operations. However, government departments and ministers are likely to be consulted on major decisions.

Using profits

The owners of sole traders and partnerships decide what is to be done with any profits generated by their businesses. Normally this decision entails whether to reinvest any surplus funds.

Companies face essentially the same decision. Most companies are obliged to publish an appropriation account as part of their annual report and accounts stating what they have done with their profits after tax and interest have been paid. Companies can choose to pay profits to shareholders in the form of dividends. Alternatively, they may hold profits within the company for reinvestment. Companies usually combine these options, distributing a proportion of profits to shareholders and retaining the rest to reinvest within the company.

Cooperatives and friendly societies distribute profits to their members. Often the share of profits members receive is proportional to the amount they have spent or invested with the society.

Legal liabilities

Sole traders and partnerships are **unincorporated** organisations. This means that they do not benefit from limited liability and the owners of the business are not legally separate from the business itself. This means that the sole trader or partners are legally responsible for the actions of the business. They are also financially responsible for any debts incurred by business and their personal possessions are therefore at risk.

Companies and cooperatives have a different legal position. They are **incorporated** and, in legal terms, the business and its owners (shareholders and members) are separate. This means that the owners are not legally responsible for all the activities of the business. In other words, if an individual or an organisation has a grievance against a company, they would take legal action against the company not against the owners of the company.

Discussion point

Research the meaning of the term 'business angel'. Discuss the reasons that might have persuaded Jane Warren (see article below) to run her business as a franchise.

How business partnerships turn sour

by Rachel Simpson

When Jane Warren took on a new business partner she hoped it would be the beginning of a beautiful friendship. At the time her educational toys firm Formative Fun (now a profitable franchise operation) was struggling in the recession. It had just made a loss of £74,000, and cash flow was dire, so she began a hunt for a business angel.

She was delighted when she found one – a man with a degree in marketing and experience of working abroad. In 1995 he invested £15,000 in the company with an agreement that as soon as the business was back on track he would be able seek to increase the business's exports. But within nine months the relationship had turned sour. The situation was eventually settled through solicitors when she paid him back the money he had invested and he quit the firm.

According to Dr Thelma Quince, a researcher at Cambridge University, such tales are all too common when relationships fail between business partners. She has been studying the subject for an entrepreneurship PhD. In her survey of 380 new firms in East Anglia she found that the level of break-ups among partners in new businesses was as high as the level of divorce – two out of every five.

A perfect partnership can turn into a business disaster. Establish the ground rules before you set up a company is the advice from many people who have taken on business partners.

"I discovered there is an awful lot of misery out there," she says. "Many of the people I spoke to told me that the break-up of a business partnership was worse than divorce – and some had even contemplated suicide."

Dr Quince was amazed to discover just how high tensions can run when such relationships fail. She came across one man who is now running his father's firm while his father is in prison for attempting to murder his business partner. She recalls another man who had set up a technical services company with his wife and his best friend. "He told me: 'My best friend is not my best friend any more. And she's now his wife'."

Dr Quince originally wanted to study firms founded collaboratively and see what was helping them do well. She says: "The myth still exists that entrepreneurs are all individuals only out for personal gain. But in fact collaboration between them is far more common than we suppose – 60 per cent of the firms I surveyed were started up jointly by people in twos or threes."

But it is when these partnerships fail that the business suffers. In her survey, 10 per cent of the firms where the partners had broken up had either been sold or closed down; and in half of these firms the problems had affected staff morale.

"This is the downside of collaboration," says Dr Quince. "The upside is that small firms where entrepreneurs are collaborating are actually more likely to survive. The key to knowing whether you'll have a successful partnership is to ask if you and your partner are both committed to the same values and beliefs." Clearly it is important that partners are pursuing the same objectives.

Stephen Alambritis, of the Federation of Small Businesses, agrees. "Enthusiasm alone is not enough," he says. "Too many partnerships start on little more than a wing and a prayer, or a handshake. But although they start rosily, they end in acrimony."

Mr Alambritis says that the cracks often start to show when a new business first experiences some success and the money starts coming in. At that point there is often tension between two partners over how the profits should be split – especially if one of them supplied the idea and the other, who put in the initial finance, is reaping a greater financial reward.

To prevent this, he says: "Partners should have an agreement between them drawn up by solicitors at the beginning. That lays down how the profits will be split as well as other issues – like what happens when one partner wants to leave."

But while solicitors can offer legal advice to business partners there is very little emotional support available to them when they split. The small business support organisations can offer the services of business angels but not of the agony aunts who are sometimes badly needed.

The Guardian, 6 July 1999

BUILD YOUR LEARNING

Keywords and phrases

You should know the meaning of the words and phrases listed below. Go back through the last 10 pages of the unit to check or refresh your understanding as necessary.

- Articles of association
- Business rates
- Certificate of incorporation
- Cooperative societies
- Deed of partnership
- Demutualisation
- Directors
- Franchise
- Friendly societies
- Limited liability
- Incorporated
- Memorandum of association
- Mutual sector
- Ordinary share
- Partnership
- Preference share
- Private limited company
- Private sector
- Privatisation
- Public limited company
- Public sector
- Quangos
- Sleeping partner
- Sole trader
- Shareholders
- Unincorporated
- Voluntary sector

Summary points

- The owners of incorporated businesses receive the privilege of limited liability, protecting their personal possessions.

- Businesses within the UK economy can be classified into mutual, public and private sectors. The private sector is by far the largest and most influential.

- Companies exist in two forms: private and public. Public companies are far larger and can sell their shares on the stock market.

- The mutual sector includes friendly and building societies. Many building societies have demutualised over recent years.

- Privatisation, the policy of selling off state-owned businesses, has reduced the size and influence of the public sector.

- Although shareholders own companies, effective control of these organisations – particularly in very large companies – lays in the hands of the directors.

Organisational functions

ALL ORGANISATIONS REQUIRE resources to carry out their functions. One way of judging the success of a business is to compare the resources it uses with the value of the product that results. We shall consider this in more detail in a later unit. For now, we shall concentrate on the resources used by business and the functions that comprise business activity.

The resources of business

One way of considering the resources used by a business is to classify them into the factors of production. The main factors of production are capital, labour and land.

- Capital refers to any manufactured product used by the business to make other products. This category therefore includes all machinery, vehicles and office equipment used in businesses. It also includes the company's buildings.

- Labour is the human resource used by business organisations during production. It refers to the input of physical or mental activity by employees.

- Land in the context of this classification is not only the site on which the business is located, but also all the natural resources it might use. So resources consumed by the business, such as coal, gas, oil and water, are classified as land.

Some economists would add enterprise to this list of factors of production. Enterprise refers to the role of the people who risk their money in establishing and operating a business. The other resources – capital, labour and land – would not be put to use without the catalyst of entrepreneurs willing to invest their money and to take a risk. Figure 1.8 shows the four factors of production contributing to business activity.

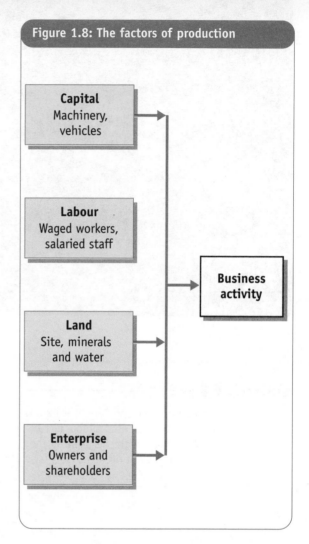

Figure 1.8: The factors of production

Of course, different businesses do not require factors of production in the same amounts or proportions to undertake their activities. The extraction of gas from the southern sector of the North Sea requires a huge investment in capital by oil companies as well as the deployment of highly skilled (and highly paid) engineers, geologists and other employees.

At the other extreme, a small craft business manufacturing furniture would also use all the factors of production, albeit in much smaller quantities. The craftsperson would use capital in the form of tools, he or she would provide the labour, and the land would be represented by the wood used in making the furniture. So, all businesses use factors of production – even if in vastly different quantities.

Discussion point

How might the quantities of the factors of production vary between a small firm of solicitors and a car manufacturer, such as Vauxhall? What rewards do entrepreneurs receive in return for taking a risk and investing their money in to a business?

▲ Oil extraction in the North Sea

A word about capital

Capital has a number of meanings in business. An economist would define it as a factor of production, as we have done above. Under this definition, capital includes money, but relates specifically to capital equipment, such as machinery, vehicles and equipment.

Accountants would use the term capital to mean the funds that are invested in a business. Shareholders contribute share capital and lenders, such as banks, provide loan capital. This capital is used to purchase assets in order that the business can operate.

There is a link here, however. Both definitions see capital as a way in which wealth is stored – whether as money or the assets that money can purchase.

The functions of business

All businesses combine factors of production as an essential part of their production activities. To combine these factors, to engage in production and to achieve their objectives organisations undertake a number of functions. The major business functions include:

- finance
- production
- human resources
- marketing
- administration
- research and development.

Not all organisations have separate departments to deal with these functions. Small businesses might merge many of these functions within their administration department, with responsibility in the hands of one or two people. As a business grows the number of people required to carry out these functions increases. Simultaneously, the business is more likely to employ specialists to carry out functions such as managing finance and marketing.

Even in large firms the relative importance of different functions varies. Large service organisations such as insurance companies do not have research and development departments to conduct scientific research, although their marketing department will undertake marketing research to discover the views of consumers on their products. Compare this with the research effort of a major pharmaceutical company such as SmithKline Beecham.

CASE STUDY

Research at SmithKline Beecham

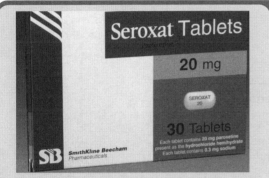

SmithKline Beecham employs approximately 5,000 scientists and support specialists at centres in Philadelphia, USA and Harlow, UK.

The company's research has resulted in drugs and treatments that have improved the lives of people suffering from a number of diseases, including cancer, arthritis, congestive heart failure, Parkinson's disease and depression. The company has also developed vaccines for hepatitis A and B, diphtheria and whooping cough.

SmithKline Beecham's research and development facilities in Europe are concentrated in the UK at New Frontiers Science Park (NFSP) in Harlow, Essex. Opened in 1997, this is a flagship research and development site and represents an investment of around £250 million. It has been designed to give employees access to the very latest in laboratory design and research and development technology.

Source: Adapted from SmithKline Beecham website
http://www.sb.com/rd

Discussion point

What are the possible advantages and disadvantages to SmithKline Beecham of investing large sums of money into research and development?

The finance function

A separate department normally carries out the finance function of the business. The finance department carries out a number of key activities. These are summarised in Figure 1.9.

- The finance department records all the financial activities of the business, listing the revenue earned by the business and the expenditure necessary for production.

- Employees in the finance department monitor the expenditure of all parts of the business and advise if expenditure appears to be too high.

- They oversee customer accounts to ensure that the business receives the money to which it is entitled and is therefore able to pay its own bills.

- Employees in the finance department may interpret financial data for senior and middle managers to ensure that decision-making is based on the most up-to-date information possible.

- The finance department also provides financial information about the company to important external bodies, including the Inland Revenue which collects corporation and income tax and HM Customs and Excise which collects VAT.

- Accountants in the finance department analyse the costs incurred by the business and compute standard costs associated with various aspects of the firm's activity. Standard costs are the normal (or average) costs associated with a particular activity, such as the typical cost of manufacturing a specific component. This data helps businesses to forecast production costs with greater accuracy.

- The finance department provides information to firms of accountants auditing the business's financial records. Auditors are employed to confirm a business's accounts are a true and fair statement of its activities.

Discussion point

Look at Figure 1.9 and identify three other departments within the company (not listed on the diagram) with whom the finance department would be likely to have close and regular contact. Why might this be the case?

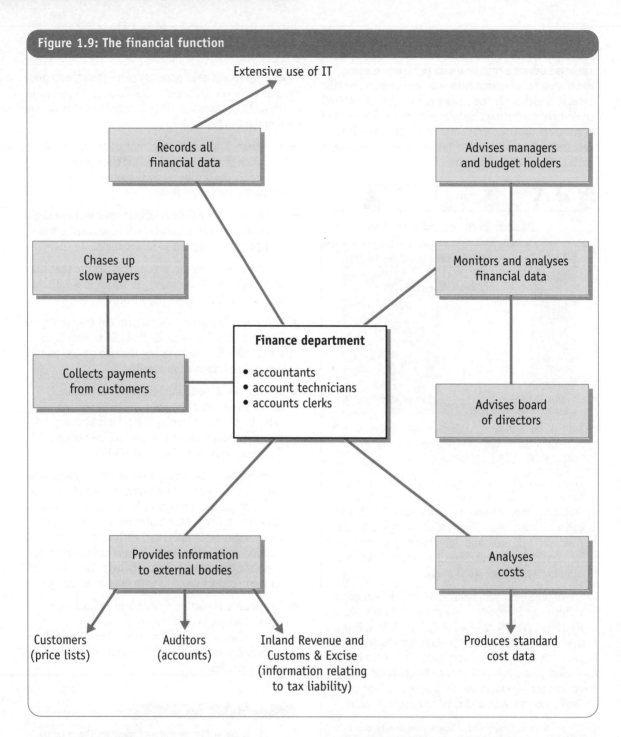

Figure 1.9: The financial function

Changes in the financial function

Clearly financial departments vary enormously from organisation to organisation. However, financial functions are changing within many modern businesses. There are two principal factors underlying the changes that are taking place: the implementation of policies intended to involve more people in the management of finance and the increasing use of information technology.

Policies like delayering, which we discuss later in this unit (see p. 51), involve more people in the finance function. Delayering involves a business reducing the number of levels of hierarchy in its organisation, often by removing middle managers from the organisational structure. This has meant that employees lower down the organisation have greater authority and greater control over their working lives. As a consequence, many relatively junior employees now have responsibility for financial management and planning within their work area. This is a significant change and means that the finance department has greater responsibilities for:

- training non-specialist employees in managing finances
- supporting colleagues on an ongoing basis
- monitoring financial decisions of a large number of colleagues.

These changes have been made possible, in part, due to advances in information technology. The use of standard computer packages such as spreadsheets, as well as more specialist software, has meant that it is possible to provide much more detailed information quickly and cheaply to employees throughout an organisation. Most businesses operate a management information system to supply financial (and non-financial information such as sales data) to all employees.

The importance of the financial function

The financial function is vital to the wellbeing of all organisations. The consequences of the failure of the financial function to carry out its duties efficiently are significant and potentially disastrous.

- Costs, if not monitored, could easily escalate causing the business to incur a loss.
- Customers may be slow to pay, or may even not pay at all. By losing income in this way, the organisation may be unable to pay for raw materials and labour, possibly leading to the business's failure.
- Directors and managers may not be able to take effective decisions without detailed information. For example, it is important to know which products are the most profitable when a business is deciding which aspects of its operation to expand.
- Slow payment (or non-payment) of the organisation's suppliers might result in the ending of trade credit, the period of grace a business is allowed before paying its bills. Suppliers may even refuse to continue to trade with a firm that does not pay promptly.

Accurate financial information is essential in allowing an organisation to maximise profits, achieve sustained growth, maximise revenue from sales and meet other business objectives.

The production function

Production covers all the activities that must be undertaken to make the firm's products, from the receipt of raw materials through to the output of the final product. The production function concentrates primarily upon planning and controlling the various stages of production so that the most efficient use is made of the business's resources.

The nature of the production process inevitably depends upon the scale and size of the business and the type of product. Production of many goods (as opposed to services) is frequently undertaken on a production line. A large-scale producer of motor vehicles, such as Vauxhall at Luton, manufactures many similar, though not identical, vehicles on a production line.

Important issues for production managers in a manufacturing environment include:

- maintaining supplies of components and raw materials to ensure continuous production – production managers use stock control systems to keep track of stocks of raw materials and finished products held by firms.
- ensuring that the precise requirements of customers are met – few modern companies can follow Henry Ford's policy that customers could have 'any car they liked so long as it is black'
- monitoring quality to ensure that finished products meet the quality standards expected by customers
- using resources – people, machinery and production space – as efficiently as possible to make the business competitive in the markets in which it trades.

Production is important within service industries as well. Although businesses such as banks, insurance companies and internet service providers do not supply physical goods that can be seen or held, they do have to organise their resources to meet customer demands as completely as possible.

One of the most important issues in production is quality. Modern businesses compete just as strongly on the quality of their goods and services as they do on price. For example, it is vital for a washing machine manufacturer to produce a high-quality product. If the machine is not reliable or does not have a wide range of functions, customers are more likely to purchase a competitor's product. Exactly the same demands are placed on a bank. It has to offer customers efficient and high-quality financial services, such as cheap banking, widely available cash machines and a range of associated financial products such as insurance, pensions and life assurance.

Many firms rely on a reputation for quality to maintain and increase their market share. Dissatisfied customers are often lost for ever, and they may persuade other consumers not to purchase from a company that has supplied an unsatisfactory product. As UK markets become more open to competition from foreign producers, quality is likely to become an even more important factor in winning business.

Another consideration for business is product differentiation. Increasingly customers expect to buy products that meet their exact needs. This complicates the production task for businesses. Companies are moving away from the mass production of standard products and adopting a more complex process of production to achieve a greater range of differentiated products.

Links with other departments

Although production has links with a number of other departments within the business, some relationships are particularly critical. The finance department has to make sure that production is carried out within agreed costs. If production costs escalate then profits may be eroded. The relationship between finance and production must therefore be strong and effective if the business is to meet its profit objectives.

The relationship between production and marketing is vital to the success of most businesses. Marketing can provide production with crucial information and what customers actually want. The marketing department can liaise with production in testing any new products on a sample of customers and feedback opinions to

Figure 1.10: The links between the production function and other departments

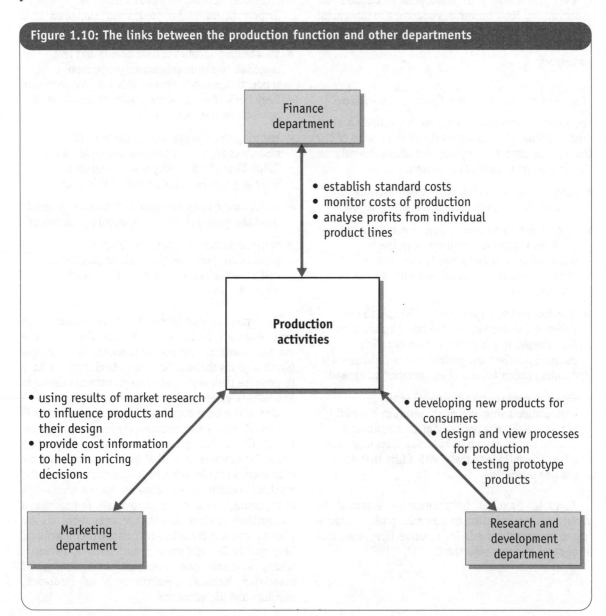

Finance department

- establish standard costs
- monitor costs of production
- analyse profits from individual product lines

Production activities

- using results of market research to influence products and their design
- provide cost information to help in pricing decisions

- developing new products for consumers
- design and view processes for production
- testing prototype products

Marketing department

Research and development department

ensure the final product is acceptable to consumers. For example, a few years ago Coca-Cola introduced a new recipe that did not prove popular with consumers. More market research and closer links between production and marketing may have avoided this situation. Communication between these two departments or functions can also assist businesses in setting prices to make sure a profit is earned.

The human resource function

In modern businesses, human resource management is now taking on the role previously carried out by personnel management. There is a very clear distinction between personnel management and human resource management. **Personnel management** considers the tasks involved in managing people – recruitment, selection and so forth – as separate elements. It does not take into account how these elements can combine to achieve organisational objectives. The personnel management approach makes decisions relating to recruitment, training and pay systems independently, without considering the impact the individual decisions have on each other aspects of management and the achievement of corporate objectives.

In contrast, **human resource management** (HRM) elevates the effective use of a business's labour force to an issue to be considered by senior managers as an essential element of the organisation's strategy. This approach has raised the profile (and salaries) of those employed in human resource management.

The human resource function engages in a number of activities to ensure employees are utilised effectively. These activities are carried out with the aim of contributing to the achievement of the business's objectives. The organisation's need for employees is regularly monitored and incorporated into a **workforce plan** (see Figure 1.11). This sets out likely future needs for labour and how (through training and recruitment) these needs might be met. In order to fulfil the workforce plan, managers responsible for human relations audit existing human resources and put into action a plan to develop the right number of employees with the correct skills to take the organisation forward.

Discussion point

Before drawing up a human resource plan, what areas of the business would need to be consulted?

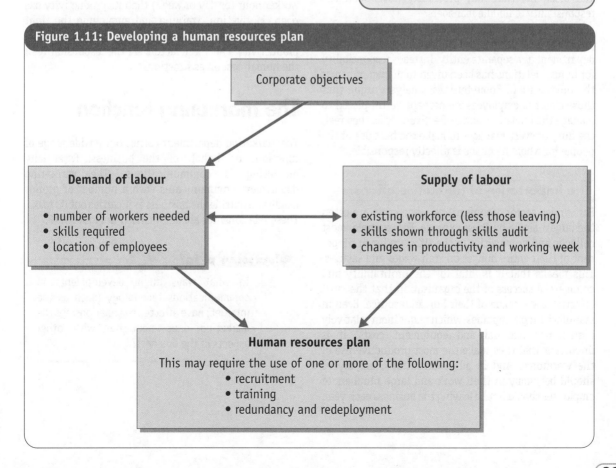

Figure 1.11: Developing a human resources plan

Corporate objectives

Demand of labour
- number of workers needed
- skills required
- location of employees

Supply of labour
- existing workforce (less those leaving)
- skills shown through skills audit
- changes in productivity and working week

Human resources plan
This may require the use of one or more of the following:
- recruitment
- training
- redundancy and redeployment

Achieving the workforce plan involves the human resource function in a number of day-to-day activities.

- recruiting employees – both internally and externally

- training new and existing employees

- paying salaries

- dealing with disciplinary matters and grievances

- overseeing industrial relations, by seeking to avoid disputes and maintain harmonious relations and constant production.

- developing and monitoring an employee appraisal system designed to assess performance, set targets for achievement and identify any training needs.

Issues in human relations

Apart from the shift away from a straightforward personnel function, human relations within businesses have seen a number of other changes. The trend for delayering (see p. 51) has changed the responsibilities of those working in human resource management. In some organisations, the human relations function must now cope with matters such as training, recruitment and discipline that may previously have been the responsibility of middle managers.

Other organisations, inspired by Japanese business practices, have decided not to have a human relations department as a separate entity. Instead, responsibility for human relations has been given to managers across the organisation. Some business analysts argue that those closer to employees are perhaps better placed to manage the human resource effectively. It is, they feel, the duty of every manager to make the best use of the people for whom he or she is directly responsible.

The importance of human relations

For service sector organisations, wage costs are often the largest single business expense. For example, most colleges and universities in the UK spend over 65 per cent of their entire budget on staff wages and salaries. This means that it is vital for the profitability and commercial success of the organisation that the most effective use is made of their human resource. Even in manufacturing companies, which might incur relatively higher raw material and equipment costs, it is important that they make the most productive use of the workforce. And in all organisations, employees should be happy in their work and large numbers of employees should not be leaving the business each year.

Productivity

Productivity is an important concept in business studies. It refers to the relationship between the inputs into a business, such as labour and capital equipment, and the outputs, the final product or service. A business increases its productivity if it can increase output from a given amount of input; or, alternatively, reduce input while maintaining the quantity of output. If the business can achieve greater output from each worker each day, its productivity will have risen. Making machines work faster can also improve productivity.

Labour productivity is calculated by use of the formula:

$$\text{labour productivity} = \frac{\text{output (per year)}}{\text{number of workers}}$$

Raising productivity offers businesses substantial competitive advantages. A business is able to reduce its prices while maintaining profit levels because its costs of production have fallen.

All businesses – both manufacturing and service companies – can therefore gain a competitive edge if their workforce is more productive than those of their rivals. The productivity of labour is a major determinant of the competitiveness of a business. If a business can be organised so that it achieves greater output per worker hour (or day or week) then its productivity has risen. Motivation, training and employing the right people are important contributors to high levels of productivity – all these factors are the responsibility of the human resources function.

The marketing function

The marketing department carries out a wide range of functions on behalf of the business. Essentially marketing is communications. The marketing department communicates with a number of groups inside and outside the business as it carries out its tasks. These relationships are summarised in Figure 1.12.

Discussion point

In what ways might developments in communications technology (such as the internet) have affected the relationships the marketing department has with other aspects of the business?

Figure 1.12: The marketing department's links inside and outside the business

Customer service
- ensuring satisfaction
- dealing with complaints

Market research
- information on consumer need
- prices to be paid

Retailers/distribution
maintain and enhance links

Marketing activities

External agencies
liaison with government departments and bodies regarding export

Promotional activity
- advertising
- PR
- sales promotions

Liaison with production
- ensure product meets consumer needs
- advice on updates and modifications to product

◀ Eagle Star Insurance sells direct to customers through its website

What benefits might Eagle Star gain from marketing its products directly to the public? In what ways might Eagle Star's marketing department have altered as a result of this change?

Lets consider some of the marketing department's relationships in more detail.

- Customers. Keeping customers satisfied is a key objective for the majority of businesses and marketing plays a central role in attaining this target. The marketing department carries out the market research to discover the needs of consumers. This research is likely to be an ongoing activity to ensure the firm is aware of changing tastes and fashions. The department is also responsible for organising advertising campaigns, special offers and other activities designed to promote the company's products. The marketing function may also deal with customer complaints.

- The production department. This is possibly the most important internal relationship between business functions. The marketing department discovers the needs of customers and advises the production function accordingly. If this channel of communication operates effectively, the business should be more able to meet the needs of consumers.

- Distributors and retailers. The marketing function normally carries the responsibility for ensuring the effective distribution of products to wholesalers and retailers. It may also liaise with retailers to gain prominent display positions for the company's products and to arrange special offers and promotions. With the development of the internet, many firms now sell their products direct to consumers. This has placed additional responsibilities on the marketing department.

- Specialist marketing firms. Some businesses, and especially small firms, are unable to carry out some marketing activities such as marketing research or designing major advertising campaigns. In these circumstances, the marketing department liaises with marketing agencies that can provide the necessary expertise.

- Government agencies. If the firm is an exporter, the marketing department may have contact with government agencies in the UK and across Europe. For example, a UK firm selling overseas may consult the Department of Trade and Industry and British Trade International as part of the process of assessing overseas markets and promoting its products abroad. These links can be particularly valuable to small businesses with limited experience of export markets.

The importance of marketing

Marketing provides the organisation with information about its customers and its markets. Effective marketing can offer businesses a number of benefits:

- early warning of changes in consumer tastes and fashions through regular market research

- knowledge about competitors and information regarding competitors' products

- the means to present the company in a positive light through public relations activities

- allowing the firm to improve the quality of its products by coordinating and analysing customer complaints

- providing a catalyst for growth by forging relationships with distributors, retailers and customers in new markets

- supplying consumers with the products they want and giving high levels of customer satisfaction, which might permit a business to charge higher prices thereby increasing its profitability.

Marketing is an influential factor assisting organisations to achieve objectives such as growth and market share. Successful marketing results in satisfied consumers and can lead to rising sales. By supplying consumers with the products they want and providing high levels of customer satisfaction, a business might be able to charge higher prices and increase its profitability.

Furthermore, by projecting a positive corporate image – the general public impression by which the business is viewed and judged by society – the marketing function helps a business to grow and prosper. It is unlikely that a business with an ineffective marketing function will satisfy consumers and enjoy commercial success.

Recent issues in marketing

There are several important trends affecting the marketing function of most businesses. First, many businesses have moved towards direct selling, cutting out wholesaler and retailers and communicating directly with customers. National computer suppliers such as Tiny have established themselves solely as direct suppliers; their products are not for sale in high street shops. The development of the internet as a vehicle for communicating with consumers across the globe has opened up enormous possibilities for selling products. The Amazon Bookshop, established by Jeff Bezos in 1994, is a hugely successful business marketing its products principally through the internet.

The internet is not just a vehicle for selling products, it can be used to deliver services too. Egg , a company owned by Prudential Assurance, provides financial services. Initially, Egg offered an internet-based credit card but it has now expanded to offer savings accounts. One interesting development is that the company has developed links with major retailers such as Tesco and W H Smith, encouraging on-line shopping using the Egg card.

▲ Financial services on the web, Egg's internet-based credit card

Japanese business practice has also had an influence on marketing practice. Much as it encouraged some firms to operate without a discrete human resources department (see p. 34), some businesses, following the Japanese example, have elected to dismantle their marketing departments and expect everyone in the company to undertake marketing activities as necessary. Some senior managers take the view that marketing is the responsibility of everyone in the business. Having a discrete marketing function, they argue, is detrimental to the business because it means that other employees do not take any responsibility for marketing.

The administration function

The scope of the administration department varies enormously between organisations. In a small business, the administration function might incorporate a number of the functions we have already discussed. For example, some aspects of finance, personnel and marketing could come under the control of the administration department. However, larger organisations are more likely to operate a specialist administration department.

A typical administration department has a number of functions.

■ The provision of information throughout the organisation. It is common for a business's information technology section to be a part of the administration function. The IT system within a business provides management information for decision-making throughout the organisation.

■ Clerical and support services. Information processing, data processing, filing and reception services can be provided to all areas of the organisation. These duties play a vital role in linking together the activities of other functions within the business.

■ Security and maintenance. These services are essential to the smooth running of the business and to the effective operation of other business functions such as production in particular.

■ In some businesses, the administration function takes responsibility for important public relations activities such as customer services.

Administration is heavily dependent upon the use of information technology. This technology allows businesses to collect information from within and outside the organisation, to analyse it and to provide important data for decision-making. However, the benefits provided by information technology have also contributed to a situation in which a discrete or separate administration department is less likely. In effect, the technology enables small and separate 'mini' administration functions to operate within other areas of the business.

The research and development function

The nature of **research and development** (R&D) varies enormously between businesses. Traditionally, the term research and development is taken to refer to scientific research undertaken by firms producing manufactured goods, high technology products or pharmaceuticals. However, R&D is equally important to firms providing services. Financial service companies are constantly developing new products to give them a competitive advantage. For example, the Co-operative Bank has spent considerable sums developing an internet bank. The bank wants to ensure that it offers a full range of banking services in an increasingly competitive market.

By investing in research and development a business seeks to maintain **competitiveness** against its rivals. Competitiveness measures a business's performance in comparison with rival firms in the same market. A highly competitive firm has some advantage over other businesses. This competitive edge can take a number of forms:

- lower prices
- more advanced and sophisticated products
- a better image with consumers
- a good reputation for advice and after-sales service
- reliability in terms of operation and delivery dates.

Discussion point

The research and development department may help a business to establish competitive advantage. We have listed five ways in which a business can gain an edge over its rivals – from lower prices to reliability. For each case, consider the possible role of the R&D function in helping to establish that competitive edge.

Types of research

Research and development can be broken down into three components:

- basic research
- applied research
- development.

Basic or fundamental research is undertaken mainly to achieve advancements in scientific knowledge that have commercial possibilities. The discovery of digital technology in broadcasting is an example of basic research.

Applied research then takes forward the scientific discovery and attempts to develop it in a way that results in a saleable product. For example, digital communications technology has been developed to the point that radio and television broadcasting and systems have been designed to deliver digital broadcasting.

The development aspect of R&D uses the results from applied research to bring the product to the stage where it is marketable. Continuing the digital example, digital broadcasting services have been tested and are now in commercial operation.

The scope of R&D

The prime function of R&D is to develop new products that can give the firm a competitive edge in the market. This necessarily involves the R&D department in close liaison with staff in market research, design and production.

- **Market research** aims to identify the needs of consumers. This information is invaluable to those in R&D, as they need to ensure that there is likely to be a demand for any products they develop. Market-oriented businesses place great emphasis on this relationship.

- Design is an important stage in developing new ideas into saleable products. Designers attempt to bring together the needs of consumers and the new ideas and processes. Good designers combine creative flair with a real sense of what the market requires.

- High quality ideas need protecting; companies do not want rival businesses stealing their ideas. The law offers protection in the form of **patents**. Patents give the creators of a new product the sole right to produce it for a limited period of time – normally up to 20 years.

- Good ideas will not necessarily result in a commercially viable product. The company needs to bring in the production department to determine whether the product can be produced both on a large scale and cost-effectively. If the new product is expensive to produce, it may not be able to be priced at a level that consumers can afford.

- However, if a company can overcome all these hurdles, new products can make high profits. A company that has a product technologically superior to those of its rivals may be able to operate a **price skimming** strategy. This company intentionally sets a high price, only attracting those consumers willing to pay that price – this is 'skimming the cream' off the market.

Discussion point

Dyson's cleaner (see case study opposite) is based on significant investment in research and development. Consider what support would be needed from other departments for a business to make the most of this kind of R&D innovation.

CASE STUDY

Dyson Cleaners

James Dyson is renowned for designing and manufacturing revolutionary vacuum cleaners. His cleaners are famous for their efficiency and the fact that they do not have a bag to collect dust and dirt. Dyson has protected his ideas with patents and has been able to use price-skimming policies to make high profits from his research and development.

R&D also focuses on new manufacturing processes as well as new products. For example, an R&D department may look for new materials to replace costly or scarce resources currently used in production. For example, many modern products contain plastics rather than more costly metals. Many drinks, such as Coca-Cola and milk, are now packaged in plastic or card containers rather than traditional glass bottles. R&D departments seek lighter and tougher packaging to reduce transport costs and the likelihood of damage to the product.

Other duties conducted by the R&D function in a business could include:

■ seeking to reduce or eliminate waste in the production process to increase efficiency and profitability

■ identifying and applying for government and EU financial support available to firms conducting research and development

■ maintaining close links with universities and other organisations conducting scientific research.

The interaction of business functions

We have considered each of the major functions of an organisation separately. However, it is the effective interaction of business functions that is essential to the success of an organisation in attaining its objectives.

As an example, consider how a business might respond to an enquiry from a potential customer. Assume that the customer is interested in placing a large order, but wants delivery quickly. This enquiry, if followed through to a sale, might involve all the business functions in different ways.

■ Marketing – responding to the initial enquiry, receiving and processing an order, distributing the product to customer.

■ Administration – adding the customer's details to the IT system, passing on details to other departments within the business.

■ Finance – investigating the financial status of the customer, offering credit terms if appropriate, invoicing for payment.

■ Production – receiving details of order and meeting the customer's demands, liaising with marketing over delivery dates, rescheduling other production as required.

■ Human resources – ensuring sufficient employees are available to meet the production requirements of the order, arranging overtime payments if necessary.

■ Research and development – liaising with marketing over possible customer requirements and reactions to product supplied.

BUILD YOUR LEARNING

You should know the meaning of the words and phrases listed below. Go back through the last 13 pages of the unit to check or refresh your understanding as necessary.

- Capital
- Competitiveness
- Corporate image
- Direct selling
- Enterprise
- Human resource management
- Labour
- Land
- Market research
- Patents
- Personnel management
- Price skimming
- Productivity
- Research and development
- Stock control systems
- Workforce plan

Summary points

- Four factors of production are used by businesses: land, labour, capital and enterprise.

- The proportions of the factors of production used by businesses vary according to their size and nature.

- Capital is a term which should be used with care as it has a number of meanings within business.

- To satisfy the needs of their customers, businesses carry out a broad range of functions.

- The finance function records, monitors and interprets financial data relating to the business. Businesses create budgets to forecast future costs, revenues and profits.

- Production relates to all the activities directly contributing to the creation of goods and services.

- Human resources relates to all issues concerning people within the organisation. This function has assumed greater importance as personnel management has been replaced by human resource management.

- The marketing function communicates with customers to ensure that the products supplied meet customers' needs and that customers purchase the firm's products.

- R&D is research undertaken by businesses. This is particularly important in industries in which advanced products provide businesses with a competitive edge.

Organisational structures

ALL BUSINESS ORGANISATIONS, from very small firms to large multinational corporations, have an internal framework or structure through which the business as a whole and the various parts of its operations can be directed, monitored and managed. A sole trader, for example, has an organisational structure, although the owner will not necessarily be aware of it in any formal sense.

In many small firms, the owner may have a very hands-on approach and may be responsible for getting customers, hiring any extra labour and acquiring other inputs and taking all financial decisions. As organisations grow, however, their structure takes on a greater significance and those at the top have to pay more attention to its formal structure and presentation. The various business functions will show an increasing degree of specialisation as an organisation expands and people will be employed to manage and take decisions in specialist areas.

In this section, we consider the different kinds of organisational structures adopted by businesses. However, we first consider the common elements of all structures. In general, an organisational structure sets out:

- major roles and job titles, showing who is in control of the business as a whole and who manages its major business functions within departments

- the level of seniority of people holding different positions and their respective positions in the organisation's overall hierarchy

- the working relationships between individuals, identifying relationships in terms of superiors and their subordinates and indicating who has authority to take certain kinds of decisions and who are responsible for carrying out the work arising from those decisions

- the extent to which decision making is concentrated in the hands of people at or near the top of the organisation or handed down to those at lower levels of management

- the broad channels through which information is communicated throughout the organisation, indicating the route by which instructions flow down the hierarchy and how information flows back up the hierarchy.

Organisational charts

An organisation's structure can be displayed diagrammatically. Organisational charts are representations of the job titles and the formal patterns of authority and responsibility in an organisation.

Figure 1.13 contains an organisational chart for the Dixon Group, showing the major features of the company's organisational structure. Note that the company has sections within departments devoted solely to areas such as design and development and community affairs. This is possible because the Dixon Group has grown and diversified to the extent that it can take advantage of the division of labour throughout its operations as employees can be kept fully occupied in increasingly specialised areas. The letters used at the ends of the organisational chart in Figure 1.13 are references to additional charts which cover the different operations within the Dixon Group in more detail. Figure 1.14 shows one of these additional organisational charts (chart G).

Discussion point

Use the charts in Figures 1.13 and 1.14 to find the different retail outlets within the Dixon Group. Find examples within Dixon's organisational structure of:

- functional roles for the group as a whole

- functional roles within a function

- functional roles in relation to products.

Businesses may produce organisational charts for several reasons. First, it is important that a company reviews its organisational structure on a regular basis to take account of any changes in the business environment. Changes such as new laws relating to environmental protection or new trends in consumer tastes and preferences may require giving managers in some departments a wider area of decision making or placing new sections into existing departments. A formal organisational chart helps the company to identify where changes need to be made and to decide the relationship between any new sections or departments and the rest of the organisation.

Figure 1.13: Organisational chart for Dixon Group plc

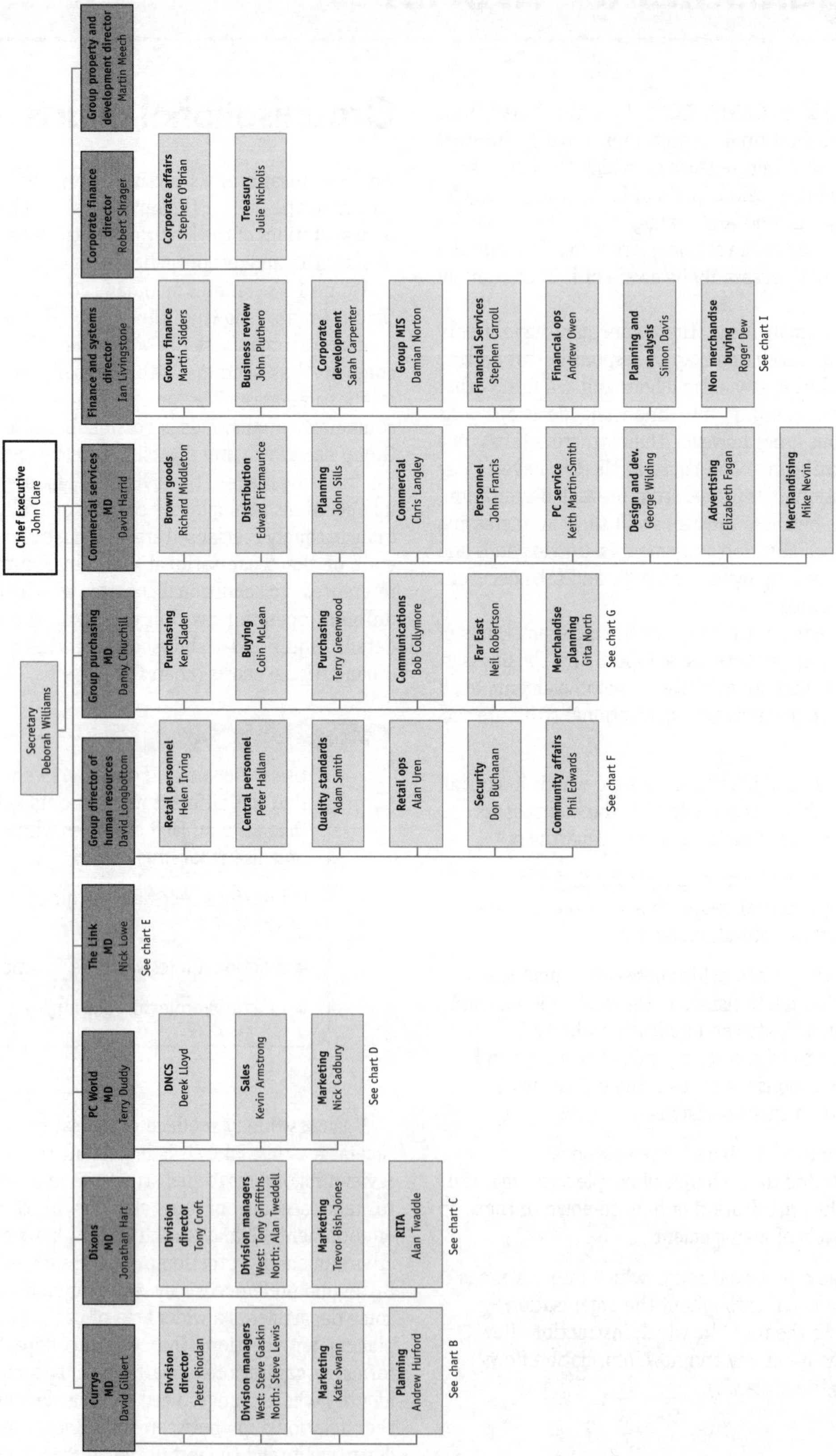

Chief Executive
John Clare

Secretary
Deborah Williams

Currys MD
David Gilbert

Division director
Peter Riordan

Division managers
West: Steve Gaskin
North: Steve Lewis

Marketing
Kate Swann

Planning
Andrew Hurford

See chart B

Dixons MD
Jonathan Hart

Division director
Tony Croft

Division managers
West: Tony Griffiths
North: Alan Tweddell

Marketing
Trevor Bish-Jones

RITA
Alan Twaddle

See chart C

PC World MD
Terry Duddy

DNCS
Derek Lloyd

Sales
Kevin Armstrong

Marketing
Nick Cadbury

See chart D

The Link MD
Nick Lowe

See chart E

Group director of human resources
David Longbottom

Retail personnel
Helen Irving

Central personnel
Peter Hallam

Quality standards
Adam Smith

Retail ops
Alan Uren

Security
Don Buchanan

Community affairs
Phil Edwards

See chart F

Group purchasing MD
Danny Churchill

Purchasing
Ken Sladen

Buying
Colin McLean

Purchasing
Terry Greenwood

Communications
Bob Collymore

Far East
Neil Robertson

Merchandise planning
Gita North

See chart G

Commercial services MD
David Harrid

Brown goods
Richard Middleton

Distribution
Edward Fitzmaurice

Planning
John Sills

Commercial
Chris Langley

Personnel
John Francis

PC service
Keith Martin-Smith

Design and dev.
George Wilding

Advertising
Elizabeth Fagan

Merchandising
Mike Nevin

See chart H

Finance and systems director
Ian Livingstone

Group finance
Martin Sidders

Business review
John Pluthero

Corporate development
Sarah Carpenter

Group MIS
Damian Norton

Financial Services
Stephen Carroll

Financial ops
Andrew Owen

Planning and analysis
Simon Davis

Non merchandise buying
Roger Dew

See chart I

Corporate finance director
Robert Shrager

Corporate affairs
Stephen O'Brian

Treasury
Julie Nicholls

Group property and development director
Martin Meech

Source: Dixons Group

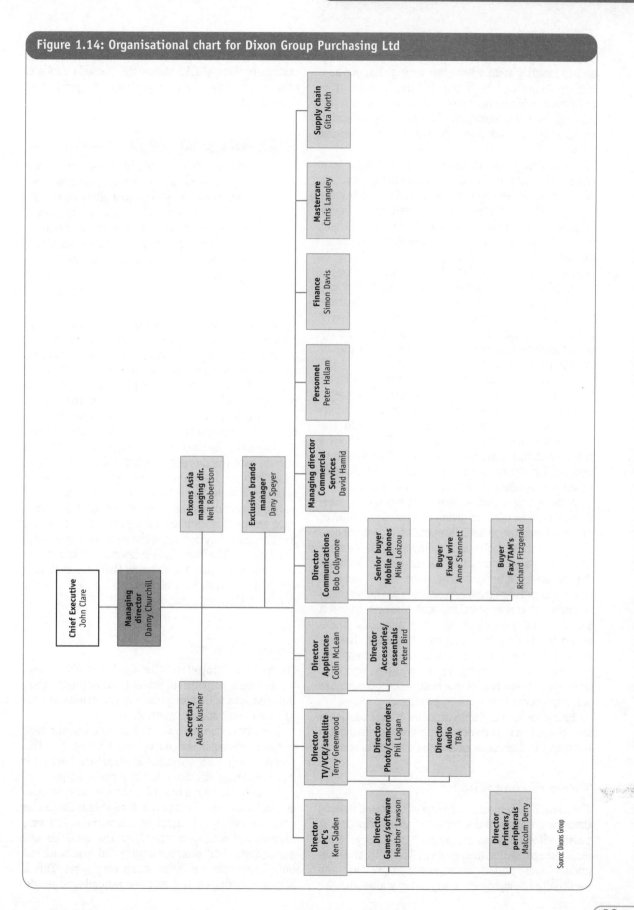

Figure 1.14: Organisational chart for Dixon Group Purchasing Ltd

Source: Dixons Group

Businesses also produce organisational charts because they allow a company to review its structure and to identify areas where cost saving changes and improvements can be made. If, for example, the business is suffering from problems associated with the internal flow of information, the chart may be useful in identifying weaknesses in the communications chain.

Organisational charts are useful when changes take place in the company. It can be updated to take account of any informal developments in its structure that have been good for the company. The updated version keeps employees fully informed of changes and makes them aware of the new working relationships in terms of authority and responsibility. If the business is restructured, the new chart will keep employees informed about the effects on their own position of any diversification into new products or a rationalisation programme that involves concentrating on fewer products. A revised organisational chart is particularly useful for informing people about the new structure of the company after mergers or takeovers.

The organisational chart can also be used during an induction period to give new employees a useful overview of the company and their own position within the structure in terms of their authority and the managers to whom they are responsible. It also shows a new recruit their links with others and allows them to compare their position and relationships with those of others in the different parts of the organisation.

Although an organisational chart has several uses, it should not be taken as giving an exact description of how the organisation actually operates. It does not give the exact nature of job responsibilities or indicate what levels of cooperation may be necessary between departments. Note also that, over time, personal initiatives and increasing experience in the job may lead to informal communications and contacts between sections and individuals existing alongside those represented in the formal organisation chart. Indeed, if the organisational structure is too rigidly applied, this may stifle the initiative of employees and slow down the introduction of new management techniques and improvements in working practices.

Before looking at different kinds of organisational structures, it is important to introduce and distinguish between the chain of command and the span of control.

Chain of command

The chain of command is the line of command flowing down from the top to the bottom of an organisation. It passes down the management hierarchy, from director and senior management levels to those in middle and junior management positions and eventually to employees in supervisory jobs who, for example, may have authority over assembly line workers or staff providing services to the organisation's customers. Figure 1.15 shows the possible chain of command within an organisation's production department.

Discussion point

Figure 1.15 shows the line authority in a typical production department. Consider the different kinds of work that are likely to be carried out within the human resource management and marketing functions. Construct organisational charts showing possible chain of command for both departments.

Organisations with a long chain of command – with a hierarchy made up of many levels of management – are said to have tall organisational structures. However, the greater the number of links in the chain of command, the further information must flow when passing up the hierarchy, and the greater the number of management layers that decisions must pass through before they achieve their desired effect further down the hierarchy. Because of this, organisations seek to operate with the shortest possible chain of command.

As well as dealing with the person immediately below them in the hierarchy, managers may also contact people further down the chain of command. Managers must ensure that their immediate subordinates do not feel threatened by bypassing the chain of command in this fashion. The immediate subordinates might gain the impression that those below them are reporting everything direct to the senior manager, thereby devaluing their responsibility.

Span of control

The span of control refers to the number of subordinates a manager is responsible for and has authority over. Organisations with a long chain of command will tend to have narrow spans of control.

Organisations with a short chain of command tend to have wider spans of control (see Figure 1.17). This produces a flat organisational structure because it has a hierarchy with fewer levels of management.

Though flat organisational structures are generally desirable, there is a limit to the number of subordinates who can be placed under one superior. Even very experienced managers who have the qualities and personalities that promote loyalty and hard work can only be responsible for so many employees. This is because exerting control over a large number of people,

Figure 1.15: Line authority in a production department

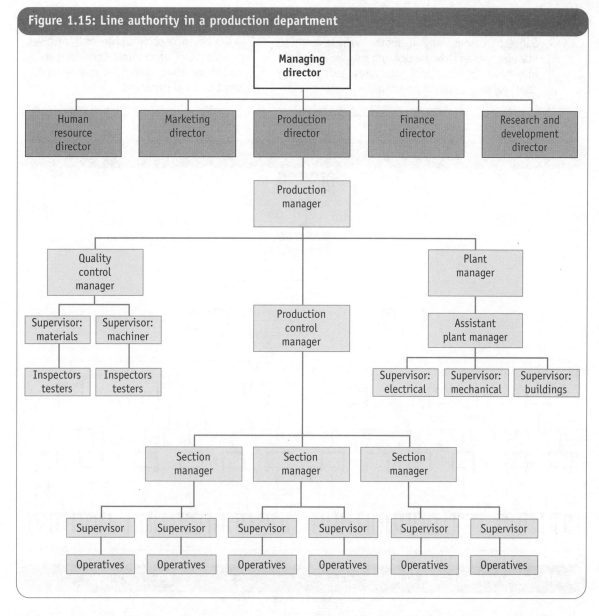

all of whom are supplying information for a decision, is bound to place a great deal of strain on the physical and mental energies of senior managers. It is difficult to coordinate the activities of a large number of people and to find time to make personal contact with them. Indeed, managers with a very wide span may not even know exactly what some of their subordinates are doing.

In some situations, however, a relatively wide span of control may be acceptable if:

- the potential disadvantages of a wide span are outweighed by the costs of employing the extra managers needed to produce narrower spans of control

- junior employees are engaged mainly in routine work and as a result the manager is required to make relatively few decisions

- managers are willing to reduce the pressure on their own time by delegating more decision making and they can identify staff who are likely to respond well to the extra responsibility.

- an effective range of financial and non-financial motivational factors produces a committed group of people who need very little supervision

- the group within the span are highly skilled or talented and are given a great deal of scope to be creative and imaginative in their work.

Figure 1.16: A narrow span of control

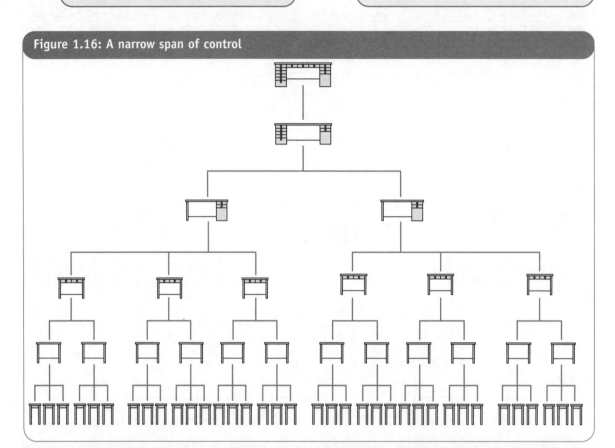

Figure 1.17: A wide span of control

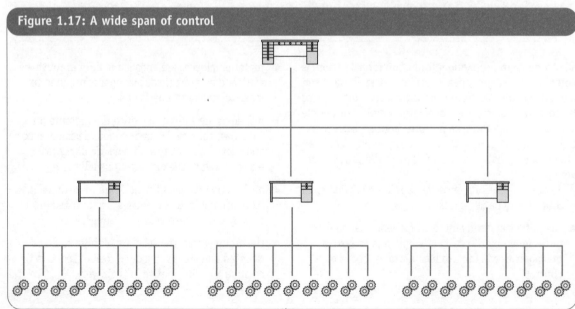

Forms of organisational structure

Organisational structures can be classified into a number of different types. In this section, we consider:

- line structures
- line and staff structures
- matrix structures
- centralised structures
- decentralised structures
- delayed structures.

However, it should not be assumed that an organisation will only contain features of one type of structure and no other. For example, an organisation's structure may have dominant features that place it clearly under one particular heading but it may also show certain characteristics associated with other kinds of organisational structures.

Many organisational structures are based mainly on a division according to departmental functions such as production, marketing and finance, or on a division according to the organisation's products or services, where each product division has its own business functions. There are, of course, other possibilities. A multinational conglomerate, for example, may be organised by country, by global region or by the companies or products that make up the group.

Some companies may have a mix of product and functional division, with some business functions being centralised and operating on behalf of products and services. For example, a leisure group involved in brewing, pubs, hotels, restaurants, fast food and health clubs may have an organisational chart based mainly on these product areas. Each product area may have its own marketing department, but there may be a central purchasing and finance division which operates on behalf of all product areas. Recruitment and training may operate on behalf of some product areas, while other product areas may have in-house departments for this work.

Line structure

In a line structure, a company is usually organised into functional departments, each headed by a senior manager, below whom there is a chain of command. This indicates that there is a line of authority and responsibility as one goes down the structure. In a production department, for example, the line may pass down from production director to production manager, quality control, plant manager, process control, production supervisors and, finally, to operatives.

Each person in the line has authority over those below, while being responsible for making sure that the work handed down to them from their immediate manager is completed. This applies even if the subordinate does not personally undertake the actual work. Assume, for example, that the quality control manager is required by the production manager to introduce changes. The quality control manager may have to delegate or pass on some tasks to the plant manager to complete this task. However, if the changes are not introduced in a satisfactory way, then the quality control manager is answerable to the production manager.

The advantages of a line structure are that:

- it is a hierarchical structure which is simple to understand – staff know precisely where they are in the structure, who can allocate work to them and to whom they are responsible

- managers have a clear understanding of the roles of people when allocating work and spend less time monitoring work because subordinates are not distracted or confused by instructions from other sources

- a well-established line authority makes it possible for work to be delegated further down the line – this can be valuable when a superior is seeking to widen the experience of subordinates and develop their management or supervisory skills.

The disadvantages of a line structure are that:

- it can involve a very long chain of command – instructions may take a considerable time to filter from the top and impact on production, which can be an important drawback if the organisation operates in a rapidly changing market

- the flow of information back up a long chain to management may be a lengthy process, causing a considerable delay before problems are identified and tackled

- individuals might only respond to requests from their superior, creating inflexibility in the organisation which may be totally unnecessary if cooperation with other managers does not effect working relations with their superior.

Line and staff structure

A line and staff structure combines both a line authority and what is known as staff authority. The term **staff authority** refers to those staff, usually at a relatively senior level, whose area of work often involves dealing with different departments. Someone with the relevant staff authority can provide services and advice to those in the line of authority of other departments. The training and recruitment activities of the human resource management department, for example, are bound to involve other departments. Similarly, senior staff in the production department may have staff authority in the purchasing department. Staff in the finance department may have staff authority across all other departments.

Managers with staff authority do not have the power to control or give instructions, but rather the authority to deal with different departments and to offer advice or support services in relation to problems or exploiting new opportunities. However, since those with staff authority are appointed because of their expertise, experience and good personal skills, their advice, though not binding, is likely to be very persuasive.

The advantages of a line and staff structure are that:

- staff authority enables the expertise and experience of specialists to be utilised more fully across the organisation

- by having access to all areas of the company, managers with staff authority can coordinate the organisation's objectives and ensure a more immediate response to changes in technology or market conditions

- it makes communication more efficient – without staff authority, communications between departments are at director level, and so any inter-departmental communication has to pass up the chain of command in one department to director level and then down the other before it reaches the appropriate level

- staff authority prevents individual departments from being too inward looking – departments remain aware of their interdependence and their role in seeking to achieve the organisation's objectives.

The disadvantages of a line and staff structure are that there is a risk that staff authority may diminish the authority of individuals in line management, particularly if those with staff functions acquire informal power and authority. This can lead to some subordinates becoming confused about whether they should take instructions from and be responsible to their line manager or to managers with staff authority. The existence of both a line and staff authority may lead to clashes of personalities and opinions. This may strain relations between staff, affecting productivity and morale.

Matrix structure

In a **matrix structure**, a senior manager heads a division or team of specialists drawn from different departments. These specialists are also located in departments where they are part of a line authority; they are therefore subject to two sources of authority. Indeed, it is possible for a specialist to be part of several teams or divisions. In a matrix structure, therefore, the simple chain of command found in a line structure is replaced by a very large number of reporting relationships as individuals report to managers in more than one department or function.

A matrix structure may be used for just some of an organisation's activities or it may cover the whole work of the organisation. It is often used for organising and managing **project teams**, where people with specialist skills, perhaps from different levels in the hierarchy, are brought together to solve complex and urgent problems. Project teams may be created to deal with issues which arise every now and again or they may be an ongoing feature of the organisational structure. For example, a project team may be brought together for a limited period of time to oversee the introduction of new technology or a performance related pay scheme. Some aspects of marketing, however, may be handled by an ongoing project team drawn from other departments, although the membership of the group may change as different marketing issues arise.

▲ A project team might work on the launch of a new product

Discussion point

Some research and development activity is suited to a matrix structure. Review the development process shown in Figure 1.18, and suggest reasons why staff with responsibilities outside the R&D department may be part of a product development team.

Figure 1.18 The product development process

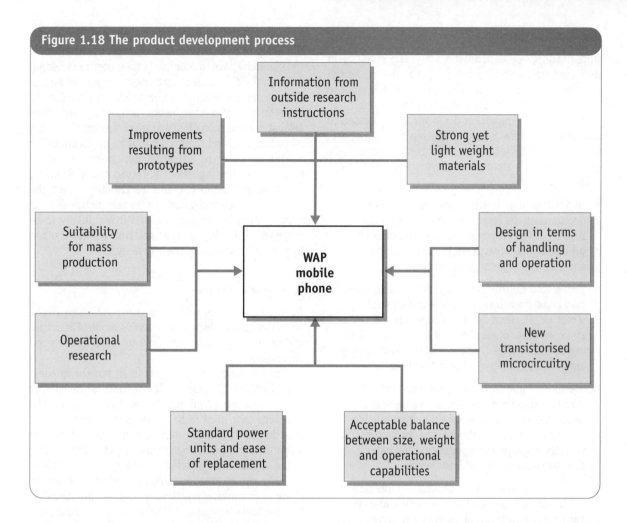

The advantages of a matrix structure are that:

- it promotes increased coordination between departments because it cuts across departmental boundaries – it encourages greater flexibility and creativity, produced by the cross-fertilisation of knowledge and skills

- it allows for the involvement of relatively junior staff, giving them valuable experience in a wider field for the expression and application of their particular skills

- staff lower down a line structure can also gain valuable management development in a project team, preparing them for promotion to higher management positions

- the involvement of specialists from different areas reduces the risk of resources being wasted on projects with no future – in non-matrix structures an idea originating in, say, the marketing department may be pursued for a long time before it comes to the attention of production which might find that it is simply not practical.

Matrix structures do have their disadvantages. The existence of a matrix structure and project teams can lead to confusion as individuals are involved in a large number of different relationships creating a complex pattern of authority and responsibility. A plant engineer, for example, may be reporting to the leader of a project team dealing with the development of a new product and also to a project group involved in a new training programme. This may involve the plant engineer reporting to some individuals who may be above his or her immediate line manager; in some cases, the plant engineer may even be reporting to managers in other departments who are at a lower grade than his or her immediate line manager.

A line manager may resent a subordinate receiving instructions from managers based in other departments, especially if they are at a lower level of management. This also raises questions as to who has priority over the subordinate's time and what information arising out of the work of the project team should also be reported through the line authority. This can be a potential source of conflict and relations may also be strained if the subordinate suffers from divided loyalty.

Centralisation

Organisations are **centralised** when the majority of decisions are taken by a few people at the top of the organisation and little decision making is delegated to those further down the organisational structure.

Even if many important decisions are delegated to subordinates, some aspects of the business are always likely to remain totally under a central control. In general, senior managers or a centralised department takes responsibility for:

- **major financial issues**, senior managers take decisions on the level and sources of external finance, dividend payments, the level of retained profits, capital investment projects and the allocation of departmental budgets

- **wages and salaries**, although recommendations may come from lower down the management structure, the final decisions on wages and salaries and conditions of employment are usually taken centrally to ensure that employees feel that they are getting a fair deal relative to others

- **manpower planning and personnel records**, these need to be centralised to ensure that a department's vacancy is not filled from outside when someone in another part of the organisation with the appropriate experience could be transferred or promoted into the job

- **purchasing**, a centralised purchasing function allows experienced staff to place bulk orders that earn a discount from the most competitive suppliers, avoids the wasteful duplication of stocks and ensures that standard specifications or styles are used throughout the organisation for items such as information technology products and office furniture and fittings.

There are many advantages of centralisation. The senior management team is aware of how both internal and external factors are likely to effect individual departments and the organisation in general. It can take decisions based on the needs of the business as whole; decisions taken further down the organisation may place too much emphasis on departmental interests. It can draw on a wealth of business knowledge, as senior managers usually have reached their positions because of their wide experience in many aspects of business and a proven record of effective decision making. They may also have proved themselves at a high level in other organisations.

By taking important decisions at the top, the management hierarchy has tight control over how the organisation ought to react to both favourable and unfavourable developments in the economic and financial environment in which it operates. This avoids the delay that might occur if managers further down the hierarchy have to coordinate their decision making.

Centralisation maintains focus on important issues. If someone at the top of an organisation identifies an important matter that needs addressing and then delegates the responsibility to subordinates, the initial momentum behind the matter and its implications for the business may be lost if decision making is passed further down the organisational structure. In addition, if decisions are only taken at the top, then the management hierarchy has a more exact picture of what is happening in the business and it is unlikely to be surprised by developments arising from decisions taken by people further down the hierarchy.

Decentralisation

An organisation is said to be **decentralised** if the authority to take decisions on a wide range of activities is delegated well down the line to managers or even supervisors.

Some decentralisation exists in all but the smallest organisations because senior managers are simply unable to cope physically or mentally with all the decisions that need to be taken. Senior management may decide to delegate decisions that do not involve major expenditure or do not seriously effect the ability of the organisation to achieve its long-term objectives. For example, an area for delegation might be plans for changes in working practices to improve productivity, training and management development techniques and customer care initiatives.

Decentralisation allows senior managers to spend more time formulating plans and actions that help the organisation to achieve its business objectives. This is particularly important in organisations where markets, competitive pressures and technology are subject to frequent change; managers must devote time to devising and implementing a business strategy

Junior managers and employees benefit from decentralisation. Motivation, self-esteem and job-satisfaction improve if employees are able to take decisions or are given the opportunity to influence the decisions of others. Involving subordinates in decision making not only helps to develop their management potential but also stimulates greater initiative and enterprise. This will not only make subordinates more effective in their existing jobs but also prepare them for promotion.

It makes business sense to decentralise many decisions down the hierarchy. Managers in relatively junior positions are close to the action, often with first-hand experience of actual production or dealing with customers. They are often the first to identify actual or potential problems and they have the experience to know how new developments will effect their area of work. This is particularly important when the organisation operates in many different geographical markets, as centralised decision making may be too remote to recognise that the organisation faces such diverse business environments.

There are several advantages in delegating much decision making to junior managers.

- The first-hand knowledge of relatively junior managers enables them to assess what does and what does not work when evaluating potential solutions to problems or exploiting new opportunities. In particular, these managers are aware of how subordinates will react to decisions that effect their work.

- Junior managers are often better placed to react to change. If information has be passed back up a tall hierarchy, there may be a long delay before a decision is communicated back down to the manager who identified the initial problem or opportunity. Events may have moved on, and the decision from senior management may no longer be appropriate.

- Decisions that come from the top have to pass through many management layers; this increases the risk of confusion and mistakes, particularly if there are weaknesses in the channels of communication.

- If control is mainly centralised and junior managers have very little authority to take decisions, they may even hesitate to decide on relatively unimportant matters. This encourages the practice of passing the buck, with people passing minor issues back up the hierarchy because they fear the consequences of taking wrong decisions.

> **Discussion point**
>
> Give possible reasons why decentralisation can raise morale and generally improve relations between management and workers.

Delayering

Delayering describes the policy of removing management layers or tiers in an organisation's hierarchy. This shortens the chain of command and, therefore, the lines of communication. The policy is designed to help accelerate decision making in rapidly changing markets and generally streamline an organisation's structure.

Delayering is likely to play a major role in a policy of decentralisation as the removal of management layers allows authority for decision making to be shifted to a lower level in the organisation. Having removed the necessary layers, authority is then shifted to **multifunctional** teams which can take decisions across departments. The aim is to get employees to identify with the needs of the organisation as a whole rather than their departments. This enables companies to respond more rapidly to market developments, ensure greater coordination of activities and a more competitive response to customers' needs.

▲ Companies need to be able to respond to unexpected events

> **Discussion point**
>
> Explain why organisations that delegate authority and decision making down the hierarchy are in a better position to react to the unexpected.

This process of delayering often involves the removal of middle management, producing a significant saving in labour costs. Delayering has been accelerated in recent years by the introduction of information technology which makes it easier for multifunctional teams to access the information to make the kinds of decisions which go right across the business functions.

Management styles

Management style refers to the approach that an organisation takes in setting objectives for its employees and the way it manages relations between superiors and subordinates. In our discussion about organisational structures, we noted that the different types of structures tend to reflect the degree to which decision making is either mainly at the top of an organisation or delegated some way down the hierarchy. The extent to which an organisation is willing to involve its workers in decision making is a reflection of the culture of an organisation and its management style.

Management or leadership styles can be categorised as:

- autocratic
- democratic
- laissez-faire.

Autocratic

A manager that adopts an **autocratic management style** takes entire responsibility for decisions and, having set objectives and allocated tasks to employees, expects them to be carried out exactly as specified. Employees are told exactly what, how and when work must be started and finished. It is the kind of management style often associated with a corporate culture centred almost exclusively around production. Power is focused at the top, and the centralised decision making is geared to getting the goods out of the factory and to customers. Little regard is paid to any non-monetary needs of employees; they are not consulted or involved in decision making.

▲ Some managers use their position at the top of an organisation to exert total control

Discussion point

What kind of organisational structure and management style allows the manager at the top of the organisation to have complete control over all aspects of its operations?

There are several situations when an autocratic style may be appropriate:

- in small organisations where the leader is very hands on and is in a position to get involved in even day-to-day decisions
- in organisations in which the workforce comprises unskilled people with little ambition and motivation beyond their pay
- in markets in which changes are so rapid and unpredictable that employee consultation is too time consuming and individual initiatives may be entirely inappropriate in market circumstances that change daily
- in working environments where there are very serious risks to health and safety when total control over all working activities may have to exerted by the leader to ensure exact compliance with legislation relating to the industry.

Employees sometimes respond to an autocratic style. If the business is successful and offers a high degree of job security, workers may have such confidence in the quality of the leader's decision making that the complete lack of consultation and delegation is more than outweighed by a regular and acceptable income. Employees may also prefer an autocratic approach as it provides a clear and consistent leadership style – they know what to expect, where they stand and their work is not complicated by interventions from several unpredictable sources.

An autocratic style does have some disadvantages:

- employees may resent every aspect of their working day being controlled by the leader and might seek every opportunity to relax their effort when not being supervised
- it encourages a lack of teamwork and social contact because there is very little reason for workers to communicate with each other
- the complete lack of consultation can produce a demotivated workforce that just follows orders.

Work till you drop

The story of Toshihide Iguchi, the trader who cost the Daiwa Bank £700 million, shocked the Japanese financial community. Iguchi frittered an average of £250,000 away on bad deals every working day for 11 years. He got away with it for so long because of the work-till-you-die corporate culture of Japanese banks.

Traders do not take time off. The fact that he was falsifying his records would have been discovered if someone else had taken over his responsibilities for a week. Iguchi, however, never took more than two or three days off in a row.

At a Western bank such a dislike of holidays would have made people wonder what he was hiding. At Daiwa, Iguchi was regarded as a very loyal and hardworking employee. To take the full holiday entitlement would have been seen as being lazy and disloyal to the company.

This attitude to work may have been suitable during Japan's post-war construction but the government now wants employees to work fewer but more efficient hours. Working hours have been cut officially but many managers make their subordinates do unofficial and unpaid overtime. It is not unknown for Japanese employees to die of karoshi – death by overwork.

Adapted from *The Electronic Telegraph*, 28 September 1995

Democratic

A democratic management style seeks to involve employees in the decision-making process, either by consulting them directly or through their representatives. This approach reflects a corporate culture which is more human resource centred and recognises the organisational benefits from meeting its employees' non-monetary needs – such as a need for job satisfaction and a sense of belonging. A consultative approach is particularly important if an organisation is planning to change product design or working conditions, methods and practices.

There are several advantages of a democratic style:

- job satisfaction, motivation and team spirit improves if employees feel that their views are valued and they are participating in decision making

- an organisation can take fuller advantage of its human resources by tapping their skills, knowledge and experience

- it encourages more personal contact between management and subordinates – they get to know each other as individuals and appreciate more fully the constraints under which they each work.

A democratic style does have disadvantages. Consultation can be time-consuming, slowing down decision making, during which time opportunities may fade and problems worsen. If management lacks the communications skills to explain the role of worker participation, the attempt at consultation may not be seen as genuine, and staff may regard the approach as both condescending and a pretence. Another drawback is that people representing employees in meetings with management may seek to pursue their own career, financial or political interests rather than express the views of those they represent.

Discussion point

Read the article about Korean Air (on p. 54). Identify the factors that suggest that the airline has a very autocratic management culture and discuss how they impact on morale and safety. What kind of management culture would you expect in a Western airline? Give your reasons.

Discussion point

Explain why the management style set out in the article 'Work till you drop' can eventually have an adverse effect on productivity. Why would this management style be inappropriate in a UK-based Japanese factory?

Survey slams culture at Korean Air

The rigidly hierarchical culture at Korean Air is seen as a major reason for it having the worst recent safety record in international aviation with five fatal crashes in 12 years. Its authoritarian management is said to put commercial considerations ahead of safety and copilots are fearful of questioning errors by captains.

A survey by Delta, the US airline, found that communications between management and pilots is very poor and administrators often try to over-rule flight crews on safety issues, such as the amount of fuel load or defects warnings, which might postpone take-off.

Morale is low as the best jobs have gone to former military pilots. No account is taken of the managerial skills needed to operate a modern cockpit in a civil aircraft.

The dominance of ex-military pilots means that copilots are reluctant to complain or speak up if they make a mistake as they feel it would damage their career prospects.

The captain's judgement is never queried by subordinates, in complete contrast to Western airline practice where there is a collaborative culture on the flight-deck and continual cross-checking of information is seen as critical to minimising human error.

The survey finds that in Korean Air cockpits there "is a volatile cocktail of complacency, arrogance, apathy and lack of self-discipline".

Adapted from *The Electronic Telegraph*, 24 December 1999

Laissez-faire style

A laissez-faire leadership style gives people complete freedom to organise and carry out their work. It is a very person centred approach. A laissez-faire approach may still impose some constraints, such as the completion dates for certain key tasks or the earliest and latest arrival times for a flexible hours working day. There is no formal structure for decision making as decisions are taken by a variety of processes depending upon the nature of the problem, the opportunity to be explored and the individuals involved.

A laissez-faire style:

■ gives wider scope for the development of individual talents, initiatives and creative thinking

■ reduces stress levels by letting people feel that they are in charge of their working lives

■ provides greater opportunity for people to choose to work with colleagues on activities where they feel they will make a productive and harmonious team

■ offers a management style and culture which is suitable for the growing number of people who work away from the office in their own homes.

▲ A creative environment like an architects' office might suit a laissez-faire style

Discussion point

Give examples of businesses which rely heavily on creative talents and where a laissez-faire management approach might be the most effective way to exploit those talents and achieve business objectives.

There are several disadvantages of a laissez-faire style:

- the more relaxed leadership style can make it more difficult to identify anyone who is exploiting the greater freedom and putting in little effort

- there is a risk that employees with the same general approach will eventually settle around a particular activity and form cliques, reducing the exchange of ideas and information in the organisation

- organisations may suffer from low productivity if methods, processes and schedules are not sufficiently coordinated

- individuals may try to build up their own area of work– this empire building may prevent an organisation from achieving its objectives.

BUILD YOUR LEARNING

Keywords and phrases

You should know the meaning of the words and phrases listed below. Go back through the last 14 pages of the unit to check or refresh your understanding as necessary.

- Autocratic management style
- Centralised organisations
- Chain of command
- Decentralised organisations
- Delayering
- Democratic management style
- Flat organisational structures
- Laissez-faire leadership
- Line structure
- Management hierarchy
- Management style
- Matrix structure
- Multifunctional
- Project teams
- Staff authority
- Span of control
- Tall organisational structures

Summary points

- All organisations need a structure of some kind through which the business can be directed, monitored and reviewed.

- Organisational charts are valuable for formally displaying and reviewing a business's structure.

- Common types of organisational structure include a line structure, a line and staff structure and a matrix structure.

- In centralised organisations, the majority of decisions are taken by people at the top, and little responsibility is delegated down the organisational structure.

- In decentralised organisations, the authority to take decisions is delegated well down the hierarchy.

- An organisation's management style describes the relationship between superiors and subordinates. Some typical leadership styles can be categorised as autocratic, democratic and laissez-faire.

Communications

THE EFFICIENT COMMUNICATION of information is particularly important for organisations that operate in competitive markets. Relevant and accurate information is needed to plan and manage efficient production, marketing, distribution and cost control. Information – whatever its nature and purpose –must be communicated as efficiently as possible.

All people in an organisation are part of an **information flow** – they are involved to varying degrees in providing and receiving information. However, there are three main levels at which information is required:

- operational level
- middle management
- senior management.

▲ Supervisors on a construction site need information to plan the building work

Operational level

At the operational level – on the factory floor, in the office or at premises where consumer services are provided – there are charge hands and supervisors who must ensure that work is planned and carried out as efficiently as possible. In a factory, for example, a supervisor giving the task of overseeing the production of a particular item needs to know:

- the quantity to be handled
- the completion date
- the availability of plant and machine capacity
- the operations to be performed
- the kinds of labour needed and its availability
- the materials and components required to produce the order.

This kind of information assists the supervisor in planning and controlling the work and it is essential for decision making at an operational level. Activities at the operational level of an organisation produce data that will be processed to provide much of the information required by middle management.

Discussion point

Describe the information that is likely to be needed by workers and supervisors on a building site.

Middle management

Middle management needs to know how efficiently work at the operational level is being carried out and the extent to which any resources under their control are being used to achieve the organisation's objectives. Much of this information relates to the productivity of labour, the utilisation of machine capacity and the rate at which materials and other inputs are being consumed.

Middle management also needs a great deal of financial information about the costs of the resources consumed in relation to output. This financial data can be used to determine and monitor total costs, revenues, profits and the achievement of business objectives. For example, it will be possible to identify any fall-off in productivity or rise in labour costs which might contribute to a rise in unit labour costs or to detect the excessive use of materials which might suggest an increase in wastage.

Senior management

So far, we have mainly considered the need for information that is processed and generated from sources within the organisation. At a senior level, however, information from internal sources often has to be supported by information derived from external sources to help managers ensure that the resources under their control are used as efficiently as possible in achieving business objectives. Decision making at senior management level has a major influence on the success or failure of the organisation. Any decisions concerned with controlling the organisation, assessing its performance, planning its future and initiating action must be supported by all relevant information.

Decision making at senior level in areas such as business strategy and planning requires information about broad trends rather than the detailed information needed to make many routine decisions on day-to-day matters at lower levels of the organisation. Senior management need information about:

- developments in internal costs and sales trends
- overall profitability, and the respective contribution of each part of the business
- capital requirements, and availability of internal funds and the cost and sources of external capital
- manpower and skills requirements
- strategies adopted by competitors
- forecasts of demand in the organisation's markets
- the impact on business of any changes in the economic, political, social and legal environment.

Communication channels and methods

The **communication channel** refers to the means by which information is communicated. The actual choice of communication channel depends upon a combination of:

- the need for an immediate feedback or response
- cost
- speed and urgency
- the number and location of the people who need the information
- the degree of confidentiality and security required
- the desired degree of formality
- convenience
- the complexity and amount of detail to be conveyed
- the type of information to be communicated
- the need to keep a record of the communication.

Business information can be communicated in many ways. Methods include:

- written reports
- instruction manuals
- letters. circulars and memoranda
- material posted on noticeboards
- in-house magazines and newspapers
- sheets of figures
- information on standard forms
- graphs, charts, drawings and photographs
- video, television and other audio-visual techniques
- meetings and interviews
- public address announcements
- electronic mail
- network messaging
- fax
- telephone and voice mail
- pager devices
- video conferencing.

▲ Information overload

Discussion point

Advances in information and communication technology (ICT) are rapid. Are you aware of any new ICT products or services that have just become available? Explain why advances in information and communication technology might encourage the provision of unnecessary information.

Whatever communication method is used, the information sent should be relevant and avoid superfluous comments and unnecessary detail. The information communicated to a supervisor in a factory may have to include an exact description of the operations to be carried out. In contrast, much broader information is supplied to middle and senior management. Senior managers may only require general indicators and a broad description of the developments that need to be considered when assessing the organisation's performance, setting objectives and deciding upon strategies.

Exception reporting

To ensure that the information provided to management is relevant, clear and concise and makes effective use of managers' time, some organisations stipulate that managers are only provided with data relating to exceptional developments. Middle management, for example, may only receive information connected with performance measurements that deviate by more than an agreed percentage from their targets. The information dealing with exceptional performance should also be supported by brief statements of the internal and/or external factors that may have contributed to any exceptional performance. Exception reporting makes more effective use of the time and skills that middle management devotes to decision making and to initiating and controlling actions.

Downward information flows

A downward information flow describes the provision of information by a superior to an immediate subordinate. It is, therefore, concerned with internal communications as part of a formal communications channel. A downward information flow can cover:

- issuing instructions on the tasks that have to be carried out by a subordinate and setting objectives, such as the target date for completing the work

- requesting information concerning the area of work for which subordinates are responsible

- communicating the organisation's procedures, working methods and practises and the rules and regulations

- giving feedback on a subordinate's performance in relation to his or her objectives and targets

- motivating people and encouraging attitudes that raise productivity and improve quality.

Some information will not come from an employee's immediate superior but from other parts of the organisation. For example, when employees first start work they receive general information about the structure and goals of the organisation from the personnel department. However, for information that relates to work undertaken by the subordinate, the communication channel should be from superior to immediate subordinate.

Upward information flows

An upward information flow along a vertical information channel is from a subordinate to a superior. This might be feedback from a downward flow or the communication may originate directly from subordinates. An upward information flow can cover:

- responding to a superior's request for information on some aspect of work for which the subordinate is responsible

- informing managers about the subordinate's own performance, problems or their personal ambitions in relation, for example, to promotion or opportunities for developing new skills

- passing on information about other employees in the subordinate's section and relations with sections with which there is a direct link

- submitting ideas on improving working methods and solving work problems.

In the interests of effective working relations, most organisations expect subordinates to report formally through their immediate supervisor or manager. However, they are likely to communicate informally with managers higher up the hierarchy and in some situations, such as a grievance procedure, may go directly to a more senior manager than their immediate superior.

Horizontal information flow

In addition to upward and downward flows, there are also horizontal information flows between people of the same status. Because many operations within an organisation must work very closely together, there must be formal arrangements for the exchange of information between sections and departments. The production department, for example, must have close contact with the purchasing department when it is considering changes to materials and components or introducing advanced machinery and equipment. Production staff also have to exchange information with employees in recruitment, training, marketing and transport.

The quality of information

The essential characteristics of an efficient information system are that the right people receive the right information at the right time. The information communicated should be:

- entirely relevant to the needs of the recipient

- accurate and concise

- comprehensive, avoiding a time-consuming request for extra information

- clear – it must be presented and communicated without ambiguity or possible misunderstanding.

The person receiving the information must have confidence in the ability of the sender and, therefore, have the confidence to take decisions based on the contents of the communication. The person sending the information must be confident that the receiver has the ability to understand, use and take effective decisions based upon the information supplied.

The information system, the communication media and the kind of information provided should be reviewed on a regular basis. The information system should be adjusted to take into account any developments within the organisation such as changes in its organisational structure or management style. This review should also take into account external factors such as advances in information technology.

> **Discussion point**
>
> What kinds of factors can effect the quality of a communication? Give possible reasons why the competitive position of a company may suffer if it fails to monitor the quantity and quality of its written communications.

Frequency of communication

Some information is required many times during the course of the working day to ensure that work is carried out smoothly and efficiently. For example, managers may want to monitor production levels in industrial or manufacturing operations on an hourly basis. However, at middle management level, much information may be prepared on a weekly or monthly basis. This applies to accounting information, for example, where a longer time period is needed in order to measure performance against targets.

Senior management also needs information on both internal and external developments that cover a much longer period. Information relating to shorter periods of time is unlikely to depict trends or problems, and the organisation would be wasting resources collecting and analysing this data.

Timing is as important as frequency. Information should be communicated at times that meet the specific needs of different levels of management and control. Supervisors require operational information to be updated and communicated on a very regular basis. Middle managers will be ineffective if the information they receive is either premature or received too late to be used for management control. For example, without up-to-date information, managers might accept an order and promise a delivery date that actually proves difficult to fulfil.

Informal communications

Vertical and horizontal information flows should be clearly defined. If individuals are not sure about from whom they should receive information and instructions, this can lead to the growth of information flows which are not part of the formal system. If there are two information flows running at the same time, there can be confusion and a fall in productivity. These informal systems can generate alternative sources of information and create a situation where the different levels of management receive inconsistent, inaccurate or even conflicting information.

Many businesses, however, accept that some tasks would not get completed if they only used formal channels of communications and chains of command. It may be necessary to short cut the formal system if a matter is very urgent or a clash of personalities is creating communications problems. Some informal channels may be tolerated if groups of workers have formed good working and personal relationships outside of the formal channels. Informal channels may even be the most effective way of communicating some kinds of information.

All organisations have a grapevine, which communicates information informally through personal contact between employees both vertically and horizontally throughout the organisation. The grapevine can be a quick way of communicating information to the workforce as a whole as it tends to operate by word of mouth. It can be used to pass on important information before an official announcement and, depending upon the feedback generated, the company may modify its intentions before the formal announcement. For example, a company may use the grapevine to test staff reaction to proposed changes in working methods or a new bonus scheme.

The problem with using the grapevine is that information can get distorted or exaggerated as it is passed on. A proposal to cut the workforce, through 10 per cent natural wastage and 5 per cent redundancies, may soon get changed to 15 per cent compulsory redundancies as it spreads through the grapevine. This may be useful as the actual announcement may prove to be much more acceptable than the distorted version on the grapevine.

External communications

Efficient internal communications are important, but an organisation's external communications are vital. Its business prospects will be seriously threatened if it neglects its external communications. An organisation needs to communicate externally with:

- customers and clients
- suppliers of materials, parts, machinery, other physical inputs and business services
- local, national and European authorities that deal with matters such as taxation, planning permission, environmental protection, competition law, investment grants, trading standards, and health and safety .
- pressure groups concerned with issues such as consumer protection, animal welfare, environmental matters and the welfare of low paid workers
- the media and the general public on matters that can either damage or enhance the company's public image.

Organisations must ensure that the quality of their external communications is as high as possible and select the most effective media for communicating information. It is obviously important that organisations maintain effective communications with their customers, and most businesses invest heavily in market research and promotion to attract and keep customers.

Discussion point

Recall recent phone conversations and face-to-face dealings that you have had with businesses. Did the staff you spoke to make you feel welcome? Did they create a good impression for their organisations? Was there any aspects of the communication that could have been improved?

Many companies now recognise the importance of providing a communication channel which allows customers easy access to the company. Some companies advertise a customer care telephone number or an e-mail address on their packaging or promotional literature. The customer care section will be staffed by people trained in the kinds of communications skills needed to deal with customers making complaints. Larger companies may employ specialist press officers and public relations officers to handle dealings with the media, pressure groups and the general public.

Organisations relying on other companies for materials and components can find themselves in financial difficulties if their external communications lets them down and orders are not placed at the right time. This may led to shortages of parts and materials, and production may be held up. Relations with suppliers may also be effected by poor verbal communications skills which can cause confusion over the exact nature and delivery of an order. It is for this reason that any changes to an order made verbally should be supported by some form of written or electronic confirmation.

▼ Organisations need efficient external communications

Open and restricted channel of communications

In most organisations, some internal channels and communication media are open to all employees; staff at all levels can access the information. Organisations want to provide some information to all their employees. This would include, for example, information on health and safety regulations, environmental management policies, incentive schemes and any response to recent adverse publicity. This downward information flow from the top of the hierarchy would be open to all.

The content of much downward and upward information flows is fairly routine, and organisations are not too concerned about people beyond the sender and recipient being aware of what is being communicated. However, access to some information and channels of communication may be restricted. Some information is sensitive – and if it becomes known to people other than the intended recipients, it could create either internal or external problems. Reasons for a communication channel being restricted include information dealing with:

- results of appraisal interviews conducted by superiors with their subordinates
- disciplinary and grievance procedures
- personal details of staff, including individual earnings and salary details
- financial and technical information that might be advantageous to competitors, including the results of R&D projects
- discussions relating to a possible merger
- initial proposals for cut backs or relocating the business.

▼ Companies need to restrict access to some information

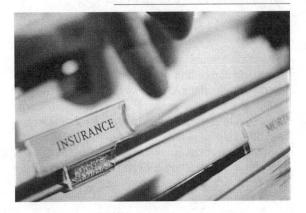

Discussion point

Consider ways in which a company can protect itself from data theft? What kind of information could create problems for an organisation if it fell into the wrong hands?

Information and communication technology

Both internal and external channels of communication are increasingly supported by information technology, with computers generating and managing information flows. A computer-based management information system provides the means to communicate, collect, store, summarise, analyse and present information in a way that best suits the controlling and decision making needs of different managers. Information received by one department or section can be further processed before it is passed onto other departments through the organisation's computer network.

Computer systems can help organisations:

- react to changes in the business environment
- process complex information
- provide administrative support
- increase job satisfaction
- collect information at source
- communicate via the internet.

Reacting to change

An organisation that can react quickly to changes in its business environment will strengthen its competitive position. Cutting down time lost through slow communications, lost messages and time-consuming searches through traditional filing systems to retrieve information reduces reaction time. Computers also save time by automating the production and analysis of complex documents.

Processing complex information

Computers can be used to process and communicate complex information. They can be used to quickly identify developments within the organisation that could threaten its business objectives. This might be, for example, a sudden rise in unit costs or disappointing sales revenue. Information technology also helps organisations analyse the market opportunities or problems caused by changes in the government's economic policies. The early identification of problems, analysis of market developments and reduced reaction times allows organisations to exploit opportunities and take action to minimise problems.

Administrative support

Higher productivity can be achieved by using electronic mail, word processing and specialist software packages for purchasing, payments, stock control, orders, invoicing and a range of accounting procedures. Computer applications reduce the time taken to communicate information between different departments and allow businesses to meet customer's requirements more efficiently.

Computerised administrative systems also help to reduce errors in the information being communicated. Unless the operator inputs incorrect data, or overrides and intervenes in the system, the level and frequency of mistakes should be reduced significantly or even eliminated.

Increasing job satisfaction

Computer technology can increase job satisfaction by reducing the amount of time spent by employees in repetitive and routine processes to extract, record and communicate information. The scope of a job can be restricted by the amount and range of information that a person has access to or is able to handle. Computer technology, however, allows employees to have much broader and more interesting jobs because all the data they require to operate in wider areas can be provided at their fingertips. This can contribute to greater job satisfaction, and the overall improvement in morale is often reflected in a rise in productivity.

"Plug the mouse into the serial port..."

Discussion point

What problems might a business encounter if it introduces advanced information technology without investing in appropriate staff training?

Collecting information at source

Computer technology allows information to be easily collected close to the source of an operation or transaction. For example, a great variety of detailed information is obtained by processing the data recorded and stored by the electronic scanners used at supermarket checkouts. Summaries of this information are communicated to senior management at the supermarket's head office, and might be used, for example, when they are reviewing their marketing strategy, and it also goes directly to the regional warehouses that supply the supermarkets within a particular area. These warehouses in turn have direct links via computer to their suppliers. Manufacturing and processing operations also use computers in stock control. Computers are used to monitor the level of parts and materials, and orders can be automatically triggered and sent to suppliers when stock falls below specified levels.

Information technology has many applications in retail environments. Travel agents can access the schedules of different airlines, check seat availability and make immediate bookings. Once a booking is received for a particular flight, the airline's database is automatically updated.

Developments in computer technology and software also allow salespeople, engineers and construction workers to communicate with a central office database, enter transactions and receive work schedules or sales leads wherever they happen to be operating at the time. These advances allow more people to work from home for at least part of their working week as well as conduct business and communicate with head office when travelling away from their main office.

Communicating via the internet

There is a very rapid growth in the number of companies marketing and selling products and services over the internet. It is estimated that, by the middle of the year 2000, about 3 per cent of retail sales are being transacted over the internet. In addition, an increasing amount of business relating to banking, investments, insurance and travel arrangements is being undertaken over the internet. Using the internet to communicate with consumers will be a major growth area for all kinds of business organisations.

Figure 1.19: Computer ownership and on-line access

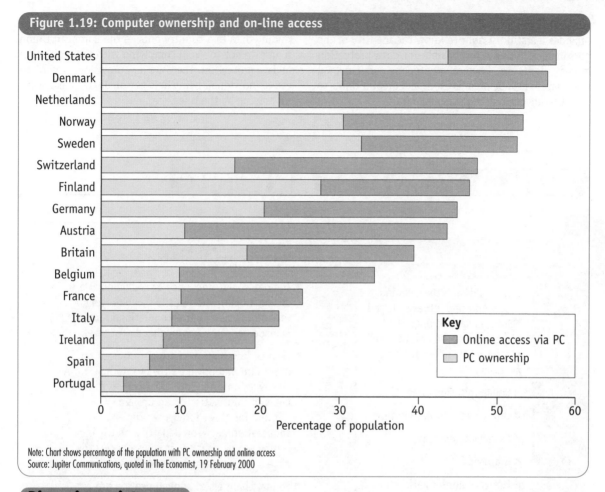

Note: Chart shows percentage of the population with PC ownership and online access
Source: Jupiter Communications, quoted in The Economist, 19 February 2000

Discussion point

Look at Figure 1.19 and suggest reasons why UK companies selling over the internet to overseas customers are relatively unconcerned that their websites are only available in English. The internet will soon be accessible through interactive digital television and mobile phones: what impact do you think this development will have on e-commerce and on businesses aiming to sell on the web?

The Data Protection Act 1984

The Data Protection Act was introduced to ensure that organisations structured and managed the data held on their computers in a responsible way. These are its main provisions.

- Organisations must register the kind of information it keeps on individuals with the Data Protection Agency (DPA).

- Data must be obtained and processed fairly. People should know if the information they give to organisations will be kept on computer and why it is needed.

- Organisations can only collect the kind of information that they have registered with the DPA, and the data must not be used outside of the purpose for which it has been registered.

- The information held on individuals must be accurate and, where necessary, up to date, and it must not be kept longer than necessary.

- Organisations must take precautions against unauthorised access to the information they hold on individuals.

- Individuals are allowed access to the personal data held by organisations and, where necessary, they can correct mistakes.

In March 2000 the Data Protection Act was extended to cover records kept on paper as well as information stored on computers and to provide additional protection for the individual. This protection includes new rights to know who holds information on you. It provides a statutory right to know the identity of the person in a business responsible for data protection issues, rights to have a photocopy of personal information held by organisations and greater rights to object to anyone holding personal data.

There are also new rules to prevent organisations sending data to a country outside the European Union in an attempt to avoid complying with the legislation on data protection. There are new provisions which can lead to individuals being held personally responsible for not abiding by the rules.

BUILD YOUR LEARNING

Keywords and phrases

You should know the meaning of the words and phrases listed below. Go back through the last eight pages of the unit to check or refresh your understanding as necessary.

- Communication channel
- Downward information flow
- Exception reporting
- Grapevine
- Horizontal information flow
- Information flow
- Upward information flow

Summary points

- The detail and frequency of communication depends upon whether the person receiving the information is at an operational, middle management or senior management level.

- Vertical information channels are used for downward and upward flow of information. A downward information flow involves different kinds of information to an upward information flow. To ensure efficient cooperation between departments within a business organisation, it is also necessary to have a horizontal information flow.

- Formal channels of communication are needed to send and receive information efficiently, however a business may use an informal information system to communicate some kinds of information.

- An efficient external communication system is needed in order to receive and send information to suppliers, customers and other stakeholders.

- The majority of an organisation's internal information flows are open channels but some information may be of a sensitive nature and this is communicated using a closed information channel.

- Advances in information and communication technology provide businesses with opportunities to make existing communication flows more efficient and scope to develop totally new internal and external communications systems.

Production and quality

Production

PRODUCTION INVOLVES ACTIVITIES which combine inputs in order to bring about the physical changes that eventually produce the desired output – the product. The product may be goods for consumers and households or parts and machinery for other producers and manufacturers. Production can create a physical change through:

- processing
- manufacturing
- assembly
- craft-based processes.

Processing

Many products are created by processing. These include foods, drinks, paper and board, chemicals, wool, paint, and building materials such as cement and plaster. Processing involves treatments such as washing, sorting, grading, crushing, grinding, milling, heating, applying pressure, and mixing with chemicals and other ingredients. This form of production is often based on a **continuous flow** – raw materials are passed through a series of processes until the desired form product is produced. For example, sugar cane is processed into packets of granulated sugar, and oil is refined into fuel, lubricants and petrochemicals.

The purpose of processing, therefore, is to change the composition, form, nature or appearance of raw materials in order that the outputs can be sold directly to households or businesses involved in a further stage

Figure 1.20: The brewing process

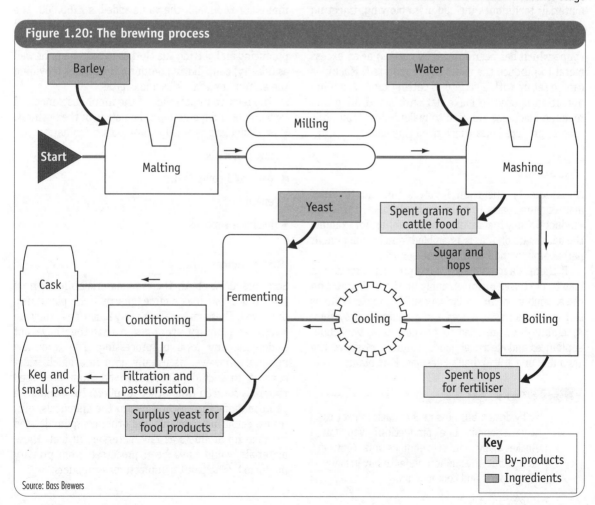

Source: Bass Brewers

of production. Navy beans, for example, are processed with other ingredients to produce baked beans; wool and cotton is processed into cloth for sale to clothing companies and soft furnishing manufacturers.

Figure 1.20 illustrates the brewing process. Beers are produced from simple ingredients – barley, water, sugar, hops and yeast. The process is designed to incur minimal wastage; by-products are reused or recycled.

> ### Discussion point
>
> Consider how the brewing process gradually adds value to the raw materials by listing the ways that inputs are treated and processed to bring about physical change – and finally produce beers.

Manufacturing

Manufacturing involves making parts and components which are then put together into a finished product. The first stage in manufacturing often involves forming, a basic shape is formed by pressing, beating or bending. This is often made easier by heating the raw material; techniques include glass blowing, injecting molten plastic granules into a mould, and casting, forging and rolling metals. Machining alters the basic shape which has been formed by cutting away excess metal to produce the exact shape required. Machines can be set up with a variety of cutting tools. A milling operation is used to make flat surfaces, drilling and reaming machines are used to make holes. Tapping is used to produce holes which need threads.

Assembly

An assembly operation involves putting together manufactured parts to make the final finished product. Production may first involve subassembly, for example the dashboard of a car is assembled from its component parts before being fitted into the vehicle.

If there is a mass market for a product, production may be organised on an assembly line basis. Workers on the assembly line fit a relatively small number of items to the product as it moves along a conveyor system. Assembly lines are used to produce cars, household appliances and electrical goods. Figure 1.21 shows the assembly line at Vauxhall's Ellesmere Port plant.

> ### Discussion point
>
> Why does a business need a mass market to use assembly line production? Vauxhall makes many of its own engines units (power units) but why might it prefer to buy in many other parts and components?

Craft-based production

Craft-based production involves making individual products by hand. It relies very heavily upon manual skills as well as an ability to create imaginative and attractive designs that suit the individual needs of customers. Craft production often involves working with materials such as wood, china, stone, glass, leather, fabrics and precious metals and stones.

Value added

A common feature of all forms of production is that they are the means by which organisations add value to their operations. Put simply, all organisations add value to the externally sourced materials and other inputs that contribute to their output. Value added is the difference between the value of an organisation's output, as measured by sales revenue, and the costs of its inputs bought in from outside which contribute to output. For example, if a clothing manufacturer spends £500,000 on inputs such as material, packaging and transport and then sells the clothes produced by these inputs for £650,000, the value added is £150,000. The inputs cost £500,000, and £150,000 – the value added – has to cover the costs of all activities involved in producing and getting the clothes to customers, as well as (ideally) contributing profit for the owners providing the entrepreneurial skills and capital.

The relative importance of the input costs incurred by a producer depend upon the nature of the business. Most businesses generally consume a combination of:

- raw materials
- parts and components
- energy
- business services.

Raw materials

Some producers obtain their raw materials directly from their source, such as a mine, quarry, field, plantation or oil well. These materials are very much 'raw', they are known as primary products in that they have not undergone any form of processing. The term raw materials, however, is usually used in a much wider context to include inputs derived from processed materials sourced from other suppliers. For example, a paint manufacturer would regard the chemicals, oils, resins, colouring pigments and other compounds used to make its products as raw materials; in fact, these materials would have been processed from primary products by the paint manufacturer's suppliers.

The production process at Ellesmere Port

The modern motor car is assembled from as many as 9000 individual parts gathered from all over the world. Up to 70 per cent of the components used by Vauxhall are sourced in the UK. Hourly, truck-loads of materials arrive at Vauxhall's factories, where the components and raw materials are assembled into cars.

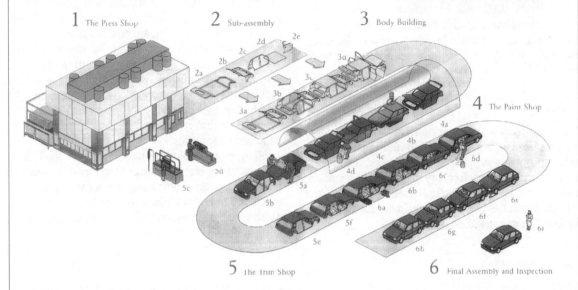

1 The Press Shop

2 Sub-assembly

3 Body Building

4 The Paint Shop

5 The Trim Shop

6 Final Assembly and Inspection

One of the state-of-the-art robots used to build Vauxhall Astras at Ellesmere Port

1.	**The press shop**	**5**	**Trim**
		5a.	Doors removed, wiring harness, glass, headlining and trim items fitted
2.	**Sub-assembly**		
2a.	Underbody pressings	5b.	Dashboard assembly
2b	Front end pressing	5c.	Door trimming
2c.	Body side pressings	5d.	Dashboard installed
2d	Roof pressings	5e.	Carpets and other trim fitted
2e.	Door pressings.	5f.	Seats fitted
3.	**Body building**	**6.**	**Final assembly and Inspection**
3a.	Underbody & front end joined	6a.	Axle, power unit, petrol tank and silencer installed
3b	Body sides added		
3c	Roof added	6b	Wheels on
3d	Doors, bonnet, wings and tailgate added	6c.	Doors re-fitted
		6d	Petrol in
4.	**Paint shop**	6e	Headlamps, brakes and wheel tracking set
4a	Body anti-corrosion protection ELPO dip	6f	Roller tests and brakes tested
4b	Spray primer	6g.	Conditioning and valeting
4c.	Spray colour	6h.	Engine underbody protection
4d.	Wash and wax protection	6i	Drive-away

Parts and components

In many cases, manufacturing organisation buy in a very large proportion of their parts and components and then assemble them to make their own particular products. Motor vehicle manufacturers, for example, buy in a wide range of parts and components from specialist suppliers. Car component manufacturers – producers of wheels, tyres, catalytic converters, shock absorbers, instruments, for example – produce their output for a large number of customers, benefiting from economies of scale and lower unit costs. Car producers, therefore, find it cheaper to buy in these parts and components rather than manufacture them themselves. Other items that must be designed to meet a car manufacturer's very specific needs, such as engines and gearboxes, may be made in one of its own factories, especially if they are going to be used in a wide range of models.

Energy

The vast majority of organisations obtain their energy supplies for heating, lighting and running machinery from an outside supplier. In a few cases, a company might consume so much energy that it may be economic to generate its own – of course, even in this case, the company still needs to buy the primary fuel inputs to be burnt in its generating plant.

Business services

Many organisations buy in business services from agencies and consultants that specialise, for example, in recruitment, advertising and design, or in providing advice on legal, financial and management matters. Companies also need commercial services such as banking and insurance, and transport, security, buildings maintenance and catering services may also be purchased from outside contractors.

The firm's own input

It is the way in which the firm's own resources of labour and capital are combined that adds value to the product as it passes through the different stages of production.

The labour input includes not just those workers who are directly responsible for making the product or providing the service but also the input of employees that provide support services in areas such as purchasing, human resource management and marketing. Consider, as an example, the manufacture of an office chair. A wide range of business functions will have been deployed to ensure that workers have the skills, materials, components and equipment to do the job, while marketing would be seeking customers

for the product. Once the chairs leave the assembly line, there are further labour inputs involved in packaging, storage and transport, for example.

In some industries, such as steel, chemicals and motor vehicle production, there is a very heavy reliance on capital items – plant, machinery and equipment – to add value. These are known as capital intensive industries. In contrast, labour intensive industries, such as many parts of the clothing industry, employ a great deal of labour relative to capital.

The term plant is generally used to describe large items of capital such as a production line in a car factory, the furnace and rolling mills in the steel industry and the complex network of containers and pipework that make up a chemical plant or a brewery. Machinery refers to capital items that are used to make or assemble parts. For example, a machine may be used for milling, drilling and other operations to turn metals and materials into finished parts. Similarly, a highly sophisticated computer controlled machine may be used to spot weld car body panels together. Equipment describes capital items used for smaller jobs such as hand and power tools.

Many capital items are bought 'off the shelf' from manufacturers offering a standard range in terms of performance and operating capacity; others are purchased from firms that specialise in making capital goods specifically designed to meet the particular needs of the user.

▲ Modern manufacture uses a range of sophisticated plant, machinery and equipment

Vertical integration

If a company is only involved in a single aspect of production, such as sawing timber into sections for sale to user industries, the value added is much lower than the saw mill could achieve by being vertically integrated. Vertical integration involves a company taking on more of the stages of production; the organisation takes on production stages previously undertaken by its suppliers and/or by its customers.

Consider the example of the wood supplier. Rather than buying raw timber, the company could develop its own managed forests and invest in a transport operation to move the timber to its own saw mills. This is known as backward vertical integration to the source of supply. The company could also build or take over a furniture factory and, eventually, open up its own retail outlets. This involves forward vertical integration towards the market. If the saw mill simply merges with another saw mill, to expand its existing timber operation, it is pursuing a policy known as horizontal integration. A vertically integrated organisation adds greater value than one which expands horizontally as the value added by greater horizontal integration does not increase much in relation to the inputs from suppliers.

Creating a service

Services meet both household and business needs. Some service industries, such as hairdressing, health and fitness and entertainment, are mainly supplied to meet personal needs, but others, such as banking, insurance, and transport, satisfy both household and business customers. Other services, such as advertising and management consultancy, are aimed specifically at businesses.

Unlike many manufacturing and processing firms, service organisations tend to use a great deal of labour as an input relative to their input of capital. In general, people have to be employed at the point where the service is provided to the customer. Technology, however, is gradually replacing labour in areas where personal contact is be considered less important. For example, there are fewer bank branches as more people use the internet to conduct banking business, and some companies use the telephone to sell and organise car insurance and have no direct customer interface.

Labour costs, however, are still a very large part of the total costs of service organisations. There are two contrasting reasons for high labour costs:

■ the knowledge and skills that service companies need tend to command a high income

■ a very large number of people must be employed to deal with the customers.

A firm of accountants or a Premiership football club employs a relatively small number of people, but they are very highly paid. In contrast, a supermarket chain employs a very large number of relatively low paid people.

As with manufacturing enterprises, the service sector acquire inputs from suppliers and then adds value. In some organisations, such as a firm of solicitors, the input costs may be relatively low, but in a restaurant chain the inputs – the food and drink bought in from outside – can be relatively high. Services may also involve some production process which adds value to their inputs. A restaurant adds value to its inputs – the food – by cooking. Some services, such as repairs, maintenance and installation businesses, may use tools or equipment at the point of delivery.

The distinctive feature of the service sector – and of personal services in particular – is that services are produced and consumed at the same time; they can not be stored for later use. For example, dentists and hotels are unable to produce and deliver a service without customers, and the customer's need is satisfied as soon as the service is provided.

Quality

Quality has always been an important competitive factor in some markets, but during the 1980s an increasing number of UK producers began to devote more attention to quality improvement. The rise in the spending power of the average household meant that consumers' choice of goods and services was no longer so dependent on price. At the same time, consumers were being offered a wider choice of products. This combination of greater spending power and wider choice obliged producers to improve and compete on quality. Because firms producing consumer goods and services sought to raise quality, their suppliers – companies producing materials, parts, machinery and business services – were also forced to improve quality.

A growing number of organisations now operate in markets where product differentiation is rapidly decreasing. For example, advances in technology mean that there is now very little difference between personal computers offered by the different manufacturers in a particular price range. A PC producer must therefore strive to gain a competitive advantage by establishing a reputation as a company with high quality and good customer care. Consider training shoes as another example. Manufacturers of trainers periodically introduce new features into their shoes in an effort to create a greater degree of product differentiation, but they all remain essentially the same design and product. If the identifying logos are removed, the average buyer might find it difficult to distinguish between brands.

Producers of both consumer goods and consumer durables must therefore place more emphasis on quality when marketing their products.

The increasing importance of quality can also be seen in the market for consumer services. The main features of services provided by airlines, banks and fast food chains are often virtually identical, and product differentiation can only really be achieved by improvements in quality.

Another factor in changing business attitudes to quality was the success of Japanese manufacturing companies. It was perceived that quality played an important role in helping Japanese companies succeed in European and US markets. By the end of the Second World War very little manufacturing capacity remained in Japan, and in the immediate post-war period Japanese products generally had a reputation as being cheap but inferior quality versions of products manufactured by US and European producers. However, by the early 1980s Japanese companies had become closely associated with high-quality products for which they were able to charge premium prices. In the early 1980s, Japan had 18 per cent of the world trade in manufactured goods, substantially more than the UK's 5 per cent share.

Meeting customers' expectations

When the word quality is used in everyday conversation, it usually suggests that the product or service being discussed is rather superior or possibly luxurious; and quality is usually associated with the upper end of the price bracket. In recent years, however, quality has taken on a more specific meaning in the context of business. It means that a product, service or process conforms exactly to the customer's requirements. There can be no such thing as high or low quality: if the product or service conforms to requirements, then it is quality; if it falls even fractionally below expectations, it is not a quality product or service.

A Mercedes, for example, may be seen as a quality vehicle because it meets a customer's expectations for performance, reliability, build quality, accessories and refinements. However, a customer may buy a small vehicle at the bottom end of the market which essentially offers no frills economical motoring. If it meets the expectations of people who want cheap motoring, then it too can be regarded as a quality product.

Satisfaction guaranteed, quickly

"What differentiates us from the competition," explains Kenny King, Kwik-Fit's customer services manager, "is that we actually entice people to call us or write to us." Indeed they do: Sir Tom Farmer's likeness is to be found all over Kwik Fit's corporate literature exhorting customers to do exactly that.

Typically a customer with a complaint dials Kwik-Fit's freephone number and an operator takes down details of the problem. This information is then relayed to an area manager – someone who oversees three or four service centres – who will then call the customer to discuss the problem and what needs to be done. If necessary, the area manager will also visit the customer in person. The area man-

ager can then take the appropriate action and prepares a report which goes back to the customer service centre. If the complaint is more serious – involving, say, the conduct of an employee – it will be dealt with at a higher level. Kwik-Fit aims to have all complaints resolved within three days of contact.

Not only does Kwik-Fit ask people to call with comments, sometimes it actively solicits them. The customer survey unit usually calls 5,000 people very evening. Should any of them come up with something along the lines of "Well ... I wasn't going to complain but to be honest I was a bit unhappy", the Kwik-Fit employee will apologise and ask if they wish to follow it up in any way. "Our aim", says

King, "is 100% customer delight. Of course in the real world it won't happen but the quicker you respond to someone's problem, the happier they'll be." And, King is quick to point out that, while happy customers are desirable, it all comes down to sound financial sense – a satisfied complainant may well become a brand ambassador. "If a customer is in the position where he or she thinks, 'Well, I wasn't satisfied earlier, but I am now', they're more likely to blow Kwik-Fit's trumpet." The efficiently rectified vehicular problem, he says, is exactly the kind of thing that pops up in conversation down the pub.

Source: Management Today, April 1999

Discussion point

How does Kwik Fit use its name to help differentiate its business from its competitors? What other non-price expectations might customers have when using the services provided by firms such as Kwik Fit?

Research shows that about 80 per cent of satisfied customers return. If, however, they have cause to complain and are then dealt with in a way that more than satisfies them, about 90 per cent of customers return. To what extent does Kwik Fit take account of these kinds of findings and use its customer care approach as part of its marketing strategy?

What do customers expect?

A company has to identify its customers' requirements exactly, if it is to satisfy them precisely and supply them with a quality product or service. What the consumer or the company buyer regards as a quality product or service is likely to depend upon their expectations in relation to a combination of factors. These include features such as:

- performance – is it suitable for the environment in which it will be used
- reliability – is it free from breakdowns
- durability – is it long-lasting
- safety – is it safe to use and does it protect the health and safety of others
- after-sales service
- ease of maintenance
- design and overall finish
- materials – are these to a sufficient standard
- delivery
- personal attention from the supplier.

Quality is customer driven

The relative importance of these product features in meeting customer needs varies both between individual customers and between various products and services. Manufacturers of music systems, for example, recognise that many people's idea of quality is based on the design and materials from which the system is made, and they are less concerned about performance and other definitions of quality. A car may be bought because of its reputation for reliability, a ready-made frozen meal for the quality of the ingredients.

Organisations buying inputs from other companies are particularly well placed to assess quality because their purchasing staff usually have many years experience dealing with different suppliers. Their staff will have an up-to-date and detailed knowledge of what is available. In many cases, a company only invites tenders from suppliers that can guarantee to meet their exact requirements, expressed in terms of clearly defined specifications. These specifications might refer, for example, to the makeup of raw materials or the design and performance of a component or item of machinery. These clearly specified aspects of quality must be met and maintained as part of the conditions for getting the contract to supply the customer. Apart from price considerations, the buyer company then takes account of other important factors such as the supplier's reputation in keeping to a delivery schedule and the quality of after-sales services.

Companies must be driven by what customers see as quality, and this can be identified by repeat orders. A quality-driven company seeks to close the gap between what customers actually expect from a product or service and what the supplier actually achieves in terms of meeting these expectations. Companies must aim for zero defects.

Exceeding expectations

As quality becomes a major factor in influencing choice between competing products and services, it is not enough to just satisfy customers' expectations. Quality is increasingly geared to exceeding these expectations, making customers feel that they have received a bonus in terms of the price, personal service, delivery and product or service features.

In the 1990s the computer company ICL, which provides hardware and systems to the business sector, introduced a quality and customer care programme. ICL aimed to 'exceed customers' expectations and to delight them with personal service'. The company's previous quality policy was to meet customers' expectations and requirements, a policy known as **conformance to requirements**. The decision to give a new definition to quality was based on ICL's research which showed that:

- a person who experiences bad service tells on average nine others about it, and 13 per cent tell more than twenty others.
- people who receive an excellent service tell three or four others about it
- it costs around five times as much to acquire new customers as it does to retain existing customers
- increasing customer retention can increase profits by up to 85 per cent.

Figure 1.22: ICL's four principles of customer care

Definition	**Exceeding customer expectations** – not merely meeting them
System	**Personal service** – not just following the process
Standard	**First choice supplier** – not we can't win them all
Measure	**What the customer says it is** – not what we think

Source: ICL training manual

Discussion point

Think of an example of a business that has recently supplied you with a product or service. Describe the extent to which you think it met all, some or none of ICL's four principles of customer care which are set out in Figure 1.22.

Quality saves on costs

Apart from improving quality as a competitive factor to increase market share, there are also some very strong financial reasons for focusing on quality. Savings achieved by reducing defective output more than offset the costs of introducing measures to improve quality. It is estimated that 25 per cent of people and assets in manufacturing companies and 40 per cent in service firms are deployed, directly or indirectly, on tackling problems connected with poor quality. In one UK organisation, each employee spent on average more than 2 hours 35 minutes in each seven hours firefighting to deal with quality problems.

The cost of poor quality can be traced and measured in every area of an organisation, from senior management down to basic administrative, secretarial and shop floor jobs. The costs associated with designing and introducing a management system aimed at a continuous improvement in quality are likely to be more than outweighed by the savings in:

- the costs of reworking or repairing faulty products

- the value of the output that cannot be salvaged and has to be scrapped

- the disruption to the flow of production caused by reworking defective items

- the effect upon production management and the organisation of the factory of having stocks of defective items and scrap taking up valuable space

- the costs of some kind of inspection department to check for defective items during the various stages of production

- labour and other resources that have to be devoted to carrying out work for customers under guarantees

- delays, lost output and maintenance costs because plant, machinery and equipment is damaged by the processing or handling of defective output

- discounts or other financial penalties paid to customers because quality, delivery or completion dates are not achieved

- the handling of the extra paper work generated by a failure to meet agreed standards with customers

- the costs – in financial and public relation terms – connected with meeting claims for compensation if a defective product is responsible for an accident or health problem.

Many of these costs have become known as the costs of conformance, the costs incurred in making sure that the product or service does eventually conform to the customer's requirements.

Apart from saving costs that are associated either directly or indirectly with faulty products or a poor level of service, an emphasis on quality can also produce other potential cost savings. Quality improvement can produce new sources of cost reductions. Almost all quality improvements come from the simplification of design, manufacturing, layout, processes and procedures. Simplification is often initially introduced by the need to reduce the incidence of errors or defects, but these changes also produce significant cost savings. The redesign of a Hewlett-Packard PC, for example, reduced from 270 to 130 the number of parts in the computer and from 120 to 50 the number of suppliers. Quality soared and costs plummeted. In addition, revenue increased from the resulting boost in sales.

Poor quality impacts on staff morale, job satisfaction, motivation and productivity because of the frustration caused by reworking products, the delays caused by machine breakdowns and the stress of having to deal with customers who have received a poor-quality product, level of service or late delivery. Improved quality brings several benefits.

- Staff morale and job satisfaction is guaranteed to rise when employees produce a consistent product or service that meets customers' requirements.

- When quality counts for more than quantity, staff become more motivated and productivity improves. This rise in productivity comes from changes in attitudes rather than demands that employees work physically harder or take fewer rest periods.

- There should be improvements in the way staff communicate with each other. This is because there should be less communication dealing with problems of poor quality – and looking to lay the blame – and more emphasis on ideas for taking quality to even higher levels.

- Companies that improve quality continuously are better places to work, and they find it easier to attract personnel and retain their existing staff.

Quality control

Quality control involves an organisation using some kind of inspection system for identifying materials, parts, components and finished products which do not meet the company's specifications. Inspection or testing may be carried out at various stages of production to ensure that faulty items do not remain in the production chain.

The operative or inspection department may check every item or just a sample of production. Processing industries, such as the brewing and chemical industries, also test regular samples of their products. Quality inspection is supported by highly sophisticated monitoring, measuring and testing equipment. This allows organisations to make adjustments to machine settings and control devices to improve quality.

There are some drawbacks to a quality inspection system. Using an inspection system to control quality encourages employees to take it for granted that some output is bound to be defective. Less attention is paid to preventing errors and defects in the first place as they will be picked up later by the inspection system.

A quality control system must ensure that there is regular contact between those departments that have a particular interest in quality matters. The marketing department for example may identify issues raised by customers, while the design and research and development departments should work with production on developing the product so that current defects are eliminated when work is being processed.

Total quality management

The concept of total quality management (TQM) was developed and first applied by Japanese manufacturers in the 1950s. The driving force behind TQM was the introduction of a just-in-time (JIT) system for managing production.

Just-in-time

Before the Second World War, the Japanese car maker Toyota operated in a very small home market dominated by imported cars. This limited market meant that Toyota could not raise output to a level where it could benefit from the economies of scale enjoyed by European and US car manufacturers. These manufacturers operated mass production conveyor-based assembly lines, a system developed by Henry Ford. Each step in the production process had to be kept supplied with a wide variety of parts. To avoid potential shortages and the production line grinding to a halt, producers kept large stocks of parts along their production line. Given the size of the Japanese market Toyota could not operate on this basis because:

- holding large stocks would tie up scarce capital during difficult economic and financial times

- stocks would take up storage space

- labour costs would be involved in handling the accumulated parts.

Toyota tackled this problem by developing a production system in which the different processes in the production and assembly sequences were only supplied with materials and components when and as they were needed – in other words, supplies came in 'just-in-time' for each sequence to be completed. This just-in-time approach obviously had a big impact on Toyota's suppliers. They had to deliver the right parts to the assembly plant exactly when they were needed.

Today, customers can specify preferences for features such as body colour, engine size, gearbox and braking system, and Toyota manufactures vehicles to about 45,000 different specifications. The JIT system continues to ensure that only the parts needed to satisfy a customer's order for a particular model are delivered to the assembly line as that model is being assembled. Because buffer stocks are not held, all items arriving at the production line must meet quality specifications. If a part is defective, a worker cannot simply pick up a replacement from stock. This means that a JIT system cannot operate without top management being committed to total quality management (TQM).

Although the essential features of TQM originated in the USA during the 1940s, the approach was mainly developed by Toyota and other Japanese manufacturers during the 1950s. It was only in the 1980s that European and US producers began to consider and introduce TQM, spurred by increased competition from Japanese imports of consumer durables in particular. Through a combination of JIT and TQM, Japanese companies had developed a reputation for being suppliers of competitively priced quality goods.

Another factor influencing the uptake of TQM in the UK was the influx of Japanese inward investment. The UK became a popular location for many Japanese producers, and companies wanting to supply them with parts and components had to adopt TQM as part of any contract.

Prevention not detection

Total quality management is an approach based upon the prevention of errors and faults in contrast to the traditional policy of error detection and correction. It is a way of managing an organisation so that every job, process and procedure is carried out correctly, first time and every time. It replaces an inspection or checking system, which looks to find and correct defects after they have occurred.

A TQM approach ensures that every aspect of the company's operations, not just the production and assembly cycle, is managed in ways that guarantee good quality products. This involves identifying the actual or potential sources of error and continuously introducing changes that improve quality. The aim is to achieve zero defects; this should be the objective of all activities that contribute to the provision of a product or service. A company can not operate TQM in isolation: TQM must be adopted by its suppliers because incoming components and supplies are expected to meet a zero defects standard of quality.

Companies operating a TQM approach should not ignore even the slightest departure from the quality of their products and services. If this happens, then TQM is no longer being practised. Having established a reputation for quality, even a small lapse can potentially cause damage in the market.

Total commitment

Total quality management is a long-term operating philosophy which requires that the entire workforce, from top management down, pursue continuous improvement in all processes, products and services. If a firm adopts this approach then it must be prepared to eat, sleep and breathe quality, and its total commitment to quality must be reflected in all aspects of management decision making.

Everybody in the organisation must be involved and accept personal responsibility for quality. It begins at the top with the chief executive, senior directors and managers; they must make it clear that they are really serious about quality. Middle managers play a vital role in spreading the TQM approach effectively throughout the organisation. They must explain TQM and demonstrate their own commitment to the people for whom they are responsible.

Changing attitudes

Quality improvements come from people and not machines. This is confirmed by the importance which Japanese companies have always placed upon involving their workforces in quality improvement. Without genuine and enthusiastic commitment by the workforce, no amount of new technology and automation can guarantee quality.

Operating TQM usually involves new systems and techniques, but the most important changes are altering staff attitudes so that the culture of the organisation is one of preventing failures rather than identifying and dealing with them. Some managers feel that they have had a good day if they have solved a series of problems and therefore helped to keep the production programme on track. They seem to enjoy the trouble shooting or firefighting aspect of their jobs. However, the management time used in solving problems does not mean that the value added is any greater than if things had been done correctly first time round.

Continuous improvement

Organisations must develop systems and procedures that ensure continuous quality improvement. TQM is not a bolt-on marketing gimmick, but a means of achieving the consistently high quality which is necessary to survive in highly competitive markets. Quality improvement has to become a never-ending process because a firm's product or service becomes increasingly less or more competitive depending upon its attitude to quality improvement. The Japanese experience shows that TQM cannot be introduced overnight – some Japanese companies worked on quality for 30 or 40 years before they developed it into a total management system.

A company adopting TQM may quickly find ways of improving quality, however after a few years there may be few obvious opportunities. Managers leading quality improvement programmes may begin to find it difficult to justify the costs. The seemingly slow progress may also damage commitment and enthusiasm. At this stage, management must maintain the momentum by finding new ways of putting life back into the drive for quality improvement.

In Japan, companies have sustained momentum for continuous improvements by introducing quality circles – these are teams of around eight workers from a particular section (often with their supervisor) that meet regularly in company time to discuss ways of improving quality and productivity. Japanese managers recognise that the experience of workers can be put to good use, and quality circles have always been a feature of Japanese factories. The teams sometimes have the authority to change the ways in which they operate without taking their ideas to superiors, and this teamwork and involvement in decision making is a vital

▲ Reputations for quality are hard won – Skoda cars were a running joke in the 1980s, but now enjoy a good reputation in the small car market

factor in motivation. In one year, quality circles at Toyota produced about two million suggestions throughout its operations, and 97 per cent of them were implemented.

Discussion point

Discuss why the adoption of total quality management is an inappropriate strategy for a business looking for an immediate solution to poor quality.

Internal customers and quality chains

Meeting the quality requirements of customers is not possible without meeting the requirements of 'customers' within the organisation itself. To achieve quality throughout an organisation, all internal suppliers must clearly define and exactly meet the needs of their internal customers. Relationships between internal suppliers and customers can be regarded as a series of internal quality chains running throughout an organisation. The external quality chain – between an organisation and its customers – breaks down if just one group of employees fails to ensure that the information, service or item which they supply to colleagues in their particular internal quality chain conforms exactly to requirements. It is not only vital that each internal supplier establishes the precise needs of their internal customers, but also that these customers make their exact requirements known to their suppliers.

Many employees never come into direct contact with the end product or service supplied to customers, but their input is still crucial. For example, if staff responsible for organising delivery schedules make mistakes, some customers will not receive the goods they ordered at the right time, and as a consequence the organisation will not be delivering a quality product or service. Those responsible for defects or errors are not generally the staff who have direct contact with dissatisfied customers; by emphasising the importance of internal quality chains, a business can help build a commitment to quality throughout the organisation. Recognising that supplier customer relationships – and quality chains – exist throughout an organisation is a key part of total quality management.

Quality assurance schemes

A quality assurance scheme is the means by which an organisation implements its commitment to quality. It helps firms to do the job properly the first time, because the scheme is designed to prevent failures rather than detecting errors once they have occurred. In this way a quality assurance scheme (QAS) differs radically from quality control systems which involve inspection procedures at various stages of production. The design of a QAS recognises that defects do not just happen; they are caused by people.

Toyota, the Japanese motor vehicle manufacturer, was the first company to adopt total quality management. A feature of TQM within the Toyota production system is *jidoka*. This is concerned with making machines respond intelligently. Examples of *jidoka* equipment include fail-safe features that prevent employees from mounting or assembling equipment incorrectly and sensors that prevent machines from operating if a defect occurs. Figure 1.23 shows a *jidoka* improvement to a machine that prevents an operative from mounting the component the wrong way round.

Assuring quality

Once an organisation has identified the reasons why people are responsible for defects and errors, it can develop a system which eliminates the causes of defects. In this way, quality is assured. There is no single format for a QAS, and an organisation chooses a system which is most appropriate to its particular product or service. What it must do is to ensure at every stage of production (or in the provision of a service) that

materials, equipment, methods and procedures are used in exactly the same way, every single time. All employees should be aware of what is expected of them, and should know how their own particular performance has to meet certain clearly identified requirements.

Quality assurance standards

The adoption of formal quality assurance systems has accelerated in recent years because of the development of internationally recognised quality standards. These are standards which are formally assessed, approved and controlled by an independent body. The best known, **BS EN ISO 9000**, is operated jointly by the **British Standards Institution** (BSI) and the **International Standards Organisation** (ISO). Companies are now increasingly looking to use suppliers that can guarantee quality assurance. The first sectors in the UK to insist that suppliers had a formally recognised QAS were the defence, aerospace and motor vehicle industries.

Setting up a QAS and securing outside recognition must be motivated by the desire to deliver continuous improvements in quality rather than to secure business through a short-term marketing tactic. An organisation could suffer damaging publicity if its quality recognition is withdrawn after a visit by an external assessor.

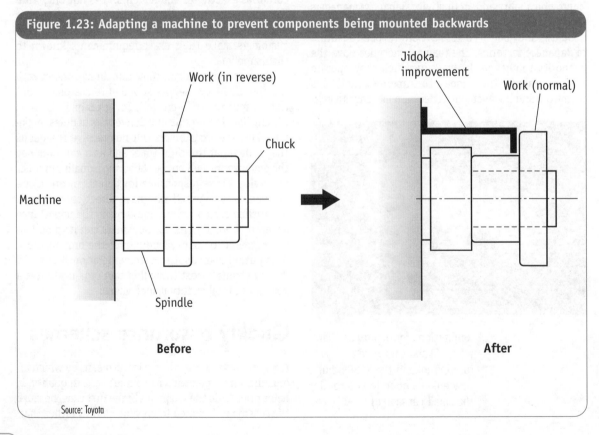

Figure 1.23: Adapting a machine to prevent components being mounted backwards

Source: Toyota

The process of designing a QAS that meets the requirements of an independent body can in itself bring quality benefits.

- The organisation must identify the kinds of attitudes and procedures that are most likely to be responsible for poor quality.

- The company must clearly identify areas of responsibility for all staff . This helps the company establish exactly who is the 'owner' of any specific problem.

- Staff gain a clear understanding of what is expected of them, ensuring that they take action to tackle the causes of defects rather than trying to pass the problem to someone else.

- The detailed work that has to be undertaken in preparation for the introduction of an externally certified QAS helps to identify a wide range of actual and potential problems that effect quality.

- The identification of the causes of quality defects is a major step towards their solution.

To gain a formal recognition of its QAS an organisation must:

- put together a comprehensive quality manual that describes the policies being followed and the systems and procedures that have been put in place to ensure the management of quality at all stages

- ensure that the manual states the way in which the organisation actually operates rather then the way it would like to operate

- satisfy the external assessor that the organisation actually works according to the systems and procedures described in the manual.

Quality standards in the service sector

In the early 1990s, the service sector also began to recognise the advantages of quality assurance systems and the need for an independent assessment. The BS EN ISO 9000 standard has now been adopted by solicitors, surveyors, architects, accountants and management consultants. Professional bodies are helping their members by writing documents to aid interpretation of the standard in their particular sector.

Standards and quality

Total quality management is a business management philosophy which recognises that customer needs and business goals cannot be separated. Achieving a quality assurance standard does not necessarily mean that a business has adopted a TQM approach. The requirements for formal recognition is decided by an external assessor, but success in meeting TQM objectives is assessed by the business itself and its customers. In BS EN ISO 9000, for example, the business sets its own standards of quality, and the external assessor simply decides if the systems and procedures in place will guarantee that standard. The award also does not mean that the producer meets a standard for quality established by any outside industry body. Accreditation to the BS EN ISO 9000 standard, however, is an excellent demonstration of a company's commitment to quality.

Benchmarking

Benchmarking is an approach to quality improvement based on the study of best practice in other organisations. A company makes an in-depth study of the production, administrative and marketing methods used by competitors in the areas which influence quality and identifies those methods which are the most successful in each particular area.

The key to benchmarking is to decide which organisations demonstrate best practice. Before making this decision, companies consider a wide range of opinion, both from customers, industry analysts and journalists working in the business and financial press. The standards adopted by the 'best practice' organisations will then be used to benchmark the company's own practice. Different organisations may be used for different aspects of quality, such as uniformity of output, delivery periods and reliability, after-sales services, efficient invoicing and payments system and customer care.

To set benchmarks, companies must collect information on how each best practice organisation carries out particular processes. This may come form the organisation's own in-house publications, articles in specialist publications or information held by research companies. This information must be analysed and assessed in relation to the firm's own performance and techniques in areas that influence quality. This analysis helps identify the processes where changes are needed and help the firm adapt the best practices of its competitors to its business.

During a benchmarking exercise, the workforce should be kept fully informed on why and how benchmarking is being used and the implications for their working methods and practices. This is not a one-off exercise: to be effective a company needs to monitor developments continuously both within and outside the business and reset benchmarks if necessary against a new leader in a particular process.

Companies must be prepared to benchmark against firms in totally different sectors to find best practice for different parts of their business. Both Ford and General Motors, for example, provide credit to their customers, so they benchmarked these financial operations against banks. The computer company IBM benchmarked its telephone operations against call centres which handle enquiries about car insurance and savings and investment schemes.

The US company, Southwest Airlines, benchmarked part of its operation against motor racing. The company was concerned that its aircraft spent an average of 40 minutes on the ground being refuelled, during which time, of course, it could not be earning revenue. Southwest Airlines benchmarked its refuelling processes against the most efficient refuellers in Formula One racing. The refuelling time was cut to 12 minutes.

▼ Formula One pit stop routines have been used to benchmark refuelling processes in the airline industry

Training and quality improvement

Quality problems can be caused by poor staff performance. In many cases this can be addressed by training, improving the manual skills of workers through training courses or improving management techniques through **management development programmes**.

Early signs that there is a fall-off in the quality of an employee's work might include:

- an increase in materials and components being scrapped

- more frequent machine breakdown

- a rise in customer complaints.

Problems can be caused by the loss of skilled workers and difficulties in finding suitable workers to fill the vacancies. A training scheme may be needed to improve the skills level of newly recruited workers. Training schemes may also be necessary in several other circumstances.

- If a capital investment project involves new plant, machinery and equipment which embodies the latest technology, then employees may need to be retrained to take full advantage of the equipment's potential for quality improvement.

- Alterations to a product or service to improve quality may involve a change in design, materials and assembly techniques. New skills or working methods may be required to ensure that the improvement in quality is consistently achieved.

Training or retraining schemes are equally important for organisations providing consumer and business services. A restaurant chain, for example, must monitor the performance of employees who serve customers to ensure that quality standards and customer care are maintained. Any signs of slippage must be addressed by an appropriate training scheme that not only deals with any manual skills or job knowledge but also the all important social and personal skills that encourage customer loyalty.

Management development

An essential part of human resource management is ensuring that there is a ready supply of trained and experienced staff who can be promoted to **supervisory positions** and higher levels of management. It is also important for the efficiency of a company the people holding existing positions of authority can reach their full potential. Productivity and quality is likely to suffer if decision making is in the hands of managers and supervisors who are not up to the job. Successful managers can:

- initiate, control, coordinate and organise activities within their area to maximise productivity and improve quality

- identify the causes of current or potential problems that threaten productivity or quality and introduce successful remedies or preventative measures

- successfully communicate to workers that they are valued and the success of the company depends very much upon the contribution of every individual in terms of competitive costs and quality.

In order to develop and improve upon these skills, an organisation needs to provide management development programmes. These might include job rotation and giving managers a special project, action learning and coaching. These on-the-job programmes may then be supported by formal management qualifications at a business school or institution of higher education.

BUILD YOUR LEARNING

Keywords and phrases

You should know the meaning of the words and phrases listed below. Go back through the last 15 pages of the unit to check or refresh your understanding.

- Assembly
- BS EN ISO 9000
- Business services
- Capital intensive
- Commercial services
- Conformance to requirements
- Continuous flow
- Costs of conformance
- Craft production
- Equipment
- Firefighting
- Forming
- Inspection system
- Internal customers
- Just in time
- Labour intensive
- Machinery
- Machining
- Management development
- Parts and components
- Plant
- Primary products
- Processing
- Quality assurance scheme
- Quality circles
- Subassembly
- Value added
- Vertical integration

Summary points

- Production combines resources in a processing, manufacturing, assembly or craft-based operation to produce goods. Services are also the result of a 'production' process that relies upon an input of both human and non-human resources.

- Value added is the difference between the costs of inputs bought in from outside the organisation and the revenue derived from the organisation's output.

- Quality can be defined as meeting people's expectations – this means that quality is determined by a firm's customers.

- The costs of introducing measures to improve quality can be more than outweighed by saving costs associated with dealing with errors and defects.

- A quality control system checks output for faulty and defective items. Total quality management is an ongoing approach which identifies the sources of errors and introduces appropriate changes to improve quality.

- A quality assurance scheme guarantees quality by introducing production methods that prevent errors and defects from occurring in the first place.

- A business can seek formal and independent recognition of its commitment to quality by having its quality assurance scheme assessed by an independent body.

- Benchmarking is an approach to improving quality based on the study and adoption of best practice in other organisations.

How to produce a detailed business report

The flow chart shows the stages you need to go through to generate evidence to meet the assessment requirements for this unit.

Construct an action plan setting out the tasks that you have to complete to write your business report.

Select a large or medium-sized company. A medium-sized company has a turnover between £1.4 million and £5.75 million, with up to 250 employees.

Collect information about your chosen business. This should cover business objectives (growth, profits, etc.), business organisation (functions, organisational charts), business type (legal status), business culture (management style and attitudes) and communications (use of IT, etc.).

Use all available sources to research your report, including annual reports and accounts, marketing materials, company visits (if possible), company publicity materials (remember to visit its website) and any newspaper articles by searching media websites such as Guardian Unlimited.

The first section of your report should describe and explain the organisation's objectives, the type of ownership, the functional areas of the business and how these help the organisation meet its objectives, the business's communications, and the production and quality assurance process.

The second section of the report requires you to write analytically and evaluatively by making judgements about the success of your organisation.

For example, you might consider whether ICT helps or hinders the organisation's communications; whether the structure and culture of the business helps it to improve its performance; whether it should adopt a different approach to quality; whether it is meeting its objectives.

Produce a word-processed business report within the timescale you stated in your action plan.

This unit provides a comprehensive overview of the markets in which businesses operate. We review the forces of demand and supply which make up markets, analysing a wide range of factors that influence market demand and market supply, and show how changes in these factors can impact on prices and sales.

Businesses are subject to many competitive pressures. The unit examines key features of the competitive environment, and considers the extent to which individual competitive features promote the interests of stakeholders. We identify some market developments which operate against the interests of consumers. There is an analysis of the motives that lie behind business expansion strategies through mergers and takeovers.

Governments intervene in markets and seek to influence the overall business environment. We look in particular at laws which target unfair trading practices and aim to protect the health and safety of consumers. There is examination of the increasing pressure on companies to minimise the environmental impact of their operations. We also consider the impact on business of government economic policies.

The expansion of world trade means that UK companies must improve competitiveness if they are to survive the increasing competition from imports and develop their export markets. We assess the impact on UK companies of movements in the exchange rate, and analyse the implications for UK business of adopting the European single currency.

The competitive business environment

How competition affects business

IN THE FIRST PART OF THIS UNIT, we look at markets in some detail. We consider the different types of market, and analyse the demand and supply side factors which shape markets.

Markets

A **market** is formed by the existence of **demand** and **supply** for goods and services. The interaction of these forces produces a market price for a particular product and determines the quantity that is traded at that price over a given period of time.

While goods can be seen and touched and services can be experienced, market forces are invisible. They can be likened to the forces that produce changes in the climate. Changes in the weather are the result of the interaction of atmospheric pressures pulling in various directions, and although we can't see these forces we most certainly experience their outcome. In a market, it is people, either as buyers or sellers, that are responsible for the invisible pressures that bring about changes both in the price of a particular product and the amount of that product that is bought and sold over a particular period of time. Each time you spend money on a soft drink, for example, you are part of the **demand side** of the market for that product. If you owned a business producing soft drinks, you would be part of the **supply side** of the market. In both cases, you are contributing to market forces.

A market registers the total strength of demand coming from people seeking to buy particular goods or services. Total demand in a market may be generated by millions of people, both in the UK and abroad. A market also registers the total amount of supply by producers. Again, goods and services can be supplied by many businesses in the UK or abroad. If it is economical to transport a product over long distances, then the total supply for a product can be generated by producers from all over the world.

Single markets

Some goods and services are identical or so similar that the boundaries that surround the market in which they are sold can be very clearly identified. Take petrol as an example. If your car takes unleaded petrol, you buy unleaded petrol – you don't choose between different brands. So an oil company which refines crude oil to produce petrol operates in the overall (single) market

for petrol because the output from its refineries is effectively identical to that of its competitors. There is no product differentiation of any real significance.

An example of a single market for services is air travel. Competing airlines fly the same routes and have an exact idea of the market in which they are operating. They can compete on price and other aspects of their service, but their basic service – transporting you in the air from London to New York, say – is identical.

Segmented markets

Many markets are not single, they are segmented to varying degrees. The market for confectionery, for example, is not made up of one type of product in a single market; there are many kinds of confectionery products. Within the overall confectionery market, it is possible to identify separate segments. Look at the vast array of sweets, chocolate bars, snack bars and boxes of chocolate displayed in a supermarket. The products are aimed at particular segments of the confectionery market, and they appeal to different types of consumer.

Each confectionery producer carefully researches the segments of the market at which each of its products is aimed. One company's chocolate covered caramel bar will compete with other bars with essentially the same ingredients or those with a similar taste and texture. The company's market research, however, may suggest that its caramel bar could succeed in markets for chocolate bars and tubes of chocolate covered caramel. It is unlikely, however, that it will compete in the segments of the confectionery market which satisfy demand for tubes of fruit flavoured sweets.

Segmented markets are very common. This is partly due to increasing product differentiation. Take cars as an example. Manufacturers develop a range of models aimed at a particular and distinct market segments. The major car companies produce a range of models including micro, mini, hatchback, family saloons, executive, multipurpose, sports and off-the-road vehicles.

The geographical size of markets

Companies in the **primary sector** supply raw materials. Many primary sector businesses operate in world markets. For example, an oil company operating in the North Sea conducts its business in the context of the world market for oil. Its output forms part of the world supply of oil, and the demand for North Sea oil is part of the world demand for oil. Oil extraction companies must pay attention to any factors likely to affect demand in any of the major oil consuming countries, and they must also monitor the actions taken by their competitors – and organisations like OPEC (see p. 86) – which could affect supply. These interactions of world supply and demand set the world price for crude oil.

In the **secondary sector**, firms turn raw materials into manufactured goods. Secondary sector businesses operate in both home and overseas markets. For example, a UK knitwear manufacturer may see the potential market for its garments extending beyond the UK, though its overseas sales might be concentrated in the larger markets of the European Union. The manufacturer, therefore, has an interest in any developments in Europe that might affect the total demand for knitwear and must take account of the styles and prices offered by its UK and overseas competitors.

Some UK manufacturers may operate solely in the domestic market. A furniture manufacturer, for example, may simply sell its products in the UK. The company may not produce styles that appeal to overseas consumers. It needs to be aware of developments in the UK market as a whole and must monitor the marketing strategies adopted by furniture makers operating in its particular market segment.

Other businesses operate in very localised markets. For example, a baker may sell bread to stores in a small geographical area and direct to customers that visit its shop. The bakery need only be concerned about very local developments in terms of market demand. However, on the supply side, it may face competition from many producers including, of course, any major supermarkets that have stores in its area.

Discussion point

How many major supermarkets are there in your area and what do you think is the geographical extent of the market in which they operate? Why might the supermarket price war be less pronounced in some areas? Suggest reasons why the costs of non-shop services continue to rise quite sharply.

Markets for services

Services are provided by the **tertiary sector**. The sector covers personal, household and business services. Personal services include hairdressing, leisure, recreation and health care; household services include dry cleaning, domestic services, plumbing and decorating.

Inflation falls to the lowest in Europe

Fierce competition between shops and lower car prices meant that consumer prices in Britain rose by only 0.8 per cent in the twelve months up to January 2000. This gives Britain the lowest inflation rate for consumer prices in the European Union. This contrasts with the previous 30 years when Britain's inflation rate was usually among the highest in Europe.

In previous years, falls in inflation have been the result of a slowing of the rate of increase of prices. The current very low rate reflects actual falls in the prices of food, clothes, cars and tobacco. The overall performance on consumer prices would have been even better had not the prices of consumer services risen by 4 per cent.

A price war between supermarkets reduced food prices by 2 per cent, and the price index for other goods such as clothes, household goods, personal articles and leisure goods fell by 3 per cent.

In the service sector the largest price rises were in non-shop services, such as insurance, rent, vehicle tax, travel costs and holidays, where the index of prices rose by 7.1 per cent.

Adapted from *The Guardian*, 16 February 2000

Companies themselves are on the demand side of the market for a wide range of specialist **business services** such as financial auditing, advertising, market research, security and transportation. Businesses also use consultants and agencies covering areas such as management, public relations, marketing, design, information technology, employment laws, environmental issues, and recruitment and training.

There are many services which meet the needs of both private individuals and businesses. Both groups make up the demand side of the market for telecommunications, banking, insurance, hotels, catering and travel facilities.

Markets for services vary from very local to global. An international airline is part of the world market for passenger transport; a small bus operator may only operate in a local market, connecting a few towns and villages. Banking and insurance services cover both national and international markets, with many banks maintaining branches and representatives in locations all over the world.

Advances in information technology now make it easier for service organisations to operate in world markets. With modern communications, they can service markets worldwide from premises in relatively few locations. Improvements in long-distance air travel also allows consultants to operate in world markets and UK architects, software engineers and financial consultants now compete in international markets with consultants from other countries.

In personal services, the potential markets are often limited to much smaller areas. Customers and clients often have to be in attendance to consume the service. So, for example, osteopaths, hairdressers and snooker hall owners are mainly concerned with developments in their local markets rather than what is happening nationally. The size of the market for a personal service is partly determined by the extent to which customers are willing to travel to use the service of a particular provider. How far would you travel for a haircut? If a provider can convince people that it offers value for money or an exceptional service, it will be able reach a larger market, particularly as consumers now have greater access to transport.

Some local services are provided by suppliers that are part of a large organisation. For example, there are many retail and restaurant chains operating on a nationwide basis. However, branch managers need to be mainly concerned about developments in the market where they are located. The performance of each branch of a retail chain is influenced by developments in both the demand and supply sides of its local market, and managers will be particularly interested in the marketing strategies adopted by similar stores in the same area.

Commodity markets

The term commodity describe the raw materials used by processing and manufacturing industries. These commodities are the output of producers involved in growing or extracting raw materials through agriculture, mining, quarrying and drilling operations. Many commodities are bought and sold on world markets, and the interaction of demand and supply produces a single world price for each commodity.

Dealings in commodities are conducted through international commodity exchanges, and some of the most important ones, such as the London Metal Exchange, are based in London. In these exchanges, dealers and brokers act as intermediaries between buyers and sellers. Many commodities are totally uniform, they have the same physical makeup and characteristics from wherever they are sourced, so buyers are not concerned about the actual source of what they are buying. This is the case for metal ores, cotton and sugar. However, different strains of wheat, varieties of coffee and sources of crude oil may have different world prices according to their relative quality.

In the short term, commodity prices can be influenced by speculators who buy and sell commodities in the hope that future price movements will make them a profit on their dealings. Speculators do not actually take delivery of any commodities they purchase. For example, a speculator may buy, and then sell on, a quantity of cotton that is still ripening on a plantation. In some cases, a speculator may even buy and sell a crop which hasn't even been planted. The cotton that is finally delivered to a company making yarn or textiles may have been bought and sold several times before it is turned into clothing or a soft furnishing product.

▲ Decisions by OPEC can have a major impact on the price of oil

One of the attractions of speculating in commodities is that the factors which influence the demand and supply sides of their markets can be very unpredictable. Sudden changes in demand or supply can produce wide fluctuations in prices. Consider, for example, recent development in the oil market. Many of the world's major oil producing countries belong to the Organisation of Petroleum Exporting Countries (OPEC) and, on occasions, they seek to increase the world oil prices through a collective agreement to cut back on production. In 1999, the oil price had fallen to $10 a barrel, but OPEC agreed that its members should cut production to 23 million barrels a day. By March 2000, the oil price had reached $34 a barrel and some OPEC members were concerned that these prices would damage growth in the major oil-consuming countries of Europe, the Far East and North America. Kuwait and Saudi Arabia favoured increasing output by 1.5 million barrels a day to achieve a price of about $25 a barrel, which they believed would be acceptable to both oil-producing and oil-consuming nations.

Discussion point

Why is the price of oil determined by demand and supply operating on a global scale? What developments can depress the world price of oil? What factors have helped to reduce the industrialised countries' reliance upon oil?

The eleven members of OPEC account for about 44 per cent of world oil production, so how might this, and other possible developments, make it difficult for OPEC to keep the world price at $25 rather than say $20 a barrel?

International trade and globalisation

Although the growth of international trade means that UK producers face more competition from foreign goods in the home market, it also brings opportunities to sell in overseas markets. As an increasing number of products become part of world markets, even relatively small firms can look for opportunities to sell abroad. Even if firms do not compete in export markets, they can not afford to ignore what foreign producers are offering. They must be able to respond to growing competition in their home market from foreign producers.

There are many reasons why international trade is likely to increase further.

- By raising productivity and achieving lower costs, more producers are able to offer competitive prices in worldwide markets even after incurring transport costs.

- Developments in mass and bulk transport systems are reducing transport costs, making it more economic to supply overseas markets

- Improvements in both packaging and transportation allows perishable goods to reach distant markets quickly and in good condition.

- Increasing economies of scale in air transportation, produced by aircraft with very large carrying capacities, means that an even higher proportion of goods can be transported to distant markets.

- Producers in the newly industrialising countries of the Far East and South America have been able to enter export markets because their low labour costs gives them a competitive advantage.

- Producers in the developed world have also shifted productive capacity to locations in the developing world to take advantage of lower labour costs. This allows them to continue to compete in world markets.

- Economic growth in the developing world has raised consumer spending power and makes it viable for producers to market their products in a larger number of countries.

- Advances in information and communication technology make businesses aware of potential suppliers in other parts of the world.

- International trade agreements are removing the restrictions which some governments place on imports in order to protect their own producers.

Many organisations now see themselves as part of a world market. This is demonstrated by the number of businesses setting up processing, manufacturing and assembly operations in different countries, giving rise to the phenomenon of the **global factory**. Organisations that have productive capacity in different countries are known as **multinational corporations**, and many use their factories and offices to meet demand from all over the world and not just the demand in the market where they are located. For example, the output from the Toyota plant in the UK is sold not only in the home market but also throughout the rest of the European Union.

An increasing number of products have become global; they are known and bought all over the world. This is particularly the case with consumer goods and consumer durables. Some of the best-known global brands include Coca-Cola, McDonald's, Budweiser, Kellogg's, Nike, Microsoft, Kodak and Sony. The globalisation of brands has been possible because developments in global telecommunications systems create consumer awareness of the kinds of products available in other parts of the world. Producers, in turn, exploit the global communications media to promote their products in new markets. Many use international sporting personalities and entertainers, like Ronaldo and Michael Jackson, to promote their products to a global market.

Building on a flaky past

John and Will Kellogg were the originators of cornflakes. They kept production in the USA for many years until Will decided to set up on his own with the Battle Creek Toasted Corn Flake Company. In 1922, it was renamed the Kellogg Company.

The company moved into Britain in 1924 and now owns five of the country's top ten cereal brands. The Kellogg's factory in Manchester produces about 1.5 million packets a day and it is estimated that about 1.6 billion bowls of Kellogg's cereals are devoured every year in the UK.

Recently however sales have fallen, not only because fewer people eat breakfast, but also because of competition from cheaper own label brands. For the first time Kellogg's has agreed to make own-label cereals for Germany's Aldi supermarket discount chain.

The company has said that the Aldi arrangement is limited only to Germany but it proves that even a well-established brand is not enough to retain the loyalty of today's cost conscious shoppers.

Adapted from *The Guardian*, 4 March 2000

Discussion point

What factors may have helped to make Kellogg's a global brand? Why has Kellogg's been able to dominate the breakfast cereal market for so long?

Why do you think that supermarkets have been able to enter the market with their own-label cereals? Why might the deal with Aldi further weaken Kellogg's brand loyalty?

Demand side factors

People have many needs and wants, but unless these desires are backed up by spending power they are not part of **effective demand**. In this section, we review the economic, financial, social, demographic and legal factors which influence the demand for goods and services. In our discussion, the term demand is used to refer to the total market demand for a product rather than the demand for a particular variety or individual brand of that product. For example, Figure 2.1 shows the total market demand for trainers, not the demand for a particular brand of trainers.

The effect of price

A rise in price generally produces a fall in demand. As the price of a product increases, it becomes more expensive relative to other goods and services which consumers can buy. The product offers less value for money, and the demand for it is likely to fall. Similarly, a fall in price generally increases demand: the product offers better value for money compared with other goods and services. This relationship between demand and price can be shown by a demand curve.

Figure 2.1: The classic demand curve

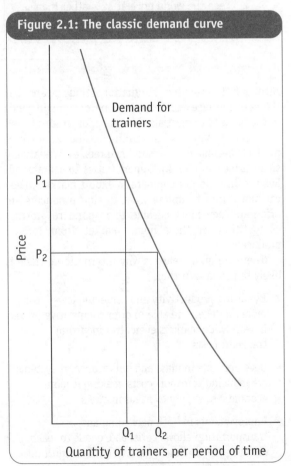

The demand curve in Figure 2.1 shows the quantity of trainers that the total market is prepared to purchase at different price levels. If, for example, the price of trainers is P_1 then the market would be prepared to purchase the quantity of trainers as shown by Q_1. However, at the lower price of P_2 consumers would be prepared to purchase more trainers, the quantity Q_2.

A wide range of goods and services compete for household spending. If producers of trainers are to increase their sales, they must offer better value for money. This means that the benefit derived from buying trainers must exceed that which could be obtained by spending the same amount of money elsewhere. To encourage people to buy extra pairs, to replace their trainers more often or to buy for the first time, trainers must be offered at a lower price so that other goods and services offer relatively less value for money.

Note that when showing the quantity demanded at various price levels, it is important that demand is described over of a particular period of time such as a month or a year. Demand is a flow; a time period is needed to assess changes in the strength of demand.

Substitutes

There is a wide range of goods and services competing for household spending. In some markets this competition is particularly strong because a specific need can be satisfied by different kinds of products. For example, there might be a relatively close relationship between the demand for frozen pizza products and changes in the prices of ready-cooked meat products. These are both convenience foods, satisfying a similar type of need, and as ready cooked meals become more expensive, consumers are likely to buy more pizzas. The products are effectively substitutes for each other.

▲ Rice is a substitute for potatos

Complementary products

Complementary products describes goods or services that must be used together to satisfy a particular need. Film and film processing, gas and gas appliances, cars and petrol, and compact discs and compact disc players are all examples of complementary products. The existence of complementary relationships means that the demand for some products is influenced by changes in the prices of related goods and services. The demand for computer games, for example, is likely to increase if there is a fall in the price of personal computers. A fall in the price of mobile phone calls will help to increase demand for the phones themselves.

Real disposable income

Disposable income is defined as income after paying tax and national insurance. In 1998, total personal (household) income in the UK was £809 billion. However after taxes and national insurance contributions, total personal disposable income was £569 billion, of which £533 billion was spent on consumer goods and services and meeting other household bills and the remainder was put aside as personal savings.

Figure 2.2: UK income tax bands, 2000–1		
Band	**Rate**	**Applies to taxable income**
Starting rate	10%	£0 – £1,520
Basic rate	22%	£1,521 – £28,400
Higher rate	40%	Over £28,400

Discussion point

If the personal tax allowance is £4,385, calculate how much income tax should be paid by someone earning £15,000.

Over a period of years, the disposable income of many households increases. However, the affect of this increase on their actual purchasing power depends on how much the cost of living has risen over the same period. The rise in the cost of living is measured by the **retail price index** (RPI). The rate of increase in the RPI is referred to as the **rate of inflation**. Once allowance is made for inflation, it is possible to measure the change in the level of **real** disposable income and, thus, actual purchasing power.

Between 1997 and 1998, total personal disposable income in the economy rose by nearly 2.6 per cent but, once allowance is made for the general increase in prices over this period, real disposable income rose by only 1.1 per cent. It is important, therefore, that money disposable income is adjusted to produce real disposable income. This is the true measure of the change in spending power.

Figure 2.3: A rise in real disposable income

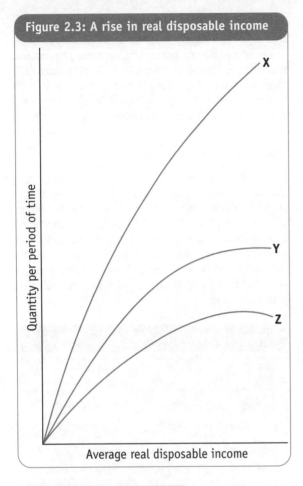

Figure 2.3: A rise in real disposable income

Figure 2.3 shows how demand for products can vary with a change in real disposable income. The demand curve X in shows a product for which demand increases as the average level of real disposable income rises. As households become better off, they can afford to buy more without having to cut back in other areas of spending. For example, people spend more on clothing, footwear, consumer durables and consumer services, such as hotels, restaurants, travel and tourism, as their real disposable income increases.

The demand curve Y in Figure 2.3 shows a product for which demand at first rises with income but then remains constant despite further increases in disposable income. This is often the case with basic food products, household cleaners and detergents, for example. Once incomes rise to the point that every household can purchase these basic items, demand becomes completely satisfied.

There are also products, as illustrated by demand curve Z, for which demand may actually fall as disposable incomes rise. This happens because greater disposable income allows the consumer to replace some existing purchases with what are regarded as superior substitutes. Demand for bread and potatoes, for example, has fallen over recent years as the gradual rise in spending power means more people can now afford more interesting and higher value added food products. Similarly, one reason for the fall in demand for public transport is that higher spending power has allowed more people to buy cars.

Figure 2.4 shows how consumer spending on some categories of goods and services has changed over time. Changes in real disposable income are likely to have been a factor contributing to these trends. Note that the figures in Figure 2.4 have been adjusted to take account of changes in prices. This is necessary because the actual amount of money spent on a product usually increases because of price rises. To show what has happened to the volume of purchases – and to therefore show changes in the demand for particular types of products – the figures are adjusted so that they are all expressed in the prices which applied in a particular year (1995 in this case).

Consumer credit

Many people are willing to spend more than their disposable income by borrowing money, using various forms of consumer credit such as bank loans, overdrafts, credit cards, store cards and hire purchase agreements. In particular, hire purchase is often used to buy expensive consumer durables such as cars, televisions furniture and kitchen appliances. A large and sudden increase in the use of credit can be a major factor in fuelling a consumer spending boom.

The willingness of households to use credit depends upon several factors. First, the repayment period granted by the finance company or bank. Over a longer repayment period monthly repayments are smaller, so it will be easier for a borrower to meet the repayments.

Figure 2.4: UK consumer spending at 1995 prices, £ billion

	1989	1990	1991	1992	1993	1994	1995	1996	1997
Food	42.9	42.4	42.4	43.0	43.5	44.0	44.0	45.7	46.5
Non-alcoholic beverages	4.6	4.7	4.7	4.7	4.7	4.9	5.2	5.2	5.2
Alcoholic beverages	28.3	28.1	27.1	26.0	26.0	26.7	26.0	26.9	27.5
Tobacco	13.8	13.7	13.3	12.6	12.0	11.8	11.4	11.1	10.8
Clothing	18.4	18.9	9.5	20.3	21.5	23.2	24.7	26.0	27.0
Electricity, gas and other fuels	14.4	14.3	15.4	15.1	15.6	15.3	15.1	16.0	15.4
Furniture, carpets and flooring	8.0	7.6	7.3	7.8	8.2	9.0	9.1	9.8	10.9
Household appliances	5.5	5.5	5.4	5.6	5.3	5.5	5.6	5.9	6.6
Car purchase	27.2	24.7	21.5	20.4	22.0	23.1	23.1	24.8	23.6
Telecommunication	6.4	6.7	6.7	6.8	7.1	8.2	9.1	9.6	9.8
Audiovisual, cameras and IT	5.9	6.2	6.2	6.6	6.8	6.8	7.5	7.8	8.6
Newspapers, books, magazines	8.0	8.6	8.3	8.2	8.7	8.6	8.3	8.5	9.0
Hotels	6.4	6.6	6.0	6.8	7.0	6.8	7.8	8.0	8.0
Personal care products	8.9	8.9	8.8	8.7	8.9	9.5	9.8	10.8	12.1

Source: Annual Abstract of Statistics 1999

Second, the size of the deposit or down payment. Some credit arrangements require a deposit: the smaller the deposit, the easier it is to buy on credit.

Third, interest rates. It is generally assumed that the demand for goods bought on credit is likely to be affected by changes in interest rates but this is not always the case. Assume, for example, you buy a music system for £1,000 using credit over three years at 12 per cent. A rise in interest rates to 16 per cent might be considered prohibitive, but this only increases the monthly payment from £37.77 to £41.11. The level of spending financed by credit, therefore, is unlikely to be substantially affected by this kind of rise in interest rates. Similarly, a cut in interest rates to 10 per cent only reduces monthly repayments to £36.11, and again this is unlikely to have much effect on sales. Fluctuations in interest rates are more likely to affect the demand for very expensive items such as new cars simply because of the large amounts which are generally borrowed.

Fourth, the general state of economy and the labour market affects the take up of credit. When the economy is buoyant, people have a greater sense of job security. Earnings may be boosted by regular overtime, bonus payments or sales commission, while a large number of vacancies suggests that alternative jobs are readily available. This makes people confident that they can meet the monthly repayments on credit agreements. A labour shortage also means that employers are under pressure to grant larger pay increases. During the onset of a recession, however, all these factors are likely to be reversed and people are less likely to take out additional credit or enter into new agreements once any outstanding debt has been cleared.

The housing market

The housing market is a major influence on the demand for the kinds of goods associated with people owning their own home or moving to another house. When, for example, a large number of houses are being bought, there is increased demand for a wide range of consumer durables and other products and services connected with home improvements.

Rising house prices also have a wealth effect, encouraging households to feel much more confident in taking on extra consumer credit. This is because more households enjoy positive equity, that is the market value of the house exceeds any outstanding mortgage on the property. They know that if their financial affairs take a sudden turn for the worse, they could always sell their house at a profit and clear their debts. Financial institutions are also likely to be more generous, both in terms of the amount they lend and the length of the repayment period, if the borrower can offer positive equity as security on the loan.

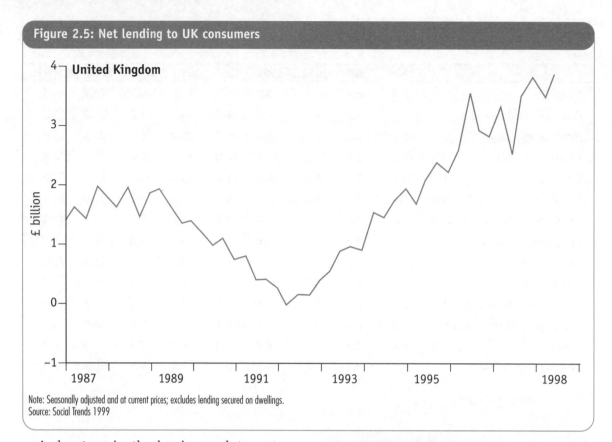

Figure 2.5: Net lending to UK consumers

Note: Seasonally adjusted and at current prices; excludes lending secured on dwellings.
Source: Social Trends 1999

A downturn in the housing market exerts a depressing effect on total spending. Many homeowners may face the problem of **negative equity**, that is the market value of their homes falls below their mortgage. During the slump in the housing market of the early 1990s, some 1.5 million households were affected by negative equity.

Discussion point

Study the recent trends in consumer credit illustrated in Figure 2.5. The graph shows new lending to consumers less repayments. It excludes mortgage borrowing. Suggest factors to explain the fall and rise in net lending seen over the period covered by the graph.

Discussion point

What kinds of small businesses do particularly well when the housing market is rising? Discuss why retailers of white goods such as washing machines and black goods such as televisions do well in a housing boom.

In March 2000, a survey showed that houses prices were increasing fastest in north-west England and Wales. What might this tell you about jobs and earnings in these parts of the UK?

▶ The state of the housing market exerts a significant influence on the demand for some goods and services

Mortgage interest rates

People borrow large sums of money to buy their homes, so even a small change in interest rates can have a significant effect on their monthly mortgage interest payments. For example, a two-point rise in mortgage interest rates, from 7 per cent to 9 per cent, increases the monthly payments on a £80,000 interest only loan by £133; in order to find this money, households will have to cut back spending elsewhere. Typically, they tend to postpone the replacement of consumer durables and home improvements, spend less on leisure and entertainment and generally cut back on luxuries. They are less likely to take on new consumer credit arrangements. A rise in mortgage repayments reduces what is called discretionary income, the disposable income remaining after a household has meet the regular fixed payments on essentials.

Consumer confidence

Consumer confidence, or the 'feel-good' factor, describes the net effect of some of the demand factors we have described. Increased job security, rising house prices, expectations of a good pay rise and improved household finances, for example, tend to raise the level of consumer confidence. People are not only likely to spend more of their disposable income but also to borrow more to buy more expensive products. Figure 2.6 shows a consumer confidence index, which is a measures of the number of people who expect their financial prospects to improve against those who expect their prospects to worsen. A positive result shows that more people are optimistic than pessimistic about their financial prospects. Figure 2.6 shows that people remained consistently pessimistic about the economy following the end of the 1980s consumer boom right up to 1996 after which the feel good factor slowly returned.

Discussion point

Suggest reasons why consumer confidence has risen since the mid 1990s.

Tastes and preferences

Tastes and preferences can be influenced by producers using persuasive advertising techniques. However, the increased demand for a particular product or service often originates with consumers themselves and the resulting trend, fashion or fad then spreads throughout the country. Market research can identify these trends and help companies produce advertising campaigns that seek to exploit changes in tastes and preferences.

Figure 2.6: UK consumer confidence index

Year	Consumer confidence index
1986	−7
1987	+5
1988	+2
1989	−17
1990	−26
1991	−17
1992	−16
1993	−13
1994	−12
1995	−11
1996	−4
1997	+4
1998	−1
1999	+1

Note: Index shows percentage balance people who expect the prospects to improve against people who expect their prospects to worsen

Source: HM Treasury Pocket Data Bank

There are many ways of filling leisure time. A fashion for certain kinds of sporting or fitness activities, such as roller blading or working out in a gym, increases the demand for the appropriate equipment and sportswear. The growth of DIY and garden centres is partly a result of the greater amount of leisure time being devoted to these interests.

Eating habits have changed as people take a greater interest in the health and nutritional value of food. For example, Figure 2.7 (on p. 94) shows how consumers have switched from full-fat milk to semi-skimmed varieties in the last few years.

Demographic changes

Changes in the population with respect to size, age, ethnic groups, social class and geographical distribution are likely to affect the demand for various kinds of goods and services. Different age groups, for example, have particular tastes in clothing and leisure activities. More people in the age group of those setting up their own homes will have a major effect on the demand for consumer durables. The distribution of the

Figure 2.7: Milk consumption, Great Britain

	1988	**1991**	**1994**	**1997**
Liquid wholemilk (ml)	1,513	1,104	870	712
Fully skimmed (ml)	177	198	207	158
Semi skimmed (ml)	350	579	863	978
Other milk and cream (ml)	240	247	252	248

Figures show consumption per person per week
Source: Annual Abstract of Statistics 1999

population between inner city, urban, suburban and rural areas affects the pattern of spending in terms of car ownership, public transport and types of clothing.

Legal changes

The demand for goods and services may be influenced by UK legislation or EU directives. Changes in the laws relating to child safety in cars has increased the demand for car seats and other kinds of restraints. The gradual tightening of the MOT test, with its greater emphasis on the safety and environmental aspects of motoring, has increased the replacement demand for tyres, exhaust systems and a range of other car parts. In recent years, health fears led to the ban of the sale of certain cuts of beef, while a relaxation of the licensing laws has encouraged more families with children to eat out together on pub premises.

Supply side factors

Firms are in business to make money. This is an overriding factor when decisions are taken on what to produce, how resources should be combined to achieve output and how much should be produced and supplied to the market. All these decisions must take account of the level of profit that will be made in relation to the level of capital investment needed and the degree of risk involved.

Once a firm has assessed the lines of business where it can deploy its capital and talents, then decisions on the quantity of goods or services it plans to supply to the market depend upon profitability. A firm seeks a level of business where the gap between its total sales revenue and total costs produces at least its target level of profit. Once this position has been established, decisions on whether to increase supply to the market are based upon how the higher level of business might affect the firm's total costs and sales revenue and, therefore, its profits.

Price

Given the market price for a product and the unit costs of production, a firm can calculate how much it must produce and supply to the market in order to achieve its target profit. Note that extra output may damage profits. A firm may not be able to increase production without a rise in unit costs and it may need to lower its price in order to sell the extra output.

If the firms supplying a market experience a rise in their unit costs as they increase production, then extra output will only be profitable if there is a sufficiently large increase in price. An increase in the demand for the product, which allows suppliers to set higher prices, will therefore encourage an increase in supply; additional units of output which were previously unprofitable, now become profitable.

Some firms may not need higher prices to justify extra output; their unit costs may remain virtually unchanged as output is increased or may even fall because of economies of scale. Eventually, however, even these firms reach a point where further increases in supply to the market requires a higher price if they are to maintain profit levels.

Buoyant market demand can push up prices and encourage an increase in market supply. In contrast, a fall in market demand can put a downward pressure on prices. This combination of declining demand and falling prices makes existing levels of output less profitable or even loss making, and this will force some firms to scale down the level of their business or leave the market altogether. So a fall in price brought about by a downturn in demand results in an eventual fall in market supply.

Discussion point

Why have the manufacturers of digital cameras and personal music systems been able to lower their prices as they responded to the growing demand?

Costs

Prices increases encourage extra supply to a market. However, if a company can find ways of lowering its unit costs, it is possible for it to increase its output and supply more to the market without a rise in price. A fall in unit costs makes additional units of output profitable that were previously unprofitable.

Unit costs can be reduced through:

- lower materials costs – such as a fall in the world prices of energy and raw materials

- greater efficiency – such as a more efficient use of energy and reduced wastage through better use of raw materials

- higher productivity – by, for example, improvements in working practices that make a more efficient use of the workforce

- new technology – such as new machinery and equipment.

Just as a fall in unit costs allows firms to supply more to the market, so a rise in unit costs eventually reduces the market supply. If producers experience a rise in unit costs and are unable to recoup these extra costs through higher prices, then existing levels of output become less profitable or even loss making. Some producers might be forced to scale down their operations or move out of the market completely. Unless the market can totally absorb a rise in price without a fall off in demand, the effect of a rise in unit costs is to eventually reduce the market supply of a product.

Subsidies

Under some circumstances, the UK government or the European Union provides organisations with a subsidy to cover part of their costs. The aim of a subsidy is to make the goods or services more affordable, and increase supply to the market. For example, subsidies are given to public transport providers to make it economic to cover certain routes and operate timetables that would otherwise not be financially viable. The government justifies this subsidy on environmental grounds, as it encourages people to make less use of cars and prevents further expansion of road freight.

Another major example is the subsidy paid to farmers by the European Union to encourage them to find alternative uses for their land. The aim this subsidy is both to cut agricultural overproduction and to reduce the damage to the rural environment caused by the excessive application of capital intensive farming methods and chemical-based fertilisers and pesticides. Many European governments have provided subsidies to encourage organic farming methods.

Organic crop prices race ahead

UK farmers can no longer keep up with demand for organic produce. As health scares about BSE and GM foods have made the public much more concerned about food safety, retail sales of organic food are increasing at 40 per cent a year. The shortage of organic foods has increasingly to be met by imports.

The strong market for organic products and the oversupply of conventional produce is leading to major price differentials. Today, the prices paid to farmers for organic crops are now three times those for conventional crops.

It takes about two years to convert to organic farming, so supply is not very responsive to demand. To encourage a switch to organic farming, the government has increased its financial support from £250 per hectare to £450 per hectare during the conversion period.

Other European governments, however, have supported organic farming more generously, and their organic food producers are in a good position to take advantage of the rising demand.

Adapted from the *Financial Times*, 23 March 2000

Discussion point

Why might the demand for organic foods be very sensitive to lower prices? What developments will help to reduce the prices of organic foods in the longer term?

Discuss ways in which the government could accelerate the shift from chemical-based to organic farming.

Taxation

The government imposes taxes on goods and services to help raise the revenue it needs to cover spending in areas such as education, health, social services, roads, education, the environment and defence.

The government also use taxes to deter certain kinds of spending and consumption which it believes to be against the public interest. For example, the government might levy 'green' tax on goods and services that are a major cause of environmental pollution. It was for this reason that the government levied higher excise duty on leaded petrol than on unleaded petrol. The decision to levy VAT on heating and lighting was defended on the grounds that it would moderate the consumption of energy, and help the government achieve its international commitment to reduce global warning.

The high excise duties on alcohol and cigarettes are not only an important source of tax revenue for the government but are also justified on health grounds. Low prices would encourage excessive consumption of alcohol and cigarettes, and impose very high costs on the National Health Service and on society in general in tackling alcohol-related social problems.

The ability to switch capacity

If a firm produces a range of goods or services which essentially use the same skills, materials and production techniques, then the supply of each of these products can be relatively responsive to a higher demand. A clothing manufacturer, for example, should be able to shift production from denim shirts into jeans if demand for jeans is rising and offers the prospect of higher profits. Similarly, a brewer may be able to increase the output of traditional beers by reducing its production of, say, lager beers, if there is a surge in consumer demand for real ale.

The availability of inputs

The ability of some firms to respond to more favourable market conditions can be restricted by shortages in inputs. A significant increase in market supply may be prevented, for example, if there is a serious shortage of the necessary skills and talents and firms are unable to recruit more labour.

It may take some companies several months, if not years, to increase their output. For example, businesses in the service sector such as hotels, restaurants, leisure and entertainment facilities may need to build more premises. A combination of strict planning regulations and a general shortage of building land in suitable locations may severely restrict their ability to increase market supply.

Production constraints

Most producers of manufactured goods can generally cope with a rise in demand by operating their plant and machinery for longer hours and by employing more labour. Companies involved in the production of raw materials, however, can not readily increase output to meet increases in demand. Agricultural production can not be easily turned on and off: production is seasonal and decisions about the amount of crops to be planted must be made at the start of the growing period.

▲ The supply of raw cotton depends on the amount planted

Consider, for example, an increase in the demand for raw cotton, caused perhaps by a growing consumer preference for cotton clothing. The supply of raw cotton coming on to the market, however, will have been decided at the beginning of the cotton growing season. Supply can only be increased by drawing upon any stocks that may have been accumulated in previous years. Once the current season's crop and stocks have been used up, the supply to the market can not be increased further. This, in turn, restricts the supply of cotton products. In the future, of course, cotton producers can allocate extra land to cotton production if they are sufficiently confident that demand will remain buoyant. For some agricultural products, such as coffee and timber, it takes several years before the bushes and trees are sufficiently mature to allow an increase in supply.

The output from the extractive industries, such as coal mining, quarrying and oil drilling, is also very unresponsive to an increase in demand once any stocks have been used up. Producers have learnt from experience that they should plan their capacity and run their operations to meet the average forecast level of demand for their output over the years ahead. A copper producer, for example, will not install plant and machinery at a mine which runs the risk of being operated well below capacity for long periods of time.

Instead, the company provides sufficient capacity to produce, say, 800 tonnes every eight-hour shift, so that when it is operated for three shifts the copper mine can meet its target output of 2,400 tonnes every 24 hours. During a period of below average demand, surplus output is put into stock and drawn upon when demand exceeds supply.

Even if demand remains high over a long period – and all the stocks are used up – raw materials producers are not necessarily encouraged to generate new capacity. It may be very difficult and expensive to install additional plant to extract more from the deposits currently being worked, and producers may not be sufficiently confident that demand will remain high enough to justify the risks. There are also very high costs connected with exploration and development projects needed to obtain and refine new output. For these reasons, the supply of many raw materials tends to remain relatively fixed once stocks have been run down. So, for example, a significant rise in worldwide demand for products which use copper, such as piping and electrical goods, may soon lead to a shortage of copper on world markets.

The time period

Several factors have already been identified which may prevent supply in certain markets from increasing in response to more favourable market conditions. These are:

- rising unit costs that soon make any significant increase in output unprofitable

- a shortage of important inputs

- the physical conditions and constraints surrounding production.

However, over a long enough time period, these constraints on market supply are likely to be eased. Indeed, producers that do not face any significant problems in expanding supply will find it even easier to increase output the longer the period that elapses after the rise in demand.

The short run is defined as a time period during which it is not possible to vary the use of both labour and capital. Output can be raised only by increasing the use of the input (either labour or capital) which can be varied most easily. In most cases, it is capital – in the form of plant, machinery and premises, for example – which tends to be the most difficult to adjust; labour is generally much more adjustable. In the short run, therefore, a producer typically seeks to increase output by adding more labour in order to use the existing productive capacity more intensively.

The long run is defined as a period of time which allows a producer to vary the input of both labour and capital and generally adjust more fully to a new level of demand. The company is no longer constrained by having a capacity and resource combination that was designed originally for a lower level of output. Because the firm is now freed from these constraints, it can introduce a more efficient combination of resources. This long-run adjustment involves investment in additional capacity, the training of new labour and the further development of management skills. In addition, the firm should be able to take advantage of economies of scale as output is increased, and unit costs should fall. In the long term, therefore, the greater supply to the market is not only made possible by increased investment in both capital assets and labour, but also by the much lower unit costs that make the much larger output more profitable.

The actual period of time which elapses before a firm embarks upon a long-run adjustment to a change in demand varies from industry to industry. A firm producing self-assembly furniture, for example, might increase output in the short run by changing working practices to make a more efficient use of labour, by overtime working and by taking on more workers. If there is a very large increase in demand, a night shift can be introduced to make an even greater use of existing machinery and equipment. It may be only a few months, however, before the firm completes a long-run adjustment by extending its premises, installing extra machinery and equipment and training new workers in the appropriate skills.

In the petrochemical industry, however, while it may be possible to squeeze extra output from existing plant in the short run, it may be years before capital projects are completed and extra plant and machinery comes on stream to cope with a substantial rise in demand. When very large amounts of capital are needed to increase productive capacity, a producer only commits to long-term adjustments if the upturn in demand is seen as being sufficiently long term to make such large-scale investment worthwhile. Business expectations are a vital factor in determining the extent to which a producer commits capital funds to a long-run adjustment in productive capacity which will increase its supply to the market.

In the agricultural sector, we have already noted that an increase in market supply in the longer term depends upon the period which it takes for crops to reach a point where they can be harvested. However, even in this sectors, other developments can increase market supply over longer time periods. If the more favourable market conditions persist over several years, productivity can be increased through the development of more capital intensive techniques, seed and plant strains that increase yields and the application of more effective fertilisers and pesticides.

If an upturn in market demand is seen as being relatively permanent, then in the longer term the market supply will be further increased by new firms entering the market. In particular, firms with existing resources of capital and labour that can be readily shifted into goods or services offering a much improved return on capital are likely to diversify into new growth areas. In recent years, for example, the growth in the restaurant trade has encouraged more brewers to develop the catering side of their operations while independent pub groups have also expanded their eating out facilities. In the information and communications sector, the spectacular growth in the demand has not only encouraged existing suppliers to increase their own provision but market supply has increased substantially through new firms entering the market with mobile phone, internet and telecommunications services.

In some cases it is relatively easy for an existing business organisation to enter a growth market because it has the funds to finance what may be a very large initial capital outlay. These funds will also see it through a potentially difficult period when its capacity is operational but its goods or services are not yet sufficiently well established to be profitable. However, the business may benefit from transferring any well-established and highly regarded brand name to its new product. Virgin did this when it moved into the expanding financial services sector with Virgin Direct.

It is generally much more difficult for a totally new business organisation to enter a market for very capital-intensive goods and service. In these markets, the costs of entry, the minimum capital outlay needed for plant, machinery and equipment, is very high. A potential new entrant would have to be confident of gaining a relatively large market share almost from the outset to ensure that it can recoup its high fixed costs yet still charge competitive prices. For this reason, few new businesses enter the chemicals, steel, air travel and motor vehicle manufacturing industries; these are all sectors with very high entry costs.

It is much easier and less risky for new producers to enter the markets for goods and service that require labour intensive methods and involve relatively low start-up costs for premises and equipment. For example, many organisations have entered the market created by the growth in the demand for day-care facilities for pre-school age children, as these new entrants can start their businesses quite cheaply by renting premises. The increased demand for landscaped gardening saw new firms entering the market, because the start-up costs do not go much beyond a vehicle and some basic tools and equipment.

The interaction of demand and supply

Having analysed the factors which influence demand and supply, we can now bring them together and examine how their interaction in a market helps to determine a market price and the quantity that is bought and sold at that price over a specific period of time.

Figure 2.8 illustrates the demand and supply curves for product X. The slope of the supply curve S in this example indicates that producers do not require a significant increase in price to encourage them to increase output. This suggests that supply is not restricted by a shortage of capacity or other factors such as the physical conditions surrounding production. This kind of supply curve could be used to represent a very large number of manufactured goods and consumer services. The slope of the demand curve D reflects a market where demand is also relatively sensitive to a change in the price. This suggests that suppliers face relatively strong competition from products that are close substitutes.

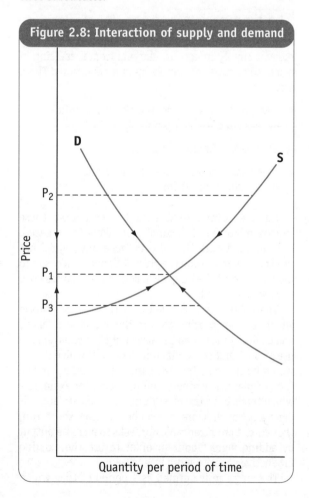

Figure 2.8: Interaction of supply and demand

Look out for any price changes in products and services which you use. Can you find recent examples of price changes which might have been caused by demand outstripping supply or supply exceeding demand.

A market is said to be in a state of **equilibrium** when the market price shows no tendency to change. At price P_2 in Figure 2.8, the supply of X to the market is greater than the quantity which consumers are willing to buy at this price – the surplus of supply over demand will cause the price to fall. This is because consumers would recognise an opportunity to obtain a lower price while suppliers would be willing to cut prices in order to sell their surplus output. As the market price falls, however, it will gradually remove the surplus supply from the market – the lower price will both stimulate a greater demand as well as discourage some of the supply.

As the price falls from P_2 the gap between the demand and supply curves gradually closes. The price continues to fall until all the surplus supply has been removed from the market. This position is reached when the price has fallen to P_1. At this price, the quantity demanded by consumers is equal to the quantity being supplied by producers. A market equilibrium has been reached because neither the price nor the quantity bought and sold will show any further tendency to change.

We can carry out a similar analysis where demand exceeds supply, for example at price P_3. This excess demand or shortage would cause the price to rise. This is because some consumers would be prepared to pay a higher price to obtain the product, and some suppliers would recognise that the shortage gives them the opportunity to charge a higher price. The resulting rise in price will gradually remove the excess demand by both encouraging a greater supply as well choking off some of the demand. Once again a market equilibrium would be established at the price P_1 where demand is equal to supply.

Changes in supply and demand

Starting from a position of market equilibrium, it is possible to identify the likely impact of changes in the factors which effect demand and supply upon the market price and the quantity bought and sold.

An increase in supply

Assume that the market for product X in Figure 2.9 is in equilibrium at the price P_1 and a quantity bought and sold of Q_1. Consider what happens if there is an increase in supply caused by the introduction of a cost-saving innovation. The effect of this increase in supply is shown by a rightward shift of S to S_1 and there is now excess supply at the original equilibrium price. The market price starts to fall, therefore, because producers are under pressure to cut prices to sell the extra output while buyers become aware that they are in position to demand a lower price. This price fall gradually removes the excess supply by encouraging greater demand. At the same time, it causes a drop in supply as some firms reduce their output because of the effect of a lower price fall on their profits. The effect of the price fall on demand can be seen by a downward movement along the demand curve while the fall off in supply is shown by a downward movement along S_1.

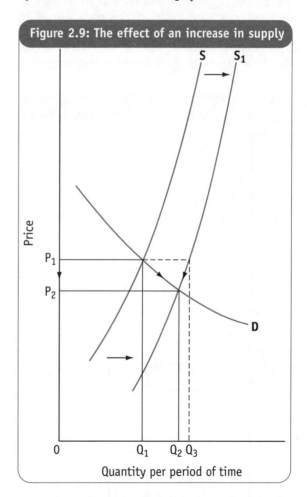

Figure 2.9: The effect of an increase in supply

Figure 2.9 shows that most of the excess supply for X is absorbed by an increase in demand ($Q_2 - Q_1$) while the fall off in supply is only relatively small ($Q_3 - Q_2$). The new market equilibrium is a relatively small reduction in price to P_2 and a relatively large increase in the quantity bought and sold to Q_2. Because demand for product X is sensitive to a price cut, in our example, it takes only a small reduction in price to encourage the extra demand needed to absorb a large part of the excess supply.

Discussion point

Demand for product X is sensitive to a change in price. Consider the impact on the price and quantity brought and sold, if there is a fall in supply of product X.

An increase in demand

Assume that the market for product A in Figure 2.10 is in equilibrium at a price of P_1 and a quantity bought and sold of Q_1. Assume that there is an increase in demand caused by a rise in the average level of disposable income. The rightward shift of demand means that at the price P_1 demand now exceeds supply, and this excess demand will cause the price to rise.

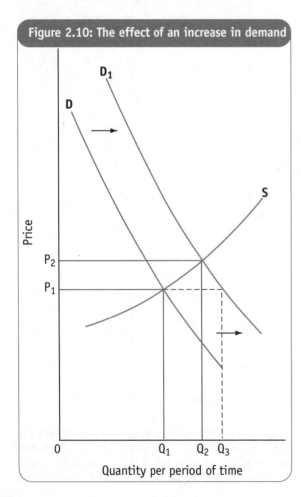

Figure 2.10: The effect of an increase in demand

The effect of this price rise is shown in Figure 2.10. Demand falls back from its peak of Q_3, shown by the upward movement back along D_1. Similarly, the extent to which the price rise stimulates a greater supply can be seen by the upward movement along S. Eventually, the rise in price removes the excess demand from the market. This occurs at the price P_2, where demand again equals supply.

In this illustration, most of the excess demand is met by an increase in supply rather than a price rise that chokes off demand. The market supply curve used in this example suggests that firms have a large amount of spare capacity and slowly rising costs, so that even a small increase in price makes a large increase in output profitable. Figure 2.10 shows that most of the excess demand is met by an increase in supply ($Q_2 - Q_1$) while only a small amount ($Q_3 - Q_2$) is choked off by a rise in price. An increase in demand, therefore, when supply is very responsive will lead to a new market equilibrium involving a relatively small price rise but a large increase in the quantity bought and sold.

The extra profits made by producers as they increase output is likely to attract other firms into the market. In the longer term, the rise in market supply may be even larger than that shown in Figure 2.10. Any entry of new firms would cause a rightward shift of the market supply curve, and the resulting increase in supply and greater competition would eventually produce a new market equilibrium at a lower price than P_2.

Commodity markets

Commodity markets operate rather differently to the markets for goods and services. Sudden changes in the demand and supply can cause wide fluctuations in the prices of raw materials.

Let's consider the market for agricultural raw materials or basic foodstuff. In these markets, supply is constrained by the amounted planted and by climatic factors which affect yields, the actual amount harvested.

Figure 2.11 shows the effect of fluctuations in the supply of wheat. The market supply is shown by vertical lines; once crops are planted supply is fixed, it cannot respond to changes in price. The demand curve is very steep because there is a lack of suitable substitutes in the majority of uses for wheat. This means that demand for wheat is very insensitive to price rises. The demand curve for wheat also shows that price falls also have relatively little impact on demand. This is because the demand for wheat-based products like bread or pizzas does not increase significantly if prices fall: lower prices do not encourage consumers to increase their consumption of bread by a significant amount.

Assume that in year one the interaction of demand and supply in world markets produces a wheat price P_1

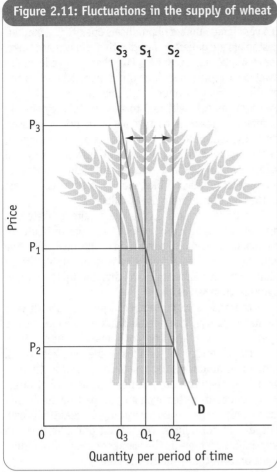

Figure 2.11: Fluctuations in the supply of wheat

Axis labels: Price (vertical), Quantity per period of time (horizontal). Curves: S_3, S_1, S_2, D. Price points: P_3, P_1, P_2. Quantity points: Q_3, Q_1, Q_2, 0.

to depress the market price below an agreed level and put it into a buffer stock. In the event of a poor crop pushing up prices above the agreed level, the authorities release wheat from the buffer stocks. This policy seeks to deliver more stable prices for consumers and incomes for producers.

In recent years, there have been more good years than bad years. Agricultural yields have risen because of higher productivity resulting, for example, in the over production of wheat in the developed world. The European Union has spent vast sums building up stocks of wheat and other agricultural products. The level of support for agricultural output has been cut to reduce 'food mountains', and instead the European Union now encourages and subsidises farmers to put their land to alternative uses.

In extractive industries, large price fluctuations are generated by changes in demand by user industries in the main manufacturing economies interacting with relatively fixed market supplies. Figure 2.12 (on p. 102) uses copper as an example to illustrate the effect of fluctuations in demand. The market supply curve for copper is very steep because it is difficult to increase supply once stocks have been used up. The demand curve is also steep because there is a lack of suitable alternatives for copper in many uses; this means that demand for copper is not very sensitive to a price rise.

Discussion point

Because the supply of raw materials is very insensitive to a price change, fluctuations in demand produce large changes in prices. How do changes in demand effect the total sales revenue of producers?

for the fixed supply Q_1. In year two, however, good weather in the major wheat producing areas leads to an increase in supply to Q_2. At the price P_1 there is now a surplus $(Q_2 - Q_1)$, and it takes a very large fall in price to stimulate demand to absorb the higher output. This is obviously good news for consumers but bad news for producers. Although producers are selling more, they have had to accept a large price reduction to sell their wheat. Their total income has actually fallen from $(P_1 \times Q_1)$ to $(P_2 \times Q_2)$.

In year three, bad weather produces a poor crop and market supply falls to Q_3, creating a shortage at the price of P_1. Because wheat is an important ingredient in many staple food products, a very large price rise to P3 is needed before demand is reduced to match the lower market supply. This is bad news for consumers but good news for producers, because although they are selling much less wheat they are now getting a very high price. The total income of producers has now rise from $(P_1 \times Q_1)$ to $(P_3 \times Q_3)$.

The unpredictable and potentially large fluctuations in the prices of many basic foodstuffs has caused the authorities in some parts of the world to introduce agricultural price support schemes. In good years, the authorities buy up surplus wheat which is threatening

Figure 2.12 illustrates a sudden increase in the demand for copper, by the shift of the demand curve from D_1 to D_2. At the initial market price P_1 there is now a shortage, and prices will rise. There is a very large increase in price from P_1 to P_2 because the higher demand is now competing for a relatively inflexible supply, which only increases from Q_1 to Q_2. Similarly, a fall in the demand for copper because of a downturn in the main manufacturing economies is shown by a leftward shift of the demand curve to D_3. In an extractive industry it is technically difficult and expensive to shut down mining and refining capacity, so supply stays relatively unchanged. The reduced demand for copper depresses the price to P_3.

To counteract fluctuations in raw material prices, some producers' associations have been set up to agree to production quotas, thus ensuring that supply does not constantly run ahead of demand. By controlling the quantity supplied to the market, producers can ensure

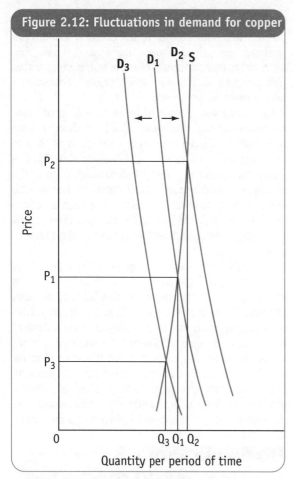

Figure 2.12: Fluctuations in demand for copper

a price that gives an acceptable profit. Users also stand to benefit from this agreement because a large price fall would put many producers out of business; any future upturn in demand could then result in a serious shortage and very high prices for users.

The factors that make markets competitive .

The strategy adopted by a firm to achieve its profit objective very much depends on the level of competition that it faces. The strength of competition is particularly important when a firm is thinking of changing its price or introducing a new or improved product or service. The actual degree of competition between producers in competitive markets depends on:

- the number of producers
- the degree of product differentiation
- non-price competition
- the rate of innovation
- the number of new firms entering the market.

The number of producers

If a very large number of producers operate in a market, customers are generally faced with a wide choice. Take, for example, the market for PCs: there is a wide choice available to consumers from different retail outlets and by direct order through magazines and the internet. Producers must be efficient to survive and they need to minimise increases in costs to moderate price increases. No individual producer can raise its prices or neglect other competitive factors without suffering a loss of sales. Similarly, if a producer can reduce prices or improve its product, it likely to win customers, at least in the short term, from rival producers.

Unofficial price cartels are much more unlikely in a market with many producers. It is more difficult for companies to come to some kind of informal collective agreement to have a quiet and very profitable life by limiting price competition and dividing up the market between themselves.

If there are a large number of producers with very similar products, the overall market demand for the type of product and the total market supply from producers tends to establish the market price. Individual producers become 'price takers' as there is very little they can do to influence the market price. Each firm contributes such a small part of the overall market supply that even a very large increase in its own output will not depress the market price. Neither can any single firm force up the market price by withholding some of its output from the market.

The degree of product differentiation

If consumers believe that there is no real difference between rival products or services, then competitive pressures are likely to be very intense. Identical (or very similar) products are extremely sensitive to price changes because consumers can react by swapping between brands. There is little product differentiation in the markets for petrol, washing powder, coffee, gas supplies and car insurance, and suppliers have to pay particular attention to their prices. If, for example, Esso cut its petrol prices it would gain market share, if it raised its prices it would lose a great deal of business.

Even relatively expensive consumer durables – such as personal computers, televisions and domestic appliances – may differ very little in technology, performance and design. The demand for one particular brand of video recorder, for example, is very sensitive to changes both in its own price and the prices of rival machines.

In industrial markets for materials, parts and components, a lack of product differentiation is also likely to promote strong price competition. This is because industrial products generally have to conform to very exact technical and quality requirements and there is no scope for product differentiation except in areas such as reliability in meeting delivery schedules and after-sales service. For example, firms seeking a contract to supply a construction company with steel and other building products have to meet precise requirements in terms of technical performance and other specifications. To win the contract, firms must be extremely competitive on price. The industrial market for the manufacture and installation of plant and machinery is similarly very price competitive because buyers have very precise and specific requirements.

With a greater the degree of product differentiation, demand is less sensitive is to price changes. Producers of consumer goods and services therefore spend large sums on advertising campaigns informing potential customers of the distinctive features of their products. Some aspects of product differentiation are very real and obvious, such as the materials used in a pair of shoes or the food and surroundings in a restaurant. In other cases, it may need very persuasive advertising to convince consumers that a particular paint, toothpaste, detergent or car tyre is different, and superior, to rival products.

If a producer can convince the market that specific features of its product make it superior to others, then it can build up a degree of brand loyalty among its customers. In building brand loyalty, it hopes to reduce the impact of competitive moves by rival producers. In the face of intense price competition, strong brand loyalty helps to minimise the loss of customers to cheaper rival products. A high degree of product differentiation and brand loyalty also means that the firm will not lose too many customers when it raises its own prices. This is particularly important if a firm is using a price rise to increase its profit margin or to pass on its high costs to consumers.

▲ Companies in the mobile phone market make huge efforts to make their service distinctive

Discussion point

Why are users of mobile phones offered such a wide choice of line rental and call charges? How else do those supplying mobile phone services try and make their service distinctive from the competition? Give examples of the ways in which the manufacturers of mobile phones seek to differentiate their products.

Non-price competition

In competitive markets, costs and prices may eventually settle at levels which leave very little room for further cuts. In these market, more attention is devoted to both indirect price competition and non-price competition.

In consumer markets, indirect price competition can take the form of a various special offers, such as multi-packs at a discount price, three for the price of two deals, money-off coupons and bigger packets offering, say, 13 per cent extra volume free. The advantage of these forms of competition for producers is that the financial implications can be carefully costed. Schemes can be introduced and then withdrawn without losing goodwill among customers. It is a better strategy than price cuts: firms may only be able to sustain price cuts for a short period and, while price cuts are soon forgotten, price increases are more likely to be remembered and resented by consumers even if the producer is simply restoring prices to previous levels.

The relative importance of non-price factors depends upon the kind of market in which a producer is operating.

- In consumer markets, non-price competition takes many forms including intensive advertising campaigns, packaging, tokens for mail-in offers, gifts, competitions, prizes for lucky purchases and give aways such as footballer cards.

- In markets for standardised machinery, equipment, parts and components, the non-price competition might stress reliability, operating capacity, technology, running costs, delivery dates and customer support services.

- In the service sector, such as the restaurant business, non-price competition (and differentiation) can be strengthened through the personal and social skills of staff. You are more likely to revisit a restaurant which has excellent service that enhance the meal.

- In markets for both consumer and business services, firms are now paying increasing attention to improving customer service as part of non-price competition.

In all highly competitive markets, firms also rely upon the knowledge and skills of its sales representatives to gain market share.

The rate of innovation

Competition between producers acts as a spur to the development of new and improved products which use the latest technology, materials and designs. In their efforts to achieve a non-price advantage, producers need to improve continuously the quality, design and features of their products. A lack of innovation and a failure to bring out new designs and styles will leave a product old fashioned and out of date.

Every effort must also be made to develop and apply new technology to production methods to ensure that unit costs are low and prices are as competitive as possible.

New firms entering the market

Over time, some producers may leave a market. Some companies may disappear in mergers and takeovers, other firms may be forced out by competitive pressures. However, as long as other firms are able to enter the market, it will continue to be competitive. The possibility of new firms entering the market increases the pressures on existing firms to be efficient and offer competitive products. If existing producers are competitive, potential new entrants may be deterred from entering their market.

Discussion point

Read the case study about health and leisure centres.

Why do think Whitbread has been moving into the leisure business and reducing its reliance on producing beer?

The large number of independently owned centres suggests low costs of entry into market. Why do you think this may be the case?

As more businesses enter the market, give examples of non-price factors that a centre might use to differentiate itself from its local rivals.

CASE STUDY

Health and fitness centres

By early 2000, Britain had about 2,500 health and fitness clubs and with an estimated membership of 2.44 million. Analysts expect the keep fit business to double in size over the next three to five years, and clubs are opening at the rate of 90 to 100 a year.

In a recent public research survey, 14 per cent of respondents said they used a health and fitness facility and a further 21 per cent said that though they not users at present, they would like to join a club.

Whitbread bought David Lloyd Leisure in 1995. By 2000, it had 41 clubs as well as health and fitness centres in other parts of its operations such as its Marriott hotels chain. Whitbread typically spends around £10 million on each of its larger, up-market clubs. Other companies expanding their health and fitness interests included Cannons, LA Fitness, Fitness First and Esporta.

Because demand is outstripping supply, it is possible for the main operators to keep prices high, and 40 per cent of the public surveyed thought clubs are overpriced. However, as the market matures and supply increases, it is expected that clubs will become more competitive.

Sir Richard Branson is planning to open 20 centres under the name of Virgin Active. Unlike most clubs which charge a joining fee as well as monthly membership fees, Virgin Active does not have a joining fee nor demand an annual commitment – its monthly fees are £42 for adults and £12 a month for children.

The factors that weaken competition

Some markets end up being dominated by a relatively small number of large firms. This can weaken competitive pressures and in particular lead to less price competition. Let's consider some of the developments that weaken price competition.

First, in a market with few firms, there is a fear of a price war and retaliatory action. If one firm cuts its prices, it will increase its own sales at the expense of just a few other producers. These rival producers can suffer a relatively large drop in sales leaving them with expensive unused capacity. A move initiated by one producer to increase market share may provoke retaliation. The other firms in the market may decide to cut their prices.

If there is no real difference between the small number of firms in a market in terms of their products, financial strength and market share, it may be difficult to predict who is likely to survive a price war. Even if the firm starting the price war survives, it may be weakened financially so that it is prey to another producer looking to enter the market. Under these circumstances, each firm may hesitate to cut prices by any significant amount because of the uncertainty concerning the reaction of its rival. Firms recognise their interdependence and seek to minimise the effect of direct price competition upon profits.

The second feature of markets with just a few producers can be some form of price fixing. It is easier for producers to reach a tacit agreement to operate a **price cartel** and refrain from price competition. If one producer is generally accepted as being the most powerful company in the market, it may emerge as the cartel's price leader or price maker. When total market demand is expanding or increased costs are squeezing profit margins, producers may seek a price increase, and they will be keen to follow any move by the price leader. If one of the firms does not follow a price rise in an attempt to increase its market share, it can be brought back into line by the price leader threatening a damaging price cut. There may also be a tacit agreement to challenge any new or potential competitors with a collective price cut in order to either deter them or to damage them when they are financially most exposed.

Markets with a small number of firms can also be vulnerable to a cartel arrangement on market shares. When tendering for orders, for example, competing firms may operate a system to ensure an agreed share of business. They might also agree to divide up geographical areas or distribution outlets between themselves, rather than competing on price to secure orders from wholesalers or retailers.

Public ripped off over soft drink prices

Pubs, hotels and restaurants are exploiting the public with extreme mark-ups on soft drinks. A government investigation has found that the average price for fruit juices is equivalent to £3.45 a pint, while beer costs on average £2.16 a pint.

Referring the matter to the Office of Fair Trading for immediate investigation, the consumer affairs minister noted that a pint of cola was £2.11 in a bar compared with 63p in a supermarket and mineral water was £2.15 a pint compared with 52p. The mark-up on beer was much less, an average pint sells at £2.16 compared with £1.23 in a store.

The report was launched in a pub managed by the Weatherspoons chain, which has some lowest prices for soft drinks, charging 50p for a small bottle of Perrier water and selling cola for the equivalent to 90p a pint.

Adapted from *The Times*,
12 November 1999

Discussion point

Why do you think that pubs, hotels and restaurants are able to charge such high prices for soft drinks, and yet still attract customers?

Suggest reasons why Weatherspoons decided to charge lower prices for soft drinks in its pubs.

These kinds of agreements to fix prices or shares of the market are illegal. If firms are suspected of these practices, they will be investigated by the Office of Fair Trading (see p. 116).

Note that the absence of price competition in a market does not necessarily imply that firms have reached some tacit arrangement on price. A lull in price competition could be explained by producers reaching a position where, in the absence of a major technological breakthrough, there is little scope for further price cuts. The firms remaining in the market after a period of intense competition may have similar unit costs and have little room to compete on price. This can explain weak price competition and a greater emphasis on non-price competition.

Pricing policies

On the assumption that a firm is always aiming for a level of sales that maximises its profits, we might expect a firm to set a price which generates a level of sales that maximises the gap between total costs and total sales revenue. In the real business world, a firm may adopt a pricing strategy which is not particularly profitable in the short run but, in the context of the competition which it faces and other market developments, will help to produce larger and possibly more secure profits in the long run. Let's review the pricing strategies that firms can adopt.

A price to maximise sales

As part of a competitive strategy, a company may seek to maximise its market share. To increase market share, it may have to make a large price cut to win business from its competitors. The company may be able to generate larger profits by charging a higher price and selling less, however it may tolerate lower profits if it is confident that it can seriously damage some of its weaker rivals. It must ensure that it has the financial reserves to survive any resulting price war before some producers are squeezed out of the market and prices can be restored to more profitable levels.

A high degree of brand loyalty

If demand is not very sensitive to a price increase, then a price rise may raise sales revenue. A company needs to ensure that the percentage increase in price is greater than the percentage fall in the volume of sales. If, for example, a firm selling 100,000 units at £200 a piece decides to increase its prices by 10 per cent, then it will increase its sales revenue – from £20 million to £20.68 million – if the price rise only leads to a 6 per cent fall in sales.

Producers that have built up a high degree of brand loyalty among their customers, therefore, may be able to increase sales revenue by raising prices; a moderate price rise should not see a significant fall in sales. Firms

with products or production processes protected by a patent may also find that demand for their goods and services is not very sensitive to a price change.

Note that in a market where brand loyalty is a dominant feature, a price reduction by a producer will not necessarily produce a significant increase in sales; other companies also have their loyal consumers, and they will not be easily attracted by a fall in the price of a competing product. In times of high unemployment, however, when money is tight, price cutting may start to eat into the market share of leading brands.

A low degree of brand loyalty

In markets with very little product differentiation, the demand for a producer's product may be very price sensitive. Here, a price cut can encourage a sufficiently large increase in demand so that sales revenue increases. If, for example, a firm selling 10,000 units at £40 a piece decides to cuts its prices by 10 per cent, and manages to generate an 18 per cent increase in sales, its sales revenue will rise from £400,000 to £424,800. This price cut is even more beneficial if the firm also enjoys economies of scale, because falling unit costs as output expands to meet the higher demand will increase profit margins. This price cut would not be a sensible strategy, however, if the firm faces rising unit costs as it tries to increase production to meet higher demand, and its total costs increase faster than sales revenue. The firm must also ensure that it has sufficient spare capacity and the necessary skilled labour to meet the increase in demand.

Even if a firm is confident that a price cut will increase demand, it must also decide if rival firms are likely to retaliate with price cuts or other measures to protect their competitive position. If the firm expects its competitors to respond with price cuts, it may opt to keep its own price at the 'market' level and allow price to play a minor role in its marketing strategy.

Changes in demand

If a company finds that demand increases for its product, it may be tempted to raise prices. First, however, it should discover the reason for the extra sales. There could be, for example, a rise in the total market demand for the product, with rival companies also enjoying higher sales. The overall increase in market demand provides an opportunity for all producers to widen their profit margins by charging higher prices. The rise in total demand may also allow them to pass on cost increases.

The extra sales, however, may have been generated because the firm has won business from its rivals – it may, for example, have introduced a new feature that makes its product more attractive. Here, the firm may decide to keep its existing price for a period to build up the brand loyalty of the new customers. Eventually, the firm may take advantage of the increased demand to charge a price which reflects the extra value which consumers attach to the product.

If the rise in demand has simply resulted from major competitors increasing their prices, then the increased demand is likely to be lost if the firm also raises its price. In this situation, the firm would decide to maintain its price to retain the new business.

If a company finds that demand for its product is falling, again it must analyse the reason for the drop in demand before making decisions about price. If there is a fall in the total market demand for a product or service, all producers will be under increasing pressure to cut prices. If the fall in demand is because the firm is losing market share to its rivals, it may cut prices to slow down the loss of business and use the breathing space to develop and introduce a longer-term strategy for improving its competitive position. Retaining market share is particularly important if the firm has very high fixed costs – it needs to sustain a large output to keep down unit costs.

Value for money

Companies need to price their goods and service at levels at which consumers feel they get value for money. If these goods or services are a regular part of household spending, then consumers will have knowledge of the prices of competing products and opinions on the extent to which they offer value for money. In these markets, consumers seek low prices and are more likely to respond to price cuts and be deterred by price increases.

New products, however, can be priced too low. Consumers can be concerned that a low price is simply indicative of inferior materials and poor workmanship. They may not think that the product will not last very long. If a new product is very well received, it may even be possible to charge a premium price and exploit the consumers' view that price is a reflection of quality. If there is little product differentiation, its price has to be set within the range determined by the highest and lowest prices charged for competing products.

Discussion point

Some commentators have argued that in today's clothing market too many shops are chasing too few customers. As the article on this pages shows, established clothing retailers are under threat. Suggest how the Arcadia Group, which has 2,000 shops and 15 chains such as Top Shop, Burton's and Dorothy Perkins, can respond to competition from the new discount outlets.

Trouble in store for old guard

The turnover of many well-established retail outlets such as Marks and Spencer, Burton's, Top Shop, Dorothy Perkins, Principles and Austin Read is under serious threat from the growing number of discount shops.

Competition comes from Matalan, New Look, the Peacock Group, Asda's George and the growing number of factory-outlet type shops which obtain and discount well-known labels.

These discount shops do not project the usual "pile 'em high and sell 'em cheap" image of the bargain basement. Their success comes from identifying trends at a very early stage and then scouring the world for low-cost producers of fashionable clothes.

Matalan now has 112 stores and makes more profit than the combined profits of stores owned by House of Fraser, Liberty, MFI and Oasis.

Adapted from The Times, 10 March 2000.

Image

High-quality products often acquire an exclusive image. Their up-market position can be sustained by a high-price strategy. As well as reinforcing a perception of exclusivity, a high price is needed to cover the costs of producing a quality product and to compensate for the low level of sales to a small but select market. The producer must ensure that the product is sold from outlets with the right image. An expensive perfume, for example, has to be sold in select department stores rather than in cut-price chemists.

Skimming the market

A **price skimming** strategy can be used when a new product is launched in a market where it faces very little competition. The strategy is based on the assumption that there will always be some consumers who are willing to pay a relatively high price to be the first to obtain the product. Once demand for the product has stabilised, the price can be lowered to a level which attracts further groups of consumers. The supplier may then use a series of further price cuts to gradually cover the potential market. This short-term strategy of using progressively lower prices as a way of skimming or creaming the market ensures that a new product is not underpriced and is not sold to all consumers at a single price.

Penetrating the market

A **penetration price** may be used when a supplier launches a new product on to an existing market where the demand is very price sensitive. A penetration price is a low price designed to get consumers to try the new product and to overcome any brand loyalty to competing products. Attracting large sales quickly is particularly important for a new product with very high fixed costs, where a high volume is needed to get unit costs down to competitive levels.

Predatory pricing

Predatory pricing is a strategy of cutting prices in the short term in an all-out attempt to inflict such severe financial problems on a rival company that it is forced out of business. Predatory pricing may reduce the company's profits – or even cause it to incur a loss – but it may be used if the company's competitor is reckoned to have higher unit costs and very small financial reserves.

This strategy is also used to deter other companies from entering a market. It is likely to be very effective if there are very high costs of entry and the potential new entrant is deterred by a low price and the prospect of high unit costs.

Discussion point

Why are airlines such as Ryanair, Easyjet, Go and Buzz able to charge lower fares than the well-established airlines? How would you expect other low-cost carriers to respond to Ryanair's price cuts?

London to Dublin for just £4

The airline price war reached a new level yesterday when the low-cost carrier Ryanair announced a million cheap seats to 21 European destinations, with a rock-bottom net return fare of £4 between Stanstead and Dublin.

The total fare with airport taxes works out at £24.99, and was described by Ryanair's chief executive, Michael O'Leary, as little more than the price of a long taxi cab journey across London.

The cheapest equivalent to Dublin offered by British Airways is £55 plus airport taxes from Gatwick and a compulsory one-night stopover on a Saturday night.

Among Ryanair's other offers are a £24.99 return fare to Glasgow, including taxes, a £29.99 fare to St Etienne and Dinard in France, £39.99 to Genoa, Turin and Rimini in Italy, and £39.99 to Stockholm and Malmo in Sweden.

The Guardian, 15 January 2000

Loss leaders

In order to attract customers to their stores, some supermarkets offer a small number of well-known brands at below cost. They highlight these bargain prices in their advertising and, in attracting customers to the store in this way, they hope that they will buy many other items. Loss leaders may also suggest to some customers that all other prices in the store have been reduced.

Price discrimination

Price discrimination is a strategy of charging different prices to particular types of customers for what is an identical or very similar product. There are several reasons why firms adopt a price discrimination policy.

- Spending power – companies adopt price discrimination to make their service available to groups with different incomes. For example, a hairdresser charges different rates for children, adults and senior citizens and rail companies often give discounts to students or family groups.

- Competition – a producer may charge different prices depending upon the strength of competition in the various markets in which it operates. Car manufacturers, for example, charge lower prices in countries where there is stronger competition.

- Geographical differences – prices may reflect variations in average spending power in different parts of the country. A pizza chain may charge more for its pizzas in better-off areas of the country.

- Peak demand – higher prices can be charged when demand is greater. There are higher charges for peak time calls on mobile phones and commuters pay more for rail travel during peak times. In hotels, weekday business users often pay much more than weekend leisure clients.

- Retail environment – the same product may be sold through different outlets at different prices. For example, a garden bench advertised in a very upmarket magazine may be much more expensive than the same product sold at a discount store. A package tour to Eurodisney may be much cheaper if bought through a special offer brochure from a ferry company rather than a travel company.

It is generally more difficult for companies that sell goods and services to other firms to practice price discrimination. Employees responsible for purchasing materials, parts and business services are likely to be experienced and knowledgeable about the prices offered by suppliers in different markets.

The effect on stakeholders

We now consider the effect of competition on the stakeholders of a business, including consumers, employees, shareholders and the community. The effects depend on the degree of competition in markets, however we can make some general observations.

Consumers

Businesses must be efficient to survive and they must moderate price increases to remain competitive. If prices rise more slowly than increases in household income, then people have greater spending power – they have more to buy additional goods and services. Strong price competition, therefore, benefits households; it raises their real incomes and their standard of living.

Strong competition, characterised by a large number of firms competing to satisfy the same need, also widens consumer choice in terms of non-price features. In their efforts to achieve a non-price advantage, producers continuously look to improve quality and other non-price features which benefit consumers, such as customer care and after-sales services.

Competition does not always benefit consumers. In some highly competitive markets with a large number of producers, there may be very little real difference between many products. For example, public transport may be served by a large number of bus companies all covering the same few limited range of routes; financial services may be offered by banks and building societies offering similar products from the same town-centre locations. With a large number of very similar products and services, there may be a wasteful duplication of resources, higher unit costs and, hence, higher prices. Consumers might have more choice if fewer firms offered more clearly differentiated products.

Suppliers

The benefits of competition extend to firms themselves, because they are customers for a very wide range of goods and services. In a competitive market, business suppliers – of materials, parts and components, machinery and business services – must seek to improve upon their competitive position in terms of both price and non-price factors.

Large producers sometimes use their powerful positions to delay payments to small businesses that supply them with goods and services. This can create cash flow problems, but many small suppliers hesitate to demand payment for fear of losing orders which can account for a high proportion of their output. However, more positively, many large companies establish very close relations with their suppliers (large and small), encouraging them to introduce quality and productivity improvements that not only help to secure future orders but makes the supplier more competitive when seeking to win business elsewhere. If a small supplier becomes more integrated into the operations of a large customer, it may become more confident of retaining orders and more likely to invest in the technology and skills that will further strengthen its competitive position.

Employees

Employment prospects can often be less secure in markets in which a large number of firm operate; this is because the competitive advantage is continuously shifting. Many producers may be constantly increasing or reducing output – with a consequent impact on jobs – and jobs can also be affected by firms entering and leaving the market. Because the future is very uncertain, some firms may be unwilling to invest in skills training as they may be worried that they will have to make redundancies in the near future.

If a large number of firms are competing strongly in a rapidly growing market, while there may be some business failures, the successful firms are likely to increase output. The overall growth in production creates a more buoyant market for key skills and increased demand for labour. This means both improved job prospects and rising pay levels as employers seek to retain and recruit workers.

In a highly competitive market, there may be a high turnover of firms, with both high levels of business failure and business creation. In contrast, the situation in a market with a few dominant producers is generally much less volatile. This provides increased job security for employees, while the large firms in this kind of market often offer a more clearly structure path for career development and promotion. These firms also have the resources to offer quality training programmes. This not only benefits the individual in terms of existing and future job prospects but also benefits the economy as a whole by raising the overall skill levels of the workforce.

A major employer in an area can bring significant employment and economic benefits. The company is likely to attract suppliers into the area to provide it with parts, components and business services. This rise in indirect employment will generate more spending in the local economy, increasing local prosperity. Other firms are also likely to be attracted by the availability of skilled labour.

Shareholders

In mature markets, some firms are able to reach a size where they are generally strong enough to withstand competitive moves by rivals. They are unlikely to suffer any terminal damage before they can respond successfully to changes in their competitive environment. Their long-term profitability means that both individuals and financial institutions holding shares in these companies benefit from regular dividends and the steady increase in the value of their shares. Their successful track record in having established a strong position in a market also makes it easier for these 'blue chip' companies to raise additional capital – through loans or share issue – to fund further expansion.

UK plc

The large producers in UK markets are responsible for a very high proportion of the exports, earning the foreign currency needed to pay for the UK's imports and to finance foreign investment. Major foreign currency earners include British Aerospace, Glaxo Welcome, ICI and British Steel. These companies have the scale of output, the investment in their workforce and their technology, and the marketing expertise both to win a large part of the UK market for their goods and services and to be competitive in world markets.

Community responsibility

Markets consisting of a few large producers – often businesses that are household names – can be sensitive to public opinion. These large companies are often among the very first to introduce environmental protection measures which benefit the local, national or global environment. Large companies are also often aware that their activities are more likely to be monitored by environmental pressure groups. As they have a greater visibility than small firms, they need to take account of environmental concerns in their decision making to avoid bad publicity and risk alienating consumers who are influenced by green issues when choosing goods and services.

Because big companies attract the attention of the media, they are also aware of the potential damage to their business if their products put the health or safety of consumers at risk. If any episodes occur, they need to respond publicly about how they intend to deal with the situation in order to avoid a loss of sales to competitors.

The high public profile of large companies makes them a target for organisations and individuals seeking financial support and sponsorship. Athletics championships and football competitions attract massive sponsorship from multinational companies, but the arts, the theatre, music and education depend very heavily upon financial support from large businesses. Companies benefit from sponsorship from the extra exposure of their name to existing and potential customers, but in some cases their sponsorship may be more altruistic, supporting activities in and around the local communities near to their offices and factories.

Mergers and takeovers

By increasing the scale of their operations, firms can improve their competitiveness, gain greater control over suppliers and gain access to new markets. Companies can achieve expansion and increased market share in two ways, either through organic growth or by mergers and takeovers. Organic growth is where a producer expands its operations by investing in larger capacity so that it can produce more and take advantage of rising demand for its output. The alternative approach, achieving expansion by merging with or taking over another company, is known as integration.

Horizontal integration

A firm expands horizontally when it increases the scale of its operations by combining with another firm in the same line of business. In other words, a strategy of horizontal integration involves continuing to specialise in the company's existing business – a baker mergers with or takes over another baker, a bank mergers with or takes over another bank.

When a firm expands organically it increases its output, thereby increasing the total supply to the market. It may therefore be forced to reduce its price to sell the extra output. If a firm merges with another company, the total supply to the market is unchanged, and there should be no need for any price cuts to maintain output.

A strategy of horizontal integration brings a number of business opportunities.

- Rationalisation programmes can be introduced to concentrate production in the most efficient factories, and high-cost units can be closed down. By concentrating capacity in this way, the most efficient centres are more fully utilised, producing a further cut in unit costs. Other areas where scope exists for rationalisation are in administration, branch and retail structure, computer and information systems, transport and aspects of distribution. When building societies merge, for example, some branches are closed to avoid the wasteful duplication of a service in the same area.

- Changes to the organisation's structure are also possible through the rationalisation of other departments such as finance, marketing and personnel. The new company may set up specialist divisions or combine operations, creating new management roles with a redistribution of responsibilities, new lines of communications and other changes aimed at trimming down management staff or removing complete layers of management.

- The larger output allows a greater advantage to be taken of the specialisation of labour. More workers can be kept occupied on a very narrow area of work both in production and elsewhere. For example, it might be viable to set up sections within the marketing department in which skilled staff can concentrate on various regions, overseas markets, market research, advertising, promotions, distribution and after-sales service.

- The larger output can lead to economies of scale which were not previously available to the separate producers. In particular, unit costs are likely fall as a result of bulk buying and the introduction of new plant and machinery. The larger organisation can raise external capital on more favourable terms than before. It can offer greater security and point to its proven record of success in establishing a stronger market position. It will be easier to attract loan capital at a lower cost with a less demanding repayment schedule.

Mergers often take place to draw on the separate strengths of individual firms. Combining these strengths produces a single, but more competitive, organisation. One firm, for example, may be strong on product innovation while the other might have expertise in marketing and production management.

Another reason for horizontal integration is to acquire well-known brand names. A company may decide to acquire a brand if it believes it can exploit more fully than the current owner. A firm may also be fearful of new technology that could produce a strong competitor, and it may merge with (or take over) a company which is in the process of developing new technologies or products and, thereby, obtain any patent rights.

▲ Lloyds TSB has grown through horizontal integration

Unilever sweet talks Ben and Jerry's

The humble Cornetto could soon be rubbing shoulders in the freezer cabinet with Chunky Monkey, Cherry Garcia and Chubby Hubby. Unilever, owner of Wall's ice-cream, is negotiating with Ben Cohen, one of the founders of Ben & Jerry's Homemade, a buyout of the Vermont-based ice-cream firm.

Founded by two eccentrics in 1978 in a petrol station in Vermont. Ben & Jerry's supports causes such as the rain-forest and helping the homeless. However, it has fought battles with big distributors to get its product on the shelf.

Ben and Jerry's makes great ice-cream. Whether what goes into the tubs justifies the full extent of the premium prices is another matter, but the company's much-vaunted ethical policies have not stopped it from making a sizeable dent in many families' household budgets.

There have been suggestions for some time that the hippy happy approach which was part of the Ben & Jerry's image, might be being tainted by commercialism. The arrival of Unilever as a big investor leaves the matter in no doubt, and it becomes clear that Ben is the commercial one and Jerry still harbours illusions. So Jerry Greenfield is bowing out of the company that he founded.

But the company is not about to abandon the pretence of public spiritedness. There is a social performance plan that will ensure that "women and minorities" are represented on the board. It seems almost inevitable that Anita Roddick turns out to be one of the backers of a fund that is putting cash into the company.

Ben & Jerry's may bring some bright ideas for Walls. But it is to be hoped that Unilever does not feel obliged to follow B&J with a 'social performance plan'.

Adapted from *The Times*,
30 March 2000

Adapted from *The Times*, 30 March 2000

Discussion point

Why might Unilever prefer to buy up an existing brand rather than develop its own premium product?

Why might Ben and Jerry's have problems in getting its products into small shops in the UK?

Describe some of the sources of economies of scale that might be gained from Unilever buying up Ben and Jerry's.

Horizontal integration can secure profits, because some of the risks of operating in a competitive market can be lessened if a company joins with a major competitor. The larger business will have a greater control over the market. A merger, for example, allows two firms to pool resources to withstand the threat from an overseas producer seeking to make inroads into the home market. During a recession, survival may also be the motive for a merger – neither firm may be sure which has the greatest potential to ride out the economic downturn.

Greater control over the market also reduces some of the risks associated with expensive investment and research and development projects. It is often a very long time before capital projects come on stream and the new products resulting from research and development reach the market and make a contribution to profits.

CASE STUDY

Rationalisation in pharmaceuticals

In early 2000, the merger between the drugs companies Glaxo and SmithKline Beecham created Britain's largest company. It produced a single company with a market value of £130 billion, combined sales of £17 billion and 7.4 per cent of the world market in pharmaceutical products.

It is estimated that the merger would result in 15,000 job losses from a worldwide staff of 110,000 in the two companies. It is expected that SmithKline's non-medical brands, including Horlicks, Lucozade and Macleans toothpaste, will be sold off.

Just a few months earlier, Warner-Lambert, one of the biggest American drugs groups, announced a merger with American Home Product (AHP). In the event Pfizer, best-known for making Viagra and the world's second largest drugs company, eventually did a deal with Warner-Lambert in February 2000.

Discussion point

Suggest why the very high costs of researching new drugs have been a major factor behind mergers in the pharmaceutical industry.

Why would you expect the new company created from the merger of Glaxo and SmithKline Beecham to benefit from marketing and distribution economies?

Vertical integration

A firm expands vertically by merging with or taking over companies involved in different stages in the production of its goods or services. The concept is best illustrated by a specific example of vertical integration. Consider a building company that specialises in constructing new houses. The company may opt for backward vertical integration by merging with manufacturers of building products and suppliers of building materials. It may integrate forward towards the market by combining with a firm that specialises in the sale or letting of new houses.

Vertical integration has a number of business advantages. It can help to lower unit costs and also make a firm more secure. Let's consider some of the benefits of vertical integration.

- By combining with companies that source raw materials, parts and components, the firm has more control and security over its supplies. This is particularly important during a period of rapidly increasing market demand, when there might be shortages and delays in supplying raw materials and basic components.

- By having greater control over the quality and design of its inputs, a firm can also ensure that its raw materials, parts and components meets its exact requirements.

- Adjustments in the productive capacities needed to cope with changes in demand can be better coordinated if more processes are under the control of a single organisation. Investment projects can be coordinated to avoid the problem of independent firms suffering from an excess or shortage of capacity.

- Some industrial processes are more efficient if undertaken close to each other. The integration of the different stages in the production of metal, oil and chemical products on to a singe site can produce substantial savings in energy, handling and transport costs.

- A firm can grow to the point at which it becomes viable to organise its own distribution. It can use its own transport to deliver direct to its customers, bypassing wholesalers. Being closer to its customers helps the firm to identify markets trends and to promote its own products more strongly.

- If growth continues, manufacturers of consumer goods may find it worthwhile to open retail outlets. This provides ultimate control over the marketing of its products to households. In the service sector, a package tour operator may take over a chain of travel agents in order to ensure that its own holidays are given as much exposure as possible.

It is through vertical integration that a company can achieve increase the added value of its products, and create a market position in which its goods and services earn higher prices. For example, an airline that serves holiday destinations may acquire hotels in order to offer complete holiday packages to consumers rather than just selling tickets for air travel. In doing so, it offers a higher value added service. A furniture retailer may join with a manufacturer to makes products to its own specifications and then move into the field of designing fitted kitchens and bedrooms for households which are then installed by another subsidiary company.

Discussion point

What are the cost advantages to Airtours of owning its own hotels?

Suggest reasons why owning its own hotels places Airtours' package tour operators in a stronger position when competing with package tour companies owned by Thomson Travel.

Lateral integration

Lateral integration is a merger or takeover strategy based on diversification. It allows firms to widen their range of products and services and compete in a range of diverse markets.

One reason for lateral integration is that the same kinds of skills, parts and plant can be used for quite different products. Honda, the car and motor-cycle producer, has gradually diversified into other consumer products such as petrol-driven lawnmowers. In the service sector, banks have taken over financial services and insurance companies because these products are suitable for marketing through the bank branches.

Companies may diversify to exploit a high degree of brand loyalty and a logo that can be used to sell other products. Nike, the producer of sports trainers, has moved into clothing and accessories. Virgin has added air travel, condoms, cola drinks and an investment scheme to its original interests that centred around the music business. The Black and Decker brand is now carried on an increasing range of products retailed in DIY stores, ranging from powered hand tools to items of garden machinery. Mars has diversify into frozen confectionery products.

Diversification may also be motivated by a desire to reduce reliance on a single product. For example, Birds Eye has reduced its reliance on what are essentially fish products, and the company now produces a wide range of frozen foods, ready meals and ice cream.

The experience gained in one market can be used to support diversification into other markets. A company with a core business of supplying and running pubs might move into other parts of the hospitality market such as restaurants, hotels and entertainment. Whitbread, for example, now has other interests such as TGI Friday, Travel Inns and David Lloyd Leisure.

Airtours buys Majorca hotel for £63.4 m

Airtours yesterday paid £63.4 million for a Majorca hotel complex and signalled its intention to buy more accommodation in key destinations used by its web of tour operators across Europe.

Tim Byrne, the new managing director, said access to accommodation was a significant issue for the tour industry, particularly in popular destinations such as the Spanish resort island of Majorca.

Airtours will buy the 1,474-apartment Bellevue hotel complex, the largest of its kind in Europe, from Spain's Banco Español de Credito for £63.4 million in cash.

The complex, situated in the popular resort city of Alcudia, will give Airtours access to one million bed nights in the peak summer season. Reports suggested that Thompson Travel, Airtours' UK rival, also submitted a bid for the complex.

David Crossland, the Airtours chairman, said: "In Majorca, quality accommodation is an increasingly scarce resource. The complex is a valuable addition to our group as it provides quality accommodation in a key destination used by all of our European tour operators."

Airtours already operates 46 hotels on its own or through associates, including the Sunwing Resorts chain. It can accommodate 400,000 guests a year.

Mr Byrne said that access to beds was essential if the company wanted to maintain its position as the world's biggest holidays group. He said the company would chase further hotel acquisitions. "We believe that there will be two or three tour operators in Europe that will be big players," he said. "The key is securing long-term access to beds."

Adapted from *The Times*, 28 January 2000

BUILD YOUR LEARNING

You should know the meaning of the words and phrases listed below. Go back through the last 31 pages of the unit to check or refresh your understanding as necessary.

- Brokers
- Business services
- Commodity exchanges
- Cost of entry
- Demand
- Discretionary income
- Disposable income
- Effective demand
- Global factory
- Market
- Market equilibrium
- Multinational corporations
- Negative equity
- Penetration price
- Price cartel
- Price skimming
- Primary sector
- Product differentiation
- Rate of inflation
- Retail price index
- Secondary sector
- Speculators
- Standard of living
- Supply
- Tertiary sector
- Wealth effect

- Markets are created by the forces of demand and supply, and they range from the very local to those which operate on a global scale.

- The overall market demand for a product is influenced by changes in prices as well a range of financial, economic, social, legal and demographic factors.

- The supply to a market is influenced by changes in prices, the cost structure of producers, the nature of the production process and the time period under consideration.

- The interaction of demand and supply in a market determines the market price of a product and the quantity that is bought and sold at that price over a given period of time.

- Competitive pressures in a market are strong if there a large number of producers and little differentiation between products. Other features of a competitive market are a high rate of product development and ease of entry for new firms.

- Competitive pressures can be weaker in a market dominated a few large producers, and there may be less emphasis on price competition in these markets.

- The pricing strategies adopted by a company depends upon the nature of its product and the type of market in which it is operating.

- Companies may seek to achieve their business objectives, for increased profits, larger market share or greater security, through mergers or takeovers, allowing them to expand through horizontal, vertical or lateral integration.

How business is affected by government policy

THE GOVERNMENT CAN HAVE a direct effect on the strategies adopted by business. It can pass regulations that constrain the ways that businesses achieve their output and influence the approach the companies take when competing in markets. On a much more general level, the government can use a range of economic policies to influence the overall state of the economic and financial environment, which can have a significant effect on the strength of demand in the markets in which businesses operate.

Monopolies and restrictive practices

Although competition forces producers to compete on both price and quality, there is always a possibility that some companies may operate, either alone or in collusion with others, against the interest of consumers. It is for this reason that the government assumes the power to intervene directly in the activities of businesses both to protect consumers from monopolies and anti-competitive practices and to encourage competition between producers.

More recently, the government has also been concerned about strengthening competitive pressures in the UK to make it an attractive location for foreign companies to set up plants and offices and to create jobs. Foreign companies might be deterred from investing in the UK if they feel that existing producers are engaging in collective anti-competitive practices that would make it difficult for foreign companies to compete fairly in the UK and European markets.

Competition Act 1998

The Competition Act 1998 came into force in March 2000, replacing the Restrictive Trade Practices Act, the Resale Prices Act and most sections of the Competition Act 1980. The new competition legislation covers a wider range of anti-competitive agreements and practices and is designed to prevent the abuse of a dominant market position. There are now much more severe penalties for offenders: they can be fined up to 10 per cent of their turnover for ever year that an anti-competitive agreement has operated. The Act grants the authorities much stronger powers to seek out evidence of anti-competitive agreements, including greater authority to enter premises, interview staff and seize documents. Businesses adversely effected by anti-competitive agreement can now claim for damages in the courts.

The **Office of Fair Trading** (OFT) is responsible for implementing the Competition Act 1998. It monitors trading practices and market developments that may be against consumers' interests and generally seeks to promote the competitive pressures that oblige producers to be more efficient. The day-to-day work of the Office of Fair Trading includes:

- collecting detailed information about consumer matters and receiving advice from consumer bodies and pressure groups

- publishing advice for consumers that sets out their rights

- considering complaints from individuals or consumer groups and, if necessary, referring them to a Consumer Protection Advisory Committee

- encouraging trade organisations to draw up voluntary codes of practice for their members

- recommending changes to close any loopholes in existing laws or to stop new kinds of unfair restrictive practices.

The Office of Fair Trading can impose financial penalties on businesses found guilty of restricting competition. Consumer protection laws and regulations are enforced by the trading standards departments of local authorities.

Anti-competitive agreements

The Competition Act 1998 applies to all informal and formal arrangements between companies, whether or not they are set out in writing. An OFT investigation does not have to uncover a written agreement between companies as evidence of an arrangement that has the effect of restricting competition, it is sufficient to produce other documents that demonstrate that such an agreement actually does exist.

An agreement is covered by the Act if it is found to have an 'appreciable effect' on competition. In many cases, this means that at least 25 per cent of the market must be affected by the agreement. However some agreements, such as those which prevent price competition or fix market shares, can be investigated with a market share of less than 25 per cent.

The main kinds of agreements covered by the Competition Act include:

- agreements between firms to limit price competition

- agreements between firms to share the market, perhaps by dividing the market by geographical area, wholesalers or retailers

- production quotas designed to limit supply to the market and force up prices

- agreements to fix the prices paid to suppliers – for example, it is illegal for construction companies to agree between themselves the price they will offer for timber and other building materials.

The Act also governs relationships between producers and retailers which can suppress competition. These include:

- supplying products to just one retailer in a particular area, so that the retailer does not have to compete on price – both the retailer and the producer stand to benefit from being able to charge high prices to consumers

- supplying products to retail outlets on condition that the retailers do not sell the goods below an agreed price – some manufacturers try and avoid selling to shops that offer discount prices

- supplying products to retailers on the condition that they do not stock certain rival products

- obliging a retailer to stock the whole range of a supplier's products when the retailer may only want to buy one or two items from the range.

There are several other anti-competitive practices governed by the Act. A producer can not give different levels of discount to buyers which are not related to the size of their orders. For example, this kind of price discrimination could be used by a brewer to dissuade some pubs and hotels from stocking any rival brands by offering them a good deal, but the same generous discount will not be given to its own tied public houses, even if they place larger orders, because they are contractually obliged to buy beer from the brewery.

Firms can not abuse the dominant position of a subsidiary which is a supplier of an important input such as a raw material. The subsidiary can not charge rival companies a higher price for the material, increasing their costs and, therefore, weakening their competitive positions.

There are also restrictions on loss leaders, the practice of charging a price below cost in order to remove rivals from the market – and then introducing much higher prices when competitors have left the

market. A supermarket group, for example, may set low prices for fresh fruit, vegetables and meat in an effort to close down independent grocers and butchers in the area. Once the shops close, the supermarket resorts to much higher prices.

CASE STUDY

Replica football kits

Football fans spend an average of £100 a year on replica shirts and other merchandise. On average adults pay £40 for a replica shirt and £55 for the full kit of shirt, shorts and socks. Children's outfits are only £5 or £10 cheaper. Annual sales of replica shirts are worth £210 million.

The high prices for replica kits have led to accusations of price fixing. This has attracted the attention of the Office of Fair Trading and, after an inquiry lasting more than two and a half years, it has won undertakings from the Football Association, the Scottish FA and Premiership clubs that they would stop resale price maintenance.

Head of the Office of Fair Trading, the Director General of Fair Trading said he had conclusive evidence that some Premiership clubs had tried to avoid discounting by retailers and that this attempt at price maintenance was unacceptable.

The DGFT said that some manufacturers had illegally threatened to withhold supplies if retailers sold cut-price kits. Retailers are now free to set their own prices, and he expected to see a variety of discounts in the future.

Figure 2.13: The price of replica kits

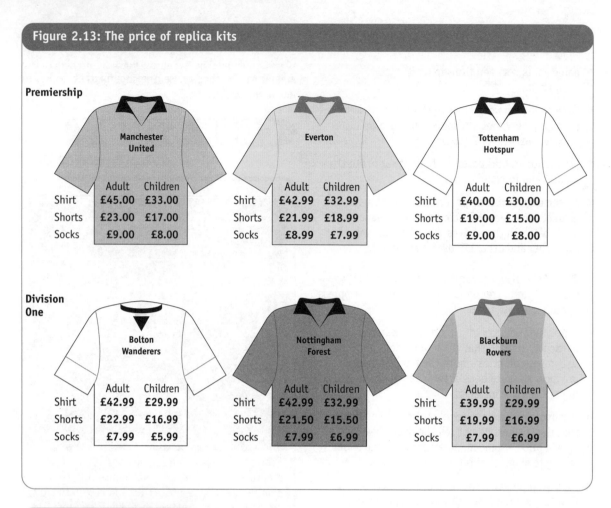

Premiership

Manchester United

	Adult	Children
Shirt	£45.00	£33.00
Shorts	£23.00	£17.00
Socks	£9.00	£8.00

Everton

	Adult	Children
Shirt	£42.99	£32.99
Shorts	£21.99	£18.99
Socks	£8.99	£7.99

Tottenham Hotspur

	Adult	Children
Shirt	£40.00	£30.00
Shorts	£19.00	£15.00
Socks	£9.00	£8.00

Division One

Bolton Wanderers

	Adult	Children
Shirt	£42.99	£29.99
Shorts	£22.99	£16.99
Socks	£7.99	£5.99

Nottingham Forest

	Adult	Children
Shirt	£42.99	£32.99
Shorts	£21.50	£15.50
Socks	£7.99	£6.99

Blackburn Rovers

	Adult	Children
Shirt	£39.99	£29.99
Shorts	£19.99	£16.99
Socks	£7.99	£6.99

Discussion point

Why would you expect the retail prices for replica shirts of well-supported Premiership clubs to be lower than the price of shirts of clubs with a much smaller following?

Give reasons why it is the interests of both the manufacturers and the Premiership clubs to avoid price cutting by retailers. Find out what penalties can the Office of Fair Trading can impose on kit manufacturers involved in price-fixing.

Abuse of a dominant market position

The Competition Act 1998 covers the abuse by one or more companies of a dominant position in a market. If a company or group of companies has a monopoly share of a market, then it can have sufficient power to damage competitors and consumers. A monopoly share is generally defined as a market share of at least 40 per cent, but the Office of Fair Trading may investigate a company with a smaller market share if the rest of the market is shared by a very large number of small companies and it is difficult for new competitors to enter the market. In both cases, however, there must be some indication that the dominant position is being abused before further action is taken.

The Office of Fair Trading can refer monopoly situations or mergers that may produce monopoly situations to the **Competition Commission** for investigation. It is the Secretary of State for Trade and Industry, however, who actually decides if the monopoly should be investigated to assess if it is against the public interest. In reaching a decision, the Competition Commission considers the level of competition in the industry and looks for evidence of competition in terms of cost reductions, the rate of innovation and the ease of access for new suppliers to enter the industry. It also considers the interests of

Consumer protection

Reputable retailers are always aware of their responsibilities to their customers. They seek to ensure that customers are satisfied with their purchases. This not only encourages customers to make repeat purchases but also to recommend the retailer to friends and relatives. Although many retailers are committed to customer care, there will always be companies that seek to sell at any cost and ignore any complaints from dissatisfied customers. Of course, it is not always the retailer that is at fault in any dispute; there are also consumers who seek to make a complaint which unfairly places the blame on the retailer.

Successive governments have introduced legislation to provide consumer protection and to set a legal framework to protect fair and responsible retailers from consumers who make unjustified claims against them.

- **Trade Descriptions Acts 1968 and 1972** – aims to prevent false or misleading statements concerning the description of a product or service, its country of origin or any aspect of its price.

- **Sale of Goods Acts 1979 and 1994 and the Supply of Goods and Services Act 1982** – covers the rights of consumers who claim that they have not been supplied with suitable goods that meet their particular needs. The 1982 Act also covers the supply of services. For example, it offers the consumer some protection against 'cowboy' building firms.

- **Consumer Credit Act 1974** – ensures that lenders inform consumers of the total cost of goods bought on credit, the annual rate of the total charge for credit (known as APR, the annual percentage rate) and any rights to cancel the agreement.

- **Consumer Protection Act 1987** – reflects a EU directive that consumers should be given certain rights to claim damages arising out of a defective product.

- **Consumer Safety Acts** – makes it an offence to sell goods which do not meet certain safety requirements. Toys for young children, for example, must be made from flame-resistant materials, have no sharp edges, use lead-free paint and have no pieces that could easily be swallowed if the toy came apart.

- **Food Act 1984 and the Food Safety Act 1990** – makes it an offence to sell food which is unfit for human consumption or to treat food in such a way that it becomes a danger to health. It also covers the labelling of food. Manufacturers must specify contents, ingredients, and artificial colorants and preservatives. The 1990 Act, in particular, is concerned with controlling all aspects of food safety throughout the food distribution chain.

- **Unfair Terms in Consumer Contracts Regulations** – came into force in 1995, these reflect an EU directive designed to remove the small print in contracts so that consumers are not bound by unfair terms. Tour operators, for example, can no longer put terms in their contracts which allow them to cancel or change holidays and limit their financial obligation to provide refunds.

- **Unsolicited Goods and Services Acts 1971 and 1975** – protects consumers from inertia selling, that is sending people goods through the post which have not been ordered and then relying upon their ignorance and apathy to extract payment if they are not returned within a certain period.

European competition policy

The creation of a true single European market (see p. 137) obviously requires the removal of all kinds of trade barriers and market distortions, such as tariffs and state subsidies, which prevent free and fair trade between members of the European Union (EU). It is also important that the EU plays a part in ensuring that competition within the single market is free from market distortions caused by restrictive trade practices and monopoly power.

In recent years there has been a move towards the harmonisation of competition policy between member states, so that companies do not experience more severe or more lenient laws according to where they are located. If some countries allow restrictive practices or the abuse of monopoly power, then companies located elsewhere may rightfully complain that they are put at a competitive disadvantage. They might find it difficult to enter certain markets or they may face unfair competition in their own markets from firms who can use the excessive profits gained from weak competition laws to subsidise prices in other EU markets.

The EU competition laws apply within the UK, however companies are only in breach of these regulations if there is a potential effect on trade between member states. The Office of Fair Trading works with the European Commission, assisting in its investigations, and comments on the evidence provided by the Commission prior to its making decisions on competition issues.

The Treaty of Rome allows the European Commission to intervene in cases of anti-competitive practice. Signed in 1957, the Treaty of Rome set up what was then known as the European Economic Community (EEC). Articles 85 and 86 of the treaty deal with anti-competitive behaviour, defined as firms acting either together or individually to use their dominant position to restrict competition between firms involved in trade within the EU. In general, the EU has been successful in implementing a common policy on competition throughout the member states; its aims are, for example, reflected in UK laws dealing with anti-competitive activities.

The rise in mergers between firms from different member states, particularly since the 1980s, has increased the risk of customers being exploited by monopoly power. As a result, the European Commission can now investigate mergers. The commission can investigate when the combined world turnover of the firms involved in a planned merger is more than 5 billion euro (1 euro is worth 61p at March 2000 rates) with each firm having a turnover of at least 250 million euros from business within the EU. If the companies generate at least two-thirds of their turnover in one member state, the merger must be dealt with according to the regulations of the relevant government. Firms must give the European Commission prior notice of any merger. It then has three weeks to decide if it should investigate.

The European Commission must also be informed of any financial aid to companies provided by central and local authorities to ensure that this does not amount to a subsidy that gives the firms an unfair competitive advantage. Aid is only be permitted if it meets very strict conditions. It is allowed, for example, if it promotes the development of poor regions, if it is for projects that promote the interests of the EU in general, and for culture and heritage conservation.

The European Commission is also seeking to persuade countries that still have state-owned industries to open up these markets to competition. This policy is aimed particularly at markets in the production and distribution of gas, telecommunications, postal services and transport. Many UK markets in these areas are now open to competition following the privatisation programme started by Conservative governments in the 1980s.

Regulating privatised monopolies

Recognising that the newly privatised industries could enjoy a monopoly position, the government has sought to open up their markets to competition. Following the privatisation of British Telecommunications, for example, it required that other telecommunications companies could use the BT network. In the energy market, the government hived off the ownership of the gas pipeline system and the national grid from the companies that supplied gas and generated electricity. This allowed other companies to compete to supply gas and electricity through these distribution systems.

Public concern, however, about the ability of privatised monopolies to increase their profits by simply charging higher prices, forced the government to create a series of regulatory agencies to monitor their prices

and to act as watchdogs to ensure fair trading. The government set up OFTEL, OFWAT, OFGAS and OFFER to monitor the activities of British Telecommunications, the water companies, British Gas and the regional power companies, respectively. They can investigate consumers' complaints.

These watchdogs can put a ceiling on price increases or even force companies to cut prices if their level of profits does not seem to justify proposed price increases. They can intervene if service levels are inadequate. Rail companies, for example, can be fined for failing to maintain reliability in keeping to timetable schedules. As more suppliers enter the privatised industries, the government anticipates that competitive forces will prevent prices increases based on an abuse of power and the role of the watchdogs, particularly in regard to prices, will no longer be necessary.

Deregulation and contracting out

Starting in the early 1980s, successive UK governments have gradually sold off the state sector industries to the private sector. They also opened up these markets to new suppliers as part of a policy of encouraging greater competition in sectors that had for many years been supplied by state monopolies.

The government also sought to give market forces a greater role in areas, such as refuse collection, transport, education and health, where central and local government services had been largely responsible for providing services. It did this by allowing private sector firms to bid for contracts to supply some elements of these services and related activities.

▲ Local transport has been deregulated, allowing competing private companies to offer bus services

It also took action on regulated markets. These markets were regulated so that once a company had been granted a right to supply a market it was protected from the entry of other suppliers. One example of a regulated market was bus and coach transport. Prior to 1980, local bus routes and long-distance coach travel in the UK was not open to free competition. Passengers were served by bus and coach companies that had been given licences to be the sole operators on particular routes. This approach sought to avoid wasteful competition, with too many buses operating vehicles on the most popular routes. There was concern that, in a free market, companies would show little interest in loss-making off-peak schedules and would compromise safety by saving on maintenance costs when faced with intense price competition.

Over the years, this regulated market for bus and long distance coach travel became dominated by local authority and state-owned bus and coach companies. Bus operators also received increasing subsidies to run unprofitable routes. However, the Transport Acts 1980 and 1985 opened up the industry to free competition in the belief that deregulation would lead to lower fares and improved services. Companies were also able to tender for routes where they would receive a subsidy. The increased use of minibuses on local routes is one of the results of deregulation.

Competitive tendering

Competitive pressures have also been introduced into many other parts of the public sector in an effort to reduce costs. This involves the practice of contracting out many of the services previously undertaken by central and local government departments. Services are put out for competitive tendering in order to give private companies an opportunity to compete for the contract to provide the service for a specific period of time. Many sections within government departments, which had previously provided services 'in house', have been turned into independent organisations and allowed to bid for contracts.

This process of competitive tendering, or market testing, now covers a wide range of services from catering, cleaning, maintenance and waste disposal to architectural and pay roll services. There are privately run prisons and private sector companies are also responsible for carrying out escort duties when prisoners are being transferred between jails or to court.

Market forces have also been introduced into the National Health Service (NHS). Hospitals supplying health care services have been converted into hospital trusts, and earn income by selling their health care services to the health authorities. This internal market is designed to lead to a more efficient use of resources within the NHS. The health authorities that buy services on behalf of patients have fixed budgets, and they will 'shop around' – hospital trusts need to offer competitive charges to get 'business' that generates income. The social services departments of local authorities are also allowed to ask private residential homes for the elderly to tender for contracts to provide accommodation for residents funded out of taxation.

The budgets of schools and colleges are more closely linked to the numbers of their students. Colleges must earn income by attracting funding from the learning and skills councils (which have replaced the training and enterprise councils) by selling courses to the business sector. This policy is expected to produce a more business-like approach as schools and colleges compete for 'customers' and funding.

Government and environmental issues

In order to maximise profits, producers continuously seek to minimise what can be termed their private costs of production, that is what they spend on labour, energy, materials and capital goods, for example. Competitive pressures, however, do not oblige firms to reduce external costs. These are costs which are not met by the firm. External costs can be generated by a firm's production methods and through the use and disposal of its end product, and they are costs imposed upon society as a whole. These costs include the harmful effects of a firm's operations on the environment, including any impact on air and water pollution, noise, traffic congestion, a deterioration in the urban, rural and coastal landscapes and any harm caused to fauna and flora. Further environmental damage may also be caused when end products, particularly those containing harmful materials, are disposed of by consumers and end users.

These spillover effects are likely to damage the health, safety and general welfare of the community. Although it may be difficult to place a precise financial value on these external costs, they still represent part of the firm's overall costs of production.

Making the polluter pay

One response to the problem of environmental degradation is to make firms pay for using the environment. For example, a company could be charged for the amount of emission its factories pump into the environment. In this way a link is established between minimising environmental damage and minimising production costs. The company would have every incentive to finds ways of reducing its emissions into the environment, in much the same way as it tries to reduce its other inputs such as labour costs. In effect, this policy seeks to reduce environmental damage by shifting a company's external costs on to its private costs, providing a direct incentive for the firm to adopt greener production methods. The policy also prevents firms that ignore their impact on the environment from gaining an unfair competitive advantage through having lower costs.

In some cases, it is possible put a direct financial cost on the impact of industry on the environment. Local and central government departments are forced to devote resources to tackling the resulting problems such as cleaning up rivers, managing landfill sites contaminated with toxic waste or dealing with respiratory problems caused by exhaust emissions. (The issue still remains, however, of assessing the extent to which individual producers and groups of consumers are responsible any particular instances of environmental damage.) However, if spillover effects go either partially or completely untreated, it is more difficult to assess the real cost to society of a product or service. It is difficult to put a financial cost on the various ways in which noise, litter and congestion, for example, affect the quality of life of individual households.

Green taxes

To date, neither the UK government or other European governments have made much progress in taxing different industries or individual companies to try and reduce their impact on the environment. In many parts of the European Union, however, there is growing support for a tax on all carbon-based fuels, given their contribution to pollution, global warming and health problems. If a carbon tax is set sufficiently high enough, it would oblige both industry and households to make more efficient use of energy. A carbon tax would also make energy derived from renewable sources a more attractive alternative than it is at the moment.

Green taxes have also been proposed for chemical-based fertilisers and pesticides, non-biodegradable containers and other pollutants. In each instance, it is argued that a tax would moderate the production of waste and pollutants and hasten the development of greener alternatives.

Regulations

Government pressure on business to improve its environmental performance continues to increase because of the growing number of voters who want

CASE STUDY

Tyres in the environment

There are over 121 million tyres on vehicles in the UK. They have a major impact on the environment, both when in use on vehicles and when they are disposed at the end of their lives.

As tyres are used small particles are worn off which can pollute the environment. Zinc, copper and cadmium from tyre wear can be washed into the ground, rivers and eventually the sea.

About 37 million car and lorry tyres reach the end of their life each year. New laws will make it illegal to dispose of tyres in landfill sites. This will make it even more urgent to recycle the material and recover energy from tyres.

Action is particularly needed to prevent illegal dumping and avoid tyre fires. In Powys, a tip containing buried tyres has been burning for nine years.

For more information access:
www.environment-agency.gov.uk/envinfo/tyres/

Disposal method	Volume (tonnes)	Percentage of all disposals
Retreading	117,200	31%
Energy recovery	102,000	27%
Landfill	97,800	26%
Material recycling	41,000	11%
Physical reuse	20,000	5%

Figures for 1996
Source: Scrap tyre working group

action on the environment. Governments have introduced legislation supported by financial penalties to provide protection for the environment. In the UK, regulations have been strengthened by the Environmental Protection Act 1990. This Act enshrines the principle that the firm responsible for any waste has a duty of care to ensure that it is disposed of in accordance with the relevant regulations. If this work is contracted out to a waste disposal firm and it is not dealt with correctly, then the originator of the waste is also liable for prosecution.

The government has established a number of bodies to shape and implement policy on the environment and pollution control. The Environment Agency deals with areas such as water resources and water quality, radioactive substances, liquid, solid and gaseous wastes, contaminated land, fisheries and conservation. The National Rivers Authority investigates and controls discharges of waste into rivers. At a local level, environmental regulations are administered by local planning authorities and environmental health authorities. These organisations are concerned with issues such as the kind of business or building allowed in a particular area, the environmental impact of both its design and the materials used for the building, the level of noise, effect on local traffic and the disposal of waste.

Discussion point

Argue the case for a disposal tax being placed on new car tyres to help fund the collection and safe disposal of used tyres by local authorities.

The uncontrolled burning of tyres damages air and water quality and contaminates soil and vegetation. Given all the external costs of tyres is there a case for subsidising companies that introduce clean ways of burning tyres to produce energy?

EU directives

UK producers also have to take account of EU directives concerning environmental protection. Apart from covering the more obvious sources of pollution the EU directives also deal with noise, non-motorised transport and sustainable cities, coastal area management, nature protection and trade in wildlife, chemicals and biotechnology, and eco-labels. The EU environmental directives help ensure that competition within the European Union is not distorted by some firms incurring lower costs because they are based in a country with less demanding laws on environmental protection.

Although EU laws apply in all member states, individual governments can still introduce environmental laws which are stricter than the European Union directives. Germany, for example, banned the use of unleaded petrol rather than joining the other countries in phasing out its use by the year 2000. Germany also introduced much stricter laws on recycling than the rest of the European Union. It requires packaging manufacturers and retailers to take back bottles, cans, cartons and other packaging in order to ensure that packaging waste is recycled.

Some of the main EU environmental regulations cover:

- exhaust emissions from cars and vans – vehicles must be fitted with catalytic converters to meet strict standards

- exhaust emissions from new heavy lorries – a directive aims to cut emissions by 50 per cent

- air pollution controls on new factories and a requirement to use the most up-to-date technology to limit emissions into the atmosphere

- reductions in emissions from power stations and factories of pollutants such as sulphur dioxide

- phasing out products that damage the ozone layer

- water quality – setting limits on the level of harmful substances including dangerous chemicals and nitrates from pesticides and fertilisers

- controls on oil pollution at sea, the dumping of waste at sea and the movement of polluting goods by sea

- standards for the treatment and disposal of sewage and a ban on discharging untreated waste into the sea or fresh water

- controls on the sale and use of dangerous chemicals such as asbestos and PCBs

- safety standards in factories using potentially dangerous products

- controls on the import or export of some 21 dangerous chemicals where the trade involves a non-member state

- the introduction of 'banks' for the collection of batteries which contain mercury, cadmium and lead – cadmium, used in plastic products such as flooring, will be phased out

- limits on noise from earth-moving equipment, compressors and pneumatic drills, tractors, lorries, cars, motorcycles and aircraft.

In order to protect the natural environment, the EU requires that projects which absorb large areas of land or which will affect the areas around must be assessed for their environmental impact before they commence. Individual governments are responsible for carrying out environmental impact assessments on the building of motorways, power stations and refineries. The EU, however, sets out the environmental aspects that must be covered by the assessment. If these procedures are not followed correctly – and any differences between the member state and the EU cannot be settled – the case goes before the European Court of Justice.

The EU aims to prevent any further growth in packaging waste. By the year 2000, it has a target to recover 90 per cent and recycle 60 per cent of packaging waste. This target is proving difficult to achieve because there is insufficient capacity for collecting and recycling the materials involved. If waste can not be recycled, the EU seeks to minimise the movement of waste. Its policy is that waste should be dealt with at local sites or incinerators using the latest technology.

International agreements

European governments are also bound by international agreements such as those reached at the Earth Summit in Rio de Janeiro in 1992 and at Kyoto in Japan in 1998. Under these agreements all EU governments are committed to stabilising the output of greenhouse gases, protecting all aspects of the natural environment such as plant and animal life and generally ensuring that economic advance is not at the expense of the environment. These international agreements also require governments to produce detailed reports on how they intend to implement the commitments. Companies need to consider the implications of these agreements for future environmental regulation and take early steps to introduce the necessary changes.

Green consumers

Companies also have to respond to the growing demand from consumers for green products. These consumers look more favourably on companies that have a reputation for seeking to minimise their impact on the environment. The extent to which a company can demonstrate that it takes greater account of the environment than its competitors is a growing factor in determining its competitive position and affects how favourably it is viewed by public opinion.

Regional unemployment

When market forces lead to the closure of a large employer or the decline of an industry as a whole, there is necessarily a large number of redundancies. If expanding firms or growth industries are located in the same area, and they need the same kinds of skills possessed by those made redundant, then people may soon find alternative jobs. If the redundant workers do not have the right kinds of skills or are too far away from firms recruiting workers, then unemployment may prove to be very long term.

Unemployment has left its mark on the UK economy for decades because of the long-term decline in the steel, shipbuilding, textile and coal mining industries. These industries provided the main sources of employment in northern England, central Scotland, south Wales and Northern Ireland. New industries and job opportunities have tended to concentrate in the South East and the West Midlands. Until very recently, therefore, the North, Scotland, south Wales and Northern Ireland have suffered from unemployment levels well above the national average.

The problem of regional unemployment is made worse because of the secondary effects on local firms which supplied declining industries with equipment and commercial services. Other (unconnected) companies are often forced to make job cuts because of the general fall in local consumer spending.

Regional unemployment is also a problem if markets are lost to overseas producers, or if technology makes a radical change to the end product. The UK motor vehicle industry, for example, suffered large-scale job losses from the mid-1970s onwards because of increasing imports. This, in turn, has affected employment in the West Midlands where there are concentrations of component suppliers, manufacturers of machine tools and engineering industry in general. Advances in technology have further reduced the demand for labour because robots have replaced workers on the assembly line, and a single computer-controlled machine tool can do the work of a whole series of traditional machine tools. The net result of these developments is that fewer people are employed either directly or indirectly in the motor vehicle and machine tool industries.

Government intervention

To tackle regional unemployment, government intervention in recent years has mainly concentrated on offering financial help to firms which either expand their existing operations in, or relocate into, areas of high unemployment. The policy has been to 'take work to the workers', rather than provide financial incentives and affordable housing for people who wish to move to areas of labour shortages.

The parts of the country in which firms qualify for a range of grants are known as assisted areas. They are classified as either development areas, in which there is much higher than average unemployment levels, or intermediate areas, in which serious unemployment is likely to arise in the near future without some form of financial assistance.

The level and scope of financial assistance has varied over the years. The current system is based upon either **Regional Selective Assistance** or **Regional Enterprise Grants**. Regional Selective Assistance is discretionary and takes the form of a grant to help with the costs of capital projects and training. To qualify for a grant, a project must be viable, create or protect jobs, bring benefits to the area or the UK economy as a whole and be one which could not go ahead without money from the government. The Regional Enterprise Grant scheme is designed to help small and medium-sized firms with the costs of capital projects and innovation. An **Enterprise Initiative Consultancy Scheme** helps firms subsidise the cost of using outside consultancies.

Urban and inner city problems

Since the late 1970s, there has been increasing emphasis on the economic, social and environmental problems of large cities and inner city areas. There has been a shift of employment and population away from the older and densely populated inner cities into towns, smaller cities and more rural areas. People living in the traditional urban areas have far fewer job opportunities. These areas have becomes centres of acute poverty, deprivation and social problems and have suffered a serious decline in their physical environment.

A variety of policies have been introduced to tackle inner city problems. One measure is the **Urban Programme** under which local authorities can obtain city grants. These can be used to help finance projects involving the private sector that are designed to create jobs, provide training opportunities, improve the physical environment and tackle problems stemming from poor housing conditions and the lack of health, leisure and recreation facilities. Another aspect of inner city policy is the **Derelict Land Programme**. This provides grants for public and private sector organisations and individuals to improve previously derelict land so that it again contributes to the local environment and economy.

The EU's regional policy

The UK receives additional financial support for regional development from the European Union. This aspect of the EU's economic policy recognises that economic growth and job prospects are not evenly spread throughout the single market. The EU has therefore introduced schemes to encourage more even economic and social development throughout the various regions and member states. The EU's assistance is aimed at:

- regions whose economic development lags behind the EU average – about 80 per cent of the EU's spending on its regional policy is allocated to these areas; in 1994, the only area qualifying for this assistance in the UK was Northern Ireland

- the restructuring of areas suffering from industrial decline in industries such as steel, shipbuilding and coal mining – in the UK about 20 million people live in areas covered by this objective compared with 53 million people in the EU as a whole

- helping agricultural sectors adapt to the reduced support from the Common Agricultural Policy and generally promoting rural development.

The European Union has three funding schemes to support its regional policy. The **European Regional Development Fund** (ERDF) finances investment in infrastructure projects such as communications, energy, water and sewerage, and environmental improvements. Emphasis is placed on supporting investment in capital projects (in manufacturing, for example) which help to replace jobs lost through the decline of traditional sources of employment. Most ERDF support in the UK has been directed to modernising and diversifying the industrial base in areas of high unemployment.

The **European Social Fund** (ESF) provides help for vocational training and retraining. As well as targeting the long-term unemployed and young people, it also aims to help women returning to work, migrant workers and disabled people. The UK has used ESF support to help tackle youth unemployment in inner cities and steel areas where retraining is an important factor.

The **European Agricultural Guidance and Guarantee Fund** specialises in financial help for projects which raise productivity in agriculture and improve the processing and marketing of agricultural products. It recognises that farmers must become more efficient. especially given the reduced financial support available through the **Common Agricultural Policy** (CAP). The EU aims to attract small and medium-sized firms into rural areas, develop tourism and leisure activities and create alternative sources of employment in agricultural areas. **Rural Development Areas** qualify for both ERDF and ESF assistance.

All support through the EU's three regional funds must be used to supplement a member state's own regional development programme and not be used as a substitute for spending by member governments. EU funding must therefore be matched by spending from national governments to produce additional resources for regional development. If a government is found to have frozen or cut its own regional spending while receiving funds from the EU, it will have its aid withheld.

Economic policy

In the economy as whole, the operation of market forces can produce a sudden and large rise in consumer spending that very soon leads to labour shortages and a rise in inflation. At other times, a downturn in total spending in the economy as a whole will produce a fall in demand which leads to firms cutting back on output, rising unemployment, and possibly even a deep recession. Because the economic environment can change very suddenly, from one of excess demand to one of a lack of demand, business have to operate in very uncertain markets.

Government economic policy is designed to remove some of the uncertainty from markets. If there is evidence that spending pressures in the economy are showing signs of pushing the rate of inflation beyond the government's target level of, say, 2.5 per cent, then a range of economic policies can be used to depress or **deflate** consumer spending. If the rate of inflation is comfortably below the government's target level but a depressed level of total spending has produced high unemployment, then economic policies can be used in the reverse direction to stimulate or **reflate** total spending.

Over the years, governments have used a variety of economic policies in an effort to either dampen down or stimulate total spending in the economy, so that there is a closer match between demand and the supply that the economy is capable of producing. It does this with measures designed to influence both the level and pattern of total spending in the economy.

Inflation

A rise in the rate of inflation is usually associated with total spending – and in particular consumer spending – rising faster than the rate at which firms in general can increase their output. To produce more and take advantage of these very buoyant market conditions, firms need more labour. Labour shortages develop and firms have to award large pay rises in order to retain and recruit workers. Increasingly, these pay rises will exceed improvements in productivity with the result that unit labour costs rise, and firms will be forced to raise prices to protect their profit margins. These price increases raise the rate of inflation further, and employees will demand even larger pay increases to compensate for the rise in the cost of living. Given labour shortages, they will be in a strong position to obtain pay increases which exceed the expected rate of inflation. This process describes the beginnings of a wage-price spiral (see Figure 2.14) which, if unchecked, can lead to a rapid acceleration in the rate of inflation.

Discussion point

Discuss why a series of interest rate cuts might eventually trigger a large increase in consumer spending leading to a wage-price spiral and rising inflation.

What kinds of firms are likely to be the first to experience skills shortages when there is a large increase in consumer spending?

If the spending boom works its way into the housing market, why might this further fuel consumer spending?

International competitiveness

The government will be particularly concerned if the UK inflation rate is out of line with inflation in other manufacturing economies in Europe, the USA and Japan. This is because a very large number of jobs can be at risk if UK firms find it more difficult to export goods and services overseas and if imports increase at the expense of home output.

If the UK's rate of inflation exceeds inflation in other manufacturing economies for a long period, then the UK's balance of trade with the rest of the world will deteriorate because:

■ a sudden and large spending boom will produce a surge in imports as UK producers are unable to meet increased demand

■ higher inflation will make imports more attractive

■ exports become less competitive in overseas markets

■ some UK producers will switch output from export markets to the buoyant home market

■ imports of consumer durables will rise, particularly if the spending boom is fuelled by rising consumer credit

■ increases in home output will be achieved, in part, through higher imports of raw materials, energy, parts and components.

The government may become concerned about the ability of the economy as whole to earn sufficient foreign currency to pay for imports. An import boom means that more sterling must be sold on foreign exchange markets to obtain the foreign currency to pay for imports. However, the demand for sterling will be relatively low because overseas customers are now buying fewer UK goods and services. The net result is

Figure 2.14: The wage-price spiral

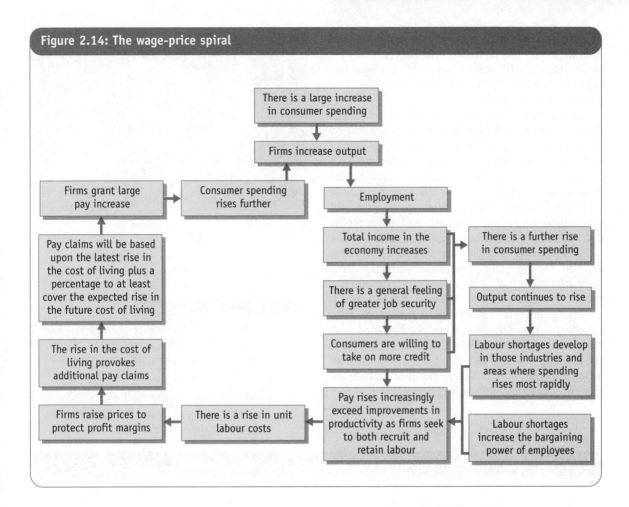

that the supply of sterling on foreign currency markets exceeds demand, and the price of the pound falls. There will be a fall in the exchange rate, the pound may fall in value from, say, $1.60 to $1.40 with severe consequences for some sectors of the UK economy.

In order to reduce the rate of inflation and improve the UK's balance of trade, the government can use either monetary or fiscal measures to deflate total spending in the economy. **Monetary policies** concentrate on changes in interest rates, while **fiscal policies** cover changes in taxation and levels of government spending.

Raising interest rates

The decision to raise (or lower) interest rates is taken by the monetary policy committee of the Bank of England. An increase in interest rates raises the cost of mortgages, loans, overdrafts and other forms of credit. This depresses the market demand for goods and services for several reasons.

First, higher interest rates impact on households. A rise in interest rates paid on home loans will have a significant effect on the monthly mortgage repayments of the typical household. This reduces discretionary incomes and, in order to find the extra money to meet the higher mortgage repayment, many homeowners will have less to spend on other items. Higher mortgage interest payments also makes it more difficult for many households to meet their repayments on other loans and consumer credit agreements. They are unlikely, therefore, to take out further loans. In particular, this reduces the demand for a wide range of expensive consumer durables which are typically bought on credit.

Higher mortgage rates also reduce the demand for houses from both first-time buyers and people moving home. This fall in the housing market, in turn, reduces the demand for furnishings, consumer durables and the kinds of services and products associated with home improvements. Falling house prices leave many households with negative equity. These households will hesitate to take on additional consumer credit: if they faced financial difficulties, they could no longer rely sell their property at a profit to clear their debts. This depresses the feel good factor.

Second, higher interest rates affect companies. Producers react to the fall in consumer spending by cutting back on production and shedding labour, causing further falls in consumer spending. Less overtime, fewer bonus payments and commissions also mean a loss of earnings for those still in work.

Firms will be forced to cut back on capital investment programmes because of depressed sales, lower profits and higher interest charges on existing loans and any future borrowing. This fall in investment depresses the demand for the plant, machinery, equipment and premises provided by firms in the capital goods and construction sectors. This means a further rise in unemployment and an even lower level of total spending in the economy. It should be noted that because investment is vital for the future prosperity of the economy, the damage which deflationary measures inflict on investment is a very serious and unwanted side effect of an anti-inflationary policy.

▲ Governments closely monitor the level of consumer borrowing

Discussion point

Why does the Chancellor of the Exchequer monitor data on consumer borrowing before taking budget decisions on changes to taxation?

Suggest reasons why the Bank of England might respond to a boom in consumer credit by increasing interest rates.

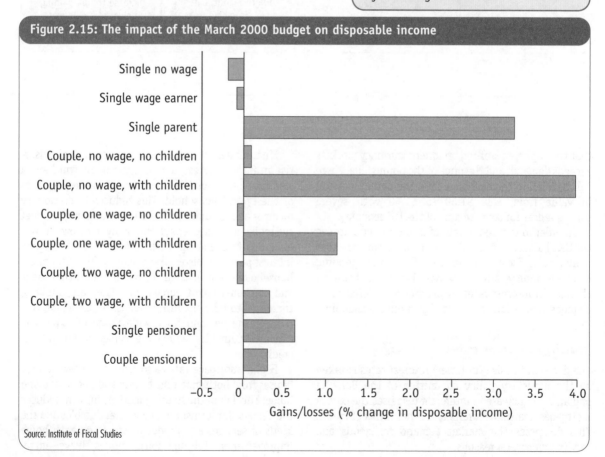

Figure 2.15: The impact of the March 2000 budget on disposable income

Source: Institute of Fiscal Studies

Raising tax levels

If the government is concerned about excessive levels of spending and rising inflation, it can raise income tax rates in order to reduce the average level of disposable income. An increase in employees' national insurance contributions also reduces disposable incomes.

An increase in income tax rates is very unpopular with voters, but the government can increase the percentage of income paid in tax without actually raising income tax rates. It can do this by freezing tax allowances and tax bands. In each budget, the government usually raises tax allowances – the income that can be earned without paying tax – in line with the rate of inflation in order to protect the real spending power of this tax-free income. It also raises tax bands, the levels above which higher rates of tax are paid, in line with inflation. By freezing allowances and tax bands, it can ensure that a larger proportion of income will be paid in tax as incomes rise in the future.

The prices which producers charge for their goods and services are also affected by changes in value added tax (VAT), excise duties and other expenditure taxes which the government imposes. These different types of expenditure taxes are called indirect taxes; taxes on various forms of income are known as direct taxes. Indirect taxes are a way of raising tax revenue from consumers when they spend their disposable income on goods and services. In effect, firms are acting as tax collectors for the government.

When VAT was first introduced in 1973 it was set at 7.5 per cent. It was raised to 15 per cent in 1979 and then increased to 17.5 per cent in 1992. In the 1994 budget, the government was defeated in its attempt to impose the full rate of VAT on domestic fuel (VAT on domestic energy is charged at 8 per cent). An increase in VAT will dampen down the level of consumer spending in the economy because it reduces real spending power. A higher rate of VAT means that the average household's disposable income does not go so far as before. In its annual budget statement, the government also has the option of extending VAT to zero-rated items. The major areas of consumer expenditure exempt from VAT are food, children's clothing and footwear, books, newspapers and magazines, and public transport.

In price terms, the actual effect of a rise in VAT can be very small. The price of a £2.35 item, for example, will rise by only 5p to £2.40 if VAT is increased from 17.5 per cent to 20 per cent. Even a product priced at £470 will cost only £10 more. However, it is the cumulative effect of these higher prices that reduces real spending power and, therefore, total demand in the economy.

Excise duties account for a very large proportion of the price of alcohol, tobacco products and petrol. Over 80 per cent of the price of a packet of cigarettes and a litre of petrol is collected in tax by the government. These items are taxed heavily because the demand is very insensitive to a price rise. When duty is increased on alcohol, cigarettes and petrol, they continue to be bought in very large quantities. Higher excise duties is a way of removing spending power from households, leaving them with less money to spend on other goods and services.

Excise duties are collected direct from the producers. This is because it is far easier for the government to collect revenue from the breweries on the basis of their beer sales, for example, than collect taxes from the thousands of outlets that sell beer to consumers. Although the breweries pay the tax, beer drinkers are effectively taxed of course, because the tax is passed on down through the distribution chain in the prices charged by pubs, clubs, off-licences and supermarkets.

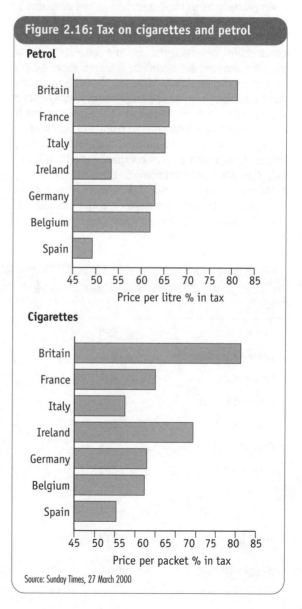

Figure 2.16: Tax on cigarettes and petrol

Petrol

Price per litre % in tax

Cigarettes

Price per packet % in tax

Source: Sunday Times, 27 March 2000

In addition to raising existing taxes, the government can introduce new taxes. In the November 1994 budget, for example, it introduced a 3 per cent tax on most general insurance premiums and a new duty on air travel, charging passengers £5 for flights within the UK and the EU and £10 elsewhere. These new taxes have since been increased, largely as a measure to raise revenue rather than deflate consumer spending. A rise in the road fund licence can also be used to withdraw purchasing power because, as with higher petrol duty, the government is not obliged to return the extra revenue back into the economy through, for example, increased spending on roads.

Restricting government spending

A very large part of total spending in the economy is accounted for either directly or indirectly by public expenditure – that is, spending by central and local government departments. In the late 1990s, for example, government spending averaged about 42 per cent of total spending. A large number of households and firms have incomes and order books which depend very heavily on public spending. If the government is concerned that total spending is rising too fast, leading to higher inflation and a growing trade deficit, it may restrict the growth of public expenditure in order to help slow down total spending in the economy. It may try to run a budget surplus, taking more money out of the economy through taxation than the amount put back through government expenditure.

If the government estimates that inflation is likely to be about 3.5 per cent in the next financial year, then central and local government departments need a 3.5 per cent increase in their budgets just to maintain spending in real terms. If, however, the government increases public spending by 1.5 per cent, then although this is still an increase in money terms it amounts to a cut in spending in real terms. For example, the money allocated to road building may increase by 1.5 per cent but, because of inflation, it actually buys fewer miles of motorway, and the construction industry receives fewer orders. Suppliers and subcontractors in the industry may be forced to lay off workers. The resulting fall in spending power will then work its way through to other sectors of the economy.

Apart from making cuts in its capital spending projects, the government can also use its power to restrict public sector wage rises. When setting budgets for central government services, and deciding on the grants it makes to local authorities, the government makes an allowance for the average pay rise for public sector employees. If it allows for a 2.5 per cent increase in public sector pay, but inflation is expected to be 4 per cent in the next financial year, then real spending power in the public sector will actually fall. This again helps to reduce the pressure of demand in the economy.

Some local authorities, when faced with what they see as insufficient funding from central government, seek extra income by increasing council tax. To prevent this, the government can use its powers to restrict rises in council tax. This capping on local authorities is a way of controlling the level of local authority spending.

Figure 2.17: UK government finances, 2000–01

Income	£bn	Expenditure	£bn
Income tax	£96	Social security	£103
Value added tax	£59	Education	£46
Excise duties	£37	Debt interest	£28
Corporation tax	£34	Defence	£23
Business rates	£16	Law and order	£20
Council tax	£14	Industry and agriculture	£15
Other income	£61	Housing, environment	£14
		Transport	£9
		Other expenditure	£59
Total income	**£377**	**Total expenditure**	**£371**
Budget surplus	**£6 billion**		

Discussion point

In the March 2000 budget, Chancellor Gordon Brown decided to use the £6 billion budget surplus to repay some of the government borrowing rather than allocate all his tax revenues to government spending programmes. What does this tell you about the Chancellor's view of the future growth of consumer spending and average earnings, and the future rate of inflation?

The effects of deflationary policies

If deflationary policies are severe, and operated for a long enough period, inflation will eventually fall. As firms react to a fall in the demand for their goods and services, increases in their unit costs will eventually slow down, thereby moderating the rate of price increases.

- As demand falls, it becomes a buyer's market and producers will face greater price competition. Profit margins cannot be protected by raising prices, so firms must be more efficient to survive.

- The need to meet higher charges on any existing borrowing also forces firms to make savings by avoiding excessive pay increases.

- Greater competition between retailers means that they will be looking for the best deals on prices from suppliers, and this pressure feeds down through the whole production chain.

- Rising unemployment also eases pressures in the labour market, weakening the bargaining power of trade unions and employees when seeking pay increases.

The gradual fall in the rate of inflation will also help to improve the UK's balance of international trade. As inflation falls below the average rate for other manufacturing economies, UK goods regain some of their lost competitiveness. This makes imports less attractive as well as making UK exports more competitive in overseas markets.

The fall in total demand in the home market eases the demand for imports of consumer goods as well as raw materials, parts and components, while the fall in investment expenditure will reduce imports of capital goods. The falling home market forces producers to pay more attention to developing export markets in order to support sales.

Firms will be left with spare capacity. The slack order book means that they can offer more attractive delivery dates, increasing their chances of winning home and export orders when competing with overseas producers.

Figure 2.18: Car and housing market indicators

	New car registrations		Housing indicators		
	'000s	increase (%)	house price inflation (%)	transactions	mortgage rate
1986	1,883	2.2	11.7	1,795	12.32
1987	2,016	7.1	14.9	1,931	10.04
1988	2,210	9.6	26.3	2,146	12.75
1989	2,305	4.3	18.4	1,566	14.44
1990	2,005	−13.0	−0.3	1,400	14.34
1991	1,600	−20.2	−1.2	1,300	11.39
1992	1,599	−0.1	−6.0	1,128	8.98
1993	1,776	11.1	−2.7	1,191	7.94
1994	1,906	7.3	0.5	1,279	7.84
1995	1,938	1.7	−1.6	1,137	7.48
1996	2,018	4.1	4.2	1,242	6.51
1997	2,157	6.9	6.4	1,441	7.58
1998	2,262	4.8	5.4	1,346	7.80

Source: HM Treasury Pocket Data Bank

Discussion point

Using the data in Figure 2.18, identify years when the demand for cars was supported by a strong feel good factor, and put forward evidence to support your answer.

What are the signs that the government used higher interest rates to depress consumer spending and deal with rising inflation at the end of the 1980s?

Present evidence that the government was trying to encourage a rise in total spending in the 1990s and that it managed to achieve this for several years without a rise in inflation.

Policies to tackle unemployment and to generate growth

The total spending in the economy can produce a level of output which still leaves a very high level of unemployment. In this case, the government may opt for measures which help to reflate total spending so that companies hire more workers. The government can select from the same range of measures used to deflate demand to deal with inflation, but in this situation it uses them in the reverse direction.

Lowering interest rates

Cheaper mortgages will increase discretionary incomes and, together with cheaper consumer credit, can play a central role in stimulating total spending, output and jobs. Once the economy begins to expand, increasing sales and profits will help to boost business confidence. Increased confidence and lower interest rates on loan capital will encourage investment spending. Firms producing capital goods will also, therefore, take on more workers.

Cutting taxes

Governments have not generally lowered income tax rates to stimulate consumer spending. They are reluctant to do so because if they are forced to reverse the tax cut in the future they risk political unpopularity. There is also the question of fairness: lower income tax rates do not help people on low incomes who pay little or no tax, but they bring

substantial benefit to those on high incomes. Another risk is that large part of extra disposable income may go on imports.

The income tax cuts made by Conservative governments in the 1980s and early 1990 were designed to encourage initiative and enterprise. It was argued that high tax rates deterred the growth of an enterprise culture. The government hoped that tax cuts would encourage small firms and the self-employed to expand their businesses, create more jobs and expand into export markets.

An alternative to cutting tax rates is to increase tax allowances and income tax bands in excess of the rise in the cost of living. This has the political advantage that these increases can be made much less generous in the future if needed, without risking the political unpopularity associated with reversing tax cuts. If tax allowances are increased, some people are taken out of taxation completely; wider tax bands mean that incomes can rise much higher before households move into the next tax band. These measures raise disposable incomes and help stimulate consumer spending and jobs.

In reality, a cut in excise duties is very unlikely as this would increase the use of products like alcohol, tobacco and petrol which are a threat to both health and the environment. Again a cut in VAT is soon forgotten, but a government would become very unpopular if future inflationary pressures forced it to restore the rate to its previous level.

Increasing government spending

The government can increase spending by running a budget deficit, spending more than it takes out of the economy through taxation. Budget deficits have to be financed by the government borrowing. The amount which it borrows in the course of the year to finance its deficit is known as the public sector borrowing requirement (PSBR). Note that if extra government spending is simply financed through taxation, by raising tax rates for example, this would defeat the aim of increasing total spending in the economy as the extra spending by the government would be offset by less spending by households.

Although it takes time before the effects of more government spending on capital projects eventually produce more jobs, this policy may be preferable to tax cuts. This is because the extra spending could concentrate on health, education, training and environmental protection measures, for example, which benefit everyone in the longer term. These projects are also labour intensive and have a relatively low import content.

Encouraging investment

The extent to which the economy can continue to push its total output of goods and services to higher levels, and achieve economic growth, depends upon improvements in productivity. Because all economies have limited resources, higher output can only be achieved if resources are used more efficiently. Producers, therefore, play a vital role in promoting economic growth because in order to strengthen their competitive positions they need to invest in the technology that raises productivity and helps to minimise their unit costs.

Because of the vital role played by investment in promoting economic growth and raising living standards, governments have always sought to encourage investment by the private sector. However, while governments have been relatively successful in encouraging consumer spending, they have found it far more difficult to stimulate the level of investment.

One of the problems facing companies when making decisions about their future strategy and investment programmes is the very uncertain nature of the business environment in which they have to operate. A major reason for this uncertainty is the effect of changes in the government's economic policy upon the total level of spending in the markets in which a firm sells its goods or services. Within a relatively short period of time, a shift in economic policy can cause major developments in markets, having implications for where companies sell their goods and where they acquire their resources such as labour and capital. If, for example, a change in economic policy produces an actual or anticipated fall in total spending in the economy, this will depress business confidence and force many firms to cut or postpone their investment and training programmes. Firms must be confident of a relatively long period of buoyant future sales before committing to multi-million pound capital investment projects.

Figure 2.19 illustrates the stop-cycle. Analysts have argued that this kind of boom-bust cycle is responsible for the relatively low level of investment in the UK and explains why its rate of economic growth has generally been below that of many other major manufacturing economies.

Discussion point

Discuss why firms hesitate to undertake long-term investment programmes even when consumer spending is rising rapidly. Why is a lack of investment in extra capacity a major reason why the government is eventually forced to depress the level of consumer spending?

The government should therefore try to avoid the sudden changes in economic policies that contribute to an unstable business climate. It needs to follow an economic strategy that produces a steady increase in total demand so that firms can respond without suffering from a lack of productive capacity or skills shortages. If this kind of market environment can be sustained for a reasonable period of time, firms have both the profits and the confidence to invest in additional capacity. This, in turn, means that future increases in demand can be met mainly by increases in total output rather than the inflationary pressures produced by a shortage of capacity and skilled labour.

Apart from the effects which higher interest rates have on sales, profits and business confidence, they also make it more expensive for firms to raise extra capital funds by borrowing. Because company borrowing often involves large sums of money, even a relatively small rise in interest rates means a large increase in interest repayments on borrowed capital. In order to meet these higher interest charges firms may need to cut back on their future capital spending programmes. The government should, therefore, seek to follow economic policies that reduce its need to resort to an increase in interest rates.

The use of public funds to help finance private sector investment plays a very minor role in the UK economy. Most of the grants that have been made available are linked to capital projects which protect or create jobs in areas of high unemployment or help to tackle the social, economic and environmental problems of run-down urban areas. Within the EU, the Commissioner for Competition seeks to ensure that member governments do not use financial assistance simply as a way of disguising the payment of a subsidy to an uncompetitive home producer.

Investment might be encouraged by a cut in the level of corporation tax which firms pay on their profits. The rate of corporation tax depends upon the level of profits. A cut in corporation tax not only increases the net return on capital but also increases the level of internally generated funds available to finance future capital projects. The government might also find ways of increasing investment by providing firms with a more advantageous system of capital allowances. These allow spending on investment projects to be offset against tax liability, making investment more attractive.

Figure 2.19: The stop-go cycle

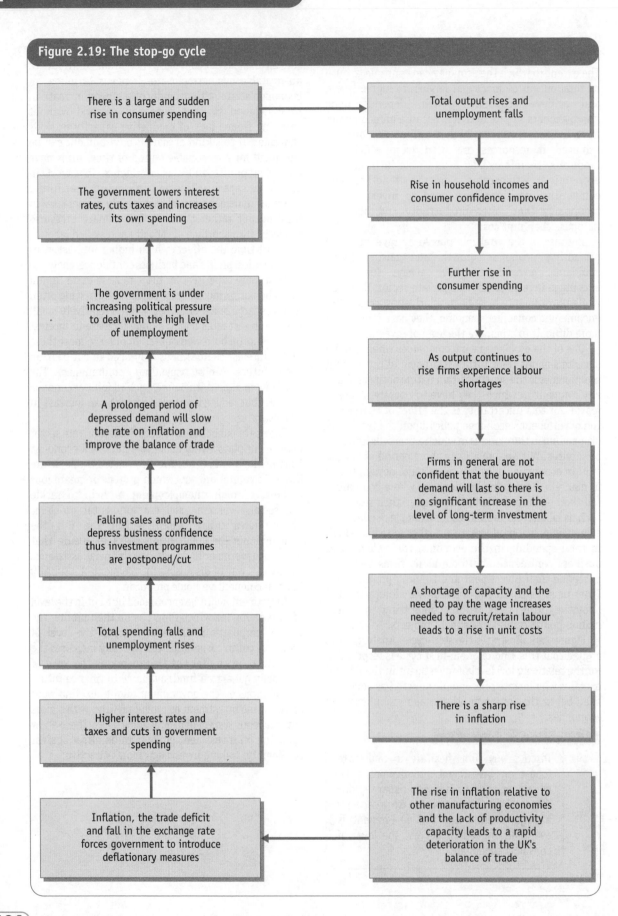

No room for complacency about long-term prospects

Despite the recent high growth rates in the UK economy relative to the rest of the EU and Japan, there is still some concern about the long-term competitiveness of many UK companies.

The growth of total output in the UK economy has been eased by the fact that firms are able to draw upon a relatively large pool of unemployed workers and the increasing number of women entering the workforce.

However, as unemployment continues to fall, future increases in output and competitiveness are threatened by a lack of investment and a growing skills shortage.

Research by the Department of Trade and Industry (DTI) shows that British manufacturers came eighth out of eleven countries in terms of the percentage of their turnover generated by bringing new or improved products to the market.

The DTI argues that UK consumers are not demanding enough and are too willing to accept poor quality products and services.

Adapted from *The Times*,
14 December 1999

Discussion point

What is the connection between a firm improving productivity and having more competitive unit costs?

Do you think UK producers would be more competitive against foreign producers if UK consumers complained more about shoddy goods?

BUILD YOUR LEARNING

Keywords and phrases

You should know the meaning of these words and phrases.

- Budget deficit
- Budget surplus
- Business confidence
- Capping
- Common Agricultural Policy
- Competition Commission
- Cost of living
- Deflate
- Direct taxes
- Economic growth
- Environment Agency
- European Agricultural Guidance and Guarantee Fund
- European Regional Development Fund
- European Social Fund
- Fiscal policy
- Indirect taxes
- Inflation
- Internal market
- Monetary policy
- Office of Fair Trading
- Public expenditure
- Public sector borrowing requirement
- Real terms
- Recession
- Reflate
- Regional Enterprise Grants
- Regional Selective Assistance
- Urban Programme

Summary points

- The law protects the public from firms that engage in anti-competitive agreements, abuse a dominant market position, neglect the health and safety of consumers or act unfairly in their dealings with customers.

- UK consumer protection legislation is supported by EU regulations designed to encourage competition and protect consumers.

- The production methods used by firms are must take account of regulations imposed by both the UK government and the European Union to protect the environment.

- The UK government and the EU implement policies to tackle high levels of unemployment and the social problems associated with the decline of key sources of employment.

- The government can use changes in interest rates, taxation and public expenditure to combat excessive rises in inflation or unemployment.

- The government seeks to stimulate economic growth by using measures that create a financial and economic environment in which companies will expand their investment programmes.

International competitors

STRONG COMPETITION IN A market stimulates efficiency and product development. If firms also have to face competition from overseas producers, this further adds to the pressure to maintain competitive prices for both consumers and business customers. Developments that encourage more companies to participate in international trade as exporters therefore increases competitive pressures at the international level.

The single European market

The very large internal market within the European Union is a major factor in encouraging competition, promoting exports and encouraging economic growth and job creation in the UK. This is for several reasons.

First, a larger 'home' market of over 360 million people allows producers to exploit greater economies of scale and benefit from lower unit costs. If they maintain prices at their current levels, profit margins will increase and provide additional profits to finance future investment projects. Of course, companies may use the opportunity provided by lower unit costs to cut prices and strengthen their competitive position at the expense of the higher-cost producers.

Second, by working towards the harmonisation of technical, safety, and environmental standards, the single market reduces the need for producers to incur extra costs in altering their products to comply with different regulations in various parts of Europe. Harmonisation allows an European producer to benefit from greater economies of scale through longer production runs.

Third, capital-intensive industries, and those which have to spend large sums on research and development, are able to undertake their capital spending programmes with a much higher degree of confidence. Investing in a new chemical processing plant or developing a new drug becomes much more worthwhile if a company sees the prospect of large sales from a potentially very large market. Advances in technology are also becoming increasingly expensive to fund, and the removal of trade restrictions and the opening up of export markets helps to generate the level of sales needed to make these projects viable.

Fourth, the removal of import controls, such as tariffs and other trade barriers to trade, within the EU increases the choice available to companies when buying raw materials, parts, components and capital goods. After taking account of non-price factors such as quality and delivery, they are able to buy components from suppliers offering the most competitive prices. It is particularly important that import restrictions do not prevent companies having access to the kind of plant and machinery which most closely meet their needs. Import controls prevent a company from selecting from the widest possible range of suppliers, and have an adverse effect upon the costs, quality and competitiveness of that company's output.

Fifth, the single European market helps prevent business complacency. If producers are sheltered behind import barriers, they may become complacent. The lack of competition from overseas companies means that they do not have to be particularly efficient to survive in their home market. If the home economy is opened up to foreign competition, home producers have to respond to the threat of imports by paying greater attention to their costs, offering more competitive prices and generally improving other features such as quality and after sales-service. Inefficient producers will not survive in this much more competitive environment; those that do are also likely to find additional markets outside the European Union.

Finally, the widespread removal of trade barriers and other restrictions on imports increases the purchasing power of households in the UK. The prices of many products may actually fall because of more intense competition. Producers in the UK may experience a greater demand for their output as households make use of their extra spending power. Output, jobs, incomes and further spending are generated by the original rise in real purchasing power.

The World Trade Organisation

Although the EU and other trading groups such as LAFTA (Latin American Free Trade Area) have made progress towards removing trade barriers within their areas, a large part of international trade is still constrained by restrictions on imports designed to protect home producers from foreign competition. The World Trade Organisation (WTO), formerly the General Agreement of Tariffs and Trade, seeks to remove barriers to international trade that make it difficult for the most competitive producers to penetrate export markets.

There are now over 130 members of the WTO and it holds lengthy rounds of talks to negotiate reductions in trade barriers. The WTO also investigates complaints against governments that have introduced new import restrictions and judges if the government lodging the complaint has the right to take retaliatory action.

The WTO rounds of talks can last for several years. during which they seek to remove:

- tariffs
- import quotas
- subsidies
- soft loans
- protection for state-owned industries.

Tariffs

Tariffs amount to a tax on imports and have the effect of making the prices of domestic products relatively more attractive. If imports enjoy very strong non-price advantages, such as quality, design or performance, then tariffs have to be very high to persuade a significant number of customers to shift from overseas suppliers to home producers. Tariffs are also known as import duties or import surcharges.

Import quotas

Import quotas protect home producers by setting a limit to the quantity or total value of a particular product that can be imported during the course of a year. (In some cases the annual quota may refer to the maximum amount that can be imported before the product is subject to an import duty.) Companies wishing to export to a country imposing quota restrictions must obtain a share of the quota, and there is no reason why the most efficient producers will necessarily gain the largest share of the quota.

Subsidies

Governments can use subsidies to help high-cost home producers charge artificially low prices and survive against foreign competition. Subsidies, unlike tariffs and quotas, not only protects home producers from imports but also allows them to compete in export markets. An attempt is generally made to hide these subsidies because of the pressure that would otherwise be placed upon foreign governments by their own producers to retaliate in some way.

Soft loans

A government may rescue a failing producer with a more generous loan, and on much softer terms, than could be obtained from a private sector lender. The terms of these soft loans could include a very long period of grace before repayments have to start, a repayment schedule spread over a very long period and interest charges well below the market rate. The producer may also be able to operate in the knowledge that the government is likely to agree to any rescheduling of the debt and it is therefore under less pressure to follow a strategy that eventually removes its reliance upon the government for its survival.

Protection for state-owned industries

Some governments continue to put large sums into supporting state-owned industries such as coal, steel, energy and rail transport. Generous financial support for these industries may then be reflected in lower prices, which are more competitive than those of businesses which receive little or no support from their governments. A subsidised steel industry, for example, has an unfair competitive advantage, both in terms of direct competition with other steel producers and in keeping down the costs of companies which use large quantities of steel such as shipbuilders and motor vehicle manufacturers. Similarly, a heavily subsidised energy sector is a great advantage to energy-intensive industries such as chemicals and synthetic fibres.

▲ The removal of agricultural subsidies is high on the WTO's agenda

One of the areas of contention in world trade is agriculture. The World Trade Organisation is seeking to remove the barriers that distort trade in agricultural products. The USA and other major food exporting countries are keen to see an end to the subsidies and other import controls which the European Union and Japan use to protect their farmers from imports of cheap foodstuffs. The USA also claims that subsidies give EU farmers an unfair price advantage when competing with US farmers in other markets in the world. The EU's position is that there is a case for protecting agriculture as it supports jobs in the countryside and directly and indirectly supports rural economies. The EU is also concerned about food safety and quality. The US government regards this as a move by the EU to restrict imports of genetically modified foodstuffs from US growers.

Discussion point

What other methods apart from subsidising farmers can the European Union use to control imports of foodstuffs?

Discuss why UK food manufacturing businesses might support the WTO in opening up export markets to genuine low-cost growers of foodstuffs.

On average, about 16 per cent of UK household spending goes on food shopping. Why will non-food businesses benefit if the WTO is successful in removing barriers to international trade in foodstuffs?

Tariffs and quotas are very obvious forms of protection, and countries using these trade barriers run the risk of retaliatory action. This has led to the increasing practice of using disguised or hidden protection to give home producers an advantage. Examples of **hidden protection** include:

- restrictive tendering
- import licences
- unnecessary standards and regulations
- inspection and testing procedures.

Restrictive tendering

Governments can put pressure on central and local authority departments and state-run industries to favour home companies when awarding contracts for materials, capital goods and construction projects. This is known as **restrictive tendering**. The government may also pay inflated prices, allowing home suppliers to earn exceptionally high profits and which they can to both subsidise exports and to gain a price advantage over imports.

Import licences

Importers may be required to obtain a licence to import certain kinds of goods. The government may then ensure that the application and approval procedures are very time-consuming and involve a great deal of red tape. This may deter potential importers. If new market is developing, the delays generated by import licences can be used to give home producers an early advantage over imported products.

Unnecessary standards

Rather than going along the route of the international harmonisation of kinds of standards, a government may retain its own particular and distinctive regulations. It may also deliberately discriminate against imports by imposing very strict and often unnecessary regulations on imported products, so that they match features of the home-produced version. Overseas producers are then obliged to make expensive modifications to their product in order to satisfy the particular regulations of a single country. Home producers on the other hand will already be producing the 'acceptable' product, and on a scale which gives them a cost and a price advantage.

Inspection and testing procedures

A government may insist upon that imported products pass inspection and testing procedures before they can be supplied to the home market. As with import licences, these procedures can be organised to frustrate and delay importers. The testing facilities may be located in different parts of the importing country. They may be organised so that an overseas producer must send its products to different inspection sites before they are able to reach the same potential market. These testing and inspection procedures may also have insufficient resources to deal with their work load, and the procedures for new products may be subject to particularly long delays to give home producers an opportunity to establish themselves in the home market.

Competitiveness and exchange rates

Movements in exchanges rate effect the international competitiveness of UK producers, as it impacts on the prices of both exports and imports. The effect on exports is not caused by UK firms changing their prices in response to changes in their costs but rather by developments in foreign exchange markets which are beyond their control.

A fall in the exchange rate

Assume that a Jaguar car is priced at £60,000 while a photocopier made in the USA is priced at $4,480. If the pound falls against the dollar, from say $1.60 to $1.40, then the price of the Jaguar on the US market falls from $96,000 to $84,000 while the price of the US-made photocopier on the UK market rises from £2,600 to £3,200. A fall in exchange rates makes exports cheaper and imports more expensive.

Although allowing a fall in the exchange rate seems to be a very easy and immediate way of helping UK producers to be more price competitive, there are several factors which may prevent the policy from having the desired effect.

- First, if producers are confident that the government will always allow a fall in the exchange rate to protect their competitive position against foreign companies, they may become complacent and they have less incentive to undertake long-term investment projects to raise productivity and keep costs down.

- Second, a fall in the exchange rate raises the production costs of companies that rely upon imported raw materials, parts and components as well as those investing in imported plant, machinery and equipment. Some of the advantage provided to exporters by the lower exchange rate can therefore be wiped out by higher import costs.

- Third, the additional cost of imported consumer goods and imported raw materials and components increases the cost of living. Trade unions may then press for larger pay rises and this can put yet more pressure on a firm's costs.

- Fourth, UK firms may not be able to take full advantage of the higher export demand or the switch away from imports, if a lack of investment in an earlier period means that they do not have sufficient productive capacity to increase output.

- Fifth, instead of exploiting to opportunity provided by the fall in exchange rates to increase exports, some UK firms may simply respond by raising their sterling prices. Similarly, UK producers competing in home market with overseas suppliers might simply raise their prices now that imports cost more.

A policy of allowing large falls in the exchange rate to help domestic producers also has implications on the foreign exchange markets. It encourages the speculative selling of the pound as soon as there are any signs of a rise in inflation or a growing trade deficit. The treasurers of large multinational corporations with deposits in different financial centres and the dealers who speculate in currency movements will move their funds out of sterling rather than risk being left with a depreciating currency. The large-scale speculative selling of sterling may then lead to a very unstable exchange rate, creating problems for both UK exporters and importers and damaging business confidence.

More fundamentally, allowing the exchange rate to fall does not deal with the underlying cause of the loss of competitiveness. It is a short-term response to the loss of price competitiveness and simply gives UK producers a breathing space during which they should undertake the investment and training programmes needed to achieve a long-lasting improvement in competitiveness.

A rise in the exchange rate

Rather than lowering exchange rates to help make UK firms more competitive, the government may even opt to allow a rise in the value of the pound. This is because a strong pound might actually help to tackle the inflation which is damaging price competitiveness.

If the government can convince firms that it will not allow a fall in the exchange rate to help offset the effects of price increases, employers will be under greater pressure to resist pay rises that raise unit labour costs. UK producers will also be need to pay more attention to other costs and ways of increasing productivity.

A strong or rising exchange rate helps to slow down inflation by keeping down the costs of imported raw materials, parts and components. As long as the exchange rate does not fall, then at least some of a firm's costs will be unchanged at a time when other pressures might be pushing up its domestic costs. Even a rise in the exchange rate may be welcomed by the government because it will lower a firm's import costs and help to compensate for any rise in its domestic costs.

Similarly, a strong pound also helps to slow down the rise in the cost-of-living by keeping down the cost of imported consumer goods. This will slow down the rise in the inflation rate and weaken the employees' case for a pay rise, helping to moderate the rise in unit labour costs.

European monetary union

If the UK adopts the euro, UK producers will no longer have their competitive position against other EU producers effected by movements in the exchange rate. They will still be effected, however, by changes in the value of the euro against the currencies of non-EU producers in, for example, the USA and Japan.

The case for and against European monetary union are the subject of considerable political and economic debate. There are many issues to be considered. If Britain adopts the euro, the UK government will no longer have the option of using a fall in the exchange rate as way of compensating for high inflation in the UK compared with the rest of the European Union. A single currency will remove the uncertainty caused by unpredictable movements in the value of the pound. The marketing strategies of UK producers will no longer be complicated by the uncertainty over imports costs, the prices of competing imports or their export prices to buyers within the European Union. UK producers will no longer incur transaction costs exchanging sterling for other European currencies or vice versa.

Interest rates in the European monetary union area will be decided by the **European Central Bank** and determined by the needs of the European Union as a whole rather than by a single member state. The UK is only likely to join the euro, therefore, when the performance of the UK economy matches closely that of the main EU economies in terms of inflation and economic growth, for example. Without converging economic performance, changes in European interest rates might be inappropriate for the UK economy. For example, the UK economy would be damaged if the European Central Bank raised interest rates to tackle rising inflation in most areas of the EU at a time when the UK had low inflation but was suffering from rising unemployment.

Note that although interest rates will be set by the European Central Bank, it would still be possible for to deal with a situation in which UK inflation or unemployment is out of line with the rest of the EU; the UK government (under current proposals) will retain the power to vary tax rates as a means of deflating or reflating total spending in the UK.

BUILD YOUR LEARNING

Keywords and phrases

You should know the meaning of the words and phrases listed below. Go back through the last four pages of the unit to check or refresh your understanding as necessary.

- European Central bank
- Harmonisation
- Hidden protection
- Import duties
- Import quotes
- Import surcharges
- Restrictive tendering
- Tariffs
- World Trade Organisation

Summary points

- Membership of the European Union means that UK producers faces greater competitive pressures from imports. Membership also provides UK producers with the opportunity to develop their export markets.

- The World Trade Organisation seeks to remove trade barriers and open up more markets to international trade. This will provide UK producers with greater export opportunities.

- Movements in the exchange rate effect the prices of UK goods and services overseas while also changing the prices of imported goods and services on the UK market.

- If the UK adopts the single European currency, this will remove exchange rate fluctuations and prevent the government allowing a fall in the exchange rate to help UK firms be more price competitive when facing foreign competition.

The British motor industry

The sale by BMW of most of Rover Group has revived fears about the health and future of the British motor industry. It has also sparked debate on wider issues, such as the vulnerability of UK manufacturers outside euroland and the role of state intervention. Yet in truth, the potential demise of Rover as a volume producer is the inevitable consequence of its poor brand image and the sustained loss of market share. In an era in which any region in any economy is susceptible to decision taken by multinational companies, further closure of British car plants cannot be ruled out. But the malady afflicting Rover, known to many within BMW as the 'English patient', does not foreshadow a terminal decline for Britain's car industry.

The last 15 years has been a good time for motor manufacturing in the UK. The volume of passenger car production reached its all-time peak in 1972, at more than 1.9 million units. But during the following decade output and exports slumped dramatically, with several plants forced to close and the controversial withdrawal of Chrysler. The industry's plight was compounded by the deep recession of the early 1980s when domestic car sales fell by a third. By 1982, fewer than 900,000 cars were produced, with only a quarter going for export.

The industry's fortunes improved dramatically from the mid 1980s, in response to a sustained revival in domestic and European sales and improved perceptions about the business climate in the UK. The late 1980s saw the arrival of three Japanese manufacturers, Nissan, Toyota and Honda, that established brand-new plants on greenfield sites. The factories at Sunderland, Derby and Swindon produced 554,000 cars last year, 31 per cent of the UK's output. They have also played an important role in improving the overall productivity of the UK's motor manufacturing sector. The latest annual survey of the productivity of European car plants conducted by the Economist Intelligence Unit found that in 1998 the three Japanese owned plants were the most productive in the UK in terms of the number of vehicles produced per employee. Moreover, Nissan's Sunderland operation was over a third more productive than any other in Europe.

With longer established manufacturers also investing to upgrade their facilities, output and exports have climbed steadily in recent years. In 1999 output reached almost 1.8 million units, having grown for eight consecutive years. Not only was production at its highest since 1972, but exports at more than 1.1 million units were more than five times the level of the early 1980s and an all-time record.

Production and exports continued to grow last year, despite the mounting difficulties at Rover. Output of

Rover cars was slashed by just over 100,000, but this was more than offset by sharply higher production by Vauxhall, Jaguar and Peugeot. With Jaguar and Peugeot between them making an additional 127,000 cars at their plants in the West Midlands, the region's output was still higher than in 1998.

Rover's difficulties stem from its inability to hold on to its position in the domestic market. Back in 1993, the year before the company was acquired by BMW, Rover Group (including Land Rover) was the third largest supplier to the home market, with a share of 13.4 per cent. By 1998, Rover had given up 5 per cent of the market and had been taken over by both Peugeot-Citroen and VW. Things went from bad to worse in 1999. The new Rover 75 was well received but didn't sell, market share fell to just 6.4 per cent, behind that of Renault, and its best-selling Rover 200 and Rover 400 ranges slipped to the lowly fourteenth and twentieth respectively on the best seller list.

Figure 2.20: UK car production ('000s)

Manufacturer	1999	1998	%change
Rover Group	367.7	465.5	–21.0
Rover	225.8	328.6	–31.3
Land Rover	141.9	136.9	3.7
Ford Group	341.9	348.5	–2.0
Ford	255.1	298.5	–14.5
Jaguar Damlier	86.3	50.0	72.5
General Motors	339.0	277.3	22.3
Nissan	271.2	288.8	–6.1
Toyota	178.7	172.3	3.7
Peugot	162.6	71.4	127.5
Honda	114.5	112.1	2.1
Total (incl. others)	1,786.8	1,748.3	2.2

Source: SMMT Monthly Statistical Review, January 2000

Under these circumstances it is hard to envisage that any commercial organisation would not resort to dramatic action. Moreover, in an industry where size definitely matters, BMW's own future and independence has been put at some risk by the huge losses at Rover. While the scaling-down of operations at Longbridge may hit the local community hard, placing at risk many thousands of jobs at component suppliers and service providers, it is far from being a knock-out blow for the

British car industry. The sector is in far better shape than it was 20 years ago, and some manufacturers, notably Nissan, Vauxhall and Honda, will continue to expand their operations.

Over the long term, the level of domestic car production is a reflection of the attractiveness of the UK as a production location and on the performance in the marketplace of those who opt to make cars here. The industry has undergone substantial change in the past decade. In both the UK and Europe, the car market has fragmented as Japanese and other Far Eastern producers have taken a significant share and as the large European manufacturers have grown in strength relative to the US heavyweights, Ford and General Motors. Rover is not the only casualty of this trend. In the UK market, for example, Ford has lost about 10 per cent of the market over the last decade. Although only three of the leading six suppliers to the European market have operations in the UK, it is encouraging that Nissan, Toyota and Honda between them now sell nearly a million cars Western Europe, a market share of about 8 per cent.

The UK's position outside the eurozone obviously carries risks, especially when multinational companies come to make decisions about where to site new plants or close existing ones. But so far this has made no difference to the flow of inward investment. The latest figures for 1999 show that the UK continued to take the largest share (40 per cent) of new investment coming into the European Union. While the level of sterling and its volatility against the euro is a problem, inward investors also attach great importance to other aspects of the business climate in the UK, including the stability and robustness of economic performance, the flexibility of the labour market and the relatively low level of social overhead costs.

The best way to restore any jobs lost at Longbridge is to ensure that the UK economy continues to perform well, and that the business environment is one which encourages investment and competitiveness.

Questions

Answer these questions in the context of the issues raised in the case study of the British motor industry.

Question 1

- Explain why the motor vehicle industry is an industry where size definitely matters.
- What kind of integration was involved when BMW took over Rover?
- Give two possible economies of scale that BMW may have expected when it took over Rover.

Question 2

- What is meant by a recession and why will it reduce demand for cars?
- Why is both the business and household demand for cars closely linked to changes in interest rates?
- Describe two other factors that contributed to the increased UK demand for cars in the late 1980s.

Question 3

- Give two possible reasons for the very high productivity at Nissan's plant in Sunderland.
- What is meant by an upgrading of facilities and why would it have helped car producers in the UK achieve record exports in 1999?

Question 4

- Describe the non-price factors which may have been responsible for the trends shown in Figure 5.20. Note that General Motors is a US car producer that owns the Vauxhall plants in the UK.

Question 5

- Why has it traditionally been difficult for a new car producer to enter the UK and European market?
- Describe factors that have helped non-European car producers gain a foothold in the UK market.

Question 6

- Why would the UK's membership of the European Union have been a factor in attracting Japanese car makers to set up in the UK?
- Give two other possible reasons why the UK continues to be such an attractive location for companies from outside the EU.

Question 7

- Explain why Japanese car producers in the UK may be concerned that the euro has fallen by over 15 per cent against the pound since its launch?
- Give two reasons why car producers in general in the UK might be in favour of the pound being replaced by the euro?

Question 8

- Apart from BMW and shareholders describe the interests of two other stakeholder groups in Rover?
- Explain how the government can help to create a business environment that encourages investment by car manufacturers and other industries.

This unit introduces the major principles and functions of marketing, covering the identification of customer needs, the anticipation of market opportunities and the formulation of a suitable strategy or marketing mix which satisfies customer needs, influences customer behaviour and enhances the customer's perception of the organisation and its products and services.

The marketing process is highly visible, and some aspects such as questioning potential customers in the street, television advertising and product placement can be seen everyday. The process involves marketing research,

effective communications, and sales and customer service. Each of these essential marketing activities are reflected within this unit.

The unit also recognises that, in carrying out marketing activities, it is important to take into account technological developments, the competition and changes in the business environment. This has to be done with reference to the other business functions if a company is to maximise its benefits in terms of income generation and profits.

3

Marketing

The principles of marketing

MARKETING IS THE MANAGEMENT process of identifying, anticipating and satisfying the needs of actual or potential customers, whether for profit or not, while also encouraging customers to make further purchases and to recommend the products and services of the organisation.

Understanding customer needs

Anybody responsible for marketing within an organisation needs to be able to identify the needs of both existing and potential customers. It is also necessary to be able to anticipate future trends and developments which could influence customers' requirements; for example, a furniture warehouse would need to increase its stock if it anticipates an upturn in the housing market.

Marketing involves constantly reviewing all aspects of a product or service in order to ensure that it continues to satisfy the potential customer's requirements. This means having the right product or service, available at the right price and at the right time and place. It is only be satisfying all these factors that a private sector organisation will be able to make a profit and a public sector organisation or charity will be effective in meeting its objectives. Ultimately, an organisation can claim that its marketing is successful when consumers make repeat purchases or are prepared to make recommendations about the organisation's products or services.

Coordinating functions to achieve marketing aims

The primary aim of marketing is to ensure that potential customers buy products or services. However, the way in which marketing is carried out varies enormously between organisations according to their size and the nature of their products or services.

In a small business, the marketing function may be carried out by a single person. Many sole traders have to make marketing decisions, along with other business decisions in functional areas such as purchasing, production and finance. The owner of a mobile hot dog stall has to purchase supplies and equipment, cook and sell the product, and control the financing of the operation, as well as make all the marketing decisions. These include deciding on the most important features of the product for target customers, such as the type and size of roll, and the variety of sausage and sauces. Other marketing decisions must be made on how much should be charged, where the mobile unit should be located, and how the business should be promoted, whether, say, through signs by the roadside or advertising.

In a much larger organisation, such as Unilever, Glaxo and Ford, there may be specialists responsible for each part of the marketing function. Figure 3.1 shows how marketing could be organised in a business which has markets at home and abroad. The most important domestic customers would be handled by a special key account manager. Some of the work connected with market research, public relations and advertising could be handled by outside agencies.

Discussion point

Figure 3.1 shows how marketing could be organised in a business which has home and overseas markets. Why is this structure likely to lead to greater efficiency?

However the marketing function is organised, it must be well coordinated and have well-defined lines of communication with other departments. If marketing is badly coordinated or lines of communication are poor, there is always a danger that problems will arise in production, purchasing and finance. Costly errors may be made about levels of production leading, for example, to over-purchasing of raw materials and components.

Adopting a marketing approach

Organisations can be categorised as being either product-oriented or customer-oriented, and this has a large effect on their approach to marketing activities.

In a product-oriented organisation, managers often become complacent about the organisation's products

Figure 3.1: The organisation of marketing activities in a large company

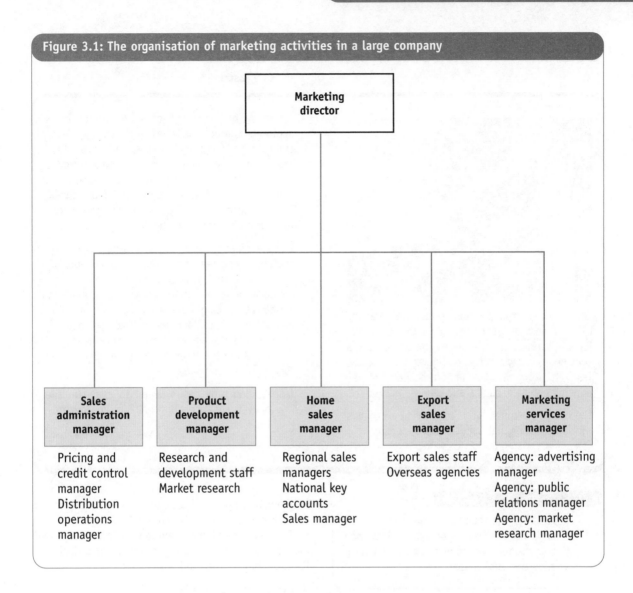

and service. By focusing on the product rather than the market, they might assume that the existing range of products is the best on the market and that sales will follow automatically; they may see no need for product change or modification. These attitudes can lead to the downfall of an organisation, particularly if it is operating in a rapidly changing, highly competitive business environment. For example, some companies producing towelling nappies were badly caught out by the introduction of the paper-based disposable nappy.

A customer-oriented organisation, on the other hand, is in a constant state of development; assessing, monitoring and responding to changes in the market in order to keep ahead of its competitors. It will have a highly developed marketing strategy, which acknowledges and is sensitive to its customers' changing needs and wants. It strives to find out what customers want, what causes them to buy products, and what the product or service really means to them as consumers. From the top down, the organisation and all its decision-makers are market led, recognising that tomorrow's profitability depends upon meeting today's needs. This attitude is exemplified by Tesco, as the following case study illustrates.

CASE STUDY

Tesco

Tesco is committed to retaining its position as the UK's largest supermarket retailer. Customer feedback forms, in-store discussion groups and a continuous analysis of sales figures has enabled Tesco to recognise the importance of the key principles of price, quality and service.

The company's objective is to 'provide customers with outstanding, naturally delivered, personal service'. This customer-oriented approach is achieved through schemes such as the Tesco clubcard, the 'no quibble money back guarantee', the 'one in front' queuing policy and the use of more customer assistants. Major Tesco stores now sell clothing, compact discs and videos, highlighting Tesco's recognition of the need for continuous innovation and trend identification.

Tesco recognises the key role staff play in promoting and conveying the company name and image. It's aim – 'to earn the respect of our staff for the company values and appreciate their contributions' – reflects its commitment to staff training and motivation. Staff are trained to be helpful, responsive and sympathetic to customer needs and to understand that their behaviour influences the success of the company.

Tesco's long-term desire is not to just earn the loyalty of its customers but their 'lifetime loyalty'.

Adapted from www.biz-ed

Discussion point

Identify the major features of Tesco's customer-oriented approach and provide two examples of other retailers that have adopted a similar approach.

Effective customer communications

Businesses need to communicate effectively with their customers if they are to satisfy their needs. **Effective communication** involves the exchange of information to achieve mutual understanding and, perhaps, to promote action. In marketing, it centres on the use of advertising, public relations, sales promotion and direct marketing activities. The aim is to influence purchasing decisions of specific customer groups (or **target audiences**). A secondary aim is to obtain positive publicity for the organisation to enhance its public image.

For marketing communications to be effective, the target audience should comprise a group of customers with similar needs and attitudes, so that each customer is likely to respond in a similar way to a particular advertisement or other promotional message.

The target audience requires different types of information before making a purchasing decision. Potential buyers need to know:

- that the product exists

- where it can be bought

- details about product or service, its price and features

- information to evaluate whether it meets the prospective customer's needs.

This information has to pass through a number of stages of communication: origination by the organisation, choice of communication format and channel, and receipt by members of the intended audience. One of the practical problems with this communication sequence is that it is essentially one way; it offers little opportunity for potential customers to provide feedback to the seller. This makes it difficult to measure the effectiveness of marketing communications: companies often have broad and rather imprecise indicators, such as a comparison of sales before and after an advertising campaign.

Another problem for organisations is that they do not have complete control of communications about their products. Potential customers don't just get product information from advertising and other marketing communications. They receive information about products from a range of sources including other consumers, critics and reviewers, television and radio programmes, and newspapers and specialist consumer magazines. These opinion leaders influence the views of others by making recommendations and giving advice. For a marketing communication to be effective, it must be received and accepted by these opinion formers. Organisations need to be aware that impartial consumer advice provided by the media and other agencies may support or damage its own marketing communications.

Constraints on marketing activities

Within the customer-oriented organisation, marketing features prominently in overall planning. Any market plan will be based on the strategic plan of the organisation. In a customer-oriented organisation, the objectives of marketing activities are determined by, and reflect, the overall objectives of the business.

Discussion point

How do you think the objectives in Figure 3.2 relate to Tesco and its customer-oriented approach.

To achieve marketing objectives, an organisation must meet the needs of customers. Unfortunately, in meeting these needs, an organisation may threaten some of its other strategic objectives. Customers generally want:

- high-quality goods and services
- low prices
- choice
- efficient and convenient distribution
- imaginatively presented, detailed information about the products
- the latest technology.

Figure 3.2: Organisational objectives

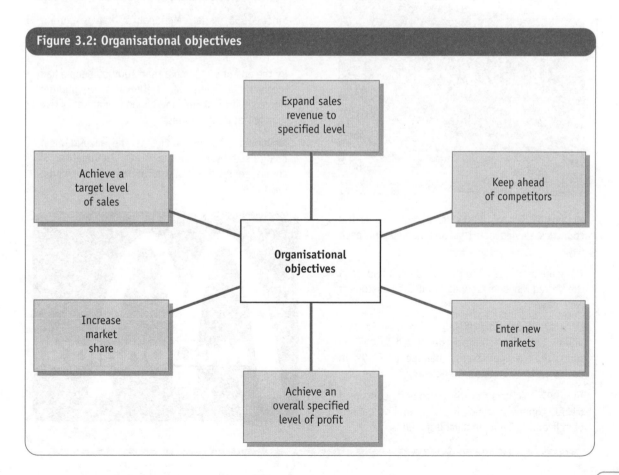

It can be expensive to meet these needs. It may require frequent changes in production methods and improvements in standards of service which may have an adverse effect on an organisation's ability to maintain its productivity and, ultimately, its profitability.

It is possible, however, for some organisations to overcome these constraints and give customers what they want as the growth and continued success of McDonald's demonstrates. As the McFacts case study illustrates, McDonald's has maintained a customer-oriented approach and achieved global dominance. It has the right fast-food products and level of service, offered at the right price and being sold at the right times in the best locations throughout the world. This is supported by its excellent communications, global promotions and close attention to staff training to ensure high standards of customer service.

Discussion point

To what extent do you think that McDonald's is oriented towards a global rather than an individual customer?

CASE STUDY

McFacts

The world's busiest McDonald's is on Red Square in Moscow, serving as many as 50,000 people each day.

Since 1955, when McDonald's first restaurant opened in suburban Chicago, McDonald's has served over 100 billion hamburgers.

By the end of 1997, more than 100,000 people had received training at McDonald's Hamburger University in East Finchley, London, or at one of five regional training centres.

McDonald's Golden Arches is the second most recognised brand in the world. McDonald's, of course, serves the best-known brand in the world, Coca-Cola.

McDonald's has over 23,000 restaurants in over 100 countries, serving more than 38 million people each day.

There are more than 850 McDonald's restaurants in the United Kingdom, serving 2.5 million customers each day.

In 1997, McDonald's UK sales amounted to £1.1 billion. Globally, McDonald's generated $33 billion sales. The average UK customer spends £2.99 on each visit to McDonald's.

In 1997, McDonald's UK customers consumed 61,500 tonnes of French fries, 7.5 million gallons of milk and 472 million hamburger buns.

BUILD YOUR LEARNING

Keywords and phrases

You should know the meaning of the words and phrases listed below. Go back through the last five pages of the unit to check or refresh your understanding as necessary.

- Customer oriented
- Effective communication
- Product oriented
- Target audience

Summary points

- The primary aim of marketing is to enable businesses to meet the needs of their actual and potential customers, whether for profit or not.

- To meet actual and potential customer needs, organisations must ensure that they have the right product or service, available at the right price and at the right time and place.

- Whether the marketing function is being carried out by a single individual or group of specialists, it must be well coordinated and have well defined lines of communication with other functional areas.

- In order to keep ahead of its competitors, an organisation needs to adopt a customer-oriented approach constantly assessing, monitoring and responding to changes in the market.

- Effective communication involves the use of advertising, public relations, sales promotion and direct marketing activities in order to influence the purchasing decisions of the target group.

- The objectives of marketing may be constrained by the other strategic objectives of an organisation.

Establishing customer needs

MARKETING RESEARCH PROVIDES information that helps organisations to recognise and respond to market opportunities and to develop suitable products to meet market needs. It enables organisations to find out which goods and services people want, the price they are prepared to pay, where they prefer to buy the product, and how products should be promoted.

By carrying out marketing research, the organisation can identify key factors which relate to customer satisfaction at three levels. These are:

- the essential or **core benefits** associated with a product – that is, what the customer seeks to obtain by buying it

- the product specification, including branding, packaging and quality

- the additional benefits associated with after-sales service, advertising, customer advice, financing and delivery.

All these factors add value to the product, increasing its competitiveness and the potential returns to the organisation. For example, research into the tastes and entertainment needs of young people has contributed to the dominance of Sony PlayStation in the computer games market.

Marketing research information is either **quantitative** or **qualitative**. Quantitative research is essentially numerical, providing data for example on how many people buy a product, how often they buy it; qualitative data relates to consumer attitudes such as their goals, aspirations and interests.

In order to develop its marketing strategy, an organisation has to explore the needs of its customers and the activities of its customers and competitors, by conducting research in a number of areas:

- product development

- distribution

- promotion

- consumer behaviour

- the market and the competition.

Let's consider each of these areas in turn.

Product research

Organisations need to undertake product research into both the development of new products and the improvement of existing ones. Before any changes are made, products are put through a series of tests to investigate features such as design, materials and ingredients, colour durability, ease of handling, fitness for purpose and operating capacity. In recent years, market research has increasingly been applied in new product development, as the article opposite shows.

One of the problems in developing and researching a new product is that customers' reaction to a prototype may be misleading. This is likely to be especially true if the product breaks entirely new ground; for example, it might use new technology to produce radically different features and services. Initially, customers may resist the unfamiliar, but as they come to recognise the benefits, the innovation may be quickly adopted. When the hole-in-the-wall cash dispenser was first introduced, many people were wary of dealing with a machine. They felt it lacked the reassurance of a human transaction. However, the use of cash dispensers grew rapidly as people came to appreciate the significant benefit of 24-hour access provided by automatic tellers.

The importance of psychology is widely recognised in product research. This is because consumers can be motivated to purchase products that they, or their friends, believe confer status or prestige. Brand labelling can play an important part in image making.

▼ The Dyson cleaner, the result of extensive product research

Research propels innovation

Innovate or die. This is the daunting challenge facing companies and it's easier said than done, given the high failure of new products introduced into the marketplace.

Market research is increasingly being used to reduce those failures and save money. Answers are needed at a number of steps in the new product development cycle and research can provide the necessary guidance.

But market research has not always been regarded as a guiding light. According to Julian Bond, new product development managing director at Research International: "Market research used to be a minor part of decision-making in the 1980s and was used to back up decisions that were already made." Bond says most manufacturers' historic use of market researchers was like a drunk's need of a lamp post. "It was used more for support than illumination," he says.

Those days are long gone.

Manufacturers are now looking to research to point out how to fine tune new products as well as predict new buyer volumes. They are listening ever more closely to their customers.

The first question a manufacturer must ask is whether or not it is reading the marketplace correctly. In other words, are new product ideas on the right track with consumers? Market research can shed light on what consumers like and don't like about a product innovation idea. This feedback can then be incorporated into the new product design to ensure it is what consumers want.

Such early testing can also be useful for helping a manufacturer choose between several alternative new product development ideas. The idea which has the most likely chance of succeeding with consumers can become a prototype.

Marketing Week, 27 January 1994

Research into distribution

Organisations need to consider how consumers prefer new or existing products to be made available. Marketing research information can be gathered to measure the effectiveness of the sales force, providing data on the cost of calls and the number and size of orders. Research can be undertaken to investigate the effectiveness of different methods of distribution, such as mail order, using a wholesaler, and direct selling, and the performance of individual distribution outlets. This research provides the information which enables organisations to build upon strong distribution and successful areas, while discontinuing unprofitable products and sales in unrewarding areas.

Research into distribution can also provide useful feedback on other aspects of an organisation's marketing strategy. By contacting people purchasing on behalf of distributive outlets or trades, researchers will gather useful opinions on the organisation's marketing techniques and some intelligence on the approach adopted by competitors.

Sales staff are generally remunerated through some form of incentive scheme. Research can be carried out to determine the most effective incentive scheme. A revised or new incentive scheme may provide additional motivation for the sales team to seek orders from customers and distributors.

Research into promotion

Organisations need to determine the effectiveness of various promotional and advertising activities in persuading consumers to buy a particular product. The impact of advertisements, brochures, exhibitions, sales demonstrations and media publicity can be assessed; for example, an analysis can be made of the number of enquiries and sales resulting from each form of promotion.

Research into consumer behaviour

Business organisations can only successfully divide the market into different groups (or market segments) and position their product by giving it a distinctive appeal to particular buyers, if they understand the wants and needs of actual and potential customers. They need to conduct research into consumer behaviour. To build up a picture of consumer behaviour, organisations might investigate:

- culture
- class
- personal characteristics
- psychological factors.

Culture

Culture refers to the set of beliefs and behaviour patterns of different groups and individuals. The main cultural influences are family, friends, teachers, politicians, religion and the media, including advertising.

Cultural influences shape our behaviour. For example, in Britain today, the typical young person expects to have a computer and a selection of computer games. This is because teenagers have been brought up in an age where they have developed the capacity to read and understand computer instructions, and they are surrounded at school by friends who are also interested in computer games. Cultural shifts take place all the time. In recent years, a greater emphasis has been placed by society on health and fitness. Consequently, market opportunities have opened up for health centres and gyms, sports shops are booming and supermarkets are stocking more low-calorie and natural foods.

Figure 3.3: Great Britain resident population by ethnic group, 1996–97

	Ethnic minority population – percentage in each group							
	Black	Indian	Pakistani/ Bangladeshi	Mixed other	Total ('000s)	White pop. ('000s)	Total pop. ('000s)	Ethnic minority as a %age of total
North East	–	–	55	31	30	2,551	2,581	1
North West	13	22	44	21	300	6,538	6,838	4
Yorkshire	11	20	53	16	263	4,730	4,993	5
East Midlands	18	53	11	18	206	3,910	4,116	5
West Midlands	22	35	28	15	452	4,812	5,265	9
Eastern	23	26	22	29	179	5,062	5,241	3
London	40	23	13	24	1,689	5,243	6,940	24
South East	16	31	19	34	247	7,479	7,729	3
South West	29	17	10	44	57	4,720	4,778	1
England	29	26	22	23	3,423	45,045	48,481	7
Wales	–	16	33	39	37	2,858	2,896	1
Scotland	–	12	50	28	54	5,015	5,070	1

Source: *Regional Trends* 1998, Edition 33

Suggest reasons why an organisation might find the information in Figure 3.3 important when drawing up its marketing communications.

Any nation or group is made up of several subcultures, holding beliefs which, in some measure, make them distinctive. For example, Figure 3.3 shows one group of subcultures, that of ethnic origin. Determining this distinctiveness and applying it to marketing is a task of research – but there are dangers.

- Irrelevance. The characteristic identified as distinctive may not be relevant. Do Catholics eat more sausages than Protestants? Probably not.

- Too general. The classification may be too crude and fail to recognise important sub-characteristics within the larger group. The ethnic minority classification masks differences between, say, people of Chinese, Caribbean and Indian descent which are much more significant than the fact that they are not white.

- Stereotyping. There is a risk of stereotyping, transferring the perceived characteristics of a group to the individuals within the group. Not all Yorkshire people like brass bands, no more than all Scots eat haggis!

Nevertheless, some cultural differences are deeply rooted – for example, Muslims do not eat pork – and generalisations can be valid.

Cultural factors may also underlie buying behaviour. For example, people from different cultures show distinct preferences in savings schemes. Figure 3.4 shows that four out of five white adults held a current account in 1996–97 compared to less than half of adults of Bangladeshi or Pakistani origin.

How might a financial institution which is considering a move into internet banking make use of the information in Figure 3.4?

Ethnic origin is not the only way of defining subcultural groups. Market researchers consider several other subcultural groups, including division by age and gender. Consider age, for example. In 1961, just under 12 per cent of the British population was aged 65 or over; by 1998, nearly 16 per cent of the population was in this age group; and it is projected that by 2031 over 22 per cent of the population will be at least 65 years old. This retired group has its own needs and patterns of consumption. It might be targeted for health care products and medical plans, retirement homes, financial packages, particular types of holidays and restaurants, and home security systems.

Figure 3.4: Adults holding selected forms of wealth by ethnic group, 1996–97

Great Britain   Percentages

	White	Black	Indian	Pakistani/ Bangladeshi	Other groups	All ethnic groups
Current account	80	63	70	45	71	79
Building society account	54	37	39	19	39	53
Premium bonds	19	4	8	2	7	19
Stocks and shares	16	8	16	3	12	15
TESSA	10	3	12	1	7	10
PEPs	8	2	5	1	6	8
Post Office account	7	4	2	1	3	7
National Savings bonds	5	1	1	1	2	5
Unit trusts	5	2	4	0	4	4
Save as you earn	1	1	1	0	–	1
Gilts	1	0	1	0	0	1
Any	89	78	82	57	80	89

Source: *Social Trends* 1999, Edition 29

Figure 3.5: Participation in physical activity, by gender, Great Britain

Great Britain	Males			Females		Percentages
	1987	1990–91	1996–97	1987	1990–91	1996–97
Walking	41	44	49	35	38	41
Snooker/pool/billiards	27	24	20	5	5	4
Cycling	10	12	15	7	7	8
Swimming	–	14	13	–	15	17
Darts	14	11	–	4	4	–
Soccer	10	10	10	–	–	–
Golf	7	9	8	1	2	2
Weightlifting/training	7	8	–	2	2	–
Running	8	8	7	3	2	2
Keep fit/yoga	5	6	7	12	16	17
Tenpin bowling/skittles	2	5	4	1	3	3
Badminton	4	4	3	3	3	2
At least one activity	70	73	71	52	57	58

Source: *Social Trends* 1999, Edition 29

Figure 3.5 provides information on the percentage of men and women participating in the most popular sports, games and physical activities. This information would be useful for a leisure centre or gym when deciding on the services and facilites to offer and when considering whether to adopt a different marketing communications strategy for men and women.

Class

In marketing, the notion of social class is used to differentiate groups according to income and occupational status. The Institute of Practitioners in Advertising uses this breakdown of class, which is very widely applied:

- higher and intermediate management, administrative or professional (AB)
- supervisory or clerical, and junior management, administrative or professional (C1)
- skilled manual workers (C2)
- semi-skilled and unskilled manual workers, those dependent on state pensions, widows without earnings, casual or low-grade workers (DE).

One benefit of having research information which places people in social classes is that it allows organisations to make generalisations about the type of jobs and, consequently, the type of lifestyle and wages of men and women, respectively. Figure 3.6 indicates that women are more likely to be in the skilled non-manual group than men, therefore an organisation might use a different advertising medium to attract their attention compared with the approach it adopts to reach largely professional and skilled manual males.

Figure 3.6: Working age population, 1998

United Kingdom	Percentages	
	Males	Females
Professional	7	2
Intermediate	27	24
Skilled non-manual	11	30
Skilled manual	28	7
Partly skilled	14	16
Unskilled manual	5	5
Other	9	16
All (= 100%) (millions)		

Source: *Social Trends* 1999 edition 29

Discussion point

Why is the gender balance between the social class classifications likely to change in the future? Consider the implications of the change on market demand.

Personal characteristics

To secure a wide picture of purchasing behaviour, it is important to gather information on personal factors such as the potential consumer's type of job, economic circumstances, lifestyle and self image. The pattern of demand for, say, clothing is significantly influenced by the type of job that people do. An office worker will buy a formal suit and shirt, a manual worker jeans or overalls.

Consumers' economic circumstances are determined by their level of disposable income and personal wealth, and this has a significant effect on the pattern of demand for a wide range of household goods. Households with less than £120 disposable income per week spend nearly a quarter of their total income on food and a further quarter on housing, fuel, light and power. By contrast, households with over £480 weekly disposable income spend 15 per cent on food and only a further 20 per cent on housing, fuel, light and power. Clearly, the wealthier group has much more available to spend on luxuries and optional leisure items.

Consumer behaviour is also influenced by lifestyle, the patterns of living expressed through their activities, interests and opinions. Research into lifestyle is important for an organisation when dividing the market into segments and identifying target groups. For example, Lucozade was traditionally sold as a drink to aid recovery from illness; through research into lifestyle trends, it has been successfully sold into another market by being promoted as a sports drink. This has been achieved by suggesting through a range of advertisements that it is an integral part of the lifestyle of sporting stars such as Linford Christie.

Research into consumers' self images is important in determining purchasing behaviour. People who see themselves as being active, sociable and outward going, and are looking for a new car, are likely to be attracted to a vehicle advertised by, or associated with, someone sympathetic to that image.

Psychological factors

Organisations need to be sure that their products match the wants of customers. Their products and services must be perceived by potential buyers as meeting their needs. It is important, therefore, that organisations should understand the psychology of needs and perception.

In his 1954 book *Motivation and Personality*, Abraham Maslow explains how people are motivated both by needs which are fundamental to existence and by those which are associated with mental characteristics or attitudes. Maslow argues that these needs can be ordered in a hierarchy (see Figure 3.7), and people try progressively to satisfy these different needs. In other words, people only try to satisfy their social needs, for example, once they have meet their safety and physiological needs.

Figure 3.7: Maslow's hierarchy of needs

Self-actualisation
Self-fulfilment, development and realisation

Self-esteem
Satisfying the ego – a desire for self respect, recognition and status

Social needs
Sense of belonging and love

Safety needs
Security and protection against present and future danger

Physiological needs
Condition affecting the human body – hunger, sleep, and temperature

Discussion point

Try to link the purchase of a package holiday to Maslow's analysis. Note, of course, that it may satisfy various different types of needs.

Obviously, any marketing strategy must attempt to link the product or service to the satisfaction of a particular need. For example, in a poor country, people may have to concentrate on the satisfaction of basic physiological needs, such as food, clothing, shelter and warmth. By contrast, in a wealthy economy, many people will have moved up the hierarchy to aspire to the ownership of status goods such as fast cars, large houses and swimming pools. They may even be buying camcorders to achieve, in Maslow's terms, self-actualisation, expressing their creativity through making home videos.

To place a product successfully, it is essential for an organisation to gather market information which accurately identifies the stage at which the majority of potential consumers are in Maslow's hierarchy. It is also important to try to take account of the potential customer's probable perception of the product or service. This is extremely difficult to achieve as it depends on the reaction to information, situations and messages associated with the product or service, some of which will be retained, distorted or rejected. For example, someone actively looking for a new car is more likely to notice, and to retain information about, advertisements for cars. However, if the person has already decided which type of car to buy, he or she may distort or reject other information to reinforce the decision that has been made.

Research into the market and competition

The market in which a business operates can be defined as the total group of all actual and potential buyers who share the same income, interests and access to sales outlets. It is important for a business to define and develop an understanding of its market. This provide a focus for its activities and the essential background to identify future opportunities and threats.

An organisation needs to gather research material not only on customer preferences but also on the state of the market. Information on the rate of growth and overall size of the market helps a business to determine whether its existing or potential market is growing, declining or saturated. Trade publications frequently carry detailed reports on the size of different markets, although they do not usually list the market share of individual competitors. Businesses can use their own sales figures to make comparisons between years and to identify any increase or fall in sales and demand.

Competitors

It is important for a business to research its competitors' performances, strengths and weaknesses to determine the potential threat they present and to identify niche opportunities. In particular, as we discussed in Unit 2 (see p. 89), the success of a new product can be influenced by the number of available substitutes. Businesses considering a product launch need to research the number of products produced by its competitors which perform the same function or satisfy similar needs to its own product. Information on available substitutes can be used to help determine a suitable price or promotion method. If a product faces competition from a large number of available substitutes, a business might decide that it needs to try and secure an advantage using a competitive pricing strategy or by adding unique selling points (USPs), additional special features relating perhaps to design, quality, availability or after-sales service, which can be used to promote the product.

Market share

Market share is used to compare the success of a business both in relation to its competitors and to the industry as a whole. The relative market share provides a direct comparison between an organisation's own market share and that of its nearest competitor in a similar market position. It is calculated using the formula:

$$\text{Relative share} = \frac{\text{Organisation's market share}}{\text{Nearest competitor's market share}}$$

Many business want their market shares to be greater than those of their competitors. A business with a lower share needs to look at both its own and its competitors' strengths and weaknesses and to identify opportunities for improvement. A business such as McDonald's has to react to changes in its competitors' market share if it is to retain its position as the market leader in the fast food market.

High market shares can be beneficial because as the business produces and sells in greater quantities, it can benefit from economies of scale in purchasing, distribution and production. A high market share does not necessarily guarantee a profitable business. To increase market share, a retail organisation might invest heavily in a number of new outlets. This expansion might increase market share but also reduce profits.

Choosing the target market

Once a business has identified its market it needs to evaluate which market area it is going to target. Essentially, a business can choose to target one of three key market types:

■ a mass market

■ a particular market segment

■ a niche market.

When making its choice, a business needs to take into account its knowledge of the availability of resources, its production capacity, overall profitability, and the firm's objectives and plans for the future. It also needs to consider market factors, such as the level of competition, the growth rate and future market potential.

Mass markets

Businesses which target the mass market do not distinguish between consumers when promoting and targeting their products and services. The mass market approach assumes that all customers have the same preferences and needs. This approach is complex and difficult as a business has to try and develop a strategy which satisfies a variety of customers. Increasingly, businesses are abandoning this approach in favour of adopting a clear focus and targeting groups of customers in manageable units or segments.

Market segmentation

In the market segmentation approach, a firm chooses to focus its activities and resources on a particular sector of the market where it might be able to excel. Market segmentation divides customers by their needs and preferences rather than the product they buy. Targeting a particular market segment allows a firm to offer a product or service which utilises its resources cost-effectively and satisfies a group of consumer's common needs.

There are several ways that a business can chose to segment its market:

- demographic: by age, class, sex, education, marital status, family members, income and religion

- geographic: by region (north, south, etc.) or by area (urban, rural, etc.)

- psychographic: by lifestyle, personality or values

- usage: by the number of purchases which are made (heavy users, light users, etc.).

Market segmentation allows a business to create a marketing strategy which is designed to satisfy specific customers' needs, in contrast to the mass marketing approach which tries to appeal to every customer in the market. For example, the car industry can be broken up into different segments. Jaguar targets image conscious consumers who want performance, power and speed; the Ford KA is aimed at young women who want a modern but practical car; the Volkswagen Sharon is a family car which targets households that want a vehicle with space and comfort.

▼ The upmarket saloon: for the managerial class and families

Niche markets

Niche markets are small markets, in which only a few competitors might operate. Niche markets can be found by dividing a market segment into smaller sub-segments. Businesses which target niche markets benefit from the fact that consumers are usually prepared to pay a premium price to have their particular needs met. Businesses targeting niche markets normally have specialist knowledge or resources that enable them to cater for the needs of a group of consumers which other businesses fail to satisfy. For example, a garage chain may provide a luxury car valeting service in a particularly affluent area.

Secondary research methods

Secondary research uses existing sources of information, which may be internal or external to the organisation. Internal sources include information about accounts, invoices, stock control levels and sales. For example, the organisation's own records of past sales may provide valuable data which could be used to establish a connection between the company's performance and outside influences.

External sources

The government is an important source of market information. The Office for National Statistics (ONS) publishes volumes of annual statistics; some of its most useful publications include the *Annual Abstract of Statistics*, the *Family Expenditure Survey*, the *General Household Survey*, *Regional Trends* and *Social Trends*. These provide data on broad aggregates in the economy such as national income and expenditure, industrial production, investment, international trade and prices as well as information on demographic and social trends. The Office of Population Censuses and Surveys (OPCS) also provides demographic and other census-related data. In all, the government publishes over 400 series of statistics. Answers to statistical enquiries can be obtained by contacting:

National Statistics Public Enquiry Service
Zone DG/19
1 Drummond Gate
London, SW1V 2QQ
Web: www.ons.gov.uk

Other external sources include the trade publications, directories and magazines that specialise in collecting market data and reporting on particular business sectors. These contain data, information and articles on subjects and developments of relevance to the industry, as well as expert opinion on political, economic and social trends. Two trade sources especially worth noting are the Joint Industry Committee for Television Audience Research (JICTAR), which produces weekly figures on commercial television audience levels, and the Audit Bureau of Circulation (ABC), which provides audited information on newspaper and magazine sales.

The journals of professional associations and institutions are also useful. These provide a good overview of developments in the business world, particularly if they are read in conjunction with news media such as *The Economist*, *Management Today*, *Marketing Week*, *Marketing* and the *Financial Times*.

Information technology

The rapid growth of information technology has made research data much more accessible and easier to analyse. This is due to the ever-increasing processing power of computers and developments, such as broadband technology, which enable large amounts of information to be moved rapidly around the world. For the first time, it is becoming possible – and commercially viable – to access and analyse data which previously was either too remote or could only be obtained in a pre-digested and simplified form. Information technology also enables data to be made available more quickly; no longer do users have to wait for printed volumes to appear. As a result, organisations have access to more reliable and up-to-date information on which to make decisions and get an earlier indication of developments which may have commercial significance, enabling then to react more quickly.

Among new developments, the use of the internet to access data sources worldwide and the use of census data for **community profiling** are worth particular note. Since 1991, census data is available by enumeration district as well as by local government ward and county. As an enumeration district comprises no more than 200 households, use of this data provides the opportunity to construct detailed profiles of local communities. Community profiling can also be achieved by analysing data by postcode.

Another significant development is the computerised model of the economy developed for the Treasury. This enables organisations to make fairly accurate economic forecasts, providing estimates of future levels of major economic indicators, such as income, expenditure, output, employment, growth, inflation and the balance of payments. It allows many larger companies to monitor movements in their own markets by putting market research information through the computer to analyse present and future trends.

There has been a significant growth in the number of organisations selling their products and services over the internet. Major companies such as Sainsbury's, Topshop, Virgin and WH Smith have launched digital shopping services which allow customers to purchase goods on-line. There are millions of internet users worldwide who can purchase their weekly shopping, keep up to date with fashion trends and satisfy their entertainment needs from their computer screens.

Internet shopping provides an accessible service, allowing companies to target customers who are unable to reach the shops at usual opening times. As well as offering the potential to increase sales, internet shopping provides companies with important research material. When customers are on-line, companies can obtain feedback on their preferences. This information can then be used to identify future sales trends and to develop a product or service which satisfies customer needs.

Marketing databases

Information technology has also contributed to the development of **marketing databases**. These are organised collections of comprehensive data, which are held on computer, covering customer profiles, products, suppliers and retailers. The demographic information about customers held on a marketing database may cover age, income, family members and birthdays, together with details of their activities, interests and opinions and a listing of products and services which they have purchased in the past. This is extremely useful information for companies, such as banks, travel agencies or airlines, which mail out offers of new products and services. The promotion may be directly targeted at people who display the characteristics and habits of the identified target market.

Organisations may also use the database to help reactivate or prompt consumer purchases. For example, a nightclub might hold details of its customers' birthdays and, at the appropriate time of the year, automatically send out a birthday card with complimentary tickets to attract people into the club. The database may also help a business to develop customer loyalty by remembering customer preferences, and sending any appropriate gifts, discount coupons and offers.

Primary research methods

Using secondary or desk research methods is economical and comparatively quick. It has the advantage that it can be conducted with complete confidentiality, and without competitors finding out, On the other hand, because the information used in secondary research is not generated for the particular purposes of the organisation, it may not be sufficiently relevant. An organisation may need to supplement secondary research by undertaking primary research.

Primary research is used when existing secondary sources of information have been tapped. To obtain additional market knowledge, organisations make fresh enquiries, such as through the use of surveys or focus discussion groups. These forms of field research yield primary data. Primary research methods enable organisations to make direct contact with potential or actual customers, and to ask them questions specific to the organisation's needs.

Sampling

Surveys may be based on a questionnaire which is conducted as part of an interview, through a discussion group, by post or over the telephone. Generally, it is too expensive and time consuming to contact every potential customer, so only a sample of customers is included in the survey. This sample has to be very carefully selected. The vast majority of people do not intentionally distort their answers in responding to a questionnaire, but the conclusions drawn from research will not be reliable if the consumer sample used is not representative of the market being investigated.

▲ Opinion polls are based on a very small sample of the electorate

One key test of the usefulness of a survey is reliability. Surveys are usually carried out using only a sample of the population to which the findings will be applied. When political pollsters want to assess the popularity of the government, for example, they interview just one or two thousand people, but they use the answers to make general statements about the opinions of the electorate as a whole. Are these results reliable? The answer involves the application of probability theory; it depends, among other things, on

the extent to which error has been contained so that users can confidently rely on the accuracy of the findings. The reliability of data depends on the size of the sample group – is it big enough to enable valid conclusions to be drawn from the results – and the extent to which its composition is representative of the wider population to which the findings will be applied.

To ensure that a survey sample is representative, researchers first determine the wider population (or universe, as they call it). They then work out the size of the sample. If it is too small, reliability may suffer; if it is too large, unnecessary costs are incurred. Ideally, the sample should be a small mirror image of the universe, in terms of its relevant characteristics, which may include gender, ethnicity, age, marital status, location, class, and so on.

The larger the number of subgroups within the universe (the wider population) that a researcher wishes to find out about, the larger the sample that is required. For example, if the universe is estimated at one million people, and the consumer sample consists of a survey of 3,000 people, a subgroup which is only two per cent of the universe will comprise 60 people in the sample. This may be too few to give an accurate indication of opinions held by the wider group which this subgroup is supposed to represent. For example, in a survey of 2,000 people representative of the UK population as a whole, just over half of this sample will be women; but fewer than 150 will be women in their twenties, and maybe no more than 12 will be women in their twenties living in Scotland. If one of the purposes of the survey is to generate information about the opinions of Scottish women in their twenties – as well as finding information on the UK population as a whole – the sample is clearly inadequate. There are two ways of tackling this problem: create an overall bigger sample or increase the number in the particular subgroup (although this must be taken into account when analysing the results as a whole).

Having decided upon the size of the sample, the researcher needs a method for selecting the people to be interviewed. There are four approaches:

■ the probability system

■ random selection

■ the quota system

■ consumer panels.

The **probability system** involves obtaining a list of the population to be researched. Names and addresses may be available from sources such as trade and telephone directories, the electoral register, magazine subscription lists and membership lists of professional and voluntary organisations. The researcher takes, say, one name in 30 from the lists and allocates them to interviewers. They, in turn, need to ensure that, as they conduct interviews, a representative cross-section is achieved. Inevitably, this means that some people who have been interviewed have to be rejected from the final sample used to compile the results, otherwise bias may develop within the sample.

Random selection involves contacting people on a speculative basis. For example, a street interviewer selects contacts by requesting the cooperation of passers-by, perhaps asking every tenth person until someone consents to be interviewed. By approaching every tenth person, say, the interviewer prevents personal preferences coming into play – for example, it removes the temptation to only approach people who look friendly. The composition of the survey group may, to some extent, be predetermined. A household survey, for example, may base the random selection upon homes which can be placed into subgroups – categorising different areas in terms of regions, rural or urban location, and types of dwelling. This may be especially useful when the sample is to contain subgroups based upon these characteristics.

The quota system is a very popular method of consumer research because it can be clearly defined.

Once the size of the sample is decided, the subgroups are defined and interviewers are allocated a quota of individuals which they must contact in each subgroup. For example, an interviewer may be required to trace and interview a specific number of households which are owner occupiers, include two children of school age, where both parents work, and which are in urban locations.

The consumer panel involves establishing a group of people which acts as a representative sample of the market. Panel members are asked to provide regular details of their household spending, identifying products, prices and sizes, the place and time of purchase, and similar information. Consumer panels are expensive to establish and require continuing attention if they are to be maintained for long enough to make the results worthwhile. The longer a person remains on the panel, the more accustomed he or she becomes to making returns. The panel members may then become less self-conscious when making purchases, ceasing to consider the implications they will have on their consumer reports. Over time, panel members act more naturally in accordance with their personal tastes and preferences, and the information submitted to the researcher becomes more valuable.

Intuition or market research

When a new product is under development, how much should the manufacturer trust intuition and how much should it rely on research? Intuition is important, but is seldom sufficient to gauge how consumers are likely to respond to a new product. Whatever the sector, it is difficult to dismiss the arguments for thorough pre-launch consumer research.

Research should inform product development from the beginning, rather than become a crutch towards the end of the process.

Traditionally, most research has been concentrated in the packaged goods sector, where the cost of entry into the market is relatively low. Before the proliferation of packaged goods, many of the strongest brands, particularly in the pre-war USA, were manufactured products, including consumer durables. Packaged goods then discovered the power of marketing and took the lead.

Meanwhile, constant improvements in technology meant that consumer durables could rely on features and functionality to sell products. Consequently, the sector put less emphasis on consumer research, failing to recognise the importance of exploring the emotional values of the brand.

But differentiation in a crowded category has always been the prerequisite for a successful brand. Recognising this, research companies are now seeking to demonstrate that by being more involved in the development process, they can cut costs and lead times rather than add to them.

BMRB International has the UK licence for IdeaMap, a research tool which introduces a quantitative element to the earliest stages of new product development when this would not normally be available.

BMRB associate director Phil Sandy explains: "A relatively small sample size – say a group of 100 people – gets taken through various elements of new product ideas on a computer screen. These might include designs, promotions or copy."

One-off ratings are given for these different features, allowing the client to get a clear idea of the strongest selling points of the proposed product, says Sandy.

Because of the small sample size, it can be a cost-effective way of narrowing down the later stages of new product development, such as concept testing. "There is no reason why the technique should not work for consumer durables, as long as you get hold of respondents when they are actually looking at the type of product in question," he says.

Marketing Week, 19 August 1999

The article opposite discusses the benefits of using small size sample groups as an alternative to other more costly methods. The small groups provide an indication of customer reactions and preferences before the product has been launched.

Discussion point

Read the article on intuition or market research. Why might it be said that it sets out the very minimum of consumer research that needs to be undertaken?

Questionnaires

The success of a sample survey depends to a large extent upon the quality of the questionnaire. Questions should be designed so that the answers allow respondents to be classified into the required subgroups of the universe or population.

Initial questions usually seek personal facts about the respondent, such as marital status, age group and occupation. Some of these questions may be designed to stimulate the interviewee's interest in the survey and create an impression that the person's contribution is important for the research. Questions of a more deeply personal nature, required to identify subgroups in terms of income and spending habits, can follow later when the respondent has become more relaxed.

When writing questions for inclusion in questionnaires, you should:

- use simple, positive language

- ensure clear meaning

- be neutral

- avoid leading questions

- keep questions brief

- avoid embarrassing questions

- avoid two-part questions.

Although the majority of people have no reason for giving false information, many may hesitate to divulge information which could show them in an unfavourable light. Where questions which may elicit these kinds of responses are necessary, similar questions should be placed elsewhere in the questionnaire so that the researcher can check the consistency of the answers given by the interviewee. This enables the researcher to test the validity of the interviewee's response.

A questionnaire comprising highly structured questions, with possible answers classified into predetermined categories, is quick to administer and the resulting data is easy to process. By contrast, a questionnaire comprising open-ended questions creates problems of interpretation and analysis, as well as in recording data.

Discussion point

Discuss the possible consequences of undertaking a consumer survey with a questionnaire that does not meet these standards?

Survey methods

The are a several ways of undertaking surveys. Here, we look at the four commonly used methods:

- personal interviews

- postal surveys

- telephone interviews

- discussion groups.

The personal interview is generally regarded as the most effective method of conducting a survey. It generally produces the best response. A personable and experienced interviewer acquires a technique which encourages participation and results in more complete and more accurate answers. The interviewer can put the interviewee at ease, the value of participation can be explained and any difficulties in understanding can be overcome by rephrasing questions. If the quota system is used, the interviewer will gain experience of different types of household and be more able to identify areas where they can be located. The interviewer may also become accomplished in identifying general characteristics of individuals or households, so that questionnaire responses may be supplemented by additional information.

Personal interviews, however, are an expensive method of conducting surveys. Probability and random selection systems are particularly expensive, as interviewers must revisit respondents who are not at home when they first call. In surveys using the quota system, a subgroup may have characteristics which makes it time-consuming and difficult to trace individuals within a particular area, and this, too, adds to costs.

Postal surveys are less expensive, but the response rate is poor – a large numbers of questionnaires have to be mailed to obtain a sufficient number of replies to produce reliable results. Because there is no interviewer on hand to assist with any difficulties, mail questionnaires must be especially well laid out, with questions and instructions clearly expressed in plain language. The method of answering the questions should require minimum effort; for example, respondents should be invited to indicate their answers by using ticks and crosses or circling items. Higher response rates to mail questionnaires can be achieved if a covering letter makes an appeal for participation and, perhaps, explains the purpose of the research and its use. Also, people are more likely to respond if they feel an affiliation with the purpose of the survey; for example, if it is about a subject on which they have strong views. However, this can introduce fresh problems, because the responses received by the research organisation may not be representative of the population as a whole.

Telephone interviews are less expensive than personal interviewing and more likely to elicit a response than mail questionnaires. They are generally representative, as over 85 per cent of families have a telephone. However, there is a danger of bias, particularly if it is found that only a certain type of person is willing to provide personal information to an unknown and unseen caller.

Discussion groups bring together a representative group of people to discuss their tastes and preferences about particular products or to give their general views on household consumer items. Usually, respondents are paid to attend and take part in focus discussion groups.

The person conducting the meeting needs to be an experienced researcher able to create an atmosphere in which the participants feel free to express their opinions. The researcher introduces topics and guides the conversation. The whole exercise may be filmed or recorded for subsequent analysis, so that researchers can assess, for example, the tone and strength of expression and body language. In some discussion groups, researchers are hidden behind a glass wall so that they can follow the proceedings without being seen. They can then relay information to the researcher leading the group, suggesting conversational leads that should be followed up. There is the danger that, in a small group, one or two people try to dominate proceedings, but an effective researcher should know how to handle this situation and be able to bring out the less forthcoming members of the group.

Test marketing

When the development of a new or improved product requires a large capital investment, some form of market testing will generally be an important precondition for a national sales effort. Market tests are carried out to help companies decide how products should be packaged, both in terms of the type of container used (where applicable) and the overall appearance.

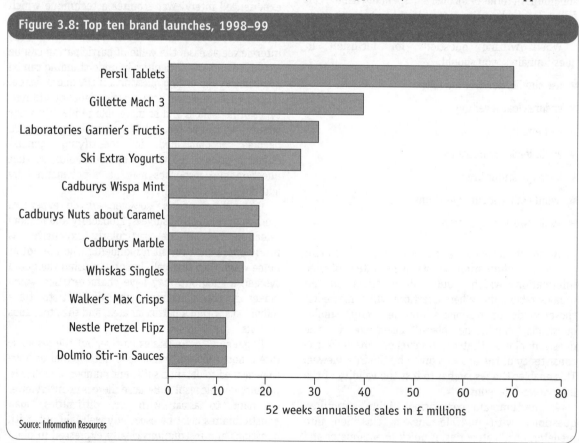

Figure 3.8: Top ten brand launches, 1998–99

Source: Information Resources

Important factors include the materials used and features such as the design, labelling, robustness, weight and ease of storage. By testing the product and its packaging, an organisation may discover features which are superfluous and might be dropped, facilitating greater standardisation in production. Tests may also be carried out on competitors' products to help pinpoint advantages or deficiencies in the new or improved product.

Test marketing applies not only to the product but also to all the marketing activities supporting it, including the sales organisation, the distribution system, advertising and promotion. It allows the company to experience the realities of competitive pressures in a market, to discover any deficiencies and to modify the product and the marketing arrangements. Test marketing has an impressive record: about 90 per cent of products launched nationally following market testing are successful. Figure 3.8 shows the top ten brand launches in 1998–99, in each case the product underwent test marketing.

Discussion point

Look at the products listed in Figure 3.8. Why do you think that the manufacturers needed to test market these products?

When conducting market testing it is important to ensure that the test area is sufficiently large and has the required characteristics to make it representative of the marketing 'universe', so that results can be a reliable guide in selling the product to a wider public. If the effect of advertising is being assessed, the product test area should, as nearly as possible, coincide with the readership of the local media.

Test marketing should not attempt to assess too many factors at the same time in the same area, as it will be difficult to disentangle the various effects. For example, if the effectiveness of promotional activities is being assessed, altering other aspects, such as packaging and price, only tends to confuse the issue. The response of competitors should be monitored, to judge whether any competition is local in nature or is likely to be repeated and sustained nationally.

The length of the test period should be long enough to provide evidence of seasonal fluctuations in demand as well as to enable confirmation of initial findings. The test area should be kept under scrutiny even after the product has been launched to a wider public. This may provide early warning of problems which may arise only after the product has been on the market for a reasonable period of time.

BUILD YOUR LEARNING

Keywords and phrases

You should know the meaning of the words and phrases listed below. Go back through the last 14 pages of the unit to check or refresh your understanding as necessary.

- Community profiling
- Consumer panel
- Core benefits
- Culture
- Market types
- Marketing databases
- Marketing research
- Probability system
- Qualitative data
- Quantitative data
- Quota system
- Random selection

Summary points

- Marketing research provides information that helps organisations to recognise and respond to market opportunities and to develop suitable products to meet market needs. It covers product, distribution and promotional research.

- Successful marketing requires a real understanding of the wants and behaviour of actual and potential customers. This requires an investigation into their culture, class and personal characteristics, the psychological factors underpinning their needs, and the market in which the organisation and its competitors is operating.

- Secondary research data may be drawn from sources internal or external to an organisation. It is available from official statistics, trade publications, directories and magazines. Organisations are increasingly using on-line information and marketing databases.

- Primary data generally comes from field research and involves the use of sampling, questionnaires, surveys and test marketing techniques.

Analysing market opportunities

THE ULTIMATE OBJECTIVE OF the marketing process is to formulate a marketing strategy which enables a business to meet the needs of its customers. The choices which a business makes when deciding which strategy to adopt need to be formed by a sound analysis of the environment in which it operates. By evaluating overall competitiveness, external constraints and influences, a business is able to identify future opportunities and adopt the strategy which best allows it to exploit its own strengths.

Assessing demand

There is considerable value to a business organisation in being able to measure and forecast demand. With knowledge of consumer behaviour and the wider social and commercial environment, it is possible to identify, measure and monitor the factors that influence the demand for products. Businesses use this information when making decisions about which markets to enter and which market segments to concentrate on.

Demand forecasts may be short term, medium term or long term; they can range from assessing local demand to world sales; forecasts may be made of the demand for individual products or an entire product range. Forecasting demand helps a business to make informed planning decisions. For example, short-term demand forecasts help in making optimal decisions about the purchase of raw materials and components, and the scheduling and financing of production. If the extent of the market is either underestimated or overestimated, extra costs may be incurred and profits lost.

The total demand in the market is a forecast of the total volume that would be purchased at a particular point in time, by a specified consumer group, in a defined geographical area, under particular economic conditions and a defined level of marketing in the industry. One of the most common ways of estimating this level of demand is to take the number of buyers in the specific market, multiply this by the quantity purchased by an average buyer in a year, and multiply the sum by the average unit price of the product. For example, if the manufacturer of a new brand of cola estimates that, within its target market, there are 800,000 potential buyers purchasing on average 75 cans of cola a year at an average price of 50p a can, the total market demand can be valued at £30 million (that is, 800,000 × 75 × 0.5). Changes in the level of total demand over time provide an indication of the growth rate in a particular market and can be used by businesses when making decisions about whether to withdraw from or enter the market.

Forecasting

Forecasting provides businesses with techniques for making predictions about how buyers may behave in a specified set of circumstances and future market opportunities. One general approach to sales forecasting involves three stages. First, a company makes an economic forecast of future levels of gross domestic product; second, it uses this forecast and other indicators in estimating future sales in its industry or business sector; and third, it bases the forecast for its own sales on an assumption that it will achieve a certain proportion of the total market.

There are other approaches that can be taken to sales forecasting. First, an organisation could carry out a survey of potential buyers' future intentions, and use the results to determine the probability of a particular group of people buying a product in the future. Second, a business can carry out a survey of expert opinion within the industry. This could involve contacting sales representatives, suppliers, distributors and trade associations to build up a composite picture of what they think might happen in the future. This approach is often taken by car producers, which survey car dealers in order to forecast short-term demand. Third, organisations can use a statistical method known as time series analysis. This enables long-term movements to be charted, offering a relatively sound basis for making projections.

Businesses which use forecasting methods have an advantage over their competitors as they are able to make predictions about customer behaviour and formulate suitable strategies to meet customer needs before their competitors.

PEST

The way businesses operate is influenced by the wider political, economic, social and technological environment. These are usually referred to as PEST factors – PEST is an acronym for political, economic, social and technological. By analysing trends and developments in their business environment, firms can spot new market opportunities and threats.

Political factors

As we saw in Unit 2 (see pp. 116–35), governments have a major effect on business and markets by creating (or dampening) demand for particular products or for consumer items in general. This is achieved by setting public spending levels, allocating funds for special programmes (such as to buy computers for schools), changes in taxation and interest rates for borrowers, and changes in laws, regulations and licence arrangements.

Increasingly, in a global economy, many important decisions are reached internationally, through the European Union, the biannual economic summit of the heads of the seven largest economies and the work of organisations such as the World Trade Organisation (see Unit 2, pp. 137–9). For example, changes in the European Union's Common Agricultural Policy has a direct influence on the opportunities for milk production by dairy farmers.

Economic factors

The United Kingdom's economic performance determines its level of national income. The distribution of national income, together with the distribution of wealth, ultimately determines the standard of living enjoyed by individual members of society. This, in turn, influences consumer spending patterns and, therefore, market opportunities.

A standard measure of a country's economic performance is **gross domestic product** (GDP). This measure defines the total value of goods and services produced by the economy, usually expressed annually and per capita – the total value divided by the population of the country. GDP is a useful broad indicator of the size of a national market, and provides a measure of comparative living standards in different countries. However, although adjustment is made for the varying price levels in different countries in calculating GDP, the figures do not show the extent to which spending power is widely spread or concentrated in relatively few hands. Nor do GDP figures reflect levels of taxation, which can substantially reduce consumer spending power.

Discussion point

How might the information in Figure 3.9 be used by a supermarket chain wishing to expand into Europe? What other information would it require?

Figure 3.9: Comparative European GDP

Rank	Country	GDP £ per capita	Percentage of EU average
1	Luxembourg	23,200	166
2	Denmark	16,100	115
3	Belgium	15,800	113
4	Austria	15,700	112
5	Germany	15,400	110
6	Netherlands	14,600	105
7	France	14,600	104
8	Italy	14,100	101
9	United Kingdom	13,900	100
10	Finland	13,800	99
11	Sweden	13,800	98
12	Ireland	13,400	96
13	Spain	10,900	78
14	Portugal	9,900	71
15	Greece	9,700	69

Source: European Commission, 1998

In the UK, GDP has increased steadily decade by decade. Total wealth created in the early 1990s was about double that of the early 1960s. Figure 3.9 shows that the UK was ranked ninth in terms of GDP per person against other European Union countries. A regional analysis of the UK's GDP (see Figure 3.10) shows that the south remains the richest part of the country. London's GDP is 23 per cent above that of the national average and nearly one and a half times higher than that of Wales and the North East. This type of information is used by supermarkets and retailers when deciding where to locate, what to stock and pricing strategies. Often, for example, prices of goods and services are lower in the north of England, reflecting the lower GDP and spending power of people living in the north.

Discussion point

Does the information in Figure 3.10 mean that the standard of living is higher for all people working and living in the south?

Figure 3.10: Regional UK GDP indices

	1986	1991	1992	1993	1994	Indices (UK=100) 1995	1996
United Kingdom	100	100	100	100	100	100	100
North East	86	85	86	86	85	85	85
North West and Merseyside	95	91	91	91	92	91	91
Yorkshire and the Humber	95	92	91	90	90	91	89
East Midlands	98	98	97	97	97	96	94
West Midlands	91	93	93	93	93	94	94
Eastern	110	109	109	108	108	108	109
London	123	124	124	127	124	122	123
South East (GOR)	109	111	110	111	112	111	114
South East	94	95	96	95	95	96	95
England	102	102	102	102	102	102	102
Wales	86	85	84	83	83	84	83
Scotland	95	98	99	99	99	100	99
Northern Ireland	79	82	82	82	82	83	81

Source: *Regional Trends* 1999, Edition 29

The national (and regional) picture does not tell us about the distribution of spending power between various groups. If you break down the UK population into five equal groups in terms of its disposable household income, then, in 1991, the top fifth accounted for slightly more than 40 per cent of overall spending, while the bottom fifth accounted for about only six per cent of spending. This disparity between rich and poor becomes even more marked when wealth (income and assets) is considered. In 1991, just one per cent of the UK population accounted for 18 per cent of marketable wealth and the richest 10 per cent accounted for half the wealth in the UK. Moreover, if you remove housing from the equation (by far and away the biggest asset for most people), the disparities become even greater, with the richest five per cent owning half of all wealth.

Differences in wealth distribution obviously have marketing implications, with greater opportunities for the sale of luxury items such as large houses, lavish furnishings, fast cars, expensive boats and exotic holidays to the top 20 per cent of households (ranked in terms of wealth). On the other hand, for the poorest 20 per cent, a market opportunity exists for basic items including food, clothing and household goods. This is reflected in the number of discount shops and street traders in poorer areas.

Changes in the composition of assets may result in market opportunities, as individuals switch between property, shares and financial assets. These changes in income and wealth normally affect overall expenditure. Figure 3.11 gives a detailed breakdown of household expenditure at constant (1995) prices, allowing comparisons to be made over time as the inflation element has been removed. Figure 3.11 shows that total household expenditure increased by 93 per cent in real terms between 1971 and 1997, which was in line with the overall increase in national income during the period.

Discussion point

Identify the major changes in expenditure indicated in Figure 3.11. Suggest reasons for these changes.

Figure 3.11: UK household expenditure

	Indices at constant prices						£ billion (current prices)
	1971	1981	1986	1991	1996	1997	1997
Household goods	100	138	180	227	266	293	86.0
Transport and communication	100	133	175	195	235	247	73.2
Housing	100	121	131	140	149	150	66.5
Food	100	104	109	115	125	127	53.5
Clothing and footwear	100	129	178	200	265	279	31.4
Alcohol	100	127	134	132	131	135	29.4
Fuel and power	100	119	135	146	146	143	28.8
Recreational and cultural	100	142	156	182	206	210	24.6
Tobacco	100	89	74	71	59	58	12.4
Other services	100	109	150	200	222	230	94.0
Household expenditure abroad	100	193	229	298	380	440	14.9
All household expenditure	100	121	144	166	185	193	500.6

Source: *Social Trends* 1999, Edition 29

Social factors

Social factors largely involve demographic changes, covering age, ethnicity and other characteristics. They are important for marketing because they reveal trends which can influence demand for particular types of products. Take age, for example. The UK has an ageing population. People are living longer and, in comparison to the boom years from the late 1940s to the early 1960s, couples are having fewer babies. By the year 2021, nearly one in five of the population will be aged over 65, compared with only one in ten in 1951. One in 27 people (and one in 20 women) are now aged 80 or older. Conversely, under-16s today comprise only one in five of the population compared to one in four in the 1960s. It is not surprising, therefore, that while in the 1960s and 1970s companies focused on the rapid growth of youth culture, with new entertainment and clothing products, more recently there has been business interest in serving the growing 'grey market'. A good example is the success of Saga Holidays, which caters specifically for older holiday-makers. Meanwhile, the baby boomers have become middle-aged, creating a lucrative market for restaurateurs, travel companies and the financial services sector, selling products such as insurance and pension plans.

Overall population trends can disguise what is happening with particular groups. For example, some ethnic minority groups have very young populations. Over 40 per cent of the UK Pakistani and Bangladeshi communities are aged under 16. Among the Afro-Caribbean population there is a disproportionate number of 16 to 29 year-olds (30 per cent of the total Afro-Caribbean population compared to only 21 per cent among whites). This reflects the wave of immigration from the Caribbean in the 1950s, with couples starting families in the 1960s and 1970s. Market evidence of the purchasing power of young black people can be seen in sales of sportswear and leisure products, but also in mobile phones and the demand for college places and educational products (a higher proportion of black young people go to college than whites). About one-tenth of the UK population now comprises 'people of colour', and this has had an influence on demand. This can be seen, for example, in the market for young people's fashions. It has also created important new product areas, such as black hair and beauty products.

Population movements within the UK also have considerable marketing significance. In the 1980s, Cambridgeshire, Buckinghamshire and Cornwall were the counties with the fastest population growth, with Belfast and the Scottish Isles experiencing the biggest decreases. These changes create opportunities (and pose threats) for construction companies, makers of furniture and durable household goods, and service and entertainment providers.

Another important social factor is household size which, as Figure 3.12 shows, has fallen considerably in the last three decades. In 1961, the average household consisted of 3.1 people, and only 14 per cent of households consisted of one person. By 1998, the average household size had dropped to 2.4 people but, more significantly, the percentage of one-person households had doubled. In part, these changes reflect the fact that more women are working and many households cannot afford to pay the child care costs associated with having a large family.

Discussion point

Discuss the factors that have led to changes in the average size of households.

From a marketing point of view, the decline in household size and the associated growth of one-person households has led to a number of market opportunities. For example, construction companies have sought to meet increased demand for flats, maisonettes and sheltered accommodation; demand has risen for home security systems, particularly from elderly people living alone; and food producers and retailers have experienced a growing demand for items packaged in smaller units, such as individual meals.

Another significant social trend is the decline in the predominance of the traditional family. Between 1961

and 1991, the proportion of all households comprising a married couple with dependent children fell from just over half (52 per cent) to two-fifths. Nevertheless, it should be recognised that a majority of people still live in this type of family unit than in any other. However, the rise in single-parent families has implications for the way products are promoted. Advertisers need to be careful not to give the impression that only traditional families buy their products.

Technology factors

Developments in technology give rise to new products and market opportunities. For example, the application of technology in the home led to the development of the white goods industry, which makes washing machines, refrigerators, dishwashers, etc. This, in turn, led to the creation of markets for the materials and services associated with these goods, such as special types of paints, new materials and plastics for food storage containers, and detergents for use in the domestic washing machines.

Many companies have research departments specifically to carry out scientific and technical work which may lead to new products. For example, pharmaceutical companies invest considerable sums on the development of new drugs and medicines.

It is not simply the technology itself which creates demand, social and market factors may spark the widespread adoption of a particular technology or create a demand for technologically innovative

Figure 3.12: GB household size

Great Britain					Percentage
	1961	1971	1981	1991	1998
One person	14	18	22	27	28
Two people	30	32	32	34	35
Three people	23	19	17	16	16
Four people	18	17	18	16	14
Five people	9	8	7	5	5
Six or more people	7	6	4	2	2
All households (=100%) (millions)	16.3	18.6	20.2	22.4	23.6
Average household size (number of people)	3.1	2.9	2.7	2.5	2.4

Source: *Social Trends* 1999, Edition 29

products. Facsimile technology was invented in the middle of the last century, but it was not until the 1980s that business uses emerged and the technology began to be widely used.

The use of new technologies can create ecological problems. New technology can pollute the environment and disturb the balance of the natural forces of regeneration. through, for example, the over-felling of trees, the intensive use of chemicals in farming and the uncontrolled emission of toxic waste products. Recognition of these environmental threats has created a marketing opportunity for green products, which are promoted to customers and consumers who are concerned about the environment.

SWOT

SWOT is another acronym, standing for strengths, weaknesses, opportunities and threats. A **SWOT** analysis enables an organisation to place itself and its products into perspective. The analysis helps to highlight the main internal strengths and weaknesses

of the organisation, together with any external opportunities and threats.

For example, A SWOT analysis may show that an organisation has strengths in research development and the use of new technologies, but it suffers from weaknesses in management and labour turnover. Opportunities may be opening up in European markets but, on the other hand, there may be threats from American competition. Under these circumstances, the company may decide to publicise its strengths and to play down its perceived weaknesses.

Let's take a real example. Virgin entered the airline industry in 1984. Before taking the decision to launch an airline, Richard Branson might have undertaken a SWOT analysis. Figure 3.13 suggests some of the key headlines that might have shown up in Virgin's SWOT analysis.

Discussion point

Study the SWOT analysis for Virgin Airlines in Figure 3.13. Given the balance between strengths and weaknesses and opportunities and threats, do you think that Richard Branson was taking an expensive risk in setting up his airline.

Figure 3.13: SWOT analysis for Virgin Airlines

Strengths	Weaknesses
• Strong brand identity • Established business track record	• No experience in transport industry • Limited access to routes • Lacked finance to cope with larger players
Opportunities	**Threats**
• Market ready for innovative, small, customer-focused provider • Development of package holidays offering transport, accommodation and entertainment	• British Airways determination to hold on to business • Monopoly hold of British Airways on major routes • Ability of British Airways to undercut Virgin on price

The findings from a SWOT analysis enable an organisation to identify where it should focus its attention. Conducting a SWOT analysis plays a key role in an organisation's strategic planning, assisting in the formulation of both short-term and long-term objectives. In addition, the findings from a SWOT analysis allow the organisation to identify the people and groups which may influence the attitudes and views of others. These opinion formers include:

- academic and commercial research organisations
- management groups
- existing, past and future customers
- newspapers, radio and television
- major suppliers
- European, national and local government officials.

The public relations team should be in regular contact with these groups in order to influence their views as, ultimately, they affect the opinions of others.

Product life cycle

In order to formulate effective short-term and long-term strategic objectives, it is important for an organisation to be able to evaluate the current and potential position of its products and services. The life cycle of products must be carefully monitored to allow the organisation to maximise its sales and profits as well as to produce the optimum amount of output. Figure 3.14 shows the typical pattern of profits and sales over a product life cycle.

> **Discussion point**
>
> Where would you place the Mini car in the product life cycle?

An organisation's marketing strategy for a product should reflect the stage it has reached in its life cycle. Different action needs to be taken at each individual

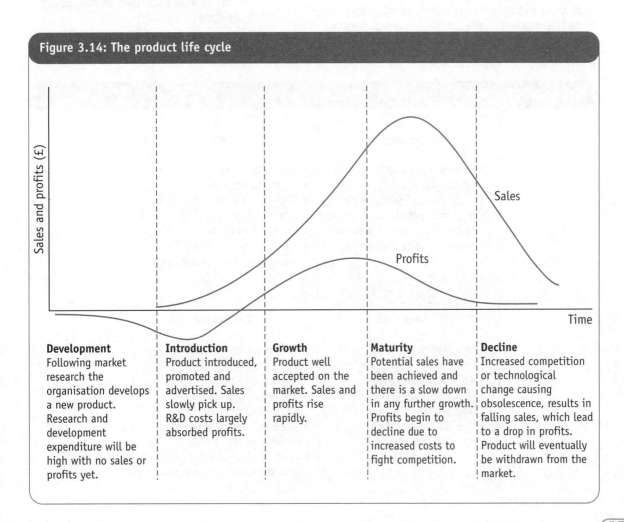

Figure 3.14: The product life cycle

Development
Following market research the organisation develops a new product. Research and development expenditure will be high with no sales or profits yet.

Introduction
Product introduced, promoted and advertised. Sales slowly pick up. R&D costs largely absorbed profits.

Growth
Product well accepted on the market. Sales and profits rise rapidly.

Maturity
Potential sales have been achieved and there is a slow down in any further growth. Profits begin to decline due to increased costs to fight competition.

Decline
Increased competition or technological change causing obsolescence, results in falling sales, which lead to a drop in profits. Product will eventually be withdrawn from the market.

stage, and the organisation typically experiences varying levels of sales and profits over the life cycle of its products.

- Development requires heavy expenditure on market research and product development, and organisations incur initial losses during this stage.

- When a new product is introduced to a market, the company should accept that it takes time for it to become established and profitable. At this stage, promotional expenses will be high to overcome slow sales.

- To sustain growth, an organisation may increase the quality of its product and add new features or models. As competitors launch their own models, promotional activities will be focused on building consumer commitment and loyalty.

- Most products are at the stage of maturity which, in some cases, may be extended by moving into other market segments or repositioning in a larger or faster growing market segment. To sustain the maturity stage, a company may modify the quality, features and style of the product, or adjust its price and the promotion and distribution arrangements.

- If the product has gone into decline, the organisation should be prepared to drop it, attempt to reposition it, or wait for the competition to go under and then pick up the rest of the market. Decline can be caused by changes in consumer tastes and technology, and by the introduction of new, more attractive products.

Boston growth share matrix

The Boston Consulting Group developed a growth share matrix, which can be combined with the product life cycle, to enable an organisation to represent its range of products in terms of market share and growth. As Figure 3.15 shows, the Boston Consulting Group matrix suggests that there are four basic types of products: question marks, dogs, stars and cash cows.

> **Discussion point**
>
> Identify products and services which might be fitted into each part of the Boston Consulting Group matrix.

Figure 3.15: The Boston matrix

Question marks	Stars
• Low market share in a high growth market • Cash required to maintain or increase their marketshare to become stars; otherwise they should be phased out	• Highly profitable • Good market share • High growth rate • Growth stage of the product life circle • Rapid growth requires relatively heavy investment
Dogs	**Cash cows**
• Low market share • Low growth rate • No longer profitable • Decline stage of the product life cycles • Need to be withdrawn	• Produce a lot of cash • High market share • Low growth rate • Maturity stage of product life cycle • Need less investment to hold market share • Cash 'milked' to finance investment in other products

Ultimately, an organisation should try to establish a balanced portfolio of products at different stages of development and different positions within the Boston matrix. This should allow for the revenue and profits generated by one product to help with the development of another, thus ensuring the future survival of the business.

The Ansoff matrix

H Igor Ansoff's product-market expansion grid, also known as the Ansoff matrix, shows the four main market growth opportunities available to an organisation (see Figure 3.16). Research information on the organisation's market, its competitors and the success of its products in meeting customer needs gathered using the SWOT and PEST models, is used to determine a suitable future strategic direction.

> ### Discussion point
>
> Relate the activities of a multinational organisation with which you are familiar to the Ansoff matrix.

Market penetration

Market penetration is often regarded as a relatively low-risk option because it focuses upon improving market share rather than changing the existing product or market. In deciding whether they can increase their market share, organisations need to focus on defining and identifying their market segment and developing their response to its needs. Generally, organisations only need to change one variable of their marketing mix – the mix of product, price, place and promotion (discussed later in this unit, see p. 180). For example an organisation might choose to adopt an aggressive pricing strategy or to improve the eff0ectiveness of its promotional expenditure. Market penetration is a beneficial option because it allows an organisation to retain its familiarity with both its products and markets, and does not require any new knowledge.

Market development

Market development attempts to find new uses and market segments for an existing product. For example, the manufacturer of Dettol has recently tried to promote the disinfectant as a medical antiseptic as well as a household cleaning product. Another market development strategy is to expand the geographical size or area of a product's market or to target different age, income or gender groups. The market development

Figure 3.16: The Ansoff matrix

	Existing market	New market
Existing product	Market penetration	Market development
New product	Product development	Diversification

strategy is moderately risky. Organisations that target a new market segment are moving into areas with which they may be unfamiliar; businesses trying to establish a new use for their products have to try and change consumers' existing perceptions of their products. Market development is best suited to products which are profitable and have future potential but are currently being offered in declining markets.

relatively small, such as changing packaging to accommodate demand for environmentally friendly materials. Alternatively, a completely new product might be introduced, requiring high research, development and launch costs. For example, Levi Strauss (see article) has had to develop its products to satisfy customers' changing demands and to avoid entering the decline stage of the product life cycle.

Product development

Product development is a continuous strategy which organisations adopt in an attempt to keep up with technological developments and changing consumer tastes and fashions. An organisation tries to develop new products for its current market. Changes may be

Discussion point

Identify two other products which are beginning to decline, and may have to adopt a similar approach to Levi Strauss.

Bottom falls out of the market for the original American jeans

Levi's 501s, the original American jeans and an indispensable fashion item for more than a century, are to be phased out in Britain after a slump in sales.

Distribution will be heavily scaled down next year as Levi Strauss aims to revamp its image with a new figure hugging range, to be called Levi's Red.

Once worn by Marilyn Monroe, James Dean and Cindy Crawford, 501s have remained unchanged for 120 years but have suffered a steep decline in their market share.

The women's range of 501s will no longer be distributed in Europe by the end of next year except in Levi Strauss stores, according to sources at the company.

Market analysts believe that the product was ill-fitting and unflattering on women, compared with fashion lines by competitors such as Diesel and Armani.

Levi Strauss, founded in 1853 as a manufacturer of denim, is the second most recognisable icon in the world – just behind Coca-Cola.

The first 501s were made in 1873 as hard-wearing trousers for pioneers and gold miners. The distinctive denim trousers with copper-riveted pockets were assigned Product Lot Number 501 in the Levi Strauss factories in San Francisco, hence their name. Designed with a straight leg for both sexes, 501s had a tiny "fifth pocket" where prospectors could keep the nuggets.

The new brand of jeans will be called Levi's Red range. These will no longer carry a stitched leather patch and will not display the brand-name anywhere. Designed to be figure-hugging, these "3-D engineered" jeans have twisted seams so that they bend comfortably with hip and knee.

The pockets have been lowered at the front and back, and will be angled at the front to allow easy access.

Kenny Wilson, marketing director for Levi Strauss in northern Europe, said: "We have not been innovative enough in recent years – but we will be pushing hard through television advertising."

Sunday Telegraph, 29 August 1999

Diversification

Diversification is a high-risk strategy because the business is attempting to introduce a new product into a new market, with which it is unfamiliar. This strategy is best suited to organisations with products operating in a declining market with a falling market share.

Virgin is an example of a company that has diversified several times. Originally established as a record shop, Virgin's first diversification strategy was concentric, moving from selling records to producing them under the Virgin record label. In recent years, the company has adopted a conglomerate diversification strategy, focusing on selling holidays, airline tickets, pensions, mortgages, beauty products, clothing and bridal wear. These products often have no relation to the company's existing business and they, therefore, have required high capital investment for research and development.

External constraints on marketing activities

In analysing market opportunities and developing a suitable strategy, it is necessary for an organisation to take account of several legal, ethical and environmental factors which may constrain and influence its activities.

Industry-based constraints

The Advertising Standards Authority (ASA) regulates the UK advertising industry. The advertising profession has adopted a code of practice which the ASA administers for all non-broadcast media. The code aims to ensure that advertisements provide a fair, honest and unambiguous representation of the products they promote, including through the use of words and impressions. The ASA gives guidance to advertisers on whether a proposed advertisement would be regarded as acceptable and deals with complaints from the general public about cases of allegedly untruthful, misleading or offensive advertisements.

The ASA is not an enforcement agency; it operates on a voluntary basis. Following an investigation, the ASA can request an advertiser to amend or withdraw an unsuitable advertisement. On the rare occasion an advertiser refuses, the ASA may seek to put pressure on the offending advertiser through the Code of Advertising Practice committee (CAP), which is made up of organisations representing all areas of the media, including advertisers and advertising agency associations. The ASA can issue a warning to CAP members and, as they are not supposed to accept advertisements which breach the code, this would make

it difficult for the offending advertiser to continue to buy space. However, if the advertisement is still being run, the ASA can fall back on the Control of Misleading Advertisements Regulations 1988, referring the advertisement to the Office of Fair Trading.

For television advertising, there are four groups that act as watchdogs over standards.

- The Broadcast Complaints Commission is a statutory body that deals with any complaints of unjust or unfair treatment. It has no disciplinary powers.

- The Broadcasting Standards Council is a statutory body dealing with issues of sex, violence, taste or decency. It also has no disciplinary powers.

- The Independent Television Commission is a statutory body set up to regulate commercial television, which monitors the use of advertisements and can enforce action, where necessary.

- The Broadcasting Advertising Clearance Centre is run by the ITV Centre and vets all advertising copy before it is screened

Ethical and social constraints

Business stakeholders and pressure groups can have a constraining effect upon an organisation's marketing activities. Organisations need to establish a balance between satisfying the demands of these two groups, while implementing a marketing strategy which increases overall development, profitability and sales.

Within an organisation there are several business stakeholders, different groups of people with a personal interest in the future direction which the organisation takes. The shareholders want assurances of future profitability and high dividends, the managers want to maximise sales to reach their own personal targets, employees want better training and a fair level of pay. Suppliers and creditors also have a direct influence upon the marketing strategy as do customers, society and the public. The marketing strategy needs to be formulated to satisfy these conflicting objectives.

Environmental pressure groups like Greenpeace can limit and influence the marketing activities of a business by generating bad publicity which damages its image. For example, oil companies can be tarnished by publicising the impact of spillages from oil tankers. Organisations that are keen to avoid accusations of unethical behaviour might adopt a promotion campaign which focuses upon their environmental friendliness. To protect their own reputation, it is important that organisations recognise the power pressure groups have to influence public opinion.

The Consumers' Association focuses upon protecting the rights of consumers in general, and its 800,000 members in particular. The association publishes regular *Which?* reports; these critically investigate the activities of organisations involved in different market sectors. *Which?* reports highlight unfair practices and can have a detrimental effect on any organisations involved in unethical business behaviour such as aggressive price undercutting or unlawful monopolisation.

Legal constraints

We have already discussed the general impact of legislation on business in Unit 2 (see pp. 116–9). It is worth noting a couple of areas which apply particularly to marketing activities. The Trade Descriptions Act 1968 makes it illegal to give a false description of a product. This covers descriptions in writing, in advertisements or in anything which the seller says when discussing the goods and services with a customer. The Act also covers the way in which goods are priced. The seller cannot charge a higher price than the one marked on the product. It is also illegal to claim that the price of a product or service has been reduced, unless it was previously offered at a higher price for a period of at least 28 days in the last six months. The Act was strengthened in 1972, introducing provisions which make it illegal to sell goods that have been manufactured abroad by trying to give the customer the impression that they were made in the UK.

As we explained in Unit 2, the Office of Fair Trading monitors anti-competitive practice. It can refer monopoly situations to the Monopolies and Mergers Commission, although the Secretary of State for Trade and Industry takes the final decision on whether a potential monopoly should be investigated to assess if it is against the public interest. Members of the Monopolies and Mergers Commission are appointed by the Secretary of State for Trade and Industry, and it functions as an independent tribunal. By considering factors such as the level of competition in the market, the quality, choice and service offered to consumers and the opportunity for other businesses to enter the market, the commission decides whether a company has gained an unfair monopoly. The Monopolies and Mergers Commission can constrain or prevent a company from expanding its market share through a takeover if it believes the company's actions might be detrimental to consumers.

BUILD YOUR LEARNING

Keywords and phrases

You should know the meaning of the words and phrases listed below. Go back through the last 12 pages of the unit to check or refresh your understanding as necessary.

- Ansoff matrix
- Boston Consulting Group matrix
- Gross domestic product
- PEST analysis
- Product life cycle
- SWOT analysis

Summary points

- In order to formulate a marketing strategy, a business needs to use market information to analyse the competitiveness of its product or service and the environment in which it operates.

- By using forecasting techniques to predict future levels of demand, a business can predict customer behaviour and stay ahead of its competitors.

- By using the PEST and SWOT models to generate information on the business environment, it is possible for organisations to analyse trends and developments and spot new market opportunities and threats.

- The Ansoff matrix may be used to evaluate the suitability of different marketing strategies, such as market penetration, new product development, market development and diversification.

- The Boston Consulting Group matrix can be combined with the product life cycle to represent a range of products in terms of market share and growth. This analysis can be used to inform a strategy of establishing a balanced portfolio of products at different stages of development.

- In developing a suitable marketing strategy, an organisation has to take account of legal, ethical and environmental factors which may constrain and influence its activities.

Creating strategies that meet customer needs

THE INITIAL RESEARCH STAGES a business undertakes allow it to match its marketing mix – the combination of product, price, promotion and place – to factors such as the socioeconomic class, age, household type, gender, personal values and geographical location of its customers. This, combined with an analysis of marketing opportunities, helps to determine the most suitable marketing strategy.

The marketing mix

In order to implement a marketing strategy which meets customer needs, businesses have to pay attention to the basic ingredients of the **marketing mix**, otherwise known as the **four Ps**. This involves matching the **product** to consumer needs, determining the **price**, deciding where and how the product or service should be **placed** (distributed) in the market and **promoting** it through publicity, advertising and sales techniques.

The marketing department develops an appropriate marketing strategy by identifying the most important components of the marketing operation, so as to determine the best marketing mix of the four Ps for its target market. By targeting a specific segment of the market, it is possible for an organisation to develop a marketing mix which satisfies the needs of a clearly defined set of customers.

Product

When designing a product strategy, it is important to identify precisely what is being purchased in terms of customer benefits and how these help to satisfy a particular need. This means that it is essential to be clear about what the product provides. For example, Theodore Levitt, a leading figure in marketing in the USA in the 1960s, noted that nobody buys drills: they buy the ability to make holes. If a more efficient and cost-effective way of making holes became available on the market, people would turn to it. In fact, as Figure 3.17 shows, a product or service may provide satisfaction at three levels.

Lets apply the model of levels of customer satisfaction to products sold by The Body Shop. In this case, the core benefits might be viewed in terms of buying natural products which make the consumer feel 'at one' with nature – a big selling point is that The Body Shop's products are made from ingredients which do not

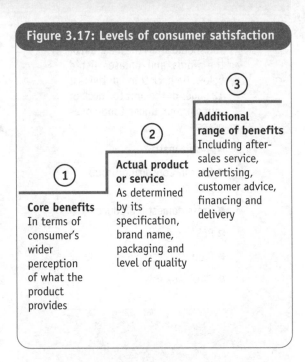

Figure 3.17: Levels of consumer satisfaction

③ **Additional range of benefits** Including after-sales service, advertising, customer advice, financing and delivery

② **Actual product or service** As determined by its specification, brand name, packaging and level of quality

① **Core benefits** In terms of consumer's wider perception of what the product provides

Discussion point

Apply the model of the levels of customer satisfaction in Figure 3.17 to the last major product you purchased.

damage the environment or infringe animal rights. The actual products are created through extensive laboratory research. They are high quality, and associated with an internationally known brand and sold in a range of sizes with the minimum of packaging. The additional benefits associated with The Body Shop's products include the advice sheets which are freely available in the shops, the product knowledge of the staff, the recycling of containers, and the fact that, through purchasing a product, consumers feel that they are supporting a business which is beneficial (or, at least, not detrimental) to the environment.

When developing a product, a marketing department must identify the three levels of satisfaction, and then design a strategy that allows customer satisfaction to be achieved at each level. This includes consideration of issues such as branding, packaging, labelling and the development of a range of products to cover all the stages of a product life cycle.

Branding

Branding helps to identify a product and differentiate it from those of competitors. It is used to establish consumer loyalty and, in so doing, makes demand more price inelastic. It also can convey a feeling of quality and reliability. For example, the name of Heinz is known by most consumers. They associate it with high-quality food products, for which they are probably prepared to pay slightly more than non-branded products or less-respected brands

Manufacturers may sometimes sell into different segments of the market under a variety of brand names. Unilever sells washing detergents under the names of Persil, Surf, Radion, Wisk, Lux and Stergene. The ultimate success in branding is when the brand name becomes associated with the product category; for example people often say Levi's when they mean jeans, Kleenex is (falsely) used as a generic word for tissues.

Packaging

Packaging can combine with branding to differentiate the product. It also helps to attract attention, describe the product and, ultimately, make the sale. A more affluent consumer is prepared to pay for the convenience, appearance, dependability and prestige that are communicated through better packaging. This is especially true in the case of expensive cosmetics and confectionery. The packaging research which QMDP conducted when launching its new added-value milk (see article) reflects a growing recognition that external appearances play a key role in attracting sales.

Discussion point

Identify three other manufacturers that have successfully differentiated their products by combining imaginative packaging with branding.

Labelling

Labelling contributes to the perceived quality of the packaging and, ultimately, the product. This is because it helps to identify the product type and the brand clearly. It might also grade the product, describe its features and provide promotion through suitable graphics; and it can add further value to the product by providing information on its usage.

Milking the packaging

Owner of the Breakfast Milk brand, Quality Milk and Diary Products (QMDP) has spent the best part of two years researching its market. Managing director Minze de Vries explains that milk tends to be a pre-planned purchase, with consumers lavishing their attention on the added-value milk shelf for an average of one eighth of a second.

The results of T-scope tests, hall tests, group discussions and 5,000 doorstep deliveries followed by telephone interviews, led to the development of a new blow-moulded pack to replace the carton. QMDP used Cambridge Foods for its research, as well as other local or specialist companies.

Designed and produced by Plysu Liquid Food, the pint bottle has a curved profile, a full-length decorated sleeve and a gold top as the ultimate quality cues. "It is possible to succeed in adding value to milk, even though it's a very functional market which presents itself in a very dull and uninteresting way," says de Vries.

Adapted from *Marketing Week*, 19 August 1999

Price

Pricing is the only aspect of the marketing mix that directly produces revenue; the other aspects all involve costs. Therefore, it is extremely important to get the pricing strategy right as this determines the financial success of a particular product and contributes to the long-term viability of the organisation. The marketing department should set the price in the context of the total marketing mix. If price is not a particularly significant factor for consumers in the target market, strategies relating to quality, promotion and distribution will strongly influence price. If, within the target market, consumers are very price-sensitive, price will strongly influence the other factors making up the marketing mix.

In developing a pricing policy, the organisation needs to consider its strategic objectives, the price elasticity of demand for the product, the costs associated with the product, and competitors' prices. Let's consider each of these in turn.

First, pricing objectives should reflect the organisation's overall objectives. If the organisation's overall objective is to maximise profits, it will estimate the potential demand and select a price which maximises current profits. But, if it is more interested in achieving security, it may set a lower price to try and obtain a larger market share. If the organisation is concerned with status and prestige, it may attempt to create an extremely high-quality product and set the price at a high level in order to cover research and development costs.

Second, through market research, the organisation needs to establish the level of demand for the product at different prices. From this analysis, it may be possible to derive a demand schedule and determine the degree of price elasticity. The more inelastic the demand for the product, the higher the company can set its price.

Third, the organisation needs to identify the costs associated with the product. Ultimately, the price must, in the long term, recover the costs of producing, distributing and selling the product, and be sufficient to generate a profit. The total costs of a particular product or service are made up of fixed and variable elements. Fixed costs have to be met regardless of the level of output, and include the costs of plant, machinery, rent and rates. Variable costs vary directly with the level of output; for example, if output increases, the variable costs associated with inputs such as labour, raw materials and energy also increase. In formulating a pricing policy, it is necessary to study the behaviour of these costs, both in the short term and the long term.

Fourth, pricing should be competitive. It is important to analyse competitors' prices and offers. Information can be gathered directly, by sending out researchers to compare prices and offers in the shops, or by studying the price lists of competitors.

Now, having undertaken these four stages, the organisation can select a pricing method. It should produce a price which reflects the organisation's objectives, the price elasticity of demand for the product, the organisation's costs and competitors' prices. It can choose one of the six main approaches to pricing:

- cost plus pricing
- target profit pricing
- perceived value pricing
- competitor based pricing
- market skimming
- market penetration pricing.

Cost plus pricing

This is a crude method of pricing. It involves establishing the total costs of producing a particular product and adding a standard margin or mark-up to produce the price of the product. For example, if it costs a manufacturer of electrical goods £12 to produce an electric kettle, it could simply add 33.3 per cent mark-up and sell the kettle to a retailer for £16. This is a method widely used by many construction companies. In some sectors a standard mark-up exists – books sold by retailers normally have a 33.3 per cent mark-up.

The major weakness of cost plus pricing is that it fails to reflect market forces. If the price has been set too high, sales will suffer; if it has been set too low, profits may be sacrificed. The system works reasonably well if all the firms within a particular industry broadly use the same method, so that prices move together.

Target profit pricing

Target profit pricing uses breakeven analysis. This is illustrated by Figure 3.18, which shows total costs and total revenues at different volumes of sales. The price must be set at a level at which the firm at least covers its variable costs, otherwise there is no point in continuing production. Profits are only made at a volume of sales above the breakeven level – this is the point at which a firm covers its fixed and variable costs for a given price.

> ### Discussion point
> Use Figure 3.18 to determine the new breakeven point if the price of the product is increased to £20 per unit.

In Figure 3.18, at a price of £15 per unit and with the given cost structure, the firm will break even if it achieves 600,000 sales. If the firm's objective is to achieve a target profit of £2 million, it would have to achieve 800,000 sales at a price of £15 per unit. It is possible that by charging a higher price the firm may achieve its £2 million profit objective with a lower volume of sales. The slope of the total revenue curve

Figure 3.18: Breakeven analysis

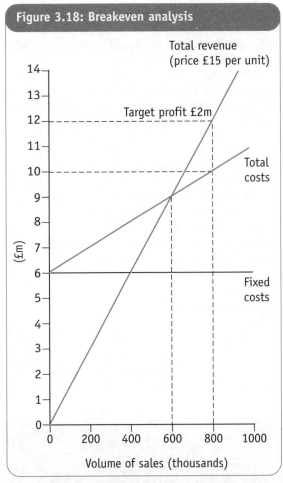

would be steeper, so the firm would break even at a lower volume of sales. Ultimately, the price and volume of sales at which the firm will achieve this target level of profit depends on its demand schedule and the price elasticity of demand. Therefore, this breakeven analysis is only useful if it is viewed in the context of the demand situation facing the firm.

Perceived value pricing

Perceived value pricing relates to the non-price variables in the marketing mix, which help to raise consumers' perception of the product and, in so doing, their willingness to pay a higher price. Take, as an example, a simple product like fish and chips. If it is served in newspaper at a fish bar, a consumer might be prepared to pay, say, £1.75 for a portion. On the other hand, if the consumer eats fish and chips as a meal in a café, a price of £3.50 might be considered acceptable. In a slightly classier restaurant, the same meal might appear on the menu at £6.50, and in a hotel restaurant a resident might pay £8 for the same dish. The higher price can be charged due to the difference in the surroundings and atmosphere in which the fish and chips are eaten.

This method of pricing relies upon accurate research into how people view a particular product and give value to the non-price variables in the marketing mix. The consumer's perception of the value of a product may, in fact, be lowered if the organisation reduces its price. This is because the consumer may consider a lower price to equate with low quality. This attitude is often taken towards electrical goods such as stereos, dish washers and washing machines; the consumer may feel that if the product is priced below the expected range, there must be something wrong with it technically, or there must be a poor after-sales service. Another illustration of this phenomena is Heinz baked beans; they are more expensive than other brands, yet consumers are prepared to pay a higher price because they think that Heinz beans are higher quality.

Competitor based pricing

Competitor based pricing is often used by smaller firms that lack the sophisticated research techniques to determine their own prices. Their solution is simply to charge what is considered to be the going market rate among their competitors. The price, then, at least reflects the collective wisdom of the industry.

Market skimming

A market skimming strategy exploits what are usually very short-term conditions in the marketplace. A company with an innovative product may initially face very little competition, and it may be possible to skim the top of the market by selling at a very high price to the relatively few consumers who are willing to pay this price. This method of pricing is common in the pharmaceutical industry. A company may spend a lot of money researching and developing a new drug; it will deliberately set high prices until rivals bring out a competitive product. Companies producing technical products such as computers also employ this technique.

Market penetration pricing

Market penetration pricing is often used by firms trying to establish themselves in the market. They may set low prices in order to build up brand loyalty and gain a share of the market. The strategy may be used by firms producing a new product or introducing an established product into a new market. By developing brand loyalty, companies hope to be able to raise their prices at a later date and retain customers. This approach can be particularly suitable for firms which anticipate high long-term sales. This pricing method does have disadvantages. It can give the product a low-price image which can be associated with poor quality. This image can make it difficult to raise prices at a later date.

Place

The marketing department has to 'deliver' the product to the consumer as and when it is required. The extent to which this is achieved depends upon decisions regarding the location of the production or service organisation, the availability of the product or service and the method by which it is distributed.

Location

Decisions on location should take account of the convenience of access for customers. The development of shopping precincts and out-of-town shopping centres and hypermarkets means that many consumers expect to be able to buy a range of products from one location. This is time-saving for consumers, who can obtain all their needs 'in one go'.

The logical development of meeting customer needs in this fashion is that businesses which provide complementary products or services will seek to locate close to each other. For example, estate agents, building societies and solicitors may prefer to be in close proximity to provide a comprehensive service in buying and selling houses. Similarly, fast-food outlets, pubs, clubs and cinemas may combine to create an area for entertainment; a component supplier may decide to locate its operations near a manufacturing organisation on a business park.

There are circumstances where customer convenience may take second place to other locational factors. Typically, this is when cost factors have a more significant effect than price in the marketing mix. These costs could include transport of the finished product, or relate to the need for special site facilities, such as storage space or a means of disposing of waste matter, or the availability of skilled labour (affecting the wages levels that organisations have to pay). To take an example, the location of a single-site chemical plant is likely to be largely determined by its requirements for access to raw materials, waste disposal facilities and the availability of suitable employees.

Product availability

Organisations make decisions regarding place which ensure the availability of products and services when customers need them and in the quantity they require. This means that the organisation of production, storage and distribution must contribute towards the

▲ Arndale shopping centre, Bradford

realisation of the consumer's expectations. For example, consumers who buy a particular make of car need to be confident that, if they visit the spares department of the main dealer, the component they require is available immediately or can be easily obtained. This is only possible if there has been an attempt to balance the production, distribution and stocking of spares with the number of finished vehicles that have been sold.

Distribution systems

The channels and system of distribution determine the way in which products reach the market. The marketing department seeks to establish the most efficient system so that the product is available at the right time and in the right place. A successful system depends upon efficient and rapid transportation, the quality of packaging, the efficiency of the stock control and storage system, and the sophistication of the ordering system.

The effectiveness of the distribution system also depends upon the channels the product may go through to reach the market. Traditionally, manufacturers have sold products to wholesalers in large quantities. These are then sold to retailers in smaller, more manageable quantities. The wholesaler is equipped to handle large shipments from the manufacturer and provide the storage for, and transportation of, the product to the retailer. In recent years, however, a number of manufacturers have decided to by-pass the wholesaler and deal directly with retailers and consumers. This enables savings to be made and provides a quicker response to market trends. Boots has taken this a stage further by having a vertically integrated operation, which controls all stages from manufacture to retailing.

Direct marketing

The place component of the marketing mix does not just comprise decisions about location and distribution. There are a range of techniques that allow businesses to approach potential customers directly. By using commnication channels like the telephone, post and the internet, a company can target potential customes anywhere in the world.

Direct marketing operates through personal channels of communication, and the target market is, in effect, a single customer. Direct marketing methods include:

- direct mail
- telemarketing
- the internet
- leafleting.

Direct mail involves posting information about an organisation's goods and services to actual or potential customers. It provides a highly targeted approach, with a mail shot to selected individuals identified by various socioeconomic and other criteria. Ultimately, the success of this approach depends on the quality of the mailing list, and these are often obtained from specialist agencies.

The most effective direct mail campaigns tend to be through a letter or promotional communication which is simple and to the point. It has both to stimulate interest and provide a means of response, such as a coupon or postage paid envelope. The response rate may be increased through the use of an inducement such as a prize draw. The use of direct mail is growing rapidly. It is used by charities, book clubs, travel and leisure companies, financial services companies and political parties.

Telemarketing involves the organisation communicating with customers directly by telephone. Interested customers may then be visited by a sales representative with a view to completing a sale. This method is used widely in the sale of double glazing, replacement windows, driveways, insurance and financial services. The success of telemarketing depends on the ability of the telephone sales staff. A team needs to be properly trained and staff have to be very methodical and well organised (usually, they work to a prepared script).

The use of telemarketing has been encouraged by technological advances such as the development of call centres. These provide a centralised service for receiving and also, increasingly, making telephone calls; a central computer carries out the dialling. The system works through the use of a target database of names and numbers. Once the call has been answered, it is routed to a salesperson. If the number dialled is engaged or an answering machine is reached, the call is routed to the back of the queue. The computer can link up with other databases to provide relevant information about the customer, such as the person's address and socioeconomic group, enabling the salesperson to adapt the sales pitch accordingly.

A similar approach can be taken in receiving calls from customers. For example, Abbey National Direct uses software that can recognise the telephone number of a mortgage customer and route the caller to the home loans adviser who dealt with the enquirer previously, thus providing continuity of service.

The internet, or information superhighway, offers new opportunities for advertising and direct selling. Large retail organisations such as the Arcadia Group have taken advantage of the development of broadband communications by promoting the interactive use of computers. Arcadia, which owns brands such as Topshop, Topman, Debenhams and Dorothy Perkins, uses its large internet site to offer customers digital shopping. Sales through the internet enable the company to target new customers and receive product feedback.

Leafleting, the door-to-door distribution of leaflets, can provide an effective way of targeting a particular area. It is often used by organisations offering domestic services, such as plumbers, electricians, builders, gardeners and painters and decorators. Many voluntary organisations deliver leaflets before making a collection.

Roadshows enable a marketing message to be communicated in a series of different locations, where representatives from the organisation can meet potential buyers. Exhibitions serve a similar purpose. They may be staffed or unattended. The purpose is to inform potential customers about products and services. Trade fairs are a particularly effective form of exhibition; manufacturers may invite a targeted group of distributors and retailers to visit the organisation's stand. Hospitality is sometimes offered.

Promotion

The purpose of promotion is to communicate directly with potential or existing customers, in order to encourage them to purchase the product or service and recommend it to others. The main promotional tools are sales promotions, public relations and advertising. Essentially, any promotional activity concentrates on the distinctive features of a product, which are known as its unique selling points.

In designing a promotional activity, the marketing department has to:

- identify and target the required market segment

- establish the purpose of the promotion

- take decisions on a suitable promotional message for the target audience

- select a suitable form of media for the target audience

- evaluate the promotional activity by measuring feedback in terms of who becomes aware of the product, uses it and expresses satisfaction with it.

In establishing the purpose of the promotion, the marketing department needs to make decisions in the context of the buying process; that is, recognition of need, consideration and evaluation of how to satisfy that need, making a choice, and evaluating the choice which may result in a repeat purchase. This will determine whether the promotion seeks to increase customers' awareness of the product, or to strengthen

their preference for it or their determination to purchase it. It also influences the choice of promotional message. In some cases, it may be appropriate to appeal to consumers' emotions; in others, to their reason.

The choice of promotional activity ultimately is determined by what the organisation can afford to spend, the type of product and market, and the stage reached in the product's life cycle.

Advertising

Advertising is an important part of an organisation's promotional activities. It is one of the most effective promotional tools and is used to inform, persuade, publicise and remind potential and existing consumers about an organisation's products and activities. Essentially, it is a means of increasing sales. It may also be used to encourage consumers to purchase products or services from a particular retail outlet.

Discussion point

Find examples of advertisements which you feel meet the objectives listed in Figure 3.19.

In deciding on an appropriate method of, or medium for, advertising an organisation needs to:

- decide on the purpose of the advertisement, whether it is concerned essentially with imparting information, persuading new consumers or reminding existing ones

- fix the budget for the campaign in the context of sales and the amount spent by competitors

- identify, design and evaluate the required message, a task often carried out by an advertising agency

- decide on the medium or media to be used, including newspapers, magazines, television, cinema, radio, hoardings, catalogues, circulars and leaflets, again a task often carried out by an agency

- evaluate the effectiveness of the advertisement in terms of communications and sales.

It is possible to measure the probable value of advertising expenditure by calculating the elasticity of advertising (EA). This is done by dividing the proportionate change in sales volume by the proportionate change in advertising expenditure. If EA is greater than one, increasing advertising expenditure is probably worthwhile, as it should create a more than proportionate increase in sales volume.

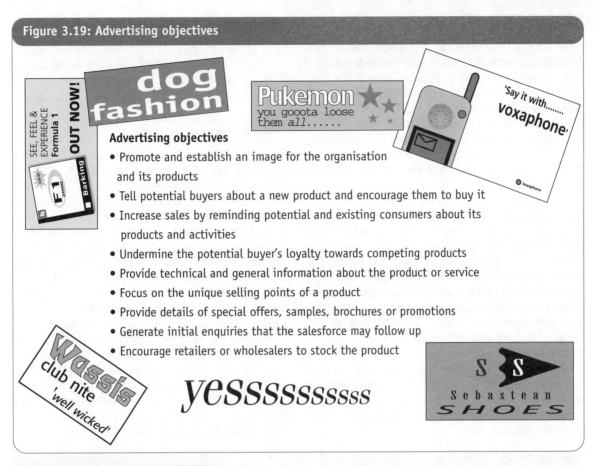

Figure 3.19: Advertising objectives

Advertising objectives

- Promote and establish an image for the organisation and its products
- Tell potential buyers about a new product and encourage them to buy it
- Increase sales by reminding potential and existing consumers about its products and activities
- Undermine the potential buyer's loyalty towards competing products
- Provide technical and general information about the product or service
- Focus on the unique selling points of a product
- Provide details of special offers, samples, brochures or promotions
- Generate initial enquiries that the salesforce may follow up
- Encourage retailers or wholesalers to stock the product

The advertising campaign

An advertising campaign must be carefully planned, with a clear view as to whether the retailer or the consumer is to be targeted and whether it is the product or the organisation which is to be promoted.

The effectiveness of advertising is often increased if the product or organisation already has a strong brand identity; this means that it has a readily recognised name, sign, logo or design. Examples are many, including Levi's jeans, Virgin, Dyson vacuum cleaners and BMW cars. High levels of recognition mean that the organisation can promote its products and publicise its activities to good effect by using these devices on sales literature, delivery vehicles, stationery or point-of-sale displays

Many medium-sized and large organisations seek the specialist services of an advertising agency. Agencies provide expert advice and carry out or manage a number of tasks, including copy writing, design and layout – advising on use of type, style and visual matter – film production for television or cinema advertisements, space buying in media and other outlets such as billboards, and evaluation.

The most successful agencies are able clearly to identify the needs of an organisation and to translate them into effective advertisements. In selecting an agency, it may be helpful to follow the advice of the Advertising Association or the Institute of Practitioners in Advertising.

Any advertising campaign usually has to adhere to a strict budget, the size of which is determined, at least ideally, by:

- the objectives of the campaign (what the organisation intends to achieve by it)
- the amount of money competitors are spending in promoting their products
- the stage the product has reached in its life cycle.

Spending on the advertising of a product is generally high when it is launched, relatively steady during its maturity, and ceases in its period of decline.

One of the major decisions associated with an advertising campaign concerns choice of media. Channels of communication include newspapers, magazines, television and radio, cinema, and outdoor displays. To ensure that the marketplace is adequately covered, it is often appropriate to use a mix of media. Details about sources of advertising media, classified by area, price and potential audience, can be found in the BRAD (British Rate and Data) directory.

Newspapers

Britain has a large coverage of national tabloid and broadsheet newspapers, with a daily readership of more than 26 million. The most popular daily is *The Sun*, which is read by one in four men and one in five women. Age is a significant indicator of readership, for example 28 per cent of those aged 15 to 24 read *The Sun* compared to 15 per cent of those over 65. Since 1971, new titles have come onto the market. Some like *Today* have not survived, others like *The Independent* have been more successful.

This sort of information helps to determine where an advertisement should be placed so as to have the most impact on its target audience. Advertising agencies can give advice by providing readership profiles for newspapers which identify typical buyers in terms of social class and income. Also, newspapers themselves give advice on the best days to place advertisements. For example, it is generally thought that mail order items should be advertised at the weekend because this is when people have the leisure to browse advertisements.

Regional and local free newspapers also provide extensive coverage. They often group advertisements in classified sections. This means advertisers can be confident that their advertisement will be read by those who are most interested.

Discussion point

On the basis of the information on Figure 3.20, where would you place an ad for a package holiday to the Greek islands.

Magazines

Britain has a wide range of magazines aimed at the mass market. Again, considerable variations exist in the age and gender of readerships (see Figure 3.21). Although many target women, in recent years the 'new lad' concept has led to the introduction of an increasing number of men's magazine titles such as FHM. Incidentally, a large number of television listings magazines have been introduced since the end of the BBC's monopoly, in 1991, on the publication of its own listings.

Advertising agencies can give advice on readership profiles and supply details of other types of magazines, such as those produced by professional associations, those aimed at particular retail and trade groups and those covering specialist hobby and leisure interests. One of the major advantages of placing an advertisement in a magazine, rather than a newspaper, is that the publication is likely to have a longer 'life': it may be reread over many months and seen by many more people among the target audience.

Figure 3.20: Readership of daily newspapers, 1997–98

Great Britain

	15–24	25–44	45–64	65 and over	Males	Females	All adults	Readership (millions)
The Sun	28	23	19	15	25	18	21	9.9
Daily Mirror	13	13	14	15	15	12	13	6.3
Daily Mail	8	9	14	13	11	11	11	5.1
The Express	4	4	7	8	6	5	6	2.6
Daily Telegraph	3	4	7	8	6	5	5	2.5
The Times	4	4	5	3	5	3	4	2.0
Daily Star	7	5	3	1	6	2	4	1.9
The Guardian	3	3	3	1	3	2	3	1.2
The Independent	2	2	2	1	2	1	2	0.7
Financial Times	1	2	2	–	2	1	1	0.6
Any national daily newspaper	52	52	61	60	61	52	56	26.0

Percentage reading each paper

Source: *Social Trends* 1999, Edition 29

Figure 3.21: Readership of most popular magazines, 1997–98

Great Britain	Percentages						
	15–24	25–44	45–64	65+	Males	Females	All
Sky TV Guide	19	17	12	3	15	11	13
M&S Magazine	6	11	12	7	5	14	10
Reader's Digest	4	8	13	12	10	10	10
Take a Break	11	12	8	7	4	15	10
What's on TV	14	11	6	6	8	11	9
Radio Times	10	7	9	9	9	9	9
AA Magazine	3	8	11	8	10	7	8
TV Times	9	7	7	8	7	8	8
Woman's Own	8	8	6	5	2	12	7
Bella	5	7	6	5	2	10	6
FHM	21	7	1	-	10	2	6
Cable Guide	10	8	5	2	7	6	7

Source: *Social Trends* 1999, Edition 29

Discussion point

Which of the magazines listed in Figure 3.21 is likely to have the longest 'life'? What are the implications for potential advertisers?

Television

Over 97 per cent of UK households have a television, making it an important advertising medium. It is particularly attractive to advertisers as it allows a combination of music, speech and pictures, as well as the use of jingles, personalities and mini-dramas as aids to the creation of brand interest and identity.

The effectiveness of television advertising depends on a large number of the target group of consumers watching the advertisement at the same time. Therefore, its placement in an appropriate programme slot is vital. Prime time programmes, especially soap operas, provide some of the most 'penetrative' opportunities for advertising to a mass market.

The growth in the number of television channels has tended to spread the viewing audience across a wider range of programmes. This makes it more difficult to target a particular market segment. The situation has been complicated still further by the widespread ownership of video cassette recorders, which enable people both to self-schedule television and fast forward through advertising breaks.

The effectiveness of newspaper and television advertisements is monitored weekly in the Adwatch survey and reported in *Marketing*. Some 500 or more adults are asked to rank advertisements according to the frequency in which they remember having seen or heard them in a given period

Discussion point

Name three products which you consider have benefited significantly from television advertising.

Radio

Radio provides a local and, increasingly, a national medium for placing advertisements, particularly those aimed at 16–24 year olds. In 1994, commercial radio accounted for four per cent of radio audiences and generated a revenue of £219 million. Three stations – Virgin, Classic FM and Atlantic 252 – accounted for 22 per cent of total commercial radio hours.

Radio is a rapidly growing advertising medium and has the advantage over television of having much lower production costs. Local radio can help to develop a strong community feeling which small local businesses may benefit from in buying advertising.

CASE STUDY

Britvic's Tango television advertising campaign

With its vision to be the number one branded soft drinks company, Britvic is intent on increasing its 20 per cent share of the ready-to-drink market. Already, a successful producer, packager and distributor, the company attributes its success to its innovative value-for-money brands and its careful monitoring and response to customer's changing tastes.

Britvic's carefully organised television advertising campaigns have enabled it to achieve its success. Hailed as the UK's favourite fruit carbonate, the Tango soft drink brand is ranked alongside Nike and Levi's as one of Britain's most respected youth brands. Tango's advertising campaigns have managed to attract the attention of its target market, the notoriously difficult 18–24 year olds. In 1992, Britvic took an innovate and award-winning approach towards advertising. Accompanied by new packaging, Britvic managed to treble Tango's sales through humorous and streetwise commercials which included the catchline 'You know when you've been Tango'd'.

By 1994, the company was selling nine cans a second, had achieved its highest market share ever and was outselling Fanta, Lilt, Sunkist and Gini combined. Tango's rapid growth derived from the fact that its adverts were both irreverent and distinctive and appealed to the target audience. In 1994, following an advert for Apple Tango, some 1.3 million people were prompted to call the Apple Tango seduction help line.

The use of television enables Britvic to provide a lively visual image of the products under the Tango brand name. Britvic's success can be attributed to the placement of its adverts in carefully selected youth slots and its ability to engage the target audience's participation.

Source: Britvic soft drinks information pack

Other media

The introduction of multi-screen cinemas and the consequent revival in cinema attendance has benefited advertising in the 1990s. Cinemas provide advertisers with a captive audience which can be reached relatively cheaply. As a medium, it is of particular value to local retailers, businesses, hotels and restaurants.

Outdoor displays are another fruitful site for advertising. Use may be made of parking meters, sandwich boards, taxis, buses and tube trains, telephone kiosks, hoardings and flashing signs.

Public relations

Public relations (PR) is a means of publicising and promoting a positive image of an organisation's achievements with a view to influencing customers to buy products, investors to buy shares, and the government and others to act in ways helpful to the organisation. Essentially, it involves using impersonal types of communication to gain favourable publicity and develop a perception that the company is socially responsible. In many cases it consists in the placement of information about the organisation in a suitable publication or obtaining a favourable presentation of its activities on radio, television or elsewhere, without having to buy advertising space.

Major retailers, like Asda, Sainsbury's and Tesco, spend a great deal on public relations to promote a responsible, caring and high-quality image. Like other major companies, they carry out public relations to:

■ promote confidence in, and create a favourable image of, the company with the general public, bankers, customers and suppliers

■ increase understanding of the company, its scope and products

■ bring the company and its products to the attention of a wider audience

■ generate more business and profits.

Organisations, or the PR agencies they hire, may decide to use one or more of a number of activities in a public relations campaign.

■ Press releases may be issued to draw attention to the successes of the organisation. These might include an announcement concerning the creation of a new product, success in securing a new order, or some other development or achievement. An advantage of a press release is that it offers the organisation's version of a particular event (and, of course, if published it is free publicity).

■ Briefings may be provided for people who speak on the organisation's behalf –either an employee or someone from outside the organisation – to ensure that its case is presented effectively on television, radio and at other events.

■ Public appearances and speeches can be used to promote the name and activities of an organisation. This may involve television and radio appearances as well as local activities such as giving a speech at a chamber of commerce lunch.

■ Sponsorship may be offered to link the name of an organisation to a particular event. Sponsorship is a popular means of publicising the name of an organisation and placing it in a favourable light. Even small local businesses can gain from sponsoring charity fundraising events, local sports clubs (with kit) or cultural events, such as helping to finance a theatre production.

Discussion point

Identify some examples of successful public relations campaigns that have been recently undertaken by businesses.

Sales promotion

A sales promotion is an attempt to communicate directly with potential consumers or distributors in order to encourage them to purchase or stock the product or service as well as to recommend it to others. It may involve both impersonal and, in some cases, personal channels of communication.

Consumer promotions are used to encourage potential consumers to try a product and, hopefully, to purchase it again. These may involve:

■ free trial samples of a product

■ discount coupons or vouchers

■ cash refund of purchase

■ bargain packs

■ free gifts with the product

■ rewards for loyalty such as air miles

■ point-of-sale displays or demonstrations

■ competitions

■ special deals such as zero per cent finance arrangements

■ loss-leaders

■ prizes, bonuses and other inducements to sales forces.

Trade promotions are aimed at distributors to encourage them to stock a particular product. They may involve the use of cash incentives to display and advertise a particular product, special prizes or bonuses paid to organisations prepared to stock the product or service, and exhibitions or product conventions aimed at potential distributors.

Sales promotions are used to:

■ introduce a new product

■ encourage consumers to buy more of existing lines

■ encourage consumers to buy at off-peak times

■ secure repeat business

■ challenge competitors

■ increase sales

■ regain former customers.

For a sales promotion to achieve its objectives it is important to ensure that it keeps within budget and clearly targets the potential group of consumers or distributors. The case study on p. 192 describes how the Pepsi Cola sales promotion achieved its required degree of targeting.

CASE STUDY

The Pepsi sales promotion

For a sale promotion to achieve its objectives it is important to ensure that it keeps within budget and clearly targets the potential group of consumers or distributors. Pepsi Cola has successfully achieved its required degree of targeting for its three brands – Pepsi, Pepsi Max and Diet Pepsi – through successful sales promotion campaigns.

Targeted at 16-24 year olds Pepsi has been promoted as 'The cola for youth'. Pepsi's sponsorship of the Pepsi Chart Show on independent radio and Channel Five has enabled the brand to associate itself with popular culture and create a favourable modern image. In recent yeas Pepsi has forged links with major celebrities such as Tina Turner, Michael Jackson, Hanson, Janet Jackson, Boyzone (pictured below), Eternal and the Spice Girls. In June 1999 Pepsi launched a sales promotion campaign supported by the popular Irish band the Corrs which was designed to ensure customers made repeat purchases. Customers were encouraged to buy large quantities of Pepsi in order to collect the necessary number of promotional ring pulls required to obtain an exclusive, limited edition Corrs CD. Offering gifts in exchange for evidence of purchases is a form of consumer promotion which Pepsi has used with great success. In early 1999 over half a million consumers claimed Pepsi radios in Pepsi's most successful promotion ever.

Targeted at 12-18 year old lads who 'want to live life to the Max' Pepsi Max was launched in 1993 to great success. When it was first launched Pepsi Max hired actors to represent those depicted in its own popular television commercials. These actors toured the country distributing free product samples in night-clubs and shopping precincts. The sales promotion was designed to increase sales and emphasise Pepsi Max's unique selling point as a full flavour cola with no added sugar. Now holding five per cent of the total cola market Pepsi Max has used event sponsorship to continue to attract the attention of its target market. Pepsi Max has sponsored The Drop at London's Trocadero and The Big One roller coaster at Blackpool as well as the 1998 Extreme Sports Festival which was attended by 65,000 people. These associations have created an image of a fast paced, exciting brand.

Since its launch in 1964 Diet Pepsi has created a sassy, streetwise image. The decision to enlist Saffron, the lead singer of the band Republica as the 1998 Face of Diet Pepsi has enabled the brand to appeal to its target 18-30 year old female market. Sponsorship of the Cosmopolitan Show provides the opportunity for the brand to offer free samples to its target market and to secure their custom.

Source: Britvic soft drinks information pack

Discussion point

List the major reasons for the success of Pepsi's sales promotion campaign.

The 1990s have seen an increase in the number of organisations which have supported sales promotion with television or radio advertising. In 1994, there was an increase of 160 per cent in the number of promotions supported by advertising. They included promotions by household names such as Weetabix, Coca-Cola, Esso, Shell and McDonald's. These organisations recognised that advertising helps to attract customers into retail outlets and encourages them to make purchases, while the sales promotional activity has a role in making people feel happy about a brand, thus making the sale promotion a success.

Selling

Once the marketing mix has been established, organisations have hopefuly arrived at a combination of product, price, place and promotion that will meet their objectives. However, goods don't just walk out of the warehouse, they still need to be sold.

Direct sales methods

In deciding upon the suitability of different sales methods, it is important to consider the strategic objectives of the organisation and the required culture of customer service and satisfaction. Basically, a decision has to be made as to whether an organisation should directly sell its own products or services or use an indirect selling method, working through an appropriate intermediary within the channel of distribution.

Direct sales methods do not use intermediaries, but involve selling direct between the producer and the customer. These methods include the direct marketing strategies we discussed on p.185.

The key feature of direct selling, as you might imagine, involves selling goods and services face to face. Typically, it takes place when the customer visits a shop, although it may occur on the doorstep or through party plan selling (that is, home-based selling events). The advantage of direct selling is that the seller is able to respond to questions, identify customers' specific needs, demonstrate particular benefits and features of the product, and secure an order immediately.

Door-to-door selling is a technique used for both domestic and industrial consumers. The sales representative either delivers the product immediately, from stocks carried in a car or van, or takes an order.

The salesperson may give advice on reorder quantities and display materials, and provide notice of future advertising campaigns. If a sales representative is dealing with stockists of consumer durables, such as electrical goods, he or she may also spend time attending to technical matters and complaints.

In retailing, many sales representatives sell directly to the purchasing departments of the large retail chains. Here, the sales reps offer advice on issues such as quality, packaging, discounts and special promotions. In selling to industrial consumers, sales representatives often need to have specialist technical knowledge of plant, machinery and computer systems – they are sometimes referred to as technical representatives.

Party plan selling is aimed at groups of domestic buyers who are brought together by a common contact or friend, who is recruited by the seller. The host receives financial or other benefits to organise the party, with sales being carried out by the organisation's personnel.

Other direct sales methods include:

- selling through television and radio, with the advertising carrying information on how to order – used often for exclusive offers such as music compilations

- selling through a mail order catalogue – used, for example, for clothes and holidays

- telephone selling, involving an initial contact followed up with a visit from a sales representative

- selling directly from factory premises – used for products such as pine bookcases and bedroom furniture.

Direct sales methods allow organisations to exert greater control over the marketing and selling of their products. However, the downside for producers of goods is that they can involve an expensive storage and distribution operation.

Indirect sales methods

Indirect sales methods involve manufacturers working through a third party or intermediary in order to sell their products. These intermediaries are part of the distribution channel, which traditionally has three operational stages:

- manufacturing – making the product

- wholesaling – holding stocks and breaking bulk supplies into retail packs

- retailing – the sale of the product to the final buyer or consumer.

The decision by a manufacturer to hand over the wholesaling and retailing activity to an intermediary is based on organisational, operational and financial considerations.

The role of wholesalers

The wholesaler provides several benefits to the manufacturer. Wholesalers buy products in relatively large quantities from the manufacturer, which they stock and sell on in smaller quantities to retailers. This allows the manufacturer to benefit from fewer but larger orders, producing economies of scale for longer production runs and avoiding a potentially high minimum outlay for storage, sales and transport facilities.

The manufacturer also avoids having to cover the delivery costs associated with small consignments to a large number of widely dispersed retail outlets. Independent wholesalers may operate a single warehouse or a chain of warehouses giving wider regional coverage and, in many cases, national distribution. In markets for perishable products, such as fruit and vegetables, specialist wholesalers are able to distribute the products more rapidly to a scattered market. Consider, for example, the role of the great London markets including Covent Garden (flowers, fruit and vegetables), Billingsgate (fish) and Smithfield (meat).

Wholesalers may concentrate on particular sectors such as beer, wines and spirits, fruit and vegetables, meat, fish, footwear, clothing, sports equipment, carpets, china and glassware, hardware, electrical goods, books and furniture. These specialist wholesalers are very important for goods which have a seasonal demand. A wholesaler that deals in swimsuits, for example, will place orders during the winter and build up stocks in the warehouse well before the summer months. The swimsuit manufacturers can therefore keep the factory going at a steady rate during the whole of the year. This helps the manufacturer to run the business more efficiently. As importantly, the wholesaler has enough swimsuits in stock to meet the very large increase in demand during the summer

▲ Wholesaling in action, New Covent Garden

months. Without the wholesaler, swimsuit manufacturers would find it very difficult to meet demand, and there would be a shortage.

Wholesale merchants act as a link between manufacturers and the firms that need raw materials, parts, equipment and machinery. This is known as selling to the trade and could involve builders, plumbers, decorators and timber merchants. Merchants are also willing to build up their stocks with items which are in seasonal demand. This is the case, for example, with building materials, as less building and decorating work goes on in the winter months compared with other times of the year.

Wholesalers may undertake specialist activities such as blending, processing or packaging. By undertaking this work for many producers, it can be carried out on a more economic scale. These specialist skills are of particular value when dealing with commodities such as tea, coffee and wool.

More generally, wholesalers know the market. So, for example, a new manufacturer with very little trading experience and limited financial resources may initially use an established wholesaler. The wholesaler is likely to have greater knowledge of local customers, knowing their credit-worthiness and the size and frequency of orders. The wholesaler can also pass on advice to the retailer regarding shelf, counter and window displays.

It may be concluded that selling through a wholesaler confers benefits to both the manufacturer and retailer. However, some criticisms are levelled at the wholesale function on the grounds that the wholesaler simply takes a cut, adds little or no value, and contributes to higher prices. This can mean that if either the manufacturer or retailer believes that it can perform the wholesaler's services, it will seek to do so in the interests both of profit and competitive sales. In fact, the development of large supermarket and DIY chains has meant that, in many cases, the wholesaling function of stocking and breaking down bulk supplies has become increasingly integrated with the retail function, with retailers taking advantage of price discounts associated with bulk buying.

Dealing with retailers direct

Some products by their very nature are distributed directly by manufacturers to retailers. These include relatively expensive products where distribution costs can be borne by manufacturers without a severe impact upon their competitive position or profit margins. It is not necessary for retailers to hold large stocks of consumer durables; they are not expected to buy television sets or washing machines in bulk. Manufacturers may perhaps conduct their own wholesaling function for those products on which they offer after-sales service; it will be necessary to have

close contact with retail units to organise this after-sales service.

Retail trends are also encouraging manufacturers to deal directly with retailers. With the development of more out-of-town shopping centres and hypermarkets, there are fewer but larger retail units. This also assists in deliveries and increases warehousing facilities. Manufacturers have also benefited from the improved motorway infrastructure and the development of larger commercial vehicles, which have reduced costs and improved the efficiency of their distribution system.

Retailers have traditionally provided a convenient point of sale, at the end of the distribution channel, for manufacturers' products. However, the relationship between retailers and manufacturers is changing. The development of supermarket and DIY chains has meant that many retailers have become much more demanding in their dealings with manufacturers. Retailers have been able to use their bulk buying power to obtain substantial price discounts from manufacturers and the larger retail groups have established an extensive own-label brand business in direct competition with manufacturers' brands. By providing retailers with the increased opportunity to use price as a competitive weapon within the marketing mix, consumers have benefited.

Agents and distributors

Agents and distributors sometimes feature within the distribution channel as another type of intermediary. The major purpose of using an agent is to generate new business contracts. In many cases, a manufacturer will employ an agent to obtain new wholesale customers, or a wholesaler will use an agent when seeking to establish new retail accounts.

Distributors are more independent than agents. They usually buy from the manufacturer at a discount and resell with a mark up. In many cases, a distributor expects and demands an exclusive sales arrangement, allowing it the sole licence to sell the manufacturer's product in a certain area. The advantage to the manufacturer of going through a distributor is that it offers access to additional sales outlets in new areas.

Agents and distributors are of particular value to companies wishing to establish a presence in export markets. The company could either sell through an export agency in the UK or appoint an agent or distributor in the country abroad. By appointing a suitable overseas agent, the business not only sells its product abroad, it also receives useful information about developments in the market, suitable promotions and the need for product modification and updating. In many cases, the agent or distributor may also supply the after-sales service on which many customers will judge the reliability of the business.

The importance of customer service

Any marketing strategy must place a strong emphasis on the achievement of customer satisfaction, and this means that an organisation must have a culture that places a premium on customer service. All employees must have the same values, beliefs and ways of communicating which reflect the needs of the customer. Employees must be trained to have an appropriate open-mindedness and readiness to act in response to customers' needs. They must strive to achieve quality in their own work and be willing to go out of their way to deliver that same level of quality to customers. This culture, of putting the customer first, must be handed down from the top of the organisation.

Organisations must develop a culture of customer service at both a strategic and operational level. Strategically, it is necessary to evaluate customers' wants and then to design a package of services which meet their expectations. For example, customers have certain expectations when they enter a dry cleaners. These must be realised in terms of the standards of the counter staff, the availability of advice, the quality of the cleaning, the treatment of the items of clothing in terms of hangers and covers, the accuracy of the bill, the methods of payment, the atmosphere of the shop and the competitiveness of the price.

Operationally, any service must be well delivered with consistent standards applied for each customer visit, across different geographical locations and by all employees. For example, an organisation like McDonald's strives to maintain the same high standards of cleanliness, speed and quality of service and food whether the outlet is in London, Paris or Moscow.

Increasingly, organisations which are committed to achieving the highest possible levels of customer satisfaction recognise that all employees must seek to do their job as well as they can for the people they serve. This extends the idea of what is meant by a 'customer' beyond the external customer, who actually buys or uses the product or receives the service, to one which includes anyone for whom an employee within the organisation provides a service, or who has a need for what is supplied. This produces the concept of the internal customer – people who work in the organisation, who have the same external customers and share the same organisational goals, and whose work is in some way dependent on that done by the employee or by others within the organisation. This is important because the service that an employee provides internally to fellow employees has a direct impact on the quality of the service delivered to the external customer.

In order to achieve a high level of quality, employees have to think in a particular way: they have to recognise that what might seem a routine duty may be of crucial significance for the effective performance of the internal customers that they serve. Under these circumstances, all employees need to know not only what they have to do and how to do it, but also why they are doing it and what the result will be for their colleagues if something is done incorrectly and not to the appropriate standard.

The commercial advantages of achieving high standards of customer service have become increasingly recognised by organisations in the 1990s. In many cases, customer service has been adopted by major business organisations as a strategic objective. These organisations have recognised that it brings significant benefits.

- Organisations that differentiate their goods and services on the basis of service can ask higher prices for comparative products or services and achieve higher profit margins.

- Good customer service is often associated with greater customer loyalty, which makes an organisation less open to attack by 'clone' competitors and ensures a measure of protection in an economic downturn.

- Due to the premium placed on customer service, organisations are likely to experience more of the benefits during an economic boom.

- Having a reputation for high-quality customer service often means that the business does not need to spend as much on advertising.

- A business which develops a culture of customer service and recognises the existence of internal customers is likely to have a more contented workforce, with lower absenteeism and higher employee retention rates

The case study opposite describes the marketing activity at Cadbury. It demonstrates how the company has developed a marketing strategy which embraces the four Ps.

CASE STUDY

Cadbury's marketing mix

Cadbury Limited was founded in 1824 in Birmingham by two enterprising brothers. The company's original success derived from its introduction of the first British edible chocolate – the Dairy Milk bar in 1905 – which broke the past French and Swiss monopoly, and is still sold today.

Since 1905 the company has extended its product portfolio by launching over thirty new products in several different sizes and by diversifying into the 'twist wrap' and moulded egg market segments.

Operating in a fast growing market Cadburys has had to develop a brand identity which enables it to differentiate itself from its competitors. The brand reflects:

- quality
- value for money
- superior taste.

When reproduced in print, the Cadbury's brand name is made easily identifiable by the use of the Cadbury's script logo. Based on the signature of William A Cadbury the script logo is key to the company's global brand strategy. The script logo is the single most important means of visually identifying a Cadbury's product. Combined with the regal purple and gold house colours and 'glass and a half' symbol the Cadbury's brand image symbolises goodness, quality, freshness and superiority.

In the United Kingdom the commercial strategy has always been to concentrate on the mid price ranges and build a wide customer base whose needs are fulfilled by the focus on quality and value. This policy has meant that Cadbury is the leader in the UK chocolate confectionery market with thirteen brands in the list of top thirty chocolate brands. In the past five years new franchise markets have opened up with Cadbury's chocolate used in biscuits, cakes, liqueur, desserts, ice creams and beverages produced by other manufacturers.

Since 1881 Cadburys has been exporting to and producing in over twenty different countries worldwide. Factories have been opened up all over the world including; Australia, New Zealand, France and Spain. Many countries continue to receive Cadbury's chocolate direct from the factories at Bournville and Somerville.

The majority of Cadbury's products are international brands, however there are some which remain unique to specific countries. The company strives to maintain its quality and value through the Globe. Packaging is sometimes altered to appeal to different cultural tastes and legal requirements but the script logo remains on all products to create a global brand identity.

The opening up of Eastern Europe provides Cadburys with new opportunities for international expansion and the opportunity to export limited quantities of some of its products to new markets.

Cadbury's marketing focuses upon the key element of taste. Supported by the bold slogan 'The Chocolate. The Taste' Cadbury's promotion campaign delivers this message through the use of; posters, magazine, newspaper and television advertising.

The product range is constructed to offer a wide range of product sizes which are suitable for all ages and all eating occasions. The wide range of bar sizes is designed to reflect changes in consumer's lifestyles and developments in the retail trade. The development of multi packs are designed to respond to the growth in demand for bulk purchases.

The recent introduction of a limited edition Star Wars Dairy Milk bar highlights the way that the company uses its association with popular cultural trends to promote its own name.

Source: Cadbury's information pack

BUILD YOUR LEARNING

Keywords and phrases

You should know the meaning of the words and phrases listed below. Go back through the last 18 pages of the unit to check or refresh your understanding as necessary.

- Advertising
- Branding
- Competitor based pricing
- Cost plus pricing
- Direct sales methods
- Four Ps
- Indirect sales methods
- Market penetration
- Market skimming
- Perceived value pricing
- Promotion
- Target profit pricing

Summary points

- A marketing strategy must embrace the four Ps, by matching the product to the consumer needs, determining the price, deciding upon where and how the product and service should be placed (distributed) and promoting it through publicity, advertising, sales techniques and customer service.

- There must be a clear understanding of the core benefits associated with a product and how these must be reflected within the brand.

- Pricing techniques include cost-plus, target profit, perceived value, competitor based, market skimming and market penetration.

- In deciding how to place the product, consideration must be given to location, availability and methods of distribution.

- The purpose of promotion is to communicate directly with potential or existing customers, to encourage them to purchase the product or service and recommend it to others. This may be done through advertising, public relations and sales promotion.

- A culture of customer service must underpin the marketing strategy.

How to produce a marketing strategy

The flow chart shows the stages you need to go through to generate evidence to meet the assessment requirements for this unit.

> Select a new or existing product in which you have a real interest.

> Undertake market research to gather information relating to the product – its features, price, promotion and distribution – and the competition. Use secondary data and gather primary data through your own investigations.

> Estimate the potential demand for the product and the possible competition.

> Analyse the PEST factors which impact upon the environment and conduct a SWOT analysis, placing the product and its prospects into perspective. If you have selected an existing product, identify where it is in its life cycle.

> Use the Boston growth share matrix and the Ansoff matrix to identify how the new or existing product might develop in the future.

> Analyse the legal constraints which may impact upon the market.

> Consider some marketing strategies for the product, ultimately making recommendations about the marketing mix under the headings of the 4Ps.

> Produce a full written and documented strategy supported by graphs, statistics, charts, diagrams and illustrations.

> Adopt the role of a marketing executive and make a presentation to your agency on one aspect of the proposed marketing strategy.

Preview

This unit provides an insight into how businesses recruit, retain and manage their human resources. It shows that if businesses are to achieve their objectives, they must plan their human resource function so that they have the right number of employees with the appropriate qualifications and training to meet the needs of the business.

Successful human resource management requires that a business takes account of changes in the labour market and employment legislation to keep its employees motivated, to monitor their performance and to help them continuously develop through additional training.

4

Human resources

Contents

Human resource planning

ORGANISATIONS UNDERTAKE **human resource planning** to determine a course of action which helps them to function more efficiently by having the right labour, in the right place, at the right time and cost. This requires accurate forecasting: organisations need to forecast their manpower needs, both in terms of the number of employees needed and the types of skills and qualities required. It is also important to monitor and assess the productivity of the existing and available workforce and recognise the impact of technological change on the way in which jobs are carried out.

An organisation's human resource planning team also needs to be able to identify and analyse the factors influencing and shaping the labour markets from which the organisation recruits staff to satisfy its manpower needs. Human resource specialists have to work within these labour markets to acquire sufficient resources to meet the productive needs of the organisation.

Let's use the simple example of a Premiership football team to illustrate what is meant by good human resource planning. Clubs like Manchester United or Chelsea need to be able to assemble a team with the potential to win football matches at a cost which still allows the clubs to make a profit. This means planning for a team with the right blend of maturity and experience, youth and energy. The labour markets for footballers are the pool of players with other clubs and young players coming through the club's youth system.

▼ Manchester United has an extremely successful human resource planning policy

Football managers, with due regard to the finances available for spending in the transfer market, are making decisions about bringing on players from the youth team, buying in players from the lower divisions or other Premiership clubs or recruiting established international names from abroad. They need to consider scouting, youth development, training, transfers, pay and performance.

> **Discussion point**
>
> Manchester United has been successful in developing young players and bringing in new talent to maintain a winning team over several seasons. Can you identify other sport teams which have met with success using a similar approach.

Levels of planning and policy making

Human resource planning takes place over different time frames, though for simplicity we can consider two time horizons: there is planning to meet short-term needs and planning to satisfy long-term intentions.

Short-term plans are referred to as tactical plans and usually contain precise, detailed, measurable objectives. Short-term planning is carried out at lower levels in an organisation, at middle manager and supervisor levels.

Long-term plans are not as detailed or measurable as short-term plans – the longer the time horizon of the plan, the less certain managers can be about outcomes. They are usually made at higher levels of management. Long-term plans are also known as strategic plans.

Responsibilities

The human resource manager is responsible for:

- manpower planning – forecasting the number and type of staff the organisation needs in the future

- attracting sufficient candidates with the right qualities so that the organisation can select the best people for jobs

- training and developing staff so that they perform to the highest level possible

- designing jobs that are stimulating and interesting so that the organisation gets the best out of people

- ensuring that organisational structures and procedures allow employees to express their views, ideas, complaints and worries

- designing ways of introducing and managing change that minimise any negative impact on individuals and groups

- providing fair and legal procedures for discipline and grievances, and ensuring that they are applied uniformly throughout the organisation

- keeping within the law on issues such as health and safety, equal opportunities, sex and race discrimination, and termination of employment

- dealing with trade unions, staff associations, disputes, industrial tribunals and other legal actions.

To successfully implement a human resource plan, a manager needs to obtain the cooperation of everybody within and outside the organisation who could affect its outcome. Getting the optimum return from each person is in the interest of the whole organisation. The human resource manager needs to motivate and enlist the cooperation of customers, suppliers, the manager's own staff, senior managers and people in other departments.

Having made a plan and put it into action, a manager constantly reviews progress to ensure that the plan is working properly – the manager needs to check that if the current activities are continued, the desired outcome will be achieved. If not, the manager makes modifications to current activities to correct the situation. The manager usually has regular feedback about progress available through management information systems (MIS) and procedures.

As in all aspects of management, and in all functions in an organisation, the quality of communication is vital to success. All staff should receive regular feedback from their managers about how they are performing against the standards demanded by the organisation.

Managers deploy resources to the different tasks that need to be done to achieve objectives. Provided that all tasks are completed successfully (that is, each meets its targets for quality, quantity, time and costs), an organisation should achieve its overall objectives. Management information systems and operating procedures are designed to give information to ensure that everyone is pulling in the same direction. Coordination is a unifying and harmonising activity.

Policy making

Human resource management takes place at different levels in an organisation. At higher levels, human resource planning is more general and strategic; at lower levels, more tactical and specific.

Senior managers and directors formulate and set general human resource strategies. These are used by human resource managers to draw up detailed plans to implement the policies, and individual human resource managers may be responsible for specific aspects of personnel management such as:

- equal opportunities policy

- equal pay policy

- non-discrimination policy

- health, safety and welfare policy

- pension arrangements

- sick pay policy

- management policies for morale and motivation

- management policies relating to changes needed for future success.

Human resource planning in a changing global business environment

Because of the dynamic nature of the modern global business environment, human resource planning is an ongoing process. A business needs to alter its objectives continuously to take account of:

- new technology

- emerging world markets

- green and ethical issues

- workforce demands.

New technology

The rate of technological change is accelerating. It permeates every aspect of business activity: design, production planning, production control, automated production, warehousing, despatch, transportation, administration systems, management information systems, and so on. Robotics, automation and information technology are still in their early stages of development. As progress continues, the nature of industry and commerce will change even more dramatically. Human resource plans should consider the

Figure 4.1: Influences on human resource planning

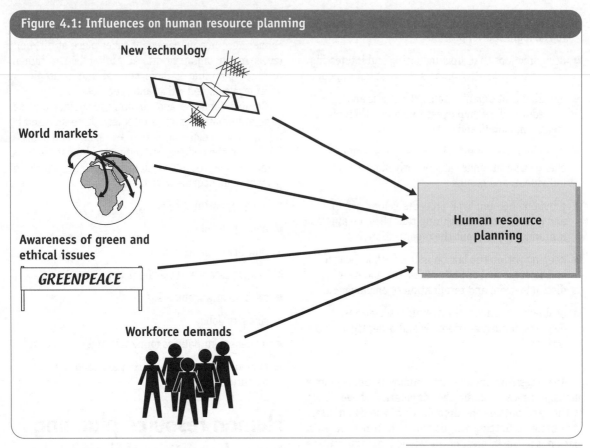

New technology

World markets

Awareness of green and ethical issues

GREENPEACE

Workforce demands

Human resource planning

likely impact of technological change on the type of employees that the organisation will require in the future as well as considering the training implications for existing employees.

World markets

International companies are able to exploit world markets, enjoying considerable economies of scale, particularly as transport costs continue to fall in real terms. Worldwide production facilities, automation and access to instant information anywhere in the world are changing the nature of companies. Businesses which do not deliver quality goods and services on time are being bypassed. Consumers demand more choice and new products. Product life cycles are shortening and product development time scales have had to speed up. Designer products are replacing traditional versions. Internet selling has become firmly established. Organisations require highly flexible workforces to survive in such an environment.

Green and ethical issues

Businesses have to maintain a good relationship with their customers and suppliers. That relationship can be threatened by bad publicity, and companies need to be

▼McDonald's is often a target for demonstrators protesting against its perceived unethical and environmentally unfriendly business practice

aware that they are scrutinised by many pressure groups that seek to publicise unfair or unethical practices. Greenpeace, for example, protests against environmentally unfriendly practices, and it sometimes targets actions against individual companies as well as putting pressure on business as a whole. The Consumers' Association, best known perhaps for its magazine *Which*, highlights unfair commercial practices such as overpricing or unacceptable levels of service.

There have been many examples of pressure groups staging high-profile demonstrations against individual companies and organising boycotts of their products. In such an environment, organisations need to consider their working practices very carefully, and they need to recruit and train their staff to be aware of, and sensitive to, green and ethical issues.

Workforce demands

Conditions at work have improved enormously, compared with say a hundred years ago, but employee expectations continue to rise. Employees demand better working conditions and a better quality of working life. They want to be consulted about matters that affect them at work. They certainly have higher expectations about work than previous generations; people are not likely to be committed and loyal to employers that do not consider their needs and expectations. They want job satisfaction, and they know how to get it. Human resource plans need to offer suitable training, development, motivation and rewards to satisfy employees and to ensure that those people with the highest skills and expertise are attracted to, and retained by, the organisation.

Manpower planning and internal staffing resources

One of the most important plans the human resource manager makes is the manpower plan. This sets out the number and type of employees that will be required by an organisation in the future. Generally, this manpower plan covers a period of anything from one to five years.

The first step in manpower planning is to conduct a skills audit and assessment of an organisation's employees. This should provide a comprehensive picture of the supply of labour available to the organisations from internal sources; in other words, it examines the skills, attributes and potential of the organisation's current employees. The audit should be based on a manpower inventory, consisting of computerised personnel records on each employee covering:

- age, gender and marital status
- date employment commenced
- how the employee first heard of the vacancy with the organisation
- job title
- department, section and job location
- employment status (hourly, full-time, part-time, shift, etc.)
- previous job titles within the organisation
- work experience within the organisation
- previous work experience with other employers
- performance and attainment
- qualifications
- training and development
- potential for transfer and/or promotion.

All the information from the manpower inventory can be analysed not only to determine the manpower resources that the organisation currently possesses but also to identify important trends which may have implications for its future labour requirements. Note that the inventory should retain the records of employees that are no longer with the organisation, and ideally include the reasons why people left.

The data in a manpower inventory provides an opportunity for measuring and analysing:

- labour turnover
- labour stability index
- sickness and accident rates
- age structure of the workforce
- succession.

Labour turnover

The labour turnover ratio is used to measure the total number of employees leaving an organisation in a given period of time, usually a year. It is calculated in percentage terms using the formula:

$$\text{Labour turnover} = \frac{\text{Number of employees leaving over specific period}}{\text{Average number of people employed}} \times 100$$

Let's consider an example. Link Computers had 4,000 employees on average in 1999. If 1,000 employees left the company during the year, its percentage labour turnover would be:

$$\text{Labour turnover} = \frac{1,000}{4,000} \times 100 = 25\%$$

A labour turnover ratio of 25 per cent is generally considered acceptable. It is when the rate approaches 30 per cent or more that alarm bells generally start ringing. High labour turnover might be indicative of a number of problems: there could be poor recruitment, with 'wrong' people being selected for jobs, low levels of motivation within a department, or employee dissatisfaction with unfavourable wage rates or working conditions. It may be that the induction process is failing and new employees are not being made to feel comfortable.

It is important that labour turnover is continuously measured to warn of potential problems so that management can take appropriate action. Replacing employees disrupts efficiency and creates recruitment and training costs. For a business to meet the objectives of its manpower plan, it is important that it minimises labour turnover.

Labour stability index

The labour turnover ratio is a rather general measure. A more subtle indicator is the labour stability index which is calculated using the formula:

$$\text{Labour stability} = \frac{\text{Number employed with more than 12 months service}}{\text{Total number of staff employed one year ago}} \times 100$$

This index denotes stability because it emphasises those employees that stay rather than leave. The importance of this index can be illustrated by developing our example. Suppose Link Computer's rival Macrosoft employs 4,000 people. In 1999, it also loses 1,000 members of its workforce. Macrosoft has a labour turnover rate of 25 per cent, the same as Link Computers. However, unlike Link Computers which lost 1,000 employees who were employed at the beginning of 1999, Macrosoft only lost 100 employees employed at the beginning of the year and replaced them (ten times on average) with a succession of short-term temps. We can use the labour stability index to show the stability of both organisations.

$$\text{Link Computer's stability} = \frac{3,000 \times 100}{4,000} = 75\%$$

$$\text{Macrosoft's stability} = \frac{3,900 \times 100}{4,000} = 97.5\%$$

Macrosoft has a far more impressive stability rate, which means it has managed to retain a much higher proportion of its experienced staff.

Sickness and accident rates

It is important that an organisation keeps a record of its sickness rates. It needs to ascertain whether staff are on sick leave for work-related or non-work reasons. Overall disruption can be minimised by identifying the cause of illness and its likely short- and long-term effect on employees' ability to carry out their tasks. Sickness rate is measure by the formula:

$$\text{Sickness rate} = \frac{\text{Number of working days lost per year due to illness}}{\text{Total number of available working days}} \times 100$$

Under the Health and Safety at Work Act 1974 an organisation is required by law to investigate and keep a detailed record of its accident rates. Accidents can be caused by factors such as insufficient safety training, stress, a lack of safety equipment or poor motivation. All of these factors can result in ineffective working practices and reduced efficiency. Keeping records enables an organisation to protect itself from legal action and to identify and deal with the causes of accidents before problems escalate.

Age structure

The information on the age structure of the workforce – analysed by different categories of employees – is useful for several reasons. It will highlight a potential staff shortage problem that might be caused by a large number of employees all reaching retirement age during a relatively short period of time in the near future. It might show that a particular age group dominates certain positions within the company, frustrating the promotional aspirations of other employees.

A detailed analysis of the age structure of the workforce, when linked to the skills audit, can also be of considerable value when deciding upon the allocation of training opportunities. For example, an organisation's short-term objective might be to train all its employees to use a new form of computer technology by the end of the year. When deciding who should receive training, the organisation needs to know which employees already possess the required skills and which employees are nearing retirement age, as training people who are shortly to leave the company would not be cost effective.

Succession

The manpower inventory also allow plans to be made that cater for the effects of retirement or possible resignation among supervisory and managerial staff. This gives rise to what is known as succession requirements. An organisation needs to know if it has the right staff to promote or transfer into the vacant managerial positions. It requires information on employees that can be lined up as potential replacements. Some may already display the qualities necessary for promotion and can therefore fill positions arising in the immediate future; others may have been identified as potential replacements after undergoing further training and development and, in this case, can fill positions arising over the next few years.

The succession requirements also have to take account of the additional staff transfers and promotions arising from the downward chain reaction caused by a single replacement further up the organisation's hierarchy. If, for example, a regional sales manager is promoted to fill a vacancy arising from the retirement or resignation of the national sales director then this has a knock-on effect; the regional sales manager position needs to be filled, with the result that the company has to plan and organise several other promotions and/or transfers.

Succession analysis identifies any managerial and supervisory posts that face a weak replacement position and, for this reason, the assessment of staff must be a continuous process.

Manpower planning and external labour market factors

As well as the continuous analysis of the internal staffing resources, manpower planning must also be supported by monitoring the availability of labour from external resources. If an organisation fails to monitor the pool of potential recruits in the working population at both local and national level then it runs the risk of not being able to satisfy any additional manpower requirements from external sources. For example, an organisation might assume that it can easily recruit web designers from the local labour market. If it discovers that people with these skills are in very short supply, it might have to set salaries at a much higher level than is anticipated in the manpower plan to attract suitable applicants. The repercussions can be considerable, and the organisation's objectives may have to be reviewed and modified.

Local external sources

When assessing the extent to which future manpower requirements can be satisfied from local labour markets, manpower planning must take account of:

- demographic trends, with particular emphasis on the overall size and age structure of the local working population

- developments in the local transport system that determine the effective catchment area for labour

- housing and the availability of different types of accommodation

- environmental developments, that influence the attractiveness of the area as a place in which to live

- the local effect of any changes in the government's regional and urban development policies

- unemployment rates, and the availability of workers with particular skills, qualifications and experience

- the availability of part-time and casual labour

- local competition for labour, and its impact on pay rates and fringe benefits

- the quality of local education and training providers.

National external sources

An organisation must also consider the extent to which its ability to meet its manpower requirements may be influenced by national factors. National policies, demographic trends and developments can affect the ability of the organisation to recruit certain types of labour, and can have implications for salary levels and the conditions of employment.

Manpower planning must therefore also take account of:

- national demographic trends, particularly any implications for the growth of the working population

- economic trends which affect the demands for different types of labour – in today's economy, for example, there is greater demand for people with practical science and technology skills and those with customer service skills required in call centres

- education and training trends, such as central government measures, which change the emphasis and structure of university courses and the provision of technical and vocational education in schools and colleges

- new legislation, including government policies and European Union directives on wage and salary negotiations, the role of staff associations and trade unions, equal pay, sex discrimination, employment protection, working time and industrial relations.

Statistical analysis

There is a great deal of statistical information, from government and private sector sources, relating to the impact of local and national factors on the labour market. For example, the case study below reports on labour market conditions in south-east England. This has been taken from a Department for Education and Employment (DfEE) briefing, one of a series of reports relating to a national skills summit focusing on a skills shortage within the regions. This type of analysis is particularly useful to any organisation drawing up a manpower plan in support of a business relocation or the setting up of a new business. The DfEE briefing clearly indicates the key industries within the south east, where the shortages exist and the strategies that are in place, and will need to be in place in the future, to meet the shortages.

Discussion point

Do you feel that an area like south-east England will ever be able to solve its skill shortage problems?

CASE STUDY

South east region skills summit

The south east is the largest region in the United Kingdom, and as one of its economic powerhouses, it is important to the improved competitive position of the nation. But economic growth here has been slower than that of European competitors.

The region has a number of key industries – advanced manufacturing, pharmaceuticals and biotechnology, and information and communications technology. Due to the technology-led nature of these industries which require rapid changes to the production process, they are highly reliant on the continual skills development of their current and future workforce to maintain their competitive edge. Although lower than at the end of the 1980s, the south east has the highest reported level of skills shortages in the UK.

The most acute skills shortages have been identified as managerial skills, professional and technical skills in advanced manufacturing and support services, information technology skills, integrated language skills, particularly for exporters and around transport nodes, and employability skills in all sectors.

Skills training was seen as concentrating on medium and low skills delivery, with a large number of competing suppliers. In many cases, high skills levels training was seen as being unmet or poorly met due to a lack of collaboration or resources. A significant amount of skills development is already taking place at national and local level, but there are a few key issues where action at the regional level would be more appropriate. The development of a regional skills strategy should resolve these issues and provide a framework for the coordination of local activities.

In the short term, there are a number of ideas for action which will enhance workforce skills and ensure that the south east region competes with the best. These ideas are:

- developing pilot centres of excellence to provide advanced manufacturing and high level information technology with the skills fundamental to the regional economy

- establishing a south east 'skills for business' unit to identify skill shortages, to transmit this information to training providers and to provide a brokerage service for employers with high-level skill needs

- coordinating a targeted regional marketing campaign to provide individual businesses with information to benchmark themselves against competitors, and link this to the provision of locally delivered management development

- developing and delivering a universal and targeted approach to the introduction of individual learning accounts (ILAs).

More generally it is felt that businesses need to be more communicative about their needs to schools and young people. They need to promote the development of key skills at school rather than ask for qualifications. There also needs to be a revolution in attitudes to instil status in vocational qualifications. Public/private sector partnerships can help by laying foundations in secondary schools for developing a good attitude to learning.

Source: Skills and Enterprise Briefing, DfEE, November 1998

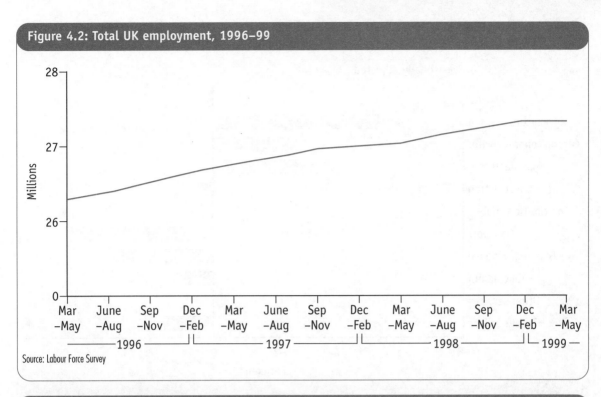

Figure 4.2: Total UK employment, 1996–99

Source: Labour Force Survey

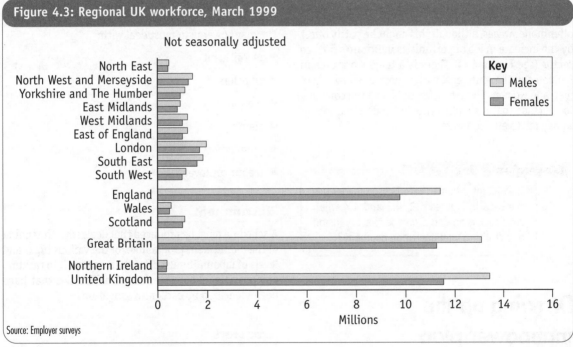

Figure 4.3: Regional UK workforce, March 1999

Not seasonally adjusted

Source: Employer surveys

Other information may be presented as statistical charts and diagrams. These provide indicators on what is happening within the wider national economy. Any manager drawing up a manpower plan would have to take into account some of the trends and associated factors shown in Figures 4.2, 4.3 and 4.4. Figure 4.2, for example, shows that total employment in the United Kingdom was rising consistently in the late 1990s.

Figure 4.3 shows the number of men and women willing and able to work in each region and country of the United Kingdom.

A Canadian insurance company considering the possibility of establishing an operation in the UK would find these tables helpful in analysing the main features of the labour market. It would note that unemployment is reducing, which might mean that it would need to

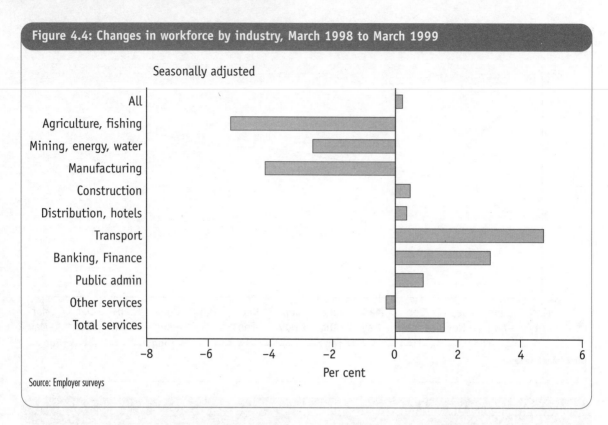

Figure 4.4: Changes in workforce by industry, March 1998 to March 1999

Source: Employer surveys

offer higher wages, although this might be partly offset by the increase in job opportunities in Britain's finance sector (see Figure 4.4). There is a large workforce in London and the south east with almost an equal mix of men and women. These factors could lead the company to conclude that it should locate in London, but expect to pay relatively high wages.

Drawing up the manpower plan

Having identified the strengths and weaknesses of an organisation's existing workforce and the external labour market factors impacting upon its ability to recruit and retain labour, a manpower plan can then be devised. This plan relates the future availability of labour to the organisation's future demand for labour.

The manpower plan must deal with:

- recruitment
- transfers
- redundancy
- training
- productivity
- labour turnover.

Recruitment

A schedule must be produced that deals with the timing of the recruitment programme for the various types and levels of labour. It must set out an approach to tackling any possible labour recruitment difficulties that have been identified by earlier investigations.

Transfers

The manpower plan needs to cover the future redeployment of existing employees between various jobs, departments, sections and locations. The plan covers not only relocations within existing premises but also any transfers involving proposed movements of employees to different geographical locations where the organisation operates.

Redundancy

If some jobs have become obsolete, or the organisation needs to reduce its activities in certain areas, it needs a programme for redundancies. This must cover the timetable and selection procedure for redundancies and/or early retirements, and the determination of redundancy payments and pensions. The plan must also specify how the organisation intends to assist redundant employees in their search for alternative employment.

Training

This section of the manpower plan deals with the duration, structure and content of training and apprenticeship courses. It should cover induction and training of young recruits and the training and retraining courses for existing employees. Details should be provided on how the training programme takes account of changes in technology, working methods and other developments that require the acquisition of new skills and techniques.

Productivity

Recruitment, selection, training and promotion measures are designed to ensure that the best possible people fill existing and future positions. However, they must be supported by action so that all employees can work more productively. There are different ways of measuring and setting targets for productivity depending upon the nature of the organisation's activities. For example, a manufacturing organisation may aim to reduce unit labour costs by a minimum of 5 per cent; a fast-food outlet's objective may be to raise the value of sales per head by 8 per cent.

The manpower plan should describe changes that will contribute to higher productivity. It needs to consider these potential sources of greater efficiency:

- the application of new technology to production methods and administrative procedures

- measures designed to reduce labour costs through the reorganisation of working methods that make a fuller utilisation of manpower resources

- the role of training programmes in raising productivity through the development of new skills and techniques

- the use of incentive schemes to encourage higher productivity, such as bonus payments for reaching higher output targets, sales commissions and profit-sharing schemes allowing employees to gain some of the benefits of higher productivity.

Productivity can also be raised by measures aimed at improving industrial and human relations within the organisation. If employees feel valued and get job satisfaction, they are likely to be better motivated and more productive.

Labour turnover

A high labour turnover is bound to affect the quality and level of output as well as incurring manpower costs associated with the recruitment and training of labour. Having identified the avoidable causes of manpower wastage, the plan may suggest some remedies to reduce wastage:

- giving pay rises to employees that might be poached by rival businesses that are offering higher pay to attract workers with skills that are in short supply

- introducing a productivity scheme so that employees' effort and attitude are more closely reflected in their earnings

- updating the pay and salary structure so that differentials are in line with the generally accepted view of the value and importance attached to different jobs

- improving career and promotion prospects and ensuring that promotion criteria are seen by employees to be fair, and that effort and excellence are suitably rewarded

- identifying sources of stress and conflict between employees, management and supervisory staff and introducing methods to improve industrial and human relations

- improving recruitment, induction, promotion and training programmes – by placing the right person in the right job and ensuring that they receive adequate support.

Having produced a manpower plan, every effort must be made to ensure that it is continually updated in the light of both internal and external developments that affect the organisation's ability to meet its demand for labour.

BUILD YOUR LEARNING

Keywords and phrases

You should know the meaning of the words and phrases listed below. Go back through the last 10 pages of the unit to check or refresh your understanding as necessary.

- Age structure
- Human resource planning
- Labour stability index
- Labour turnover ratio
- Manpower plans
- Sickness rates
- Succession requirements

Summary points

- Human resource planning helps an organisation to operate more efficiently by having the right labour, in the right place, at the right time and cost.

- Human resource planning operates in a changing business environment which is influenced by technological, market and environmental developments, and workforce expectations.

- The manpower plan sets the number and type of employees that will be required in the future.

- Manpower plans should be based, in part, on an internal manpower inventory which provides data for the analysis of labour turnover, the labour stability index, sickness and accident rates, age structure and succession.

- The plan also has to take account of external labour market factors, including local and national demographic trends, transport, housing, the environment, education, training, government and EU policies, and the state of the economy.

Recruitment and selection

NO MATTER HOW SOPHISTICATED the technical means of production, the ultimate success of an organisation depends upon the quality and contribution of its workforce. It follows that an organisation must have both an efficient recruitment policy and an efficient selection procedure to ensure that it has a workforce of the highest possible quality. This is as important for the highly capital-intensive industries as it is for the more labour-intensive sectors of the economy such as retailing and the service industries. In capital-intensive industries, such as petrochemicals and power generation, a failure to maintain standards (in terms of either skills or attitudes) in a relatively small workforce can have huge repercussions both on the level and quality of output and the safe operation of the plant.

Companies may need to recruit for several reasons. The growth of an organisation can generate additional demand and therefore create a need for extra labour. External influences such as technological developments can change job roles within the organisation, creating a need to recruit new people with specific skills. Alternatively, vacancies can be created through resignation, retirement and dismissal.

Before embarking on the recruitment process, it is essential to ensure that there is actually a need to recruit somebody in the first place. Too often, organisations can assume that a change in working methods or staffing levels, or the introduction of new technology, means that another member of staff is required. A closer investigation may reveal that this is not the case. Perhaps the component tasks of the new job could be shared by other members of the department, through job enhancement, job redesign or job enlargement. Maybe some element of the job could be dispensed with all together. If new equipment and new technology is being introduced, it may be possible and even preferable to retrain existing members of staff, rather than recruit people who already possess the necessary skills or knowledge required.

So, companies should first consider whether it is actually necessary to recruit anyone at all.

The recruitment process

Once the need to take on new staff has been properly established, however, it is then necessary to go through the recruitment process. Figure 4.5 illustrates a tried and tested process that aims to reduce the risk of selecting the wrong person for the job.

Discussion point

Discuss the stages in the recruitment and selection process in the light of any job applications that you have made.

By following the logical approach set out in Figure 4.5 organisations can ensure that information is gathered in the right order, is relevant and that conclusions are based on sound reason. Organisations are encouraged to adopt a step-by-step approach, proceeding in this order:

- job analysis
- job description
- person specification
- finding suitable candidates
- choosing the best person
- taking references
- making appointments.

Job analysis

The first stage is to conduct a detailed analysis of the job, which may involve questioning the current job holder or observing the job holder at work. The information gathered is carefully recorded and analysed. Further information might be obtained through discussions with the job holder's manager or supervisor. The job analyst compiles a description of the main responsibilities of the job by asking:

- what are the main tasks of the job and how often do they need to be completed
- are any specialist technological skills required
- what mental processes are required to do the job
- is the job holder required to take decisions and use initiative
- what are the limits of the job holder's authority
- is the output from the job a part or a whole
- does the job holder have to work with others, or control the work of others
- what are the required performance standards and how are they measured?

Figure 4.5: The recruitment and selection process

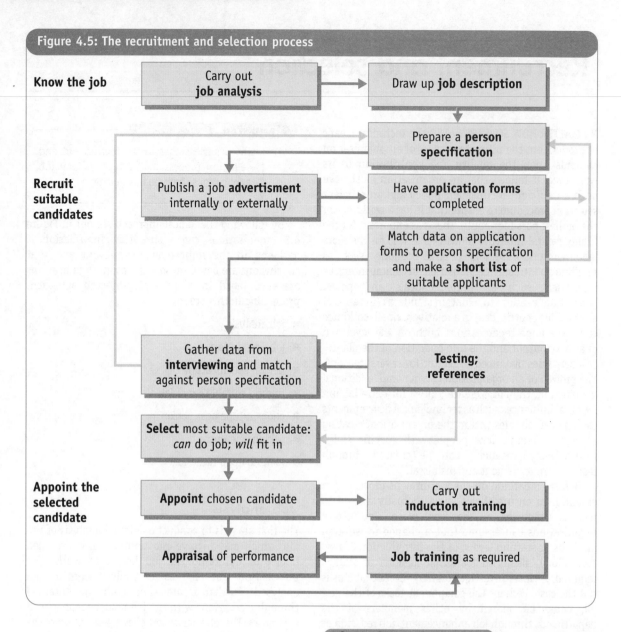

Job descriptions

When the job analyst has gathered all this information, it should be written down in a summary report setting out what the job entails. This summary report is normally called a job description. It contains two types of information: it describes the tasks of the job and it describes the behaviour necessary to actually do these tasks satisfactorily. This can clearly be seen in the example in Figure 4.6; this job description is typical of the type of part-time job held by many students.

Discussion point

Do you feel that the job description in Figure 4.6 provides a clear indication of the tasks associated with the job and gives sufficient indication of how they should be carried out?

Person specification

A person specification (sometimes called a personnel profile) describes the characteristics and attributes which a person needs to be able to do the job to the required standards. There are several ways of setting out this information. One approach is to follow a six-point plan, listing the requirements under broad headings:

- physical make-up – what should the job holder look and sound like

- achievements – what education, qualifications and experience does the applicant need

- specific skills – what special skills and talents are needed by the applicant

- interests – what sort of pastimes or hobbies would the ideal applicant follow

- personality – what motivation and temperament and attitude should the applicant have

- personal circumstances – what personal and domestic arrangements might the ideal person have?

Finding suitable candidates

The next stage of the recruitment process is to attract only those people who fit the company's person specification. The first task is to identify, accurately, where the ideal people can be found. They may be found doing a different job within the company itself; they may be found through the families and friends of present staff. If someone straight from school or college, or on a youth training programme, would be ideal, the company may want to contact the careers service. However, in many cases, it may be necessary to advertise the position more widely.

If a company needs to advertise for staff, it is important to think about the type of people it is trying to attract and the publications they read. For example, are the people the company is trying to attract more likely to be readers of *The Times* or *The Sun*? If the job is a very technical position, or highly specialised, it is

Figure 4.6: Job description for a part-time sales assistant

Job description

Job title: Part-time sales assistant

Directly responsible to: Store manager

Direct responsibility for: No one

Contact with: Manager, other sales assistants, personnel department, central service department, other stores and customers.

Job outline: To help to meet customer requirements by providing them with a high level of service and ensuring that they remain satisfied. To deal with customer complaints and requests efficiently, to offer advice when required and to process sales using the till system.

Job responsibilities: The sales assistant needs to maintain an up-to-date knowledge of all product ranges and new developments. As a company representative a professional, polite and sensitive manner should be adopted at all times. Whenever possible the company's own brand products should be promoted over those of its competitors.

Job requirements: All customer orders must be processed and logged correctly using the company system as soon as the order is received. Overall and individual sales targets must be met. Complaints must be dealt with politely and without delay.

Figure 4.7: Person specification for a part-time sales assistant

Physical apperance:
Smart personal appearance. Clear, articulate speech.

Achievements:
Four GCSEs at Grade C or above. No previous sales experience required, but would be an advantage.

Specific skills:
Good communication skills. Ability to listen to problems and offer practical suggestions. Willingness to learn. Competent with money.

Interests:
Any position of social responsibility or participation in team-related activity.

Personality:
Polite, pleasant and cheerful. Ability to deal calmly with aggravated customers and to cope under pressure. Good team worker.

Personal circumstances:
Reliable person, good time-keeper, living locally and willing to do additional overtime during the holiday periods.

more likely to attract suitable candidates if it is advertised in specialist and technical journals. For specialist and management jobs, the most popular medium for advertising is the relevant professional and trade press.

Job advertisements have to be carefully worded in order to attract the most suitable candidates for the job. Research suggests that there are four things that most applicants look for in a job advertisement. They are:

- details about the organisation – who would I be working for
- a clear description of the job – what would I be doing
- the location – where would I be doing it
- the salary scale – what financial reward would I get?

The advertisement should also make it quite clear how any interested person should apply, and state whether applicants need to submit a copy of their curriculum vitae (CV).

Advertising can be expensive. A quarter-page, black and white newspaper advert in the *Sunday Times* costs about £12,000. It is important that an advertisement is clear and precise so that a company gets a good return on its investment. In drafting advertisements, employers must respect the laws that relate to employment and recruitment.

- The Disability Discrimination Act 1995 states that an employer of more than 20 people must not discriminate against a disabled person in relation to the recruitment process, training, promotion opportunities or dismissal.

- The Equal Pay Act 1970 requires that equal pay is given to men and women doing the same sort of work or work of equal value.

- The Sex Discrimination Acts 1975 and 1986 make it unlawful to discriminate against persons, directly or indirectly, on the grounds of gender or marital status.

- The Race Relations Act 1976 requires that equal access to jobs and promotion is provided to people of equal ability irrespective of race, colour or creed.

- The Employment Rights Act 1996 set out employees' statutory rights from the point when they initially submit their CV or application to the point at which they leave the organisation.

Penalties for breaching these laws can be severe. Courts can impose heavy fines and companies have to meet the legal costs involved. Companies that fail to comply with the law can attract adverse publicity. The job advertisements shown here demonstrate how much care has to be taken when drawing up a suitable advertisement. None of these examples reflect any bias in terms of race, gender, age, marital status or disability.

Discussion point

Identify the possible legal pitfalls that a company might face with the type of job advertisements shown here.

▼ Job advertisements have to be carefully worded to comply with the law

Yard Person

Builder Center, one of the country's leading trade suppliers of building and timber products require a Yard Person to join the busy Hinchley Wood branch.

Duties include serving customers with general heavyside building materials, assisting in the general smooth running of the yard, receiving goods in and loading our delivery vehicles. Knowledge of the heavyside industry would be a definite advantage, and a fork lift truck licence is essential.

Please apply in writing with full cv to date, to: Peter Mayhew, Branch Manager, Builder Center, Station Road, Manor Road North, Hinchley Wood, Surrey, KT10 0SP.

BUILDER CENTER

Wolseley Centers is an equal opportunities employer and operates a 'no smoking' policy.

Blooming Marvellous

A successful mail order company specialising in child and maternity clothing, nursery products and services seek additional warehouse team members.

Successful applicants will possess a good understanding of various warehousing duties. These posts would best suit young enthusiastic individuals willing to learn about the mail order business and Supply Chain Operation.

In the first instance, applicants may telephone the Warehouse Manager on 020 8391 6806 for a quick appraisal of the post. Application forms will be sent out on request, alternatively, CVs can be sent to the following address

The Warehouse Manager
Blooming Marvellous Ltd
Unit C61 Barwell Business Park
Leatherhead Road, Chessington, Surrey KT9 2NY

You may also e-mail your application to:
Admin@bloomingmarvellous.co.uk
marked for the attention of the Warehouse Manager.

SECRETARY

Required for busy Accountants Office based in Twickenham

General Practice requires Audio Secretary for expanding business (min 69 WPM)

No experience of Accountancy required. You need to be accurate and computer literate. Knowledge of Word an advantage.

Full or Part time considered.

Please send C.V to:

**D.K Poynter & Co.
Enterprise House
5 Briar Road
Twickenham
Middlesex TW2 6RB**

Senior Data Installation Engineer

Sound and proven experience in voice, fibre optic and structured cabling systems coupled with effective site management skills and a 'customer care' approach.

This is a permanent position working for a large organisation dedicated to providing best of breed solutions for their customers and supported by a technically experienced and committed networking division. The positions will predominately be based on project sites in the S/SW/W London areas. Salary and Benefits negotiable and dependant on experience.

Please send CV to PO Box 1472, Newspaper House, 34-44 London Road, Morden, Surrey, SM4 5BR.

Figure 4.8: A standard application form

Standard Application Form (SAF) AGCAS/AGR approved form			Name of Employer		
Please complete this form in BLACK ink or typescript. Check employer literature or vacancy information for correct application procedure.			Vacancies or training schemes for which you wish to apply Job function(s) Location(s)		
Current/most recent University/College					
First name (BLOCK LETTERS)			Surname (Dr, Mr, Mrs, Miss, Ms) (BLOCK LETTERS)		
Out of term address (BLOCK LETTERS): give dates at this address			Term address (BLOCK LETTERS) give dates of address		
Postcode Telephone			Postcode Telephone		
Date of birth	Age	Country of birth	Nationality/Citizenship	Do you need a work permit to take up employment in the UK?	
Secondary/Further Education Name of Schools (s)/ College(s)	From	To	Subjects/courses studied and level (eg GCSE, O, A, AS, H, IB, BTEC, GNVQ) Give examination results with grades and dates		
First degree/diploma University/College	From	To	Degree/diploma (BA, HND, etc.)	Class expected/ obtained	Title of degree/ diploma course
Main subjects with examination results or course grades to date, if known					
Postgraduate qualifications University/College	From	To	PhD/MA/ Diploma etc.	Title of research topic or course Supervisor	

Choosing the best person

Once a business has attracted applicants who match the person specification, the next stage is to gather information on each applicant. The main sources of information are:

- application forms
- curricula vitae (CVs)
- interviews
- testing
- taking references.

Application forms

The purpose of an application form is to gather information about the candidate that will give definite clues about personal attributes, qualifications, experience, and so on.

Businesses make decisions about which candidates to short-list by comparing the information on application forms to the person specification. Promising candidates are then requested to attend an interview; unsuccessful applicants receive a letter explaining that they have not been successful with their application on this occasion. The interview process is costly; it is time-consuming and disrupts managers' normal duties. It is important, therefore to short-list applicants both to minimise costs and to ensure that the expectations of unsuitable candidates are not falsely raised.

The completed application form is regarded as part of a candidate's contract of employment. It is important that no false claims are made or any deliberate misinformation is included, otherwise the contract of employment could be rendered void, resulting in dismissal.

Discussion point

Suggest how you might check on the accuracy of the information included on an application form.

Discussion point

Look at the CV in Figure 4.9. What type of work do you feel might suit Rachel Flencher?

Curriculum vitae

A **curriculum vitae** (CV) is a document usually initiated and prepared by a job seeker. It serves a similar purpose to an application form. It supplies a prospective employer with the job seeker's details. It should include information on:

- personal details
- education
- qualifications
- work experience
- interests
- ambitions.

In addition, the CV should include any other information that would be likely to persuade a prospective employer to consider granting an interview. It should also offer at least two referees who will corroborate what has been claimed – one should be a character reference and the other a work reference. The CV should provide a pen picture of the values and skills a job seeker can bring to any prospective employer.

Selection interviews

The structure of the selection interview depends on the nature of the vacancy and the size of the organisation. For some jobs, applicants may be interviewed just once on a one-to-one basis; for others, they may be seen by a succession of people or by a panel made up of people from the organisation who are likely to be involved with the person who eventually fills the vacancy.

In large organisations, it is usual for the applicant to be interviewed by a member of the personnel department, and by the manager of the department in which he or she will work if selected. It may also be considered important for others within the organisation to be included in the selection procedure, such as supervisors, directors or heads of department, and this to some extent may govern the type of interview chosen. In a small organisation that does not have a specialist personnel department, the interview may be conducted by a senior member of the staff from the department that has the vacancy needing to be filled.

The purpose of the interview is to find the right person for the job. The interview has two main objectives:

- assessing the suitability of the candidate for the position
- providing information abut the job and the company.

Figure 4.9: An example of a curriculum vitae

Curriculum Vitae

Rachel Flencher
14 Fosters Avenue
Founder
Brighton
Sussex
BN1 SJ2

01273 452453
Rachelflencher@abc.com

D.O.B. 16 06 1979

Education

1997–2000 University of Bridgetown, Suson, Herts

BA Single Honours in English and Business Administration
Projected Grade: Upper second

1990–1997 Finhill School, Ickfield Road, Founder, Brighton

June 1997	A level	Business studies	A
		English literature	C
		Spanish	B
June 1995	GCSE	Art	B
		Business studies	A
		English language	A
		English literature	A
		Geography	C
		History	C
		Maths	C
		Science	C
		Spanish	B

Additional achievements

- University swimming team captain
- Participant in local community work
- Secretary for university council
- University magazine editor
- Participant in several piano concerts

Previous Employment

Life Guard	Souson Leisure Centre The Lanes Souson Herts	I obtained my gold life saving certificate and was responsible for maintaining pool safety. I helped teach some classes and dealt with queries. I also helped to launch the monthly family fun evening.
Sales Assistant (9 July 1996 – 14 July 2000) Brighton	Rosenights 6A Central Approach Founder	I received extensive till training and assisted with stock checks and cashing up procedures. I dealt with customers on a one-to-one basis and liaised with other branches when compiling special orders.
Pizza Assistant (12 May 1995 – 8 July 1996)	Pizza House Broadway Lane Founder Brighton	I had to take customer orders and produce pizzas to time. I was in charge of short shelf tests and assisted with both stock checks and the waste procedure.

Hobbies and interests
Sport, in particular swimming and tennis, reading, listening to music, going to the cinema and cooking

Career aspirations
My main interest are in creative and persuasive writing. I feel that these skills would be of particular value in the following areas:-
a) Producing advertising copy
b) Customer communications
c) Magazine work
d) Public relations

I appreciate that my degree is only a starting point and I am both willing and anxious to pursue further studies in my chosen speciality.

References

Character references

Mr J Jones (previous emplyer)
Souson Lesiure Centre
The Lanes
Souson   BN1 S11

Academic references

Professor Julian Stevens
Combined Studies
University of Bridgetown
Souson   SG3 4HN

It is important to understand that the interview is a two-way process. The applicant is assessing the suitability of the job and the company, just as much as the company is assessing the suitability of the applicant. If the company's staff fail to communicate effectively in the interview, the organisation might have its job offer rejected by a potentially suitable candidate who gains the wrong impression about the company and the vacancy.

▲ It is important to realise that a job interview is a two-way process

In human relation terms, the interview is an interaction between people. The applicant behaves in response to the environment and the behaviour of the interviewer(s). It is therefore worth spending some time creating an atmosphere in which the interviewee feels at ease and free to talk. The interviewer's questions should be designed to get the candidates to talk about their work experiences and their lives. However, it is important to avoid asking any questions that may discriminate against a person or group of people. It is illegal to ask a question such as 'do you intend to start a family' which may suggest that the company might discriminate against applicants on the grounds of gender or marital status.

It is important to use open questions, which invite interviewees to give more information in their answers. Words like what, why, when and how help to keep questions open. An open question like 'how did you do your stocktaking' invites a very different answer from a closed question such as 'did you do stocktaking'. Phrases such as 'tell me about ...' or 'can you explain ...' should produce answers that give a great deal of useful information. Questions should not imply the answer by inviting a 'yes' or 'no' answer. For example, a question like 'I expect you were very busy in your job' will almost certainly get the answer 'oh yes, I was', leaving the interview none the wiser about the candidate. Answers to open questions can reveal clues about whether interviewees can do the job, whether they are motivated, and give some indication of how they cope in a variety of situations – including those where they are likely to be under pressure and stress.

Two further useful interviewing skills are probing for clues and active listening. If interviewees are to reveal their ability, experience, and motivation, they, not the interviewer, must do most of the talking. If an applicant's answer leaves doubt, or raises an interesting issue, it should be probed further. A response like 'I was responsible for the stock' may mean that the candidate kept the records up to date, or it could mean that he or she had full budget responsibility. The interviewer should aim to let the interviewee speak for at least 60 per cent of the interview. To do this, interviewers need to ensure they have prepared carefully.

Following recruitment, the interview may be used during a person's period of employment as an important tool to ensure that he or she is happy and performing well in the job. This may be part of an appraisal system. Some companies also give formal exit interviews when a member of staff leaves, which provides information on labour turnover and informs the recruitment process for a replacement.

Testing

Interviewing is an inexact process, and may not give sufficient information about some aspects of an applicant's ability, experience and personality. Additional data can be gathered by setting applicants tests.

Some people consider testing an invasion of privacy, others simply doubt its value. However, if tests are to be used, there is a strong moral obligation on the organisation to ensure that the tests chosen are valid and reliable for the purpose for which they are used. They should be conducted by a person who is competent, trained and qualified in their use and in the interpretation of the data collected. (Some testing systems require that the tester holds a licence before the tests can be conducted.)

Tests must be valid – that is, they must test what they are intended to test. If they do not, the test cannot be described as a valid predictor of successful job performance. Tests must be reliable – that is, they must be consistent in measuring what they are supposed to measure whenever they are repeated. In other words, you should obtain the same type of results if applicants are asked to retake the test.

There are several different types of test.

- **Aptitude tests**. These are used to discover the mental and physical capabilities of people who have no formal qualifications, or perhaps to establish whether someone has the potential for doing a particular job before placing him or her on a costly training programme.

- **Achievement tests**. In contrast to aptitude tests which seek to measure potential ability, achievement tests measure the skills and knowledge a candidate has already acquired. Keyboard knowledge, forklift truck driving and translating are examples of skills that can be tested in this way.

- **Intelligence tests** measure a person's intelligence quotient (IQ). People whose scores fall below a known minimum IQ for the job being filled would not be interviewed. It is important that intelligence tests are used precisely as directed, and they should always be conducted under the control of a psychologist.

- **Personality tests**, otherwise known as psychometric tests, assess a person's emotional make-up. They attempt to predict an individual's behaviour under different circumstances. Personality is described by plotting an individual's score against a series of factors.

- **Assessment centres**. These are used mostly today in the testing and selection of potential managers. The applicants spend time together – often one or two days – working on a problem and set exercises. Their behaviour is closely monitored during their time at the assessment centre and personality traits and leadership qualities are identified.

References

A reference is an opinion, usually in writing, of a person's character, ability, honesty and reliability in support of a job application. The problem with references is that it is usually impossible to obtain a detailed and accurate report on how candidates are performing in their present jobs from their current employers.

- It is unethical to contact an employer who may not be aware that an employee has applied for another job.

- Some employers do give references to current employees – for example, teachers and local government staff can get references from their current employers – but it is hard to know if these are accurate and unbiased.

- Personal relationships influence some referees more than job performance, even to the extent of writing a glowing reference to get rid of someone they do not like!

Employers are often cautious when writing references. There is no legal obligation to provide references on request, but most employers do. References must be accurate. Any false information, or any omissions that might cause a candidate to fail to be offered a job which he or she would have been offered had the correct information been given, may make a case for damages against the writer of the reference.

Making appointments

In the entire recruitment and selection process, it is illegal to set any standards, or ask for qualifications, experience or personal qualities that discriminate unfairly against men or women, minority racial groups, and the disabled. It is important for a business to keep a record of its reasons for appointing or rejecting candidates to show that legal obligations are being met. If the selected candidate is offered and accepts the job, the other candidates should be informed and thanked for their time and interest.

Ethical obligations

The personnel and development profession has a ruling body – the Institute of Personnel and Development (IPD) – which sets out codes of practice which should be followed by all practitioners, whether members of the institute or not. The institute published a code of professional conduct in 1995. This includes individual codes on:

- recruitment
- psychological testing
- secondment
- employee data
- redundancy
- career and outplacement consultants
- employee involvement and participation
- equal opportunities.

Figure 4.10 sets out the standards that the institute expects its members to respect. These IPD standards and ethics are demanding on the integrity of organisations and individuals, but there is no excuse in the normal course of events for failing to observe them.

Figure 4.10: IPD standards

IPD MEMBERS MUST RESPECT THE FOLLOWING STANDARDS

Accuracy
They must maintain high standards of accuracy in the information and advice they provide to employers and employees.

Confidentiality
They must respect their employer's legitimate needs for confidentiality and ensure that all personnel information remains private.

Counselling
They must be prepared to act as counsellors to individual employees, pensioners and dependents or to refer them, where appropiate, to other professions or helping agencies.

Developing others
They must encourage self-development and seek to achieve the fullest possible development of employees in the service of present and future organisation needs.

Equal opportunities
They must promote fair, non-discriminatory employment practices.

Fair dealing
They must maintain fair and reasonable standards in their treatment of individuals.

Self-development
They must seek continuously to improve their performance and update their skills and knowledge.

Source: The Institute of Personnel and Development Code of Professional Conduct

Discussion point

What costs might an organisation incur if its human resources staff fail to meet the IPD standards?

The success of a business depends very much on getting the right person in each job. It is important that expertise and experience should be deployed to achieve this goal. Businesses with effective recruitment processes gather information by a variety of means, from application forms to testing, and weigh the evidence very carefully against the person specification before arriving at a decision as to who to appoint.

Evaluating the recruitment process

Recruitment is a costly and time-consuming practice and it is essential that an organisation implements a means of evaluating its effectiveness and success. Recruitment success should not be determined by a simple measure of the number of recruits that remain with the organisation after a specific period of time (say one or two years) after appointment – although this measure contains useful information. Organisations need to evaluate every stage of the process.

The labour turnover rate can be used to indicate weaknesses or strengths in the recruitment process. For example, if labour turnover is high it may be that 'wrong' candidates are being selected or applicants are being misled about the requirements of a job. Low labour turnover, on the other hand, might suggest that the recruitment and training procedures are working successfully. However, evaluation is essential to ensure mistakes are rectified and costs reduced.

Getting the recruitment policy right can lead to significant improvements in an organisation's performance. This can be clearly seen in the Littlewoods' case study.

CASE STUDY

Littlewoods puts equal opportunities policies at the heart of its business objectives and has a long-established reputation as a leading-edge employer. It has begun a scheme, called Local Equal Opportunities Employment Strategies (LEOPUS), to ensure that recruitment at new stores matches its community.

The policy is linked to the business needs of Littlewoods, as the idea of the scheme is that this will increase the potential customer base.

LEOPUS was pioneered for the opening of a Littlewoods Index store in Oldham in 1996.

Littlewoods first established the number of full-time and part-time vacancies needed in the store. Once this was known, it approached local community and religious organisations, women's and disabled groups, Race Equality Councils (REC), jobcentres, the local authority and the regional training and enterprise council. Each of these groups provided information about the local population.

Fliers were then translated into the relevant ethnic community languages for the Oldham area, with the assistance of the REC. These included telephone numbers of the organisations which had aided Littlewoods, so a potential applicant could ring and speak to someone in their own language. The fliers were also dropped in certain residential areas with high ethnic minority populations and displayed in jobcentres. Littlewoods also hosted a freephone telephone number and held an open day at a local hotel. The approach led to 938 applications for the 60 jobs. The average at previous stores was 200.

One in three applicants were from ethnic minorities, as compared to 5 per cent normally. One quarter of these were subsequently employed. During the first six months of trading, sales performance at the store was higher than comparable stores.

Littlewoods estimates the performance improvement as a result of the scheme amounted to £123,499. Staff turnover at the new store is 5 per cent, compared to 25 per cent at comparable Littlewoods stores in the region.

As a result, the LEOPUS scheme is now used for all Christmas and new store recruitment by Littlewoods.

Source: *Personnel Today*, 23 September 1999

Discussion point

Why has Littlewoods' recruitment policy improved its performance?

The recruitment of a flexible workforce

The recruitment and maintenance of a flexible workforce is vital for an organisation if it wants to stay competitive. In recent years, the general composition of the workforce has altered to create a demand for more flexible working practices, such as flexitime, multiskilling (that is, employees trained in a variety of tasks) and job sharing.

Full time

Full time or 'core' employees are those staff that work what is considered to be a standard week, of $37^1/_2$ hours or more. Full-time workers benefit from increased pay and benefits and, until recently, had more employment rights. It is advantageous for an organisation to employ full-time employees because they can be trained more quickly to become multiskilled. The fast food restaurant chain McDonald's states that it takes four months to train a full-time crew member with basic skills, but eight months to train a part-time employee. Increasingly, organisations employ a select group of highly skilled core workers, and then supplement their workforce with cheaper part-time and temporary workers.

Part time

The rise in part-time workers can be attributed directly to the growth in the number of women choosing to work. Figure 4.11 shows that there are four times as many part-time female workers as there are male. Growing demand for more flexible hours has arisen as employees attempt to balance working with raising children. Although it is not a legal requirement, some employees allow mothers to return to work part-time after maternity leave or to participate in a job share scheme with another employee.

Discussion point

Suggest reasons for the different proportions of part-time working between regions.

Part-time positions are sometimes taken by employees as a 'hobby', to supplement other jobs or because there is no full time work available. For employers, the attraction of part-time working is that it can offer more flexibility. The standard nine-to-five

working day is becoming outdated, as businesses need to work more flexible hours to meet ever increasing customer demands. Part-time workers, students or school employees are beneficial because they can be used to cover evening and weekend shifts. Government legislation has been introduced to protect the rights of part-time employees and give them similar rights to full-time employees.

Temporary or casual

Temporary employees are used by businesses to:

- cover another employee's maternity leave
- assist with large orders or special projects
- cover periods of sickness or unforeseen absence
- help cope with seasonal changes in demand.

Employers are not responsible for training temporary workers and it is up to individuals to ensure that they maintain up-to-date skills and knowledge. Organisations can save time and money on recruitment by obtaining temporary workers through specialist employment agencies. The agency takes time to select suitable workers and deals with basic administration such as sorting out pay and national insurance. Recruitment agencies charge a fee for their work.

Figure 4.11: Part-time working, by region and gender, 1997

	Men		Women	
	Part-time workers (thousands)	As a percentage of employment	Part-time workers (thousands)	As a percentage of employment
North East	52	9.0	233	48.3
North West	129	7.9	583	44.1
Yorkshire and the Humber	102	8.4	465	47.5
East Midlands	78	7.3	426	48.8
West Midlands	104	7.7	473	45.8
Eastern	104	7.4	499	45.3
London	191	10.9	483	33.8
South East	200	9.6	778	46.1
South West	125	19.1	533	52.0
England	1,085	8.8	4,474	45.0
Wales	51	7.9	249	48.2
Scotland	93	7.7	433	41.9

Source: Labour Force Survey, Office for National Statistics

Contracted staff

In recent years there has been an increase in the number of people employed on fixed-term or fixed-task contracts. Fixed-term contracts offer employment for a specified period of time; fixed-task contracts offer employment until a particular task or project has been finished. By employing workers using fixed-term or fixed-task contracts, an organisation can ensure that its labour costs are no higher than they need to be, as it only employs people for specific projects or periods of high demand.

Contract of employment

In all recruitment procedures, an organisation needs to understand the **contract of employment**. The rights of employers and employees – the legal relationship between them – rests solely on the contract of employment. A contract is an agreement between two parties. The contract of employment sets out the basis on which the employee carries out the legitimate work of the employer in return for the payment of wages. The contract of employment is not a single, written document but a combination of both express and implied terms, and may be verbal as well as written. (An exception is an apprenticeship contract, which must be set out in writing.)

Express terms

Express terms are stated plainly, exactly and unmistakably during the making of the agreement. Usually, a letter of appointment is given to a new employee. This is a very important document because it sets out the details of the agreement between the two parties in writing, and it is usually accepted by the new employee in writing. The letter of appointment becomes the cornerstone of the contract and may be called upon in the event of a dispute between the employer and employee about the nature of the agreement.

In the event that a verbal offer is made, and a verbal acceptance is given, the agreement is based upon what was said during the interview and what was agreed during any discussions between the employer and prospective employee. Any additional detail about what the job entails – such as a job description, work rules or employee handbook – may also be called upon to clarify the details of the contract. So what is written, and anything that is said which the two parties intend to be binding upon them, is part of the contract of employment.

Fundamental rights of employees were first set out in statute law in 1963 and 1971. (Statute law is law enacted by Parliament and is the highest law in the land.) In 1978, the law was amended by the Employment Protection (Consolidation) Act. This gives employees the right to receive written particulars of the terms of employment. Under this Act, most employees are entitled to receive a written statement of the main terms and conditions of their employment within 13 weeks of starting work. In April 1993, a European Union directive reduced this time period to eight weeks. The written statement must include:

- the employer's and the employee's names
- the date upon which employment began, including any previous period of employment that is to be considered continuous
- the job title
- the payment scale or rate and the frequency of payment
- hours of work
- holiday entitlement and holiday pay
- sick pay and allowances
- pension schemes
- the amount of notice to end the contract
- disciplinary and appeal procedures, and grievance procedures.

If an employer fails to provide a written statement of the main terms and conditions of employment, an employee could exercise his or her legal right to ask an industrial tribunal to decide what ought to have been in the written statement. This is then imposed upon the employer. Employers with more than 20 employees are also obliged to ensure that every employee has a copy of (or access to) the disciplinary and grievance procedure.

Implied terms

It is impossible to predict the changes which might occur in the relationship between an employee and employer during the period of employment. To overcome this difficulty, the legal courts read implied terms into contracts which are necessary to allow the contract to work.

Some implied terms are reasonably straightforward. For example, all contracts of employment will be deemed to include common law duties, such as the duty of care (safety); in other words, each party has a duty not to jeopardise the safety of the other.

Employees also have a common law duty of obedience. The duty of obedience (although modified by both UK statute law and European Union laws and regulations) remains fundamental to employment relationships. If an order given by a supervisor is within the contractual authority of the employer, the employee has an obligation to obey or run the risk of losing his or her job.

Other implied terms are less clear. In many cases, we must look to the courts for precedents to give direction. In the 1970s, Lord Denning – then Master of the Rolls – suggested the test as to whether an implied term is to be read in, should be: 'has the law already defined the obligation or the extent of it? If so, let it be followed. If not, look to see what would be reasonable in the general run of such cases, and then say what the obligation shall be.' The obligation in such a case would be an implied term.

It is usually very difficult for a manager or employee to determine whether an employer is in breach of the implied terms of a contract. It is likely that a lawyer would be required to examine case law and advise the firm or individual. Case law is based on decisions given by a judge in one case, which then become precedents, providing guidance in all other similar cases. As a general guide, however, there will be implied terms in all contracts relating to:

- a duty to act with good faith towards the employer

- a duty of care, each party for the other

- a duty to maintain confidence and trust between the employer and the employee

- a duty of the employer to provide work, and a duty of the employee to carry it out conscientiously

- a duty of the employer to give reasonable support to all employees so that they can carry out their work

- similarly, the employer has a duty to support managers in their managerial duties.

There are some contracts into which particular implied terms are read. For example, a skilled craftsperson would be expected to know his or her craft and to practise it to an acceptable standard of quality and safety. This implied term about competence, expertise and due care not only applies to craft occupations but also to professional people as well. For example, teachers are expected to know their subjects and be able to communicate them to students in an acceptable fashion.

Some firms also negotiate agreements with trade unions. These collective agreements usually relate to wages and conditions of work. For example, a teacher's salary might be agreed between his or her employer and the National Union of Teachers during the annual pay negotiations. These agreements are not legally binding between an employer and the union but, once they are incorporated into an employee's contract of employment, they are binding upon both the employer and the employee.

There may be occasions when custom and practice is considered to be an implied term in the contract. Custom and practice is the term given to unofficial working practices operated by the workforce which are not covered by a specific rule or procedure. They are condoned by management but have never been 'agreed' by management. Custom and practice is hard to establish and courts tend not to be sympathetic to arguments that it constitutes an implied term of contract. The case *Devonald* v. *Rosser* [1906] defines a custom as something 'so universal that no workman could be supposed to have entered into this service without looking to it as part of the contract'. The definition in this case is still used by courts to determine whether something is custom or practice.

Statutory rights

In order to clarify matters, and to ensure that employee rights are protected from abuse by powerful employers, governments have introduced numerous employment laws in the past thirty years.

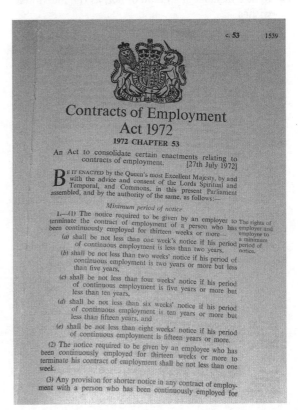

▲ Employment legislation sets out the statutory rights of all employees

It is not possible to waive these rights, so they are read into (or implied in) the contract of employment of all employees in the land. The main Acts of Parliament that relate to employment are:

- Equal Pay Act 1970
- Fair Employment (NI) Act
- Health and Safety at Work Act 1974
- Sex Discrimination Act 1975
- Race Relations Act 1976
- Employment Protection (Consolidation) Act 1978
- Employment Act(s) 1980 to 1996.

These Acts give employees the legal right:

- not to be discriminated against on grounds of race, gender or marital status
- to receive equal pay for work of equal worth
- to receive a written statement of the main terms of the contract
- to be a member of a union or not, as the individual wishes
- to receive notice of termination of employment
- to be paid redundancy payments depending upon age and length of service
- to work in safe and healthy conditions
- to receive sick pay
- not to be unfairly dismissed
- to be given a written reason for dismissal.

UK law is continuously being amended or supplemented to meet European Union (EU) regulations and directives, and human resource managers, therefore, need to maintain an up-to-date knowledge.

To summarise, a contract of employment consists of:

- the offer and acceptance of the job
- the written statement of the terms and conditions
- any other written and agreed documents
- common law duties and rights
- other implied terms
- collective agreements
- custom and practice
- UK and EU statutory rights.

Collectively, this has an impact on business in that the contract of employment gives both employers and employees rights and confers duties, one to the other. The notion of British justice applies as much in the workplace as in any other walk of life. The average manager and employee does not usually have (or need) a detailed knowledge of law. So, they need some sort of structure to work within – and some set of procedures to guide them.

Recruitment and the internet

Finally, before leaving the subject of recruitment, it is worth noting that traditional procedures and practices may be all set to change. As the article reproduced here suggests, the whole process of recruitment – and the legal framework supporting it – could be revolutionised in the future by the wider use of the internet by recruiters and job seekers.

Discussion point

Discuss the possible downside of on-line recruitment.

A site for sore heads

In the six weeks since its introduction, six people have found jobs through Talent Market in the US, the first "live employment auction" in the world. They have ranged from a low-level data entry position to a senior PR executive. The system works by job seekers registering their occupation, region, time, commitments and the duration they are willing to let the auction remain open and employers then "bid" for them.

Once the candidate has registered an interest in an offer, contract details can be swapped. There are no fees for anyone until there is a successful match. Thereafter, Talent Market takes a cut, based on the value of the contract: $250 for contracts up to $5,000, up to a maximum of $1,000 for contracts up to $15,000.

Troy Hatlevig, director of new markets for Monster.com, the on-line recruitment giant behind Talent Market, claims to be unconcerned about the slow take-up. "When you have something as fundamentally different, it will take people a while to

catch on. Monster.com had one success story in nine months."

Hatlevig might just have a point. Monster.com is believed to account for one third of on-line recruiting in the US. It has 226,000 job openings on its books, 1.5 million CVs tucked away in its memory banks.

So are human auctions the future of recruitment? British experts swing between cautious and dismissive.

"I very much doubt the British market is ready for such a product," says Mark Brewer, a partner in specialist HR recruitment firm Frazer Jones.

Talent Market claims otherwise. Once it has found its feet in the US, it promises "aggressive expansion" globally.

These days, there is little interest in whether the internet will transform the recruitment game, only in how. No one quite knows in what direction the market will lurch next, so many are wary of adventurous chancers with brash and apparently unworkable ideas. Despite this, it might just catch on.

By general consensus, UK employers are using the internet as a supplement to existing channels – the electrification of classifieds if you like, The Institute of Personnel and Development's recruitment survey launched in May found that in no sector is the internet the primary tool for attracting new blood. Just 1 per cent cited it as the most effective means.

Typically, the internet offers job seekers an alternative to picking up the phone. Given the choice of ringing up for an information pack or downloading it with a mouse click, 90 per cent will pick the latter. Job specs, background checks and even links into client websites are increasingly available on-line.

Yet the evidence of its rapidly rising stature is overwhelming. According to a Georgia Institute of Technology study, 64 per cent of managerial and professional job seekers have used the internet. A survey by Softworld found that 54 per cent of employers will use the internet to recruit by 2001.

The IPD research found that three years ago 14 per cent of respondents used the internet. By 1998, 19 per cent were using it. Yet , by this year, the figure had raced to 32 per cent. The internet is used most for professional jobs – 29 per cent – and for managers – 18 per cent. But even for skilled manual workers, 9 per cent of respondents said that they used it. For new graduates, the internet has significantly overtaken both the local and national press for publicising vacancies.

Personnel Today, 26 August 1999

BUILD YOUR LEARNING

Keywords and phrases

You should know the meaning of the words and phrases listed below. Go back through the last 17 pages of the unit to check or refresh your understanding as necessary.

- Achievement tests
- Aptitude tests
- Assessment centres
- Contract of employment
- Curriculum vitae
- Express terms
- Implied terms
- Intelligence tests
- Job description
- Person specification
- Personality tests

Summary points

- The ultimate success of an organisation depends upon an efficient recruitment policy and selection procedure in order to ensure that it has a workforce of the highest possible quality.

- The first stages of the recruitment process involve analysing the job, describing the main tasks, identifying the characteristics of the desired applicants through a person specification, and attracting the right candidates through suitably placed advertisements.

- The selection process involves weighing up the evidence which comes from application forms and CVs, ranking performances at interviews, evaluating the results of any aptitude, achievement, intelligence and personality tests, studying the results of any assessment activities and weighing up the opinions given in the references.

- The legal relationship between employers and employees rests on the contract of employment, which sets out the basis on which the employee carries out the legitimate work of the employer in return for the payment of wages.

- The contract of employment is a combination of clearly written express terms as well as implied terms which allow the contract to work.

Training and development

AN IMPORTANT PART OF manpower planing is the continual review, identification and update of training and development programmes. Factors such as the introduction of new technology or new working methods create training needs that have to be met if an organisation is to remain competitive. In recent years, there has been a growing employer awareness that training can play a significant role in developing a flexible and multiskilled workforce. As Figure 4.12 shows, in 1999 some 15.9 per cent of the UK population received job-related training.

Companies organise training and development programmes for many reasons. For example, training and development programmes may be introduced to:

■ motivate employees and increase job satisfaction, thereby reducing absenteeism and labour turnover

■ reduce wastage and accident rates by creating a consistent performance across the workforce

■ develop the skills of existing employees to cope with labour shortages

■ establish the most effective and efficient working methods in order to maximise productivity and remain competitive

■ reduce employees' resistance to change, perhaps deriving from the introduction of new equipment and the application of new technology.

The resources devoted to training can create substantial costs. It is important that training needs are correctly identified and the desired standard of skill is established. The training programme needs to be

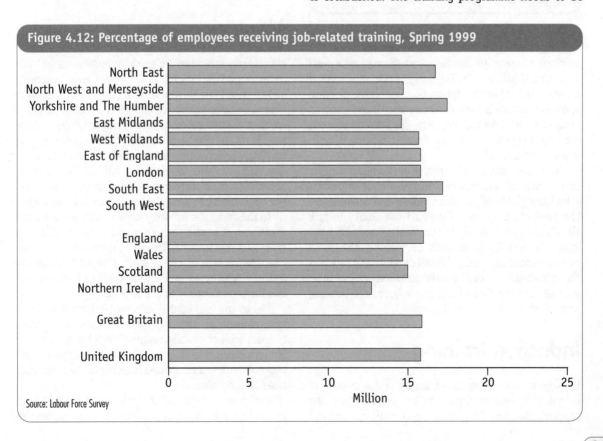

Figure 4.12: Percentage of employees receiving job-related training, Spring 1999

Source: Labour Force Survey

administered efficiently and evaluated – the results achieved by employees that have received training should be compared with the standard of performance it was hoped to achieve.

CASE STUDY
Mortgage Express

The mortgage lender Mortgage Express recognises the importance of careful monitoring and evaluation to ensure that the training and development process is cost effective.

When identifying a training need a manager at Mortgage Express consults with the employee. This initial consultation enables both the employee to take an active role in his or her own self-development and the manager to identify any untapped skills the employee may possess.

The manager writes a brief report on the employee's knowledge and skills level before training is undertaken and uses this report as a means of evaluating performance before and after training.

This process helps to ensure that the training is delivered in the most cost-effective way.

When making a decision about the skills which an employee needs to develop, many managers will conduct a skills analysis. The analysis takes the form of a very detailed job description that covers the physical and mental activities and necessary knowledge involved in the various tasks that comprise the job, and sets out the required performance standards – in terms of both quality and quantity.

Television sales assistants, for example, require certain manual and service skills: an ability to process sales through the till, an ability to use and demonstrate the products they are selling and the ability to talk clearly and persuasively to customers. They also have longer-term skill requirements; for example, they need to know about new technological developments such as the introduction of digital television. Employees can be assessed against these skills and appropriate training developed to cover any skills gaps.

Induction training

Employers use induction training as a means of introducing new employees to the organisation and ensuring that they have the necessary information and skills to perform their tasks to the required standard. Induction training can help to minimise labour turnover among new recruits by ensuring that they are made to feel welcome and are fully aware of what the job entails.

Induction training provides new employees with information about:

- the organisation's policies and objectives
- future career opportunities
- pay, training and fringe benefits
- health and safety
- the organisational structure and layout
- the requirements of the job
- colleagues and managers.

Good induction training programmes successfully balance the amount of information that needs to be conveyed with the length of time employees can sustain their concentration. An organisation makes the vast amount of information it needs to convey more digestible by varying the means by which it is communicated. It can develop an imaginative programme by using a combination of videos, OHPs, face-to-face discussions and printed matter such as company handbooks.

Mentoring

Mentoring schemes are used by businesses both to develop good working relationships between employees and to provide employees with the opportunity to learn new skills. Employees are allocated a mentor, usually an older or more experienced existing employee, whose role is to advise and answer their concerns. The employee benefits from advice on issues such as career development and managing change. The mentor benefits from an increased sense of responsibility and the opportunity to pass on their personal knowledge.

In the computer industry, organisations like ICL use mentoring schemes to help new graduates adjust in their first few months. These organisations recognise that the success of the scheme is dependant on the trainees' willingness and commitment to learn and the mentors' commitment to the scheme.

Mentoring is regarded as a cost-effective and less time-consuming training method because external trainers are not usually required. Mentoring schemes are less disruptive than off-the-job training methods because employees continue to perform their everyday tasks as they learn.

For some professional and senior posts, it has been found that mentoring is more effective if the mentor comes from an external organisation. The mentor would be expected to have a wide range of professional skills and experience and be able to offer independent advice and support.

Coaching

Coaching involves regular informal meetings between a manager and an employee, which allow discussion of the employee's performance in relation to the achievement of any objectives or targets. These informal performance assessment sessions enable a manager to identify an employee's strengths and weaknesses.

Managers should not use coaching solely as a means of criticising employees for their lack of progress or mistakes. Coaching sessions should be positive and employees should be encouraged to discuss any current problems with their manager. During the coaching session managers and employees should work together to identify potential solutions to any problems. Employees should be encouraged to explain the reasoning behind any solutions that they propose to use and managers should offer advice on possible implementation of the solutions. The employee and manager should work together to formulate a plan of action for the employee's future development.

Coaching provides managers with a means of both assessing an employee's suitability for promotion and analysing the way an employee has coped with any additional responsibility or extra authority. In order to be effective, coaching sessions should be properly structured. The manager's counselling and coaching skills clearly effect the success of any coaching programme, and managers should be encouraged to develop their skills if necessary. In order to maximise employee motivation and confidence, the manager should not simply issue instructions and make decisions on behalf of employees. Instead, the manager should fully explain any proposals they make and they should encourage employee participation.

In the 1990s, ICL's employee development programme recognised the contribution a manager's expertise and experience make to staff development. ICL encouraged managers to take an active role in the coaching process.

In our industry in particular, managers must understand that profits are made by people, not by products. Consequently they must effectively manage, invest in and develop their people if they and ICL are to enjoy long term success.
The ICL Way

This approach requires ICL managers to coach their staff by:

- rehearsing them through an important presentation and providing feedback during and after the presentation

- identifying and encouraging them to take on a new task which extends their job scope and provides experience in a new area

- discussing the qualities of a role model and getting them to identify the reasons for that person's success

- allowing them to go through a manager's in-tray and asking them to suggest how they might deal with each item

- discussing how the working environment can affect job performance and the factors that influence such an environment

- encouraging them to seek information relevant to their job and working environment by reading books, newspapers, magazines and internal publications

- delegating more responsibilities.

In-house training

In-house training schemes, often referred to as on-the-job training, provide employees with training and development using resources within the organisation. In-house training is used when the skills that an employee needs to acquire, or the nature of the task that needs to be performed, are not too complex. The trainee is placed in the actual working environment and uses the same materials and equipment that they will be required to use once the training has been completed. On-the-job training is advantageous because the trainee is not being taught in the artificial environment of a training establishment and then expected to perform the same tasks and use the skills they have developed on different machinery and equipment in the real working environment.

The success of in-house training schemes is dependent upon the teaching skills of the instructors. These may be supervisors or experienced employees. Instructors need to possess good communication skills and be able to break down, explain and prioritise each section of a particular task. It is vital that instructors are able to devote a sufficient amount of time to the training programme and that they do not appear bored with their role. Instructors should offer trainees encouragement and practical criticism to keep them motivated.

Compared with external training programmes, in-house training provides an organisation with greater control over both the content – the type of skills and information covered – and the structure – the way employees are taught – of the programme. The fast-food retailer McDonald's has developed a highly effective and organised in-house training programme. McDonald's recognises the importance of standardising the quality and appearance of its products so that a customer can be guaranteed a product that is of equal quality to products sold in every other McDonald's restaurant throughout the world. Each McDonald's restaurant trains new employees in areas such as health and safety, customer care and food hygiene using the same company manuals, techniques and videos. In-house training is used by McDonald's to enable the company to ensure that the training given to employees is directly relevant and that employees perform their tasks in the most effective way.

> **Discussion point**
>
> Identify other organisations which adopt a similar approach to staff training and development as McDonald's.

External training

Externally run training schemes are normally used by smaller organisations, as they usually have too few employees requiring training to justify expenditure on specialist training facilities and full-time instructors. In a small production company, there may be one manager, two supervisors and fifteen employees. Clearly, if the manager requires specialist performance management training it would not make sense to establish an internal training centre. Larger organisations may use external training courses for some off-the-job training, but the size of their labour forces and their financial resources make it more viable to set up their own specialist training facilities staffed by trained instructors.

External training courses, by definition, take place away from the real working environment. Employees may be taught new skills and learn to perform new tasks with equipment (and in situations) that may be different to that they will use and experience when they go back to work. The problems of transferring the skills learnt in the training environment back into the workplace environment can be overcome by providing a supplementary period of on-the-job training to enable trainees to gradually adapt their skills. Externally run courses are often more lengthy than in-house training programmes, but they can contribute to higher productivity and an increase in the quality of output.

McDonald's supplements its in-house training programmes with externally run courses. The company has established external training centres that provide training away from the normal restaurant environment. McDonald's has developed its own hamburger university in the USA, a national training management centre at East Finchley in the UK and several regional training centres.

The national training system

Training and enterprise councils

First established in 1990, **training and enterprise councils** (TECs) help businesses to identify their training needs. Sponsored by the government and led by local people, there are some 80 TECs in England and Wales. Their mission is to encourage economic growth through effective training and enterprise.

TECs can help finance company training programmes for young employees (people up to 24 years old) by providing training credits. The value of these credits depends upon the level of training being supplied by the company and can also be used to help with the costs of internal training. TECs also contribute to the training costs associated with modern apprenticeships.

In 2001, TECs are being abolished, and many of the their duties will be absorbed by the new **learning and skills councils**

Investors in People

TECs are also responsible for assessing firms that wish to be recognised publicly as **Investors in People**. The idea behind the initiative is that investing in people is one of the most effective ways of improving business performance. To gain recognition as an Investor in People, companies must meet exacting training standards.

Regardless of its particular business objectives, a firm is likely to benefit from being an Investor in People. Improvements can be expected in areas such as quality, motivation and customer satisfaction. A firm should gain a reputation for being a well-organised and efficient company. This can enhance the company's standing and help it to recruit employees.

Individual learning accounts

Individual learning accounts (ILAs) are designed to help individuals manage, plan and invest in their own learning and, therefore, take charge of their career and future. They are a sort of bank account into which the government, the individual and the employer all make a contribution, and the money is used to buy training and education, both now and in the future.

The scheme is generally targeted at people on low incomes who are in work, or about to enter employment, with a small or medium-sized enterprise. The ILAs are used to encourage people from a wide range of backgrounds to take part in education and training and, in so doing, generally reduce dependence on welfare, increase employability, raise the skills of the workforce and support responsible citizenship. By encouraging people to save for their own education and training, the government hopes that they will value it more highly and will become lifelong learners.

Individual learning accounts have been tested in a number of pilot schemes run by TECs and the further education sector. A national scheme was introduced in April 2000.

Modern apprenticeships

Modern apprenticeships provide young people with a means of obtaining a nationally recognised qualification while gaining valuable work experience.

Open to young people aged between 16 and 19, although those up to 23 years old can be considered, modern apprenticeship schemes provide young people with the opportunity both to gain experience working in their chosen profession and to study for qualifications.

The modern apprenticeship scheme is very flexible and can be structured to meet the specific needs of different employers. Working on a day-release system, the young trainee typically spends most of his or her time being paid to work for a company and the remaining days studying at college.

Providing an employee with the opportunity to become a modern apprentice is beneficial to employers, because it means that at the end of the apprenticeship period the apprentice is trained to at least NVQ level three and has the potential to progress to a technician, supervisory or managerial level. The apprentices benefit from the opportunity to earn while they learn and to combine both on-the-job and off-the-job training.

Figure 4.13: The NVQ framework

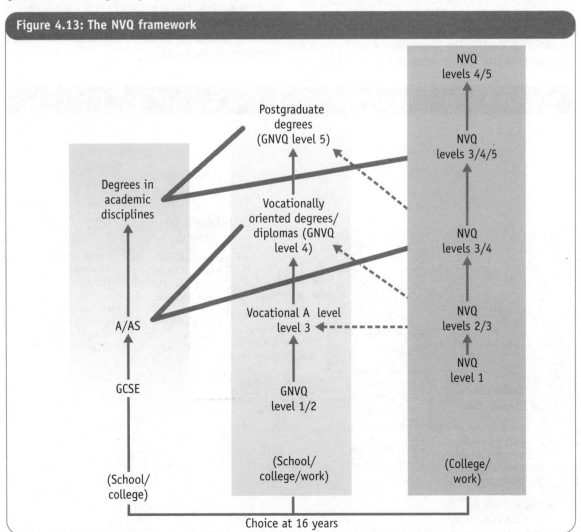

National vocational qualifications

National vocational qualifications (NVQs) are occupational qualifications based upon an employee's ability to reach defined levels of skill or competence in carrying out various tasks connected with their particular occupation. The basis for awarding an NVQ is an assessment of an employee's level of competence, and any necessary underpinning knowledge. The assessment is based on evidence collected from his or her workplace.

Since NVQs take account of performance in the workplace rather than academic knowledge and ability, they should also motivate more mature employees to develop their skills and competence. NVQs have now been developed to meet the needs of all groups of employees from operative levels through to senior management. Figure 4.13 shows the NVQ framework.

The education system

Education is as important as training in improving the quality of the workforce. In the 1990s, there was a 100 per cent increase in the number of people in higher education in the UK. The percentage of young people graduating from university is now nearly as high as that in Japan. There has also been a 5 per cent increase during the last decade in the number of people staying on in full-time education after their compulsory schooling. Despite these developments, however, more young people stay on in full-time education and training in the USA, Japan and most other European Union countries than in the UK.

The growing number of full time students following full-time vocational course – such as this business course – also plays a vital role in raising the quality of the workforce. These courses not only provide the essential knowledge aspects of a particular occupation, but are competence-based and develop the core skills which allow young people to play an effective role in other areas of employment.

National learning targets

To support the training and education structure and to encourage wider participation by providers, employers and employees, the government has set targets for training achievement. Figure 4.14 shows the national learning targets for England, which the government wants to achieve by 2002.

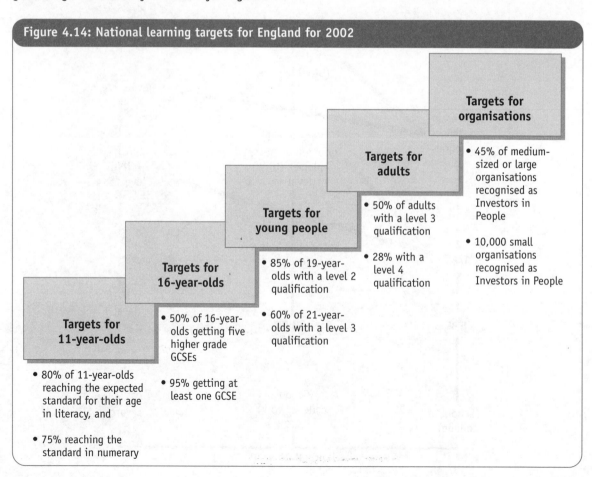

Figure 4.14: National learning targets for England for 2002

Targets for 11-year-olds
- 80% of 11-year-olds reaching the expected standard for their age in literacy, and
- 75% reaching the standard in numerary

Targets for 16-year-olds
- 50% of 16-year-olds getting five higher grade GCSEs
- 95% getting at least one GCSE

Targets for young people
- 85% of 19-year-olds with a level 2 qualification
- 60% of 21-year-olds with a level 3 qualification

Targets for adults
- 50% of adults with a level 3 qualification
- 28% with a level 4 qualification

Targets for organisations
- 45% of medium-sized or large organisations recognised as Investors in People
- 10,000 small organisations recognised as Investors in People

BUILD YOUR LEARNING

Keywords and phrases

You should know the meaning of the words and phrases listed below. Go back through the last six pages of the unit to check or refresh your understanding as necessary.

- Coaching
- Individual learning accounts
- In-house training schemes
- Investors in people
- Learning and skills councils
- Modern apprenticeships
- Mentoring schemes
- National vocational qualifications
- Training and enterprise councils

Summary points

- In order to remain competitive, organisations need to constantly review and update their training and development programmes.

- Effective training depends upon the correct identification of training needs, establishing the desired standard of skill, administering the training programme efficiently and fully evaluating its effectiveness.

- Employers use induction training to introduce new employees to the organisation and to ensure that they have the necessary information and skills to perform their tasks to the required standard.

- Mentoring and coaching schemes are used by businesses to develop good working relationships between employees, provide them with the opportunity to learn new skills on the job and to constantly review performance.

- Training is often delivered in-house using resources within the organisation. External training provided by specialists is considered more suitable for the development of higher level specialist skills.

- Nationally, training is encouraged through the activities of training and enterprise councils and initiatives such as Investors in People, modern apprenticeships and individual learning accounts.

Performance management

A BUSINESS NEEDS TO MANAGE the performance of its employees effectively if it is to remain competitive. This means that there must be effective management control exercised at both individual and organisational level.

A range of processes and techniques need to be in place which allow individual employees to know how well they are doing and for managers to be able to monitor how well their subordinates are performing. Performance monitoring provides information which is of value for identifying future training or promotion opportunities and areas where insufficient skills or knowledge could be deemed a threat to an employee's efficiency.

Managers exercise control at an individual and organisational level through:

- planning by setting objectives and targets

- establishing performance standards

- monitoring actual performance

- comparing performance against targets

- rectifying mistakes and taking action.

Management by objectives

The process described above contributes to management by objectives, in which the performance of the individual and organisation is consistently being measured against objectives and targets which have been agreed jointly by managers and employees. An objective relates to something which is to be achieved by a team or an individual. For example, a shoe manufacturer may have an objective to sell shoes through the internet. This objective may then be quantified as a target: the company wishes that 10 per cent of its annual sales should be generated from the internet in the next financial year. This may be further refined in qualitative terms as a standard of performance: goods will be delivered to the customer within 24 hours of being purchased on the internet.

Objectives should be determined through discussions between managers and employees. This involves both a top-down and a bottom-up approach. The manager presents the corporate objectives and the individuals and team members then state what they feel can be achieved. A compromise is then be struck.

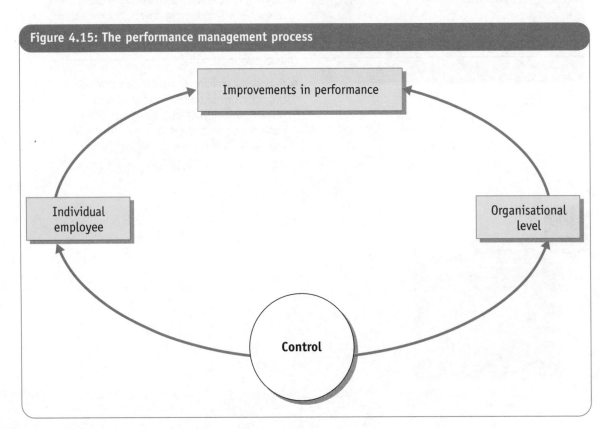

Figure 4.15: The performance management process

Improvements in performance

Individual employee

Organisational level

Control

This process is more likely to be successful if the objectives meet the SMART criteria. They should be:

S specific
M measurable
A agreed
R realistic
T time-related.

Monitoring performance

The monitoring process requires the measurement of performance and then linking these performance measurements against the achievement of objectives (and targets).

Measurements may be made indicators such as output, sales and profits over a specified period. When comparing performance with targets, account has to be taken of the general context in which a particular operation is taking place. For example, a director who just falls short of his or her target profit figure may in reality have performed very well because, say, the company was operating in the face of a major economic downturn. The monitoring of quality standards is very often done against set criteria defining different levels of quality standards. These criteria are used to form the basis of a customer opinion survey, which could be undertaken by sending a questionnaire to a cross section of customers or through a telephone survey.

Organisations may also find it helpful to make behavioural assessments, which measure an employee's approach and attitude towards his or her job.

Essentially, this focuses on the process of the job, on what an individual actually does. This is obviously more difficult to assess and measure. Very often a rating system might have to be used. For example, Figure 4.16 shows a proforma an office supervisor might use to rate his or her staff.

Discussion point

Do you think that a performance assessment based on observation and rating using a proforma like the one in Figure 4.16 is fair?

The data that is collected as part of the monitoring process is compared against the targets and contributes to any judgement regarding the overall performance of the organisation and the identification of where rectifying action needs to be taken at an organisational or individual level.

Individual performance review

For individual employees, the monitoring process we have outlined is usually complemented by some or all of these review systems:

- appraisal
- self evaluation
- peer evaluation
- 360 degree evaluation.

Figure 4.16: Performance assessment proforma

Post: Administrative Assistant

Attribute	Excellent	Very Good	Rating Good	Average	Poor
Timekeeping					
Appearance					
Communications					
Customer care					
Organisational Skills					
Relationship with manager					

Appraisal

An **appraisal system** is used to review the standard of work being undertaken by people within an organisation and to assess the value or contribution of individual employees. Appraisal and performance review interviews are used by employers to:

- reinforce company goals
- identify training needs and career opportunities
- recognise good performance
- review and set targets.

Good appraisals have a positive effect on an employee's motivation, but bad appraisals can be costly, time consuming and have a negative impact on the manager-employee relationship. A poor approach is to simply appraise employees by rating their performance against specific factors such as knowledge of the job, accuracy, reliability and output capability. This system discourages employee involvement and does not identify the means of overcoming weaknesses. Much better is the personal performance review interview; this allows solutions and objectives to be identified by both the manager and employee. Under this system, the formal appraisal interview should cover:

- a review of performance against objectives over the previous year
- an assessment of an employee's strengths and weaknesses based upon key job-related criteria
- a personal job improvement plan
- a career development plan
- a performance rating
- comments from the employee and reviewing manager
- agreement or reconfirmation of the objectives for the next year.

It is important that consideration is given during the appraisal interview to the extent to which an employee has reached objectives agreed at an earlier meeting (such as the previous year's appraisal interview). Organisations such as ICL categorises these objective into three areas:

- key results – reviewing the employee's contribution to the business objectives of his or her unit
- performance standards – contributing to an improvement in the employee's job performance
- personal development – objectives relating to increasing the knowledge or skills of an employee.

ICL requires that objectives should be SMART. The company recognises the need to have a system for measuring the extent to which the various objectives have been achieved. ICL suggests that organisations should observe these guidelines when conducting performance appraisals.

- Appraisals should be regular. At ICL, formal appraisals are held annually, while informal appraisals are treated as an ongoing process.
- Managers should be trained in conducting interviews and make an effort to place the employee at ease.
- The interview room should be neutral and a timetable should be organised to allow both parties time to prepare.
- Managers should assess if targets are still relevant and realistic, by considering how the company has changed and whether unavoidable factors such as inadequate resources have affected performance.
- Targets should be SMART and any numerical targets should be realistic. At ICL managers negotiate between six and eight targets.
- Both parties must feel satisfied with the outcome and be clear about what is going to be achieved.

Following the appraisal interview, the manager needs to help the employee to determine a suitable strategy and plan of action in order to help them to achieve their objectives and take advantage of future opportunities. This often involves the drawing up a personal job improvement plan and a career development plan.

The **personal job improvement plan** recognises that all employees can improve their performance. The plan deals with areas for improvement and considers the need to respond to new demands. It is effectively taking an overview of where the employee is now and how he or she needs to change in order to embrace the new context in which he or she is likely to be working in the future. For example, a marketing manager may be required to improve his or her strategic planning, and in particular to do this in the context of a future which recognises the importance of internet selling.

The **career development plan** helps to identify the most suitable job progression for the employee. Career development takes account of the employee's aims but will also take into account the needs of the business. Development is not just concerned with promotion. An employee may aim to develop vertically through promotion or to move horizontally through the career structure by moving into different sections and functional areas or taking on a different role at a similar level. Career development might involve gaining beneficial experience or considering ways of increasing job satisfaction. Someone who has worked successfully as an administrator within the personnel function might be placed in another functional area in order to provide a broader range of experience that will eventually lead to move into management.

Self evaluation

Before attending performance review interviews, individual employees might be asked to consider their own view of their performance. This normally starts with identifying the extent to which they have achieved the targets which they have been set and then evaluating the factors which have either encouraged or hindered the achievement of performance targets. Self-evaluation enables an employee to decide what his or her objectives are and identify training and development needs.

The main problem with self evaluation is that it can be highly biased. Some employees overestimate their performance through a fear of admitting their weaknesses; others underestimate their performance because they do not want extra responsibility or because of false modesty. Employees might propose objectives which they are interested in but do not have sufficient ability to achieve. Managers can use self evaluations to gauge employees' expectations but must recognise the potential for bias.

Peer evaluation

To inform the performance review process, many organisations also look at peer evaluations of the individual. This is based on the idea that the best people to provide feedback on an individual's performance are those who operate at a comparative level. Obviously this can only work if it is carried out in complete confidentiality, so that the people making the peer evaluation do not feel that there can be any come back.

Again, there is a danger about objectivity: peers may be in competition for a promotion or they may favour a friend in order to promote their own interests.

360 degree evaluation

The ultimate form of employee evaluation is where an organisation put its staff, especially managers, through a 360 degree review. This provides an opportunity for receiving feedback on their effectiveness from people that they have contact with at all levels. These perceptions are very useful for evaluating management style and in clarifying development needs.

The review is normally carried out through the completion of a series of questionnaires by the employee under scrutiny, together with their peers,

their line manager and the people that they line manage, and may also involve customers and suppliers. The respective responses are then collated and compared. If there is a consistent response, the question has to be asked whether this represents a strength or limitation. The review normally reflects on the skills the manager under scrutiny brings to:

- managing during difficult situations
- building relationships
- organising
- applying business judgements
- leading and inspiring people
- dealing with emergencies and remaining effective.

An analysis of the results should highlight:

- the personal strengths that are recognised by others, which can be best deployed and built upon
- the personal strengths that are not rated highly by others, which may point at areas for development and training
- personal limitations which are well regarded by others, which may mean a member of staff has been excessively self-critical
- personal limitations identified by others, which need to be worked on to improve performance.

Obviously, the process suffers from the same potential weaknesses as the peer review, but because so many different views are incorporated into the assessment the danger of bias is reduced. It also helps to identify clearly the areas of individual performance which need attention and so an appropriate training and development plan can be established.

Managing performance in the modern business environment

Approaches to performance management have to reflect the modern business environment which is dominated by the impact of consistent change factors and the effect of new legislation.

Managing change

Successful organisations must constantly adapt to new ways and adopt new methods in response to the changes in the labour, consumer, world and technological markets. It is the manager's job to ensure that these changes are implemented smoothly and effectively, and that the level of employee resistance is minimised. Organisations need to embrace change to:

- improve profits
- respond to, or get ahead of, the competition
- adopt new technology
- introduce new products or services
- improve efficiency
- comply with UK and European Union regulations.

The organisational benefits of implementing change are clear – increased profitability, better products and faster growth than competitors, good public relations and more power in the marketplace.

It is important, however, that a manager understands why people resist change before devising a plan for its implementation. Failure to take into account and address people's fear can make the change more costly and time consuming, reduce employee morale and cause the business to receive the benefits of the change later than its competitors. Resistance to change is common and is not just a fear of the unknown but derives from an employees fear that:

- they might lose their job
- additional responsibility might be too hard to handle
- they might lose their status and the success they have in their current job
- they might have to do work that they dislike or that they feel devalues their skills
- they might have to change their work and social group
- the change is futile and will not work
- they might have to work harder and will be under greater pressure.

Managers need to overcome the conflict between an organisation's need to change and human nature's fear and resistance of the unknown. Managers need to develop a successful implementation strategy. The plan should ensure that information is made available on how the change will affect people from the first stages of implementation to the end. Employees should be encouraged to ask questions and, if possible, managers should provide any guarantees that can be given about job security, transfers, retraining, etc. Simple language should be used to avoid excluding or misleading people through the use of technical jargon. The manager

should not present the change as necessary because of past bad performance but as something that will contribute to continuing good performance. In implementing any programme of change, the manager's objective should be to deliver the change as quickly as possible with the least waste of time and money.

Employee welfare

An organisation has a duty to provides its employees with a good and safe working environment and must respect employees' statutory rights and interests. In order to be able to fulfil this obligation, an organisation must respond to new government legislation and regulation. If an organisation fails to comply with the law it can face prosecution or financial costs.

Some employers and business organisations have argued that recent legislation on working hours and working conditions has reduced their capacity to operate flexibly and made it more difficult to achieve improvements in performance.

Working Time Directive

The Working Time Directive was introduced into the UK in October 1998 as a measure designed to protect the health and safety of employees. The directive covers seven areas:

- maximum working weekly hours – the average working time for each seven- day period should not exceed 48 hours, however employees have the right to opt out of the regulation
- daily rest – employees are entitled to a rest period of 11 consecutive hours in each 24-hour period
- rest breaks – an employee that has worked six hours is entitled to a 20-minute rest period
- weekly rest – employees are entitled to an uninterrupted rest period of 24 hours in each seven-day period
- annual leave – an employer has a duty to provide an employee with at least four weeks paid annual leave
- patterns of work – an employer should ensure that employees takes regular breaks and that they are not subjected to any monotonous or high-risk tasks
- night work – night workers should not work more than an average of eight hours in any 24 hour period and they should have the option to move to day jobs if they become ill.

The Working Time Directive recognises that working hours are a health and safety issue and provides protection for employees. Organisations such as the retailer Morrisons have been able to weaken the effect of the directive by encouraging its employees to sign an opt out form. However, the opt out only applies to weekly working hours. The added annual leave entitlement clearly increases an organisation's financial costs.

Maternity and paternity leave

The **Sex Discrimination Act 1975** and the **Employment Rights Act 1996** entitle pregnant employees to maternity leave regardless of their length of service or the number of hours they work. Under 1999 legislation, the maternity leave period has been extended from 14 to 18 weeks. The latest time leave can be taken is the expected week of childbirth itself, and the earliest 11 weeks before the baby is due. By law, employees must take at least two weeks maternity leave immediately after the birth of the child. Employers must continue to grant employees their statutory and fringe benefits (such as company car, health insurance, holiday entitlement) during the maternity leave period. Employees must be free to return to work after maternity leave.

At present, there is no legal requirement for organisations to grant paid paternity leave to the partners of pregnant women. To satisfy employee demand, however, some companies and local councils do grant paid leave. The average paternity leave period is currently ten days.

The minimum wage

The **national minimum wage** was introduced in April 1999 in order to provide employees with basic protection from exploitation. The minimum wage covers any UK employee who is aged 18 or older. The legislation covers agency workers, homeworkers, temporary and casual employees, and people on fixed-term or freelance contracts as well as all full-time and part-time employees. No exclusions are made on the grounds of region, size of company or type of industrial sector and employees cannot be excluded because of their hours, employment patterns, length of service or contract status.

At present (April 2000), there are three bands for the minimum wage:

- a rate of £3.60 per hour for those aged 22 and over
- a rate of £3.00 per hour for those aged 18 to 21 (inclusive)
- a rate of £3.20 per hour for those who are 22, are within the first six months of a new job and taking part in accredited training.

Some people are not entitled to the minimum wage. These include:

- the self employed
- people less than 18 years old
- voluntary workers who are only paid expenses
- prisoners
- people who normally work outside the UK
- the armed forces
- people living in their employer's home
- members of an employer's family
- people on voluntary work experience.

The implications of ignoring the minimum wage legislation are severe. Employers can face a fine of up to £5,000 and criminal prosecution.

The minimum wage can distort the market for labour, especially if it is higher than the real market rate for particular jobs. Opponents of the initiative have argued that it may reduce employment opportunities and lead to higher costs, which will be passed on to the consumer in the form of higher prices.

Improving performance through raising employee motivation

Motivation describes the extent to which an individual makes an effort to do something. Organisations are likely to improve performance, in terms of productivity, attendance rates, cooperation and quality, if they can find ways of increasing the willingness of their employees to make even greater efforts at work. This may be achieved through a variety of means – which, as we discuss in this section, are all aimed at increasing an individual's job satisfaction and are underscored by a different theoretical premise.

Job satisfaction is achieved through the work environment, and is influenced by factors such as target setting, responsibility, independence, teamwork, interaction and achievement. Motivation may be generated by a pay increase, by promotion or simply by the status and satisfaction associated with possessing a new skill and using the most up-to-date machinery and equipment. Managers use both financial and non-financial means to motivate employees. In doing so, they hope to minimise labour turnover, attract new recruits and create an effective, productive working environment.

Figure 4.17: Pizza Hut's employee satisfaction equation

Employee satisfaction = Progression + Package + Experience

internal promotion	salary	rewards
recognition	bonus	working conditions
	benefits	

For example, Pizza Hut recognises that in order to achieve its strategic objective to be the UK's favourite restaurant brand it needs to be the UK's favourite employer. Pizza Hut's employee satisfaction equation (see Figure 4.17) aims to show employees that rewards can be achieved through good performance. Pizza Hut's annual WOW awards and management bonus schemes provide recognition and rewards, and the emphasis it places upon internal recruitment and promotion provides the opportunity for advancement.

Herzberg's two factor theory

Pizza Hut's WOW awards are designed to increase job satisfaction. Comparisons can be made between Pizza Hut's recognition approach to management and the ideas of Frederick Herzberg, which he set out in his book *The Motivation to Work*.

In the 1960s, **Herzberg** identified two different sets of factors that influence job satisfaction. Herzberg stated that the first set of factors are those that induce job satisfaction, known as **motivators**. These factors are:

- achievement in the job
- recognition of good performance
- satisfaction deriving from the work itself
- the opportunity for advancement at work
- being granted additional responsibility.

Managers must focus upon these factors if they want to increase job satisfaction and motivate employees.

The second set of factors that Herzberg identified are referred to as **hygiene** factors. These are the necessary conditions to prevent dissatisfaction but, in themselves, they are not sufficient to motivate employees. Hygiene factors include:

- an employee's salary
- supervision and technical conditions
- company policy
- interpersonal relations
- working conditions.

Herzberg's theory suggests that an increased salary might only have a short-term effect upon employee efficiency and satisfaction. However, if employees are given additional responsibility, such as being placed in charge of a specific project, this would have a long-term motivating effect. This form of **job enlargement** contributes to **job enrichment**. Another strategy for long-term motivation is **job rotation** which involves exchanging tasks between workers to provide greater variety. The fundamental aim is to give employees greater control over the planning and execution of their work. Herzberg felt that this motivates employees as it means that their abilities and potential are utilised more fully.

This philosophy of utilising employees' abilities more fully also lies behind the idea of **quality control circles**. These are part of the total quality management (TQM) approach we discussed in Unit 1 (see pp. 73–5). The car manufacturer Honda, for example, embraces the TQM principle by offering employees equality and responsibility and emphasising their involvement in the company. Honda circles are made up of employees who meet on a regular basis to discuss problems and propose their ideas. Encouraging employee input enables Honda to correct problems before they escalate and to consider ideas which may be more cost and time effective. It also provides a more satisfying working environment for employees.

McGregor's Theory X and Theory Y

The motivation of employees is normally the responsibility of the manager. He or she makes assumptions about an employee's basic needs when deciding on a suitable motivation method. **Douglas McGregor's** 1960 study, *The Human Side of Management*, suggests that two types of employee exist, each possessing different needs. McGregor argues that the type of employee a person becomes is influenced by management style.

Theory X conveys a negative view of human nature, portraying employees as lazy, unambitious people who dislike work and need to be controlled through punishment. McGregor argues that if a manager treats employees as if they are naturally inclined to be idle and disinterested and believes that they do not want responsibility, then they will fulfil this role. It is a self-fulfilling prophecy.

Theory Y argues that employees are not money motivated but gain reward from the job itself. Theory Y presents employees as self-disciplined, work appreciative people who crave responsibility and creative fulfilment. McGregor's Theory Y is significant because it suggests that given the right conditions and management style employees can be motivated to work efficiently and productively.

Clearly, Theory X and Theory Y workers will react in contrasting ways to different management attempts to increase motivation. The manager's role is to determine which approach and style should be adopted in order to satisfy the needs of workers. For example, the Theory X employee is more likely to respond to financial inducements, the Theory Y employee would be stimulated by job enrichment, job enlargement, job rotation and quality control circles.

Maslow's hierarchy of needs

We have already discussed the work of Abraham Maslow in relation to marketing (see Unit 3, p. 157). His work, *Motivation and Personality*, also has lessons for performance management. It suggests that people are motivated both by needs which are fundamental to their existence and also by those which are associated with mental characteristics or attitudes. These needs can be presented as a hierarchy (see Figure 3.7), and Maslow assumes that, within the workplace, employees will strive to move up the hierarchy.

This means that, initially, an employee's physiological needs may be satisfied through the basic pay and comfort of the working environment. He or she will then want to satisfy security needs by gaining greater job security and perhaps pension arrangements. Membership of a lively team may help to satisfy social needs. A flash title and large company car may help to meet his or her need for self-esteem, and increasing levels of responsibility and control may satisfy self-actualisation needs. By recognising where people are on Maslow's hierarchy, employers can tailor their package of financial and non-financial rewards in order to increase staff motivation.

It is interesting to note that Maslow's lower order needs correspond with the hygiene factors in Herzberg's two-factor theory. The higher order needs of esteem and self-actualisation correspond to Herzberg's motivators.

Taylor's principles

Frederick Taylor in his 1911 work *Principles of Scientific Management* advanced the view that employees are basically motivated by money. The job of management was to provide formal order and control in the working environment. Management did the planning and provided the support to show the workforce how best to do the job. Taylor felt that, with this clear line and staff organisational structure, productivity would increase because the employee would recognise that higher output would lead to higher pay. Obviously, this approach tends to address what are perceived to be lower level needs and, by its very nature, is far more relevant to labour intensive industries.

Taylor's principles would support the use of these three pay systems.

- **Performance-related pay** (PRP) is a scheme which links output and performance to pay. Employees receive bonuses which are dependent on their ability to reach specific targets. PRP rewards good performance, so it should motivate employees to work harder. However, some critics argue that factors beyond an employee's control, such as the breakdown of machinery, could effect their performance. Critics also argue that PRP categorises employees as good or bad performers and this can have a demotivating effect upon those who fail to achieve their targets. To overcome problems, managers need to consult with employees and ensure the targets they set are specific, measurable, achievable, realistic and timed (that is, SMART).

- **Piece rates** provide employees with a variable income; payment is directly linked to output. Employees are encouraged to produce as much output as possible and maximise productivity. The piece rates system allows employers to identify good performers. However, by paying for quantity not quality, standards can be sacrificed as employees strive to gain rewards.

- **Commission-based pay** is often used for sales staff and employees are paid a percentage of the value of the goods they sell. Commission-based pay motivates employees because the level of their salary is determined by their own performance and ability to sell the company's products.

BUILD YOUR LEARNING

Keywords and phrases

You should know the meaning of the words and phrases listed below. Go back through the last eight pages of the unit to check or refresh your understanding as necessary.

- 360 degree review
- Appraisal system
- Career development plan
- Commission-based pay
- Herzberg's two factor theory
- Hygiene factors
- Job enlargement
- Job enrichment
- Job rotation
- McGregor's Theory X and Theory Y
- Management by objectives
- Motivation
- Motivators
- National minimum wage
- Objectives
- Peer evaluation
- Performance-related pay
- Personal job improvement plan
- Piece rates
- Quality control circles
- SMART objectives
- Standard of performance
- Targets
- Working Time Directive

Summary points

- Performance management at both individual and organisational level is important if businesses are to remain competitive.

- Management by objectives measures performance against objectives and targets which have been agreed jointly by managers and employees.

- Individual performance review involves appraisal, and can include self, peer and 360 degree evaluation. It leads to the drawing up of a personal job improvement plan and career development plan.

- In managing performance in the modern business environment acknowledgement has to be given to the constant state of change.

- Managers also need to consider the impact of legislation such as regulations governing working hours, maternity and paternity leave and the minimum wage.

- By improving employee motivation, employers can raise productivity, attendance rates, cooperation and quality of work.

- Motivation may be raised by improvements in the working environment, extending opportunities and introducing different reward systems.

- The theoretical arguments that underpin motivation strategies have been developed by Herzberg, McGregor, Maslow and Taylor.

How to produce a report on managing human resources

The flow chart shows the stages you need to go through to generate evidence to meet the assessment requirements for this unit.

> Select an organisation in which you or a family member has worked or which is keen to support your study.

> Identify and collect a range of information from primary and secondary sources which is relevant to human resources planning. This may involve research into organisational structures, the impact of the global environment, the manpower inventory, and national and local market factors.

> Present your research on a series of charts, diagrams and illustrations and construct a suitable manpower plan for the future.

> Conduct research into your chosen organisation's existing recruitment and selection process. Evaluate its effectiveness.

> Conduct research into the existing training and development process. Assess how it fits into the nationally recognised training structures and contributes to the government's education targets. Analyse its impact on the performance of the organisation and its staff.

> Identify how performance management is conducted in general and how this may be influenced by motivational theories.

> Identify and explain any conflicts which may exist between the human resource and other functions within the organisation

> Produce a word-processed business report which covers all of these issues. (This should be fully action planned.)

The management of finance is of prime importance in business survival and success. Money is the lifeblood of any business, circulating through it to keep it alive and allow it to grow and prosper. Money is required to set up and establish a business, to purchase equipment and supplies and to pay for the ongoing running costs of the business. It is vital, therefore, that businesses establish systems for controlling and recording the movement of money and operate these systems with accuracy and integrity.

This unit investigates the significance of finance, by starting with individual transactions and moving through to the accumulation of these transactions in the presentation of year-end final accounts. Public confidence relies on good accounts and businesses are under an onus to produce accounts that represent a true and fair view of their activities.

The unit looks at how to interpret these accounts accurately and to make judgements about organisations' effectiveness. It recognises the importance of not only monitoring and control of financial transactions but also the impact of forecasting and planning in managing finance.

5

Finance

Recording financial information

FINANCIAL INFORMATION IS vital in planning and controlling the activities of a business. The finances of a business must be monitored effectively. Some monitoring involves examining the historical financial records of the business, such as profit and loss accounts and balance sheets, to determine how it has performed over time and to assess the current situation. The accurate recording of financial information is the starting point for planning and controlling the business. Without accurate records, how would an owner or manager know how the business had performed? Or even who owed the business money?

Another form of monitoring involves comparing what is happening in the business with what was predicted to happen. This is known as budgeting. It requires managers to estimate sales and expenditure over the coming months (or years) and, therefore, predict the performance of the organisation. This estimation is known as a budget. However, no comparison of performance against budget can take place if there is no reliable and accurate record of events. This, therefore, is another of the main motivations for recording financial information. Other reasons include:

- generating accounts, such as profit and loss accounts and balance sheets

- meeting legal requirements, for taxation purposes, for example

- forming a basis for understanding between buyer and seller

- meeting the requirements of internal stakeholders

- meeting the requirements of external stakeholders.

Let's consider these reasons in more detail.

Generating accounts

It is essential that every transaction is recorded, accurately and completely, in order to generate complete and accurate accounts. Everything the business has bought or sold, no matter how small, must be taken into account when calculating profit (or loss). Likewise, everything the business owns or is owed by others (its assets) and everything it owes to others (its liabilities) must be shown on the balance sheet. In this way, the final accounts achieve their purpose and give a fair and true view of the financial affairs of the business.

Meeting legal requirements

There is an enormous amount of legislation governing the way businesses conduct their affairs, including the way financial information is recorded, displayed and made available to interested parties.

All businesses are required to keep financial records in order that their liability for tax can be accurately determined. Information must be recorded and made available to the Inland Revenue and Customs and Excise. These agencies have legal rights to inspect the accounts and check that they are accurate and represent a true and fair view of the business.

The Companies Acts (of 1985 and 1989) relate specifically to limited companies. These require companies to follow specific procedures in the preparation and presentation of accounts and the disclosure of financial and other information.

If a business pays employees, it must keep accurate payroll records, including any deductions made with respect to income tax (PAYE) and national insurance. The Employment Protection (Consolidation) Act 1978 requires all employers to provide itemised, written pay slips to their employees in respect of their wages or salaries. Obviously, this cannot be done if accurate records have not been kept.

Forming a basis for understanding

The use of written documents allows both buyer and seller to have a clear understanding of the trading arrangements. They confirm each stage of the transaction:

- the buyer's requirements

- the prices to be paid to the seller

- the delivery of the goods or services

- the amount owed by the buyer

- the time within which payment must be paid

- the amount paid.

Documents can constitute evidence of transactions in cases of dispute. They also fulfil the requirement of proof that a transaction took place in the event of an audit.

Financial information used by internal stakeholders

Owners

Owners are interested in examining the financial records of their business to determine whether or not it is being properly managed. They are also interested in the profitability of the organisation, its financial stability and the return they may make on their investment. Analysis of financial information allows the owners to examine the accounts in great detail. It provides mechanisms by which shareholders (or other owners) can compare returns over a period of time, make comparisons between organisations and against the current rate of interest.

Their main interest is in the final accounts (see p. 274). However, owners will be interested in all the firm's activities and accurate records may well be the only way they can actually see what is happening, especially if the organisation is large.

Owners also have a particular interest in the amounts of money owed to the business, and how long it takes debtors to pay. When deciding whether to trade with another company, whether buying or selling, the business's past records will provide invaluable information about that company's reliability. Have you ever loaned someone some money and then forgotten about it? Keeping accurate records prevents this sort of circumstance from occurring.

Directors

Directors use the final accounts to justify the decisions they have made. A limited liability company uses its final accounts to explain the financial position of the business to the shareholders and to set out its future plans. Financial accounts can be analysed to evaluate past decisions and to identify possible areas of strength, weakness or inefficiency within the organisation. Again, accurate recording allows the board of directors to extract much detail from the accounts about the performance of the business and analyse its financial stability.

Recording financial transactions helps directors to examine areas of the company they may have little or no contact with in day-to-day activities. It enables directors to measure performance, analyse trends and, most importantly, make decisions based upon information rather than intuition.

Managers

Managers run an organisation on behalf of the owners and, within the business, often have specific responsibility for an area or department. Junior and middle management may well use financial information to pinpoint areas of inefficiency within their departments and to help them stay within their budgets or achieve targets. Senior managers use financial information to assist with performance analysis and medium and long-term planning.

Employees and trade unions

It can be an advantage for employees to have an understanding of the financial situation of the company for which they work for several reasons.

First, knowledge of the company's profit level can help in formulating demands for higher wages or improvements to working conditions. Second, if employees can see that their company has financial stability, this can add to their feelings of job security and motivation; the opposite, of course, is also true, but if the company is financially unstable it might encourage employees to look for new jobs. Third, involving employees in the compilation and management of budgets can again act as a major motivator, enhancing responsibility and job satisfaction.

The recording of financial information allows companies to set targets and operate bonus systems for their staff. For example, the best salesperson of the month would be calculated from records of sales invoices.

External stakeholders

Governments

Governments primarily use private organisations' final accounts for the assessment of corporation tax and value added tax (VAT). However, financial information is also used by government agencies to make sure that businesses are operating legally and ethically. For example, financial records could be used to detect fraud or unfair pricing policies.

The government also needs to analyse the performance of public corporations, agencies and other publicly owned bodies, such as the Royal Opera House. It may use different methods to analyse the financial performance of public sector organisations, but they need to record financial events just as accurately as the private sector, if not more so.

Financiers

Business financiers need to be able to assess an organisation's profitability, stability, efficiency, activity and the comparative return on their investment. Just looking at a company's profit level is not enough. Institutions and individuals providing finance want to determine the 'profit quality' as well as judging the level of risk an investment entails against the possible return they are likely to make. Accurate financial records and accounts allow financiers such as banks and venture capitalists to undertake detailed examinations. Their prime interest will be in the final accounts, working capital and ratio analysis.

Creditors

Companies that are going to supply goods on credit terms will examine the financial accounts of their customers. This gives information such as the customer's ability to pay, its financial stability and how long, on average, it takes to pay its debts. This information is invaluable in determining whether or not to offer credit to a customer, how much credit to

allow and what credit period the customer should be given. A company can also assess the credit worthiness of a potential customer by looking at its working capital position against its profit.

Potential investors

No two organisations are exactly the same. There are many differences in, for example, size, profits and capital structure. Comparing different organisations to try to decide which one offers the best investment opportunity is therefore a very complex task. The recording and presenting of financial information in common formats makes it easier for these comparisons. Potential investors use a range of ratios to help them decide the best opportunities for investment.

Discussion point

Study Figure 5.1. Identify two other groups that could be considered stakeholders of a business. Why might they be particularly interested in the finances of a business organisation?

Figure 5.1: Stakeholder analysis

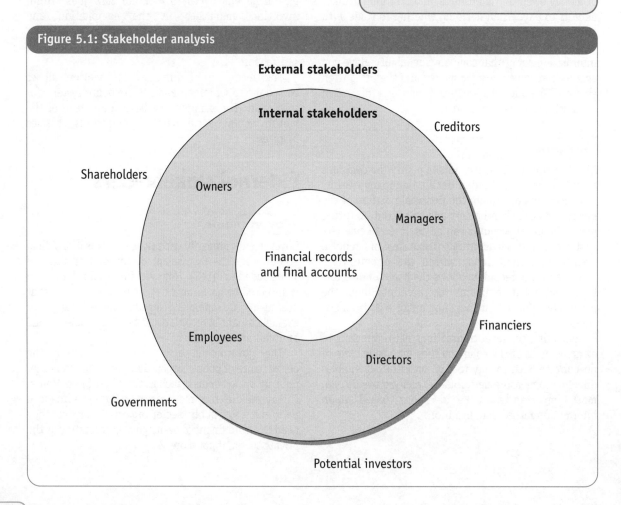

External stakeholders

Internal stakeholders

Creditors

Shareholders

Owners

Managers

Financial records and final accounts

Financiers

Employees

Directors

Governments

Potential investors

To summarise, financial information is put to a range of uses, from profit assessment and determining the financial stability of a company, to taxation and making individual decisions. The financial information produced by an organisation is going to be used by every category of stakeholder when making decisions about the likely future of, and their involvement with, the business.

Financial documents

Now that we have an understanding of why financial transactions need to be recorded, we can look at the documents used in the process. Most of these documents are required when goods are purchased and supplied on credit. This is because as there is a delay between exchange of goods and payment being made, an exceedingly accurate record needs to be maintained by both suppliers and customers.

Purchase order

The purchasing process begins when the customer sends an order form to the supplier, detailing what he or she wants to purchase. Each **purchase order** shows:

- name, address, telephone and fax details of the customer

- delivery address, used if the goods are to be sent to a different address such as a warehouse

- unique order number, used for reference on subsequent documents and for filing

- date of order

- a full description of the goods required, including any product code or catalogue numbers

- the quantity required, including units where applicable such as box of 30, pack of 2, a ream

- unit and total price(s), as quoted by the supplier

- authorised signature, the order must be signed and dated by someone authorised to place orders

- required delivery date

- whether quality/certification documentation is required.

Figure 5.2 shows an order placed by Morgan Publishers with one of its suppliers – Banville Business Supplies Limited. Look at the list of features of a purchase order form and locate them on this example.

Orders are normally checked and approved by an authorised person, who has both the authority to approve purchases and the responsibility for justifying why they were made. The authorised person then signs the order, making it official. Authorised persons may be the managers of different departments or individual budget holders, or there may be a central purchasing department where all orders are issued and authorised.

Remember that a signed order form is a legal commitment to purchase what you have ordered, so errors could be very expensive. Additionally, receiving the wrong goods from a supplier may mean that you, in turn, are unable to supply your customers on time. That could prove even more expensive – especially if your customers find a new (and more reliable) supplier and stop buying from you.

Delivery note

Having received an order, the supplier checks that the goods are available and arranges for them to be delivered, with an accompanying **delivery note**. This is issued by the supplier and lists the items that are being delivered.

When a delivery arrives, the customer checks the goods to ensure that what is listed on the delivery note has actually been delivered in good condition and then signs the delivery note to confirm receipt of the goods. If the goods are packaged in such a way that a full inspection is not possible at the time of delivery, the person receiving the goods should write 'unexamined' on the delivery note before signing it. In this way, the customer retains the right to notify the supplier if goods are found to be faulty or missing when the packaging is opened. Figure 5.3 shows a delivery note from Banville Business Supplies Limited to Morgan Publishers detailing a delivery of stationery.

Once the goods have been signed for, there is a legal obligation to pay for them. It is important, therefore, that the number, specification and condition of the goods are checked against the original order and match the delivery note before the delivery is accepted. This responsibility usually rests with the warehouse supervisor or manager.

Goods received note

Some organisations also prepare an internal document called a **goods received note**. This lists what has actually been received and is used by the accounts department to check that the purchase invoice, when it arrives, is correct and that the company is only being charged for goods it has actually received. Figure 5.4 shows the goods received note drawn up by Morgan upon receipt of its delivery of stationery from Banville Business Suppliers.

Figure 5.2: A purchase order

 Morgan *Publishers*

103-107 Dorien Park Road,
Hammersmith, London W6 5TL
Telephone: 0181-643 5542
Fax: 0181-307 3556
Vat No: 267 7453 03

To   Banville Business
Supplies Limited
Manor Park Road
Weybridge
Surrey
KT11 4TM

PURCHASE ORDER
Date: 1-4-00
Reference No: TRA/C136
Order No: 21/2455

Both the Order No. and Reference No.
must be quoted on all correspondence.

Please supply:

Quantity:	Description	Cost centre	Price (exc. VAT)
30 boxes	Punched Pockets A4 Clear (100 Pockets Per Box)	174.2	63.00
10 boxes	Nyrex Folders (Yellow) (25 Per box) - 022233	140.6	72.60
10 boxes	Nyrex Folders (Red) (25 Per box) - 022235	140.6	72.60
10 boxes	Nyrex Folders (Green) (25 Per box) - 022236	140.6	72.60
10 boxes	White self-seal Envelopes with windows - SE9112	174.2	49.80
10 boxes	Manilla, self-seal Envelopes - SE2103	174.2	63.00
		Total	393.60

Deliver To Morgan Publishers
103-107 Dorien Park
Road
Hammersmith
London
W6 5TL

Delivery Required   A. S. A. P.

Authorised Signature   *Jane Cook*

Invoice to   Purchase Ledger Department
Morgan Publishers Ltd
North Hill Road
Glasgow G67 1RT

Registered as Morgan Publishers Ltd (Scotland 1948 No. 53987), North Hill Road, Bishopbriggs, Glasgow, G67 1RT

Figure 5.3: A delivery note

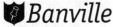 **Banville**

Manor Park Road
Weybridge
Surrey KT11 4TM

Tel: 01831 657553
Fax: 01831 558427

Van Route: 7

Site:

INVOICE TO:

Morgan Publishers Ltd
Purchase Ledg Contract (811)
North Hill Road
Glasgow
G67 1RT

DELIVERY TO:

Morgan Publishers
103-107 Dorien Park Road
Hammersmith
London
W6 5TL

DELIVERY NOTE

REF 1/DT3573   PAGE 1   ACCOUNT Morgan   DATE 5 April 00

STOCK LOCATION	PRODUCT	DESCRIPTION	PACK SIZE	OUR REF	YOUR REF	QUANTITY SENT	QUANTITY TO FOLLOW
BA32	127529	PUNCHED POCKETS A4 CLEAR	100	ON7264	TRA/C136	3000	0
BL44	022233	NYREX FOLDERS (YELLOW)	25	ON7264	TRA/C136	250	0
BL44	022235	NYREX FOLDERS (RED)	25	ON7264	TRA/C136	250	0
BA44	022236	NYREX FOLDERS (GREEN)	25	On7264	TRA/C136	250	0
BA30	SE9112	WINDOW WHITE SELF-SEAL ENVELOPES	500	ON7264	TRA/C136	5000	0
BA33	SE2103	MANILLA ENVELOPES SELF-SEAL	250	ON7264	TRA/C136	2500	0

Goods for credit must be returned within 14 days and
in original packaging and of resaleable condition

Packed and checked by: SMS

Figure 5.4: A goods received note

 Morgan *Publishers*

Goods Received Note

Supplier:
Banville Business
Supplies
Manor Park Road
Weybridge
Surrey KT11 4TM

GRN No 69211
Date 5 April 00

Quantity	Description	Order No.
30 Boxes	PUNCHED POCKETS A4 CLEAR	21/2455
10 Boxes	NYREX FOLDERS (YELLOW)	21/2455
10 Boxes	NYREX FOLDERS (RED)	21/2455
10 Boxes	NYREX FOLDERS (GREEN)	21/2455
10 Boxes	WHITE, SELF-SEAL ENVELOPES WITH WINDOWS	21/2455
8 Boxes	MANILLA, SELF-SEAL ENVELOPES	21/2455

Carrier: Thompson Deliveries

Received By:

Checked By:

Condition of Goods:
good condition ✓
damaged
shortages: *2 boxes manilla*
self-seal envelopes

Invoices

Having confirmed receipt of the goods, the customer can now expect to receive an **invoice** from the supplier, stating how much money needs to be paid. These are normally sent by mail and usually arrive a few days after the goods are received.

As far as the supplier –in our example Banville – is concerned this document is a sales invoice. However, from the customer's – Morgan Publishers – viewpoint, it is an incoming purchase invoice detailing what has been bought and how much is due to the supplier. In other words, the same document serves two purposes depending on which side of the transaction you are, supplier or customer. Figure 5.5 shows the purchase invoice issued to Morgan Publishers by Banville.

The invoice shows details about the supplier, the customer, the date of sale, the details of goods or services supplied and the terms of trade. It has names and addresses of the supplier, the customer – to whom the invoice should be sent –and the delivery destination of the goods (if different to that of the customer).

The invoice date is the start of the credit period and it therefore determines when payment is due. If VAT is included in the transaction, the invoice date is also known as the tax point because it is the date at which the sale officially takes place and at which VAT is charged for tax purposes. For recording purposes, a transaction is deemed to have taken place if terms have been agreed and goods exchanged irrespective of when payment actually takes place. The section on constructing profit and loss accounts later in this unit (see p. 278) discusses this point in greater detail.

The invoice usually has several reference numbers. These include:

- invoice number, an unique number which is usually pre-printed

- order number(s), enabling the customer to match the invoice to the original order form(s)

- delivery note number(s), enabling the invoice to be matched to the delivery note(s) and goods received note(s)

- customer's account number, for reference in the supplier's accounting system.

It contains details of goods supplied, including:

- code or catalogue numbers of the goods delivered, as shown on the original order(s) and delivery note(s)

- full description of each item of goods supplied

- quantity of each item supplied – this should agree with the quantity ordered and delivered

- unit (such as ream, box)

- unit price of each item

- total price per item (unit price multiplied by quantity)

- trade discount, the discount usually given to regular customers in the same line of business

- net amount due after deduction of trade discount

- goods total, the total of the net amount column

- cash discount, an amount which may be deducted by customers if they pay within specified terms

- value added tax (VAT)

- invoice total, the final amount due after all the above has been taken into account.

Figure 5.5: An invoice

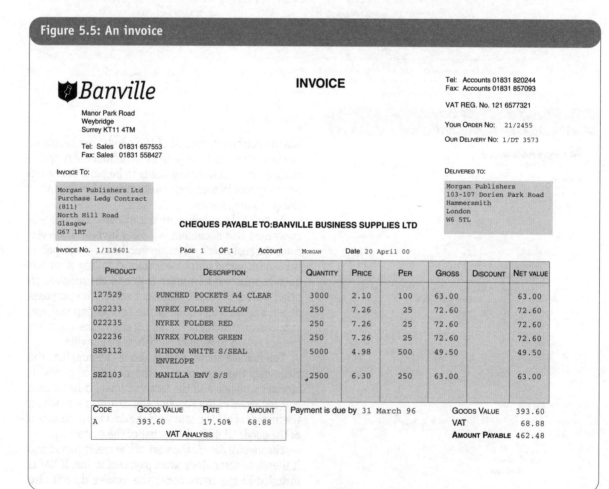

PRODUCT	DESCRIPTION	QUANTITY	PRICE	PER	GROSS	DISCOUNT	NET VALUE
127529	PUNCHED POCKETS A4 CLEAR	3000	2.10	100	63.00		63.00
022233	NYREX FOLDER YELLOW	250	7.26	25	72.60		72.60
022235	NYREX FOLDER RED	250	7.26	25	72.60		72.60
022236	NYREX FOLDER GREEN	250	7.26	25	72.60		72.60
SE9112	WINDOW WHITE S/SEAL ENVELOPE	5000	4.98	500	49.50		49.50
SE2103	MANILLA ENV S/S	2500	6.30	250	63.00		63.00

Banville
Manor Park Road
Weybridge
Surrey KT11 4TM

Tel: Sales 01831 657553
Fax: Sales 01831 558427

INVOICE

Tel: Accounts 01831 820244
Fax: Accounts 01831 857093

VAT REG. No. 121 6577321

YOUR ORDER NO: 21/2455
OUR DELIVERY NO: 1/DT 3573

INVOICE TO:
Morgan Publishers Ltd
Purchase Ledg Contract
(811)
North Hill Road
Glasgow
G67 1RT

CHEQUES PAYABLE TO: BANVILLE BUSINESS SUPPLIES LTD

DELIVERED TO:
Morgan Publishers
103-107 Dorien Park Road
Hammersmith
London
W6 5TL

INVOICE NO. 1/I19601   PAGE 1   OF 1   Account   MORGAN   Date 20 April 00

CODE	GOODS VALUE	RATE	AMOUNT
A	393.60	17.50%	68.88
	VAT ANALYSIS		

Payment is due by 31 March 96

GOODS VALUE	393.60
VAT	68.88
AMOUNT PAYABLE	462.48

Finally, the invoice shows what terms of payment apply to the supply. For example:

- **net 30 days** – means that the supplier expects the invoice to be paid in full (with no cash discount) within 30 days of the invoice date

- **10% 7 days** – means that the customer can deduct a 10 per cent cash discount (as shown on the invoice) if the invoice is paid within seven days of the invoice date

- **carriage paid** – means that the price of the goods includes the cost of delivery

- **E & O E** – standing for errors and omissions excepted, this means that if there is a mistake on the invoice, or something has been left out, the supplier reserves the right to correct the mistake and demand the correct amount.

If the supplier is registered for VAT, the invoice must also show the supplier's VAT registration number.

Credit note

Sometimes the goods that are ordered do not arrive in good condition. They may have been damaged or lost in transit, incorrect items or quantities may have been sent or they may be faulty. When this occurs, the supplier sends the customer a **credit note**. A credit note is very similar to an invoice but, instead of increasing the customer's debt to the supplier, a credit note reduces the debt. In other words, it is the opposite of an invoice for accounting purposes. Credit notes detail very similar information to invoices, usually with the addition of an explanation of why the credit is being issued. To avoid confusion, credit notes are often printed in red so that they are not easily mistaken for invoices.

Occasionally, deliveries are incomplete or damaged. Banville left two boxes of manilla envelopes off Morgan's order. Figure 5.6 shows Banville's credit note acknowledging this error and showing that Morgan does not have to pay for this part of the order. Credit notes are also issued if the customer has been overcharged on an invoice or if the customer has decided not to purchase some of the goods (provided the supplier is prepared to take them back).

Figure 5.6: Credit note

CREDIT NOTE — Banville, Manor Park Road, Weybridge, Surrey KT11 4TM

Tel: Sales 01831 657553 / Fax: Sales 01831 558427
Tel: Accounts 01831 820244 / Fax: Accounts 01831 857093
VAT REG. No. 121 6577321
Your Order No: 21/2455
Our Delivery No: 1/DT3573

Credit To: Purchase Ledger Department, Morgan Publishers Ltd, North Hill Road, Glasgow, G67 1RT

Delivered To: Morgan Publishers, 103-107 Dorien Park Road, Hammersmith, London, W6 5TL

Credit No: 1/C58227 PAGE 1 of 1 ACCOUNT MORGAN DATE 25 April 00

Product	Description	Quantity	Price	Per	Gross	Discount	Net Value
SE2103	Manilla Envelopes Self-Seal	500	6.30	250	12.60		12.60

Code	Goods Value	Rate	Amount
A	12.60	17.50%	2.20

VAT ANALYSIS

Goods Value 12.60
Vat 2.20
Total Credit 14.80

Statements of account

At the end of each month, a supplier issues a **statement of account** to each of its customers. This lists all the invoices and credit notes that have been sent to the customer during the month, together with any payments that have been received from the customer. The total of the statement, therefore, is the outstanding amount currently owed by the customer. In effect, the statement is a summary of all the transactions that have taken place between the two organisations during the month and a reminder to the customer of how much remains to be paid.

Figure 5.7 shows the statement received by Morgan in respect of the order it placed with Banville Business Supplies Limited. Morgan may pay on receipt of a regular statement such as this rather than paying each invoice. In practice, it is likely that a statement received by Morgan would contain details of a number of invoices rather than a single one. You will also note that details of any credit notes are also recorded, denoted by the initials CN on the statement.

Making payments

Before any payments are made in response to an invoice or statement of account, checks are carried out to ensure that the goods were ordered by an authorised person and received in good condition. Usually, this is undertaken by matching the invoices received from the supplier to the original purchase orders (and goods received notes if used). Any discrepancies or errors are notified to the supplier and the invoice held until the matter is resolved (usually upon receipt of a credit note or the outstanding goods). These security checks ensure that no supplier is paid in error.

Provided that everything is correct, the invoices then need to be approved for payment. A senior accountant or manager usually has responsibility for approving payments. Sometimes an 'authorisation box' is rubber-stamped on the front of the invoice, which is signed when it is approved for payment. Ensuring that different people are responsible for the receipt of goods and the payment for goods reduces the opportunities for fraud. This is known as segregation of duties.

Figure 5.7: Statement of account

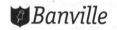

Banville

Manor Park Road
Weybridge
Surrey KT11 4TM

Tel: Sales 01831 657553
Fax: Sales 01831 558427

STATEMENT

ACCOUNT DATE 28 MAY 2000 ACCOUNT MORGAN 3/96

Morgan Publishers Ltd
North Hill Road
Glasgow G67 1RT

REMITTANCE ADVICE
Banville Business
Supplies Ltd
Manor Park Road
Weybridge
Surrey
KT11 4TM

ACCOUNT: MORGAN 3/96

Please indicate items you are paying (√) and return this advice with your remittance

Date	Type	Reference	Value	Outstanding	Reference	Outstanding	√
20 Jan 96	INV	1/I19601	462.48	447.68	1/I19601	447.68	
25 Jan 96	CN	1/C58227	14.80				
			Total	447.68	Total	447.68	

If the customer is satisfied that the statement of account is accurate and there are no items under dispute, a payment is sent to the supplier to settle the account. Sometimes the statement includes a tear-off section called a **remittance advice**, which is detached and returned by the customer with the cheque to confirm what is being paid. Some customers prepare their own remittance advice to be sent with their cheques.

Cheque

A **cheque** instructs a bank to pay a specified amount of money to a named person (or organisation). The bank issues cheque books – sets of printed cheques – to its account holders for use when they need to pay money to other people or organisations. Printed on the cheque is the name, address and sort code of the bank at which the account is held, together with the name of the account holder and the account number.

The person writing out the cheque is known as the drawer, and person to whom it is payable is known as the payee. Cheques must be written clearly, in ink, with the amount written in both words and figures to avoid mistakes. The name of the payee must appear and the cheque must be dated and signed by the drawer. Any changes made on the cheque must be initialled by the drawer. In the UK, the cheque is valid for a period of six months, after which time it becomes invalid.

Most cheques are marked 'A/C Payee only'. This means that the cheque can be paid into a bank account held in the payee's name. This provides some measure of security against fraud and allows cheques to be sent safely through the post. Payments can normally only be authorised by senior staff and only 'authorised signatories' can sign cheques. The authorised signatories give the bank specimens of their signatures. Banks will not make payments unless cheques are signed by one or more of the authorised signatories. Some organisations specify that two signatories must sign each cheque, reducing the risk of embezzlement and fraud (theft of money from the business). The cheque sent by Morgan Publishers to Banville (see Figure 5.8) has two signatories.

Cheques are used for the majority of transactions. However, occasionally small purchases – such as postage stamps or a box of tea bags for the office – are made in cash. When this happens, the receipt is submitted to the person in charge of **petty cash**, who reimburses the purchaser for the expense. Each transaction is recorded on a petty cash voucher, which details the date, the amount spent and what was bought. The person in charge of petty cash signs the voucher to authorise payment; the person who has been reimbursed signs the voucher to confirm receipt of the money. Petty cash transactions are recorded in the petty cash book, which forms part of the double-entry accounting system. Businesses would not expect to spend large sums through petty cash.

Figure 5.8: A cheque

Normally only one person has access to petty cash funds. He or she is responsible for ensuring that the contents of the petty cash box are correct at all times. Only small purchases can be paid through petty cash; usually firms set an upper financial limit. Larger items are referred to someone with greater purchasing authority.

Receipts

When a cash transaction is made – that is, the exchange of goods and payment is simultaneous – a **receipt** is normally issued to the customer as proof that the payment has been received. There is no need for further documentation or any record of the customer's details because there is no outstanding debt. Credit and debit card transactions are treated in exactly the same manner as cash, except instead of exchanging notes and coins, the card holder signs for the value of the transaction to be deducted from his or her account. Account details are taken by 'swiping' the card.

There are many different receipt formats; you are probably most familiar with the till receipt issued by retail stores. Because many stores now use computerised tills, these often show exactly what items

have been bought, in addition to the price and total amount. Alternatively, some retailers issue a handwritten receipt.

In either case, the receipt should show the name and (where applicable) the VAT registration number of the supplier, the date, the amount paid and the VAT amount. Not all till receipts show the amount of VAT charged, so an additional handwritten receipt, showing VAT, may be issued if required.

Paying-in slips

Regardless of whether money comes into the business in the form of cash or cheques, it needs to be deposited in the business's bank account; a **paying-in slip** is used for this purpose.

Books of blank paying-in slips are issued to account holders by the banks. When a deposit is made, the account holder completes the paying-in slip, listing the cash and cheques to be paid in to the bank. Most businesses receive payments by cheque. Figure 5.9 relates to an account held by Morgan Publishers. You can see that Morgan is paying in three cheques and some cash. Note this is the same account that was used to issue the cheque to Banville (see Figure 5.8).

Figure 5.9: A paying-in slip

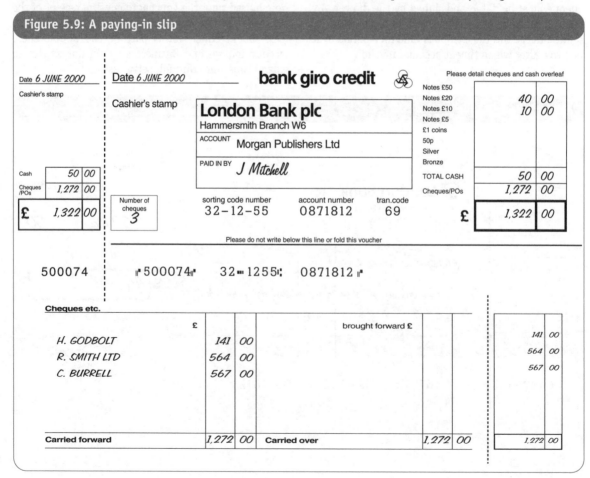

Figure 5.10: A bank statement

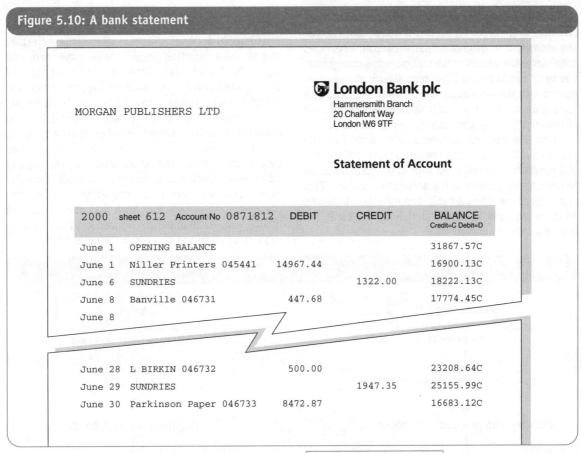

London Bank plc
Hammersmith Branch
20 Chalfont Way
London W6 9TF

MORGAN PUBLISHERS LTD

Statement of Account

2000 sheet 612 Account No 0871812	DEBIT	CREDIT	BALANCE Credit=C Debit=D
June 1 OPENING BALANCE			31867.57C
June 1 Niller Printers 045441	14967.44		16900.13C
June 6 SUNDRIES		1322.00	18222.13C
June 8 Banville 046731	447.68		17774.45C
June 8			
June 28 L BIRKIN 046732	500.00		23208.64C
June 29 SUNDRIES		1947.35	25155.99C
June 30 Parkinson Paper 046733	8472.87		16683.12C

These details must normally be included on a paying-in slip:

- the date of deposit

- name, branch and sort code of the bank where the account is held

- account name and number into which the money is to be paid

- the amount of cash being deposited (listed by denomination)

- the number of cheques being deposited

- the total amount of the cheques being deposited (entered on the front of the slip)

- a list of cheques and their amounts (entered on the back of the slip)

- the total amount (cash plus cheques) being deposited

- the counterfoil is completed (this is a record retained by the account holder)

- the person making the deposit signs the slip.

Bank statements

On a regular basis (usually weekly or monthly), banks send each account holder a **bank statement**. This is a statement of account which lists all the transactions that have taken place in the period since the previous statement was issued. The first entry shows the balance brought forward from the previous statement. All the deposits paid into the account are listed in the credit column, all payments from the account are listed in the debit column and the final column shows the balance (how much is left in the account). The balance is updated after each transaction – this is known as a *running balance*.

Items such as bank charges and interest also appear on the bank statement. Bank charges may include a monthly fee and a fee per transaction or they might be calculated on the amount of money passing through the account. Interest can be either paid to the account holder (when the account is in credit) or charged by the bank (when the account is overdrawn).

Figure 5.10 shows an extract from a bank statement received by Morgan Publishers for its account number 0871812. It drew a cheque on this account to pay Banville Business Supplies Limited. The company also paid in some cheques and cash to the account. These details and other transactions are recorded on its bank statement.

The letter C beside the balance indicates that there is money in the account; a letter D would indicate that the account is overdrawn. When an account becomes overdrawn, the account holder is borrowing money from the bank and is charged interest. Overdrafts must be agreed with the bank in advance. This should only be a temporary measure because it as an expensive method of borrowing money and interest charges are high.

When the business receives a bank statement, the entries are checked against the firm's records of receipts and payments. This record is kept in the cash-book, an important component of the accounting system. This is known as preparing a bank reconciliation. It should be done regularly to ensure that both the bank and business records are correct.

Completing documents

The financial documents we have examined are the first step in the accounting process. As we have seen, and Figure 5.11 illustrates, there is a complex flow of documents between customers and suppliers even for straightforward transactions. It is essential, therefore, that they are prepared clearly, accurately and completely. Each document, whether written by hand, typed or prepared on computer, should be checked before issue, to ensure that all details are correct and all necessary information has been entered. Particular care must be taken in preparing handwritten documents, to ensure that both text and figures are legible and unambiguous. Figures must be written neatly and clearly to avoid them being misread.

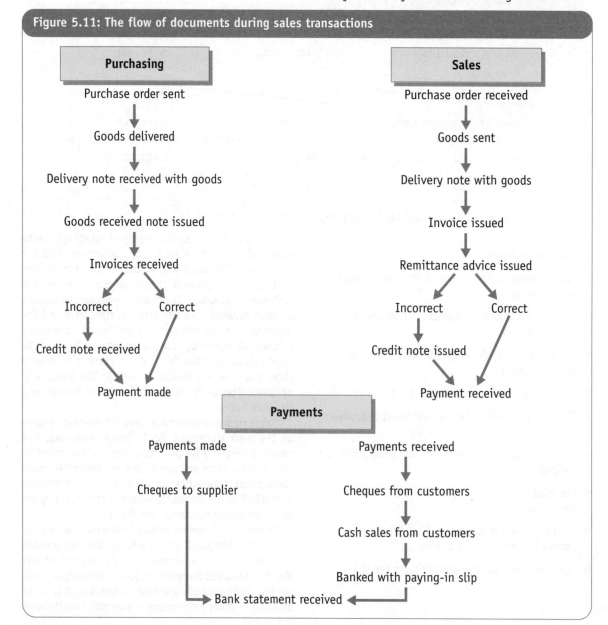

Figure 5.11: The flow of documents during sales transactions

Failure to complete documents correctly results in inconvenience, expense and incorrect accounting records. Relationships with other businesses may be affected, especially if suppliers are not paid promptly or customers fail to receive deliveries. Incorrect accounting records result in incorrect final accounts. These will no longer reflect a 'true and fair' view of the business or its performance. Profits may be understated or overstated in the profit and loss accounts, while assets and liabilities may be incorrectly stated on the balance sheet.

At best, inaccurate documentation leads to inconvenience and wasted time. At worst, inaccurate accounting records may cause incorrect decision making, resulting in business failure, or lead to charges of false accounting, resulting in prosecution.

Discussion point

Why do you think it is necessary for organisations to keep such detailed records? List three consequences a business faces if it keeps inaccurate or incomplete financial records.

Figure 5.12: Use of financial documents

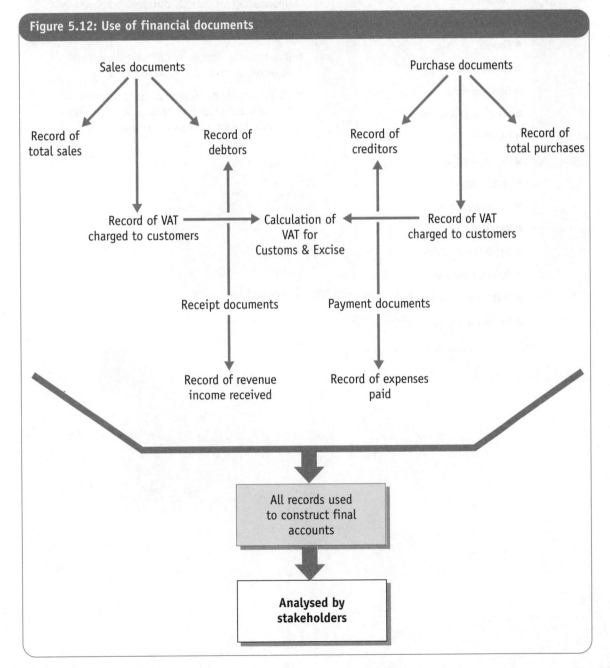

BUILD YOUR LEARNING

Keywords and phrases

You should know the meaning of the words and phrases listed below. Go back through the last 14 pages of the unit to check or refresh your understanding as necessary.

- Bank statement
- Cheque
- Credit note
- Delivery note
- Goods received note
- Invoice
- Paying-in slip
- Petty cash
- Purchase order
- Receipt
- Remittance advice
- Running balance
- Statement of account
- Tax point

Summary points

- Every business has to meet internal and external information needs so that stakeholders are able to make accurate and informed decisions.

- Different stakeholders examine the same information for entirely different purposes and interpret the data contained in different ways

- Business use a range of different documents to record purchases and make payments.

- These documents help businesses maintain accurate and secure procedures, and provide the information to draw up accounts.

Constructing accounts

WE HAVE LOOKED AT THE MAIN documents used in financial transactions and explained how and why they are used. Now, in this section, we begin to look at the accounting system used to record these documents and transactions and produce the final accounts that summarise the financial affairs of a business.

As discussed, much documentation arises from the fact that many transactions take place on credit. Organisations need to keep records not only of what and how much is bought and sold, but also by whom. Accountants have special terms for those involved in credit transactions:

- **debtors** are companies (or individuals) that owe money to a business – they have been sold, but not yet paid for, goods (credit sales)

- **creditors** are companies (or individuals) owed money by the business – the business has purchased, but not yet paid for, supplies (credit purchases).

The general idea behind recording transactions and constructing accounts is to classify transactions into different categories and summarise the results to provide a numerical picture of the organisation.

Books of original entry

Also known as books of prime entry or journals, the books of original entry are used to record all the details of original documents, including invoices, credit notes, cheques, etc. These journals list the transactions that have taken place in chronological order. In order to keep matters simple, therefore, different types of transactions are listed in separate books: all sales are listed in one book, all purchases in another, and all bank and cash transactions in a separate book.

The books of original entry are used to complete the individual account entries required by the **double-entry** system of recording transactions. All transactions are listed first in books of original entry, and these lists are then transferred to the relevant accounts (ledgers).

Books of original entry are more commonly referred to as journals and the books where individual accounts are kept are called ledgers. The main books of original entry are:

- **purchases journal** – used for credit purchases only, records the invoices a business receives from its suppliers for its purchases

- **sales journal** – used for credit sales only, records the invoices a business sends to its customers for sales

- **returns in journal** – records the credit notes issued to customers for goods they have returned

- **returns out journal** – records the credit notes received from suppliers for goods that the business has returned

- **general journal** – sometimes known as the journal proper, used for other items such as purchases of fixed assets and writing off bad debts

- **cash-book** – records receipts and payments of cash and cheques.

Note that only the cash-book forms part of the double-entry system. It is both a book of original entry and a ledger book. This is because cash transactions happen quickly unlike credit transactions. Because it is vital that a business keeps track of its available finance, cash and bank transactions are entered immediately in the ledger

The books of original entry list events in chronological order. The information in the books of original entry is then transferred to the appropriate ledger accounts. This is known as posting to the ledger. All postings to the ledger consist of two entries, hence the term **double entry**.

Purchases journal

The purchases journal is only used for credit purchases. Cash purchases are not entered here. A business should receive an invoice from the seller for all credit purchase. Note this invoice is a purchase invoice when it is entered into the accounts of the buyer; this same document is a sales invoice when entered into the accounts of the seller. As each invoice is received it should be stamped with a reference number and filed. Figure 5.13 shows an example of entries in a purchases journal.

Figure 5.13: Entries in the purchases journal

Purchases journal				page 22	
Date	**Description**	**Invoice ref.**	**Folio**	**Amount**	
12/10	L. Bones	624	PL 22	970	→ To personal
13/10	K. Smithers	625	PL 35	1,880	accounts in purchases
14/10	M. Hodgers	626	PL 10	720	ledger (credit
24/10	L. Barker	627	PL 14	610	entries)
	Transferred to purchases account		GL 2	4,180	

To the purchases account in the general ledger (debit entry)

GL - general ledger

PL - purchase ledger

Discussion point

Why do you think it is important that entries are listed in chronological order? Try and give three reasons for listing purchase invoices in this way.

This purchases journal records the date on which the invoice was received, the name of the company (or individual) it was received from and the invoice amount. All the information entered into the accounting system is linked using folio numbers. The folio number acts a reference to where an entry came from and where it went. The folio numbers in Figure 5.13 show where the entries were posted, for example M Hodgers was posted to page 10 of the purchase ledger. If you turned to page 10 of the purchase ledger, the folio number against the entry for Hodgers would read PJ 22, indicating that the original entry can be found on page 22 of the purchases journal.

This referencing system is vitally important when errors need to be traced or an audit is being undertaken. Auditing is a process of checking the whole accounting system of a business for accuracy and authenticity. The law requires that limited companies must be audited by an independent person, but it is good practice for all businesses to do so. By using folio numbers, it is possible to track each transaction through the system from the original document to entries in the books of original entry and ledgers.

Figure 5.13 shows that each entry is posted to its individual account in the purchase ledger, and the total is posted to page 2 of the purchases account in the general ledger. So, in effect, each entry has been posted to two different destinations, completing the double entry.

Sales journal

The sales journal is only used for credit sales. Cash sales are not entered here, as there is no need to know the names and addressees of people who pay for goods by cash.

For any credit sale, the seller should provide the buyer with a sales invoice. Sales invoices should run in numerical order, and the seller should make a copy of all sales invoices processed and enter up the details of sales made into the sales journal. Figure 5.14 gives an example of an extract from a sales journal. This is very similar to the purchases journal; however, note the folio numbers.

Discussion point

Why are only records of sales made on credit terms listed in the sales journal? Why not list the cash sales as well?

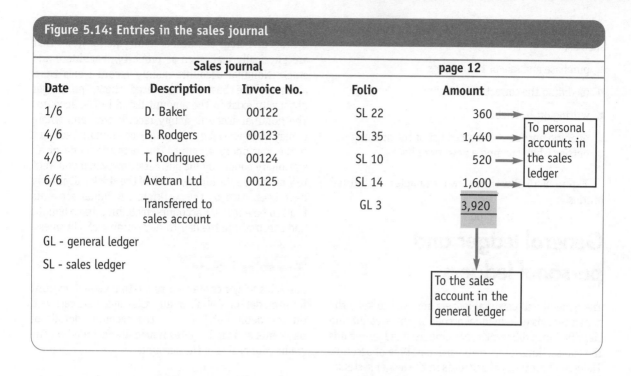

Figure 5.14: Entries in the sales journal

Sales journal				page 12
Date	Description	Invoice No.	Folio	Amount
1/6	D. Baker	00122	SL 22	360
4/6	B. Rodgers	00123	SL 35	1,440
4/6	T. Rodrigues	00124	SL 10	520
6/6	Avetran Ltd	00125	SL 14	1,600
	Transferred to sales account		GL 3	3,920

To personal accounts in the sales ledger

To the sales account in the general ledger

GL - general ledger

SL - sales ledger

Note that although some customers might receive trade discounts, the entry in the sales journal only records the actual value of the sales invoice. However, a different approach needs to be used for discounts offered for prompt payment. By definition, these can only be made after the invoice has been issued. There must be a separate record of these discounts, otherwise the amount received from the customer will not tally with the amount charged and recorded.

Returns journals

Returns journals are laid out in exactly the same fashion as the purchases and sales journals shown in Figures 5.13 and 5.14. Each credit note is posted to individual accounts in purchase and sales ledgers, and the totals are posted to the returns inwards and outwards accounts in the general ledger.

- Credit notes issued are recorded in the returns in journal, then posted to individual sales ledger accounts of customers and the returns inward account, which is kept in the general ledger.

- Credit notes received are recorded in the returns out journal, then posted to individual purchase ledger accounts of suppliers and the returns outward account, which is kept in the general ledger.

The journal proper

Other items that usually are much less common, and can therefore be rather more complicated, are listed in the journal proper. Due to the uncommon nature of these items, these entries are far more detailed than entries in the other journals. For each transaction, there is a record in the journal proper of:

- the date

- the name of the account to be debited and the amount

- the name of the account to be credited and the amount

- a description of the transaction taking place – this is called the narrative

- a reference number of the source documents giving proof of the transaction.

The journal proper is not used by all businesses, as many would have too few items to warrant a separate book. However, the use of a journal proper lessens the chance of fraud by bookkeepers and reduces the risk of errors in accounting.

The journal proper should be used for transactions such as:

- purchase and sale of fixed assets
- recording the correction of errors
- writing off bad debts
- opening entries – a recorded list of the opening entries when opening a new set of books.

Figure 5.15 illustrates two examples of journal entries.

General ledger and personal ledgers

The general and personal ledgers are used to keep the actual records of individual accounts. The accounts are classified into different types, and each ledger records the transactions for its own particular type of account. There are four types of accounts in the ledger system:

- personal accounts for debtors
- personal accounts for creditors
- real accounts
- nominal accounts.

Personal accounts are accounts for a business's debtors and creditors. Real accounts are for items that are physically real, such as property, machinery and stock. Nominal accounts mainly record items that, although the business has used them, no longer physically exist in the amount listed in the account. The nominal account simply records why and where money was spent. A good example of a nominal account is the stationery account. This lists the value of all stationery bought by the business; however, if you went to look for the stationery, much of the stock will already have been used by the workforce. Nominal accounts tend to be expenses accounts, recording items bought and consumed in the day-to-day running of a business.

The sales ledger

The sales ledger contains a separate personal account for each debtor. Details of any sales made are recorded on the debit (left) side of the account; details of payments and credit notes issued are recorded on the credit (right) side of the account.

The purchase ledger

The purchase ledger contains a separate personal account for each creditor. Details of any purchases made are recorded on the credit side of the account; details of payments and credit notes received are recorded on the debit side of the account.

Figure 5.15: Entries in the journal proper

The Journal

Date	Description	Folio	DR.	CR.
1/6	Purchase of new vehicle registration W675 NVF on credit			
	Capital purchases invoice 3456 from N.J.Motors Ltd			
	Vehicle	GL 14	6,500	
	N.J. Motors Ltd	GL 26		6,500
23/6	Debt written off as bad. See letter of notification in file ref PD3.			
	Bad debt	GL 32	820	
	A. Bandit Ltd	SL 15		820

The general ledger

The general ledger contains the remaining accounts of a business, both real and nominal. Some businesses may have a separate ledger for real and nominal accounts, depending on the volume of their transactions. The general ledger is used to record all details of fixed asset purchases and expenses paid. The capital account – funds invested by the owner(s) – is also listed in the general ledger.

You may wonder why the purchase and sales accounts – which detail the total credit purchases and sales of the business – are located in the general ledger, rather than the purchase and sales ledgers, respectively. The answer is that accountants classify these two accounts as nominal accounts and, as such, they belong with the other nominal accounts in the general ledger.

The cash-book

The cash-book shows the bank and cash accounts together. This has one prime advantage, other than just being more convenient to use, in that it allows us to see how much money has been paid out or received in any one day.

Sometimes a business may want to take cash out of the bank and put it into its cash account or vice versa. As it can record this transaction without referring to another ledger or journal (both parts of the transaction are shown on the same page of the cash-book), it does not need a folio number. This type of transaction is known as a contra item. This tells us that the second entry is on the same page of the book.

The cash-book is also used to record cash discounts. A firm may agree to accept a smaller payment in return for prompt payment, or within a certain time period. The amount that the original invoice is reduced by is called a cash or settlement discount. As we discussed earlier (see pp. 256–7), the rate of a cash discount is usually stated as a percentage on the terms and conditions of an invoice; a typical period during which discount may be allowed is one month or thirty days from the date of the original transaction. These discounts are taken into account in the cash-book. There are two types of cash discount:

- discount allowed – discounts allowed by the company to its customers

- discount received – discounts received by the firm from its suppliers.

Discounts allowed are always debit entries in the discount allowed account and always credit entries in the cash-book. Discounts received are always credit entries in the discount received account and debit entries in the cash-book.

Private ledgers

Some companies keep details of capital, funds invested by the owner, and drawings, funds withdrawn by the owner, in what is termed a private ledger. This is so that office staff cannot see details that the proprietors want to keep secret.

The double-entry system

Having looked at the subdivisions of the ledger, and what accounts it contains, we now look at the double-entry system of accounting. The double-entry system has been in use for centuries, and nobody has yet found a better way of recording financial information. There are many books that deal specifically with double-entry bookkeeping and you may find it worthwhile to examine the process in greater detail. However, we shall cover the basic principles in this unit.

The fundamental principle of double-entry bookkeeping is that two entries are made for every transaction. The accounts in the ledgers are split into two sides: the debit side (traditionally the left-hand side, abbreviated Dr.) and the credit side (traditionally the right-hand side, abbreviated Cr.). For each transaction, one entry is made in the left-hand column and one in the right-hand column. This provides a self-checking device to ensure that accounting records are error free. At the end of an accounting period, the total of the left-hand column should equal the total of the right-hand column; that is, they should balance. If they don't, then a mistake has been made somewhere.

There is a simple rule of bookkeeping: for every transaction that takes place, there is an equal and opposite reaction. In other words, every transaction has two effects; one that is of benefit to the organisation, listed on the debit side, and one that creates a burden, listed on the credit side. For example, if a business purchases a new vehicle for £12,000, the benefit that it receives is obviously a new vehicle. However, a burden has been created as the business now has £12,000 less in its bank account. The entries for this transaction would be:

- debit the vehicle account (left-hand side, showing benefit) with the value of the transaction, that is £12,000

- credit the bank account (right-hand side, showing burden) with the value of the transaction, that is £12,000.

Using the double-entry system, all transactions are recorded twice once on each side. There are five main classifications of items that are involved in transactions:

- assets
- liabilities
- capital
- expenses
- revenue.

But what are assets, capital, liabilities, expenses and revenue?

Assets

Assets are anything that is good for the business, such as the resources it owns . Assets can be classified into three different types.

- Fixed assets are assets the business plans to hold for a year or more and which can be used repeatedly such as vehicles, computers or other machinery.

- Current assets are assets whose value changes repeatedly during the course of a year or are items intended for resale. Examples of current assets are stocks of finished goods, cash and bank accounts.

- Other assets are assets that do not naturally fall into the fixed or current categories. Examples include investments, such as shares and deposits.

Liabilities

Liabilities are anything that the business owes such as debts to suppliers, loans, mortgages. Liabilities can be classified into two types.

- Long-term liabilities are money (or debts) owed by the business that have to be paid in more than one year's time. Examples include mortgages and long-term loans.

- Current liabilities are money (or debts) owed by the business that have to paid in less than one year's time. Examples include money owing to creditors and wages owing to the workforce.

Discussion point

Note the similarity between the definition for current assets and current liabilities. Are there any other similarities between the other definitions?

These rules apply when making bookkeeping entries for assets and liabilities:

- assets increasing – debit the account, obviously an increasing asset is a benefit
- assets decreasing – credit the account, creates a burden for the business
- liabilities increasing – credit the account, creates a burden of more debt
- liabilities decreasing – debit the account, has the benefit of reducing debts.

In two cases, we debit the account and in two cases we credit the accounts. For each transaction, we must make an entry on each side; it is impossible to have a transaction that involves two credit entries or two debit entries. For example, buying some stock for cash involves increasing an asset (Dr. purchases) and decreasing an asset (Cr. cash).

Let's look at another example. Consider a company buying £300 of stock on credit from DJ Supplies Limited. This transaction involves the increase in the asset of stock (Dr. entry) and the creation (or increase) in liabilities, as the company now owed DJ Supplies Limited £300 (Cr. entry). Figure 5.16 demonstrates the double-entry required for this transaction. Note the folio numbers on each account list back to the purchases journal where the original invoice would have been recorded.

The same rules apply to every posting to the ledger. Regardless of how many entries are made or which accounts are involved, the value of the transaction entered on the debit and credit sides must balance. Now consider a slightly more complicated example. Assume that VAT is payable on the goods the company purchased from DJ Supplies. Figure 5.17 (on p. 272) shows how the entries should now be made. Note that there is an unequal number of accounts and entries. However, the totals of the Dr. column entries and the Cr. column entries still balance.

Discussion point

Why is it necessary to have a separate account for VAT? Do all businesses have to charge VAT on every product they sell?

Capital

Capital in financial terms means anything invested by the owner(s) such as money and vehicles. This is a very specific definition, and is not to be confused with the more general usage of the term in which capital refers to money, machinery or other assets used by a business.

Figure 5.16: The ledger entries for DJ Supplies

General ledger, page 4   **Purchases account**

Dr

Date	Details	Folio	Amount
09/03	DJ Supplies Ltd	PJ 14	£300.00

Cr

Date	Details	Folio	Amount

Purchase ledger, page 26   **DJ Supplies Ltd account**

Dr

Date	Details	Folio	Amount

Cr

Date	Details	Folio	Amount
09/03	Purchases	PJ 14	£300.00

Note that capital is treated as being a liability. This is because the funds invested in the business actually belong to the owner(s). It can be difficult to understand why money invested by the owners should be treated as a liability. This reflects a concept in accounting called the business entity concept. This asserts that a business and its owners are two separate legal identities. Any money invested in the business by the owners is therefore liability, as at some point it theoretically should be paid back. In reality, money invested by the owners is only likely to be paid back in event of the business ceasing to trade or being sold to another party.

Expenses

Expenses is used to describe all the general running costs incurred by a business. An expense is an item that is purchased and used up in day-to-day activities. Expenses include:

- wages and salaries
- rent and rates
- insurance costs
- heating and lighting
- motor expenses
- administration expenses
- telephone
- printing, postage and stationery
- advertising
- sundry expenses
- distribution costs
- bad debts
- provision for bad debts
- depreciation.

Most of this list is self-explanatory. However, there may be a few terms with which you are unfamiliar. For example, sundry expenses – sometimes referred to as miscellaneous or general expenses – is used as a category to put in any small items of expenditure which don't fit in other areas, such as purchasing tea, coffee, biscuits, etc. for the office.

Bad debts is money which can't be recovered. During the course of the financial period, some companies who owe the business money may go into liquidation, in which case it does not get paid. This can be written off against profits as bad debts. Provision for bad debts is

Figure 5.17: The three ledger entries for DJ Supplies with the VAT account

General ledger, page 4 **Purchases account**

Dr

Date	Details	Folio	Amount	Date	Details	Folio	Amount
09/03	DJ Supplies Ltd	PJ 14	£300.00				

Cr

General ledger, page 16 **VAT account**

Dr

Date	Details	Folio	Amount	Date	Details	Folio	Amount
09/03	DJ Supplies Ltd	PJ 14	£52.50				

Cr

Purchase ledger, page 26 **DJ Suppliers Ltd account**

Dr

Date	Details	Folio	Amount	Date	Details	Folio	Amount
				09/03	Purchases	PJ 14	£352.50

Cr

an allowance that a business makes against an assumption that a certain percentage of debtors outstanding at year end will not pay. Therefore, it deducts the money that it does not think it is going to receive as an expense. Bad debts, and provision for bad debts, are against sales recorded in the trading account. If debtors are not going to pay up (in full), a business should legitimately be able to knock that money off its total sales figures.

Transactions involving expenses are dealt with by:

- debiting the expense account – wages, postage, utilities, etc.
- crediting the payment account – bank, cash or supplier.

Revenue

Revenue is any income generated by the business through sales or from other sources. It could include rent received, commission received from selling other companies' products, interest received as well as direct sales revenue.

For revenue transactions:

- credit the revenue account – sales, rent received, commission received, etc.

- debit the asset account – cash, bank or create a debtor.

Balancing accounts

The fundamental principle of double entry is that the two sides of the whole ledger system must balance. The main challenge is to learn which entries go on which side. This can only be learned through practice.

Totalling accounts is more properly called balancing off. This is done periodically by the business as a summary of its position to date. In addition, the personal accounts of debtors and creditors need to be balanced at least monthly to determine the amount of debtors and creditors that are outstanding. How is this done?

First, add up the biggest side of the account – this can be either the debit or credit side, and enter the total. Second, carry the total across to the opposite side. Third, enter the difference between the total and the sum of the entries on the opposite side. This difference is called the balancing figure, it is the remaining balance on the account. As the remaining balance, this figure

is to be taken forward into the next period; it is labelled the balance carried forward (balance c/f).

To reopen the account for the beginning of the next period, the balance c/f is transferred across to the opposite side to become the opening balance. This is labelled the balance brought forward (balance b/f), as it is the balance brought forward from the previous period. This figure is important as it the figure that is used from each account in compiling the trial balance. Figure 5.18 shows this in action. The balance b/f shows that the company has £800 in its bank account

The trial balance

On a regular basis (usually at least monthly), the accountant draws up what is known as the trial balance. This is a summary list detailing the accounts in the ledger that have an account balance brought forward. Accounts that balance off, that have a zero balance, are ignored. This is primarily a checking device as the figures from these ledgers will eventually be used to produce the company's final accounts.

The trial balance is used to make sure that the entries in the ledgers are correct before calculating and drawing up the final accounts of the company. Remember it is vital that these accounts are accurate, as they will be subjected to analysis from many different stakeholders.

We check the double-entry system by adding up the all the Dr. balance b/f and all the Cr. balance b/f. If we have used double entry correctly then:

Dr. b/f = Cr. b/f

Figure 5.18: Balancing ledger accounts

Bank account

Dr						Cr
Date	Details	Amount	Date	Details	Amount
10/9	Capital	1,000	11/9	Rent	300
	+				
20/9	Sales	200	15/9	Purchases	150
	+				
21/9	Sales	100	25/9	Wages	50
			③	balance c/f	800
Total	①	1,300	②		1,300
Balance b/f	④	800			

This is formally known as a trial balance. It is compiled by transferring all the individual Dr. and Cr. balance b/f's from the ledger accounts and totalling the Dr. column and the Cr. column. Figure 5.19 shows an example trial balance. In reality, there would probably be many more accounts than those shown in the figure. However, Figure 5.19 does detail the main ones you are likely to come across. Note that each individual debtor and creditor is not listed. The reason for this is simple, imagine the length of the trial balance for a company like Marks & Spencer if it had to list every customer account individually.

The main purpose of the trial balance is to check the firm's bookkeeping. However, some errors can occur that will not be identified by a trial balance, this is because they do not result in the two sides of the ledger being unequal. For example, there may be no entry for a transaction on either side; in other words, it is missed off the accounts completely. Other errors can occur if a bookkeeper misreads a document and enters the wrong amount on both sides by, for example, entering £256 on the Dr. and Cr. side instead of £265. This is called transposing a figure.

When the accountant is satisfied that the trial balance is correct and error free, the account balances in the trial balance are used to compile the period end final accounts.

Final accounts

Final accounts are prepared at the end of **accounting periods**. These might be quarterly (every three months), half yearly or annually. Quarterly and half-yearly final accounts are drawn up by some businesses; annual accounts are prepared by all businesses. The **final accounts** summarise all the transactions that have taken place in the accounting period. These consist of a **manufacturing account** (if appropriate), **trading account**, **profit and loss account**, **balance sheet** and an **appropriation account** (if required).

Final accounts are prepared using a set of governing principles, referred to as concepts and conventions. They are laid down by the governing bodies of accountancy, such as the Accounting Standards Board (ASB). One of these principles is that all income and expenditure of the business should be matched to the period under review. Sometimes this means that adjustments need to be made to ensure that the correct amount is included in the appropriate financial period. For example, if an annual insurance policy is taken out halfway through an accounting year, only half the insurance premium (six month's worth) belongs in the current year's final accounts. The remaining six month's premium needs to be included in next year's final accounts. This is because half the benefit received from the insurance policy accrues in the current financial period, and half in the next. An adjustment therefore needs to be made to the trial balance figure to take this into account.

Figure 5.19: A trial balance

Trial balance for [company name] as at 31 March 2000

Account	Dr £	Cr £
Bank	1,000	
Purchases	400	
Sales		800
Capital		1,150
Loan		500
Rent	600	
Rates	300	
Debtors	1,000	
Creditors		850
	3,300	3,300

All businesses produce profit and loss accounts and balance sheets, and these are examined in detail in this unit. Appropriation accounts and trading accounts are used by a great majority of businesses, so we also look at the purpose of these accounting statements. However, manufacturing accounts are a particular form of statement used by those businesses involved in the manufacture of finished goods and components. This is a specialist area of accountancy and is not examined here.

Trading, profit and loss accounts

Before examining the construction of these accounts in detail, it is necessary to introduce a few key terms:

- **profit and loss account** – an accounting statement that shows a firm's revenue generated over an accounting period and all the relevant costs experienced in earning that revenue
- **profit** – the difference that arises when a firm's revenue is greater than its total costs
- **loss** – the difference that arises when a firm's sales revenue is less than its total costs.

The trading profit and loss account is designed to provide financial information based on the performance of a business over an accounting period. Usually a business wants to know how successful it has been and needs some kind of measure of its performance. Profit is one of the main criteria by which a business monitors its success or failure in the marketplace.

Other bodies need this information as well. Government agencies such as the Inland Revenue need to have financial reports in order to be able to calculate how much a business needs to pay in tax. Suppliers also want to be able to establish a business's creditworthiness, although this is often done by taking up credit and bank references.

Discussion point

Imagine you are managing a business. Would you supply another company with thousands of pounds worth of goods or services if you weren't sure it would be able to pay. What information would you want to know about your client?

If you are a potential investor, what information would you wish to know in order to help you decide whether or not to risk your money in a particular company?

A profit and loss account is the tool or engine which organisations use to determine their level of profits. It

provides a measure of how successful the business has been compared to other businesses, and it can be used to see how the business's actual performance compares with the owners expectations – expected results don't always equate with actual results. The measurement of profit can also be used to:

- obtain loans and finances from banks or other lending institutions – lenders want some evidence that the business is capable of paying back loans
- determine the value of the business if the owners wish to sell – a profitable business is usually worth more than an unprofitable one.

Measuring profit

A profit is made if revenue is greater than total costs for a given period. Revenue includes all income received by the company, not just that generated by sales. For example, a large department store not only receives revenue from sales to customers but may also receive income from renting out some of its floor space to other companies, and may receive additional income from interest charges on customers' store credit card accounts. This additional income must be accounted.

Of course, the sales revenue figure is not necessarily an accurate representation of the amount of money a company actually makes. Some customers may have returned purchased products because they were faulty or damaged, on the wrong size and colour. These customers expect a refund or an exchange. Goods brought back to a company are called **returns in**, and the value of these returns must be deducted from the sales figures.

Sales (less returns in) is called **turnover**. So if a company has £50,000 sales, but £2,500 worth of goods are returned by customers, its turnover is £47,500. When calculating turnover, a company also excludes any sales taxes such as VAT. Although, customers pay this tax to the company – as part of the purchase price – it is merely being collected by the business on behalf of the government. The company therefore does not receive money from these sales taxes, and so they are not included in the sales figure.

In accounting terms, profit is the excess of turnover over costs and expenses. If the turnover is greater than the company's costs and expenses, the difference is its profit. Note that the calculation of profit is not based upon the amount of money received or paid out by a business. Sales revenue is recorded when the sale is realised, not when the payment is made. It is perfectly possible, therefore, for an item to be purchased by a customer in one financial period and the money received from the sale to be received by the company in the next period.

Profit classification

In accounting terms, the word profit on its own has very little actual meaning. Profit needs to defined more carefully to enable comparison and analysis of company performance, detailed examination of year-by-year variances and in-depth monitoring of the differences between expected and actual results. It is important, in particular, to understand the difference between gross profit and net profit.

Gross profit is measured on the trading account. It is defined by excess of revenue generated by selling goods over the costs of providing those goods for sale. In other words, it measures the success of a business's trading activities. Not all companies measure gross profit; service businesses, such as solicitors and hairdressers, are not involved in buying and selling activities.

Gross profit = Turnover – Cost of sales

Net profit measures the overall success of the business during the period. It takes into account all the other costs incurred by the business in its day-to-day running.

Net profit = Gross profit – (Expenses + Overheads)

The difference between gross and net profit can best be demonstrated by considering an example. Brian and John are both milkmen. They have similar sized milk rounds, and sell similar amounts of milk for the same price. They both purchase their milk from the same dairy and pay the same price for their supplies. The only difference is that Brian delivers his milk on an electric milk float, while John uses his Ferrari. Figure 5.20 summaries the gross and net profitability of both businesses.

Discussion point

If you are John's accountant, what financial advice would you give him about the way he runs his business? What are the advantages of measuring two forms of profit?

From an examination of Figure 5.20, you should be able to see that if we are just given the profit figures with no explanations we might mistakenly believe that Brian is a much more successful businessman than John. However, in reality, their trading positions and gross profit are identical; it is just in the area of expenses that Brian's business outperforms John's, for reasons that should, hopefully, be obvious.

Examining profit and loss accounts

The first important piece of information included on a profit and loss account is its title. The title provides some very important information at the outset. First, the company name lets us know what type of business we are dealing with, as Figure 5.21 illustrates.

Figure 5.20: A tale of two milkmen

	Brian £	John £
Sales	80,000	80,000
Purchases	54,000	54,000
Gross profit	26,000	26,000
Less expenses		
Motor insurance	300	2,500
Electricity	4,000	Nil
Petrol	Nil	10,000
Net profit	21,700	13,500

Figure 5.21: Company names

Company name	Type of business
L Birkin Decorating	Sole trader
Watson, Hope and Carlyle	Partnership
Matlock Ltd	Private limited company
Lewis Barnthorpe plc	Public limited company

By knowing the type of company, we can start to form an idea of what we should be expecting to see on the profit and loss account.

We are also provided with the year end date. This is an important factor to take into consideration when comparing company accounts, as many types of businesses and markets suffer from trends and fashions and seasonal booms and slumps.

Discussion point

What are the problems of comparing the final accounts of two shops, one with a year end of 30 November, and the other with a year end of 30 January?

The profit and loss account is divided up into three sections:

- the trading account – concerned with profit on trading activities (gross profit)
- the profit and loss account – concerned with the overall level of profit (net profit)
- the appropriation account – concerned with the distribution of any profits made by the business.

Note that sole traders do not need an appropriation account. All profits belong to the sole trader, as the single owner of the business. However, if there is more than one person involved in the ownership of a business, then an appropriation account is needed, as the owners will need to be told where the profit has gone. For example, a public limited company needs to show how much profit is being distributed to shareholders and how much is being retained within the business.

The trading account

The trading account shows how much revenue has been earned. An example of a trading account is shown in Figure 5.22. It embodies two key calculations.

Gross profit = Turnover – Cost of sales

Cost of sales = Opening stock + Purchases – Returns out + Carriage inwards – Closing stock

Figure 5.22: An example of a trading account

D Bagley Trading Account for the period ended 30 May 2000

	£	£	£
Sales		57,200	
Less Returns in		410	56,790
Less Cost of sales			
Opening stock	4,736		
Add Purchases	23,748		
Less Returns out	644	23,104	
Add Carriage in		620	
		28,460	
Less Closing Stock		5,892	22,568
Gross profit			34,222

The cost of sales is trying to establish how much it cost to make or buy the products that have been sold in the current financial period. Unless it is their first year of trading, companies actually start an accounting period selling stock left over from the previous period, this is called opening stock; the cost of this stock is brought into this accounting period as this is when it is going to be sold.

We then need to add the cost of purchases made during the accounting period which are used to produce new stock. These should include the cost of delivery, carriage in, of purchases. This is sometimes shown as a separate line on the account.

From this figure, we deduct returns out; that is, the value of any purchases sent back to suppliers because they were faulty or damaged in some way.

Finally, we deduct the value of closing stock. This is the amount of stock left over at the end of the accounting period, which is available for sale in the following accounting period. Closing stock at the end of the current accounting period becomes opening stock in next period's final accounts.

Discussion point

Consider the account in Figure 5.22. Assume Bagley's sales are 10 per cent higher than shown, and the purchases are 5 per cent higher. If all other figures stay the same, what is Bagley's gross profit? Draw up a revised trading account.

The profit and loss account

The profit and loss account starts directly under the trading account (see Figure 5.23). This is because we need the gross profit figure to calculate net profit, so we just continue the account we've already started.

The trading account only considers revenue received from trading activities. The profit and loss account needs to take into account income from other areas as well, such as rent, commission and interest. Remember these are denoted as income rather than expenses by being followed by the word received. The business could have sold some of its assets, and any profit from this sale is also recorded here.

Now take a look at Figure 5.23 and examine how a profit and loss account is presented for analysis.

Profit quality

An important aspect to take into consideration when examining a trading profit and loss account is not only the level of profit made but also the quality of that profit. High-quality profit is considered to be profit that is made from sustainable sources; low-quality profit comes from one-off events that cannot be repeated to generate profits again in future years.

Discussion point

Read the article below. Discuss the quality level of the profit being made by BA.

BA's future on the line

British Airways' chief executive, Bob Ayling, yesterday admitted for the first time that his job and the jobs of thousands of his staff were at risk if he failed to achieve radical changes in the company.

Mr Ayling also admitted that hundreds more staff would be voluntarily leaving BA by March, in addition to the 1,000 voluntary departures already announced.

Mr. Ayling's candid statements came as BA announced pre-tax profits for the six months to the end of September of £240 million, compared with £385 million, down almost 40 per cent.

The total was swollen by the inclusion of £191 million in profits from disposals, primarily from the sale of business interests, of which the most important was BA's ticketing organisation.

The City responded positively to the announcement, convinced that BA is taking positive measures to deal with its current crisis. The results were actually marginally better than the City had forecast. In spite of the problems, BA's board decided to pay an interim dividend of 5.1p per share.

The Guardian, 9 November 1999

Figure 5.23: A profit and loss account

D Bagley Trading, Profit and Loss Account
for the period ended 30 May 2000

	£	£	£
Sales		57,200	
Less Returns in		410	56,790
Less Cost of goods sold			
Opening stock	4,736		
Add Purchases	23,748		
Less Returns out	644	23,104	
Add Carriage in		620	
		28,460	
Less Closing stock		5,892	22,568
Gross profit			34,222
Add Other income			Nil
Less Expenses			
Wages and salaries		3,046	
Motor expenses		1,842	
Rent		700	
Heat and light		479	
Distribution		656	
Printing, postage and stationery		184	
Advertising		1,460	
Insurance		200	
Bad debts		154	
Provision for bad debts		62	
Depreciation		1,240	
Sundry expenses		104	10,127
Net profit (loss)			24,095

The appropriation account

The purpose of the appropriation account is to show the owners – which in the case of a public limited company could be thousands of people – exactly how the net profit has been shared out. Net profit can be used in two main ways. It can either be distributed or retained.

Distributed profit provides a share of the net profit to the owners. In a partnership, partners receive their share of net profit directly; in a company, shareholders receive their allocation of net profit through dividends. Some profit may be used by the business to reinvest for the future. The retained profit could be allocated for specific projects such as investment in new assets.

Limited companies may also choose to transfer some profit to reserves. These are profits that are kept by the company to use in future years; for example, reserves may be used to pay a dividend in years when profits are low. Rather than being termed retained profit, this item is usually shown as a transfer to general reserve. Completed profit and loss accounts for a public limited company are shown in Figure 5.24. The appropriation account, at the foot of the figure, shows how much profit has been shared out as dividends, how much has been kept by the company, as well as the amount of tax paid. Note that the profit and loss account balance from last year – the retained profit – is bought into this year's account.

Figure 5.24: Final accounts for internal use

Vitador plc Profit and Loss Account for internal use
for the period ending 31 March 2000

	£	£	£
Turnover			1,530,000
Less Cost of goods sold			
Opening stock		210,000	
Purchases		920,000	
		1,130,000	
Less Closing stock		272,000	858,000
Gross profit			672,000
Other income			
Rents		8,000	
Commission		6,000	14,000
			686,000
Less Expenses			
Sales and distribution expenses			
Wages and salaries	100,000		
Motor expenses	42,000		
General expenses	30,000		
Depreciation	14,000	186,000	
Administration expenses			
Wages and salaries	88,000		
Directors remuneration	40,000		
Motor expenses	16,000		
Sundry expenses	5,000		
General admin expenses	61,000		
Depreciation	10,000	220,000	
Finance expenses			
Interest	10,000		
Bank charges	2,000	12,000	418,000
Profit on ordinary activities before tax			268,000
Tax on ordinary activities			98,000
Profit on ordinary activities after tax			170,000
Retained profit from last year			25,000
			195,000
Transfer to reserves		30,000	
Proposed ordinary dividend		90,000	
Proposed preference dividend		30,000	150,000
Retained profits carried to next year			45,000

Discussion point

Obtain a set of company accounts; you can find copies in firms' annual reports. Compare the information with the type of details shown in Figure 5.24. What are the major differences? Can you suggest reasons why the published accounts contains a different range of information.

Public limited companies

Public limited companies are required by law to publish their accounts. The Companies Act 1985 gives specific instructions about the minimum information that must be included and the format in which the accounts must be presented. When a company draws up its profit and loss account for internal use – for the eyes of directors and management only – they look very similar to

Vitador's accounts in Figure 5.24. However, when the accounts are drawn up for external publication, a company usually only reveals the minimum amount of information required by law. This is because these accounts could be examined by competitors as well as the owners and potential investors

Figure 5.25 shows a version Vitador's prepared for external publication. It can be seen that the account for external use does not provide as much information as the one for internal use. This minimises the information competitors might be able to use to gain an advantage.

Companies do not have to publish to the minimum standard. They can include any extra information they wish, but not less. Many plcs are not individual companies, but form part of a group. These companies are required to produce consolidated accounts. These are the type of accounts you often see in company reports. They show both the financial position of the individual company and also the financial position of the group.

When examining company reports, it is important to not only to look at the main accounts themselves but also to read the notes to the accounts. These often contain more detailed explanation of the figures, and include a description of financial events that have taken place over the period. For example, the notes list:

- exceptional items – one-off transactions that have the effect of distorting the company's trading account

- extraordinary items – transactions that have occurred during the period that are not part of the usual activities of the business, again they have the effect of distorting the published accounts.

Discussion point

Read the article on p. 282 about the problems of being a listed public limited company. What are the 'heavy and permanent burdens imposed for access to the market' and why they are of concern, especially for smaller companies?

Figure 5.25: Final accounts for external use

Vitador plc Profit and Loss Account for external use for the period ending 31 March 2000

	£	£
Turnover		1,530,000
Less Cost of goods sold		858,000
Gross profit		672,000
Other income		14,00
		686,000
Less Overheads		
		418,000
Profit on ordinary activities before tax		268,000
Tax on ordinary activities		98,000
Profit on ordinary activities after tax		170,000
Retained profit from last year		25,000
		195,000
Transfer to reserves	30,000	
Proposed ordinary dividend	90,000	
Proposed preference dividend	30,000	150,000
Retained profits carried to next year		45,000

Never a bed of roses

Never believe that life for directors of a plc is bed of roses. Unless, that is, the petals have yet to be stripped from their thorny stems. The current trend for delisting smaller companies from the Stock Exchange in Britain reflects a growing disillusion with life in the public eye.

Markets typically generate a wave of publicity that attract private firms to the Stock Exchange like bees to a financial honey-pot. Entrepreneurs and backers sense the chance to cash in on years of private labour and risk.

Stock exchanges exist to facilitate the raising of new capital and the easy exchange of ownership. For many firms their need for these facilities is temporary or infrequent; but the burdens imposed for access to this market are heavy and permanent. They are also overlooked in the rush to go public.

The hard costs of being a plc can be high, but they can be calculated and taken into account when deciding the relative merits of differing ways of raising finance from going public. It is the soft costs – of disclosure of financial information, scrutiny by auditors and competitors and accountability – that are often underestimated and take their toll on capital in listed companies.

The Guardian, 1 April 1999

Depreciation

Fixed assets have a limited life, even though some equipment might last for decades. Accountants write off some of the value of fixed assets each year. This appears as a charge on the profit and loss account before tax is paid. This charge is called **depreciation**; it is not a cost, it is a **provision**. In effect, depreciation reduces the book value of an asset; it does not reflect the value of monetary transactions.

The book value does not have to reflect the true market value of the asset. The book value depends on the method used to calculate depreciation. The only time that depreciation can be accurately calculated is when the firm disposes of the asset, and the difference between its purchase cost and its value at the time of sale be calculated. However, as this is known by selling the asset, for accountancy purposes it is impractical.

Causes of depreciation

Depreciation of assets can be caused by many factors normally these are:

- wear and tear – through normal use the asset eventually wears out

- decay – rust, rot, erosion, etc.

- inadequacy – an asset is no longer useful to a company due to changes in company size, structure or purpose.
  Causes of depreciation could also include:

- technical obsolescence – a machine will be replaced by faster more efficient models, although the old machine may still be in perfect working order

- market obsolescence – some products have a limited lifetime, so the machinery used to produce the products may become obsolete

- depletion – some natural assets, such as the contents of a quarry or mine, will run out, therefore they can be depreciated in value.

Some assets, such as patents or leases, actually have a set legal lifetime. They therefore lose value as the expiry date gets closer. The process of depreciating assets with fixed legal lifetimes is called amortisation.

Of course, some assets can actually increase in value; this is called appreciation. Normal accounting practice is to ignore appreciation as, in many cases, the value is very subjective. A company may own a painting, for example, which is displayed in the boardroom. Some people may be prepared to pay £30 million for the painting, others may think it worthless.

There is no single approved method for calculating depreciation. The simplest and easiest approach is the **straight-line method**. This reduces the book value of the asset by the same amount each year over the asset's useful life. It is calculated using the formula:

$$\text{Depreciation charge} = \frac{\text{Cost of asset} - \text{Expected residual (scrap) value}}{\text{Useful life}}$$

For example, suppose a machine costs £20,000 and is expected to be used for four years, at which point the company will hope to sell it for £6,000.

Annual depreciation = (20,000 − 6,000)/4 = £3,500

The annual depreciation is charged to the expenses section of the profit and loss account. This straight-line method is useful when the business is expecting constant returns over the life of an asset.

The **reducing balance method** recognises the fact that few assets decline in value by the same amount each year. This method reduces the value of an asset by a fixed percentage. This means that depreciation is highest in the early years and lower in later years. The method takes into account the fact that as a machine gets older it requires more maintenance, and costs are liable to increase as its earning power decreases.

Again consider an example. A company buys a vehicle costing £8,000 that is expected to be resold after four years for £2,500. Depreciation is to be charged at an annual rate of 25 per cent.

- Year 1: depreciation charge is £2,000 (£8,000 x 0.25); net book value is £6,000 (£8,000 − £2,000)

- Year 2: depreciation charge is £1,500 (£6,000 x 0.25); net book value is £4,500

- Year 3: depreciation charge is £1,125 (£4,500 x 0.25); net book value is £3,375

- Year 4: depreciation charge is £844 (£3,375 x 0.25); net book value is £2,531.

Note that the net book value in Year 4 is £2,351; this is not the exact scrap value but it is near as we are likely to get unless we use an extremely awkward percentage.

There is no hard and fast rule about which method should be used. A general guideline is to try to match the method with the amount of benefit received in each year. For consistent returns use the straight-line method. For high initial returns, which gradually decline, use the reducing balance method. In each case, the depreciation charge in each year is charged to that year's profit and loss account (as part of expenses). The unallocated portion – the cost of the asset less the total depreciation charged to date – is the net book value. This is treated as an asset and appears on the balance sheet.

Balance sheets

After the revenue accounts have been prepared, and the net profit figure has been determined, the remaining balances on the books need to be shown on the **balance sheet**. Before we proceed with a detailed examination of balance sheets it is useful to define a few key terms.

- **Balance sheet** – An accounting statement that shows an organisation's assets and liabilities at a given point in time, usually the last day of the accounting year. A balance sheet also shows where and how an organisation has obtained and spent its capital.

- **Assets** – Items which can be ascribed a monetary value and that bring benefit to the organisation. Assets can be thought of as the being resources owned by the organisation.

- **Liabilities** – Debts or money owed by the organisation to other parties. Liabilities are sources of finance, and provide the means by which assets can be acquired.

- **Capital** – Money or resources invested by the owner(s) in the organisation. This is another source of finance used by the business to acquire assets.

Balance sheets provide information about a business that isn't available on the profit and loss account. The balance sheet is a statement that records the sources of finance for the business. It also lists the assets possessed by the company. A balance sheet, therefore, enables the stakeholders to look at the make up of a company's finances and make decisions about the companies stability, ability to pay debts and ability to expand. A balance sheet shows you the strength of business built up over years of trading; in contrast, a trading, profit and loss account only shows what has happened during the current accounting year.

The accounting equation

The accounting equation is the formula that forms the basis for the balance sheet and all balance sheet operations. It is this formula that actually balances the balance sheet. The formula states that:

Assets = Capital + Liabilities

To begin with let us simplify this to:

Assets = Capital

This formula states that all the resources or assets in the business are equal to the amount of money or resources that the owners have invested. For example, imagine Bill Godfrey is about to establish a business as a window cleaner. This is a fairly simple (and cheap) form of enterprise. Bill puts up all the capital required for the business. This start-up capital is used to pay for ladders and equipment, and any money left over would be put into a bank account to pay expenses and bills as the business starts trading.

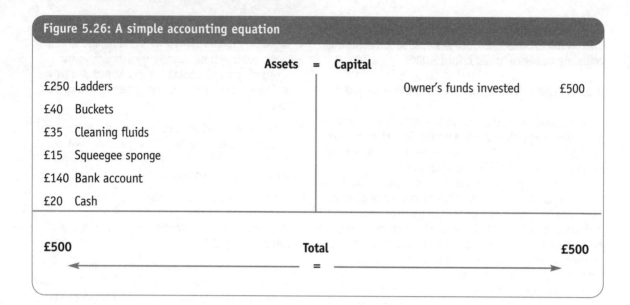

Figure 5.26: A simple accounting equation

Assets	=	Capital	
£250 Ladders		Owner's funds invested	£500
£40 Buckets			
£35 Cleaning fluids			
£15 Squeegee sponge			
£140 Bank account			
£20 Cash			
£500	Total		**£500**
	=		

As Figure 5.26 shows, Bill Godfrey starts his business with £500 that he has managed to save over the last few months. He buys a set of ladders costing £250, several buckets cost £40, some cleaning fluids cost £35 and a squeegee sponge cost £15. He then puts £140 into a business bank account and holds £20 in change. Figure 5.26 shows a very simple balance sheet in operation; the two sides balance at £500.

Now, let's consider the full form of the equation and introducing liabilities. Bill Godfrey decides that his window cleaning business would be much more successful if he could get to see more clients. To do this, he needs to purchase a van to transport himself and his equipment. He used all his own savings to start the business, so he approaches the bank for a loan. As Figure 5.27 shows, he manages to obtain a loan for £3,000 repayable over the next two years and purchases a van costing £2,700. Note that the extra £300 from the loan has been deposited in Bill Godfrey's bank account.

From Figures 5.26 and 5.27, we can see that the

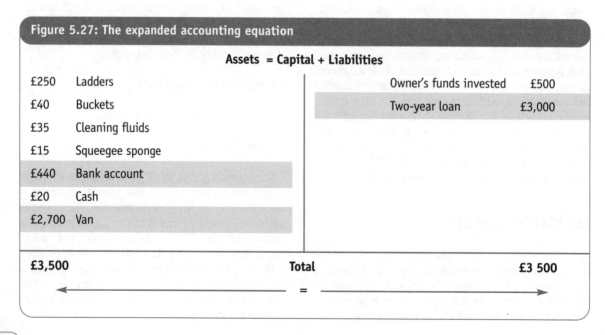

Figure 5.27: The expanded accounting equation

Assets	= Capital + Liabilities	
£250 Ladders	Owner's funds invested	£500
£40 Buckets	Two-year loan	£3,000
£35 Cleaning fluids		
£15 Squeegee sponge		
£440 Bank account		
£20 Cash		
£2,700 Van		
£3,500	Total	**£3 500**
	=	

accounting equation will always hold true as any money invested in the business is either spent, in which case we record what it is spent on, or it is left within the business in the form of bank or cash deposits. Part of a financial accountant's role is to classify and summarise financial data. If we just continue list randomly all the resources purchased and all the finance invested, we would end up with a huge list of items. This would make very little sense to anyone attempting to read it. It would also be virtually impossible to make sound business decisions. A balance sheet is a much more formal document, breaking down assets and liabilities into distinct areas. This makes it much easier to determine where and how a business obtained its resources, and to make informed judgement about the performance of the business.

Balance sheet format

A balance sheet can be compiled in two formats: horizontal and vertical. The horizontal format is the easier to follow and understand, but the vertical format contains much more information. For this reason, the vertical format is more commonly used in business today. Assets and liabilities are defined in exactly the same manner on both formats. The divisions that are used are on the balance sheet (in both formats) are:

- fixed assets
- current assets
- other assets
- owners' funds and capital
- long term liabilities
- current liabilities.

We have already defined these terms, but it is worth considering these component parts of the balance sheet in more detail.

Fixed assets can be divided into tangibles and intangibles. Tangibles include:

- freehold land – land over which the owner has sole rights
- freehold buildings – premises to which the owner has sole rights
- leasehold land or buildings – a lease is a contract between the owner and another party granting the use of the property for an agreed period
- plant, machinery and equipment – anything from manufacturing machinery to computers and faxes
- fixtures and fittings – furniture and telephones
- vehicles – cars, vans, trucks and lorries.

Intangibles include:

- goodwill – the prestige a business enjoys which adds value over and above the value of its physical assets
- patents and copyright – exclusive legal rights to manufacture or sell a particular invention, design or work
- trademarks – these have a value as they encourage consumers to purchase products through brand loyalty.

Fixed assets are listed in order of permanence: assets that are held longest are listed first.

Current assets include stock, debtors, prepayments – expenses that the business has paid in advance such as rent and rates, cash at the bank and cash in hand. Current assets are listed in order of liquidity. The most illiquid are listed first: that is, asset which is most difficult to turn into cash without a loss in its value.

Long-term liabilities include loans, mortgages and debentures – a form of fixed repayment and interest loan stock issued by the company and secured against fixed assets. Current liabilities include creditors, accruals – goods and services which have been used and not yet paid for. such as electricity and gas – provision for repayment of debts expected to mature, such as loans falling due, taxation owing and dividend payments proposed but not yet paid. Current liabilities are listed in this order: creditors, accruals, provision for repayments.

The horizontal balance sheet

The horizontal, or 'T', balance sheet is probably the simplest format. Figure 5.28 shows its broad scheme. If we assign each classification a value, as shown in the shaded boxes, we can see that the two sides balance. Note that although assets equal liabilities, it is unlikely (and even undesirable) that current assets and current liabilities should be the same.

The figure that we get when we add up both sides of the balance sheet is called the balancing figure. This figure supposedly represents the value of the business. It shows the value of all the assets added together, and is meant to represent how much the business is worth. In reality, this isn't strictly true, as we shall see when we look at the vertical format. The value a business assigns to the assets on its books may be totally different from their current market value. Assets are recorded at their purchase value less accumulated depreciation. This may not reflect their true market value at all. Figure 5.29 shows a fully worked example of a horizontal balance sheet for a sole trader.

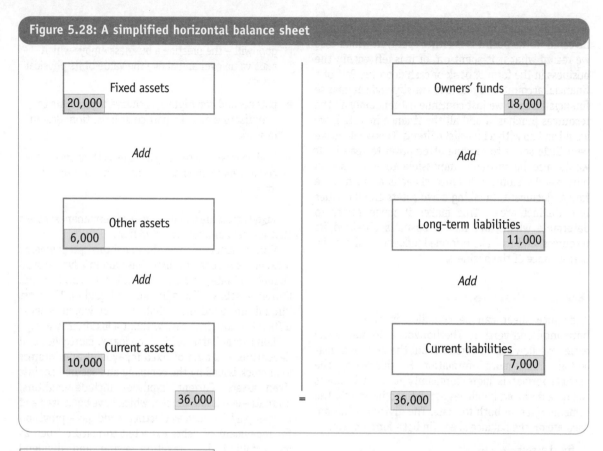

Figure 5.28: A simplified horizontal balance sheet

Fixed assets			Owners' funds	
20,000				18,000
Add			*Add*	
Other assets			Long-term liabilities	
6,000				11,000
Add			*Add*	
Current assets			Current liabilities	
10,000				7,000
	36,000	=	36,000	

The vertical balance sheets

The vertical balance sheet is more complicated than the horizontal format, yet it is the one most widely used in business today, so it is worth trying to become familiar with this format. Figure 5.30 shows a vertical balance sheet in simple layout.

Discussion point

On the horizontal balance sheet, the business in our simplified example is worth £36,000. On the vertical balance sheet, using exactly the same figures, it is apparently only worth £29,000. Which do you think more accurately reflects the true worth of the business?

Compare the two formats (Figures 5.28 and 5.30). We can see that the balancing figure in the vertical format is much lower than the balancing figure given by the horizontal format. This is because current liabilities have been moved from the liabilities section to the asset section, and deducted from current assets. Why should a business do this?

First, current liabilities are short-term debts. The argument is that these should be taken away from the balancing figure, which supposedly shows the worth of the business, as they have to be repaid fairly soon, thus reducing the value of the business. Short-term debts need to be repaid with short-term, or current, assets. The net effect of repaying these debts ought to be taken into account when drawing up the balance sheet.

Second, as current liabilities need to be repaid, hopefully using current assets; by taking the current away from current assets we get a figure termed working capital. This shows an organisation's ability or inability to pay its short-term debts. If current assets exceed current liabilities, the business has enough short-term assets to pay short-term debts. However, if current assets are less than current liabilities, the business does not have enough short-term assets to pay short-term debts. The balance between current assets and liabilities is a very important figure. Consider what action a business's suppliers might take if they do not receive their due payment.

Figure 5.31 shows in vertical format the same balance sheet we illustrated in Figure 5.29. Note there are several other changes: the balancing figure is now labelled capital employed, this represents the total assets actually owned by the organisation and shows the sources of finances used to obtain these assets. Note that the extra space provided by using a vertical layout, allows more detail to be shown about the composition of the fixed assets. It must be realised that the fixed assets owned by a business are of major importance.

Figure 5.29: Horizontal balance sheet for a sole trader

Balance Sheet of J Mullings as at 13 June 2000

Assets			Liabilities		
Fixed assets	£	£	**Owner's funds**		
Freehold premises		70,000	Capital invested	46,000	
Fixtures and fittings		8,000	Profit for the year	14,000	60,000
Motor vehicles		3,000			
		81,000	Less Drawings		8,200
Other assets			Capital as at 13/06/2000		51,800
None					
			Long-term liabilities		
Current assets			5 year loan		40,000
Stock	8,000				
Debtors	3,000		**Current liabilities**		
Prepayments	1,000		(Debts due within one year)		
Bank	2,000		Creditors	3,000	
Cash	800	14,800	Accrued costs	1,000	4,000
		95,800			95,800

Figure 5.30: A simplified vertical balance sheet

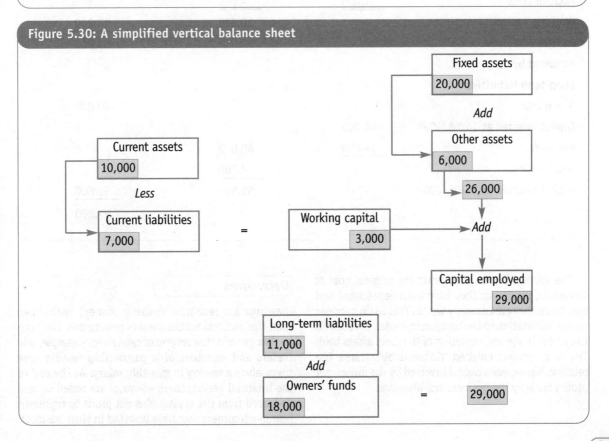

Figure 5.31: Vertical balance sheet for a sole trader

The balance sheet of J Mullings as at 13 June 2000

	£	£	£
Fixed assets	Cost	Accumulated depreciation	Net book value
Freehold premises	70,000	Nil	70,000
Fixtures and fittings	9,400	1,400	8,000
Motor vehicles	6,000	3,000	3,000
			81,000
Other assets			
None			
Current assets			
Stock	8,000		
Debtors	3,000		
Prepayments	1,000		
Bank	2,000		
Cash	800	14,800	
Current liabilities			
(Debts due within one year)			
Creditors	3,000		
Accrued costs	1,000	4,000	
Working capital		10,800	10,800
Capital employed			91,800
Financed by:			
Long-term liabilities			
5 year loan			40,000
Capital invested at 14/06/1999	46,000		
Net profit	14,000	60,000	
Less Drawings		8,200	
Capital invested at 13/06/2000		51,800	51,800
			91,800

The vertical layout also shows the original cost of the assets, how much they have been depreciated and how much they are currently worth. This again provides useful information to the competent reader, as it details the probable age and condition of the fixed assets held. The last section, entitled 'financed by', shows the relationship between capital invested by the owner, net profits made by the business and drawings.

Drawings

Drawings are resources (usually money) withdrawn from the business for the owner's private use. They can be thought of as the reverse of capital. For example, sole traders and members of a partnership usually give themselves a weekly or monthly salary. At the end of the financial period, these drawings are added up and deducted from the capital plus net profit to represent how much owners now have invested in their business.

Balance sheets for sole traders

Figure 5.31 shows that the net profit made by the business is added to the capital invested by the owner. This makes sense as people run most businesses so that they can make and keep the profits. However, it must be recognised that this profit is not a lump sum that is handed to the owner at the end of the year. It is the sum total of the excess of sales over expenses made up thousands of individual transactions that have taken place during the course of the year's trading.

However, the net profit does belong to the owner, so it is shown as increasing the amount of capital the owner has invested in the business. If a business makes a net loss instead of a profit, this figure is inserted instead of the net profit figure and deducted from the original capital balance, showing that the value of the owner's investment in the business has fallen.

Balance sheets for partnerships

The balance sheets for partnerships are very similar to those shown in Figure 5.31. They details:

- fixed assets
- other assets
- currents assets
- current liabilities
- long-term liabilities.

The component parts of these classifications, and the order in which they are listed, are exactly the same as for a sole trader. It is only the 'financed by' section which is different. The reason for this is simple. A single person owns a sole trader, but a partnership is owned by between two and 20 people. So, while on a sole trader's balance sheet one capital account is recorded and all the net profit and drawings are credited and debited to that account, on a partnership's balance sheet a capital account for each of the partners is shown. This is because partners may have invested different amounts of capital and completed different amounts of work throughout the year: each partner is therefore entitled to a different share of the profits.

A partnership's balance sheet shows the same details as a sole trader, but for each individual partner. This is recorded together with any other items set out in the partnership agreement about the way in which profits (or losses) are to be shared.

Balance sheets for limited companies

Limited companies follow the same broad layout, but as limited companies tend to be larger and more complex organisations, this is reflected in the structure of their balance sheets. Limited companies are much more likely to have intangible assets such as patents, trademarks and brand names. It is also common for companies, and especially public limited companies, to hold other assets such as shares in other companies and deposit accounts with financial institutions.

The structure of the bottom half of a company's balance sheet recognises that companies are able to raise finance in more ways than a sole trader or partnership. It is much easier for limited companies to obtain loans. Limited companies are also able to sell loan stock like debentures to raise long-term finance. Limited companies can also issue differing types of shares to raise capital.

> ### Discussion point
>
> Explain why a business may want to retain some the profit generated. What will shareholders receive instead? Explain the difference between authorised and issued share capital. Why might a company not issue all of its available shares?

The balance sheet for a limited company therefore tends to have more entries and is more complex. Figure 5.32 shows a balance sheet for a limited company. You might be unfamiliar with some of the terms used on the balance sheet, so these are explained here.

- Authorised share capital – the value of share capital that a company may issue. It does not necessarily equal issued share capital, depending on whether the company has sold all its authorised capital.

- Issued share capital – shows the types and number of shares that have been sold. This is the capital raised through the sale of shares and is included in the balance sheet calculations.

- Share premium account – the additional revenue gained from the sale of shares over and above their nominal or face value.

- Revaluation reserve – a book adjustment, balancing any fixed assets that have been revalued on the lower half of the balance sheet. It has the effect of raising the value of shareholder investment in the company.

- Profit and loss account – this takes the place of net profit. Profits are distributed to shareholders through dividends. However, some profit is retained by the business. This belongs to the shareholders, increasing the level of their investment, but it would be impossible to show individual accounts for each shareholder; so profits retained and reinvested year by year are recorded in one profit and loss account.

Figure 5.32: Balance sheet for a limited company

Balance Sheet for Dunnes Limited as at 31 December 2000

	£ Cost	£ Accumulated depreciation	£ Net book value
Fixed assets			
Intangible			
Goodwill	40,000		40,000
Tangible			
Premises	380,000	40,000	340,000
Plant and equipment	440,000	180,000	260,000
Vehicles	100,000	20,000	80,000
Fixtures and fittings	100,000	10,000	90,000
			810,000
Current assets			
Stock	116,000		
Debtors	65,000		
Prepayments	4,000		
Bank	39,000	224,000	
Current liabilities			
Creditors	80,000		
Proposed dividend	24,000		
Corporation tax	10,000	114,000	
Working capital		110,000	110,000
			920,000
Less			
Long-term liabilities			
5 year loan		40,000	
10% debentures		80,000	120,000
Net assets			800,000
Financed by:			
Authorised share capital			
100,000 6% preference shares £2 ea.		200,000	
1,200,000 ordinary shares £1 ea.		1,200,000	
		1,400,000	
Issued share capital			
40,000 6% preference shares £2 ea.		80,000	
600,000 ordinary shares £1 ea.		600,000	680,000
Share premium account		12,000	
Revaluation reserve		20,000	
Profit and loss account		88,000	120,000
Shareholders funds			800,000

BUILD YOUR LEARNING

Keywords and phrases

You should know the meaning of these words and phrases. Go back through the last 26 pages to check your understanding.

- Accounting periods
- Appropriation account
- Balance sheet
- Books of original entry
- Capital employed
- Cash-book
- Consolidated accounts
- Cost of sales
- Depreciation
- Distributed profit
- Double-entry system
- Final accounts
- General ledger
- Journal proper
- Loss
- Nominal accounts
- Profit
- Profit and loss account
- Profit quality
- Purchases journal
- Purchase ledger
- Real accounts
- Retained profit
- Sales ledger
- Sales journal
- Trading account
- Trial balance
- Turnover
- Working capital

Summary points

- The information in financial documents received and issued by a company is recorded first in books of original entry

- These entries are transferred, posted. to the ledgers using the double-entry system;

- A trial balance is extracted to check the entries are accurate and these records are then used to compile the businesses final accounts.

- Final Accounts of a business consist of the trading, profit and loss account, the appropriation account (if applicable) and the balance sheet.

- The trading account is used to calculate gross profit. This is profit made on buying and selling activities only. Note service companies do not have trading accounts.

- The profit and loss account takes into account all other costs, including depreciation, incurred by the business during its day-to-day activities.

- The appropriation account is a statement attached to the profit and loss account that shows where and how net profit has been distributed. Sole traders do not need an appropriation account.

- The balance sheet is a snapshot of a business on a given date showing its long-term financial position. It shows what the business owns (assets), set against what the business owes, (liabilities and capital).

Interpreting financial information

FINANCIAL INFORMATION IS vital in planning and controlling the activities of a business. Managers need to know whether the business is making a profit or a loss, how much money is available for equipment, whether they need to alter the way the organisation operates, and so on. Only if accurate and up-to-date financial information is available can they make important decisions about the business or plan for the future.

Monitoring business performance allows informed decisions to be made by owners and managers. Better decisions are made when people are well informed. There are a number of important issues that the interpretation of financial information can identify or address. These include:

- performance
- solvency
- profitability.

However, the results gained from a comprehensive financial analysis mean absolutely nothing unless the organisation's objectives are also taken into consideration. Different businesses have different objectives. These have an influence on whether or not we consider the results of any financial analysis to be acceptable.

Consider, for example, a sole trader that makes an annual profit of £100,000. This could be considered a healthy return. But would a partnership with 10 partners be equally satisfied? A more extreme example would be to contrast the objectives of a major plc such as the Halifax Bank with a leisure centre run by a local authority. Halifax may have a range of objectives including maximising profits, being the market leader and corporate growth. The leisure centre may well be trying to provide an efficient service to the whole community within a given budget. So remember to consider what an organisation is trying to achieve when interpreting financial accounts.

There are various ways in which the final accounts can be investigated including:

- initial reading
- vertical analysis
- horizontal analysis
- trend analysis
- ratio analysis

An initial reading is used to gain a broad understanding of the company's financial position, including the type of industry and market in which it is operating, and provides a rough idea of its recent financial performance. Vertical analysis is used to analyse the linkages between figures from accounting statements for a given period. This analyses the interdependence of one figure to another. For example, gross profit is not only determined by sales but also by the cost of sales. Horizontal analysis is used to compare current financial statements with previous financial statements. This is done on an item-by-item basis, to determine whether there have been any particular areas of change.

In trend analysis, the figures from the current accounting statements are compared with those from several previous periods in an attempt to determine the presence of any significant trends. This can be done on a horizontal basis or a vertical basis, or both. For example, we could use horizontal analysis to see if there has been any significant change in the level of sales over two years. We could then use vertical analysis to see if this change has had a knock-on effect on the level of reported gross profit and to establish the relative sizes of the changes. This could then be investigated through several years' accounts to try to establish any trend.

One of the main ways in which a business monitors its performance is through the use of ratio analysis. Ratio analysis can assist in interpreting financial information and help managers in analysing performance. solvency and profitability. Ratio analysis is the use of accounting ratios to compare and interpret financial statements. This method allows for in-depth monitoring of financial performance from one period to another, comparisons over time, comparisons with other companies and analysis of current financial performance

In reality parties trying to glean information from accounts will use a combination of the above methods not just a single one. To undertake a full and detailed analysis of the information contained in a set of final accounts, a logical and thorough process must be followed. This process is shown in Figure 5.33.

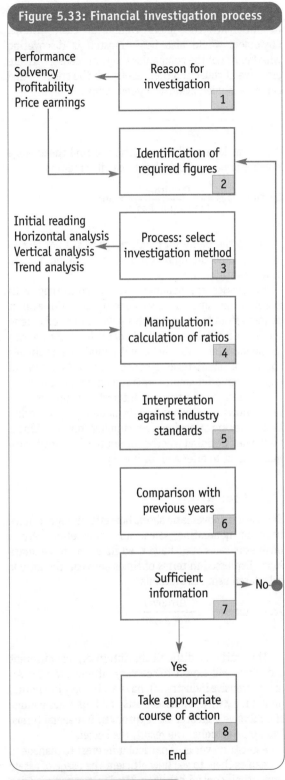

Figure 5.33: Financial investigation process

Performance
Solvency
Profitability
Price earnings

Reason for investigation
1

Identification of required figures
2

Initial reading
Horizontal analysis
Vertical analysis
Trend analysis

Process: select investigation method
3

Manipulation: calculation of ratios
4

Interpretation against industry standards
5

Comparison with previous years
6

Sufficient information
7 → No

Yes

Take appropriate course of action
8

End

Types of ratio

Like everything else in accounting, ratios can be classified according to type. By grouping ratios according to type, we actually make the identification stage of the investigation process much easier. Once the reason for the investigation is established, the appropriate range of ratios can be deployed. For example, if a shareholder is considering whether or not to invest in a company he or she may start by examining price earnings ratios and then move on to a consideration of the profitability ratios.

There are three main types of ratio. which we examine in greater detail in this section:

- **performance ratios** – used to assess the overall performance of a business, these tell how much it costs a business to make its sales, how hard its assets are working and how good its credit control is

- **solvency ratios** – used to investigate the financial stability of the firm by examining the relationships between assets and liabilities, these are sometimes also called liquidity ratios

- **profitability ratios** – used to examine the relationship between (gross and net) profit and sales, assets and capital employed.

Performance ratios

Stock turnover

The stock turnover ratio measures the number of times in one year that a business turns over its stock of goods for sale. From this, we can also establish the average length of time (in days) that stock is held by the company. The ratio is expressed in terms of however many times, and is given by the formula:

$$\text{Stock turnover} = \frac{\text{Cost of goods sold}}{\text{Average stock}}$$

$$\text{Average stock} = \frac{\text{Opening stock} + \text{Closing stock}}{2}$$

We can undertake a comparison with previous years or with other firms of a similar size in the same market. As a general rule, the higher the rate of stock turnover the better. The quicker a business is selling its stock, the quicker it is going to realise the profit on its activities. A decreasing stock turnover figure can indicate falling sales levels or it may suggest that the company is holding a large amount of obsolete or slow-moving items. It could also result from an inefficient purchasing system, that isn't effectively matching purchasing to selling. A note of caution though: the rate of stock turnover can be increased if a firm decides to selling off stock cheaply (below the normal market price). In many circumstances, this would be undesirable.

This ratio can be converted to show the average number of days stock is held. It is also possible to express stock turnover in terms of weeks or months. The ratio for stock turnover (expressed as the average number of days stock is held) is given by either of these formulae:

$$\text{Stock turnover (in days)} = \frac{365}{\text{Stock turnover (times per year)}}$$

$$\text{Stock turnover (days)} = \frac{\text{Average stock}}{\text{Cost of goods sold}} \times 365$$

This stock turnover ratio is of particular interest to managers and suppliers. It allows managers to examine the rate at which sales are been made and year-on-year comparisons can be used as a performance indicator. Suppliers will also be interested in this ratio as it can provide an indication of how frequently a company is going to need to reorder. Note that the stock turnover ratio cannot be used for service industries as service companies do not sell stocks of goods.

Debtors' collection period

It is vitally important for a business to know how long debtors are taking to settle their accounts. This is known as the debtor collection period or debtor days. Good credit control should ensure that customers pay their bills on time but should a firm's credit control slip, the length of time customers take to pay could start to increase over and above the company's agreed terms. This can have important implications on the firm's cash flow.

$$\text{Debtor collection period (in days)} = \frac{\text{Debtors}}{\text{Credit sales}} \times 365$$

Often the figure for credit sales is not actually provided on the profit and loss account. In this case, the sales or turnover figure should be substituted in the formula and used instead.

Different industries allow varying amounts of time for debtors to settle invoices. Standard credit terms are usually range from 30 to 120 days. The debt collection period figure should therefore be compared against the official number of days the organisation allows for settlement. Obviously, the shorter the debt collection period the better.

This ratio is of particular interest to managers and customers. Financial managers can use this ratio to

determine the effectiveness of their credit control and to anticipate the likely timing of cash inflows. Customers would also be interested is discovering whether or not the companies they are dealing with are effective at collecting their debts or if the credit period can be extended over the agreed terms.

Creditor days

We can make a similar calculation to find the average number of days a firm takes to pay its creditors.

$$\text{Creditor days} = \frac{\text{Creditors}}{\text{Credit purchases}} \times 365$$

Again the figure for credit purchases is not always available, and the figure for purchases should be used as a substitute.

Businesses are generally not as concerned with keeping this figure as low as debtor days. However, it cannot afford to let its creditor payment period extend too far or it will lose any trust that it has built up with suppliers. While extended credit periods are a valuable source of short-term finance, the willingness of suppliers to offer credit terms should not be abused.

This ratio is of particular interest to suppliers. This ratio allows a company to determine how good other businesses are at paying their suppliers on time. This is vital when deciding whether or not to offer credit, how much credit to offer and for how long.

Asset turnover

The asset turnover ratio shows how effective assets have been in generating sales, and how effectively a business's sales staff have used its assets to generate sales. Expressed in terms of times per year, the ratio is calculated using the formula:

$$\text{Asset turnover} = \frac{\text{Turnover}}{\text{Net assets}}$$

This ratio is difficult to interpret, as different industries will expect to see very different results. An asset intensive industry will have a relatively low figure; an industry with low asset costs and high sales volume should have a greater asset turnover. In general terms, though, the higher the result, the better.

Asset turnover is of particular interest to managers. It enables them to see how efficient the usage of assets under their control has been. Used in comparison with previous years, it can be an indicator of increasing or decreasing efficiency.

Selling

The overheads as a percentage of turnover ratio expresses the amount of sales absorbed by overheads as a percentage. It is sometimes referred to as the expenses to sales ratio. It is calculated using the formula:

$$\text{Overheads as a percentage of turnover} = \frac{\text{Overheads (expenses)}}{\text{Turnover}} \times 100$$

This ratio tells us the level of overheads compared to sales. It is a measure of how efficiently an organisation is being managed. The lower the result, the better. Comparisons need to be made with the ratios calculated for previous years to determine if the company is becoming more or less efficient. Obviously, the smaller the amount of revenue being absorbed by expenses, the more there is left for profit.

This ratio is of particular interest to managers and owners. It is a measure of efficiency for an organisation. For example, it is no good increasing sales by 20 per cent, if this achieved by a 40 per cent increase in overheads. This would indicate that the company is obviously becoming less efficient. Managers and owners therefore use this ratio to determine if any rise in the level of sales has been achieved effectively and not just through increased costs, such as substantial advertising expenditure.

Solvency ratios

Solvency ratios examine the financial stability of the organisation. They are mainly concerned with an organisation's working capital and whether or not it is being managed effectively. Working capital is needed by all organisations in order to finance their day-to-day activities. If the company has too little working capital, it may not be able to pay all its debts. Too much, and it may not be making most efficient use of its resources.

Current ratio

The current ratio looks at the relationship between current assets and current liabilities, it is sometimes called the working capital ratio and examines the liquidity position of the firm. It is calculated by the formula:

$$\text{Current ratio} = \frac{\text{Current assets}}{\text{Current liabilities}}$$

This is expressed as a ratio, for example 2:1 or 3:1. A result of 2:1 would show that there is two times as many current assets as current liabilities. This means that for every £1 of debt the company owes, it has £2 of assets to pay them. This company is therefore in a position to pay its short-term debts.

Conventional wisdom is that an 'ideal' current ratio should be approximately 2:1. Any higher than 2:1 and the organisation has too many resources tied up in unproductive assets; these should really be invested more profitably. A low current ratio means a business may not be able to pay its debts. For example, a result of 0.6:1 would mean that it has 60 pence of current assets to pay every £1 it owes, and so is not actually able to cover all its short-term debts.

The current ratio can be improved in several ways. However, this is dependent on the direction the business wishes to go. If the current ratio is too high – such as 6:1, for example – the business is holding far too many resources in either stocks, cash, its bank account or has too many debtors. If the ratio is too low, the company may well be have to sell some of its fixed assets (or sell and leaseback) to obtain a more liquid position, or it may have to seek additional long-term sources of finance.

The current ratio is of particular interest to managers, banks and suppliers. This is because it is an indicator of the short-term financial stability of the business. It is important for all parties to consider this ratio when deciding whether or not to borrow and/or lend funds.

The acid test

Sometimes also called the liquidity ratio, the acid test also examines the business's liquidity position by comparing current assets and liabilities, but it deducts stock from the total of current assets. The reason for this is that stock is the most illiquid current asset, it is the hardest to turn into cash without a loss in its value. For example, to convert stock into cash or bank deposits quickly, a company may lower its prices and sell its goods cheaply. It can also take a long time to convert stock into cash; consider a garage that stocks used cars, its stock may sit on its forecourt for months. The stock may also be too old and unsellable.

By removing stock from the equation, we are able to obtain a measure that directly relates cash and near cash equivalents (cash, bank and debtors) to current liabilities. This provides a much more accurate measure of the firm's liquidity. The acid test is calculated using formula:

$$\text{Acid test} = \frac{\text{Current assets – Stock}}{\text{Current liabilities}}$$

The acid test is expressed in the form of a ratio such as 1.7:1. Conventional wisdom states that an ideal result should be approximately 1.1:1, showing that the organisation has £1.10 to pay every £1 of debt. The company can pay all its debts, and has a 10 per cent safety margin as well.

A result lower than 1.1:1 indicates that the firm may well have difficulties meeting short-term debts. However, some businesses are able to operate with a very low level of liquidity; supermarkets, for example, have much of their current assets tied up in stock. This can be a dangerous situation for most businesses, however, whose short-term debts consist mainly of suppliers (creditors) and utilities (electricity and gas). How would companies continue trading without being able to purchase new stocks or without electricity?

Like the current ratio, this ratio is of interest to managers, banks and suppliers. This ratio is a more stringent test of the company's short-term financial stability.

Profitability ratios

Profitability is a measure of how much profit the business is making for its owners. It is usually measured in relation to the size of the business, by comparing the profit made with:

- the value of the firm's assets
- the amount of capital invested
- the level of turnover.

The most important ratios for measuring profit performance are the gross profit margin, net profit margin and the return on capital employed.

Gross profit margin

This ratio looks at the relationship between gross profit and turnover (or sales). It measures how effective a business is at trading. It is expressed as a percentage, calculated by the formula:

$$\text{Gross profit margin} = \frac{\text{Gross profit}}{\text{Turnover}} \times 100$$

$$\text{Gross profit margin} = \frac{\text{Gross profit}}{\text{Sales}} \times 100$$

In simple terms, it is obviously better for a business to have a high gross profit margin. However, the level of gross profit margin varies considerably in different industries. So any result must be looked at in the context of the industry in which the firm operates, and by comparing the results of direct competitors. The firm can also make comparisons with previous year's figures to establish whether or not it has become more or less efficient in its trading activities.

Generally speaking, the gross profit margin should be relatively easy to control, given that a business should know how much it pays for the goods it sells. However, should the gross profit margin start to fall, the cause must be investigated.

This ratio is of particular interest to owners and managers. This is because it is a measure of how well the company undertakes its trading activities. It enables owners and managers to see how well the main activities of the business are performing against its competitors.

Net profit margin

The indicator considers net profit against turnover or sales. Again expressed as a percentage, it is calculated in a similar way to the gross profit margin:

$$\text{Net profit margin} = \frac{\text{Net profit}}{\text{Turnover}} \times 100$$

$$\text{Net profit margin} = \frac{\text{Net profit}}{\text{Sales}} \times 100$$

Net profit margin is used to establish whether the firm has been efficient in controlling its expenses. Once more, the higher the result, the better. Net profit margin is slightly harder to control than gross profit margin. This is because any one of the overhead and expense categories can effect the net profit figure. If the net profit margin falls the business needs to consider whether the gross profit margin has also fallen, causing a knock-on effect.

It needs to ask if one or more expense items increased significantly. And, if so, why? This in itself can be investigated by ratio analysis:

$$\text{Expenses to sales ratio (labour costs)} = \frac{\text{Wages and salaries}}{\text{Turnover}} \times 100$$

$$\text{Expenses to sales ratio (promotion)} = \frac{\text{Advertising}}{\text{Turnover}} \times 100$$

It should investigate if the non-trading sources of business income have fallen significantly. Again, if so, why? If any of these investigations show significant changes in comparison with previous years, the business may have an indication of the cause of the problem.

The net profit margin is of particular interest to owners and managers. Net profit is the profit after all costs have been considered, and the net profit margin is of prime importance in determining the performance of the organisation as a whole. It allows owners and managers to analyse business performance, and by considering individual expenses ratios, it can be used to pinpoint areas of good or bad performance in comparison to previous years and to competitors.

Return on capital employed

Return on capital employed (ROCE) is sometimes referred to as the primary ratio and is considered to be one of the most important ratios. This ratio measures the efficiency of funds invested in the business at generating profits. This ratio is expressed differently for different types of business. This is because various types of business can raise capital in different ways.

For a sole trader or partnership, return on capital employed (expressed as a percentage) is given by the formula:

$$\text{ROCE} = \frac{\text{Net profit}}{\text{Total capital employed}} \times 100$$

For a limited company, return on capital employed (expressed as a percentage) is given by the formula:

$$\text{ROCE} = \frac{\text{Net profit before tax and interest}}{\text{Total capital employed}} \times 100$$

Note that:

Total capital = Ordinary share capital
    + Preference share capital + Reserves
    + Debentures + Long-term loans

Total capital = Total assets employed

The idea of this indicator is to try to determine how much profit has been made for distribution from the total assets employed by that business. This is why we ignore tax and interest charges when calculating ROCE for a limited company. These items are beyond the control of business, and fluctuate subject to the policies of the government and the Bank of England. If we measure profit after tax and interest, we would not reflect actual changes in the performance of the business but external factors.

The higher the value of the ratio, the better. A higher percentage means owners receive a greater return. As with the other ratios, this indicator needs to be compared with the results for previous years and for other companies to determine whether result is satisfactory or not.

The percentage return on capital employed (ROCE) should be compared with the return offered by interest-bearing accounts at banks and building societies. Ideally, the ROCE should be higher than any return that could be gained from interest-earning accounts.

This ratio is of particular interest to owners as it is the measure by which they determine whether their business is a better investment than other possible alternatives. Owners can use the ratio to compare the performance of their business against the possible returns to be made if their capital is invested elsewhere.

Limitations of financial accounts

So far in this unit we have expounded at length about the value of financial records and final accounts. However, it must be understood that they do not possess the answer to every question or problem a business may face. Interpreting financial statements has some major drawbacks.

Accounts cover financial and numerical information only. They make no assessment of workforce morale, management style or developments in market technology. A company might have accounts showing exceptional performance, but it may be facing a strike from a discontented workforce, the loss of an experienced managing director who is about to retire, and a product that is about to become obsolete due to a technological advancement by a competitor. All these developments would suggest that the company could not sustain its current level of performance.

The information contained in a set of accounts is historical. The accounts show what has happened, not what will happen. They do not reflect current developments in the economy. For example, changes in the exchange rate can have dramatic effects on the profitability of many businesses. An awareness of current economic policy and political developments is a useful tool when trying to assess the future performance of a business.

The figures actually presented in the accounts may not necessarily be an accurate representation. For example, the accounts may list assets such as buildings at their purchase cost, though this may not be a true reflection of what they are worth now. Similarly, the record of depreciated assets in the accounts is only a book value that may have no relation to their true market value. Remember that value is subjective, cost can be proven.

There is also the issue of **window dressing**. This is the practice of massaging profit figures and balance sheet valuations to make a company look as if it has performed better than it actually has in reality . One of the main problems in interpreting balance sheets is that they only show the financial position at a single point, usually on the day that marks the end of a company's financial year. Businesses may try to window dress the accounts for this day. Three months down the line, the balance sheet may show a completely different picture of the financial situation of the company.

There is also a problem is making valid comparisons between companies. Although ratio analysis is tool for making inter-firm comparisons, it is actually rather difficult to find two or more companies that make and sell exactly the same product. Which company would you choose to compare with Heinz, given the wide range of different products it sells? Similarly how do make comparisons for Coca-Cola: the obvious answer, you might think, is Pepsi, but Coca-Cola is actually part of the Coca-Cola Cadbury's Schweppes group, which has a wide product range in many markets.

For major businesses like public limited companies (plcs), the picture can become even more muddied. Plcs often own intangible assets such as brand names and copyrights. However, how do you accurately determine what a brand name like Coca-Cola or Heinz is actually worth? The difficulty of obtaining a true and fair valuation for these intangible assets makes it entirely possible that businesses can drastically overstate or understate their value on the balance sheet.

This poses a problem for investors. They are primarily concerned with assessing the level of return they might gain from an investment in a particular company. This can be difficult as the value of shares – their market price – can vary quite considerably. Some mechanism is required in order for accurate comparisons to be made between companies. So let's consider how investors make these judgements by examining the relationship between profit, share prices and dividends and looking at the use of price earnings ratios.

Share prices

When a limited company is formed, the board of directors must decide how much capital is needed to finance the business's trading activities. This capital is divided up into smaller equal units called shares. Each share, therefore, represents a small stake in the business, and these shares are sold to raise money for investment into the business.

If you buy shares in a company, you become an official owner of part of the company. Most shares carry voting rights, enabling the holders to have a say in how the company is run. Obviously the more shares you have, the more say you have. If you own over 50 per cent of the shares, you are in effective total control. This allows a person or group of people to control a company without having to own the entire business.

Discussion point

Obtain the financial section from a national newspaper. What information about share prices is shown for individual companies? Suppose you are considering making a £100,000 investment in a company. In your opinion, is there sufficient information in the newspaper to make a sensible and informed investment decision?

Shares and securities

A security is simply a written or printed document that acknowledges that the holder has invested some money in the issuing company. Securities can be classified into two main types:

- stocks – loans that carry a fixed rate of interest and must be repaid in full

- shares – which carry a variable rate of return depending on the company's performance and are not repaid by the company, but can be sold to other people.

Shares can be of various denominations – 50p, £1, £10 are not unusual. An important note to make at this point is that shares are always listed at their nominal value on a company's balance sheet irrespective of their market value on the stock exchange. The nominal value is the face value (original value) of the share). It is not uncommon for shares which are listed on the balance sheet as worth £10,000 to actually be worth considerably more on the stock exchange. Note that only shares in public limited companies are listed on the stock exchange.

There are different types of share, and not all give the holder the right to vote at company meetings to decide on future policy. Ordinary shares usually carry voting rights, which is only fair as they carry the most risk. Preference shares normally carry no right to vote as they are fairly low risk. Debentures have no rights, as they carry no risk. Debentures are not shares they are loan stock. Even if the company goes into liquidation, debenture holders are paid out first by the official receivers, after meeting any liabilities to the Inland Revenue and any outstanding wages to employees.

The share price is an important indicator of company performance: a rising share price indicates a healthy confident company with good prospects for future profits; a falling share price, however, can indicate that a company is beginning to struggle.

Investors benefit from share ownership in two ways: from making capital gains if the shares increase in market vale and from dividends. Let's first consider capital gains. This is an important feature of share dealing. The market value of a share can fluctuate considerably, with obvious consequences for the value of shareholders' investments. Many investors and share dealers hope to purchase shares that will increase in market price. They can then sell the shares and make a substantial profit on the transaction. As Figure 5.34 shows, the profits to be made from speculation can be far greater and quicker than the returns from saving money in a bank; however, so can be the losses.

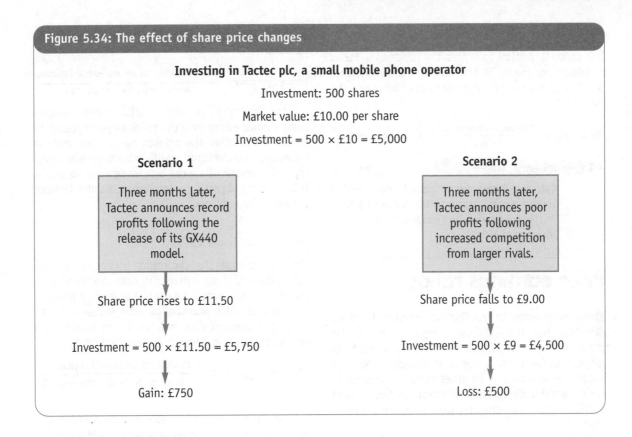

Figure 5.34: The effect of share price changes

Investing in Tactec plc, a small mobile phone operator

Investment: 500 shares

Market value: £10.00 per share

Investment = 500 × £10 = £5,000

Scenario 1

Three months later, Tactec announces record profits following the release of its GX440 model.

Share price rises to £11.50

Investment = 500 × £11.50 = £5,750

Gain: £750

Scenario 2

Three months later, Tactec announces poor profits following increased competition from larger rivals.

Share price falls to £9.00

Investment = 500 × £9 = £4,500

Loss: £500

Discussion point

Calculate the percentage gain and loss made by the investor in the two scenarios in Figure 5.34. Compare the results to the returns that can be obtained by investing £5,000 for three months in a bank deposit account.

Investors must be careful not to judge a company's performance solely on the basis of its share price. Economic policies and booms and slumps in the trade cycle can effect the value of shares on the stock exchange. Company directors also try to keep the share price (often artificially) high, as low share prices causes shareholders unrest. Indeed, most directors have shares (and share options) in their companies and have no wish to make a capital loss. This, in part, leads to pressure window dress accounts, release misleading statements and pay dividends from reserves, even when profits are low.

Dividends

Shareholders are entitled to a share of company profits. This is known as a divided. The size of dividend is dependent upon the amount of profit made, and how much profit the directors wish to retain for reinvestment in the company. Dividends are usually paid annually, but companies can pay a dividend more frequently if they wish.

The size and frequency of dividends is an alternative way of measuring business performance. Larger dividends suggest that the company is the more profitable and successful. As dividends are paid from the **distributed** part of net profit, it follows that the company must have made a considerable net profit to be able to pay out a substantial dividend. However, a note of caution needs to be introduced, as companies often pay out dividends to shareholders even if it has been a disastrous year for profits. Each year limited companies can transfer part of their **retained** profit to reserves; these can then be used to pay dividends in future years when profits are poor.

Look back at the article about BA (see p. 278). This shows that BA still issued an interim dividend even though profits were lower than expected. This is done to maintain confidence in the business and the board of directors: the board is trying to convince shareholders and the City that although profits are not very good, they still have enough confidence in the business to pay out an extra dividend during the year. It is a tactic to try and keep the share price high.

Calculation of dividend

It is common practice to express the dividend in terms as pence per share. To calculate the total dividend payable on any type of share by the company, use the formula:

$$\text{Dividend payable} = \frac{\text{Total nominal value of shares}}{100} \times \text{Percentage dividend}$$

Price earnings ratios

There is a potential conflict of interest between directors and shareholders; companies are under pressure from shareholders to maximise short-term returns, while directors may want to retain profits for long-term investment. In other words, shareholders seek a greater distribution of profits in the form of dividends, the company may wish to retain a greater share.

Price earnings ratios explore the relationship between the profits available for distribution to shareholders and the market value of the shares. They are used to analyse potential investment opportunities by comparing the number of shares issued, dividends paid, market value of shares and the overall level of company profits.

Earnings per share

Earnings per share is very simple ratio that measures the amount each individual ordinary share earns for its investors. Usually expressed in pence, it is given by the formula:

$$\text{Earnings per share} = \frac{\text{Net profit after tax and preference dividends}}{\text{Number of issued ordinary shares}}$$

This indicator is only useful when making comparisons; either with the previous year's results to determine whether the amount earned per share is increasing or decreasing, or with other organisations to try and establish where the best investment might lie. It is therefore of particular interest to shareholders and potential shareholders.

Price earnings ratio

This ratio analyses the relationship between how much each individual share earns and its current market price, that is, how much each share is really worth. It provides the basis on which shares of differing values and with varying degrees of dividend can be compared on a common basis. It is calculated using the formula:

$$\text{Price earnings ratio} = \frac{\text{Market share price (in pence)}}{\text{Earnings per share (in pence)}}$$

The ratio describes the relationship between the value and the last reported earnings for that share. For example, if the price earnings ration (P/E) is 6, this means that the market price of the share is six times that of its earning. Investors looks for high P/E results: the higher the P/E value, the better the share when compared to others with lower P/E values.

The price earnings ratio provides a measure for shareholders and potential shareholders to compare the actual cost (market price) of share with the level of earnings that can be achieved from that investment.

Figure 5.35: Calculating a dividend

	Example 1	Example 2
Number of shares	200,000	1,000,000
Denomination (nominal value)	50p	£1
Total nominal value (share capital)	£100,000	£1,000,000
Dividend	20%	5%
Total dividend	£20,000	£50,000
Dividend per share	10 pence	5 pence
Dividend on a 1,000 share holding	£100	£50

Dividend yield

Dividend yield ignores that part of the profits that, though they actually belong to shareholders, are retained by the company. Expressed as a percentage, it is calculated using the formula:

$$\text{Dividend yield} = \frac{\text{Ordinary share dividend (in pence)}}{\text{Market share price (in pence)}} \times 100$$

Again, high results are good. However, the dividend yield needs to be compared against results for previous years and for competitors. This indicator enables shareholders and potential shareholders to measure the expected returns, in terms of dividend payments, against the cost of the shares.

A worked example

Figures 5.36 and 5.37 show the final accounts and balance sheet for Meredith plc. To conclude this section on interpreting financial statements, we show here worked calculations of all the financial indicators we have covered using Meredith's financial data as a case study.

$$\text{Gross profit margin} = \frac{\text{Gross profit}}{\text{Turnover}} \times 100$$

$$= \frac{294{,}400}{679{,}000} \times 100 = 43.36\%$$

$$\text{Net profit margin} = \frac{\text{Net profit}}{\text{Turnover}} \times 100$$

$$= \frac{193{,}130}{679{,}000} \times 100 = 28.44\%$$

$$\text{ROCE} = \frac{\text{Net profit before tax and interest}}{\text{Total capital employed}} \times 100$$

$$= \frac{193{,}130}{920{,}000} \times 100 = 20.99\%$$

$$\text{Stock turnover} = \frac{\text{Cost of goods sold}}{\text{Average stock}}$$

$$= \frac{384{,}600}{(47{,}360 + 100{,}000)/2}$$

$$= 5.22 \text{ times} \ (\text{every 70 days})$$

$$\text{Debtor collection period} = \frac{\text{Debtors}}{\text{Credit sales}} \times 365$$

$$= \frac{126{,}000}{679{,}000} \times 365 = 67.73 \text{ days}$$

$$\text{Creditor days} = \frac{\text{Creditors}}{\text{Credit purchases}} \times 365$$

$$= \frac{84{,}000}{437{,}480} \times 365 = 19.2 \text{ days}$$

$$\text{Current ratio} = \frac{\text{Current assets}}{\text{Current liabilities}}$$

$$= 334{,}000{:}227{,}000 = 1.47{:}1$$

$$\text{Acid test} = \frac{\text{Current assets} - \text{Stock}}{\text{Current liabilities}}$$

$$= (334{,}000 - 100{,}000){:}227{,}000 = 1.03{:}1$$

$$\text{Earnings per share} =$$

$$\frac{\text{Net profit after tax and preference dividends}}{\text{Number of issued ordinary shares}}$$

$$= \frac{140{,}130}{600{,}000} = 23.36 \text{ pence}$$

$$\text{Price earnings ratio} = \frac{\text{Market share price (in pence)}}{\text{Earnings per share (in pence)}}$$

$$= \frac{250.00}{23.36} = 10.7$$

$$\text{Dividend yield} = \frac{\text{Ordinary share dividend (in pence)}}{\text{Market share price (in pence)}} \times 100$$

$$= \frac{15}{200} \times 100 = 6\%$$

> **Discussion point**
>
> Obtain a set of financial accounts for a public limited company and prepare a financial analysis for a potential investor. Compare your results with those of a colleague and determine which company you would invest in.

Figure 5.36: Final accounts for Meredith

Meredith plc, Trading, Profit and Loss Account
for the period ended 31 December 2000

	£	£	£
Sales		720,000	
Less Returns in		41,000	679,000
Less Cost of goods sold			
Opening stock	47,360		
Add Purchases	437,480		
Less Returns out	6,440	478,400	
Add Carriage in		6,200	
		484,600	
Less Closing stock		100,000	384,600
Gross profit			294,400
Add Other income			Nil
Less Expenses			
Wages and salaries		26,460	
Motor expenses		18,420	
Rent		7,000	
Heat and Light		4,790	
Distribution		6,560	
Post and packing		1,840	
Advertising		6,600	
Insurance		2,000	
Bad debts		1,540	
Provision for bad debts		620	
Depreciation		12,400	
Sundry expenses		1,040	
Loan interest		4,000	
Debenture interest		8,000	101,270
Net profit for the year before taxation			193,130
Less Corporation tax			53,000
Profit for the year after tax			140,130
Add Profit and loss account balance			72,000
			212,130
Less Transfer to general reserve		34,130	
Ordinary dividend		90,000	124,130
Retained profit carried forward to next year			88,000

Figure 5.37: Balance sheet for Meredith

Balance Sheet for Meredith plc as at 31 December 2000

	£	£	£
Fixed assets	Cost	Accumulated depreciation	Net book value
Intangible			
Goodwill	60,000		60,000
Tangible			
Premises	360,000	40,000	320,000
Plant and equipment	460,000	180,000	280,000
Vehicles	100,000	40,000	60,000
Fixtures and fittings	100,000	10,000	90,000
			810,000
Current assets			
Stock	100,000		
Debtors	126,000		
Prepayments	14,000		
Bank	79,000		
Cash	15,000	334,000	
Current liabilities			
Creditors	84,000		
Proposed dividend	90,000		
Corporation tax	53,000	227,000	
Working capital		110,000	110,000
			920,000
Less			
Long-term liabilities			
5 year loan		40,000	
10% Debentures		80,000	120,000
Net assets			800,000
Financed by:			
Authorised share capital			
1,400,000 ordinary shares £1 ea.		1,400,000	
		1,400,000	
Issued share capital			
600,000 ordinary shares £1 ea.		600,000	600,000
Share premium account		27,870	
General reserve		84,130	
Profit and loss account		88,000	200,000
Shareholders funds			800,000

Note: The current market price of the ordinary shares is quoted at £2.50 per share.

BUILD YOUR LEARNING

Keywords and phrases

You should know the meaning of the words and phrases listed below. Go back through the last 12 pages of the unit to check or refresh your understanding as necessary.

- Acid test
- Asset turnover
- Creditor days
- Current ratio
- Debtors' collection period
- Distributed profit
- Dividend yield
- Dividends
- Earnings per share
- Gross profit margin
- Market share value
- Net profit margin
- Nominal share value
- Performance ratios
- Price earnings ratio
- Profitability ratios
- Retained profit
- Return on capital employed
- Solvency ratios
- Window dressing

Summary points

- Financial data provides vital information about the solvency, profitability and performance of a business.

- Accurate financial data and interpretation give owners and managers an opportunity to make informed decisions to avoid insolvency, maximise profits and improve performance.

- Comparisons can be made between accounting periods of the same firm or to compare the performance of two separate firms in the same type of business.

- Ratio analysis provides insight into business performance. However, it should not be used in isolation – qualitative factors based on business experience can prove just as valuable in determining business success.

- Price earnings ratios can be useful for assessing the potential returns to be gained from investing in different public limited companies.

Cash flow management

AS WELL AS RECORDING and analysing financial information, businesses need to manage their finances. The main elements of financial management are budgeting and cash flow.

Budgeting

Budgeting is an important technique for all businesses. Budgets are based on forecasts of future events. Forecasts can only be best guesses as to what may happen in the future, but there are techniques that firms can employ to help base their guesses on the most reliable information.

- A business can base its forecasts on what has happened in the past by extending the trend into the future. This process is known as extrapolation.

- Businesses can also undertake research. For example, a forecast of next year's sales figures may be based on research into consumers' buying habits.

In business, forecasts are generally referred to as budgets, though the term projection may also be used. Forecasts are made of both the income that the business expects to earn and different types of expenditure that the business is to undertake.

The purpose of budgets

A budget is a forecast of costs and revenues. It is intended to provide a target for management, a means of controlling expenditure and the basis for a future performance review. Budgets need to be prepared for an identified purpose – there must be a specific set of objectives or targets that both informs the preparation of the budget and guides the actions of managers that will have to operate within the budget. The purpose of a budget will also shape its actual content.

Budgets are usually prepared for specific business functions such as:

- sales
- marketing
- production
- finance
- administration.

However, budgets can also be prepared for individual projects, departments, branches and cost centres. These individual budgets within an organisation can be collated into a single budget for the whole business, called the master budget. By compiling together all the budgets for individual functions and projects, a business can make an overall forecast about its future profits and financial stability. A master budget is therefore laid out as a forecast profit and loss account and balance sheet. Ratio analysis can then be undertaken on these projected or forecast accounts.

Organisations (and individuals) that lend money to businesses require some indication of how the owners expect the business to perform in the coming months or years. Forecasts, and the budgets prepared from these forecasts, allow managers to set out how they think the business will develop. It is one way of assessing the possible success of the business and it is an important step in persuading potential investors to lend money. Drawing up forecasts in this way is an important part of preparing a business plan. Banks and other financial institutions require a company to submit a business plan before they will advance a loan.

Types of budgets

It might be assumed that most business planning has a one year horizon, and certainly one-year budgets are the most common. However, businesses have long-term plans as well as short-term plans. Longer-terms plans are called corporate plan. A business has three short-term budgets: a revenue budget (or sales budget) relating to planned sales within the short-term – usually over the forthcoming year – expenditure budgets detailing likely short-term costs and expenses and a capital budget (or capital expenditure budget) associated with capital investments in the same period.

Capital budgets

Expenditure on capital items, such as premises or machinery, is likely to be substantial. It is important that businesses remain within their budgets when undertaking capital expenditure. However, it is equally important for businesses to appreciate the likely extent of this expenditure.

The capital expenditure budget outlines planned expenditure on fixed assets for the budget period, usually month by month. In a manufacturing organisation, it is normal to compare planned production levels and existing production facilities. If the facilities are inadequate, planned expenditure on fixed assets (for example, new premises and equipment) will have to take place over the budget period.

Figure 5.38: Rusholme's capital budget

	Planned	Actual
Premises	775,000	803,500
Vehicles	96,000	89,000
Equipment	135,750	129,000
Machinery	85,000	85,000
Total	**1,091,750**	**1,106,500**

Figure 5.38 shows a sample capital budget for Rusholme Engineering Ltd, a Suffolk-based business producing components for use in the motor vehicle industry. A column for actual expenditure is included to allow managers to measure whether the business is performing to expectations. This allows planned and actual figures to be easily compared. For a medium-sized organisation such as Rusholme Engineering, capital budgets may be drawn up after the departments or areas that comprise the business have submitted bids for capital.

Capital budgeting entails planning the total amount of capital spending over the next year or two on items such as premises, equipment, vehicles and machinery. Because the sums are large, the timing of capital expenditure is often critical to allow for the arrangement of suitable financing. Capital budgets are often updated quarterly, since both amounts and timing of payments can change quickly.

A number of financial techniques are available to help firms take decisions on whether to invest in capital items, or to help them choose between alternative capital investments. These techniques are called investment appraisal and compare expenditure on capital items with their estimated earnings.

Sales budget

Forecast sales revenue is a key figure for any business. A sales forecast is the start of the budgetary process. Sales budgets are notoriously difficult to estimate as they are subject to many influences, including changes in tastes and fashions. When compiling a sales budget, businesses need to consider:

- market research – this can be used to assess consumer demand for their products and provide the basis for an estimate of sales revenue

- economic trends – firms need to assess whether the state of the economy is likely to lead to improving or deteriorating sales levels

- trend analysis – an assessment of sales trends can be made from an examination of their own accounts and industry statistics

- the competition – a review of the expected actions of competitors and the degree of market competition.

Figure 5.39 shows a monthly sales budget for Rusholme Engineering.

Discussion point

Obtain the published (or reported) sales figures for a company over the last quarter. Try to make an accurate forecast of the company's sales for the next month. Explain the reasoning behind your prediction.

Expenditure budgets

Businesses need to keep records of, monitor and plan for their likely costs, including wages and raw materials. All manufacturing businesses require raw materials if they are to produce and sell goods. Raw materials are a variable cost, that is they rise and fall in line with the level of production. This definition of raw materials can also extend to businesses such as retailing; here, the raw materials are the products that shops and supermarkets purchase to resell to customers.

Wages are an important cost faced by any business, particularly those in the service sector. In recent years, there has been a significant trend within the UK and other advanced economies for more people to be employed in tertiary or service industries. Because service industries, such as health and education, buy relatively few raw materials (by definition they do not produce goods but offer services) their major expenditure is on wages.

Like raw materials, wages are a variable cost. There is a close correlation between expenditure on wages and the level of sales achieved by a business. Forecasting wage costs can be complicated for a number of reasons. If employees suffer ill health and receive sick pay, then wage costs increase as replacements have to be paid. If workers are less productive than anticipated, or are successful in obtaining higher than expected pay rises, then wage costs can exceed the forecast figure.

Figure 5.39: Rusholme Engineering monthly sales budget

Rusholme Engineering Sales Budget
Analysis by monthly sales

Product type	Value of sales March 2000 £	Forecast share of market growth	Sales target March 2001 £	Actual value of sales
Brake components	65,000	2%	66,300	
Body parts	120,000	10%	132,000	
Electrical	40,000	5%	42,000	

Wages costs are subject to other influences. There is a trend for what is termed flexible staffing. This involves greater use of part-time staff, with companies also employing more people on short-term contracts and using more self-employed personnel. This gives businesses greater flexibility to cope with short-term staffing needs caused, for example, by sudden changes in the level of demand for a firm's products. An additional advantage of flexible staffing arrangements is that the overheads incurred by the business are reduced.

Firms face a variety of other costs. Some of these costs are fixed and some will be variable. They include telephone expenses, postal charges, stationery costs and interest payments. All businesses have to pay overheads. These costs are usually fixed and include rent and business rates, water rates and the salaries of managers. These costs are not generated by the production process. The importance of these costs varies according to the nature of the business.

Figure 5.40 shows an example of a monthly expenditure budget for Rusholme Engineering.

Figure 5.40: Rusholme Engineering monthly expenditure budget

Rusholme Engineering Expenses Budget
Analysis by monthly expenditure

Expenditure item	Expenditure March 2000 £	Budgeted expenditure March 2001 £	Actual expenditure March 2001 £
Raw materials	45,000	46,000	
Wages	37,000	40,000	
Other			
Telephone expenses	1,200	1,100	
Postal charges	600	450	
Stationery costs	250	250	
Interest payments	950	600	
Rent and business rates	2,000	2,200	
Salaries	30,000	32,000	

> Imagine you work for a travel agency. List ten categories of expenditure items that you think would be incurred by this type of business.

Benefits of budgeting

Managing a business involves making decisions and choices. Forecasting can help businesses decide between alternatives. Consider, for example, the choice faced by a restaurant owner who has to decide whether to open a new restaurant or to expand the existing one. Forecasts and budgets play a key role here. The owner will want to have some estimate of the likely sales in both scenarios and the potential costs in terms of wages and raw materials. It will also be useful to have some indication of possible expenditure on fixed assets in both circumstances. The process of forecasting and the creation of budgets bring a quantifiable aspect to the decision between alternative courses of action.

Budgets are, therefore, an important tool in the business manager's repertoire. Further reasons for using budgets include:

- budgets allow the directors to coordinate the activities of the organisation, which is especially true for those that have several divisions and which operate over a wide geographical area

- by setting targets managers can identify the extent to which efficiency gains or improvement levels have been met

- budgets make managers think about the effects of their actions, and the implications for their future operations and the rest of the business

- budgeting should improve management control simply because staff are aware that their performance is monitored against pre-set targets

- budgets can be used as a motivational aid, by setting salaries and rewards on the basis of meeting targets

- budgets can be delegated to subordinate personnel, providing additional motivation by giving employees additional responsibility.

Most businesses, therefore, set objectives and targets for a number of reasons. However, the usefulness of budgets depends upon the forecasts; the targets have to be reasonable and attainable. If they are not, then employees at all levels within the company can be demotivated. Accurate forecasts are of crucial important in setting targets.

Variance analysis

Variance analysis is a financial management tool that enables an organisation to compare its actual performance over a period of time against its budgeted expectations for that period. The purpose of variance analysis is to highlight and pinpoint areas of poor performance over the period being examined, as well as emphasising areas where performance has been good.

Variance analysis can be used to calculate the differences between any two actual and budgeted figures. In particular, though, it is used to examine:

- material price variance – this highlights any changes between the budgeted cost of raw materials and supplies and the actual costs incurred

- material usage variance – this examines the difference between the intended (budgeted) quantities of raw materials and supplies against the actual quantities used to meet production targets

- labour rate variance – the budgeted pay bill compared to the actual wages paid out over the period

- labour efficiency variance – the budgeted number of man-hours or time to complete given tasks in comparison to the actual amount of time taken

- profit variances – the expected or forecasted level of profit for a period, project or activity measured against the actual profit.

Variance analysis is usually undertaken fairly frequently. This is to allow managers and budget holders to take prompt corrective action if necessary and to adjust their future budgetary expectations and targets in line with actual events. If, due to unforeseen circumstances, your original yearly forecast budget turns out to be inaccurate after three months, there is little point in continuing with it. Variance analysis allows budgets to be adjusted so that they become a more accurate planning tool with more realistic targets. It enables more effective monitoring of performance and tighter coordination and control. Adjusting the budgets in light of variance analysis results is known as flexing the budget.

In all applications, variance analysis is used to quantify the difference between what managers thought should happen and what actually happened. The key to variance analysis is the interpretation of these variances: if major differences occur between expected and actual results, you need to ask why did these differences occur.

In essence, then, variance analysis compares the actual cost or revenue generated against what we thought it was going to cost, and compares the actual sales income against the amount of revenue we thought we would receive. Figure 5.41 shows a simple method for calculating variances.

Discussion point

Discuss the possible causes of the results in Figure 5.41. Suggest some remedies to prevent the situation from reoccurring.

Interpreting variances

The key to using variance analysis effectively is to determine why the variance occurred: managers need to identify the cause of the variance and suggest remedies to prevent it happening again. There are two main scenarios:

- **favourable variance** – the actual performance of the organisation has been better than expected

- **adverse variance** – the actual performance of the organisation has been worse than expected.

Don't assume that adverse variances are bad and that favourable variances are good. This is not actually the case as any major variations between budgeted and actual figures, no matter what the direction, show poor planning and forecasting by those responsible for compiling the budget. For example, buying cheaper lower-quality materials could cause a favourable material price variance. This is not necessarily a good development – it could have implications for material usage and labour efficiency variance as the lower-grade materials are harder to use and generate more waste. Figure 5.42 shows some remedies for tackling variance.

Good budgeting seeks to produce variance results that are neither adverse nor favourable but minimal.

Cash flow forecasts

A cash flow forecast is a detailed estimate of a firm's future cash inflows and outflows over a specified period. This is usually calculated on a monthly basis and by adding together the monthly figures the firm's cumulative cash position can be calculated.

Figure 5.43 is a simplified summary cash flow statement covering four months. Cash inflows represent the earnings of the business, resulting from sales of its goods or services. These inflows could be the results of cash sales in the month in question, or the payment for credit sales that may have taken place in previous months. Cash outflows represent the costs faced by businesses. These can be as a result of capital expenditure on fixed assets, or of current expenditure on, for example, rent and rates.

The net cash flow is simply the monthly balance between outflows and inflows. For January the net cash flow is £120,000 minus £130,000, which is minus £10,000 or (£10,000). Note that accounting convention places brackets around negative figures. The cumulative

Figure 5.41: Calculating simple variances

Production budget for March 2000	Grade of labour	Budgeted £	Actual £	Variance £	
50 tonne press	Setters	7,200	7,300	(–100)	Adverse
	Setter/Operator	1,200	1,800	(–600)	Adverse
	Operators	4,000	3,500	+500	Favourable
100 tonne press	Setters	10,440	10,520	(–80)	Adverse
	Operators	10,000	10,100	(–100)	Adverse
Total production variance				**(–380)**	**Adverse**

Figure 5.42: Some remedies for tackling variance

Possible causes of variances	Possible remedies
Material price variance	
Increased tax	Not much managers can do other than try to increase efficiency
Supply and demand variations	Plan for price fluctuations at low supply or peak demand points
Supplier price rises	Negotiate new suppliers or new long-term contracts
Changes to design or specifications	Plan budgets and forecast more accurately
Quality of raw materials	Change supplier or change quality
Material usage variances	
High wastage level	Training and better stock control
Poor quality materials	Change supplier
High reject rate	Better quality standards
Labour rate variance	
Excessive overtime	Improve motivation and production per employee
Wage rises	Add fringe benefits, automate processes to use fewer staff
Wrong grade of labour	More efficient human resource planning
Labour efficiency variance	
Unskilled workers	Training
Poor raw materials	Change supplier or grade of material
Poor morale and production levels	Improve working conditions

cash flow is simply calculated by adding the net cash flow for any month to the business's cash position at the beginning of that month. We can see that the company began January with a cash balance of £100,000, its net figure for the month was (£10,000) and so at the end of the month the firm had a cash balance of £90,000.

Both profit and cash flow are important to all businesses, but it is important to understand that they are not the same things. A profitable company can experience cash shortages and, in extreme cases, these can result in liquidation. Small businesses, especially, can face short-term cash difficulties due to a temporary decline in sales or an increase in charges. They are particularly at risk from the desire to overtrade. This puts a strain on the financial position of the firm, although fundamentally the businesses may be profitable. Unfortunately, a large number of small businesses go bankrupt due to cash flow difficulties.

The difference between profit and cash

Profit is a surplus earned in respect of a period of trading, after deducting all business expenses from sales turnover and any other income earned. Cash is a liquid asset owned by a business that enables it to purchase goods and services. Cash includes bank accounts and deposits.

Figure 5.43: A cash flow summary

Burrell Electronics

(All figures in £000s)

	Jan	Feb	Mar	Apr
Cash at start	100	90	70	95
Cash inflows	120	130	175	195
Cash outflows	130	150	150	145
Net cash flow	(10)	(20)	25	50
Cumulative cash	90	70	95	145

If a business sells its products for more than they cost, it has earned a profit. However, if its customers have purchased on credit and not yet paid for these goods then it may have no cash available.

When a firm purchases fixed assets, for which it may pay in cash or credit, it does not deduct the whole cost of the assets from the profit made in the period in which payment is made. Instead, the company's accounts usually charge only a proportion of the cost of the fixed assets as a depreciation expense in each period of the asset's life.

Profit, therefore, looks at the overall balance of income and expenditure, cash flow analysis (and of course cash flow forecasts) take into account the timing of payments and receipts. Cash flow analysis looks at the flow of money into and out of the organisation.

The purpose of a cash flow forecast

Cash flow is an important part of financial planning for any business. Monitoring cash flows can ensure that the working capital for a business is sufficient and that funds are available to undertake day-to-day transactions. This planning and management ensures that cash is available to maintain growth in the business. As an example, an expanding business may need to purchase additional stocks to allow higher production levels and to meet increased customer demand.

Cash flow forecasts can confirm that cash will be available to meet a variety of financial requirements. Expenditure may be necessary to meet the demands of capital budgets, ensuring that suitable fixed assets are available as and when the business requires them. Cash flow forecasts also indicate by how much a business may have to increase its sales or reduce its costs to meet the impending capital outlay. Alternatively, the cash flow forecast may highlight that some staging of the capital

payments is essential: that is, payment for the fixed assets should be spread out over a longer time period. The business may also have to consider undertaking increased borrowing to meet its planned capital commitments.

Evidence of this kind of cash flow planning is likely to be helpful in attracting prospective investors and providers of finance. A positive cash flow position is likely to generate confidence in potential lenders. It will provide evidence that the business is well managed and has the ability to repay the debt.

Cash flow forecasts will also highlight the times at which funds are available to meet the current costs associated with trading. They identify when finance is available to pay major costs, such as rent and the purchase of raw materials. Equally, they make clear the timing of the receipts from the sale of goods or services.

Monitoring cash flows can also reduce the bank interest paid by the business. By monitoring and managing its cash flow, a business should have less need to use its overdraft facility or to require expensive short-term finance. This reduces the costs of the business and should improve its profitability. Control of cash flows is a critical determinant in the success of a business.

Cash flow forecasts should also indicate the timing of cash surpluses. This can help firms to schedule projects in the anticipation that sufficient funds should be available. It is not in a firm's interests to have a very large surplus of cash; tying up resources in unproductive assets such as cash will not enhance profitability.

Each spending decision taken by a business should be dependent on the availability of cash: all business decisions should be considered from a cash flow perspective. Once a cash flow becomes negative, it can threaten the life of a business unless more cash is made available to the business. Cash flow forecasts can provide advance warning that a business may face a cash shortage. This enables a business to reschedule payments, if possible, or to arrange alternative short-term finance well in advance.

The structure of cash flow forecasts

The precise format of cash flow forecasts can vary, although the basic principles remain the same. The format set out in Figure 5.44 is one that is in common usage by business.

Discussion point

Can you identify the two reason for net cash outflows in January and March in Figure 5.44? Is there anything the company could do to lessen the impact of these transactions?

Figure 5.44: A cash flow forecast

	Jan	Feb	Mar	Apr
Cash inflows	£000s	£000s	£000s	£000s
Sales cash	26	22	18	25
Sales credit	330	450	490	520
Receipts from loans	50	0	0	0
Capital introduced	150	130	0	0
VAT recoveries	0	40	0	0
(a) Total cash inflow	556	632	508	545
Cash outflows				
VAT payments	0	0	198	0
Salaries	115	125	125	125
Wages	17	19	23	18
Raw material costs	60	65	60	65
Drawings	0	0	0	23
Heating and light	25	27	27	26
Rent and rates	100	100	100	100
Mortgage payment	20	34	34	34
Interest on loan	52	97	97	97
Fixed asset purchases	275	0	0	0
(b) Total cash outflow	664	467	664	488
(c) Opening bank balance	**245**	137	302	146
(d) Net cash flow (= a − b)	(108)	165	(156)	57
Closing bank balance (= c + d)	137	302	146	**203**

The cash flow forecast in Figure 5.44 comprises three sections. The top section records the cash inflows into the business and the middle section the outflows from the business. The final section shows the net cash flow from the business; this is the balance between inflows and outflows over the month in question. This final section also records the cash position at the beginning and end of each month. Frequently cash flow forecasts have two columns for each month – one to record the forecast and the second to give the actual figures for the month. This allows a business to see whether it is performing as well as expected. This is a format that we encountered when discussing capital budgets.

Cash inflows

The cash inflows to a business can take a number of forms:

- capital introduced
- receipts from loans
- sales receipts
- VAT recoveries.

Capital introduced is capital put into the business by the owners of the business. A company might raise capital for a specific purpose, for example to finance the purchase of some machinery or new premises. When capital is introduced at the beginning of the life of a business, it is referred to as start-up capital. This might be required to alter and adapt premises before trading commences or for development and advertising costs to launch the new product. For a new business, this start-up capital could be the only cash inflow for some time until the business begins to earn revenue from selling its goods and services.

All businesses take out loans at some time or another. This is an alternative to raising funds from shareholders and owners. The balance between capital raised through loans and through the sale of shares is a sensitive one. This balance is known as capital gearing. The company illustrated in Figure 5.44 took out a loan in January and the business received £50,000 as a consequence. This is shown against 'receipts from loans' in its cash flow forecast. Loans are likely to be a very common feature on cash flow forecasts in the early stages of business trading

Sales receipts can fall into two categories: cash sales and credit sales. This is an important distinction when considering cash flow. Cash sales are transactions for which payment is received in advance or at the time of purchase. These are likely to be sales to customers which the firm does not know well or to companies (or individuals) that have a bad track record in paying bills. This benefits the selling firm because it does not have to wait for payment when, of course, it has already had to pay many of the costs associated with production. Credit sales occur when the supplier allows the customer to purchase goods and services without making an immediate payment. For example, it might allow reliable customers 30 days grace before payment has to be paid. In effect, it is granting customers an interest-free loan.

The income received from sales is recorded on the cash flow forecast at the time the money flows into the business not when the sale is made. So, if a credit sale is made in February of £30,000 but payment is not received until March, the £30,000 is recorded as an inflow in March.

Businesses are charged value added tax (VAT) on most items that they purchase. Similarly, businesses must charge VAT on the products that they sell, unless the particular goods and services are zero-rated or the business is exempt from VAT. (Companies do not have to charge VAT if their annual turnover is less than a prescribed amount, currently around £50,000.) Businesses have to pass on the VAT that they collect from their customers, but they are allowed to reclaim the VAT that they pay on their supplies. VAT recoveries are the repayments that a business receives from HM Customs and Excise (which administers the VAT system) and can appear in the cash flow forecast as shown in

Figure 5.44. It is usual for businesses to pay VAT on a quarterly basis and also to receive VAT recoveries on the same basis. This explains why there is only a single entry for VAT recoveries during the four-month period covered by the cash flow forecast.

It is usual for businesses simply to pay the net amount of VAT that is due. That is, they pay the amount of tax they have charged on their sales less the amount they paid to suppliers. In this case, VAT recoveries would only appear as a separate item on a cash flow forecast if, for a particular VAT quarterly period, a business reclaimed more VAT from its suppliers than it collected from its customers.

Cash outflows

There are a number of forms of expenditure that can lead to a business incurring a cash outflow including:

- payments for assets
- purchase of raw materials
- wages
- interest and loan payments
- VAT payments
- other running costs.

Payments for assets refers to the purchase of fixed assets such as buildings, machines and vehicles. These appear in the capital budget; you may wonder why they should also appear in a cash flow forecast. The answer is that the capital budget is designed to tell managers if they have sufficient funds to purchase the assets, but the cash flow forecast looks at the timing of the expenditure. It is important for businesses to plan major items of expenditure to make sure that they occur at a time when the business has sufficient funds available.

Purchase of raw materials is often a particularly expensive item for manufacturing businesses. They can hold large stocks of raw materials, particularly if suppliers are unreliable. Manufacturers may also hold large stocks as a hedge against inflation, particularly if they expect the price of raw materials to rise in the near future. However, part of the art of successful management is to order raw materials as they are required. and to avoid tying up a large amount of cash in large stocks.

Recently European industry has been influenced by and adopted a number of Japanese management techniques (see pp. 73–4). One, known as just-in-time manufacturing, involves minimising the level of stocks (including raw materials). Benetton, which is renowned for its controversial advertising campaigns, only produces knitwear once orders are received from stores. Benetton dyes its knitwear after the garments have been knitted to avoid holding large stocks of different coloured wool. This method relies upon a very efficient ordering system to ensure raw materials and components are available as required.

The purchase of raw materials can be treated in two ways in a cash flow forecast depending upon whether they have been purchased with cash or on credit. If purchased with cash, they should be recorded in the forecast immediately. If they are purchased on credit, they should be recorded when payment is made and the transaction is completed. This is likely to be two or three months later.

Wages are a major expense for many businesses. The timing of these payments are, to a great extent, beyond the control of a business. Delaying the payment of wages would do little to enhance industrial relations! Most cash flow forecasts will record an expenditure figure against wages in each month. It may be, in the early stages of a new business, that the owner of a business will draw the minimum amount possible to help his or her business establish itself.

Most businesses take out loans, particularly in their early years. This, of course, means that a business has to pay interest on the loans as well as repaying the loans themselves. Interest payments will be made each month and may be fixed. However, if a business takes out variable-rate loans, the amount of interest charged will rise or fall with variations in the general level of interest rates.

We have explained that most businesses have to charge VAT on the products that they sell. They have to pass on the net VAT payments they have collected to HM Customs and Excise on a quarterly basis. Most small businesses are registered for VAT on a cash payment basis. This means that they make VAT payments to HM Customs and Excise each quarter based on the actual VAT paid and received during the quarter. So, if a business makes a credit sale, it does not include the VAT on the sale in its quarterly return until it has actually received payment from the customer.

Businesses face a range of other costs that will require expenditure at various times. In addition to the expenses listed above, most businesses also have to pay telephone charges, a mortgage and/or rent, business rates charges for gas and electricity, stationery costs and marketing costs.

Net cash flows and cash balances

Let's now look at the last three rows of a cash flow forecast. First, it is necessary to deduct the total cash outflow for the month from the total cash inflow for the same month. The resulting figure – which may be positive or negative – is termed the net cash flow figure (reference D in Figure 5.44). This, in turn, is added to the opening cash balance which the firm had at the beginning of the month or year (reference C in Figure 5.44). By adding the net cash flow to the opening balance, the closing balance for the firm is calculated. This is then carried forward to become the opening balance for the following month or year.

To illustrate this process, you can see that in Figure 5.44 the net cash flow figure for January is (£108,000) – in other words, during this month £108,000 more cash flows out of the business than flows in. The cash available to the business at the start of the month is £245,000 – this is the opening balance. By adding together the net cash flow and the opening balance we arrive at the closing balance – in this case, it is (£108,000) plus £245,000, that is £137,000. This closing balance becomes the opening balance for the next month (February) and the process begins again.

Cash flow management

By now, you should be aware that the timing and receipts of payments are very important to a business. If you look at Figure 5.44, which shows the four-month cash flow forecast, you will see that, in addition to receipts from sales of £356,000, the business received £200,000 in January. This figure is made up of £150,000 capital introduced and £50,000 from an arranged loan. What would have happened had this money not been received until March? In particular, what would have been the closing balance at the end of January?

It is part of the task of management to manage the inflows and outflows of cash so that the business is not short of cash and, perhaps, unable to pay its creditors. Nor is a large surplus of cash desirable; this means the business has assets tied up in a form that is not earning any money. Management attempts to have sufficient, but not too much, cash available.

By negotiating purchases of items such as raw materials on credit terms, the business can improve its cash flow position. Credit terms often give between one and three months grace before payment is required. However, this benefit may be counterbalanced because many businesses have to offer similar credit terms to their customers. If they fail to do so, customers might take their business elsewhere.

The fact that VAT is payable on a quarterly basis can help the cash position of a business. As we discussed earlier, a business will normally make a net VAT payment at the end of each quarter. This does, however, mean that the funds may be available to a company for a period of up to three months. Increasingly, financial institutions are offering services to help businesses improve their cash flows.

Remember that it is the timing of cash flows into and out of a business that are critical, not the total amount of cash generated. Many experienced managers hold the view that companies do not go bust because they make a loss, rather they fail because they run out of cash. Having sufficient cash is essential for commercial success.

The consequences of poor forecasting

Incorrect cash flow forecasting can lead to a number of difficulties. The managers of a firm may receive a misleading impression that a business has more (or less) cash available than is actually the case. As a consequence, a business may arrange short-term loans or decide to invest in assets at times when these actions are not appropriate. Good decision-making by managers depends upon having good quality information on which to base decisions. Incorrect cash flow forecasting will not provide good quality information.

A potentially dangerous implication of incorrect cash flow forecasting is that a firm may have insufficient liquid assets for the day-to-day operation of the business. If this is the case, the business may not be able to pay its suppliers as their invoices arrive. This may result in suppliers being unwilling to continue to supply the business and they may take legal action to recover their debts. This lack of liquidity could lead to the business becoming insolvent and ceasing trading.

Working capital management

Working capital is the day-to-day finance needed to run a business. Once a business has all the fixed assets needed for operation, managers have to consider the requirements for working capital. Figure 5.45 summarises the need for, and purposes of, working capital.

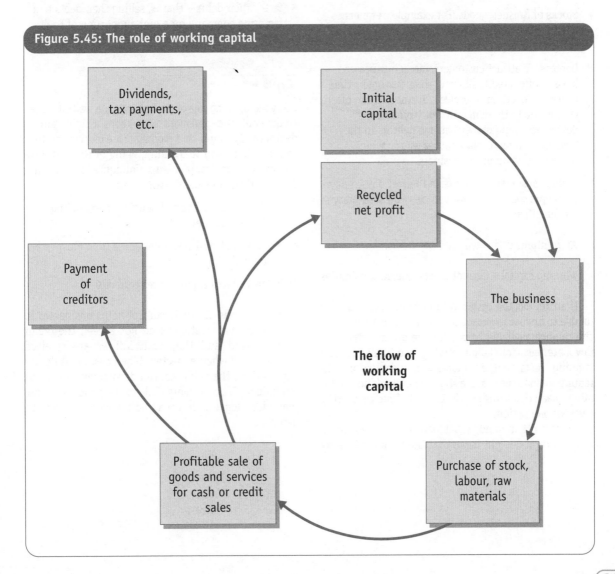

Figure 5.45: The role of working capital

Working capital is necessary to establish and operate a business. Working capital is needed for many different purposes.

- Raw materials and components. This can be a significant cost particularly for manufacturing businesses.

- Work in progress. Semi-completed goods will be on the production line of a manufacturing business at any time. The business has paid for the materials and components in work in progress but has not yet received any income from this work. In industries with long production times, such as house building, work in progress can tie up large amounts of capital.

- Labour costs. These can be very high for service industries; for example, health care organisations` employ large numbers of people but spend relatively little on raw materials.

- Stocks of finished goods. For example, retailers need to hold large quantities of stocks to offer sufficient choice to their customers.

- Debtors. To attract customers, many businesses have to offer credit, allowing their customers time to pay for goods and services. Businesses can often wait for up to three months for payment. Customers owing money become debtors to the business and represent another way in which money is tied up in the business.

- Cash. A business requires cash to meet day-to-day payments such as fuel for vehicles and stationery for the office.

Accountants define working capital as:

Working capital = Current assets – Current liabilities

If a firm has too little working capital, it might be unable to finance increased production. It may not have the finance available to pay for the greater stocks of raw materials, more labour services and higher general running costs that an increase in production will require. In extreme cases, a shortage of working capital might mean that a business is unable to finance existing levels of production.

On the other hand, too much money tied up as working capital might mean that the business is short of asset finance. Money on deposit in bank current accounts earns very little return, too much working capital can mean that the business is not maximising its opportunities. These excess funds could be working harder if invested elsewhere.

Managers can take a number of actions if they need to improve the working capital position. They can:

- shorten the time between the purchase of raw materials and the sale of finished goods, so that cash is not tied up for a long time in stocks and work-in-progress

- delay payment to suppliers by retaining the cash within the company for longer.

- raise extra cash by arranging loans or selling fixed assets that are surplus to requirements

- strictly control stocks, so avoiding tying up too much cash in the form of stock

- factor their debts – that is, selling their debts to a factoring company for a high proportion of their total value – so they can raise cash immediately.

Credit control

A key factor is the role of credit control. A well-managed credit control department that keeps a tight rein on debtors and ensures that payments are received on time can go a long way to avoiding many of the cash flow and working capital problems highlighted in this unit. A good credit control department will:

- establish clearly defined policies on extending credit to customers

- request bank and trade references from prospective customers

- follow collection procedures correctly.

This process of credit control helps businesses to make sure that customers do not exceed the credit terms agreed and that cash inflows are received regularly and when expected. When customers do not pay on time, the credit control department sends out reminders. If customers fail to respond to these reminders, legal action may be taken to recover the debt.

BUILD YOUR LEARNING

Keywords and phrases

You should know the meaning of the words and phrases listed below. Go back through the last 12 pages of the unit to check or refresh your understanding as necessary.

- Adverse variance
- Capital budget
- Cash flow
- Cash inflows
- Cash outflows
- Expenditure budget
- Extrapolation
- Favourable variance
- Flexing the budget
- Master budget
- Revenue budget
- Sales budget
- Variance analysis
- Working capital

Summary points

- Forecasts help a business obtain finance, assist in choosing between alternative plans and projects, and can be used to provide targets and motivate staff.

- Forecasts also give managers a yardstick against which to measure the success of their enterprises.

- The compilation of budgets into a forecasted profit and loss account and balance sheet is called a master budget.

- Variance analysis is a tool to compare the expected (budgeted) performance of a business with the actual outcomes.

- A business needs to determine possible causes and remedies of variances to improve both the businesses future performance and the accuracy of budgets.

- It is crucial that businesses plan and time cash outflows to cash inflows to protect their financial stability and working capital position.

- The management of working capital and credit control ensures that companies have enough day-to-day capital to meet expenses.

- Most businesses do not fail due to low profitability but from bad working capital management and cash flow problems.

Audio Direct

Set up in 1978 importing records from the USA and eventually diversifying into international music products, Audio Direct has grown into one of the largest mail order CD and music companies in the UK. On the back of its success in a booming market, Audio Direct went public in 1985 under the leadership of Bryon Kavanagh, who is still the company's managing director. The company has an authorised share capital of 5,000,000 ordinary shares at £1.00 each, and the current market value of its shares is 128 pence per share.

Bryon Kavanagh has expanded operations throughout the 1990s, adding telesales, video and specialist music book divisions. However, following the compilation of this year's final accounts (see Figure 5.46), the directors are becoming concerned about the performance of Audio Direct plc.

Although a large organisation with a good asset base and customer reputation, Audio Direct has found itself coming under increasing competition from direct-selling internet-based companies. In recent months, the sales team has reported a downturn in sales figures, particularly in CDs, as more and more traditional customers go 'on line'. One of the biggest problems is that the internet companies do not face large staffing and warehousing costs as they operate just-in-time stockholding policies, ordering from manufacturers as and when they receive orders. Audio Direct tries to keep prices competitive through bulk ordering popular lines and negotiating preferential rates from manufacturers. However, its smaller internet-based competitors do not have the massive overheads of a company like Audio Direct and are able to compete effectively on price.

Bryon has asked his senior staff to put forward suggestions about how Audio Direct can combat this situation. Several ideas have been forthcoming.

- Changing Audio Direct's traditional selling methods to compete directly with the smaller operators on the internet.

- Reorganising the outdated warehousing and distribution service by upgrading the IT system and improving communications within the company.

- Selling off non-core areas such as the specialist books divisions in order to concentrate on securing Audio Direct's reputation as a key player in the mail order music market. The money raised could be used to fund an intensive marketing campaign.

Bryon has called a board meeting. He is concerned with financing any proposal as the company accounts show falling levels of retained profits. However, he needs to develop a sound strategy for presentation to the shareholders at the impending annual general meeting.

Bryon also believes that it is his responsibility to lead from the front and he has been considering some possible ideas himself. His instinct is to consider options that involve expansion or diversification rather than rationalisation. However, in the past, this has dangerously over extended the company.

His main idea now is to explore the possibility of acting as a wholesale distributor for independent music retail outlets. This would take time to establish, but would maximise the company's existing warehousing and distribution functions. It would also allow Audio Direct to benefit even further from the economies of bulk purchasing.

If Audio Direct starts to offer wholesale services to independent retailers, many would expect favourable credit terms to convince them to change existing suppliers. Currently all mail orders received are accompanied by the customer's payment.

Questions

Help Bryon Kavanagh and finance director Michelle Culverhouse prepare for the annual general meeting. First, identify five stakeholders of Audio Direct plc. Explain their financial interest in the final accounts.

- Explain the term working capital. Analyse Audio Direct's liquidity position for the two years shown.

- Calculate Audio Direct's profitability ratios across the two years. Using your results, comment on the current financial position of the company.

- Using appropriate analysis, comment on the three proposals from senior staff. Make specific reference in each case to any likely effects on working capital and to the specific stakeholders that could be affected by these plans.

- Outline any limitations that should be considered when using financial information to plan future business strategy.

Before pitching his idea – of offering wholesale services to independent retailers – to Audio Direct's other directors, Bryon has approached you to provide him with reliable background information.

- What types of additional documentation and ledger systems would Audio Direct need to set up in order to offer credit terms to customers?

- Using a suitable diagram, explain to Bryon the information flow between organisations and within Audio Direct itself before being used to prepare final accounts.

- Consider the implications to Audio Direct's cash flow if Bryon's plan is accepted.

Figure 5.46: Accounts for Audio Direct plc

Audio Direct plc
Profit and Loss Account for the period ended 31 December 2000

	This year £000	This year £000	Last year £000	Last year £000
Turnover		357,418		393,746
Cost of goods sold		271,786		309,282
Gross profit		75,732		84,464
Distribution costs	48,514		53,124	
Administration costs	26,762	75,276	19,156	72,280
Operating profit		456		12,184
Interest receivable		1,286		500
		1,742		12,684
Interest payable		(7,312)		(10,662)
Profit/(loss) after interest		(5,570)		2022
Taxation due (rebate)		(2,032)		930
Profit after tax and interest		(3,538)		1,092
Retained profit b/f		4,848		4,476
Dividends		Nil		720
Retained profit c/f		1,265		4,848

Audio Direct plc
Balance Sheet as at 31 December 2000

	This year £000	This year £000	Last year £000	Last year £000
Fixed assets		34,829		32,746
Current assets				
Stock	59,123		58,047	
Debtors	255		364	
Bank	6,472		15,056	
Current liabilities				
Creditors due within one year	57,179		64,344	
Net current assets		8,671		9,132
		43,500		41,878
Creditors due after one year		36,735		31,530
		6,765		**10,348**
Financed by				
Called up share capital	4,000		4,000	
Share premium	1,500		1,500	
Profit and loss account	1,265		4,848	
		6,765		**10,348**

This unit takes you through the stages of producing a business plan for an enterprise that you are establishing. This involves identifying the information you need to complete the various sections that make up a business plan. This includes a thorough analysis of the market for your product, supported by information on the role, contents and structure of a marketing plan.

It is important that you know exactly how you intend to produce your product and have identified and quantified your resource requirements. This needs to cover finance and labour as well assets such as premises, plant and equipment. You need to be aware of any constraints on how you produce and market your output. The unit outlines some of the main legal, financial, social, environmental and technological constraints.

Potential investors need financial information to assess the viability of any business proposal. This unit sets out the areas that must be covered in your financial plan. It advises on how to use information technology to prepare and present financial projections.

Business planning

The purpose of business planning

A **BUSINESS PLAN** IS a detailed statement about the proposals for a new business or plans to develop an existing business. The plan includes details on an organisation's objectives, proposed operations, resource requirements and financial forecasts. Business planning involves researching and collecting information, evaluating and analysing that information and then presenting the relevant findings in a format which can be used to improve decision making. It helps to ensure the success of a new business and to improve the future performance of an existing business.

Business planning is not a static, or one-off, process. A business plan must be reviewed on a regular basis and updated, if necessary, to take maximum advantage of actual or anticipated developments that will help an organisation achieve its business objectives. A business plan also has to be amended in the light of adverse developments in the market environment that can threaten the achievement of any business objectives. By updating the plan in this way, the document forms the basis for the actions needed to help an organisation respond as effectively as possible to developments that are likely to have an adverse effect on its performance.

Since the mid 1980s, an average of half a million businesses have been started up each year. They range from builders to florists, software specialists to garden centres, recording studios to haulage firms. Generally, 40 per cent of these businesses fail within the first three years of operation. In many cases, the reason for failure is poor initial planning. Once established, companies still need to plan very carefully when expanding or changing the direction of the business.

Discussion point

This Practikal handle (see case study) shows that inventions do not necessarily require specialist knowledge or advanced technology to be successful. Discuss any ideas you may have had about a totally new product or design and its potential market.

CASE STUDY
Protecting an invention

The Practikal handle is a new device that takes the pain out of those plastic bag handles that cut into your fingers. It is made from moulded polypropylene, and has been designated a millennium product by the Design Council. Developed by Paul Conway Stuart, the handles have moulded undulations that fit all fingers and a groove that takes the weight of several bags and prevents them from cutting into your hand.

Mr Conway Stuart has taken out a patent on his invention. He can sue anyone who infringes his patent by making a copycat product. The patent also gives him the right to grant a licence to (and receive payment from) other organisations to manufacture and distribute the product.

If your business plan is based on a proposal that involves an entirely new (or significantly developed) product or manufacturing process, you can apply for a patent to the Patent Office. If you are granted a patent, you have the sole right to make the product or use the process for twenty years. The Patent Office (www.patent.gov.uk) also deals with the registration of design rights and names and symbols used as trademarks.

Preparing a business plan for a new business

A well-researched business plan describes the foundations upon which a new business is to be built. It acts as a kind of map to help the business reach its desired destination. In this section, we describe the activities and processes involved in collecting the information that generally has to be included in a business plan that can presented to a bank to secure start-up finance. In tackling the groundwork for a business plan, you should also recognise the intrinsic benefits – to yourself and to your proposed business – of carrying out the exercise.

To cover the essential elements required for a business plan you have to:

- find out about the market for your product and produce a marketing plan in line with your findings

- predict the potential demand for your product by analysing and developing an understanding of the market within which your business will operate

- decide upon the production process for your goods or service and relate your production decisions to the finance and marketing elements of the plan

- identify the resources needed for the production and marketing of your product and include these findings in your business plan

- investigate the financial aspects of your business and prepare a financial plan for your product or service

- be aware of any legal, financial, social, environmental or technological constraints that might affect the way you produce or market your product

- understand and use financial information to assess the viability of your idea, using IT, such as spreadsheets, to present your financial projections effectively

- clarify, identify and justify the legal status of your business

- use a range of techniques to evaluate the viability of your business plan.

The objectives of a business plan

The main reason for producing a business plan is the vital role that it plays in the decision making of the different potential stakeholders in the business.

The owners of the business

The very process of thinking about the contents of a business plan, and undertaking the necessary research and analysis, obliges the people behind the business proposal to actually put down in writing, perhaps for the first time, all their ideas about the business. Until then, the reasons for starting the business, and the practicalities of how to set it up and how it should be run, may have been gone over in their minds many times or discussed with others but nothing may have been put into an organised written format. Having to produce a business plan concentrates the mind and this

is especially useful when financial matters have to be identified and listed. The process of business planning may actually cause a project to be abandoned at an early stage; or it might suggest that the project could be even more profitable than at first thought.

It is all too easy to believe that you are the right person to set up your own business. Few of us want to admit that we are better suited to being bossed than being boss. We tend to gloss over our faults – even if we are prepared to acknowledge that we have any. However, there is nothing to be ashamed about in facing up to the fact that you might not have what it takes to run a business. Deluding yourself will only prove harmful in the end – emotionally and financially. Figure 6.1 contains a questionnaire prepared by the HSBC bank which encourages you to take a long, hard look at yourself.

Discussion point

Tick the statements in Figure 6.1 which best match your outlook. Discuss which answers might be expected from somebody who is likely to make a success of running a business.

Raising money

In most cases, raising money is the single most important reason for a new business to produce a well-presented and carefully researched business plan. Although sole traders or people who set up a partnership may be able and very willing to put their own money into their business venture, they may also need to raise money from outside sources. If they do, it is imperative that they provide banks and other potential lenders with important information concerning the market for their product(s), a cash flow forecast and profitability projections.

The business plan should aim to make a good overall impression, creating an image of a new and exciting venture with a good potential market. On first reading, it should convey the drive and enthusiasm of the owner, of someone who has confidence in both the product and his or her ability. You must be seen as someone who is completely aware of what is involved in running the business and is realistic about its future.

The information should be presented in a style, language and format that attracts and sustains the attention of the reader. If the reader is to be encouraged to get as far as the more detailed financial information, then these earlier part of the plan must sustain interest; it should not be filled with superfluous and excessively detailed comment.

Figure 6.1: Starting a business self-evaluation

1 Are you a self-starter?

(a) I use my initiative. ☐

(b) Once someone's told me what to do, I get on with it. ☐

(c) I only put myself out when I want to. ☐

2 How do you get on with other people?

(a) I make sure I get on with everybody. ☐

(b) I have a close circle of friends. I don't need other people. ☐

(c) I'm never at ease in company. ☐

3 Can you lead and motivate others?

(a) Most people follow my lead. ☐

(b) I can give orders if I know what's required. ☐

(c) I'll join in once something is already started. ☐

4 Can you take responsibility?

(a) I like to take charge and see things through. ☐

(b) I'll take over if I have to but I'd prefer someone else to be responsible. ☐

(c) There's always an eager beaver waiting to show off. I leave them to it. ☐

5 Are you a good organiser?

(a) I like devising a plan – then sticking to it. ☐

(b) I'm OK when everything goes to plan. ☐

(c) I take things as they come. ☐

6 Can you make decisions?

(a) I often make snap decisions that work out. ☐

(b) If I have time to think about them. ☐

(c) I prefer others to make decisions. ☐

7 Can you stay the course?

(a) Once I have a goal, nothing will stop me. ☐

(b) I usually finish what I start. ☐

(c) If it doesn't go right, I lose interest. ☐

8 Do you take care of your health?

(a) I look after myself so I'll stay that way. ☐

(b) What will be, will be. ☐

(c) It's my mind, not my body, that's the thing. ☐

9 What experience do you have in your proposed area of business?

(a) I've been in the trade for years. ☐

(b) I need to train to learn new skills. ☐

(c) Experience isn't that important. ☐

10 Do you have the support of family and friends?

(a) My family know the risks. They are happy to get by on a reduced income for a while. ☐

(b) They're not sure what's involved, but think it's worth a try. ☐

(c) My family and social life are all-important. ☐

Source: HSBC

The description of the key features of the business should be supported by thoroughly researched and well-reasoned data. The figures should be realistic and achievable in the context of what is written about the business in the earlier parts of the plan. The manager at the bank responsible for lending to small businesses is likely to hold a relatively senior position and will be very experienced in evaluating business plans for new ventures. The manager will have handled the affairs of many small businesses and is likely to be concerned about the viability of any proposal that is based upon rather optimistic financial forecasts. If the business plan is poorly presented, has gaps and makes claims which are not supported by carefully researched figures, then the potential lender might make unfavourable assumptions about the way the business is likely to be run. If you can't make a convincing case to a bank for finance, then this suggests you might face similar problems when trying to convince potential customers about the value of your product.

Monitoring performance

When the business is up and running, the owner and managers will need to monitor its overall performance. They should compare actual sales, costs, turnover and profits with the forecasts made in the business plan. This will point to the extent to which the business is developing in line with the plan's cash flow forecast. This comparison may trigger a review of problem areas or, ideally, confirm that the cash flow forecast was based on good market research and accurate costing.

Identifying resource requirements

A business plan needs to identify the kinds of human and physical resources required to set up and run a business. This is because, in the early stages of the business, a high proportion of these resources will have to be financed from external sources. Including the resource requirements in the business plan helps to focus the mind on many of the practical aspects of the business: it ensures that you think through how you actually intend to produce your product.

The plan should quantify and cost the human resources initially needed by the business, setting out the number of employees required and their rates of pay. Unless you intend to live on your savings, as the owner, you will also need to draw some income from the business for your personal living costs. Physical resources include the premises, machinery, equipment and any vehicles as well as stocks of raw materials, parts and components, and consumables such as packaging and stationery.

Once these resources have been identified, quantified and costed, it is possible to calculate the financial resources needed to meet the initial capital outlay on fixed costs as well as the working capital needed to finance production once the business is up and running. This detailed research into start-up costs and running costs is not only important for a potential lender but will force you, perhaps for the first time, to look at the financial viability of your new business. In the process of calculating these costs you may reconsider your proposal and look for an alternative market opportunity. Alternatively, the costs may support your initial decision that your business has a profitable future.

Attracting key personnel

Your venture may depend very heavily upon attracting scarce skills or talents to fill important posts. People with these skills may command high salaries. Before any potential employees leave their existing jobs, they need to have important information about the venture which they are thinking of joining. Much of the information contained in the business plan can be put into a format that can help ensure that both you and your new employees meet each other's expectations.

Attracting finance for further expansion

If the business performs beyond the expectations contained in the initial business plan, then the organisations (and individuals) that provided some of the initial finance are more likely to provide additional funding as and when required. They may also be prepared to offer further finance on more generous terms – with lower interest charges and longer repayment periods – if the business is seen to be doing better than expected.

Applying for grants

If the proposed business is seeking a grant from a central or local government department, then a case has to be made to qualify for this financial assistance. The relevant application process is made substantially easier if much of the information required has already been put together in a business plan. The government department responsible for awarding financial assistance is also likely to be influenced by an applicant that has already produced a business plan that has secured external funding from the private sector.

BUILD YOUR LEARNING

Summary points

- A business plan must be based upon very thorough investigation of your market.

- The plan needs to set out how the goods or services will be produced and should identify all the resources and finance needed by the business.

- Owners get benefit from producing a business plan both before the business is set up and when it is up and running.

- The business plan is also useful for potential employees and for public sector bodies that award business grants.

Market analysis and marketing planning

A MAJOR PART OF YOUR BUSINESS plan should focus on what you have found out about the market for your product. A comprehensive understanding of the market is vital if a business proposal is eventually to be turned into a successful and profitable business venture. You must therefore undertake a thorough market analysis of the potential market for a new product or the extent to which your version of an existing product is likely to penetrate the current market. This analysis of the market allows you to make a forecast of the volume of sales and sales revenue. Your business plan should also include a marketing plan, based upon the findings of your market analysis.

Market analysis

To undertake your market analysis, you will almost certainly have to obtain some primary data on the market. Information about the market can also be gleaned from secondary data. Primary data will need some form of field research, while secondary data can be obtained from desk research by extracting important information from existing published sources.

The market analysis should provide information on:

- changes in customer tastes, preferences, fads, fashions and spending power

- the market potential for new, improved or existing goods and services

- the market segment or niche into which the product or service will be sold

- the size of the market, and its past growth and projections for future growth

- the extent to which the market will support a new business

- how to position the product in the market

- the approximate price that the market can sustain after any introductory offer

- the importance of non-price factors such as durability, quality, design and after-sales service

- the contribution of price and non-price factors to customer perceptions of value for money

- the need for further development to differentiate the product from existing goods and services

- the strengths and weaknesses of potential competitors

- the likely response of competitors to a new product launched on to the market.

Market analysis should also provide important information about your potential customers. You need a profile of the customers for your product. If it is a consumer product, you need to build up a picture of likely customers in terms of sex, age group, household and family size, level of education, socioeconomic class and other factors which are important for promotional activities. For business goods and services, you need to identify the kinds of businesses that are your potential customers. Find out about the characteristics of potential customers: what image do they like to project, what is their social standing and personal values, how and where do they like to buy your type of product? All this will help to determine aspects of your marketing mix.

You can glean a lot of information from secondary sources. For example, suppose your product is designed for children. Figure 6.2, taken from the government publication Social Trends, shows the most popular magazines and newspapers read by children up to 14 years old. Other readily available statistics tell us that nearly three times as many girls as boys make purchases of clothing and footwear, although boys make the most expensive purchase: an average of £11 per week for boys who buy these items compared with less than £7 for girls (1997–98 figures). Similar proportions of boys and girls spend money on leisure goods, but the average amount spent by boys is double that of the girls: an average of £5.60 for boys who bought leisure goods compared with £2.70 for girls. All this helps to build up a picture of the market.

> ### Discussion point
>
> Using the information in Figure 6.2, and reviewing our discussion on children's spending habits, discuss the kinds of products that might be offered on mail order in magazines and newspapers read by children.

Figure 6.2: Most popular magazines and newspapers for children

United Kingdom			Percentages
Aged 7–10		**Aged 11–14**	
Males		**Males**	
Match	29	The Sun	19
Beano	28	Shoot!	16
Shoot!	20	News of the World	13
Dandy	15	Match	13
Sonic the Comic	15	Beano	12
Females		**Females**	
Girl Talk	34	Sugar	47
Smash Hits	30	Smash Hits	40
Live and Kicking	17	It's Bliss	34
Barbie	13	Seventeen	31
Beano	11	Big!	27

Source: *Social Trends*, 1999

To analyse the factors that will influence the demand for your product, you have to undertake two kinds of research. First, you need to consider factors which will influence the **total market demand** for the kind of product offered by your proposed business. This will involve investigating and analysing your proposal in the context of the wider **business environment** in which your business will be operating. Analysis of economic, financial, social and legal developments, for example, can help to confirm whether the business environment is suitable for the launch of your business. Trends and changes in the business environment have a dual effect. They can generate business opportunities but they can also create threats and pitfalls for new businesses. New firms may have little in the way of financial resources to survive a sudden and serious jolt to their business prospects. Timing in launching a new business venture is all important, because it is best to start any new business at the beginning of an actual or forecast upturn in the economy.

Second, you must take account of factors which will influence the **specific demand** for your own particular product within the market. This will help you estimate the extent to which you are likely to win over customers. You need, therefore, to conduct a thorough analysis of data gained from both your field and desk research and, in particular, use secondary sources to assess the marketing strategies of your competitors in terms of their price and non-price features.

Total market demand

In Unit 2, we reviewed the demand side factors which influence the total market demand for particular goods and services (see pp. 88–94). Here, we consider the importance of some of these factors in planning a new business venture.

The price of substitutes

A rise or fall in the price of substitutes can increase or reduce the total market demand. If, for example, you have decided to open a sandwich bar then your trade is likely to be influenced by price competition between outlets which specialise in pizzas, burgers and other kinds of fast food. Similarly, if you intend to grow and market organic vegetables, then sales may be further encouraged by a green tax on chemical fertilisers and pesticides which increases the price of non-organic produce.

Complementary goods and services

A boom in the demand for particular products can create market opportunities for complementary goods and services. Time spent researching areas where consumer spending is increasing most rapidly may reveal market opportunities for related products and services. For example, the boom in the health and fitness market, with an increasing number of people now using gyms as a way of keeping fit, has increased demand for sportswear, drinks with energy supplements and specialist fitness magazines. Consider another example: it has become fashionable over the last few years to have fish ponds in gardens. This has encouraged the development of water garden centres stocking a wide range of products such as fish, aquatic plants, pond ornaments and fountains, water filters and fish food.

Tastes and preferences

You may have based your business proposal on a product which exploits the market opportunity created by changes in tastes and preferences or by new fashions and fads. You should find out if sales to this market are still rising rapidly. If they are beginning to level off, you run the risk of your own goods and services being launched when market demand is actually falling. If you are setting up a business that seeks to take advantage of sudden, and what may be very short-lived, fashions, then you need to identify them at the earliest possible stage. You need to have confidence in your ability to spot the next fashion or fad so that you can shift resources into a new product as soon as possible. Areas where a new business can exploit new market opportunities include the latest trends in eating habits, leisure, entertainment, recreation, clothing, footwear and other aspects of personal appearance and grooming.

▲ The Pokémon craze: how long will it last?

In some cases, trends may be gradual and more permanent – the market reaches a peak before falling to a relatively stable level of people who have become regular consumers of the product. For example, the boom in the numbers visiting clubs for late night leisure and entertainment has been running for some years now. However, in 1999, there were signs that this boom had peaked and more people – particularly in the younger age groups – were opting for pubs with music, many owned by the large breweries and pub groups. The clubs will continue to do good business, but the peak demand appears to be over.

Disposable income

Changes in the average level of disposable income can result from the government's decisions on income tax rates, tax bands and tax allowances. This can cause significant changes in consumer spending. Changes in VAT and excise duties can also impact on the purchasing power of consumers. These changes in government economic policy are particularly important if you are launching a product in a market where total demand is sensitive to a change in spending power. If, for example, you intend to run a landscaping and garden maintenance business, then your research may show a definite and positive link between average levels of real disposable income and spending on these kinds of services. If you set up in business when average spending power is no longer rising, or is even falling, then your initial business forecasts may prove to be rather optimistic.

The feel-good factor

There are regular published surveys which measure levels of consumer confidence. These surveys give you information about the respective proportions of consumers who expect their financial position to improve and those who expect it to deteriorate. If the measures show rising levels of consumer confidence then consumer spending may soon start to rise more rapidly. This is because the feel-good factor will be reflected by more people spending a higher proportion of their income as well as borrowing more to finance extra spending.

Consumers retain confidence in the British economy

The sixteenth annual British lifestyles survey published by Mintel concludes that Britain has entered a period of "solid confidence".

Consumer spending is set to rise. "People have built up a cushion against adversity," said Paul Rickard, head of market research at Mintel.

However, although consumers are ready to spend, they will not do so at any price. "The third millennium consumer will wait for the sales or for prices to go down to a level they are prepared to pay. In short they want value for money," said Peter Ayton, Mintel's chief statistician.

"People are more savvy: they know that if they wait longer the price will come down – the 'hurry hurry hurry' sales mentality no longer holds."

The internet and other new technologies will become crucial, said Mr Rickard. The web will have an impact on prices. Some sectors, such books and CDs, have already responded more bullishly than others. "The web will create consortia of buyers who will drive prices down; the balance of power will shift more and more to the consumers," he said.

Gross domestic product

In order to find out what may happen to the overall trend in spending power over the next two or three years, you have to investigate forecasts of gross domestic product (GDP). This measures the total value of all the goods and services produced in a single year. The data on GDP is usually adjusted to take account of price increases so that changes can be seen in real terms. The rate at which the UK's GDP is increasing is generally referred to as the rate of economic growth. If GDP is rising rapidly – and is forecast to continue to do so – then this is a sign of a buoyant and expanding economy.

In periods of economic growth, more jobs are created and those in work have increased earning potential. Because consumers have greater spending power, periods of strong economic growth are particularly good times to start a new business. As a benchmark to assess current and forecast rates of economic growth, note that over the last fifty years the UK economy has experienced an average rate of economic growth of about 2.25 per cent.

Consumer spending

It is important to analyse recent trends in consumer spending, because a more rapid rise in GDP – and therefore a higher rate of economic growth – is usually triggered by an upturn in consumer spending. Once this process is underway, it can develop a self-reinforcing momentum. The rise in spending stimulates increased supply, and if this is largely sourced from UK producers rather than from an increase in imports, then eventually this will mean more jobs as well as increased earnings for those in work. The economy experiences a period of rising prosperity through a cycle of higher spending, increased output, stronger economic growth, more jobs, higher spending, and so on.

Unemployment

A fall in unemployment is usually a sign of an improved rate of economic growth, rising prosperity and higher consumer spending. However, this is not always the case. It is possible for consumer spending to rise without a significant fall in unemployment. Consumer spending may be increasing at a time when producers have spare capacity and are achieving productivity improvements. In this case, there is likely to be a time lag before increases in consumer spending produce a fall in unemployment.

Private sector investment

The level of private sector investment is also a valuable guide to the future level of economic activity. Increased spending by firms on capital projects such as buildings, plant, machinery and equipment will increase GDP, create jobs in the capital goods sector and eventually increase consumer spending. The willingness of firms to invest in fixed assets is also evidence of increased confidence in the business sector as a whole. Firms do not spend large sums of money on increasing their capacity and introducing new technology unless they are generally optimistic about the future level of demand in the economy. Surveys which monitor the level of business confidence and investment intentions are a valuable guide to the future level of economic activity.

Interest rates

When considering the timing of a new business, it is important to consider the future trend and current levels of interest rates. Changes in interest rates will effect the cost of bank loans and overdrafts. A rise in the cost of borrowed money can have a significant impact on a business during its early life. Higher interest rates will also effect your customers because of the impact of higher mortgage repayments on discretionary incomes. If you are selling your product to other companies, they will also be effected by the fall in consumer spending and the impact of higher interest charges on their own loans and bank overdrafts.

The rate of inflation

Inflation is a key economic indicator, and influences economic decisions on interest rates, taxation and government spending. If, for example, the latest inflation figures suggest that the government's inflation target – currently 2.5 per cent – is likely to be breached, then the government or the Bank of England may use fiscal and monetary policies to deflate total spending in the economy. A new business will be particularly interested in the outcome of the monthly meeting of the Bank of England's monetary policy committee. If this group of economists judge that there are no serious inflationary pressures in the economy, then interest rates are likely to remain unchanged or even be cut. This may be a good time to launch a new business. If, however, inflation is rising, then interest rates are likely to be increased and this may not be an appropriate time to start a new business.

Each month the government publishes key economic indicators. These can be used to establish movements in the factors which are likely to influence total demand in the market in which your new business will be operating. Some of these indicators will also be used by the government and the Bank of England to decide whether or not they need to take action to dampen down consumer spending in the economy in order to keep inflation down to an acceptable level. Figure 6.3 lists some of these key economic indicators.

Discussion point

Explain why output data can be used to assess what is happening to total spending in the economy. What does data on business investment tell you about profitability and the overall level of business confidence?

Figure 6.3 shows the level of several key economic indicators at the beginning of 2000. Discuss whether these indicators suggest that it would be a good time to launch a new business.

The exchange rate

Recent and expected movements in the exchange rate are important for some new businesses because of their effect on the foreign currency prices of exports and the sterling prices of imports. A rise or fall in the value of the pound will effect a business that is hoping to make an early entry into export markets, faces competition from imports or relies upon imported materials, parts and components.

Exports and imports

The UK's international trading performance can also provide an indication of the general direction of the economy. If exports are increasing faster than imports, then this suggests that UK firms are generally competitive: this is good for jobs, incomes and consumer spending. If imports are rising faster than exports, then this may eventually mean a loss of jobs and reduced consumer spending power. A growing trade

Figure 6.3: Key economic indicators

Indicator	Latest figures
Output (1995 prices)	
GDP (Q4)	Up 0.8% on the previous quarter and up 2.9% on a year earlier
Service sector output (Q4)	Up 0.9% on the previous quarter and up 2.9% on a year earlier
Industrial production (Q4)	Up 0.3% on the previous quarter and up 1.8% on a year earlier
Manufacturing output (Q4)	Up 0.7% on the previous quarter and up 1.9% on a year earlier
Demand (1995 prices)	
Household consumption (Q4)	Up 0.8% on the previous quarter and up 4.5% on a year earlier
Retail sales (three months to Jan)	Up 1.8% on the previous 3 months and up 5.3% on a year earlier
Whole economy investment (Q4)	Up 1.1% on the previous quarter and up 3.1% on a year earlier
Business investment (Q4)	Up 1.2% on the previous quarter and up 3.8% on a year earlier
Real household disposable income (1995 prices)	
Income (Q3)	Down 0.8% on the previous quarter and up 2.9% on a year earlier
Households saving ratio (Q3)	4.5% down from 7.0% in the previous quarter
Labour market	
UK ILO unemployment (Sept–Dec)	Down 4,000 on the previous 3 months to 1.718 million giving a rate of 5.9%, down from 6.2% a year ago
UK claimant unemployment (Jan)	Down 9,800 on December to 1.158 million, giving a rate of 4.0%, down from 4.2% a year earlier
Headline average earnings (GB)	Annual earnings growth of 5.5%
Inflation	
Headline inflation (Jan)	All-items RPI inflation of 2.0%, up from 1.8% in December
Underlying inflation (Jan)	RPI ex MIPs inflation of 2.1%, down from 2.2% in December
Halifax house prices (3 mths to Feb)	Down 0.9% on the previous 3 months, and up 15.0% on a year earlier

Source: HM Treasury, Pocket Data Bank, 21 January 2000

deficit is also likely to trigger economic policies aimed at deflating consumer spending, so that less is spent on imports and UK firms are forced to look abroad for markets.

Demographic and social changes

Demographic and social changes tend to take place over a relatively long period of time. A new business is unlikely to be threatened by any sudden change in demographic factors. If, however, a new business fails to take account of demographic and social trends, then over the years it may find itself in a declining market.

Information on demographic and social trends can be used to identify market opportunities for a new business. The total market demand for certain kinds of products and services can be affected by changes in:

- the total size of the population

- its age structure

- social groups

- ethnic and cultural groups

- geographical distribution between inner city, urban, suburban and rural areas

- rate of household formation

- composition and size of household units

- social attitudes to, for example, marriage, sexuality, health and fitness, the environment

- level of education.

▲ Old people make up an ever increasing proportion of British society

These demographic developments create opportunities and, in some cases, pose threats for organisations developing new business proposals. For example, as older age groups are forming an increasing percentage of the population, there is increased demand for a range of leisure and travel services that generally appeal to older people. There is also a greater demand for retirement accommodation, including both sheltered and residential care homes. A fall in the birth rate, on the other hand, reduces demand for many kinds of goods and services, such as crèches and nurseries.

Legal changes

Legal changes can either enhance or possibly reduce the market for your business. This is a huge area, but let's consider some specific examples.

Tougher environmental controls increase demand for less harmful alternatives for CFCs and other propellants and coolants. They change the market environment for waste collection services, recycling and disposal companies. Environmental controls boost the market for energy conservation equipment and materials, for instruments to measure and monitor emissions and provide work for consultants in environmental management.

Health and safety is a focus for much new legislation. Laws aimed at improving the safety of consumer goods and durables may increase demand for new materials, paints, power systems and cut-off devices as well as increasing the demand for design consultants. Motor vehicle manufacturers have been obliged to devote more attention to the safety features of their cars, increasing the demand for products such as air bags, new braking systems, passenger restraint equipment and impact absorbing materials. Food safety and hygiene regulations have expanded the market for alternative ingredients, higher-quality animal feed, food storage facilities, packaging, clothing and equipment as well as providing work for specialist food hygiene training agencies.

A strengthening of health and safety regulations in the workplace has increased the demand for more effective protective clothing and equipment, devices for extracting dust and other emissions, more sophisticated heating, lighting and ventilation systems, and better designed office furniture and work stations. Firms providing training in health and safety are in greater demand as well as consultants offering advice on how improvements to the physical working environment can help to reduce stress-related problems.

Of course, new laws also generate an increased demand for legal firms. Specialists in employment law are likely to get more work as new legislation is introduced regulating areas such as equal opportunities, the maximum working week and employment protection rights.

Advances in technology

Technological changes also bring new market opportunities as well as possibly threatening the market for some existing goods and services.

New technological processes can help to lower production costs. This may help lower the entry costs to markets. Advanced production technology can reduce sources of defects and errors, improving the quality of products and helping you to compete on quality. Many large-scale producers are able to establish a reputation for quality because they can afford to devote resources to extensive quality systems. New technology that helps to improve quality can now be incorporated into machinery and equipment suitable for small-scale producers, allowing new producers to compete very strongly on quality with established producers.

The development of new, or much improved, products may give you access to markets previously dominated by large well-established producers. For example, developments in materials technology –leading to new kinds of plastics, fibres and other materials – may open up new market opportunities because these allow companies to produce economically many household and consumer goods on a relatively small scale.

The processes, capital goods, products and materials that stem from new technology can create a huge range of new market opportunities. The technology that produced personal computers, for example, not only resulted in the market for the computers themselves, but produced new markets in business, educational and entertainment software, peripherals, the internet, consultancy and support services, PC magazines and specialist retail outlets. The computer revolution has

been supported by many small companies providing training courses to help individuals acquire the skills to make the best use of their computers. It also created opportunities in more traditional sectors such as furniture manufacture, as demand increased for desks, seating and storage facilities for computer work stations in both offices and homes.

Specific demand for your product

If you are satisfied that the overall business environment and the total market demand are favourable – and are expected to remain favourable – you must then consider factors that are likely to effect the demand for your particular product. You must establish an effective combination of price and non-price features to ensure, in time, that your sales and revenue reach forecast. Financial investors will be particularly interested in knowing how you intend to make your goods and services different from those already on the market.

You may be operating in a market which is very price sensitive, with very little customer loyalty. This occurs in markets with very little scope for product differentiation; consumers see no reason to choose between different suppliers except on the basis of price. In this situation, you will attract customers if you can set lower prices than your rivals. You must pay a great deal of attention to unit costs to ensure that your price can be as competitive as possible. Investigating the scope for cost savings must be an ongoing process, so that you can either gain a price advantage to boost sales or have the scope to reduce prices if necessary in response to a price cut by a competitor.

There is the possibility, of course, that you can identify ways of introducing a degree of product differentiation. Your market research may have suggested areas for product differentiation which have not been adopted by your rivals. If you can introduce a product that offers something different from what is already available, you should be able to attract customers and even gradually raise prices over time.

If the market is already differentiated in various ways, then the market research you undertake to obtain primary data should seek to identify the relative importance of the different product features in consumer choice. This will allow you to incorporate these features into your own product and to give them prominence in the promotional aspects of your marketing mix. Researching the relative importance of factors that contribute to product differentiation can also help avoid the costs of building in features that play little or no part in determining consumers' choice

Organic food takes root

Foodies and faddies have been fans for ages, but in the last few months organic produce has entered the mainstream diet in a big way.

Where supermarkets once paid lip service to those who were thought of as cranky customers with a few knobbly organic carrots and undersized apples in their fruit and veg section, they are now giving over whole swathes of their sales area to chemical and additive-free food.

Marks & Spencer has introduced special sections, Sainsbury's reports a record £2.8m sale of organic products each week and Tesco is shelling out £250,000 a year for four years to help fund the Aberdeen University Centre for Organic Culture while reporting a dramatic increase in pure food sales.

Waitrose, in the meantime, can boast that it has once again been voted the organic supermarket of the year in the Soil Association's 1999 awards.

The main complaint about organic food is the cost. It is more expensive than other produce because of specialist production. Organic crops are produced under strict European legislation and for a farm in this country to clear its land of pesticides under Soil Association regulations takes a two-year transitional period and careful accreditation. Seventy per cent of organic food is still imported into Britain but this country is developing its own sources, especially in Scotland, where there are also organic fish farms.

But cost is weighed against purity.

Sustain, the Alliance for Better Food and Farming, says that a test found traces of 32 different agrichemicals in apples. And there is also the matter of additives, suspect animal feed and the legacy of BSE and new variant CJD to consider.

Another virtue of organic food which makes it attractive to those who buy with a conscience is that it is often produced by small suppliers. Organic foods mean that ethics can enter your shopping basket along with pure food.

Fairtrade, whose aim is to get a better deal for Third World growers and producers, has under its banner a number of organic products, with the Hampstead Tea and Coffee Company's Darjeeling the winner of a Soil Association award. Fairtrade also markets organic cocoa, chocolate and honey.

Waitrose, as a supermarket leader in the organic field, has more than 500 products in its stores, including pet foods, beers, wines, ciders, meat and fish, with such treats as organic brown trout. Tesco sources from registered growers and farmers. Its suppliers include Shipton Mill where wheat is traditionally stone-ground, Caledonian Brewery, which uses organic Scottish barley and organic hops from Kent and the Yeo Valley Organic Company, which is its principal yoghurt supplier.

The Guardian, 11 March 2000

between rival products. In general, the greater the degree of product differentiation that you can achieve, the less you will be affected if competitors lower their prices to win back customers.

Discussion point

Explain the factors that have contributed to the rapid increase in the sales of organic food.

Suppose you are planning to set up a wholesale or retail business to sell organic products. What topics might you investigate in a market research questionnaire to assess likely demand for your business?

Identifying and analysing competition

In seeking to estimate the demand for your particular product, you must also take account of the degree of competition which you will face from existing producers as well as assessing the possibility of new firms entering the market.

The demand for your product may be influenced by how rival firms react to your entry into the market. If the market comprises a large number of competing suppliers, then you are likely to win customers from many different firms. Because the impact of your entry into the market is spread over a large number of firms, your presence is less likely to trigger your competitors to make large price cuts. If, however, you are entering a market currently served by very few firms, then – if your business is successful – each company in the market may experience a significant decline in sales. They are unlikely to simply let this happen without making a response. The competition may react by introducing a combination of lower prices and increased spending on promotional activities. Your marketing strategy has to take account of how you intend to respond to any competitive moves by existing producers.

Having decided upon your product, and given serious consideration to your start-up costs, you should have a good idea of how easy or difficult it is to enter the market. This needs to be considered when devising a marketing plan because, if you are particularly successful, then other (new or existing) businesses may diversify into the market. If there are low costs of entry, then strong initial sales for a very new product may soon be hit by other firms entering your market.

The questionnaire used for field research is the opportunity to obtain primary data that allows you to get more information about your competitors and the popularity of their products. Responses to questions designed to discover the relative importance to consumers of price and non-price factors when making purchasing decisions also provide valuable information on what are the main strengths and weaknesses of competing products.

Discussion point

Use the same headings in the table in the case study to compare your proposed business with those which are already operating in the same market.

Having made the comparison are you persuaded to change any features of your product.

CASE STUDY

Tom Star's minicab business

Tom Star was planning a mini-cab business, so he compared his proposed service with two existing ones in the area.

Tom concluded from this comparison that Ace Cars wouldn't pose much of a threat. Their charges were slightly lower, but the cars were older and rundown. However, he noticed that their parcel delivery service got them some business customers and he decided to investigate offering a similar service.

The other competitor, Len Brown, was new to the area, had high standard cars and charged higher rates for special occasions, such as weddings. Tom felt he couldn't compete with this service, but could use his better cars for chauffeuring business people. This led him to include stepping-up contacts with businesses in his plan, to reduce his dependence on the less predictable domestic trade.

Source: Barclays Bank

	Tom Star	**Ace Cars**	**L. Brown**
Price	On average £1 per mile	On average £1 per mile	On average £1 per mile
Quality	Good	OK	Very good
Availability	5 a.m.–2 p.m. 7 days a week	24 hours 7 days a week	24 hours 7 days a week
Customers	Mostly domestic	Domestic and account work	New
Reputation	Good	Mixed	New
Advertising	Newsagents, supermarkets, door-to-door	Door-to-door	Ad in Thompson Directory
Delivery	n/a	n/a	n/a
Location	Local and airports	Local and airports	Local, airports weddings
Special offers	None	None	?
After-sales service	n/a	n/a	n/a

Data from field research also allows you to identify the 'place' component of your rivals' marketing strategies. This will help you to decide upon the most effective distribution method for your product. If you intend to set up your own premises to deal directly with your customers, then this research should help you decide on the location – and style – of your business premises.

Important information about other aspects of your competitors' marketing strategies can be obtained by obtaining their promotional material. Look, for example, at their advertisements, sales brochures, merchandising and packaging. This provides useful information on the various elements of the marketing mix used by each of your competitors. If you are likely to be in direct competition with one or more large companies, then find out more about these competitors from any relevant articles in the business sections of the newspapers. These articles may give you some useful information about product development, recent sales performance and changes in their marketing strategy. Information about the recent performance of large companies, and their plans for the future, can also be obtained from their annual reports and accounts; these can be a further valuable guide when formulating your own marketing strategy.

The marketing plan

The information from your market analysis is used to produce a marketing plan. This part of your business plan is very important as it helps to demonstrate to a bank or other source of finance that your company has a good understanding of the market, that there is a demand for your product, and that it is possible to trade successfully in the current market.

The first step in compiling the marketing plan is to assess where the business is at the moment. Your venture, clearly, is not actually trading. To assess the position of the business before setting up in production and entering the market, you need to carry out a SWOT analysis (see Unit 3, p. 172–3). This identifies your internal strengths and weaknesses and the external opportunities and threats. A lender will be particularly interested in a clear and full description of the strengths of your product and its unique selling points. This can be supported by information about the prices charged by competitors and why your combination of price and non-price factors will allow you to gain sales at the expense of rival suppliers.

A marketing plan should be constructed with a clear idea of where you want your business to be at some point in the future. Your marketing plan, therefore, should include some financial targets relating to your business objectives such as sales volume. These financial targets should be based on short-term objectives (up to a year), medium-term objectives (one-to-three years) and long-term objectives (up to five years).

For very small businesses, and especially for sole traders, it is often appropriate to include both personal and business objectives. These personal objectives may include, for example, the desire to be one's own boss, to have an outlet for a creative talent, to travel and meet people, and other non-monetary objectives that are important for your quality of life. These personal objectives are likely to be taken into account when a potential lender is assessing what may appear to be relatively modest financial targets.

Many people are tempted to set up their own business based on a hobby, sporting or recreational activity that is an important part of their leisure time. In this situation, it is even more important that the marketing plan is informed by proper market research: the budding entrepreneur needs to assess whether other people may be as easily persuaded that the product is something worth spend their money on. This need to use market findings rather than personal experience and intuition is an important part of putting together a successful marketing and business plan.

Most new business start-ups have limited financial and human resources, and the first period of trading can make or break a new venture. It is important, therefore, that the marketing plan is based on detailed research to ensure that resources are used as effectively as possible. If human and physical resources are devoted, for example, to aspects of product differentiation which are of little importance to consumers and financial resources are wasted on inappropriate forms of promotion, this can seriously reduce the business's chances of achieving financial targets.

The marketing plan should include an outline of the means by which you intend to achieve your targets and business objectives. This involves generating an effective marketing strategy so that the marketing mix – the combination of product, price, promotion and place (that is, the channel of distribution) – contributes to the achievement of your business objectives. Much of the information used to decide the marketing mix will come from an analysis of the data generated by your field and desk research.

The marketing strategy may also involve changing the balance between the various elements that make up the marketing mix once the business has been running for some time. For example, when your product is first put onto the market a great deal of emphasis may be placed upon a special introductory price; you may use other promotion techniques once sales reach a certain level.

CASE STUDY

Do it yourself point of sale

Do it yourself

There is a lot of effective advertising which you can do yourself. Start with your sign. A good sign is a great investment. A catchy slogan (WEE-MIX, YOU LAY. Just enough readymix for your job) gets you remembered.

Simple A-boards outside premises will attract customers. Try to think of ingenious ways to remind them of your name at times when they need you.

An enterprising plumber called on the homes in his area with his business stickers, and said: "You don't need me now, but stick this on your central heating boiler for when you do." A simple but effective way to get his business message over in the right place at the right time. Distributing leaflets within a local area is also a very good way of advertising the product or service you are offering.

Signs at point of sale

Tests carried out by a large US supermarket suggest that:

- stores using simple handwritten signs with 'as advertised' on them to promote products on shelves increased their sales – this is compared to products in stores with no signs.

- using 'new item' signs increased sales of powered bleach by 73 per cent.

These are just two examples of point of sale tests which show the power of signs. even if you cannot use them in your business, they prove the principle – point of sale pays.

Source: NatWest Bank

The marketing plan is particularly important once the business is up and running. You need to compare your actual performance with the marketing objectives and financial targets included in the marketing plan. As long as your targets are based on a thorough analysis of the market, you should review the market environment and make any necessary adjustments to the marketing strategy if your performance is not going as you expected.

If a bank has lent you money, it may require a periodic review of your performance. The bank will pay particular attention to your situation in relation to the financial aspects of your marketing objectives. This is another reason why forecasts in your marketing plan should be realistic and achievable, because the bank will be concerned if actual performance is significantly below the forecast.

No matter how much hard work goes into preparation, the business performance can be very dependent upon the attitudes of employees who are involved in production or in dealing with customers. If employees are made aware of your marketing plan, they are more likely to appreciate how their particular efforts can make a contribution to the future of the business. They will understand the reasoning behind any changes you might make to the product or any changes to the way in which they do their job, if they are based on a marketing plan that is adapted to any market developments that impact on business performance. You are more likely to run a successful business, if you can secure the commitment and motivation of employees. They are more likely to respond favourably if the business knows where it is going.

Your marketing plan should give the reader a good impression of how you are going to run the business. If the plan is very customer oriented, then a potential lender may also sense that other all other business activities are also customer driven. This will help them to feel more confident that you can reach your financial targets and meet your loan repayments.

Discussion point

Produce a small-scale version of a possible sign for your business. Apart from the name of the business and other essential information, you might also include a catchy slogan and a logo.

If you are proposing to set up a retail, catering or other kind of service where customers come to your premises, then design point-of-sale signs for some of your services.

BUILD YOUR LEARNING

Keywords and phrases

You should know the meaning of the words and phrases listed below. Go back through the last 12 pages of the unit to check or refresh your understanding as necessary.

- Business environment
- Consumer confidence
- Desk research
- Discretionary income
- Economic growth
- Field research
- Gross domestic product
- Market analysis
- Marketing plan
- Marketing strategy
- Price sensitive
- Primary data
- Product differentiation
- Secondary data
- Total market demand

Summary points

- A market analysis must be carried out to gain a thorough understanding of your potential market.

- Market analysis should be based on both field and desk research and be supported by a detailed understanding of the factors which effect the total market demand.

- A start-up business needs to identify factors which are likely to influence the demand for its particular goods and services, including price and non-price factors and the level of competition.

- A marketing plan should be based on a SWOT analysis. It should include sales targets, details of the marketing mix and other information which indicates that the business has a clear idea of how to market its product successfully.

- The marketing plan will be used to review the business's performance against its marketing objectives.

Production and resource requirements

POTENTIAL FINANCIAL BACKERS will be very interested in the part of your business plan that details how you intend to produce your particular product. You must be capable of producing the goods or services described in your marketing strategy at a unit cost that allows you to charge a competitive price. If you are making goods, you – and any key production personnel – must be able to demonstrate that you have a very sound understanding of the manufacturing process . If your enterprise is a service business, you need to show how you will provide and organise your services.

The nature of your product will determine the way that production is organised. An important factor is the volume of output: are you going to supply a small number of customised goods and services or larger quantities of a standardised product? This has a bearing on the kinds of manual skills required and the type of machinery and equipment needed. The level of output also has implications for the lay out of the production area, including the handling of materials and work in progress and the storage of finished product.

Job production

Job production is a process specifically designed to meet the individual requirements of each customer. Examples of products that are produced on a job production basis include made-to-measure clothing, machine tools and equipment designed to meet the exact, non-standard specifications of a specialist user, and tableware and furnishings made to the individual materials and design requirements of a restaurant.

Features of job production include:

- few raw materials and parts will be stocked by the business, as many jobs use non-standard components

- there will be few stocks of the end product, as each product is tailored for individual customers

- the business needs a variety of machinery, equipment and tools, because many of the jobs are likely to be very different

- the factory layout and workforce must be flexible to deal with individual orders and relatively short production runs for each customer

- labour costs are likely to be high because the work needs skilled and versatile workers who are likely to command high wages.

Job production is likely to be very labour intensive, because it requires considerable staff input to organise production to meet the particular needs of each customer. Output is likely to be relatively low. Making a small number of different products, one at a time, also has implications for sales revenue. A relatively long period may elapse between receiving an order, incurring production costs and receiving payment from the customer. A long lead-time must therefore be built into the revenue forecasts.

Batch production

Longer production runs, in which a number of products are passed through one or more production operations or processes, is known as batch production. In batch production, the manufacturing operation or process is repeated but is not continuous. Batch production is particularly suitable for making a range of products. For example, a furniture manufacturer may make a batch of desks, followed by batches of bookcases, cupboards, tables and then chairs. By working on this basis, the firm can build up a stock of the complete range of its products.

The size of each batch is determined by the demand for the particular product and on cost considerations. A company must take account of the changeover costs, such as the time spent resetting machinery, before switching production to another product. Account must also be taken of the cost of holding stocks of finished items, particularly if the batch runs are relatively large.

The actual size of a batch may also depend upon the need to even out the workload in different parts of the production operation. If batch sizes are too large, this can produce a situation in which some employees at different stages of production are under a great deal of pressure, while others are not being fully utilised because their respective jobs involve different batches of products.

In comparison with job production, batch production can be maintained with relatively unskilled (and therefore) cheaper labour; the longer production runs mean that greater use can be made of labour specialisation. Workers at each stage of the manufacturing or assembly process can be kept more fully occupied on a small number of simple routine tasks, which can be performed with little training.

Although batch production is used to make a range of products, the different products will be made using the same basic operations and processes. For example, a rug manufacturer will produce a range of different rugs and carpets in different designs, colours, sizes and materials using the same basic manufacturing processes. Batch production, therefore, enables a company to operate with fairly standardised machinery and equipment, and it requires less variety of equipment and production processes than job production.

Flow production

Flow production – known also as mass production – is used when demand for the product requires continuous supply. It is often used by firms producing consumer durables for the mass market and is a common production method in industrial sectors like food processing, brewing and chemicals. As a new business, it is very unlikely that you will be making a product that requires flow production to satisfy a mass market. New entrants into mass markets are often offshoots of already well-established large organisations that have the resources and management expertise to diversify into markets that require flow production methods. However, some smaller firms though starting with batch production may find that their products become so popular that it is viable to set up separate flow production lines or processing operations.

It is also possible that your market analysis identified a very large gap in the market and your product has so many new features that your market research provides convincing evidence that demand will be extremely high. In this case, flow production may be viable even for a new business, particularly as new technology now enables flow methods to be introduced on a relatively small scale. For example, organic beer can be produced on a flow basis using essentially the same technology used by large brewers but on a smaller scale. There may not be the economies of scale that can be gained from large-scale flow production levels, but if the product is sufficiently innovative and is well-designed for a niche market, you may be able to charge a price that covers relatively high unit costs.

Flow production usually involves considerable investment in skills, machinery and equipment and layout so that continuous output can be maintained. Investment in this type of single-purpose capacity generally involves very large start-up costs and it is vital to maintain a level of sales to ensure that productive capacity is fully utilised. The inflexible nature of the plant used in flow production makes it difficult to transfer production to other products if the market does not live up to expectations.

Flow production lends itself to an even greater application of specialised labour and further increases the scope to employ relatively unskilled labour. This type of production also requires that all parts of the operation are supplied with the appropriate raw materials and components. A shortage of the necessary inputs at one stage in the production sequence can hold up the whole of the manufacturing, assembly or processing operation.

An efficient purchasing, stock control and materials handling system will also have to be supported by an effective maintenance programme to avoid breakdowns in equipment and machinery and to take full advantage of flow production.

Plant, machinery, equipment and vehicles

Our discussion of job, batch and flow production methods suggested that the anticipated volume of sales is a crucial determining factor in the plant and equipment needed for a new business. This determines whether you have to acquire a range of different machines, for example, or whether you can operate effectively with standard items of machinery which perform a relatively limited range of operations.

The information in your business plan on your capital equipment requirements will help the reader establish that you are fully conversant with how to produce your product. The business plan should include the following:

- a brief description of the plant, machinery, equipment and vehicles needed for start-up

- details of their functions in the production process, including information on operating capacity and expected useful life

- costs, including the reasons for choosing outright purchase (new or used) or leasing, and details on the method of payment

- the insurance, maintenance and replacement requirements of all capital equipment

- reasons for the choice of particular equipment and models, including an indication of any competitive advantage provided by the equipment you will use

- longer-term needs for capital items.

You should avoid the temptation to acquire capital items that may have operating capacities, functions and levels of technology which are very much in excess of the needs of your business. For example, buying an item of machinery that employs the latest computer-aided manufacturing techniques may be a very expensive luxury when you are only likely to use a fraction of its capacity and range of functions.

If your machinery and equipment needs are relatively straightforward – and is not likely to be quickly obsolete due to frequent and significant improvements in technology – then it may be worthwhile looking at the second-hand market. Trade journals often carry adverts for used items from businesses that are either closing down or trading up to the latest model. It is not unusual, for example, for new catering establishments to acquire items such as fridges, freezers and cooking equipment from the used market. It is important, however, to have any second-hand capital items checked to ensure that they comply with health and safety regulations and meet any other legal requirements that apply in your line of business.

▲ The government has introduced tax advantages to encourage e-commerce

You should also be aware of any tax advantages that apply to the purchase of capital equipment. For example, in the March 2000 budget the government introduced plans to encourage small firms to take advantage of the opportunities offered by e-commerce. This allows small companies to write off the full cost of computer hardware and internet technology against tax in the year it is purchased. Usually, small companies are only allowed to claim a 40 per cent capital allowance on their spending on plant and equipment.

Discussion point

What is the advantage to small companies of the new 100 per cent tax allowance on computers and internet technology.

Will it encourage you to invest in e-commerce for your proposed business?

Do you think there is case for giving some kind of tax relief to companies that lease rather than buy computer hardware?

The production plan

Your plan should demonstrate that you have the knowledge and expertise relating to all the practical aspects of the production process for your product. As part of your preparation, you will have put together a production plan to show how production will be organised to achieve goods and services that conform precisely with those described in your marketing plan. You need to describe how the product passes through the various stages in the production process.

The whole of production must be carefully planned so that each part or stage in the process operates at optimum levels and the various operations are coordinated to avoid either bottlenecks or idle capacity in both machines and labour. You can extract information from your production plan and condense it into a concise format to be included in your business plan. This part of your business plan should cover:

- production methods and processes
- raw materials
- production layout
- subcontracted operations
- production capacity.

Production methods and processes

The plan should describe the methods and processes involved in producing goods and services and the sequence in which they will be carried. This should also include references to the items of capital used at each stage in the process as this can support your section on the need for finance to acquire plant, machinery and equipment.

Raw materials

You should give a description of the raw materials, parts and components required, and details of which companies will supply them and on what terms and conditions. This is also an opportunity to highlight any aspects of these inputs and sources of supply which will help you to achieve lower unit costs and a quality advantage over your competitors

Production layout

The description of the production process can be supported with a sketch of the layout of the manufacturing or service unit within your premises. This will show the overall size of the production area, the positioning of machinery and equipment, the path of materials and finished goods and where any stocks will be held. Handling costs in a manufacturing firm can be a high proportion of total costs. Your layout should show that you recognise the importance of an efficient handling system and the need to ensure that all items move smoothly between operations. This might start, for example, with the receipt of raw materials and parts, moving on to their treatment and processing, the manufacture of components, their assembly and final finishing and packaging.

Subcontracted operations

You need to identify any operations that will be subcontracted out to other firms. It makes sense, for example, to subcontract a process that needs an expensive piece of machinery if your production levels would not enable you to operate the machine at full capacity . The process may also require a highly skilled operative whose wages could not be justified by the limited number of times that particular part of the production process would be carried out.

It is sensible to subcontract out jobs to specialist companies if they can undertake the work for a lower costs. It may be that the specialists can achieve economies of scale because, by undertaking work for many other firms, they can carry out the operation on a much larger scale.

Production capacity

Your production plan should demonstrate that production is organised to achieve the targets in the marketing plan. If the forecast volume of sales in based on a thorough market analysis, then labour and productive capacity must reflect the sales forecast. If you are unable to meet the demand for your product, then you will quickly gain a reputation with customers for being unreliable and having long delivery periods. This is a reputation that can be difficult for a new business to shake off and can seriously threaten its survival. However, the productive capacity of plant, machinery and equipment must not be too far in excess of your sales forecast as this will push up unit costs and reduce your profit margin. Once the business is operating, the production plan must continue to reflect any changes in the marketing plan.

Labour requirements

The size of the workforce – the skills of the people that you employ – must reflect your production and marketing plans. The amount of labour allocated to the production process must allow you to achieve sales targets. These employees must also have the appropriate skills to use the machinery and equipment

and to deliver the quality of work required by the marketing plan. You must also avoid employing people who are more highly skilled than is necessary; skilled labour tends to be more expensive, so this will be an unnecessary expense.

If you are providing a business or consumer service, then your employees need appropriate job skills as well as good social and personal skills and an acceptable standard in terms of personal care.

Your business plan should set out labour requirements by providing:

- a description of the major tasks to be carried out as outlined in the production plan

- a summary of the job descriptions for key positions

- details of the basis on which people are to be employed, such as full-time, part-time, casual, fixed-term contracts or consultant

- the salaries to be paid to employees and how they compare with the going rate in the local labour market.

- details of any performance-related pay such as piece rates, bonus schemes and sales commission and any provision for paying overtime

- a brief statement concerning other employment costs such as national insurance and pension contributions.

In setting wage and salary rates, it may be tempting to look at the lowest rates that appear in the recruitment sections of your local paper or the pay offered for jobs registered at the jobcentre. You might be better advised, however, to pay a decent salary to attract reliable workers with the kind of positive attitude that will help to get your business off to the best possible start. Paying the bare minimum may mean you hire inflexible workers with little motivation. This might lead to a high labour turnover during the first period of business.

Quality assurance

Apart from convincing potential financial backers that you are capable of meeting a realistic sales target at a competitive unit cost, you also have to persuade them that you can do so while also assuring quality. This requires that you understand what is meant by quality from the customer's point of view.

Your market analysis should have produced some indication of why your potential customers are currently choosing one of the products provided by your competitors. These findings will help you decide upon which features of your product are an essential part of your marketing strategy. If these product features succeed in attracting and retaining customers in line with your forecast – and at the price you set for the product – then your product is meeting the expectations of your target market. You will have achieved sales because customers regard your product as representing quality: it conforms to their requirements for the price they are prepared to pay.

The key point is that the quality level required for your business is determined by your ability to satisfy the expectations of potential customers. These expectations are created by your marketing strategy, but the decision on whether your product is the right quality is taken by your customers and not by you. If you are not meeting their expectations, then you do not have a quality product – and you cannot run a business for long on the basis of any other level of quality.

Quality is what your customers say it is. For example, in their own ways, both a downmarket café and a classy restaurant can aim to offer a quality catering service. If the café is increasing its trade while the restaurant is struggling to survive, then the café must be meeting its customers' expectations while the restaurant is not. The café is delivering quality while the restaurant is failing to do so.

Playing to strength: Wow Toys takes off

Imagine spending eight hours a day pursuing a passion that turns over millions of pounds a year. Add to that flexible hours, trips abroad and the constant feeling that you're at leisure rather than work.

Nadim Ednan-Laperouse doesn't need to dream. The founder and managing director of toy design business Wow Toys says he manages to combine all of these benefits in his job. It's not something that fell into his lap.

With a passion for cartoons and a creative flair inherited from his mother, Nadim concluded that his true vocation lay in product design. His inspiration was his friend's father who designed consumer goods like funky pens for a living. "Meeting him introduced me to another world beyond what I knew at school. It was something totally off the wall and I thought, crikey, that's more me."

Nadim decided to go to art school. But with three A-levels in maths, electronics and physics and not a piece of art work, he was turned down by every institution he applied to. Undeterred, he did a one-year evening course in art and built up an impressive portfolio. Chelsea School of Art gave him an interview and he hasn't looked back.

After art school he took a degree in industrial design at Manchester Polytechnic. Then came his first job designing a range of products including beer pumps for Swan Beer.

"I thought my job was going really well, then after seven months I got slapped round the face with redundancy and escorted out of the building within minutes of learning my fate."

It was four months before he landed another job. He worked for a small firm designing products such as cashpoint machines. After his next job, in 1992 he decided to take control of his working life and go freelance.

Nadim's freelance design portfolio included toys, which soon accounted for 90 per cent of his output. "I did Sindy dolls, play dough and Action Man. As I got one product done more work would come in, so I set up as a sole trader under Nadim Associates and hired 12 people to help me."

With the business booming life was getting manic for Nadim and his staff. "The quality of work could be dubious sometimes because people wanted toys in two days," he admits.

"We were working like maniacs to fulfil marketing values we didn't believe in. These were to do with the culture of big business which is to sell it on the strength of TV advertising rather than on the strength of a product's quality. I wanted to create a successful business from great creativity and not from a mediocre product."

So Nadim launched Wow Toys at the Olympia Toy Fair in January 1997. This opportunity arose after a call to Toy and Hobby Association, organisers of the event. "We had a tiny stand, [there] wasn't even room to put a chair in it," recalls Nadim.

The stand cost £1,000 for five days, but Nadim more than made his money back. "We got £45,000 worth of orders, [from] John Lewis and little toy shops. We realised it was a winner."

Nadim says Wow Toys are aimed at pre-school children. His toys are tested by children at four nursery schools in West London. Around 6,000 stores now stock the toys, while 70 per cent of production is exported. First year toy sales were £850,000 on a £2 million turnover. In 2000 it is on target to achieve sales of £12 million. But massive growth is not a priority.

"We don't want to be the biggest toy company in the UK but the best. It's important not to want to be the biggest because we would lose sight of our original mission, which is to make the best educational pre-schools toys."

Read the article about Wow Toys. How has Nadim managed to balance both business and personal objectives? What role did formal training play in Nadim's change of career direction?

What segment of the toy market did Nadim aim for with his new company in 1997 and why? What do you think were the unique selling points of Wow Toys?

Why do you think Nadim's choice of below the line promotion proved so successful?

Your marketing mix communicates information about your product to potential customers. Your marketing communications sets out how it will satisfy their needs in some way, so you must ensure that the product you produce actually delivers – and can totally satisfy these needs. There must be no errors or defects that could cause customer expectations not to be met in full. This covers not only the product itself but also any expectations that you might have created in terms of customer care and after-sales services.

You need a strategy for quality assurance which might include:

- recruiting employees with the necessary skills and competencies to work to the required standard

- ensuring that all items of plant, machinery and equipment can perform (and continue to perform) to the required standard

- providing detailed procedures for each part of the process so that employees complete their tasks error or defect free first time

- ensuring that inputs of raw materials, parts and components from suppliers always meet your specifications

- identifying the sources of any errors or defects and introducing the changes to working methods or processes as necessary

- encouraging employees to contribute ideas on both quality assurance and quality improvement.

You might also try to create a working environment in which employees treat each other as a kind of internal customer. This means that each employee in the internal chain is supplied with the information and/or work that conforms exactly to their requirements at the right time. This allows each employees to do their job to the standard that allows them to meet the needs of the person who represents their customer in the internal customer chain.

Until the whole of your firm's operations are aimed at satisfying customers' needs, it may be necessary to introduce some kind of inspection system to prevent faulty products being processed and going out to customers. A reputation for failing to satisfy customers' expectations during the first period of business tends to stick: unfortunately first impressions do count, and it may be difficult to recover from this position.

If you are providing a service, the quality is even more crucial. If the service is poor and below customers' expectations it is particularly damaging because, while a faulty product can be identified and intercepted during an inspection process, in this case the customer has already been affected. Recruiting the right people, and if necessary training them to met the particular requirements of your clients, is a vital part of assuring quality in service businesses.

In order to expand your sales without cutting prices, you can introduce new product and service features that might attract new customers. A café, for example, might introduce new furnishings and fittings and improve the décor; if this attracts new customers, and retains the existing ones, then quality has improved. The expectations of existing customers are more than satisfied because, if they like the new décor, they now see the café as offering even better value for money than before. The new customers, however, simply enjoy a quality service in that it meets their expectations and provides value for money.

Premises

If you are going to deal directly with consumers, then the choice of premises is very much part of your marketing strategy. Your choice of premises will be influenced by the findings from your market analysis. If, however, your product is being distributed by other retail outlets or is a service or product being supplied to other businesses, then you are likely to have a much wider choice when deciding on the type and location of your premises.

Your business plan needs to contain information about your premises. Potential lenders will want to ensure that the financial and physical aspects of the premises have been carefully considered in the light of the nature of your business. Premises are likely to be a major fixed cost of your business and you may have to take out a lease with the owner of the premises for a relatively long period of time. This is a cost that you will have to pay, even if you cease trading before the end of the period of the lease.

When drawing up a list of possible locations, and possible premises in those locations, you need to consider a range of factors. First, you need to decide upon a general area for your business such as a town centre or a commercial area where offices and small business units are located. Second, you then need to assess specific sites within your chosen area. The relative importance of the location factors we discuss here will depend upon the nature of your business.

Pedestrian flows are important for retail outlets or services such as catering. Being close to rival outlets can be an advantage, because when people are shopping around they are unlikely to leave an area where there is cluster of shops to look in a single retail outlet some distance away. A good passing trade can also be produced by being close to well-known **multiple shops** such as Boots, W H Smith, McDonald's and Dixons. Bus stops or regular crossing points can also generate a good pedestrian flow. You can increase opportunities for passing trade by attracting motorists if there is nearby kerb-side parking or other parking areas not too far away.

If you are offering a specialist product range or service – one that people are willing to go out of their way for – then your premises do not have to be in a main shopping area. However, you may need to have a location which is attractive and gives a good first impression when your prospective customers enter the neighbourhood. Premises may be cheap in a run-down area but any sign of dereliction and anti-social behaviour, such as vandalism and graffiti, can be off-putting for prospective customers and clients.

Your premises might have to be accessible for commercial vehicles that deliver your supplies or transport your products to customers. Deliveries to and from your premises will require room for loading and unloading as well as space for reversing and turning. Local noise regulations may govern the times when heavy vehicles can use the site.

Before using your own home or signing up for any other premises, you should check that they can be used for your particular business. Do you need an application for **change of use?** Will it be granted? There may be restrictions on the kinds of alterations you can make to premises if it is subject to a **conservation order** or if it is a listed building. You should also assess the premises to see if they are suitable for expanding your business. Room for expansion may be restricted by the size of the existing site or building by regulations.

The cost of premises will depend upon location, the condition of the buildings and the nature of the accommodation provided. You must also take into account the cost of any alterations, modernisation, fittings, rent, business rates and any fees paid to surveyors and solicitors. When assessing the costs of premises you need to take account of the relative advantages and disadvantages of different locations. If the rent is low, for example, there may be a surplus of accommodation in relation to the demand. Low rents for retail outlets may suggest that most shoppers go elsewhere to large supermarkets. High rent for some premises may be more than compensated by the extra business generated by a particularly good location. It is also possible that good quality office or factory accommodation is cheap simply because developers have overestimated demand and there is plenty of surplus property. You must therefore investigate the reasons for differences in rents at different locations.

▲ Meadowhall, Sheffield, attracts thousands of consumers

Legal aspects

In carrying out your market analysis, you will have taken account of actual or expected developments in the overall business environment that can influence total market demand. In addition to your assessment of the potential business opportunities or threats, you must also take account of any environmental factors which can have a more direct effect upon the way you run your business. In particular, you must comply with any laws and regulations which prescribe how you produce and market your product or service.

Consumer protection

We have discussed the consumer protection legislation in Unit 2 (see pp. 118–9). This is an important area if you are planning to start a business which will sell goods directly to consumers, indeed the legislation also regulates trade between businesses. Here, we review some of the main pieces of legislation and describe some of the implications for new businesses.

- The **Trade Description Acts** make it an offence to apply a false or misleading description to your goods or services and a false or misleading indication of the price.

- The **Fair Trading Act 1973** has many provisions to protect consumers' interests. One area deals with restrictive trade practices, and you must avoid any temptation to join an agreement with other suppliers to fix prices or fix market shares

- If you have a license to offer goods and services on credit then you must be aware of your customers' rights under the **Consumer Credit Act 1974**. This allows customers the right withdraw from a consumer credit arrangement after signing the agreement, to complete payments ahead of time and to terminate the agreement. You must also make clear the total charge for credit by publishing the annualised percentage rate (APR).

- Under the **Unfair Terms in Consumer Contracts Regulations** you must avoid any complex small print in contracts which give you unfair exclusion clauses or stipulate reasons for you not having to fulfil all or parts of the contract.

- The **Weights and Measures Act 1985** sets out the legal weights and measures to be used for trading purposes. If you are selling a product by weight, dimensions or volume, you might have all your measuring devices checked by an inspector.

- The **Sale of Goods Acts** require that your goods are 'as described'; that is, they comply with the description given to them. They must also be 'fit for the purpose' for which they are intended or for the use described to the customer when making the purchase. They must be of 'satisfactory quality', this allows consumers to return goods for relatively minor defects which may not necessarily have compromised their fitness for purpose.

- The **Sales of Goods and Services Act 1982** requires that companies and tradespeople must use 'reasonable' care and skill in providing services.

- The **Consumer Safety Act 1978** allows the government to introduce or update regulations concerning the safety of goods to reduce the risk of personal injury. You must make sure your product's design, labelling, container, materials, parts, wiring, paint finishes and the way it operates meet the relevant safety regulations. You can be sued by consumers for any damages connected with your product being defective.

- The **Food and Drink Acts** concern catering businesses as well food and drink producers. These cover food hygiene, food ingredients and the labelling of ingredients, artificial colorants and preservatives.

The **Food Safety Act 1990** control all aspects of food safety and hygiene throughout the food distribution chain, including locations where food is manufactured, prepared and sold.

Apart from abiding by the Trades Descriptions Acts and the Sale of Goods Act when promoting your business, you also need to take account of the codes for advertising and sales promotion laid down by the Advertising Standards Authority (ASA). Although the ASA's Codes do not have the force of law it is possible that the courts may also make a ruling on matters covered by the codes. In 1999, the ASA dealt with 12,141 complaints relating to 8,617 advertisements. Some 1,812 advertisements required investigation, and just less than 10 per cent of those investigated were found to break the codes. Some interesting examples of advertisements that attracted complaints can be found at www.asa.org.uk.

Figure 6.4 sets out part of the ASA's codes. These stress that, in putting your advertising and sales promotion campaigns together, it is important to avoid using pictures or information which may make you seem insensitive to the feelings of particular groups of people or which may mislead potential customers.

Figure 6.4: Extracts from the ASA code

Decency

Avoid causing offence on the grounds of race, religion, sex, sexual orientation or disability.

Substantiation

Documentary evidence must be available to prove all direct or indirect claims about the product or service but obvious untruths or exaggerations that are very unlikely to mislead are generally allowed.

Honesty

Advertisers should not exploit the lack of knowledge or inexperience of consumers.

Truthfulness

The advertisement must not mislead by inaccuracy, ambiguity or exaggeration.

Fear and distress

Avoid using shocking claims or images to attract attention unless they are used to encourage sensible behaviour or to discourage dangerous or ill-advised actions.

Safety

The showing of unsafe practices is only allowed in the context of promoting safety and particular care should be taken with advertisements aimed at young children.

The environment

The **Environmental Protection Act 1990** has implications for the way in which you produce goods and services. It seeks to prevent pollution of air, water and land from emissions resulting from the production process. It controls waste disposal methods, litter, odours, vibration, noise and other side effects of business that may damage the environment or create a public nuisance.

The **local planning authority** will be concerned about the potential impact of your business on the local environment. You will have to pay attention to any restrictions on the kind of business that can be carried out in particular premises as well as building controls relating to extensions and modernisation. You will also have to satisfy the authority about the impact of your business on local traffic.

Setting up your business

The **Companies Act 1985** governs the setting up and registration of limited companies. If you are setting up a partnership then you need to take account of not just the Companies Act 1985 but also the **Partnership Act 1890** and the **Limited Partnership Act 1907**. You can run your business under your own name. However, if you intend to run the business under a different name, you must obey the provisions of the **Business Names Act 1985**.

Employing labour

The **Employment Protection (Consolidated) Act 1978** deals with the fundamental rights of your employees, including their right to receive written particulars of the terms of employment. Your employees' contracts of employment must recognise **statutory rights** covered by:

- Disabled Person's (Employment) Act 1944 and 1958
- Equal Pay Act 1970
- Fair Employment (NI)
- Health and Safety at Work Act 1974
- Sex Discrimination Act 1975
- Race Relations Act 1976
- Employment Acts 1980 to 1990.

By collecting all the material that needs to go into a business plan, you should begin to appreciate what is really involved in setting up and running your own business. Perhaps now is the time to see if you are really ready to go ahead. Figure 6.5 is a questionnaire designed to help you assess your desire and preparation to run a business.

Figure 6.5: Do I really want to go into business?

1   Do I really want to go into business?
- What is my business idea?
- Have I set business and personal goals?
- What motivates me to start my own business?
- What do I hope to get out of it?
- Does it suit my skills, experience or ambitions?
- Have I any friends or relations in business?
- If so what do they get out of it?
- If my family behind me?
- Am I confident I can cope.

2   My market
- Have I researched my market thoroughly?
- Who might be interested in buying from me?
- Who do they buy from now and why?
- Why do I think they will choose me rather than someone else?
- Do I know what my market share could be?
- Have I got a plan to promote my product?

3   My costs
- Have I got the proper cost information?
- Have I added up all the costs?

4   My profit
- Will I make a profit?
- When will I break even?
- Do I have a target?
- Do I know what my margins are?
- What profits will it give me?
- Is there a safety margin in my plans?

5   My capital and cash
- How much money do I need?
- Can I manage with less?
- Have I made a cash flow projection?
- Do I have the proper facts?

6   My assets
- Have I listed everything I need?
- Have I thought about leasing?

7   My premises and equipment
- Do I need premises to get started?
- If so, what size and type?
- Am I happy with the location?
- Have I taken legal advice?
- Do I have security of tenure?

8   My staff
- Will I need to employ staff?
- Can I find people with the right skills?
- Do I need to provide any further training?
- Do I know all the legal requirements?
- Have I taken out employers' liability insurance?

9   My banking needs
- Do I need financial support?
- Where will I get it?
- Will the bank approve of my plans?
- Have I checked whether I can get a grant?

10   My business and the law
- Have I decided on the legal form of my business?
- Have I taken legal advice?
- Do I have a licence if I need one?
- Should I register for VAT?
- Do I need planning permission?
- Have I told the Inland Revenue about my business?

11   My business systems
- Is my book-keeping system ready?
- Have I got an accountant?
- Have I opened a business bank account?
- Is my cash control good enough?
- Can I control debts?
- Can I monitor my business performance?
- Is my stationery printed?
- Do I have a realistic timing schedule?

Am I determined to go ahead?

BUILD YOUR LEARNING

You should know the meaning of the words and phrases listed below. Go back through the last 10 pages of the unit to check or refresh your understanding as necessary.

- Batch production
- Business Names Act
- Change of use
- Companies Act
- Consumer Credit Act
- Consumer Safety Act
- Employment Protection (Consolidation) Act
- Environmental Protection Act
- Fair Trading Act
- Flow production
- Food and Drink Act
- Food Safety Act
- Job production
- Lead time
- Local planning authority
- Multiple shops
- Partnership Act
- Pedestrian flows
- Sale of Goods Act
- Sale of Goods and Service Act
- Trade Descriptions Acts
- Weights and Measures

Summary points

- You need to include a production plan within your business plan which explains how you intend to organise production.

- The production plan must give information about the plant, machinery and other equipment you need and their functions in the production process.

- Information must be supplied about your labour needs including the size of the workforce, skill requirements, job descriptions for key positions, wages and salaries, and other employment costs.

- You need to demonstrate the quality assurance procedures and policies that you will use to ensure that you consistently satisfy customers' expectations.

- You must justify your choice of premises, both its location and its suitability as a venue for conducting your business.

- You must take account of any laws and regulations which impact on your marketing activities and production operations.

- You must recognise the need to set up your business and recruit and employ staff in accordance with the appropriate laws and regulations.

Financial analysis and planning

POTENTIAL INVESTORS WILL LOOK very carefully at the section of the business plan that contains a financial analysis of your proposals. In some cases, they might actually decide to ask for an independent financial analysis of the venture. This section, therefore, must be thorough and convincing, and any financial forecasts should be very realistic. Any assumptions should be explained and accompanied by a statement indicating why they are felt to be valid and what alternatives may be followed if they are not achieved.

Many of the techniques for the presentation and analysis of the financial data are covered in Unit 5. You may find it helpful to refer to Unit 5 as you study this section.

Five sets of financial data and forecasts need to be produced:

- start-up capital and working capital, an estimate of the capital required to finance the business initially

- a breakeven analysis, providing some indication of the level of sales necessary to earn a profit

- a start-up balance sheet, listing the assets and liabilities of the business when commencing trading

- a trading profit and loss forecast, showing the forecast profit (or loss) to be made by the business over its first period of trading

- a cash flow forecast.

These should be familiar concepts. We came across breakeven analysis in Unit 3 (see pp. 182–3). We covered balance sheets, profit and loss accounts and cash flow forecasts in Unit 5. Figures 6.12 and 6.13 (see pp. 368–9) show standard forms on which you can present a trading profit and loss forecast and a cash flow forecast, respectively.

As a first step, entrepreneurs need to consider where and how they will raise the finance required to actually get their business up and running.

Sources of finance

There are a number of ways in which a business can raise the finance necessary to purchase assets and fund working capital. The method chosen depends upon:

- the amount of money required by the business

- the risk that the business represents to potential lenders

- the time period over which the loan is required.

The time period over which the loan is required can be used as a means of classifying methods of finance into three categories:

- short-term finance

- medium-term finance

- long-term finance.

In deciding on the length of a loan, a business wants to ensure that finance is repaid within the life of the asset purchased. For example, if a company needs a loan to fund the purchase of a machine that is expected to last for four years, the loan period should be of four years or less. Otherwise the company will end up still having to pay for an asset that is no longer generating any income.

Let's now look at the sources of finance available to someone starting a business. Remember that you need finance for both start-up and working capital. **Start-up capital** is required to purchase essential fixed assets such as property and machinery. **Working capital** is the finance required to fund day-to-day operations such as purchasing raw materials and paying wages.

Short-term finance

The importance of working capital to a new business is easily underestimated. A new business will be expected to pay its suppliers promptly to prove that it is being managed responsibly. It may be some time before suppliers are prepared to offer credit to a new firm. At the same time, a new business might have to allow customers time to settle their debts. Customers might be allowed up to 90 days (three months) to pay their bills. This is known as offering **trade credit**.

By paying its bills promptly and letting customers have time to settle their invoices, a new company usually requires considerable amounts of working capital to keep the business running. It may need to arrange a substantial overdraft with the bank. It must also have the cash to cover other contingencies; customers might delay paying for goods and services, sales might be unexpectedly low, there may be a sudden increase in the cost of raw materials.

New businesses need access to short-term finance to meet their requirements for working capital. Short-term finance is usually repayable within a one-year period. There are two principal methods of short-term finance: overdraft and trade credit.

Overdrafts

Overdrafts are perhaps the best-known method of short-term finance. An **overdraft** is a facility offered by banks allowing businesses to borrow up to an agreed limit without notification and for as long as they wish. Overdrafts are a very flexible form of finance as the amounts borrowed can vary as long as they are within the agreed overall limit. They are also simple to arrange;

established business customers can often arrange an overdraft, or increase their overdraft limit, without too many formalities.

Figure 6.6 illustrates how a small firm might use its overdraft facility. It shows a scenario in which the firm receives a £10 000 order for its products and the effect this might have on its day-to-day funds.

> **Discussion point**
>
> Look at the scenario outlined in Figure 6.6. What evidence is there to show that this business has managed its working capital well? In what ways might it improve its management?

Figure 6.6: A typical small firm cash-flow scenario

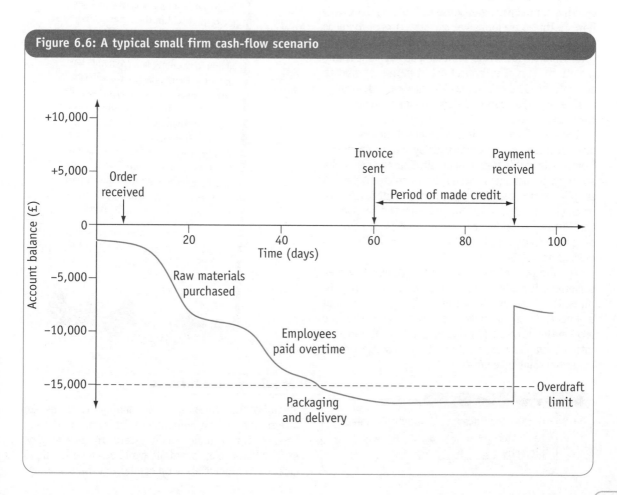

Overdrafts are quite expensive. Interest is charged at between 2 per cent and 4 per cent above the bank's base lending rate. This is not usually a problem unless a business seeks to use an overdraft facility over a long period of time. In these circumstances, a business would be well advised to convert its overdraft to a longer-term method of finance.

It is unusual for an overdraft to be a secured loan. That is, banks and building societies do not normally require a business to provide security (the deeds to property, for example) before agreeing to an overdraft. Secured loans require businesses to offer security or collateral against the loan. Property is frequently used as collateral because these assets are less likely to fall in value over time. In the event of the loan not being repaid, the bank sells the collateral and uses the money raised to repay the original loan plus any outstanding interest.

Trade credit

Many firms grant their customers an interest-free period in which to pay for the goods and services they have received. From the customer's point of view, this is a useful form of finance: it helps fund the customer's working capital at the expense of the supplier's cash flow. In Unit 5 we looked at the structure of invoices (see p. 255–7); invoices usually include a statement concerning credit terms, for example 'payment is due within 30 days'. The typical credit period offered to customers is 30 days. In practice, however, on average businesses take nearer 75 days to make payments to their suppliers.

The use of trade credit is widespread. However, it is open to abuse; some businesses delay making payments beyond the agreed period of credit. This can be a risky strategy. If customers exceed the trade credit period, suppliers may demand that payment is made in advance or may simply refuse to supply goods and services in the future. New businesses may find it difficult to negotiate trade credit until they are established as a creditworthy firm.

This form of credit is attractive to business. However, sometimes it might make financial sense to settle bills promptly. Some suppliers offer a discount for prompt payment. It might make more sense to settle and receive the discount (particularly if it is substantial), rather than delay payment and have to settle a much larger bill some time later.

Discussion point

Outline the advantages and disadvantages to a business of paying its creditors promptly.

British firms pay up more promptly

British businesses have been paying their bills much more rapidly. They are now ninth in a league of 21 European countries, according to a recent survey.

Since the first survey was conduced in 1993, the average payment times to small business have fallen from 52 days to 46 days. This compares with an average of 55 days throughout the European Union.

The improvement predates new legislation allowing businesses to charge interest on invoices which are not settled within the agreed credit term.

However, there are doubts that legislation preventing late payments has any effect on businesses. Greece, with an average payment period of 87 days, and Italy, at 81 days, both have late payment laws.

Other European countries have also improved their payment record. Fastest payers are still the Scandinavians, with the Finns top of the European league at only 26 days, followed by Norway on 31 days.

Adapted from *The Electronic Telegraph*, 8 March 1999

Medium-term finance

Medium-term finance is commonly used as an alternative to, and replacement for, some short-term finance. For example, medium-term finance may be sought because an overdraft may become difficult to clear or to provide start-up capital to establish a new business. Medium-term finance is usually repayable over a period of between two and eight years.

There are three principal methods of medium-term finance: leasing, hire purchase and bank loans.

Leasing

Leasing can be used to acquire a wide range of assets, including property and equipment. A business simply leases (or rents) a fixed asset (such as a vehicle) rather than buying it outright. Throughout the period of the lease, the ownership of the asset is retained by the finance company, and the amount of rent payable on the lease provides the finance company with a level of profit. Fixed assets that are often leased by business include vehicles and office equipment such as photocopiers and computers.

Businesses often lease assets, rather than purchasing them outright, to avoid the need for a large outlay of capital that can be used for other, more profitable, purposes. Leasing also enables firms to update their equipment at relatively little extra charge. Some lease agreements allow the firm to purchase the leased asset for a relatively low price at the end of the lease period. It is common for a leasing agreement to include a maintenance contract to ensure that the asset is kept in good working order.

As with all methods of finance, leasing has disadvantages. Because the finance company providing the asset has to make a profit, it is inevitable that, over a period of time, leasing an asset will be more expensive than purchasing it outright. Furthermore, because the asset is never owned by the business, it does not appear as an asset on the balance sheet; this can make the business look less attractive to a potential investor.

▲ Assets that need replacing regularly such as computers and photocopiers are commonly leased

Hire purchase

Hire purchase is a credit agreement enabling a business to purchase an asset by making an initial down payment as a deposit and paying the remainder in instalments over an agreed period of time. In any hire purchase arrangement, the purchaser only owns the asset when the final instalment is paid.

As a method of finance for new businesses, hire purchase has similar advantages to leasing. Assets can be acquired without a large outflow of capital, improving the cash position of the business. In contrast to leasing agreements, the business's balance sheet position is improved because it owns the asset once the final payment is made. The principal disadvantage of this method of finance is that the final cost of the asset is considerably higher than if the business purchased it outright.

Bank loans

It is common for businesses to purchase assets by raising loans with banks and building societies. The financial institution advances the business a set figure and the business makes repayments over an agreed period of time. Bank loans are relatively straightforward to arrange if the business seeking the credit is solvent and has a satisfactory financial history. If the bank lending the capital considers that the loan is in any way risky, then it is likely to charge a higher rate of interest. Small businesses, in particular, suffer from this policy. Normally, banks charge about 2 per cent above their base rate of interest for business loans. In some cases, banks may also charge an arrangement fee for setting up a business loan.

Banks often require security for their loans. Borrowers usually secure loans against their property. If a business defaults on a loan, the bank can sell the property and recoup the money that it is owed. In this way, banks lower the degree of risk they incur in making loans to businesses.

The interest rates charged on bank loans can either be fixed or variable. Some businesses prefer fixed rates; because the interest payments and repayment schedule are fixed, they find it easier to plan and manage the business finances. Others are reluctant to take out fixed-rate loans; interest rates may fall after the loan is agreed, leaving those with fixed-rate loans paying higher charges than is necessary. Firms taking out variable-rate loans hope to benefit from cuts in interest rates.

When taking out loans firms have to be careful that they do not end up borrowing too much and leave themselves vulnerable to rises in interest rates. This can cause many businesses to collapse, as they no longer can afford their loan payments and financiers close in to try to regain their money. Remember many loans are secured against assets and, if the company fails to pay, the financier can remove the securing asset in lieu of payment; this can then make it very difficult to continue trading.

Long-term finance

Most businesses need to raise long-term finance to purchase major fixed assets such as land and buildings. There are a number of ways in which businesses can raise long-term finance including mortgages, share capital and venture capital.

Mortgages

Mortgages are long-term loans granted by financial institutions for the purchase of land and buildings. The land or building is used as security for the loan. Typically, mortgages can be for up to 85 per cent of the value of the property. These loans can be for long periods of time – often in excess of twenty years. They can have fixed or variable rates of interest. Mortgages are particularly suitable when a business wishes to raise a large sum of money. It is an obvious way to purchase any property required to establish a business.

Small and new businesses with large mortgages can be vulnerable to rises in interest rates. Evidence shows that an increase in business failures can be linked to rising interest rates. For example, between January and March 1999, when interest rates were rising, 3,729 companies failed, up almost 10 per cent from the final three months of 1998.

Discussion point

What reasons can you think of to explain why newly established businesses are especially vulnerable to rises in interest rates?

Some businesses may choose to remortgage their premises to raise capital. A remortgage either increases the value of the existing mortgage or establishes a mortgage where one did not exist before. This source of finance is particularly used by small businesses.

Share or equity capital

Shares are a very common form of finance, providing both start-up capital and also additional capital in a later stage of a business's life. Firms raise capital by selling a share in their business to investors. A share is simply a certificate giving the holder ownership of part (or a share) of a company.

Investors gain in two possible ways from purchasing shares. First, if the business is successful, the price of the shares might rise allowing them to be sold at a profit. Second, the company usually pays the shareholders a proportion of its profits, known as a dividend. This dividend is paid on every share, so the more shares an investor or shareholder has, the more he or she receives. A newly established business is likely to form a private limited company mainly because this protects investors and is relatively cheap to establish.

By selling large numbers of shares, companies can raise significant sums of capital. However, shareholders usually have the right to voice an opinion in the running of the company and, by selling too many shares, the owners can lose control of the company. Issuing shares is often administratively very expensive, which means it is only appropriate for raising very large sums of capital. Private limited companies (denoted by the letters Ltd after their names) are restricted in the ways in which they can sell their shares, which makes it more difficult to raise finance through increasing their share capital.

There are a number of benefits from raising capital through the selling of shares or equity. In particular, a company is not committed to meeting fixed interest payments when raising finance in this way. Although companies are expected to pay an annual return to shareholders, the level of this payment is not fixed and in an unprofitable year it may be possible for the company to avoid making any dividend payment.

Venture capital

There are a number of organisations that specialise in providing venture capital to small and medium-sized businesses, particularly private limited companies and, sometimes, newly established businesses. Venture capital is regarded as a relatively high risk investment; the borrower is not a large firm and usually requires significant sums. It is not unusual for sums in excess of £750,000 to be raised in this way. Venture capitalists frequently provide a package of loans and purchase of shares.

Merchant banks (specialist commercial banks such as Rothschild, Lazards and Hambros) commonly get involved in lending, or arranging, venture capital. There is also a specialist venture capital provider called 3i plc (formerly Investors In Industry); this was originally a government-sponsored agency set up to promote economic growth by providing venture and risk capital to industry. There are several initiatives which try and encourage contacts between venture capital companies and new businesses. For example, the First Tuesday Club provides a forum for internet entrepreneurs and venture capitalists to meet.

The charges associated with venture capital can be quite high, but they are offset to some degree by the fact that most venture capitalists offer management support to the companies that they back.

Other sources of finance

There are some other sources of finance available for starting a business. In particular, businesses should investigate the availability of grants from the government and independent trusts. These sources are either the first to be investigated by a prospective business or, it seems, are forgotten and ignored entirely.

Government grants can take a number of forms. Some financial assistance is only available in designated areas of the UK. These tend to be parts of the country which suffer the highest levels of unemployment and the lowest levels of prosperity.

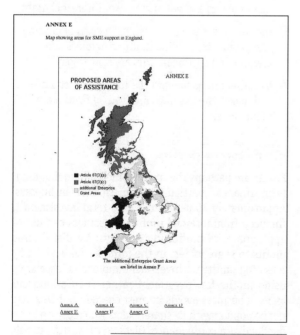

▲ Areas of assistance for government support to business

As we discussed in Unit 2, companies in the designated areas can benefit from several schemes offered by the government or by agencies on its behalf.

- **Regional Selective Assistance.** Under this scheme, the government offers grants to firms who move to a designated area and create jobs.

- **Regional Enterprise Grants.** These grants are for firms with less than 25 employees that create jobs in development areas. The aid can help with investment up to a maximum of £25,000.

- **Consultancy Initiative.** Available to firms with fewer than 500 employees in all assisted areas. They can claim 66 per cent of the cost of hiring consultants.

- **Enterprise zones.** Designed to revitalise inner cities, these are areas of a few hundred acres. Firms can receive financial incentives to locate within these zones. Benefits include tax incentives and subsidised premises.

The government also plans to introduce a new tier of enterprise grant areas in England, where assistance will be available to businesses employing up to 250 people. Small businesses have a crucial role to play in regional development and the new enterprise grant areas are intended to encourage the growth of small businesses. Under devolution arrangements, the Scottish and Welsh administrations are deciding whether to introduce similar designated areas.

The government also offers some financial support irrespective of the location of businesses within the UK. There is a business start-up initiative providing training and financial assistance to people who were previously unemployed and who wish to start businesses. These schemes vary from area to area, but applicants are normally expected to make a substantial capital investment into their business; in return, they receive a weekly wage and appropriate training from a local government agency.

Many local authorities also offer financial support to new businesses. These can include:

- grants for business start-ups

- innovation grants

- job creation grants

- rent and rates free period

- guides to sources of finance

- loans to businesses.

Lastly there are several independent trusts that exist to help people in particular circumstances start their own business. Perhaps the best known is the Princes

Trust. which provides a range of support to help young people get a start in business.

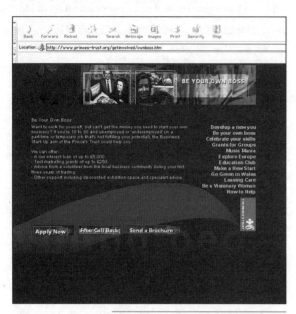

▲ Page from the Prince's Trust website

Personal capital

By far the easiest way to raise the finance to start a business, of course, is for entrepreneurs to provide it from their own personal resources. This is impractical if not impossible in many cases.

However, most financiers want to see that entrepreneurs are also willing to risk some of their personal capital in the venture. If entrepreneurs are able to raise and invest some of their own capital, banks and other financial institutions will take the business proposition more seriously. Personal capital can also be raised from friends or family. It is not always necessary to offer friends and family a stake in the business. An advantage of this form of finance is that friends and relatives may be willing to loan funds at more favourable rates and terms than a bank.

Ongoing sources of finance

New businesses are usually only concerned with raising the capital to finance their start-up. However, businesses require ongoing sources of finance for a variety of reasons, including:

- to expand the company
- to overcome cash flow difficulties
- for research and development
- to replace fixed assets.

Although the main focus of this unit is business planning and business start up, it is poor management to only consider the business's financial requirements for its first days or weeks of trading. So we have outlined here some of the sources of finance that are available to a business that been trading for some time. Of course, the sources of start-up finance are also available as ongoing sources of finance.

Debt factoring

Debt factoring is a service offered by financial institutions – known as factors – to help businesses recover debts quickly and to improve their cash flow. The factor – often a bank or building society – provides up to 80 per cent of the value of an outstanding invoice as an immediate cash advance. It then organises the collection of the debt and makes a further payment to the business. It is usual for the factor to retain about 5 per cent of the value of the invoice to cover its costs.

Many small firms consider that to lose 5 per cent of the value of their earnings makes factoring uneconomic. However, as a means of raising short-term finance, factoring does offer a number of benefits:

- the factor takes the risk of bad debts, ensuring that the firm receives at least a proportion of all its debts
- the immediate cash provided by the factor means that the firm is likely to have lower overdraft requirements and will incur lower interest charges
- the firm saves the administration costs of chasing late payments, sending multiple invoices and telephoning customers who are slow to pay
- factoring brings forward the timing of cash flows and makes the earnings received by firms more predictable.

Reinvesting profits

Profits are perhaps the major source of ongoing long-term finance, particularly for smaller businesses. Approximately 70 per cent of long-term investment is financed from retained profits. A business can use or appropriate its profits in two ways: by distributing profits to shareholders in the form of dividends or by retaining profits for investment and capital assets. By using profits for investment rather than taking out loans, a business avoids interest charges, but this may not be popular with its shareholders who receive a lower dividend as a consequence. Obviously investing profits is a method of finance only available to firms during profitable trading periods, and even then it may not provide sufficient funds to purchase the more expensive capital assets.

Selling shares

Public limited companies can use rights issues as a means of raising finance. A rights issue allows shareholders in the company the chance to buy new shares at a reduced price in proportion to their existing holdings (say, one new share for each ten shares already owned). The company can afford to sell shares at a reduced price because the administrative costs of rights issues are relatively low. This, in effect, is just another means of raising additional finance from the existing owners of the company.

As an alternative to a rights issue, a company may make a general shares issue to attract additional investment. Public limited companies employ a merchant bank to advertise a share issue in the hope of attracting funds both from other companies and from members of the public. A prospectus is published giving details of the company and setting out its financial position as positively as possible. (There are, however, strict rules to prevent companies issuing misleading statements.) Adverts are usually placed in financial journals and newspapers. This is an expensive method of raising finance and it is only undertaken by a large company seeking to raise a substantial sum of capital.

Internal sources of finance

Although retained profits are a major source of finance for many businesses, there are also other ways in which companies can use their own resources to provide capital.

Companies may sell any assets that are surplus to their requirements in order to raise capital. For example, the recently privatised water companies have sold off large parcels of land for which they have no use. The capital raised is available to finance investment in other aspects of their business.

Some companies use the technique of sale and leaseback. They sell major assets, often property, and then lease back the asset. In this way, they continue to have the use of the asset but receive a large injection of capital at the same time.

Finally, company directors may provide interest-free loans to the business from their personal resources. This tends to only happen in certain industries (for example, football clubs) and there are usually some strings attached. Company directors will expect something in return for an interest-free loan.

Figure 6.7 summarises the main sources of funds that are available to each type of business organisation.

Figure 6.7: Sources of business finance

Type of business organisation	Examples	Sources of finance
Sole trader	Corner shop, window cleaner, painter and decorator	Owner's savings, banks, suppliers, government grants and loans
Partnership	Accountants, lawyers, dentists	Partners' savings, banks, suppliers, government grants and loans, hire purchase and leasing companies
Private limited company (Ltd)	These are generally small firms operating in many areas of the economy, but can also include larger nationally-known businesses, such as the Virgin Group	Dependent upon the size of the private limited company, suppliers, banks, factoring, leasing and hire purchase companies, government grants and loans, venture capital institutions, private share issues
Public limited company (plc)	Larger companies enjoying the benefits of selling shares on the Stock Exchange, major plcs include J Sainsbury plc and British Nuclear Fuels plc	Suppliers, banks, factoring, leasing and hire purchase companies, government grants and loans, venture capital institutions, public share issues via the Stock Exchange

Budgets

Unit 5 considered budgeting in some detail. However, there are some special considerations that need to be taken into account when starting a business. In particular, you need to know how to prepare a start-up budget.

Start-up budgets

A start up budget sets out the forecast expenditure of the business and its expected revenue. The start-up budget needs to be presented in the business plan so that it is clear to prospective investors how much finance is required, what proportion is to be put up by the owner and what assets are available for security. These headings may be used:

- resource needs – shown as a list of capital items, these include premises, plant, machinery, equipment, fittings, furniture and vehicles

- finance required – shown as a list of the capital items that have been financed from external sources and the amounts involved in each case

- own financial resources – shown as the difference between the resource needs and the finance required

- collateral – shown as a list of the assets available for security and their value.

The information relating to resource needs should be collected and analysed on business planning sheets. Figure 6.8 shows an example of how this information is presented in a business plan for Build-it Limited, which is a small building firm specialising in renovations, alterations and extensions.

> **Discussion point**
>
> Imagine you are a bank manager considering making a loan to Build-it Limited. What factors would encourage you to make a positive reply to an application for a loan?

However, businesses not only need to consider capital expenditure in the start up budget but also projected working capital needs. It will take time for a new business to establish a client base and a regular flow of orders and cash. Working capital is required for:

- raw materials and components – this can be a significant cost particularly for manufacturing businesses

- labour costs – these can be very high for service industries

- stocks of finished goods – retailers, for example, need to hold large quantities of stocks to offer sufficient choice to their customers

- cash – businesses require cash to meet day-to-day payments, such as fuel for vehicles and stationery for the office.

▼ The Millennium Dome at Greenwich suffered from a shortage of working capital

Figure 6.8: Extract from Build-it Limited's business plan

Build-It Limited – Business Plan

An outline of the resources needed

(a) Resources needs

Capital item	Cost (£)
Builder's yard and mobile building	75,000
Plant and equipment	60,000
Office computer and other equipment	15,000
Vehicles (lorry plus van)	25,000
Materials and working capital	20,000
Total	**195,000**

(b) Finance required

Capital item	Source of finance	(£)
Yard and building (freehold)	Bank mortgage	40,000
Plant and equipment	Bank loan	30,000
Materials and working capital	Bank overdraft	20,000
	Total	**90,000**

(c) Own financial resources — 105,000

(d) Collateral

Assets	Value (£)
Yard and building (freehold) (value at 1/1/90)	80,000
Other fixed items (at cost)	100,000
Total	**180,000**

If a firm has too little working capital, it might be unable to finance continuing or increased production. It may not have the finance available to pay for stocks of raw materials, labour services and general running costs. On the other hand, too much money tied up as working capital might mean that the business is short of asset finance.

Businesses need to make an estimate of their working capital requirements to see them through their initial start-up period. This estimate is also included on the start-up budget. This budget enables a prospective business to determine its start-up finance needs in full, and to determine whether sufficient funds are available from the possible sources of finance.

Even large concerns can underestimate their working capital needs. The Millennium Dome encountered working capital problems within a few days of opening to the public on 1 January 2000. The managers of the Dome managed to negotiate a £60 million loan from the Millennium Commission to get them out of cash flow difficulties. The loan has to be paid back out of the Dome's operating surplus at a later date.

Discussion point

Why, given the huge publicity it has received, might a new project such as the Millennium Dome encounter difficulties with working capital?

This budget is used in conjunction with other forecasts. Predictions relating to sales and cash flow can then be used to help secure the sources of finance needed to start the business.

Breakeven analysis

It is important that a business knows how much its goods and services cost to produce. Businesses also benefit from knowing how many products they have to produce and sell in order to cover all of their costs over a certain period of time. This level of output is known as the breakeven point. At this level of output, the revenue or income a firm receives from its sales is (just) sufficient to cover all its costs. In other words, at this level of output, the business concerned is neither making a profit nor a loss – it is breaking even.

You should note that to calculate the breakeven point you need information on costs and, to forecast the firm's income, its prices too. As we see later, either a change in costs or a change in the firm's pricing policy alters the level of output at which the firm breaks even.

Digital aims to break even

ONdigital, the digital television company backed by media companies Carlton and Granada, has revealed that it needs two million subscribers to break even.

The company is competing fiercely for digital television subscribers with rival BSkyB and its service Sky Digital. ONdigital is expected to break even during the year 2000.

Discussion point

Why might it be particularly difficult for a new business to break even in a market where rivals are competing strongly for customers?

Breakeven analysis is a fairly simple forecasting technique for businesses. It is also a valuable one, particularly in small businesses where the managers may not be able to employ more sophisticated techniques. Businesses can use breakeven analysis:

- to set the level of output they need to produce (and sell)

- to assess the impact of price changes upon profit and the breakeven output

- to assess how changes in costs may affect profits and the breakeven output.

Breakeven analysis is therefore essential in business planning to demonstrate that the business idea is viable and profitable, and has realistic prospects of survival in the market.

Breakeven output can be calculated or, by using chart, can be determined graphically. First, we show how to forecast breakeven output through calculations before looking at breakeven charts.

Calculating breakeven

In order to calculate the breakeven point for a single product, we need to know the selling price of the product and its fixed and variable costs.

Fixed costs do not vary with the level of output. Fixed costs have to be met even if a business is not producing any goods or services, and a business is usually only able to take long-term action to change its fixed costs. Examples of fixed costs include business rates, administration, management salaries, interest charges and depreciation.

Rent on premises is another example of a fixed cost. This can be paid monthly or annually, but its level is fixed regardless of the level of a company's output. If a manufacturer can double output within the same premises, the amount of rent does not alter – it is a fixed cost. Similarly, the rent must be paid even during the period when the factory is closed – say, for the annual summer holiday – and there is no production.

Businesses obviously benefit from using their facilities (and especially their premises) intensively. This is because their fixed costs do not alter as facilities are used more intensively but, because they are increasing their output, they should be able to generate more revenue in higher sales.

In the long term, fixed costs can alter. A manufacturer may want to increase output significantly. This may not be achievable in the existing facilities; it may require additional factory space and the negotiation of loans for additional capital equipment. So, rent will rise, as will interest payments. In this way, the long term fixed costs may alter but, in the short term, they are – as their name suggests – fixed.

Variable costs are those costs that vary directly with the level of output. They include payments made for the use of inputs such as labour, fuel and raw materials. If a manufacturer doubles output then these costs rise significantly. A business does not incur variable costs if it is not trading.

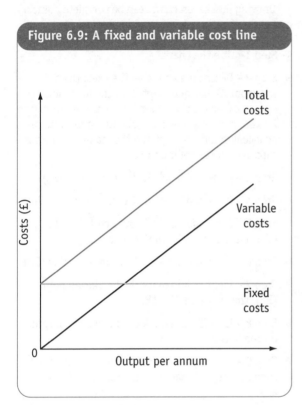

Figure 6.9: A fixed and variable cost line

Discussion point

What would be the shape of the variable cost line if the business received discounts for purchasing raw materials in bulk?

This classification of costs – into fixed and variable costs – is simple and very convenient. In business, however, not all costs can be classified in this way. Take the example of a delivery vehicle used by a business. Costs such as insurance and vehicle excise duty (road tax) do not alter no matter how much the vehicle is used. On the other hand, if the business increases its output and more deliveries are necessary, fuel and maintenance costs will increase. The cost of operating

the vehicle is therefore semi-variable; it is part fixed and part variable. Can you think of any more semi-variable costs? When added together, the fixed costs, variable costs (plus any semi-variable costs) give the total costs of a business.

We can calculate the breakeven point by comparing the total costs and total revenues of the firm. As an example, consider a pleasure boat used by Jim Court to take tourists on sightseeing trips. The boat makes one trip a day and Jim estimates that the cost of each trip is £200 in fuel, harbour dues, depreciation and wages for the crew; these costs remain the same no matter how many passengers he takes. The trip includes a meal and wine for all the passengers and a landing fee charged by the owners of the island. These items cost an additional £5 for each passenger on the boat. Jim is allowed to take a maximum of 30 passengers on each trip. Jim charges £15 per passenger for the day trip.

We can use these equations to calculate the breakeven number of passengers for the day trips:

Total cost (TC) = Fixed cost + Variable cost
Total revenue (TR) = Price × Quantity sold (Q)

For Jim's boat:

TC = £200 + (£5 x Q)
TR = £15 × Q

Here, Q is the number of passenger places sold. To break even, Jim needs sufficient passengers that he will not make a profit or a loss on the trip. In other words, his total revenue should equal his total costs. At breakeven output:

TR = TC

Now we need to find the value of Q (which is the number of passengers, remember) when total revenue equals total costs. This can be worked out by simple algebra. Total revenue equals total costs, so:

£15 × Q = £200 + (£5 × Q)

(£15 × Q) – (£5 × Q) = £200

15 Q – 5 Q = £200

10 Q = 200

Q = 200/10 = 20

In other words, Jim needs 20 passengers on each of his day trips to break even.

In undertaking breakeven analysis, it is important to understand the concept of contribution. **Contribution** is the amount of money left from sales revenue once the variable costs have been paid. Contribution can be used for two purposes:

- to pay fixed costs (overheads)
- to provide profits for the business.

Consider an example. A small brewery has annual fixed costs of £8,000. It sells its beer for £20 a keg. The variable costs of producing a single keg are £12, so the contribution from each keg is £8. The contribution from the first 1,000 kegs sold each year are used to pay the brewery's fixed costs (£8 × 1,000 = £8,000). Any further sales of kegs provide contribution, that is profit, for the brewery.

The concept of contribution provides an alternative way to calculate break even. We can calculate the contribution from each sale by subtracting the variable costs from the selling price. This gives us the amount each individual product can contribute to the running of the business over and above its own individual cost of production (that is, its variable cost). Now, if we divide this figure into our fixed costs, we will have calculated how many sales we need to pay all fixed and variable costs, that is, to break even.

Now, we can calculate Jim's breakeven number of passengers using this method.

Contribution per sale = Selling price – Variable cost

$$= £15 - £5 = £10$$

$$\text{Breakeven output} = \frac{\text{Fixed costs}}{\text{Contribution per sale}}$$

$$= 200/10 = 20$$

Not surprisingly, and reassuringly, we arrive at the same answer using this contribution method of calculating breakeven.

Breakeven charts

As we have shown, breakeven output can be calculated using simple equations. However, more understanding of the sensitivity of the relationships between costs, sales and production is achieved through the use of **breakeven charts**. A breakeven chart is simply a graphical representation of a business's breakeven point.

A breakeven chart is constructed on a graph by first drawing the horizontal axis to represent the output of goods or services for the business. The vertical axis represents the values of costs and sales, usually in pounds sterling. On the horizontal axis, we mark output for a given time period – usually monthly or annual output.

Drawing breakeven charts can be completed quickly and easily if broken down into simple steps.

- Step 1– Title the chart.
- Step 2 – Determine and label the axes; the X (horizontal) axis goes from 0 to the maximum output capacity; the Y (vertical) axis goes from 0 to maximum cost or revenue. (Maximum revenue can be calculated by multiplying the maximum output capacity by the selling price.)
- Step 3 – Draw and label the fixed cost line (FC).
- Step 4 – Draw and label the variable cost line (VC).
- Step 5 – Draw and label the total cost line (TC). (This must be parallel to the VC line.)
- Step 6 – Draw and label the sales revenue line (SR).
- Step 7 – Identify and mark the breakeven point (BE), this is where TC = TR.
- Step 8 – Identify and mark the breakeven output on the X axis.
- Step 9 – Add any additional information required, such as margin of safety and areas of profit and loss.

Our first breakeven chart is based on this business scenario. Mark Cushion Limited manufactures confectionery. One of its most popular lines is Chewies – a fruit flavoured chew. These sweets sell for £1 a kilogram. The variable (or marginal) cost of production is 60p per kg. The fixed costs associated with this product are estimated at £50,000 a year. The company's maximum output of Chewies is 250,000 kg a year.

Now, let's go through the steps of producing a chart. After putting a title on the chart, we need to put scales on our axes (Step 2). The output scale needs to extend to the company's maximum annual output; this is 250,000 kg. The vertical axis records values of costs and revenues. Since revenue is usually the higher figure, we

Figure 6.10 Constructing a breakeven chart for Chewies

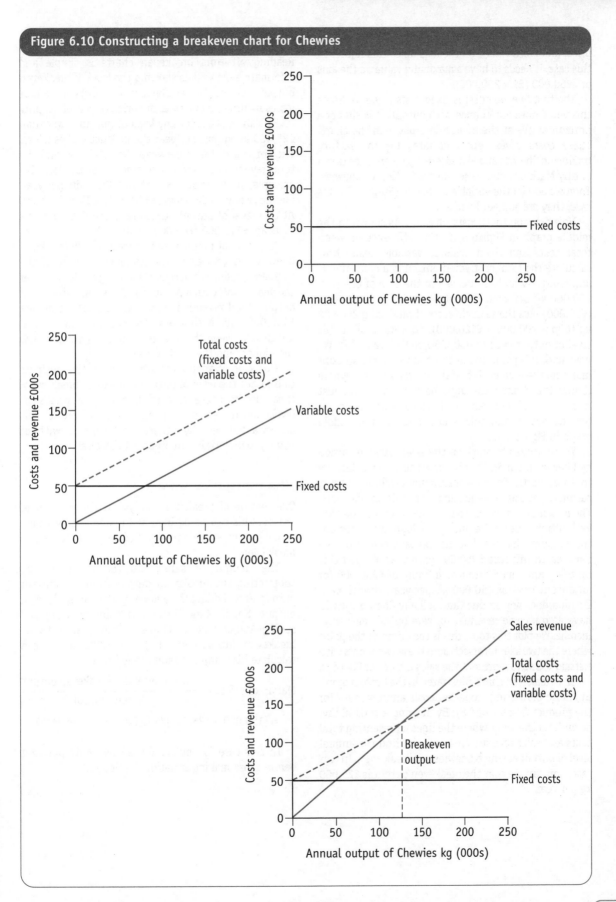

simply multiply the maximum output by the selling price, and place values on the axis up to this figure. In this case, it needs to have a maximum value on the axis of £250,000 (£1 × 250,000).

The first line we enter is fixed costs (Step 3). Since this value does not change with output, it is simply a horizontal line at the appropriate place on the chart. These costs cover rent and rates for the factory producing Chewies and also interest paid on loans taken out by Mark Cushion to set up production of Chewies. Then we add on the variable costs line (Step 4). In this case, they are 60p per kilogram.

Now draw on total costs (Step 5). As shown in the middle graph in Figure 6.10, the difference between total costs and fixed costs is variable costs. Now calculate the total cost when output is a convenient, and relatively high figure, say in the case of Chewies, 200,000 kg per year. The total cost is the fixed costs (£50,000) plus the variable costs of producing 200,000 kg (60p × 200,000 = £120,000). So, total cost at this level of output is £170,000 (£50,000 + £120,000). We now mark this point on our chart. If we draw a straight line from the extreme left of the fixed costs line (where it hits the Y axis) through the point we have just marked, it will represent the total costs of production for Chewies. Again, this is illustrated in the middle graph in Figure 6.10.

We now need to mark on the sales revenue earned by Chewies (Step 6). We can draw this in a similar way to total costs. For the maximum level of output, calculate the sales revenue and mark this on the chart. The maximum annual output of Chewies is 250,000 kg; we multiply this by the price per kilogram to work out the maximum income that the company can earn from Chewies, in this case £250,000 each year. We plot this on the graph, mark an income figure of £250,000 for an output level of 250,000 kg per year. Now if Mark Cushion does not produce and sell any Chewies, it will have zero income revenue: so, zero output means no income. We plot this too – this is the origin or the point where the two axes intersect. Join these two points with a straight line to represent the sales income of Chewies.

The breakeven chart, illustrated in the bottom graph in Figure 6.10 brings together costs and revenues for the product(Steps 7 and 8). By drawing a vertical line down from the point where the lines representing total costs and sales revenue cross, we can find the annual level of output at which Chewies will break even. In this case, you can see that the breakeven output is 125,000 kg per year.

Using breakeven charts

Reading off from breakeven charts is simple and informative. As well as showing the level of breakeven output, we can also see the level of profits earned, or losses incurred, by Chewies at various levels of output.

We can see that for any level of output lower than 125,000 kilograms per year the product makes a loss. The vertical distance between the total cost and the total revenue line shows the amount of the loss. For example, at an output level of 100,000 units per year, Chewies would make a loss of £10,000 for Mark Cushion. At this level of output, sales are worth £100,000 but costs are £110,000 (£60,000 + £50,000).

Any level of production in excess of 125,000 kg of Chewies per year earns the company a profit. If the company produces and sells 150,000 kg of Chewies over the year, it will earn a profit of £20,000. At this level of output, total revenue is £150,000 and total costs are £130,000. This is shown on the chart by the vertical distance between the total revenue line (which is now the higher) and the total cost line.

This kind of analysis allows a prospective business to find out the level of output it needs to break even. It can use its market research to assess potential sales levels and to assess the possible level of profit. This allows a business hypothesis to be tested without having to undertake any financial risk at all.

The margin of safety

One feature of breakeven analysis is the margin of safety. This can be defined as the amount by which actual output exceeds the level of output necessary to break even.

The margin of safety can be calculated by subtracting the breakeven output from the current output, and dividing the answer by the current level of output. So, if Mark Cushion is manufacturing and selling 150,000 kg of Chewies each year, with its breakeven output remaining at 125,000 kg, we can calculate his margin of safety as follows:

$$\text{Margin of safety} = \frac{\text{Current output} - \text{Breakeven output}}{\text{Current output}}$$

$$= (150,000 - 125,000)/150,000 = 0.166 \text{ or } 16.67\%$$

In this case, output could fall by 16.67 per cent before a loss-making situation developed.

Breakeven relationships

If costs remain unchanged and prices fall, then a business is faced with a higher breakeven level of production. Lower prices mean that more has to be produced and sold before a profit-making position can be reached. Conversely, a rise in price results in a lower breakeven level of production.

Costs have an equally important impact on breakeven levels. A rise in either fixed or variable (marginal) costs will result in a higher level of breakeven output. Similarly, a fall in costs reduces the amount necessary to be produced and sold (each year, say) in order to break even.

If there is a rise in fixed costs, then the effect on the total costs line is to shift it upwards by the same amount at each level of output. In effect, the two total cost lines are parallel. This is because the rise in fixed costs is unaffected by the level of output. For example, a rise in rent for a factory has the same impact on total costs regardless of whether the firm is producing at half or full capacity. In contrast, a rise in variable or marginal costs increases the slope of the total costs line. These relationships enable us to make contingency plans to cover circumstances such as prices falling or costs rising unexpectedly.

Why use breakeven analysis?

As with most financial control techniques, breakeven analysis has advantages and disadvantages. Breakeven analysis is simple to conduct and understand and it is cheap. It can show profit and loss at various levels of output, particularly when it is presented in the form of a chart. This may be of particular value when a business is first established. Indeed, financial institutions may require this sort of information before lending any money to an aspiring entrepreneur.

As we have seen, breakeven analysis can be used to show the effect of price changes: with a rise in price the total revenue line will pivot upwards, and the company can break even at a lower output. Conversely, a fall in price will cause the line to pivot downwards increasing the breakeven output. A change in costs can also be shown, with rises in costs shifting the cost function upward and falls in costs lowering it.

However, breakeven analysis does have some drawbacks. It assumes that the firm sells all its output. This may well not be true and, if so, would result in an inaccurate breakeven estimate. In times of recession, a firm may have difficulty in selling all that it produces.

Although breakeven analysis can cope with changes in prices and costs, in the real world it is difficult to forecast costs and prices accurately.

The model also assumes that costs increase constantly and that firms do not benefit from economies of scale. Similarly, it assumes that a firm sells all its output at a single price. In reality, firms frequently offer discounts for bulk purchases. Finally, breakeven analysis is only as good as the data on which it is based: poor quality data can result in inaccurate conclusions being drawn.

We have considered breakeven analysis in some detail, as it is not covered in Unit 5. Other elements of financial planning, which we review here, should be studied in conjunction with the relevant parts of Unit 5.

Start-up balance sheets

As we showed in Unit 5, a balance sheet is simply a picture that shows what a company owns and owes at a given point in time. It records the assets (what a business owns) and the liabilities (what a business owes) on a particular date. It is a snapshot of a business's financial position and gives an indication of its long-term financial stability. Balance sheets are published in a company's annual report and accounts along with other important financial information.

The purpose of a start-up balance sheet is to draw together, in a simple summary, the financial position of the company at its outset if everything proceeds as outlined in the business plan. The start-up balance sheet is used to provide information to prospective investors. It seeks to show that their investment would be a satisfactory risk. It also informs providers of finance that if the business's assets are financed in accordance with the start-up budget and start-up balance sheet, then the business is a viable proposition.

A business will find it easy to source finance if it has a strong start-up balance sheet position. This is because providers of finance will see the proposition as less of a risk. For example, if the owners of the new business are putting in a lot of their own money, this makes the start-up balance sheet stronger, and might make the enterprise a more attractive proposition. Even if the start-up position isn't one of great strength, financial institutions will find a certain degree of security and reassurance in the fact that a start-up balance sheet has been prepared. Well-researched and accurate financial documentation makes it easier to secure the finance required by the business.

Figure 6.11: Start-up balance sheet for Andrews Plumbing

	£	£	£
Fixed assets			
Equipment			8,000
Fixtures and fittings			12,000
Vehicles			42,000
Current assets			
Stock	35,000		
Debtors	Nil		
Prepayments	Nil		
Bank	–		
Cash	1,500	36,500	
Current liabilities			
Creditors	24,000		
Accruals	Nil		
Bank overdraft	5,000	29,000	
Working capital		7,500	7,500
			49,500
Financed by:			
Long-term liabilities			
3 year loan J. Andrews		10,000	
5 year loan Bank		12,000	
HP owing on vehicle		10,000	32,000
Capital			17,500
			49,500

Discussion point

Study Figure 6.11. How might this business increase the amount of working capital it has available?

- No depreciation has been included in the fixed asset section. This is because the business has not started trading yet, and the fixed assets have not been used by the business, even if they have been purchased as second hand. Therefore, no depreciation can be charged.

- In the 'financed by' section, there are no entries for net profit retained or any drawings. Again as the business has not started trading, profits have not been generated nor have any drawings been made by the owners.

Figure 6.11 outlines a start-up balance sheet for Andrews Plumbing Services. This business provides household plumbing services and a retail outlet for DIY plumbing. It may be a good idea at this stage to remind yourself of a normal balance sheet layout by looking back at Unit 5 (see pp. 283–90). Hopefully, you should see some important differences.

Alongside the start-up balance sheet, a projected balance sheet for one year in the future should also be presented. This allows potential investors to make a good assessment of the business's growth potential and it also highlights any areas of strength and weakness where future financial problems may occur.

Projected profit and loss accounts

Projected profit and loss accounts should be drawn from the budgets and forecasts produced by the business. We looked at this in some detail in Unit 5. The main budgets providing information are the **sales budget**, based upon the companies marketing plan, and the **expenditure budget**. The **marketing plan** (covered in Unit 3) is very important in constructing the profit and loss account. It helps to demonstrate to a bank or other financial provider that the organisation has a good understanding of the market and that demand exists for the firm's products. It shows that the organisation is in control of the crucial success factors that will enable it to enter the market and reach its sales goals and financial targets.

The evidence from the analysis of the business environmental trends and from the desk and field market research should provide sufficient market information to draft an outline plan. This should cover:

- brief details of the size of the marketing budget
- a sales forecast and estimate of revenue for the first year
- an indication of the level of sales necessary for the business to break even.

The sales forecast is used to provide the estimated total sales revenue figure for the profit and loss account. The expenditure budget is used to complete the forecast profit and loss account. Figure 6.12 contains a standard layout to help you prepare a forecast profit and loss account.

Discussion point

Imagine you have to complete the form in Figure 6.12. How might you find out the likely levels of expenditure on overheads and salaries?

It is worth noting here that the same figures used to compile the start-up budget, start-up balance sheet and projected profit and loss account should also be used to compile a cash flow forecast. It is important, therefore, to use accurate and realistic information. Any attempt to improve one set of figures, such as underestimating the business's costs to produce a higher profit result, will have a knock-on effect. You may be refused a vital loan because the bank believes you don't really require additional finance if your profit projections are realised.

The circumstances of new business ventures vary enormously. The business you start may be offering a new innovative product with few competitors. Alternatively, it may be serving a relatively small market in which there exists a particular niche for your product. In any scenario, it is not necessary that the business shows a huge profit on its projected profit and loss account. Indeed, many businesses make no profit at all in their first year of trading.

The idea of a projected profit and loss account is to show that the business has the potential to generate sufficient profit in the future to warrant investment now. Potential investors and financial backers want to see if any profit is likely to grow, or at least be sustained, over future years. A projected profit and loss account can show a loss in its first year: if investors have faith in the long-term future of the business, they may be willing to invest in the enterprise. Accurate and pessimistic is a better starting position than inaccurate and optimistic.

Simple cash flow forecasts

Cash flow forecasting is covered in detail in Unit 5. For the purpose of business planning a cash flow forecast can be presented as a standard form, and these are available in most business start-up packs. Figure 6.13 provides an example of a standard format for a cash flow forecast.

Cash flow is particularly important because managing cash badly is one of the main reasons for business failure. By monitoring cash flow properly, a business is able to identify when there may be a shortage, recognise when extra cash may be generated, and ensure that there is sufficient cash to cover any necessary capital expenditure.

Discussion point

What is the difference between a cash flow forecast and a profit and loss forecast?

Cash flow forecasts record the inflows of cash into a business over a period of time. This cash results from sales of products, though if the firm offers its customers credit it may have to wait for payment. Offering too much credit (known as trade credit) is one cause of cash flow problems. New businesses often face a dilemma in relation to trade credit: they need to offer it to attract customers but they may not be in a position to wait too long for payment.

Figure 6.12: Profit and loss forecast

Profit & Loss Forecast

BARCLAYS

Year beginning _____

	Month		Month		Month		Month		Month		Month		Sub totals	
	Budget	Actual	Budget	Actual	Budget	Actual	Budget	Actual	Budget	Actual	Budget	Actual	Budget	Actual
Sales (a)														
Less Direct Costs														
Cost of Materials														
Wages														
Gross Profit (b)														
Gross Profit Margin ($^b/_a$ x 100%)														
Overheads														
Salaries														
Rent/Rates/Water														
Insurance														
Repairs/Renewals														
Heat/Light/Power														
Postage														
Printing/Stationery														
Transport														
Telephone														
Professional Fees														
Interest Charges														
Other														
Other														
Total Overheads (c)														
Trading Profit (b) – (c)														
Less Depreciation														
Net Profit Before Tax														

*These headings may vary according to the needs of your business. You may therefore need to amend any that are not applicable.

Figure 6.13: Cash flow forecast

Cash Flow Forecast

Year beginning _____

BARCLAYS

	Month		Month		Month		Month		Month		Month		Sub totals	
	Budget	Actual	Budget	Actual	Budget	Actual	Budget	Actual	Budget	Actual	Budget	Actual	Budget	Actual
Cash Sales														
Cash from Debtors														
Capital Introduced														
Total Receipts (a)														
Payments														
Payments to Creditors														
Salaries/Wages														
Rent/Rates/Water														
Insurance														
Repairs/Renewals														
Heat/Light/Power														
Postage														
Printing/Stationery														
Transport														
Telephone														
Professional Fees														
Capital Payments														
Interest Charges														
Other														
VAT payable (refund)														
Total Payments (b)														
Net Cash Flow (a–b)														
Opening Bank Balance														
Closing Bank Balance														

*These headings may vary according to the needs of your business. You may therefore need to amend any that are not applicable.

The outflows of cash result from the business's expenditure. Some of this expenditure is on fixed costs or overheads such as rent and rates. Other expenditure varies directly with the level of the business's output. Examples of variable costs include expenditure (or cash outflow) on fuel, transport costs and raw materials.

The cash flow forecast is a tool that can be used to monitor the effect that the timing of cash inflows and outflows have on the short-term financial stability of a business. Financial analysis and planning are also major steps in the monitoring and control process. By comparing actual figures against budgeted statements, it should be possible to spot any difficulties or unforeseen events and expenditure early on. This may enable timely remedial action to be taken. In the long-run, the discipline imposed by cash flow forecasting and financial planning should not only help to get the business started but also act as an invaluable aid for improving business performance.

Presentational aspects

A business proposal needs to be professionally presented if it is to have a good chance of success. You should make use of word processing and spreadsheet packages to give your business plan a professional look.

Word processing packages

Word processing packages are extremely helpful in presenting business propositions. An entrepreneur may have the best idea in the world, but if the business plan contains grammatical errors, misspelled words or is written poorly, potential investors may misunderstand, misinterpret or miss the point of the presentation entirely. Modern word-processing packages help you explain your proposal clearly, concisely and thoroughly. They also allow you to make additions and amendments to the proposal quickly and easily. One of the main advantages of the technology is the speed with which extra copies can be made and circulated.

Spreadsheet packages

Spreadsheet packages are a form of software developed for the manipulation of numerical data. They are invaluable in the financial analysis of the proposal. They enable calculations to be carried out automatically and the results to be displayed either as numerical reports or charts and graphs. A spreadsheet can be tailored to the specific needs and layout of each individual business, enabling financial information to be modelled quickly and clearly with very little chance of error.

A spreadsheet application performs any mathematical calculation using the appropriate units so long as the formula is entered correctly. It can be used to calculate percentages, fractions, perform routines, and you can enter text as well. Many start-your-own-business packs have ready set-up spreadsheets for cash flows and profit and loss accounts.

The legal status of a business

There are a range of factors which should influence your decision on the best form of organisation and legal status to adopt for your business venture.

- The amount of capital required. As the amount of start-up capital required increases, more people and organisations will be involved in raising and providing finance. This tends to require a more complicated – or at least, more formalised – legal structure.

- The amount of projected profit. Consider an example. An annual £60,000 net profit is a very nice result for a sole trader or even a partnership of two people. For a partnership of four people, or a limited company with 20 shareholders, this is unlikely to provide a sufficient return.

- Personal preference. Many people do not make the move to partnership or limited company status as they would rather work for themselves. Conversely, others wish to share the burden of responsibility and will actively look for people to share in the running of the business.

- Professional constraints. There are restrictions on the legal status of some trades and professions.

Sole trader

Many new businesses start as sole traders. This means that a single person provides the capital, takes the decisions and assumes the risks of the business. The attraction of operating and working as a sole trader is that it is relatively easy to set up, and it provides considerable scope for the development of the owner's ideas and initiatives. However, this can often be at the cost of having to work very long hours, accepting heavy responsibilities, taking considerable business risks and experiencing financial problems.

Partnership

When planning and developing a new business, it is often easier to work with a partner. It allows for the sharing of responsibilities, the pooling of financial resources, the opportunity to discuss important issues, and the bringing together of complementary business and technical skills. Partners provide additional capital for the business, sharing the resulting profit or loss.

Care should be taken in selecting a suitable business partner because, ultimately, if the partners fall out the business is unlikely to prosper. Personalities must match, skills should complement each other, and relative strengths and weaknesses need to balance out.

Family's £40 million breadwinner

A baker and his family are nearly £40 million richer following the sale of their Sheffield-based bakery to Northern Foods.

Paul Fletcher and his daughters own nearly all the shares in Fletcher Bakeries. The family business grew rapidly after a change of direction.

They decided to move away from running local bread shops, and to start supplying supermarkets with bread and cakes instead.

The business has become a national supplier to supermarket chains.

Adapted *The Electronic Telegraph*, 24 April 1999

Discussion point

What legal form of business is Fletcher Bakeries? Why do you think the move to supplying supermarkets with bakery products proved so successful?

Family businesses

The growth in small family businesses has provided a very useful training ground for budding entrepreneurs. Typically, these businesses are in retailing, personal services and small-scale engineering.

Starting a private limited company as a family business can have several advantages:

■ there is scope to tailor roles and responsibilities to meet the precise needs, strengths and interests of the owners and staff, thus providing better training and more satisfying work

■ the owners of the business benefit from the protection of limited liability

■ family members should be more committed, more flexible, less inclined to defraud and easier to induct into the working ways of the business

■ it can be easier for a limited company to raise larger amounts of capital.

In the long term, future survival of the business can also be ensured by handing it on to the next generation However, a recent survey (conducted in 2000) suggests that many small business owners do not want their children to take over the firm. The survey, by accountants Grant Thornton, found that 73 per cent of business owners in the UK would not encourage their children to step into their shoes. The reasons given include stress and long working hours.

There can be a number of difficulties in working for a close relative. Family relationships do not necessarily transfer easily into business relationships. In some cases, resentments may develop – some people may find it difficult to work for an older brother or sister or a parent. Conversely, an older relative's judgement may be clouded by their emotional relationship with the younger family members. They may, for example, be too easy going or too critical. Also, you might not get a good deal on pay. Family members may be paid less than the going rate for the job. This may be justified on the grounds that they will be compensated in the future when they inherit the business.

Businesses need a constant injection of new ideas to flourish and grow. The danger is that a family member may be less inclined to criticise and more accepting of the traditional family way of doing things. Other employees, who are not relatives, may resent the position, and what may be viewed as the preferment, of family members.

Franchise

A **franchise** is a business based upon the ideas, image and activities of an existing business. When purchasing a franchise it is possible to acquire a complete business package including national advertising. A **franchiser** is the person or business selling the business package. **Franchisee** is the term given to entrepreneurs who purchase franchise businesses.

To reduce the danger of business failure, it is often worthwhile buying into a franchise. This involves a contractual licence granted by the franchiser to the franchisee. The licence is normally purchased for an initial franchise fee (usually exclusive of future royalty payments). The franchisee then receives a complete business package from the franchiser, including expertise and market research, financial planning, training, and the use of the corporate name and its promotion through advertising. This allows the franchisee to operate the business to the same standard and format as all the other units in the franchised chain. Essentially, this means that someone can run his or her own business to a format with a proven track record.

Franchises often are well-established household names, offering brands backed in many cases by national and international advertising. Under these circumstances, there is a far higher probability that the business will be successful. Franchised operations can be found in retailing, catering, fast food, print shops, parcel delivery, home maintenance, cleaning, drain cleaning and plumbing. McDonald's, for example, operates franchises through the UK. This form of business operation has proved very profitable and has been one of the factors leading to the exceptional growth of the company, with McDonald's outlets opening throughout the world.

Discussion point

> List three advantages and three disadvantages for an entrepreneur of purchasing a franchise in McDonald's rather than starting his or her own fast-food restaurant.

If you are considering purchasing a franchised business, you should carry out a very careful evaluation of the franchise contract and arrangement. You should consider:

- the exact terms, conditions and responsibilities under the contract
- whether the market for the franchised product is growing, static or declining
- whether the franchised product is competitive in your local market
- the proximity of the nearest operator of the same franchise

- the history, track record and performance of the franchiser
- the true cost of the franchise in terms of initial fee and royalty payments on turnover
- whether the franchise is backed by national advertising
- whether there is any provision for promoting an individual outlet
- who pays for training and what it provides
- how often the operating manual is changed and updated
- whether the franchiser is a member of the British Franchise Association.

▲ The British Franchise Association's website

Discussion point

> The British Franchise Association offers training for potential franchisees and accredits responsible franchisers. What are the benefits of contacting the British Franchise Association for someone considering starting a business?

Some people may not enjoy running their own business as part of a franchise. This is because it may limit the opportunity to express their personal initiative in terms of product, service and design. They are not in full control of all aspects of the business. If franchiser's product receives bad publicity, this will obviously have an effect on the franchisee. Finally, the failure of a franchiser may leave a franchisee with a business that is not viable on its own.

BUILD YOUR LEARNING

Keywords and phrases

You should know the meaning of the words and phrases listed below. Go back through the last 23 pages of the unit to check or refresh your understanding as necessary.

- Breakeven analysis
- Breakeven chart
- Collateral
- Contribution
- Debt factoring
- Factors
- Fixed costs
- Franchising
- Hire purchase
- Leasing
- Margin of safety
- Merchant banks
- Mortgages
- Overdraft
- Share capital
- Start-up budget
- Start-up capital
- Trade credit
- Variable costs
- Working capital

Summary points

- New businesses require finance to purchase fixed assets and to provide capital to cover day-to-day trading expenses.

- There are a range of finance options including short-term finance (overdrafts and trade credit), medium-term finance (bank loans, leasing and hire purchase) and long-term finance (mortgages or share capital).

- Other sources of business start-up finance include government grants, support from independent trusts and entrepreneurs' personal sources of finance.

- Breakeven analysis allows firms to forecast the number of sales they require to ensure that earnings match their expenses.

- Breakeven points can be calculated or illustrated on charts. Charts are more complex to construct but allow entrepreneurs to see the effects of changes in sales on profits (or losses).

- Businesses need to provide potential investors with a start-up budget, start-up balance sheet, projected profit and loss account, a cash flow forecast, and a breakeven analysis.

- Information and communications technology enables people starting their own businesses to produce accurate and professional business proposals.

- It is possible to establish a business in a number of legal forms. New businesses are more likely to be sole traders, partnerships, family-run companies or franchises.

- Working with other family members offers advantages and disadvantages. Family businesses often experience frequent arguments and disputes.

- Purchasing a franchise can be more successful than establishing a new business from scratch. However, purchasing a well-known franchise can be very expensive.

Evaluating a business plan

ONCE A BUSINESS PLAN IS complete it is important to develop some criteria to judge whether the plan is likely to be a success. It may be that entrepreneurs have their own targets for their businesses. These may not necessarily be financial targets. People may set up in business to meet personal goals, such as:

- providing a means of earning a living as your own boss

- generating an income to supplement a pension taken following early retirement

- offering an opportunity to develop a hobby into a full-time business interest.

If entrepreneurs feel that their personal targets are likely to be met by the enterprise described in their business plan, they may consider that it is likely to be a success. However, other people who are considering establishing businesses may use more rigorous measures of success. Certainly any organisation or individual that is planning to lend money to, or invest in, a new business will want some quantifiable means of evaluating the business plan. We shall consider a number of criteria that might be employed in these circumstances.

The return on capital employed

As we saw in Unit 5, one way to assess the financial performance of a business is to use ratio analysis. It is also possible to apply ratio analysis to forecast accounts to make some judgement on the likely performance of the business. Clearly, the value of the technique is limited by the fact that the figures are forecast rather than actual. Nevertheless, having some notion of the likely return on an investment allows those proposing to put money into a business to make comparisons with other investment opportunities.

Return on capital employed (ROCE) compares the profits generated by the business (or in this case, the forecast profits) with the amount of capital available to the business. Measuring profits against the capital available to the business makes it possible to compare the financial performance of businesses of varying size.

ROCE is referred to as the primary ratio. It is considered one of the most important ratios available.

This ratio measures the efficiency of funds invested in the business at generating profits. It is calculated using the formula:

$$\text{ROCE} = \frac{\text{Net profit before tax and interest}}{\text{Total capital employed}} \times 100$$

CASE STUDY

Robin's dilemma

Robin Lawrence is in a quandary. Two of his relatives are planning to start businesses and both have invited him to put money into their enterprises. Robin isn't sure that he can afford to invest in both, so he has to make a choice.

Looking at the two business plans in front of him, it appears that cousin Mike's business looks the more attractive. Mike is an architect. He is forecasting a net profit before tax and interest of £150,000 at the end of his first year of trading. Robin's niece Paula is planning to open a flower shop and her plan indicates an expected profit of £20,000 at the end of the first year.

"This is simple," thinks Robin. "I'll invest my money in Mike's business as he will generate the greater profits." But then a thought struck him: Mike's business is being set up with much more capital than is available to Paula. Robin decides to calculate the return on capital employed for each business.

Mike's business is being established with £1,500,000 capital.

$$\text{Mike's ROCE} = \frac{150,000 \times 100}{1,500,000} = 10\%$$

Paula's business is being established with £160,000.

$$\text{Paula's ROCE} = \frac{20,000 \times 100}{160,000} = 12.5\%$$

So, Robin decides to invest his £10,000 into Paula's business. "After all," he reasons, "I should earn a greater return on my investment in the flower shop."

In addition to calculating ROCE, what else might Robin take into account when making his investment decision?

In general, a higher figure for ROCE is preferred as it represents a greater potential return for investors if the figures in the business plan prove correct. Anybody considering investing in a business will compare its return on capital employed with:

- the return on capital employed of other, similar businesses
- the rate of interest offered on interest-bearing accounts at banks and other financial institutions.

The average figure for return on capital for an established business is 20–25 per cent. It is likely that a business plan will forecast a lower figure for a start-up business. The ROCE for a new business might be relatively low for a number of reasons.

- All emerging businesses are attempting to break into a market and sales may be low for the first year or two until businesses become established and known by potential customers.

- New businesses can face high start-up costs. For example, a new business might incur considerable marketing costs in its attempts to establish its name and products.

- It is not uncommon for new businesses to charge low prices to tempt customers away from existing suppliers. This may reduce the level of profits.

Some new businesses are unlikely to forecast any profits for their first few years. For example, the Prudential has run its internet-based Egg credit cards and savings accounts at a loss for several years. So return on capital employed could actually be negative for newly-planned businesses. It could be argued that the expected return on capital for the first year or two is not a good measure of a business's success and that investors should take a longer-term view of the enterprise. A better measure might be to compare sales revenue with the value of assets available to the business.

Profit margins

The forecast profit figures in the business plan can be used in other ways to evaluate the future success of a business. One alternative financial measure of success is to consider the profit margin earned by the firm. We looked at profit margins in Unit 5, and you should recall that a profit margin simply expresses profit as a proportion of sales revenue.

There are two basic types of profit margin: gross profit margin and net profit margin. Gross profit margin relates the gross profit earned by a business over a trading period to the sales revenue generated over the same period of time.

$$\text{Gross profit margin} = \frac{\text{Gross profit}}{\text{Sales revenue}} \times 100$$

The **gross profit** earned by a business is the sales revenue less the cost of sales (direct costs such as raw materials) in the same trading period. Overheads are not taken into consideration, therefore gross profit is higher than operating profit.

Net profit is gross profit less overheads and depreciation. If you are unsure about any of these concepts you should look again at the relevant sections of Unit 5.

$$\text{Net profit margin} = \frac{\text{Net profit}}{\text{Sales revenue}} \times 100$$

As with most means of analysing profits, a higher figure is preferable to a lower figure; so a higher profit margin figure is a preferable result. The expected gross profit margin varies according to the type of business and the size of its overheads. An established business might show a gross profit margin of up to 50 per cent if the overheads are a large proportion of costs. It is unlikely that a small business will achieve a figure anywhere near as high as 50 per cent in its first year or two of trading. Inevitably it takes a business time to build up its sales volume and to generate high levels of sales revenue.

The net profit margin figure is normally lower. A normal return for an established manufacturing business is 8–10 per cent, while a retail outlet might only run on a 5 per cent net profit margin. A new business might deliberately set a low profit margin to build up its share of a local market, attracting customers as a result of its low prices. If a new business predicts very high profit margins, this might suggest that the sales revenue forecasts are optimistic. If very high profits are achievable, then the new business will almost certainly attract competition from established firms.

CASE STUDY

Robin's dilemma continues

Robin is having second thoughts. He discovers that other ratios can be used to compare the expected performances of his relatives' new businesses. Robin decides to calculate the net profit margin for the two businesses.

Mike's business is expected to generate £150,000 net profits on an anticipated turnover of £1,875,000.

Mike's net profit margin = $\dfrac{150,000 \times 100}{1,875,000}$ = 8%

In comparison, Paula's shop forecasts £20,000 profits and she anticipates £140,000 sales revenue over her first trading year.

Paula's net profit margin = $\dfrac{20,000 \times 100}{140,000}$ = 7%

Now Robin is less sure. Paula's ROCE is better but her net profit margin is less than Mike's. Robin wonders which is the most important measure of success in a business plan.

Discussion point

Which measure do you think is the most important? Why do you think that Robin chose to calculate the net profit margin rather than the gross profit margin?

The ability to reward investors

A simpler way to assess the viability of a business plan is to consider whether the business is able to offer a return to its investors, whether they be shareholders or institutions that have loaned the business money.

Rewarding owners

If a business is established as a sole trader (having just a single owner) than one measure of success is whether the owner will earn sufficient income to make the business worthwhile. In making this judgement, bear in mind that many sole traders accept long working hours and low pay while establishing their businesses.

Similarly, partnerships may be adjudged according to the expected returns for each of the partners setting up the business. Once again initial returns might be expected to be low. It is not unusual for people involved in creating a new business to accept an income below £10,000. This is much less than they would be prepared to accept when working for someone else. However, all entrepreneurs hope that their business will make them very rich one day.

Rewarding shareholders

A new business may be established as a private limited company. In this case, the owners are the business's shareholders. One way of assessing the viability of the business is to measure the return that shareholders can expect on their investment. Most companies pay a part of their profits to their shareholders in the form of dividends. We can use a ratio – in this case the dividend share ratio – to measure the worth of the dividend.

Dividend per share = $\dfrac{\text{Dividends} \times 100}{\text{Number of ordinary shares}}$

This measure takes the amount that the company intends to distribute to shareholders in the form of dividends and divides this by the number of ordinary shares issued by the company.

Note that the dividend per share ratio gives the amount a shareholder receives for each share he or she earns. However, a new business may not pay any dividends for its first few years. This may be because the business may not generate a profit or because the directors decide to retain all profits within the business to invest in new assets and to provide working capital.

Repaying creditors

Creditors, you should recall, are those individuals and organisations that are owed money by a business. Anybody who is seriously considering making a start-up capital investment will look closely at the business plan to check whether there is a good chance that they will be repaid. Investors will expect that the payment of interest on their loan – as well as some repayment of the principal – forms a central part of the business's financial planning. If the business is projecting a significant loss, creditors may be concerned that they will not be repaid.

It is also likely that creditors will scrutinise the business's cash flow forecasts carefully. It is important that a business earns sufficient revenue to repay creditors; equally it is important that earnings arrive in time to satisfy the demands of creditors. Investors will want to be assured that the business has made arrangements to pay interest (and principal) instalments on loans even at times when cash may be in short supply.

CASE STUDY

Robin's dilemma: the final chapter

Still undecided, Robin is looking to see what return he might get on his investment from his relatives' businesses. The situation is a little complex in that Paula intends to run her business as a private limited company, but Mike is establishing his business as a partnership with two colleagues.

Paula expects to have profits of £14,000 after she has paid tax (£4,000) and interest (£2,000). She has indicated that she will pay this profit to shareholders in the form of a dividend. The flower shop has 100,000 shares each sold for £1. In these circumstances the dividend per share is:

$$\text{Paula's dividend} = \frac{£14,000 \times 100}{100,000} = 14\text{p per share.}$$

If Robin buys 10,000 shares in Paula's business, he would expect to receive £1,400 in dividends at the end of the first trading year, if her forecasts proved accurate.

A partnership normally distributes profits according to the proportion of capital contributed by each partner. Even if he invests £15,000 in Mike's business, Robin would have contributed only 1 per cent of the capital. He could, therefore, only expect 1 per cent of the profits. If Mike and his fellow partners decided to distribute all their profit, Robin would only receive 1 per cent of £150,000 , in other words £1,500. Receiving £1,400 from Paula for an investment of £10,000 suddenly seems very attractive.

Discussion point

Why might it be rather simplistic for Robin to only focus on the profits earned by the two businesses in their first year of trading?

Market share

The **market share** gained by a business is the percentage share achieved by its products of total market sales for the type of product. In 1999, for example, Coca-Cola had approximately 51 per cent of the world market for soft drinks. If a business is to establish itself and be successful, it is important that it gains a foothold in the market. Many new businesses will not be seeking to conquer the world, or not even a national market. New businesses normally target local markets. As an example, a new local fast-food restaurant might seek to gain a 10 per cent market share of the local fast-food trade. If this target is achieved, it means that £1 in £10 spent on fast food in the locality will be spent in the new fast-food restaurant.

Businesses can adopt a number of strategies to gain market share. New businesses may elect to use a policy of **price penetration**. By setting a price below the established market price, they can attempt to win new customers. This is a difficult policy for new businesses to maintain as it reduces their forecast sales revenue and expected profits.

Another approach is to go down the route of a major advertising campaign or sales promotions such as two-for-one offers. As with most methods of gaining market share, marketing can be an expensive option.

A more effective approach is to introduce a new product significantly different from those offered by existing suppliers. This can give a new business an identity distinct from established firms and allow it to gain a foothold in the market. In 1999, Richard Branson announced the launch of Virgin Mobile, a new company set up to compete with the established mobile phone service providers. To differentiate the service, Richard Branson has promised potential customers a clear and transparent pricing policy. The success in this new venture, in time, can be measured by the market share achieved by Virgin Mobile. Figure 6.14 shows the leaders in the mobile phone service market before Virgin Mobile entered the market.

Figure 6.14: Share of mobile phone market

Mobile phone operator	Market share
BT Cellnet	31.1%
One2One	14.8%
Orange	16.6%
Vodafone	37.5%

Source: Financial Times, 5 January 1999

Discussion point

In what other ways, apart from market share, might a firm's performance in a market be measured?

A final way of assessing the viability of a business plan is to consider whether the forecast financial outcomes will allow the business to meet the objectives the owner(s) have set themselves. For example, if the owners have expressed the intention of achieving a high rate of growth over the first few years of trading, ask whether the business plan suggests that the enterprise can generate sufficient profits to provide capital for future growth.

BUILD YOUR LEARNING

Keywords and phrases

You should know the meaning of the words and phrases listed below. Go back through the last four pages of the unit to check or refresh your understanding as necessary.

- Creditors
- Gross profit
- Market share
- Net profit
- Price penetration
- Profit margin

Summary points

- There are a number of techniques to evaluate the potential of a new enterprise from its business plan, including measures of return on capital employed, profit margins and rewards for investors.

- A fundamental measure of the viability is the return on capital employed (ROCE). However, it is important not to take a short-term view, and to consider ROCE over a reasonably long period of time.

- Investors will want to judge whether the business will be able to repay them or to provide a return on their investment.

- A good measure of the potential of a business is the market share that it forecasts to win after the first year or two of trading.

How to produce a business plan for a new product

The flow chart shows the stages you need to go through to generate evidence to meet the assessment requirements for this unit. The work on developing ideas and creating a business plan can be undertaken in small groups but each individual must write up his or her own business plan for assessment.

> You need to come up with a practical business idea. This product or service will form the basis of your business plan.

> Undertake research to provide the essential market information to write your plan. This will require primary research to question potential customers as well as a trawl of relevant secondary sources of data. This should be used to complete a comprehensive market analysis.

> Use the market analysis to write the marketing plan, setting out in detail your choice of the four Ps: product, price, place and promotion.

> Describe how you are going to produce and deliver your product or service by writing a production and quality assurance plan.

> Produce a comprehensive financial plan including sources of finance, a budget, a breakeven analysis, a cash flow forecast, a project profit and loss account and a start-up balance sheet. Use spreadsheets to present your financial data in a professional manner.

> Provide an evaluation of all components of your plan, by describing and justifying your approach and indicating any alternatives you considered.

Index

Race Relations Act 1976 217
radio advertising 189
random selection 162
rate of inflation 89, 126, 129, 131, 330
ratio analysis 292
rationalisation 111
raw materials 66, 313–14, 341
real accounts 268
real disposable income 89–90
real terms 130
receipt 260
recession 126
recruitment and selection 210, 213–30
redeployment 210
reducing balance method 283
redundancy 211
references 222
reflate 126
Regional Enterprise Grants 125, 355
Regional Selective Assistance 125, 355
registering a company 19, 347
Registrar of Companies 19
reinvesting profits 356
remittance advice 259
remortgage 354
replica kits 117, 118
research and development 29, 37–8, 171–2
resources of a business 27–8
restrictive practices 116–21
restrictive tendering 139
retail price index (RPI) 89
retailers 195
retained profit 277, 279, 299
return on capital employed (ROCE) 297, 374–5
returns in 275
returns in journal 265, 267
returns out journal 265, 267
revenue 273
revenue budget 305
roadshows 186
role culture 11, 12, 13, 14
Royal Ancient Order of Buffaloes 20
RPI (retail price index) 89
running balance 261
Rural Development Areas 125
Ryanair 108

Safeway 7
Sainsbury's 7
Sale of Goods Acts 1979 and 1994 119, 346
Sale of Goods and Services Act 1978 346
sale and leaseback 357
sales budget 305, 306, 307
sales journal 265, 266–7
sales ledger 268
sales promotion 191–2
sampling 161–3
satisficing 6
secondary business objectives 6
secondary data 326
secondary research methods 159–60
secondary sector 85
securities 298–9
segmented markets 84, 159
selection interviews 219, 221
self evaluation 241
service businesses 276
Sex Discrimination Act 1975 217, 243
Sex Discrimination Act 1986 217
share capital 289, 354
share prices 298–9
shareholders
    competition and 110
    divorce of ownership from control 24
    limited liability 16
    rewarding 376
    voting 24
shares 18–19, 298–9
    selling 357
Shell 9
short-term finance 350–1
short-term plans 202
sickness rates 206
simplification 73
single markets 84
    single European market 119, 137
skill shortages 208
sleeping partner 17
SMART objectives 239
SmithKline Beecham 29, 113
social changes 332
social class 156
soft drink prices 105
soft loans 138

sole trader 16–17, 370, 376
    balance sheet 289
    financial information 251
    franchise 19
    legal liabilities 24
    liability for debts 16, 17
    sources of finance 23
    using profits 24, 277
solvency ratios 293, 295–6
sources of finance 22–3, 350–7
Southwest Airlines 78
span of control 44–6
specialisation of labour 111, 339
specific demand 327, 333–4
speculators 86
sponsorship 110, 191
spreadsheet packages 370
staff authority 47–8
stakeholders
    definition 4
    effect of competition on 109–10
    financial information 251–3
    satisfying needs of 4–5
Standard Life Assurance Society 21
standard of living 109
standard of performance 238
standards 139
start-up balance sheet 350, 365–7
start-up budget 358–60
start-up capital 350, 370
state-owned industries, protection for 138–9
statement of account 258
statutory employment rights 227–8, 347
stereotyping 155
stock control systems 31
stock turnover 293–4
stocks 298
stop-go cycle 133, 134
straight-line method 282–3
strategic plans 202
subassembly 66
subsidies 95, 138
substitutes 89, 327
succession requirements 206–7
supervisory positions 79
suppliers, competition and 109
supply 84
    changes in 99–102
    interaction with demand 98–9
Supply of Goods and Services Act 1982 119
supply side factors 94–8
survey methods 163–5